Electronic Resource Management in Libraries: Research and Practice

Holly Yu
California State University, Los Angeles, USA

Scott Breivold
California State University, Los Angeles, USA

INFORMATION SCIENCE REFERENCE

Hershey · New York

Acquisitions Editor:	Kristin Klinger
Development Editor:	Kristin Roth
Senior Managing Editor:	Jennifer Neidig
Managing Editor:	Sara Reed
Copy Editor:	Erin Meyer
Typesetter:	Sean Woznicki
Cover Design:	Lisa Tosheff
Printed at:	Yurchak Printing Inc.

Published in the United States of America by
Information Science Reference (an imprint of IGI Global)
701 E. Chocolate Avenue, Suite 200
Hershey PA 17033
Tel: 717-533-8845
Fax: 717-533-8661
E-mail: cust@igi-global.com
Web site: http://www.igi-global.com

and in the United Kingdom by
Information Science Reference (an imprint of IGI Global)
3 Henrietta Street
Covent Garden
London WC2E 8LU
Tel: 44 20 7240 0856
Fax: 44 20 7379 0609
Web site: http://www.eurospanonline.com

Library of Congress Cataloging-in-Publication Data

Electronic resource management in libraries : research and practice / Holly Yu and Scott Breivold, editors.

p. cm.

Summary: "This book provides comprehensive coverage of the issues, methods, theories, and challenges connected with the provision of electronic resources in libraries, with emphasis on strategic planning, operational guidelines, and practices. Its primary focus is management practices of the life-cycle of commercially acquired electronic resources from selection and ordering to cataloging, Web presentation, user support, usage evaluation, and more"--Provided by publisher.

Includes bibliographical references and index.
ISBN-13: 978-1-59904-891-8 -- ISBN-13: 978-1-59904-892-5 (ebook)

1. Libraries--Special collections--Electronic information resources. 2. Electronic information resources--Management. I. Yu, Holly. II. Breivold, Scott.

Z692.C65E425 2008

025.2'84--dc22
                    2007036853

British Cataloguing in Publication Data
A Cataloguing in Publication record for this book is available from the British Library.

All work contributed to this book set is original material. The views expressed in this book are those of the authors, but not necessarily of the publisher.

Table of Contents

Section I
Historic Overview, Strategic Planning, and Usage Statistics

Section II
Workflow Management and Competencies of Electronic Resource Librarians

Section V
Electronic Resource Management Systems (ERMS)

Detailed Table of Contents

Section I
Historic Overview, Strategic Planning, and Usage Statistics

Traces the history and major developments of electronic resources in libraries in the United States. The chapter discusses the rapid changes and underlying issues which have affected the evolution of library electronic resources from the 1960's to the early 2000's. It is the author's hope that this historic overview may lead the reader to a better understanding of the current situation and provide lessons for the future.

Addresses the subject from the perspective of planning, policy, and workflow management issues experienced by libraries. The authors suggest ideas and methods to address these management challenges.

Provides an overview which includes methods of defining, collecting, and using usage data. A survey of some of the systems of estimating journal usage in the print environment is followed by a description of the development of electronic usage practices. The important contributions of the COUNTER and SUSHI projects are reviewed, along with examples of other ways statistics can assist in decision-making throughout a product's life cycle.

Section II
Workflow Management and Competencies of Electronic Resource Librarians

Provides an in-depth analysis of the workflow for electronic resources from selection to acquisition. It addresses major steps, processes, procedures, and issues in selecting and acquiring electronic resources and covers the selection process including tools, challenges, and selection criteria.

Illustrates that while management of electronic resources is often seen as a strictly technical services endeavor, it should be approached as a multifaceted process requiring all areas of the library. This chapter offers a detailed account of how one library handles the electronic resources management workflow collaboratively.

Chapter VI

Bases its research on the premise that existing electronic resource management guidelines are conceptually linked to actual management situations. This chapter describes how a business and industry method called process mapping can be applied to the management of electronic resources in libraries. A case study is presented to illustrate the process.

Examines the emergence of the electronic resource librarian specialty within academic libraries as a result of increasing demands for library professionals trained in the planning, selecting, implementing, and evaluating of electronic resources. The authors discuss the core competencies of these positions by analyzing job advertisements published in the *College & Research Libraries News* and *The Chronicle of Higher Education* between July 2001 and June 2006. Implications for library education and organizational structures are also discussed.

Section III
Copyright and Licensing

Provides a comparative analysis of 35 licenses created prior to 2000 (and their 2006 equivalents) to reveal how license agreements have evolved to meet the principles set forth in recent years by the American Association of Law Libraries, the International Federation of Library Associations, and the NorthEast Research Libraries. The results of the study indicate that efforts in the library community to encourage the development of licenses that meet the needs of most institutions are having a positive impact.

Begins with an examination of the sections of copyright law that impact electronic resource management. Copyright is discussed in relation to particular types of electronic resources and their unique characteristics and challenges. The chapter incorporates information gathered from a survey of professionals working in a variety of libraries—providing a practical view of how librarians are approaching copyright in the daily reality of their increasingly electronic environments.

Chapter X

Provides the reader with an overview of basic contract law as it relates to electronic resource licensing. The chapter also discusses the negotiation process as well as license agreement terms and clauses. By sharing tips and lessons learned in the negotiation process, the author hopes to provide librarians with a practical understanding of the resource licensing process.

Section IV
Working with Electronic Resources

Chapter XI

Heather Christenson, California Digital Library, USA
Sherry Willhite, California Digital Library, USA

Describes how the California Digital Library (CDL) supports the thousands of electronic journals, databases, collections and reference works that are licensed by CDL on behalf of the ten campuses of the University of California (UC). It indicates that three key components were vital to CDL's success: involvement of librarians at all campuses; internal processes for working with vendors; documentation which emphasizes technical standards and best practices.

Chapter XII

Janet Crum, Oregon Health & Science University, USA

Advocates providing a unified, seamless, interface for the full range of journal literature available to library patrons. The author reviews the tools available for making journal collections accessible, and then analyzes the categories of journal literature to which a library could provide access. It closes with a brief look at future trends that will affect the ability of libraries to provide coherent, seamless access to journal literature.

Chapter XIII

George Boston, Western Michigan University, USA
Randle J. Gedeon, Western Michigan University, USA

Provides an overview of the existing techniques for reference linking of scholarly research materials and discusses some of the new techniques designed for advanced linking. The discussion also includes information about the impact of Web and Library 2.0 tools on resource linking.

Chapter XIV

Juan Carlos Rodriguez, California State University, Sacramento, USA
Bin Zhang, California State University, Sacramento, USA

Opens with a discussion of the need for libraries to provide users with local and remote access to electronic resources. It discusses authentication and authorization mechanisms currently in use by libraries, their parent organizations and electronic resource providers. The chapter concludes with a look at considerations and directions libraries and e-resource providers may take in the future to provide secure and seamless access to electronic resources.

Points out that there are no accepted standards governing naming electronic resources in A to Z lists or electronic resource management (ERM) systems. Current practice superficially resembles cataloging standards and guidelines, but is substantially ad hoc, and reliant on local adaptation and innovation. The issues related to naming electronic resources are discussed and a draft set of principles and conventions is offered.

Section V
Electronic Resource Management Systems (ERMS)

Chapter XVI

Built to manage all steps in the lifecycle of an electronic product, ERM systems must interoperate with existing integrated library systems (ILS), public service, and financial software already in use within the library. The importance of ERM standards is discussed, including efforts like SUSHI and the License Expression Work Group to define new standards and protocols for ERM systems.

Discusses problems encountered at an institution during the installation and utilization of ERM systems, such as Ex-Libris SFX and III ERM. The author's objective is to provide readers with a balanced understanding of ERMS pros and cons from a librarian's perspective.

Discusses the Electronic Resource Management Initiative reports, various library-developed systems, and how existing and developing standards help with the continued development of ERMS and with their integration into integrated library systems.

Chapter XIX

The development of "home grown" tools at several academic institutions is traced, with a focus on the aspects of how the systems are unique to each university. As a result of locally development systems, community-wide efforts to identify key elements for managing electronic resources have begun to emerge.

Chapter XX

Examines ways in which collection analysis and other functionality might be facilitated by the use of data stored in electronic resource management systems. The author suggests that as ERMS evolve, their utility should expand to include collection analysis as well as the source for critical access and license data for patrons wherever they access the library's electronic resources.

Chapter XXI

Describes how libraries have struggled to rethink policies, procedures, systems, and their own roles, to meet the information seeking and research demands of their patrons. The chapter discusses ways in which ERMS should evolve to help libraries meet the challenges of the future. They conclude that ERMS represent the "new ILS"—the next "heart" of library management systems, and believe that it's imperative libraries direct ERMS development in ways that support and advance, rather than undercut, their missions.

Foreword

I am delighted and honored to provide a foreword for this fine collection of richly informative articles on a wide array of topics within the emerging field of electronic resource management. I think the book will be just as useful to relative beginners as to those like me who have been working in this area for some time.

It is no longer news that libraries continue to invest more and more heavily in e-journals, e-journal back files, "traditional" databases, e-books, and newer types of e-resources of every description—or that something like 500 libraries have now purchased and are implementing e-resource management ("ERM") systems to help them manage these collections more effectively. As director of the Digital Library Federation's E-Resource Management Initiative that helped shape many of these systems, I came to realize during "phase one" of that project both how complex they need to be in order to support the many different facets of ERM work and how flexible they will need to be to adapt to changing technologies, business models, and other variables we may now only dimly envision.

With such a challenging and unpredictable environment, what is needed is a collection of articles that strikes a balance between providing background and practical information for the "here and now" and helps build toward and bring order to the future; this volume succeeds in doing this remarkably well. To focus briefly on some immediate and practical organizational concerns, several articles discuss such crucial issues as workflows, roles and collaboration, or explore how strategic planning or less familiar approaches like "process mapping" can be used to promote orderly and efficient operations. Others deal thoroughly and helpfully with more readily defined but still challenging problems like processing and making optimal use of usage statistics for decision-making, how to present journal holdings, or how to work productively with vendors on quality control issues—even across a large and complex consortium like the University of California's.

Few will dispute that another important and problematic area for libraries, publishers and vendors these days is licensing; while licenses must be understood and negotiated in the present, evolving business models and legal developments are likely to have serious implications for the future environment that libraries will work in. Serious and continuing attention must therefore be paid by librarians to this part of the landscape, and those seeking a deeper understanding of it will be pleased to see three substantive, complementary articles that deal, respectively, with the evolution of license terms over the last several years, the role of copyright, and the negotiation process.

The book also provides much of interest on what might be called the "technical" front, as well. There are, for example, two helpful articles concerning ERM systems—as well as excellent discussions of linking technologies and authentication. In addition, there is a nice survey of standards relevant for ERM systems that describes and explains the important existing and emerging ones and provides useful ideas about how new standards might further simplify and automate needlessly time-consuming tasks. Lastly, two additional articles focus more directly on and discuss possible but achievable ERM "futures"—including one that argues that ERMs can and will provide the core or essential functionality for future integrated library systems.

That is quite a remarkable notion, since not many years ago there was a pervasive sense among librarians involved in managing electronic resources that they were on their own and had to "make things up as they went along!" Now it seems much clearer that there is firm ground to stand on while we deal with our day to day management and operational issues, and one of the great strengths of this collection is that it helps solidify that place while contributing a basis for intelligent discussions and planning for the future. That is no mean accomplishment!

Tim Jewell
University of Washington Libraries, USA
June 2007

Tim Jewell *has coordinated the Digital Library Federation's Electronic Resource Management Initiative—which has helped to encourage and shape the development of electronic management systems and related data standards—since its inception in 2002. He is currently director of information resources, collections and scholarly communication with the University of Washington Libraries in Seattle, where he has worked since 1983. Active in regional consortium activities for a number of years, he also served as visiting program officer for electronic resources at ARL from 1996 to 1998. He holds an MLS from SUNY-Albany and an MA in sociology from Pennsylvania State University.*

Preface

Since the advent of Dialog in the 1960's, the proliferation of computer-based bibliographic resources has dramatically changed the way library collections are processed and accessed. In the 1980's, we witnessed the parallel development of online and CD-ROM databases. Then, with the entrance of the World Wide Web in the early 1990's, came a radical shift in the way users access information and vendors responded by developing new Web-based platforms and search interfaces. In the early years of the new millennium, further developments such as meta (cross-interface) database searching, link resolvers, openURL standards, and so forth began to emerge.

These developments, coupled with the new expectations of the Internet-savvy user, affected all types of libraries who had to rapidly shift from print-based to electronic resources. Whether the electronic resource comes from a commercial publisher or a local digitization effort, this trend is also rapidly changing library operational and organizational practices. Along with the increase in electronic resource acquisitions, librarians have had to quickly adapt and address an ever complex set of new challenges and changes related to: workflow management and planning; selection and acquisition procedures; copyright and license negotiation; cataloging practices; public access interfaces; and utilization of usage statistics. Libraries must now come to terms with how to better evaluate, acquire, store, and manage this wealth of electronic resources. The proliferation of electronic resource management systems (ERMS) presents an additional problem for libraries, that must now develop in house resource management solutions or acquire one of a myriad of emerging turn-key solutions and implement them in an evolving organizational setting.

Many librarians and managers have begun to understand that issues related to electronic resource management are far-reaching, complex, and changing the very nature of what we collect and how our users access it. A typical scenario for acquiring print resources in an academic library for example, might involve the selection of materials by subject-specialist librarians or bibliographers; order placement by library acquisitions; cataloging and processing by library technical services; and shelving by the circulation unit. In the electronic realm, this traditional workflow could potentially be an entirely different process or be handled in whole or in part by an ERMS.

Electronic resources may take many forms, from e-books or journals to full-text resources from aggregators, or index/abstract databases from publishers. The way in which electronic resources are managed is becoming more distinct from print with new approaches to planning, tasks, workflow and communication. The planning process encompasses policy-making, budgeting, and staffing. Tasks may include things like setting up trials, license negotiation, authentication, troubleshooting, evaluation, and renewal. Workflow covers the entire process from initial product consideration, making the resource available to patrons, to renewal or cancellation. Communication includes a variety of interactions from local administrators to vendors, IT staff, public service personnel, and users.

In conducting a literature review on this subject, we found a number of "how-to" manuals or guides, but few comprehensive research volumes on the topic of electronic resource management in libraries. Several of these texts are worth exploring however, and provide useful information to librarians involved with electronic resource management. A summary of some of the key texts follows.

In an attempt to be as inclusive as possible, Jewell (2001) identifies ten primary issues and practices in *Selection and Presentation of Commercially Available Electronic Resources: Issues and Practices*, a report published by the Digital Library Federation (DLF) and Council on Library and Information Resources (CLIR). From a broad perspective, Jewell stresses two fundamental factors to sustainability of electronic resources: pricing and management operation. He examines emerging strategies for exerting economic pressure within the marketplace for electronic resources. He also points out that because substantial staff time is required, sustainability is an important operational issue. Jewell's report was one of the most comprehensive available at the time of its publication in 2001.

Building an Electronic Resource Collection: a Practical Guide by Lee and Boyle (2004), discusses the reasons for buying electronic resources, and provides information on delivery options, collection development policies, and usage evaluation. They also present an overview of the major technical issues that arise when working with electronic resources, such as: remote versus local access, authentication, linkage services, and archiving issues.

In his *Buying and Contracting for Resources and Services, A How-to-do-it Manual for Librarians*, Anderson (2004) emphasizes the importance of establishing successful vendor relations. The book provides insightful and noteworthy tips on building and maintaining the library-vendor relationship.

Discussions on management, assessment, budgeting and planning, collection development, acquisitions, licensing, and more can be found in Conger's *Collaborative Electronic Resource Management: from Acquisition to Assessment,* published in 2004. The author emphasizes the disruptive effect of digital resources on workflow as library professionals strive to address an array of management challenges. She points out that "digital resources, by their nature, have proved to be slippery and their management requires innovation, creativity, and collaboration" (Conger, 2004). She suggests that, "a discussion of electronic resource management quickly becomes a discussion of the overall management of a typical library" (Conger, 2004). The author demonstrates how the management of electronic resources fits into the new collaborative management model that relies on learning more than control to respond to change.

In *E-Metrics for Library and Information Professionals: How to Use Data for Managing and Evaluating Electronic Resource Collections,* White and Kamal (2006) introduce electronic usage statistics (e-metrics). Section 3 of the book in particular, focuses on how to use and customize vendor-supplied data, and how to build local metrics.

The revised edition of *Selecting and Managing Electronic Resources, A How-to-Do-It Manual for Librarians*, by Gregory and Hanson (2006), provides a list of useful selection tools and includes a "Selection criteria worksheet for electronic resources," which serves as a model for libraries in need of implementing such procedures.

The most comprehensive effort on electronic resource management can be found in the *Report of the Digital Library Federation Electronic Resource Management (DLF ERMI) Initiative.* ERMI grew out of Jewells' research discussed earlier. In May 2002, the National Information Standards Organization (NISO) and DLF sponsored a workshop on Standards for Electronic Resource Management. Participants included librarians as well as representatives from EBSCO, Endeavor, ExLibris, Fretwell Downing, Innovative Interfaces, SIRSI, and Serials Solutions. The main purpose of the workshop was to bring librarians, publishers, and vendors together to create and test standards for electronic resource management. ERMI incorporated information from the workshop and went on to develop common specifications and tools for managing license agreements, related administrative information, and internal processes associated with collections of licensed electronic resources. The report and working documents from this initiative provide detailed specifications, standards, and best practices; invaluable for drafting system specifications, directing vendor development efforts, and informing librarians. These guidelines have now been largely adopted by commercial ERMS vendors.

These publications, along with numerous published journal articles, provide a framework for the management of electronic resources in libraries. We believe there are many important issues and questions still to be explored in this field, however. For example: why do many institutions continue to be reactive rather than proactive, lack policies and procedures, and retain antiquated workflow systems for the handling of electronic resources? We believe to fundamentally address these concerns, administrators, library professionals, and support staff, need to more fully understand the issues and challenges associated with the provision of electronic resources and the importance of proper management and strategic planning.

This book provides comprehensive coverage of the theories, methods, and challenges, research and practices connected with the provision and management of electronic resources in libraries. It can serve as a practical guide that emphasizes and supports strategic planning, operational policies and procedures, workflow and organizational structure. It addresses strategic planning for electronic resource management from the perspective of planning, policy, and workflow management. It also provides an authoritative analysis of electronic resource management systems including their challenges and trends, and the latest development in electronic resource management standards, such as SUSHI and COUNTER, and the impact of Web 2.0 and Library 2.0 applications. The book also provides a comprehensive review of the evolving license terms, practices and agreement negotiation techniques of electronic resources, and impacts of copyright in relation to electronic resources and their unique characteristics and challenges. It examines evolving roles and core competencies for electronic resource librarians as a result of increasing demands for library professionals trained in the planning, selecting, implementing, and evaluating of electronic resources. Discussions are also provided on practical issues encountered by librarians that have not been well addressed in the literature, such as naming conventions for electronic resources, or the various types of authentication and authorization mechanisms currently in use.

In an attempt to provide the reader with comprehensive coverage of the core topics related to electronic resource management, this book consists five sections including an historic overview, strategic planning, and usage statistics; workflow management and competencies of electronic resource librarians; copyright and licensing; working with electronic resources and electronic resource management (ERM) systems.

Chapter I "History of Electronic Resources" traces the history and major developments of electronic resources in libraries in the United States. The chapter discusses the rapid changes and underlying issues which have affected the evolution of library electronic resources from the 1960's to the early 2000's. It is the author's hope that this historic overview may lead the reader to a better understanding of the current situation and provide lessons for the future.

Chapter II "Strategic Planning for Electronic Resource Management" addresses the subject from the perspective of planning, policy, and workflow management issues experienced by libraries. The authors suggest ideas and methods to address these management challenges.

Chapter III "Electronic Usage Statistics" provides an overview which includes methods of defining, collecting, and using usage data. A survey of some of the systems of estimating journal usage in the print environment is followed by a description of the development of electronic usage practices. The important contributions of the COUNTER and SUSHI projects are reviewed, along with examples of other ways statistics can assist in decision-making throughout a product's life cycle.

Chapter IV "Selecting and Managing Electronic Resources" provides an in-depth analysis of the workflow for electronic resources from selection to acquisition. It addresses major steps, processes, procedures, and issues in selecting and acquiring electronic resources and covers the selection process including tools, challenges, and selection criteria.

Chapter V "Sharing the Albatross of Electronic Resources Management Workflow" illustrates that while management of electronic resources is often seen as a strictly technical services endeavor, it should be approached as a multifaceted process requiring all areas of the library. This chapter offers a detailed account of how one library handles the electronic resources management workflow collaboratively.

Chapter VI "Process Mapping for Electronic Resource Management— A Lesson from Business Models" bases its research on the premise that existing electronic resource management guidelines are conceptually linked to actual management situations. This chapter describes how a business and industry method called process mapping can be applied to the management of electronic resources in libraries. A case study is presented to illustrate the process.

Chapter VII "Evolving Roles for Electronic Resource Librarians" examines the emergence of the electronic resource librarian specialty within academic libraries as a result of increasing demands for library professionals trained in the planning, selecting, implementing, and evaluating of electronic resources. The authors discuss the core competencies of these positions by analyzing job advertisements published in the *College & Research Libraries News* and *The Chronicle of Higher Education* between July 2001 and June 2006. Implications for library education and organizational structures are also discussed.

Chapter VIII "The Evolution of License Content" provides a comparative analysis of thirty-five licenses created prior to 2000 (and their 2006 equivalents) to reveal how license agreements have evolved to meet the principles set forth in recent years by the American Association of Law Libraries, the International Federation of Library Associations, and the NorthEast Research Libraries. The results of the study indicate that efforts in the library community to encourage the development of licenses that meet the needs of most institutions are having a positive impact.

Chapter IX "Copyright Implications and Applications for Electronic Resource Management" begins with an examination of the sections of copyright law that impact electronic resource management. Copyright is discussed in relation to particular types of electronic resources and their unique characteristics and challenges. The chapter incorporates information gathered from a survey of professionals working in a variety of libraries—providing a practical view of how librarians are approaching copyright in the daily reality of their increasingly electronic environments.

Chapter X "Negotiating Licenses for Electronic Resources: Tactics, Terms, and Process" provides the reader with an overview of basic contract law as it relates to electronic resource licensing. The chapter also discusses the negotiation process as well as license agreement terms and clauses. By sharing tips and lessons learned in the negotiation process, the author hopes to provide librarians with a practical understanding of the resource licensing process.

Chapter XI "Working With Database and E-Journal Vendors to Ensure Quality for End Users" describes how the California Digital Library (CDL) supports the thousands of electronic journals, databases, collections and reference works that are licensed by CDL on behalf of the ten campuses of the University of California (UC). It indicates that three key components were vital to CDL's success:

involvement of librarians at all campuses; internal processes for working with vendors; documentation which emphasizes technical standards and best practices.

Chapter XII "One-Stop Shopping for Journal Holdings" advocates providing a unified, seamless, interface for the full range of journal literature available to library patrons. The author reviews the tools available for making journal collections accessible, and then analyzes the categories of journal literature to which a library could provide access. It closes with a brief look at future trends that will affect the ability of libraries to provide coherent, seamless access to journal literature.

Chapter XIII "Beyond OpenURL: Technologies for Linking Library Resources" provides an overview of the existing techniques for reference linking of scholarly research materials and discusses some of the new techniques designed for advanced linking. The discussion also includes information about the impact of Web and Library 2.0 applications.

Chapter XIV "Authentication and Access Management of Electronic Resources" opens with a discussion of the need for libraries to provide users with local and remote access to electronic resources. It discusses authentication and authorization mechanisms currently in use by libraries, their parent organizations and electronic resource providers. The chapter concludes with a look at considerations and directions libraries and e-resource providers may take in the future to provide secure and seamless access to electronic resources.

Chapter XV "Using Consistent Naming Conventions for Library Electronic Resources" points out that there are no accepted standards governing naming electronic resources in A to Z lists or electronic resource management (ERM) systems. Current practice superficially resembles cataloging standards and guidelines, but is substantially ad hoc, and reliant on local adaptation and innovation. The issues related to naming electronic resources are discussed and a draft set of principles and conventions is offered.

Chapter XVI "Standards: The Structural Underpinnings of Electronic Resource Management Systems." Built to manage all steps in the lifecycle of an electronic product, ERM systems must interoperate with existing integrated library systems (ILS), public service, and financial software already in use within the library. The importance of ERM standards is discussed, including efforts like SUSHI and the License Expression Work Group to define new standards and protocols for ERM systems.

Chapter XVII "Challenges and possibilities in the time of ERMS" discusses problems encountered at an institution during the installation and utilization of ERM systems, such as Ex-Libris SFX and III ERM. The author's objective is to provide readers with a balanced understanding of ERMS pros and cons from a librarian's perspective.

Chapter XVIII "Panorama of Electronic Resource Management Systems" discusses the Electronic Resource Management Initiative reports, various library-developed systems, and how existing and developing standards help with the continued development of ERMS and with their integration into integrated library systems.

Chapter XIX In "The Impact of Locally Developed Electronic Resource Management Systems" the development of "home grown" tools at several academic institutions is traced, with a focus on the aspects of how the systems are unique to each university. As a result of locally development systems, community-wide efforts to identify key elements for managing electronic resources have begun to emerge.

Chapter XX "The Future of Electronic Resource Management Systems: Inside and Out" examines ways in which collection analysis and other functionality might be facilitated by the use of data stored in electronic resource management systems. The author suggests that as ERMS evolve, their utility should expand to include collection analysis as well as the source for critical access and license data for patrons wherever they access the library's electronic resources.

Chapter XXI "In the Eye of the Storm-ERM Systems Guiding Libraries' Future" describes how libraries have struggled to rethink policies, procedures, systems, and their own roles, to meet the information seeking and research demands of their patrons. The chapter discusses ways in which ERMS should evolve to help libraries meet the challenges of the future. They conclude that ERMS represent the "new ILS"—the next "heart" of library management systems, and believe that it's imperative libraries direct ERMS development in ways that support and advance, rather than undercut, their missions.

In order to provide up-to-date coverage of research, practices, and challenges related to electronic resource management in libraries, we invited researchers and practitioners to submit proposals describing their suggested topics and contributions in the field. All proposals were carefully reviewed by the editors for suitability in scope and coverage. Each chapter submission was then subject to a double blind, peer review process.

We hope that this book helps library managers, professional librarians, and library personnel involved in electronic resource management come to a realization that with the increase in electronic resources, the types of processes libraries have traditionally employed in print collections are no longer suitable, and the workflow of electronic resources has a tremendous impact on the overall structure, strategic planning of the library. It also helps to learn how libraries can manage electronic resources in a more streamlined workflow and collaborative effort. It assists in foreseeing key issues and challenges encountered during the installation and utilization of ERM systems, and impacts of the Web 2.0 and Library 2.0 tools on resource linking, and the latest development in tracking usage statistics of electronic resources. It is our sincere hope that the research and analysis by our expert contributing authors provides a comprehensive and practical tool with which to better understand electronic resource management in research and practice.

Holly Yu and Scott Breivold, California State University, Los Angeles, USA

REFERENCES

Anderson, R. (2003). *Buying and contracting for resources and services: A how-to-do-it manual for librarians*. New York: Neal-Schuman Publishers.

Conger, J. E. (2004). *Collaborative electronic resource management : From acquisitions to assessment*. Westport, CT: Libraries Unlimited.

Curtis, D. (2005). *E-journals : A how-to-do-it manual for building, managing, and supporting electronic journal collections*. New York: Neal-Schuman Publishers.

Gregory, V. L., & Hanson, A. (2006). *Selecting and managing electronic resources: A how-to-do-it manual for librarians*. New York: Neal Schuman Publishers.

Jewell, T. D. (2001). *Selection and presentation of commercially available electronic resources: Issues and practices*. Digital Library Federation & Council on Library and Information Resources. Retrieved November 16, 2007, from http://www.clir.org/pubs/reports/pub99/contents.html

Jewell, T. D., Anderson, I., & Chandler, A. et al. (2004). *Electronic resource management: Report of the DLF ERM initiative.* Washington, DC: Digital Library Federation. Retrieved November 16, 2007, from http://www.diglib.org/pubs/dlf102/

Lee, S. D., & Boyle, F. (2004). *Building an electronic resource collection: A practical guide.* London: Facet Publishing.

White, A. C. (2006). *E-metrics for library and information professionals : How to use data for managing and evaluating electronic resource.* New York: Neal-Schuman Publishers.

Scott Breivold *is an associate librarian at California State University, Los Angeles. He is the University Library's Media, Communications, & Arts Librarian and oversees the Music & Media Center. He recently took on the role of Library Web Administrator, and will be responsible for coordinating the development and maintenance of the library's web site. As a member of the web team, he played a lead role in the library's current site design, OPAC interface, and online Information Literacy Tutorials. He has presented at local and national conferences on topics ranging from media collection development to library web and tutorial design. He is the editor of Howard Hawks: Interviews published by the University of Mississippi Press in 2006.*

Holly Yu *is an associate librarian and Electronic Resources Coordinator and reference librarian at the University Library, California State University, Los Angeles. She is responsible for providing overall coordination for all aspects of library electronic resources, including selection, budgeting, contracts, troubleshooting, remote access, and more. As the former Library Web Administrator, she coordinated the development and maintenance of the library's web site. She also provides curricular support, library instruction and reference service to students and faculty. She is the editor of Content and Workflow Management for Library Websites: Case Studies, and has authored and co-authored articles on library web interface design. She has presented at American Library Association conferences and regional conferences, as well as the Internet Librarians' conference on the topics of web site usability and library web development. She is active in the Library Information & Technology Association (LITA) and the American Library Association (ALA).*

Acknowledgment

The editors would like to acknowledge the assistance of all involved in the compilation and review process for this book, without whom this project could not have been accomplished.

We are grateful to the exceptional members of our Editorial Advisory Board: Adam Chandler, co-ordinator, service design group of the Information Technology and Technical Services of the Cornell University; Sharon E. Farb, director of Digital Collections Services of the UCLA Libraries; Lisa A. Moske, director of System-Wide Electronic Information Resources for the California State Universities; Kimberly J. Parker, head, Electronic Collections of the Yale University Library; and Angela Riggio, head, Digital Collection Management and Digital Collections Services of the UCLA Libraries.

Many thanks go to our dedicated team of reviewers, several of whom also served as contributing authors: Ivy Anderson, director of collections for the California Digital Library; Kitti Canepi, head, Information Resources Management of the Morris Library at Southern Illinois University in Carbondale; Ellen Finnie Duranceau, scholarly publishing and licensing consultant for the MIT Libraries; Sharon E. Farb, director of Digital Collection Services at UCLA; Kristine Ferry, research librarian for business at the University of California, Irvine; Ted Fons, senior product manager for Innovative Interfaces Inc.; Patricia Hults, coordinator of technical services for the Research Libraries of the Rensselaer Polytechnic Institute; Smita Joshipura, acquisitions librarian at Arizona State University; Marie R. Kennedy, head, Metadata and Content Management, Norris Medical Library of the University of Southern California; Ted Koppel, Verde product manager for the Ex Libris Group; Lisa A. Moske of California State Universities; Marvin Pollard, unified information access systems project manager for the California State Universities; Angela Riggio of UCLA; Juan Carlos Rodriquez, director of Library Systems & Information Technology, California State University, Sacramento; Robert M. Russell, electronic resources coordinator, Northern State University; and Aline Soules, library faculty and professor, California State University, East Bay.

We greatly appreciate the publishing opportunity and efforts of our team at IGI Global Publishing. We especially want to thank Kristin Roth, our development editor for this project, for her invaluable assistance, guidance, and patience throughout this entire process.

Special thanks go to Tim Jewell, one of the pioneers of the electronic resource management realm, for inspiring this project and generously offering to write the foreword.

Finally, but most importantly, we wish to thank all of our insightful and expert authors for their excellent contributions to this book and to the field of library electronic resource management.

Section I
Historic Overview, Strategic Planning, and Usage Statistics

Chapter I
History of Electronic Resources

Dalene Hawthorne
Emporia State University, USA

ABSTRACT

This chapter describes the history of the development and use of electronic resources in libraries in the United States. It provides an overview of the major developments in the field with a focus on library catalogs, electronic databases, e-books and e-serials. The chapter is intended to convey the broad sweep of change that has characterized these electronic resources from the 1960's to the early 2000's, as well as a sense of the underlying issues that remain the same. The author hopes that an understanding of the history of the development and use of these resources may lead to a better understanding of the current environment and provide inspiration for the future.

INTRODUCTION

The library profession recognized the potential of computers to make library resources more accessible early in the development of computer technology. Librarians were often enthusiastic and sometimes early adopters of technology. The use of electronic resources in libraries began with the development of the machine-readable cataloging (MARC) format in the mid-1960's, a full 30 years before the introduction of the World Wide Web and its subsequent ubiquity. Bibliographic databases became available at approximately the same time.

Libraries provided access to data sets such as census and survey data as early as the 1970's. During the microcomputer revolution of the 1980's, libraries acquired software and data on diskettes and offered databases on CD-ROM. Databases on CD-ROM began to contain full text. Search interfaces became more straightforward and simpler to use. Online catalogs became more common, and libraries began to offer them through the pre-World Wide Web Internet.

Tim Berners-Lee created the World Wide Web in 1990. The subsequent development of the Mosaic browser in 1992 led to widespread use of the Web beginning in 1993. The graphical interface and the later development of Web search engines such as Yahoo! made resources on the Internet more accessible to average patrons.

Web-based electronic resources were widely available beginning in the mid-1990's. Libraries offered Web-based catalogs, bibliographic and full-text databases, electronic journals, and eventually electronic books through the Web. Patrons no longer had to go to the library to do a significant amount of their research.

This chapter is intended to convey the broad sweep of change that characterized the development of library electronic resources from the 1960's to the early 2000's as well as a sense of the underlying issues that remain the same. An understanding of the development of library catalogs, databases, electronic serials and electronic books may lead to a fuller understanding of the current environment and provide inspiration for the future.

BACKGROUND

The pursuit of electronic resources by libraries was driven by the core values of library science. It is possible to recognize in Ranganathan's five laws of library science the motivation that drove libraries to incorporate electronic resources into services and collections. Paraphrased to better suit electronic resources, the laws read: resources are for use, every person his or her resource, every resource its user, save the time of the user, and the library is a growing organism (Ranganathan, 1963).

Each technological development in library electronic resources during the 20th century was intended to make access to resources more direct, convenient, and timely for the user. The implementation of electronic resources made the library a growing organism as libraries adapted processes and reorganized staff repeatedly to accommodate the changes inherent in the use of constantly changing technology.

ONLINE CATALOGS

Electronic resources began to dramatically change the way patrons accessed library resources in the mid-1960's. The card catalog, a standard fixture in libraries for a century, faced its demise. One of the major developments during the 1960's was machine-readable cataloging (MARC). The MARC format dramatically changed the way library resources were processed and accessed. The library professionals who created MARC recognized the need for automation and a supporting data standard at a critical juncture in the development of technology, and took the necessary steps and risks to develop one. The flexible and expandable MARC format demonstrated the foresight and vision of those who developed it over 40 years ago.

MACHINE-READABLE CATALOGING

In 1964, the Council on Library Resources commissioned a study about capturing cataloging data in machine-readable form. A report called *The Recording of Library of Congress Bibliographic Data in Machine Form* resulted from the study, and was used as the basis for the first Conference on Machine-Readable Catalog Copy in 1965. Participants at the conference determined the requirements for a machine-readable record and discussed how it might be used in libraries. The Library of Congress' Information Systems Office developed and distributed a report based on this meeting titled *A Proposed Format for a Standardized Machine-Readable Catalog Record* (Avram, 1968).

During a second conference held at the Library of Congress, the MARC Pilot Project was conceived. Planning for the project began in February 1966. The MARC I format was created, codes for place of publication, language, and publisher were developed, computer software was designed, and procedures were developed and documented (Avram, 1968).

In November 1966, the Information Systems Office of the Library of Congress began to distribute magnetic tapes of MARC records to 16 libraries that agreed to participate in the pilot project. The tapes contained English language Library of Congress catalog records that were formatted in MARC I. During the pilot project, the Library of Congress converted 35,000 records (Avram, 1968). Some of the libraries that participated in the pilot project were able to use MARC records to automate some aspects of their library operations. Some of the pilot libraries, however, struggled with a lack of computer programming knowledge as well as a lack of experience with complex bibliographic data (Torkington, 1974). The pilot project officially ended June 30, 1967, but distribution of records continued into 1968 (Avram, 1968).

The Library of Congress decided that the pilot project was an overall success and began to work on the MARC II format in March 1967, while the pilot project was still being carried out. The MARC II format was developed based on feedback from libraries that participated in the pilot project. The Information Sciences and Automation Division of the American Library Association formed a Machine-Readable Cataloging Format Committee to review the MARC II format (Avram, 1968).

MARC II was designed to serve as a communication or exchange medium. The Library of Congress began general distribution of MARC II records in March 1969. Responsibility for creating MARC records was transferred from the Library of Congress' Information Systems Office to a newly created department called the MARC Editorial Office. At first, coverage was limited to American imprints, but this was later expanded to include current English language imprints. By the end of 1972, the MARC database contained more than 300,000 records, and projects to develop MARC systems began in several other countries including Great Britain, France,

Italy, West Germany, the Netherlands, and Japan (Torkington, 1974).

The development of the MARC format laid the foundation for libraries to share bibliographic data. Databases and services were subsequently created to support that sharing.

SHARED CATALOGING

The Ohio College Association hired Frederick G. Kilgour in 1967 to establish the Ohio College Library Center (OCLC), which was the world's first computerized library network. In 1971 OCLC introduced a shared cataloging database, now called WorldCat, to support 54 academic libraries in Ohio. This online cataloging system allowed libraries to achieve dramatic cost savings by sharing bibliographic records. One library could create an online bibliographic record and other libraries could use that same record to create cards with local information for their print catalogs. The Alden Library at Ohio University increased the number of books it cataloged by a third and simultaneously reduced its staff by 17 positions in the first year of use. Word of this increase in efficiency spread, and the network quickly expanded to include libraries from all 50 states and around the world (Librarian...educator...historian...entrepreneur, 2006).

ONLINE PUBLIC ACCESS CATALOG (OPAC)

In 1975, Ohio State University Libraries installed computer terminals in its main lobby so that patrons could directly search its library control system without help from a librarian intermediary. The library control system became one of the early online catalogs. The catalog was searchable by author, title, author and title, call number, and Library of Congress subject headings. There was also a computerized shelf list that patrons could browse (Norden & Lawrence, 1981). Most of the library systems that were available in the 1970's performed a single function, such as circulation, and this information was also made available to library patrons.

Computer-output-microform (COM) catalogs were another alternative to the card catalog that developed as a result of shared online cataloging. Libraries that used these catalogs generally had large collections (over 25,000 volumes, with a growth rate of at least 1,000 titles per year), needed the catalog in at least 20 locations, and were having difficulty managing the logistics of maintaining a card catalog because of the large volume (Boss & Marcum, 1980). COM catalogs enjoyed only a brief period of popularity due to patrons' clear preference for online catalogs over microform.

Online catalogs began to replace existing library card catalogs in significant numbers during the 1980's. A study of users' reactions to four of these systems indicated that the users preferred online catalogs to card catalogs (Moore, 1981). This clear preference led to further development of the online catalog. Online catalogs provided more advantages to patrons than simply improved searching capabilities. These systems were integrated with acquisitions and circulation processing so that added information about on-order, in-process, and up-to-date circulation status information was available to patrons for the first time (Horny, 1982).

By 1989, 50% of all library systems purchased had a patron access catalog that was implemented (Boss, 1989). Many card catalog cabinets were discarded or sold. To ease the transition between card catalogs and online catalogs, online catalogs were designed to mimic the functionality of the card catalog. Text-based catalogs were available remotely using the TELNET protocol, but only relatively sophisticated computer-using library patrons accessed library catalogs this way. That changed significantly with the advent of the World Wide Web.

WEB-BASED CATALOGS

Vendors developed Web-based versions of online public access catalogs to satisfy the demand of librarians, but these catalogs replicated text-based catalogs, which were in turn based on the card catalog. Web-based catalogs, although presented through a graphical interface, relied on Boolean searching, which was "still a retrieval technique designed for trained and experienced users" (Antelman, Lynema, & Pace, 2006, p. 128).

Many libraries added catalog records for Web pages, but it quickly became clear that it would be impossible for librarians to catalog the Web in the way they had traditionally described print resources. Before librarians could fully respond to this new technology, the first Web search engines such as Aliweb, WebCrawler, and Lycos and Web directories such as Yahoo! were created. Libraries became more selective about adding catalog records with links to Web resources and focused more on electronic resources for which the library paid.

Some libraries created catalog records for individual titles in Web-based databases, only to find that database vendors' title lists changed frequently, causing significant cataloging backlogs and inaccurate links that were frustrating to users. Other libraries created html lists of electronic journals and databases rather than catalog records. As databases and electronic journals proliferated, this task became a time-consuming chore. In response to both the need for catalog records and what were often referred to as A-Z lists, vendors emerged that provided services that tracked the individual electronic journals from databases and supplied MARC records for libraries to load into their databases.

In many cases, the library catalog was no longer the main discovery tool for library patrons. The catalog became for many users simply a way to look up call numbers for items they found elsewhere. Despite the fact that researchers in information retrieval developed several experimental catalogs, such as RLG's Red Light Green, that provided features such as spell checking, subject heading and keyword suggestion, and term weighting, these features were not incorporated into catalogs developed by library vendors (Antelman et al., 2006)

Libraries grappled with ways to incorporate social computing into their Web presence. Podcasts, blogs, and wikis appeared on library Websites. Ratings, social tagging, and reviews were included in library catalogs by vendors. Still, many patrons overlooked the library catalog.

In May 2005, The North Carolina State University (NCSU) Libraries purchased Endeca Technologies' Information Access Platform (IAP) and made a new catalog available using this software in January 2006. The new catalog allowed NCSU to offer its patrons relevance-ranked results, new browsing capabilities, and improved subject access (Antelman et al., 2006). The NCSU catalog caused such a stir in the library world that vendors began to create search platforms with similar capabilities.

Standards development, which started with the MARC format, continued to be critical in the new Web environment. Librarians used XML and developed metadata schemas to describe collections. Metadata schemas and the metadata they carried made it possible for search engines to find and expose these collections to users through digital Web-based libraries. METS (metadata encoding and transmission standard), MODS (metadata object description schema), and EAD (encoded archival description) became familiar to catalogers and archivists. An XML version of MARC was created, along with crosswalks to and from these different schemas, to allow data to be converted from one to another. These new metadata schemas were used to markup online collections of born-digital works as well as digitized photographs, artwork, musical scores, and historical documents.

Many libraries found themselves at the beginning of the 21st century with the unenviable task of maintaining multiple catalogs and systems of information, including Web-based catalogs for traditional sources, A-Z lists of electronic serials and databases, and digital repositories. Patrons found themselves with a sometimes confusing and overwhelming array of resources with no clear path to searching them all.

BIBLIOGRAPHIC DATABASES

While the MARC format was under development at the Library of Congress, the first electronic bibliographic databases were being created on the opposite coast. These databases were originally created to provide access to scientific and government information resources. The first Dialog database software was created under Roger K. Summit's leadership at Lockheed in 1966 (Dialog invented online, 2006). Lockheed and Bunker-Ramo both won funding to develop software that NASA could use to access its database. Lockheed won the contract in 1967 and retained the rights to the Dialog software it created. In 1968, System Development Corporation (SDC), led by Carlos Cuadra, won a contract from the United States Office of Education for research and dissemination of educational information (ERIC). In 1969, SDC created a retrieval program for the National Library of Medicine called ELHILL, which was the precursor to MEDLINE (Bjorner & Ardito, 2003).

Computer-based bibliographic services revolutionized bibliographic research in the 1970s. The ramifications of this revolution continued to impact libraries and electronic resources into the 21st century. In *The Electronic Library: Bibliographic Data Bases, 1978-79*, Christian (1978) attributed the development of these databases in great measure to issues around scholarly communication. These issues included the proliferation of journals and journal articles due to tenure and promotion requirements, increased discipline specialization, and significant price increases for scholarly journals.

Another driver in the development of these databases was the trend in the publishing industry toward computer-aided production techniques. Techniques such as photocomposition left publishers with a by-product in the form of machine-readable bibliographic data that could be sold to supplement traditional product lines. Finally, the National Science Foundation's Office of Science Information Service (OSIS) was legally charged with fostering and disseminating scientific and technical information through technological transfer. "OSIS funded the foundation of new information services and regional centers to provide data base services on a not-for-profit basis; the conversion to computer-readable form of a number of substantial files of scientific and technical bibliographic data, and a host of other significant innovations" (Christian, 1978, pp. 2-3).

Online information retrieval was a new concept for many libraries, but one that coincided with the core library values of saving the time of the user and providing access to information. Convey (1992) defines information retrieval as "the searching for, and the retrieving of, selected information from the data held on a computer." In the early days of online access to databases, connections were made through leased telephone lines. In 1972, Tymnet set up a commercial telecommunications network, and database providers began offering services via the network (Bjorner & Ardito, 2003).

By 1975, there were already more than 100 machine-readable databases, although less than half of those were available online. Many of them were distributed on magnetic tape and the tapes were searched from a local computer. By the late 1970's, the number of databases had grown to more than 360 and there were at least 40 abstracting and indexing services (Christian, 1978).

These databases were very expensive to use. In the mid 1970's, Lockheed Information Systems and System Development Corporation (SDC) were the two major nationwide vendors of collections of online databases. The average cost of each online search for bibliographic citations was approximately $50.00 per search. By late in the decade Bibliographic Retrieval Services emerged and offered competitive rates for high-volume users. Lockheed and SDC were forced to lower their prices to remain competitive, and prices dropped to an average of $25.00 per search (Christian, 1978).

Because of the high cost per search and the arcane searching protocols that varied from database to database, searches had to be carefully constructed using Boolean logic before the search was conducted. This was not something that could be done by the uninitiated layperson. Jobs were redefined. Reference librarians became gatekeepers to this information and were called online searchers or information brokers.

Some libraries charged their patrons fees for database services. This was a controversial topic at the time and there was much emotional debate about whether it was appropriate, especially in public libraries. The entire library community, partly due to the cost of these resources, did not immediately embrace databases. However, resource sharing in the form of consortial purchasing became more common in this decade and helped make it possible for more libraries to provide access to these databases. Since the content of most of the databases at the time was scientific or technical in nature, most of the libraries that used these databases were academic or special libraries, although a few large public libraries provided access to these databases.

The rate of change in the use of library electronic resources began to increase during the 1980's. Databases were designed for the end user, licensing of electronic resources became common, and the full text of articles began to appear in databases.

CD-ROM DATABASES

Vendors began to distribute electronic databases on compact disc-read only memory (CD-ROM) in the mid 1980's. CD-ROM technology was touted as the "new papyrus" (Roose, 1988). Vendors also designed interfaces for the end user for the first time. The first commercially available CD-ROM product designed specifically for libraries was Library Corporation's BiblioFile. BiblioFile contained Library of Congress MARC cataloging records and was exhibited at the American Library Association's midwinter meeting in January of 1985 (Eaton, MacDonald, & Saule, 1989).

Databases on CD-ROM quickly became popular for several reasons. CD-ROM databases with user-friendly interfaces put online searching into the hands of the end user. Patrons no longer had to request the assistance of a librarian to gain access to these electronic resources, resulting in a service model that was more closely aligned with core library values than mediated searching. Another benefit to CD-ROM databases was that users could search them as much as they wished without concern for per search or per minute charges. Libraries could budget more easily for database use since they did not have to predict the amount of online searching that would be requested.

Optical discs provided high-density storage compared to other media available at the time, such as floppy discs and magnetic tape. They were also more durable and could not be altered or erased (Tenopir, 1986). Library patrons stood in line to use *Magazine Index* through the InfoTrac interface on CD-ROM. The ability to print citations from a computer rather than having to write them down was very convenient for patrons (Roose, 1988). When full-text began to be offered on CD-ROM products in addition to bibliographic citations, these products became even more popular.

While there were advantages to this new media, there were also some disadvantages. It was more costly for libraries to start using CD-ROM data-bases since they had to invest in a computer and CD-ROM drive for each database they purchased, at least before CD-ROM networking was developed. The annual lease for each database could be quite expensive, especially in the beginning when database producers were trying to establish pricing formulas. Therefore, libraries had to determine whether the CD-ROM database would be more cost-effective or provide more value than online searching of the same database before they could justify purchasing one. After some years, prices became lower as information providers became more comfortable with the medium and perceived the need to increase their subscriber bases.

Some librarians had concerns about investing large sums of money in the computer hardware required to use these databases when with some foresight it was possible to imagine that another medium might soon replace CD-ROM technology (Roose, 1988). CD-ROM databases were not updated as frequently as online databases could be, since the CD-ROMS had to be produced, copied and shipped to the library. Some databases were updated monthly, some quarterly, and others annually.

Along with the introduction of CD-ROM databases, librarians found themselves dealing with a new purchasing model that they were somewhat slow to accept. Vendors frequently offered these CD-ROM database products as annual serials subscriptions, although some were available for outright purchase. The result of purchasing databases on a subscription basis was that instead of buying a resource that could be added to a library's collection indefinitely or paying for an online search on demand, libraries paid significant amounts of money for data that was leased for a limited time (Pooley, 1990).

Librarians were faced with having to interpret complex, legal documents generally referred to as license agreements. These documents specified terms which libraries were required to enforce. These included terms such as whether out-of-date discs had to be returned to the publisher, the conditions for single- or multiuser access, the conditions under which lost or damaged discs might be replaced, and whether or how much data could be downloaded from the CD-ROM product (Pooley, 1990). Librarians and their institutions identified objectionable clauses in these licenses and worked with publishers to find more favorable alternatives. One of these objectionable clauses required libraries to monitor the number of print copies that could be made or the amount of data that was downloaded. Librarians who worked in state institutions had to be aware of state laws that dictated which state's laws would be used to govern the agreement or where a contract-related lawsuit would be held and then negotiate license agreements to meet those requirements (Nissley, 1990). License agreements continued to be of concern into the early 2000's.

One of the early disadvantages of CD-ROM technology was that libraries had to dedicate a workstation, which generally included a computer, CD-ROM drive, and printer, to each copy of a database. The development of networking hardware and software and CD-ROM servers, colloquially referred to as jukeboxes, gave libraries the ability to offer more than one database at each workstation. Libraries were also able to remove the CD-ROM discs themselves from public areas, which reduced problems with 'missing' discs. However, these networks were difficult to design and install, and could be quite temperamental. The networks generally had to be set up and managed by a network administrator, and often added to the overall cost of these databases to libraries (Flanders, 1990).

ONLINE DATABASES

Online databases were still very much in use in the 1980's. Full-text articles began to be added to online bibliographic databases toward the middle of the decade, which made these databases even more useful. Online searching at this time was generally done via the TELNET protocol and private, for-profit networks, not the Internet.

Some of the disadvantages to using online databases during the late 1980's did not change significantly when these databases became available on the World Wide Web. These disadvantages included the difficulty of identifying and locating relevant sources, the problem of each resource having a different search interface, and the difficulty of moving search results from one system to another for consolidation and analysis (Lynch & Preston, 1990).

WEB-BASED DATABASES

Once the Web became available, online database interfaces were improved to make searching easier. More full text and multimedia became available. However, because most of these resources were subscription based and licensed, libraries were responsible for controlling access to these databases. In addition, these resources were part of the deep Web, along with the library catalog, and it was not possible to discover them with Web search engines. Since most users started looking for information with these search engines, they were not finding these expensive and very useful resources. Librarians responded with expanded library instruction, A-Z lists, searchable databases of databases, and MARC records in the catalog, but this issue continued to be of great concern into the early 2000's.

Early in the development of Web-based databases, access to them was controlled through the use of logins and passwords. It quickly became clear that this was an awkward, if not impossible, way to manage access to Web-based databases. Authentication by IP (Internet protocol address) became the main method used by libraries and database providers to provide resources to computers in the organization, and libraries used proxy servers to authenticate remote users. Library information became easily accessible to patrons outside the library, which led to a greater demand for full-text resources.

The problem of the appropriate copy of a full-text resource began to be of concern to librarians. Library patrons performed searches and often found only the options to purchase an article from the database provider or request it through interlibrary loan. All too often, the library had the full text of the article available in another electronic resource or in a print collection. Most patrons did not know enough about library resources to anticipate that they might find that resource immediately and at no direct cost to them in another of the library's databases.

Some database providers cooperated with each other to create links from bibliographic records in one database to full-text in another database, but these partnerships were relatively few. When the OpenURL specification became available in 1999, link resolvers were developed to utilize OpenURL to provide the most appropriate copy of a resource to library patrons. Link resolvers used a knowledge base to store information about the library's resources. When a search was performed in a database, another search was conducted in the background against the library's knowledge base. The patron was presented with options for retrieving the resource, fulfilling the core library values of providing the specific resource required by a specific user and saving the time of the user.

Various metasearch or federated search engines were developed in the late 1990's, but none provided truly satisfactory results. This was primarily because each database provider labeled fields differently and search mechanisms behaved differently. Many libraries invested in metasearch engines even though they required improvement because these metasearch engines furthered the core value of saving the time of the user.

In the 2000's, Google and Microsoft helped libraries expose database and electronic journal collections through the use of link resolvers, openURL and services such as Google Scholar and Microsoft LiveAcademic.

ELECTRONIC SERIALS

Internet

Experimental electronic journals were available as early as 1982 through the Electronic Information Exchange System (EIES), which was sponsored by the Division of Information Science and Technology of the National Science Foundation. There were four prototypes of electronic journals available on this system. The four prototypes included a newsletter, a "paper fair" which was a totally unrefereed journal, a peer-reviewed journal where articles were published when they were ready, and an interactive journal that consisted of inquiries, responses, and briefs (Turoff & Hiltz, 1982). Electronic journals continued to be created, mainly in scientific fields, and were made available through ftp and gopher sites, but their proliferation was destined to await the development of the Web.

Some types of serials, such as newletters, were distributed by electronic mail and fax in the 1980's and early 1990's, but this was only practical for shorter serials with limited graphics. The primary method for libraries to access serials electronically during this time was through aggregated databases.

World Wide Web

The Web became the environment where electronic serials flourished. Hitchcock, Carr, and Hall found that there were 115 e-journals in existence in 1995. Within the next three years, the same authors discovered 1,300 electronic journals (Hitchcock et al., as cited in Cole, 2004). Serials publishers were fearful of the potential loss of revenue stream, but benefited from the experience of online database providers and learned to use subscriptions and licensing terms to make libraries responsible for controlling access to e-journals in the same ways libraries authenticated patrons who used online databases.

Initially, many publishers offered online access free with a print subscription. While many publishers continued to offer this model into the early 2000's, others charged an increased price for print plus online or a somewhat reduced price for print only or online only journals. Some publishers offered special pricing for libraries that purchased large "packages" of journals, often referred to as "The Big Deal." Many smaller libraries found these packages to be completely unaffordable. Some larger libraries decided that "The Big Deal" was unacceptable because the high number of low-usage titles that were often included in them did not seem to justify the overall cost.

Electronic serials were available to libraries in a variety of ways. Some publishers offered their journals through their own sophisticated and proprietary search and retrieval platforms on the Web. Other publishers offered their journals through platforms such as Project MUSE and Highwire Press. Project MUSE began in 1993 with Johns Hopkins University Press titles and later added titles from other nonprofit publishers (General overview, 2007). Highwire Press, a division of Stanford University Libraries, offered over 1,000 electronic versions of high-impact journals in partnership with scholarly societies, university presses and publishers by 2007. Still other publishers offered their journals through subscription vendors or on simple Websites.

The open access movement took shape during this time in response to decades of double-digit price inflation and the early promise of the Web to provide free access to information. This movement advocated making scholarship, especially that which was paid for by public institutions, available freely on the Web. The viability of the economic models to support open access was not proven by the early 21st century. Open access business models in general either charged

the author or the author's institution or grantor a fee to publish an article. BioMed Central and the Public Library of Science were examples of early open access publishers.

By 2004, the number of e-journals was estimated at 30,000 titles (Cole, 2004). Such growth clearly demonstrated the popularity of electronic journals. There were some disadvantages to this medium, however, that were not yet resolved. Electronic dissemination in itself did not solve the problem of the rising cost of serials, although the open access movement sought to limit costs or move the costs from libraries to the entities that generated the research. In fact, as publishers invested in hardware and programming to make their journals available on the Web, costs continued to rise. In addition, there were no established workflows between publishers, vendors, and libraries to manage electronic serials, and libraries were ironically forced into manual processes to track acquisition and access provision. Some libraries created databases to better manage these processes, and vendors responded to the efforts of the Digital Library Federation's Electronic Resource Management Initiative by creating products such as electronic resource management (ERM) systems. Still, electronic resource management workflows were very immature when compared with the imperfect, but well-established processes for print serials.

ELECTRONIC BOOKS

Internet

Project Gutenberg was the first electronic book project. It focused on documents and books that were in the public domain. Project Gutenberg began in 1971 at the Materials Research Lab at the University of Illinois. Michael Hart began the e-book project in part to fill up the spare time of computer operators in the lab. The philosophy behind this project was to create texts that were easy to use and inexpensive to create. Every book was freely available to the public on the Internet, and then on the Web. This was accomplished by using volunteers and by creating the files in "plain vanilla ASCII" (Hart, 1992). Volunteers converted the original ASCII files to other formats such as html and .pdf as there was demand for them.

CD-ROM Books

The first commercial packages of electronic books became available at about the same time as other CD-ROM products. The Library of the Future was one of these products, and it contained about 300 public-domain literary works in ASCII format, and sold for $695.00 in 1991 (Mullin, 2002). As late as 2007, The Library of the Future 4th edition was listed on Amazon.com and contained more than 5,000 titles. Customer reviews were very favorable, and seemed to focus on the amount of information available on one disc as well as the usability of the software, but the item was no longer available. It was still available on eBay at the same time for $32.00. Other popular electronic book collections on CD-ROM included reference works such as the International Dictionary Unabridged on CD-ROM, published by Merriam-Webster Inc. in 2000. It included a thesaurus and illustrations as well as multimedia functions such as audio pronunciations and interactive features such as bookmarks and spelling help.

Despite these early success stories, books did not make the swift transition from print to electronic that was predicted by many in the late 1990's. There seemed to be a variety of reasons for this, but the one most often cited was that reading books on a backlit screen was an unpleasant experience for many people. There was even some confusion about the definition of what an e-book was during this period, as both the reading devices and the text were referred to as e-books.

In addition, there were obvious advantages to electronic serials and databases over their print equivalents, which included the ability to search for and retrieve information more quickly and easily than in print and the ability to do these things from any location. These advantages did not seem to transfer as readily to electronic books, with the notable exception of reference books. While the improved search and retrieval advantages of the electronic format helped users find the books they wanted to read, they usually wanted to read them in print. Most people in the transitional generation between the print world and the electronic world printed items of any real length that they wanted to read. Articles and database records tended to be much shorter and therefore less expensive to print in terms of paper and toner. It was also easier to handle one-sided printouts of 15 pages that could be stapled together than to carry around one-sided unbound printouts of a several-hundred-page book.

There were potential advantages to electronic books, both for publishers and readers. By the 1990's, most books were born digital and had to be transformed into print at a fairly significant cost. In addition, it was often wasteful to print copies in advance. Gall (2005) wrote, "It is estimated that 10 percent of texts printed each year are turned to pulp, although, fortunately, many are recycled. The BBC reported that more than two million former romance novels were used in the construction of a new tollway." Gall also pointed out that the cost of printing caused specialized titles to become out-of-print quickly because fewer copies were printed. So, one potential benefit of electronic books was that publishers would not have to estimate the number of copies of a particular book that would be sold in advance. Some potential advantages to electronic books for readers included the ability to carry several books at once in a small space, a potential benefit to students and travelers, the fact that e-books required little or no space on shelves, and that they could be used with text-to-speech software (Gall, 2005).

The potential advantages to electronic books were undermined in part by the early business models used to sell them. Most of the early commercial business models for electronic books were focused on sales to individuals, and usually tied customers to a particular e-book reader. E-book readers themselves were expensive, costing from $300 to $700 each, and consumers could only purchase e-books that were available in the proprietary format for that particular reader. Additionally, the files could not be transferred to another reader of the same type, but could only be used on the specific reader to which the file was originally downloaded. So, for example, a family that purchased two readers was not able to buy one e-book and share it between e-book readers. The RocketBook was an early example of this business model.

Publishers selected these business models precisely because it made it very difficult to copy or share an e-book. Most publishers were concerned about losing revenue to file sharing. This in turn made it particularly difficult for libraries to offer e-books to their patrons. Many libraries invested in e-book readers such as the RocketBook, and downloaded several titles to each reader. The problem with that model was that as long as that reader was checked out, none of the e-books on the reader were available for other patrons to read.

There were some publishers, however, namely The National Academy Press, The University of California Press, and Baen Books, who saw e-books as a way to increase print book sales. The National Academy Press, for example, made all of their titles freely available to download and after doing so sold more print copies of those same books than it did before they were available online (Mullin, 2002). Baen Books, which published mostly science fictions books, created the Baen Free Library where it offered authors the option to put copies of their books online. Baen limited authors to one or two books in a series or four or five books overall so that less known authors would have a better chance to be discovered by potential readers (Flint, 2000). This

program began in 2000 and was still in existence in early 2007.

NetLibrary joined the e-book market in late 1998 and developed yet another business model that was based on the way libraries check out one copy of a book to one patron. ebrary joined the market at about the same time, and with a similar business model. Libraries and businesses could purchase collections of electronic books that were hosted on the company's server. Patrons associated with the institution could check out electronic books for a period of time. Printing was deliberately set up to be inconvenient, and software controls prevented users from printing more than a few pages at a time. Publishers that worked with these companies insisted on a one book, one patron model rather than a simultaneous user model, once again out of fear of losing the print revenue stream.

There was significant upheaval in the electronic book market during the dot.com bust of the early 21st century, and very few of the original electronic book publishers survived. NetLibrary was rescued by OCLC, which already had an agreement with NetLibrary to archive each customer's collection of e-books. ebrary also continued to operate, but most of the big names in e-books in the late 1990's were gone by 2001.

After 2000, the e-book market gradually began to regenerate. New companies such as Mobipocket, which became a subsidiary of Amazon.com, and OverDrive entered the market with business models that were not hardware specific. OverDrive developed a business model that was library friendly. Libraries purchased specific e-books or digital audiobooks and provided links to these electronic books in their catalogs. Library patrons checked these books out for a period of time, using the OverDrive software, and downloaded them to their computers or MP3 players.

In 2004, Google entered into partnership with major libraries to digitize their print book collections and make them searchable through Google Book Search http://books.google.com/. Titles that were out of copyright were made available in their entirety. Titles still under copyright displayed bibliographic information and perhaps the table of contents and a few pages of text (Google milestones, 2006).

Sony developed a new e-book reader that it released in 2006. The new Sony Reader used E Ink screen technology, which for the first time did not rely on backlighting and provided a screen resolution similar to print. The new readers supported various file types including .pdf and even Word documents. It also allowed users to listen to MP3 files at the same time they were reading an e-book. The cost was still over $300 for the reader, but the E Ink technology seemed to address one of the major objections to e-books, which was the issue of readability.

While electronic books did not dramatically change the way people read by the early 21st century, they did offer one more way to search for and find information quickly. As a result, these resources were more successful in academic libraries than with the public or public libraries.

FUTURE TRENDS

It seems apparent that library catalogs must evolve quickly if they are to remain an integral piece of the library electronic resources puzzle. Vendors have already begun to respond to innovative efforts such as the NCSU catalog by creating library portals that include federated searching, relevance ranked results, and improved browsing capabilities.

It is almost certain that databases will continue to increase in both number and type of content. Users will continue to demand full-text resources. Federated searching and linking must continue to improve, and libraries will encourage the further development of these tools. Libraries will continue to work to make their resources available where their users can find them through Google and other Web search engines.

Electronic journals will continue to proliferate and it is likely that they will evolve as the Web becomes the primary publication medium. For example, T. Scott Plutchak, speaking at the 2006 North American Serials Interest Group 2006 conference, suggested that the serials container, that is the title, volume and issue number, and publication date, will become less important because publishing on the Web allows individual articles to be published as they are ready. If open access develops into a successful and accepted mode of publishing, more scientific and scholarly information will be freely available to all.

Except for reference works, electronic books will likely only become popular when e-book readers become more similar to print books and when the price of these devices drops significantly. As mentioned earlier, E Ink technology may be the key to that development. Or perhaps the generation that has grown up with the Web will find e-books acceptable as they exist. Then again, it might be that books will have to evolve to better suit the technology.

Until there are adequate means for archiving electronic resources, it would be irresponsible of the library community as a whole to move exclusively to electronic serials and books. The community must come to some consensus about how to archive these resources. In 2005, the National Archives faced the challenge of archiving government documents and awarded a contract to Lockheed Martin to develop a system to preserve documents created by any United States government entity in any format (Reagan, 2006). Perhaps this project will present a solution to this difficult problem that libraries can implement.

CONCLUSION

This brief history of library electronic resources demonstrates that librarians provide access to electronic resources as a way to realize core library values. While certain problems have persisted throughout the development of these resources, such as the inability to adequately search across a variety of resources, there is hope that these problems will be resolved with time and effort from librarians and vendors. It is certain that whatever new electronic resources or ways of accessing them become available in the future, libraries will enter the fray with both enthusiasm and trepidation, along with the will to provide the best possible resources and services to their patrons.

REFERENCES

Antelman, K., Lynema, E., & Pace, A.K. (2006) Toward a twenty-first century library catalog [Electronic version]. *Information Technology and Libraries, 25*(3), 128-39.

Avram, H.D. (1968). MARC: The first two years. *Library Resources & Technical Services, 12*(3), 245-250.

Bjorner, S., & Ardito, S.C. (2003). Online before the Internet: Early pioneers tell their stories [Electronic version]. *Searcher, 11*(6), 36-46.

Boss, R.W. (1989). Current uses of automated systems: A review and status report. In A.P. Trezza (Ed.) *Changing technology: Opportunity and challenge* (pp. 99-102). Boston: G.K. Hall & Co.

Boss, R.W., & Marcum, D.B. (1980, September-October). The library catalog: COM and on-line options. *Library Technology Reports, 16*, 443-527.

Christian, R. (1978). *The electronic library: Bibliographic data bases, 1978-1979.* White Plains, NY: Knowledge Industry Publications, Inc.

Cole, L. (2004). Back to basics: What is the e-journal? *The Serials Librarian, 47*(1/2), 77-87.

Convey, J. (1992). *Online information retrieval: An introductory manual to principles and practice* (4th ed.). London: Library Association Publishing.

Dialog invented online information services. (2006). Retrieved November 10, 2007, from http://www.dialog.com/about/

Eaton, N.L., MacDonald, L.B., & Saule, M.R. (1989). *CD-ROM and other optical information systems: Implementation issues for libraries.* Phoenix, AZ: Oryx Press.

Flanders, B.L. (1990). Spinning the hits: CD-ROM networks in libraries [Electronic version]. *American Libraries, 21*(11), 1032-1033.

Flint, E. (2000). Introducing the Baen Free Library. Retrieved November 11, 2007, from http://www.baen.com/library/home.htm

Gall, J.E. (2005). Dispelling five myths about e-books [Electronic version]. *Information Technology and Libraries, 24*(1), 25-31.

General overview. (n.d.). Retrieved November 11, 2007, from, http://muse.jhu.edu/about/muse/overview.html

Google milestones. (2006). Retrieved November 11, 2007, from http://www.google.com/corporate/history.html#2005

Hart, M. (1992). Gutenberg: The history and philosophy of Project Gutenberg by Michael Hart. Retrieved November 11, 2007, from http://www.gutenberg.org/wiki/Gutenberg:The_History_and_Philosophy_of_Project_Gutenberg_by_Michael_Hart

Horny, K.L. (1982). Online catalogs: Coping with the choices. *The Journal of Academic Librarianship, 8*(1), 14-19.

Librarian...educator...historian...entrepreneur. (2006). *NextSpace, 3*, 2-7.

Lynch, C.A., & Preston, C.M. (1990). Internet access to information resources. In M.E. Williams

(Ed.), *Annual review of information science and technology* (Vol. 25, pp. 263-312). Amsterdam: Elsevier Science Publishing B.V.

Moore, C.W. (1981). User reactions to online catalogs: An exploratory study. *College & Research Libraries, 12*(4), 295-302.

Mullin, C. (2002). A funny thing happened on the way to the e-book [Electronic version]. *PNLA Quarterly, 67*(1), 20-27.

Nissley, M. (1990). CD-ROMs, licenses and librarians. In M. Nissley & N.M. Nelson (Eds.), *CD-ROM licensing and copyright issues for libraries* (pp. 1-17). Westport, CT: Meckler Corporation.

Norden, D.J., & Lawrence, G.H. (1981). Public terminal use in an online catalog: Some preliminary results. *College & Research Libraries, 12*(4), 308-316.

Pooley, C. G. (1990). CD-ROM licensing issues. In M. Nissley & N.M. Nelson (Eds.), *CD-ROM licensing and copyright issues for libraries* (pp. 31-43). Westport, CT: Meckler Corporation.

Ranganathan, S.R. (1963). *The five laws of library science.* Bombay, India: Asia Publishing House.

Reagan, B. (2006, December). The digital ice age [Electronic version]. *Popular Mechanics, 183*(12), 97-94, 139.

Roose, T. (1988, October 15). Computerized reference tools of the next decade: Taking the plunge with CD-ROM. *Library Journal, 113*, 56-61.

Tenopir, C. (1986, March 1). Databases on CD-ROM. *Library Journal, 111*, 68-69.

Torkington, R.B. (1974). MARC and its application to library automation. In M.J. Voigt (Vol. Ed.), *Advances in librarianship* (Vol. 4, pp. 1-23). New York: Academic Press Inc.

Turoff, M., & Hiltz, S.R. (1982). The electronic journal: A progress report [Electronic version]. *Journal of the American Society for Information Science, 33*(4), 195-202.

Chapter II
Strategic Planning for Electronic Resource Management

Robert L. Bothmann
Minnesota State University, USA

Melissa Holmberg
Minnesota State University, USA

ABSTRACT

This chapter addresses electronic resource management from the perspectives of planning, policy, and workflow issues experienced by libraries. Many libraries attempt to transfer and incorporate the print workflow onto electronic resource management. The result is a feeling of chaos and lack of control. The challenges, methods, and impacts on electronic resource management perceived by libraries are described. The authors suggest methods and ideas to address these topics that may help libraries create a sense of order for electronic resource management.

INTRODUCTION

An overarching theme with electronic resource management is the rapid growth of electronic resources. Because of this growth libraries are experiencing issues related to time management, staffing, and the time-honored task of deliberating the set-up of logical workflow systems for such resources. Unlike the traditional library workflow of ordering and paying for print resources, cataloging those items, and processing them for the shelves—a workflow in which the different library units know their roles and responsibilities—most libraries consolidate all things electronic such as A-Z title lists, federated search engines, e-journals, abstract-and-indexing databases, dark archives and electronic resource management tools, and allow an electronic resources librarian to handle most, if not all, responsibilities from pre-order activities to access set-up and maintenance.

When all these activities are left in the care of one or two people in a library, many of these librarians are unsure what to do. Chaos reigns. The managers of electronic resources are putting out fires rather than conducting fire prevention activities and education. They need to break down the chaos into pieces that can be controlled and managed. They need to let some fires rage and work on preventing the next ones from happening. They need to step away, get some fresh air, and find some calm in the chaos.

This chapter reviews electronic resource management, defined as overseeing all aspects of electronic resource management from pre-selection activities such as trials and initial vendor inquiries to renewal/cancellation decisions, from the perspectives of planning, policy, and workflow issues experienced by many libraries. Each of these topics discusses some of the challenges perceived by libraries, the methods libraries use to address these challenges, and the impact of these challenges on electronic resource management.

BACKGROUND

Electronic resource management may be defined in various ways. The definition may be as narrow as an A-to-Z list of serial titles (Marshall & Kawasaki, 2005), a focus on an approach to budget management (Jasper & Sheble, 2005), or a broader concept like a content management system to create Web pages, provide administrative functions, and track license agreements (Brown, Nelson, & Wineburgh-Freed, 2005; Robbins & Smith, 2004). While there is a great deal of literature devoted to various types of electronic resources, particularly to electronic journals (Burrows, 2006; Curtis, 2005; Curtis, Scheschy, & Tarango, 2000; Fowler, 2004; Islam & Chowdhury, 2006), very little has been written about electronic resource management in a more holistic sense, with the exception of two books on the topic.

Conger's (2004) book provides an in-depth discussion on collaborative learning, management of staff, and group participation related to electronic resources work. She addresses leadership and management, budgeting as planning, the infrastructure and tools of electronic resource management, as well as cataloging and technology needs. The purpose of the book is to instruct library professionals on the incorporation of electronic resource assessment as a continuing learning process, and how to use that learning process to make electronic resource management more stable within a library. Gregory's (2006) revised edition of *Selecting and Managing Electronic Resources* provides descriptions and checklists for policies, selection, budgeting, cataloging and access, and assessment. It supplies a number of details that are helpful in the formation of effective electronic resource management workflow.

As Collins (2005) notes, the growing number of electronic resources requires more sophisticated workflows and is changing the nature of work for many professional librarians into that of workflow managers for updating and maintaining A-to-Z lists, vendor MARC records, and openURL. She foresees the electronic resource management tools as a means to allow the OPAC to become the comprehensive access point for library resources again. In particular, Collins stresses the importance of implementing various management tools and allowing flexibility in cataloging practices and workflow, such as what a library will accept in the OPAC. For example, brief MARC records may be a better option for the cataloging of electronic resources because they allow for a faster, timelier entry into the system that also streamlines the cataloging workflow (Curtis, 2005, pp. 288-289).

Beyond the cataloging part of the electronic resources workflow, there are other workflow functions unique to electronic resources management. These tasks include licensing, access set-up, troubleshooting, link maintenance, inter-database linking (e.g., between catalogs, abstract-and-indexing databases, federated search tools, openURL resolvers), vendor negotiation—the list is extensive, but has been summarized by Curtis (2005, pp. 97-98) from Duranceau and Hepfer's survey results (2002) on electronic resource management staffing. Obviously workflow for electronic resources is quite different from the traditional resource management workflow.

The traditional library workflow for tangible resources such as monographs, serials, audio, and video materials is a systematic process of review and selection by subject bibliographers, order placement with a vendor and verification upon receipt by acquisitions, description and processing by catalogers, and proper shelving by circulation. This flow from one library unit to another works well for tangible resources and much of this work is accomplished through the use of paraprofessional library employees (Congleton, 2002). Professional librarians oversee the process, assign much of the routine work to paraprofessionals, and typically resolve problems or complete professional work such as the assignment of funds to budgets or the creation of original catalog records (Graves & Arthur, 2006). This workflow also may be managed entirely within a library's integrated library system (ILS) for the purposes of order tracking, budget encumbrances and payments, catalog access, and inventory.

The ILS is ideal for this workflow management because it has been constructed with this workflow in mind. The ILS can alert a library when the receipt of a resource is overdue, display all of a library's holdings accessible in the catalog, and inform the patron via the catalog of the availability of a particular resource through a status notice in the circulation system. With the exception of computer software, tangible library resources require very few extraordinary treatments for the purposes of acquisition, catalog access, and circulation.

Electronic resources, however, do not fit well within this traditional workflow. Resource selection, ordering, and payment may be easily managed within the traditional ILS workflow, but the similarity ends there. Once an order is placed, there is no mechanism in an ILS to notify a library of nonreceipt or the availability of a resource to the library user. There is nothing tangible for

acquisitions to send to cataloging for the provision of access. The ILS cannot handle licensing issues or patron authentication, and many look to the electronic resource management system (ERMS) to fix the gaps in what the ILS can do (Allgood, 2006; Harvell, 2005).

While a library may provide a catalog record for an electronic resource, the nature of many of these resources such as abstract-and-indexing databases or full-text aggregators may be "lost" in the catalog for the purposes of patron use. Thus many libraries provide access to aggregators and indexing databases from their library's Website, often from some kind of pathfinder or guide to electronic resources (Brown, Nelson, Wineburgh-Freed, 2005; Shorten, 2006), as well as providing additional full-text access points via openURL, creating yet another difference in the workflow.

The variety of resources encompassed in the idea of electronic resource management is also very different in nature from traditional resources. Libraries are faced with products that aide in resource access for patrons such as A-to-Z lists, openURL servers, and abstract-and-indexing databases, federated search engines, and resources that provide full-text content such as a publisher's electronic-journal content, journal-content platforms such as Project MUSE® or JSTOR,® and content aggregators such as Ebsco's Academic Search Premier. Yet there are other products not used by library users that also fall into the realm of electronic resources. These resources include analysis tools such as Gold Rush reports or OCLC's collection analysis, ERMS, and proxy servers or other authentication tools.

With all of these choices, each with different benefits and unique issues, it becomes difficult for libraries to effectively plan the management of these resources. Libraries are faced with the challenges of strategically planning and managing their collections of electronic resources, providing cross-training or redundancy to cover temporary and permanent staff changes, and designing new workflows for electronic resources, rather than adapting from print policies and procedures.

To get a sense of where libraries stand in electronic resource management, the authors conducted an informal survey (Bothmann & Holmberg, 2006) that was posted to the ERIL discussion list. Forty respondents completed the survey and another seventeen respondents provided partial responses. The survey consisted of 26 multiple-choice and open-ended questions. The questions posed in the survey asked electronic resource librarians to identify resources for which they have planned, developed procedures, and documented their workflow. Additionally, the survey requested comments on the challenges and the impacts related to planning, procedures, and documentation. Demographic questions included library size and type, electronic resources offered, total numbers of professionals and paraprofessionals, and numbers of professional and paraprofessional librarians involved with electronic resources.

The results of the survey revealed four common themes related to electronic resource management that libraries perceive as challenges. These themes include lack of adequate staffing levels, constant change in resources, budget issues, and communication with vendors, colleagues, and users. The survey responses present the many distinctions in management that are different from the workflow designed for print resources. Electronic resources come with demands that may also be barriers to some libraries. These demands include licensing issues and patron authentication, bibliographic control and access questions, and overall management for purchases, renewals, and license tracking.

Excluding electronic journal titles, many respondents indicated that they now provide access to a great number of electronic resources, typically between 50 and 250 separate resources. Regardless of size, most of these libraries employ only one to three professional librarians to manage electronic resources, often with little or no paraprofessional support. Thus these tasks

fall to a few librarians to manage upwards of 50 different license agreements, vendors, renewals, statistics, verification of access, authentication, and catalog access, as well as any other aspects of work entailed by electronic resources.

PLANNING

Planning for electronic resources is perhaps the most important and least practiced activity in libraries. Electronic resources present a number of challenges to the traditional library operations and workflow that must be addressed in order to provide smooth management. The challenges faced by many libraries include operational issues such as the number of staff assigned to electronic resource management duties, staying in-step with technological and vendor changes in electronic resources, budgeting limited resources for the acquisition of resources, and communication with vendors and amongst librarians and administrators. Other challenges relate to access issues such as management tools like openURL knowledge bases, federated searching, catalog records, and authentication.

Staffing for electronic resources is perhaps the biggest challenge most libraries face. The results of the authors' survey indicate that the majority of libraries, regardless of total staff size, typically have only one or two professional librarians involved in electronic resource management. Paraprofessional involvement varied widely with one-third having no paraprofessional involvement, a tenth having more than five, and the rest having one to three paraprofessionals involved in the workflow. In response to challenges related to planning for electronic resources, one librarian answered: "How can you plan if you don't have enough people to do the work?"

Some libraries address the challenge of limited staffing by distributing work among existing staff, prioritizing projects according to staff availability, and emphasizing the need to invest more staff time in the electronic resource environment. Others have developed a team structure to meet the staffing need, delegating specific tasks to paraprofessionals. Another common technique is to create a committee of individuals to examine choices for a particular resource, narrow the choices and present a limited set of options from which the library may choose. However, once a resource is chosen, the investigation often continues as libraries research alternatives and new technological developments for a given resource.

Respondents indicated that the impacts of staffing issues center on training and time. One respondent said "when the organization of the workflow is not managed efficiently and completely, it is nearly impossible to teach others in how to manage it." One library indicated that staffing levels prevent them from implementing many resources, thus limiting their choices only to those resources that come with vendor back-end management. Implementing new technologies, such as openURL, can be labor-intensive and take time away from other job responsibilities. Some libraries indicated time-management issues related to developing in-house management tools which then have little or no support once completed, and spending too much time on things that could be better addressed with "out-of-box software."

Change was another planning challenge indicated by respondents. One librarian commented, "just about everything related to e-resources management changes too quickly to do any planning," and another said they do not have time to plan; "instead we play catch-up all the time." Many libraries use various tools to address the challenges of electronic resource changes. One method is to use a shared email system and a database of tasks to track and manage changes in resources. Other libraries only implement those services that can be supported by their small staff size or that have significant vendor support. Still others limit the number of vendors from whom they acquire electronic resources to help limit the number of changes.

Respondents indicated that the budget available for the acquisition of resources was another planning challenge. "Some planning (e.g., purchasing new tools/services) requires money that isn't available," is one comment that demonstrates this theme in survey responses. Other libraries noted that cancellation of some resources is the only way to acquire a new resource. Libraries address their budgetary issues by diverting funds from their print resource budgets or rearranging budget priorities when necessary. Cancellation of microform or print subscriptions duplicated by online content was one method of rearranging the budget. Another option is making use of consortial opportunities and discounts. Many libraries indicated constant requests to administration for more money.

The fourth major challenge cited by respondents was communication related to knowledge and understanding of electronic resources. Vendor communication is often frustrating because some try to work with librarians to improve their products and services and to create win-win situations, while other vendors are simply trying to earn a particular dollar amount. Publishers who are breaking into the electronic resource environment sometimes create communication problems as they lack an understanding of the access requirements libraries have (e.g., openURL, IP authentication). Couple these issues with an often-mistrustful attitude on both sides and communication becomes a big issue in electronic resource management.

Communication with administrators usually involves justifying the expense of resources, proving the need for resources, and obtaining budgetary support. Communication with users typically involves instruction on the use of resources and re-instruction as the resource interfaces constantly change. However, communication with other librarians tended to be the most problematic issue. Communication issues with fellow colleagues cited by electronic resources librarians were the acceptance of the need for particular resources, a lack of realistic expectations of what one electronic resource librarian can do with the large number of resources and vendors, as well as of the technological capacities of electronic resources, agreement on resource needs, and assistance with the work from other staff.

Libraries address communication through various methods, such as asking questions on discussion lists, developing promotional materials for librarians to use for patron instruction, and sending continuous emails to library staff about projects and tasks related to electronic resources. With regard to vendor communication issues, some librarians and vendors can overcome the challenges. Librarians must simply keep working at communication until they find a style that works and until they can discern which vendors have problematic representatives and which have problematic organization cultures. Whenever possible, librarians should meet with the representatives and develop the communication and partnership. And, whenever possible, support those vendors who try to work with librarians and quit supporting those who do not. It is also worth ensuring that vendors meet with library administration, even if that meeting is brief. This can help with administration understanding any vendor representative problems as well as communicating the importance of the vendor's product by the administration showing some interest.

The responses from libraries regarding planning for electronic resources demonstrate the reactive nature of electronic resource management, rather than work defined by any sort of plan. While it is not necessary and is probably impossible to create any kind of comprehensive plan, most libraries would benefit from developing a prioritized list of goals for electronic resources to guide their work. Creating a small electronic resources committee of key players in a library's electronic resource management work is the first step in a good planning process. These key players should come from various divisions of the library, such as public services, cataloging, and systems,

as well as a library's electronic resources librarian, when such a role exists.

A first task of the committee should be to identify all of the staff involved in electronic resources workflow, from administrative support personnel to administrators (Mi & Sullenger, 2006). Often some of the work created from electronic resource management may be accomplished by a rigorous examination of staff workload and reassignment of duties to create a core group of individuals to focus on electronic resources within the existing organizational structure. Librarians should always make note of repetitive tasks that may be delegated to paraprofessionals and begin delegating that work. Another option is to evaluate and plan for a major reorganization of library units, which may or may not be feasible depending upon the current staff size and the organizational structure (Curtis, 2005, 98-99). Regardless of the path a library takes, the examination of specific tasks in relation to existing positions is a beneficial exercise for assessing the current situation and planning for the future.

For budgetary concerns, the committee may create a list of electronic resource types, such as A-to-Z lists, openURL, assessment tools, abstract-and-indexing databases, full-text databases, and so forth. The list may be used to identify and prioritize what a library has, what it needs but is lacking, and what it wants to have but is not essential for service to patrons. Inquiries and cost quotes are easy to obtain from vendors and may be added to the list to show the dollar amounts required to obtain a desired resource. Although such an exercise does not achieve acquisition of the desired resources, it provides an easy plan libraries can use if and when funding is available. A comprehensive assessment of the materials budget, particularly of serial subscriptions may provide a number of opportunities for targeted cancellations to free funds for desired resources.

Another important task for an electronic resources committee is to work on communication issues. Identifying specific people to interact with vendors aides in communication and understanding for both libraries and vendors. Another important communication task is the development of a vision, definition of common goals related to a library's mission, and the involvement of staff (J. White, 2005) in the process. Communicating changes and new developments in a variety of different ways, such as email, newsletters, staff meetings, and one-on-one interaction helps staff to feel like they are in the loop and a part of the process.

By creating an electronic resource committee, nonelectronic resource librarians can gain a greater understanding not only of the complexity of managing these resources, but also of the many ways others unintentionally sabotage the management of electronic resources. Often fear is at the root of these various biases: librarians refusing to attend training to avoid realizing how little they know; librarians complaining constantly about the problems with electronic resources and wearing on the morale of those managing them; or librarians working hard to limit the number of resources to either limit the number of interfaces they need to keep up with or to protect the much smaller print budgets. Having more librarians, such as those on an electronic resource committee, seeing these biases can possibly build more support and morale for those managing the resources. Furthermore, librarians may start to realize the difficult situation they have placed electronic resource librarians in: we never tell collection developers that they can only order books and other materials from only 10 publishers; we do not complain incessantly about how bad a particular book is; we do not ignore librarians when they are pointing out how helpful a particular reference book is for certain questions. By overcoming the different biases and fears, more librarians can participate in the management of electronic resources, will understand the various issues and the impact of these on the library's services, and hopefully will strive to view electronic resources within the larger organizational planning process. For

example, librarians across the board could start considering:

- How much time should a library invest in its Website for displaying its electronic resources, if it believes it will migrate to a next-gen OPAC
- Whether to add a next-gen OPAC or a federated search tool upon reaching a threshold for electronic resource interfaces (when librarians and patrons start complaining frequently, the library has probably reached the threshold)
- Which tool(s) are needed to improve services, access, and management; migration to these tools; and internal and external training, including instructing patrons at the desk, in drop-in sessions, via traditional instruction sessions, through online tutorials, and promotions of these new resources

POLICIES

The development and use of policies is critical in electronic resource management and for communicating a library's goals. Policies set guidelines of practice that aid in electronic resource management (H. White, 2005). Aside from collection development policies, libraries need policies that address issues such as types of resources to support, licensing issues, and user access. Other policy topics include how and which resources should be cataloged, placed in a content management system or subject guide, or added to an ERMS.

Staffing and time are one of the challenges that libraries face with policy development. Libraries indicated that the lack of sufficient staff requires all of their time for managing electronic resources and does not allow any time for the consideration and development of policies. Change was also cited as a problem for policy development because vendors, products, and staff opinions are inconsistent and change too often. Decisions are often made when there is not an ideal solution, which causes the need to remake a decision after seeing how things work out or when the technology evolves to meet a library's needs. Communication is another barrier to policy development, particularly because of the time required to educate other librarians on the issues.

Respondents addressed policy challenges in differing ways. Less than half of the respondents have developed any particular policy, and most policies relate to electronic resource trials, inclusion of resources in the A-to-Z list, and the addition of resources with access restrictions. Some libraries create task forces to deal with policy development issues. Others send emails with justifications for decisions, or simply deal with issues as they arise rather than creating and following a specific policy.

The perceived impact of a lack of policies on electronic resource management was also varied. Some respondents see policy writing as cumbersome and time-consuming. Others felt that policies may be too restrictive or may make some management tasks more difficult. Still others feel that there is no way to create a universal policy or that their management practice is non-standard and therefore their policies would not be valid. Another impact of the lack of policy development indicated in survey responses was the pressure to keep up with peer institutions, which a policy might prohibit or even become meaningless if the administration does not buy into the policies.

While at times painful and time consuming, policy and procedure development are essential for electronic resource management. The time invested in the creation and writing of documentation will provide benefits now and in the future. A library that has a policy concerning the requirements of specific types of electronic resources can use that policy to eliminate investigation or consideration of vendor products that do not meet desired standards. For example, if your policy states that only those resources that are openURL

compliant will be added to your collection, then time can be saved by not adding nonopenURL resources. Additional policies that libraries may want to consider writing include:

- Who can contact vendors under what circumstances?
- What sorts of troubleshooting should be done prior to contacting vendors?
- Should you go with the lowest cost vendor every year or should you try to stay with fewer vendors?
- What will you do about password-protected resources: not use them at all; use them by only via mediated access; use a scripted Webpage to display passwords (and if so, how often will you change those passwords); program your proxy access to input the passwords upon local authenticated access
- Will you provide access via OPAC and/or Website: all electronic resources only via Website or via both; just ebooks in the OPAC the others on the Website

While many would like to write a policy and consider it done, librarians must remember that what works now may not be feasible as more electronic resources are added to a collection. Thus, strategic planning, workflow, and policies remain intertwined.

Furthermore, communicating this decision to the vendor lets them know the specifics of what your library desires in a resource, and may influence their development of the product. Another reason to create policy and procedure documents is to assist with training and answering of questions. Brisson (1999) and H. White (2005) both note the benefits of documentation for these purposes, and describe methods libraries can use in the development of documentation. However, once documented, it is also important to maintain and update those documents. As Wisniewski (2006) observes, the largest benefit from an intranet for online documentation is the allowance of all participants to be authors. Some libraries have begun using this methodology for communication and documentation through Web logs and wikis for documenting and instructing technical services workflow (Traill & Huismann, 2004).

WORKFLOW

Related to planning and policy development, workflow and the documentation of the workflow is a crucial aspect of electronic resources management. Some of the librarians who responded to our survey indicated that they documented part or all of their electronic resource management workflow in order to determine what is not getting done. Others did so to create consistency, particularly in terms of requests from other librarians. Others found the documentation to be comforting to other employees, even if the workflow changed and made the documentation outdated. Some found documentation necessary to ensure each step is completed in a particular process, to better prepare for staff changes and leaves, or to begin a database trail. Still others believed documenting the workflow led to a better understanding of what is going on and improved communication of workflow tasks to others in the library.

While the reasons for documenting the workflow are numerous, several libraries perceived compelling reasons to not take on this task. Some believed the workflow is too cumbersome to document. Others work in libraries in which most electronic resource management is done on a case-by-case basis because there are too few common issues to make workflow documentation relevant. Some cited lack of time and personnel, while others indicated that the organizational culture precludes the documentation process (e.g., no one documents anything; cannot use the documentation in benchmarking; turf issues). Some also stated that the workflow is still undetermined and therefore cannot be documented.

Starting the workflow documentation process can be daunting because some sections can be problematic. For example, licensing is something that is done at all libraries, regardless of whether they accept all licenses as is or actually negotiate every one before signing. While most libraries have written or verbal priorities, few actually have lines drawn in the sand that will prohibit them from signing an agreement with a vendor. As such, writing the workflow for license negotiations can be difficult when it is far from an ideal situation and when it is beyond what most librarians thought they would be doing when getting their MLS degree. Furthermore, every vendor seems to have different requirements, both legal and technical, that make a documented workflow quite difficult to develop or follow. Conger (2004, pp. 127-132) stresses the importance of developing guidelines and provisions for licensing to assist electronic resource librarians with vendor negotiation. Documentation allows librarians the ability to reference specific needs and to verify specific aspects of a license when questions arise. Gregory's (2006, pp. 79-101) chapter sections on licensing include a number of considerations and helpful questions for any library to development documentation on licensing.

Once the licenses are signed, other workflow issues present themselves. How do libraries communicate license information to their patrons, to their own staff in other units, to their administrators? Should they cut and paste the exact terms of the license into an ERMS or Web page, or should they interpret the terms and rewrite them in more understandable language? Should libraries only communicate to one group and not the others? What if the library does not have an ERMS—how can information be tracked and updated easily? If a library does have an ERMS, how will the short-staffed area populate and maintain the ERMS? Will a library ever be able to retrospectively add in the terms from ongoing licenses that were negotiated five years ago? Should libraries start with those and work their way up to the licenses negotiated this fiscal year? As these questions suggest, documenting aspects of workflow may involve a number of tough questions to answer; however, leaving these questions unanswered will only allow the confusion and lack of control many libraries have about electronic resource management to grow.

Control, or lack thereof, also influences the documentation of workflow. When parts of the workflow are outside the realm of electronic resources management, it is difficult to document that workflow. When other librarians and staff do not agree with the current workflow, documenting it can generate some heated discussions. The constant change through acquisitions and mergers in the vendor and publisher realm, new or changed license terms, new statistics metrics and/or accessibility, and the myriad other things that affect electronic resources management workflow daily all contribute to the feeling of not having any control.

Despite the difficulties and barriers to documenting workflow, libraries must do so if for no other reason than to help the new people that will inevitably manage the electronic resources. A library's current state of electronic resource management chaos may dictate the starting point for documentation of workflow. For example, if a library is unsure of what is not getting done, start with an outline of the entire lifecycle of electronic resources, from pre-selection activities to renewal/cancellation (for assistance with this task, see the Digital Library Federation's ERMI workflow in appendix B [Jewell, et al., 2004]). In the outline, also list who is currently doing each activity and note which areas are lacking assigned responsibility. Such an exercise may help with reassignment of responsibilities among library staff or possibly provide justification for increasing staff size. The outline will also point out tasks that are not currently being done, are not assigned and not attended to consistently, or even point out tasks that are superfluous. If on the other hand the electronic resources staff find

that certain steps are forgotten, then documenting those particular procedures in the workflow will help bring more control and organization to that workflow, from which a library may create a checklist of activities that must be completed and further standardize the workload.

If a library can maintain an ERMS, the tool can be helpful with improving workflow. Currently, the different ones offer different features. Some libraries are choosing their OPAC vendor's ERMS to help them manage the acquisitions module, payments, and so forth. Others are choosing an ERMS that is from another vendor to have access to other features or to have the ERMS interact better with their selected openURL and/or federated search tool. Eventually, librarians would like to see ERMS, federated search, ILS, openURL, and statistics all interacting seamlessly. For now, libraries must discern what their greatest needs are (workflow knowledge is helpful here) and to then select the ERMS that will help cover those needs best. Some advantages to ERMS, if maintained, include:

- Multiple staff can access information about vendors and decisions: so, if a library has decided to cancel several databases for a more comprehensive one, that decision can be documented in the ERMS and save folks the challenge of remembering what they did and why or of searching through meeting minutes to find the explanations
- Vendor usernames and passwords can be stored in a central place
- Information about trials can be included

CONCLUSION

Many libraries currently have some variation of the electronic resources librarian as a professional position. The placement of this position within the organizational structure often varies. Some libraries place the position in public services, others in technical services (Ginanni, 2006), and some centralize the work of electronic resources management, whereas others have the workload distributed throughout the organization (Fischer & Barton, 2005). Too many libraries appear to make little or any use of paraprofessional staff for routine electronic resource workflow tasks. And many libraries are caught between the print and the electronic worlds of information organization, with a primary focus on acquiring and holding print resources (McDonald, 2006). Their organizational and workflow structure is heavily influenced by the print workflow and little attention has been given to reforming that structure for electronic resources, as evidenced by the survey responses regarding planning, policies and workflow.

Planning, policy making, and documenting workflow and procedures are intertwined activities that are hallmarks of professionals. Ignoring them, waiting for the ideal situations to arise, and hoping for best practices to arise will not prevent the inevitable need for libraries to begin treating electronic resource management now before the perceived chaos of electronic resources takes over and inhibits user services and access. Libraries must regularly work towards creating policies, documenting their workflow, and planning in all areas of electronic resource management. Attending a workshop can upstart the process. Writing some outlines on the plane home, while everything is still fresh in the mind, can start wonders at libraries. Gathering some colleagues together with a particular task in mind or pounding something out during a slow hour on the reference desk or a really boring meeting can also get a new leaf turned over.

Managing electronic resources need not be the daunting, chaotic state that so many libraries described in their survey responses. As librarians, we have an affinity to structure and order that is clearly evident in our print resources workflow. What we have to remember is that this order did not just happen—our predecessors created that order. We as electronic resources librarians can also create that order and efficiency for the electronic resources era we now enjoy. We simply have to address one issue at time, one policy at a time, one workflow task at a time, chip away at the chaos we perceive and if not order, then at least a clear path, with documented decisions and policies will develop out of this process and lead to better electronic resources management. Just remember to keep communicating with all interested and biased parties along each step. It will be the only way to discern our best practices as a profession in this new area of librarianship.

REFERENCES

Allgood, J.E. (2006). Friend or foe?—Digital resources within library collections. *Against the Grain, 18*(2), 24-30.

Bothmann, R.L., & Holmberg, M. (2006). *Electronic resources planning and management.* Unpublished electronic survey conducted on ERIL from 27 November to 1 December 2006.

Brisson, R. (1999). Online documentation in library technical services. *Technical Services Quarterly, 16*(3), 1-19.

Brown, J.F., Nelson, J.L., & Wineburgh-Freed, M. (2005.) Customized electronic resources management system for a multi-library university: Viewpoint from one library. In G. Ives (Ed.), *Electronic journal management systems: Experiences from the field* (pp. 89-102). New York: Haworth Information Press.

Burrows, S. (2006). A review of electronic journal acquisition, management, and use in health sciences libraries. *Journal of the Medical Library Association, 24*(1), 67-74.

Collins, M. (2005). The effects of e-journal management tools and services on serials cataloging. *Serials Review, 31*, 291-297.

Conger, J.E. (2004). *Collaborative electronic resource management: From acquisitions to assessment.* Westport, CT: Libraries Unlimited.

Congleton, R. (2002). Re-evaluating technical services workflow for integrated library systems. *Library Collections, Acquisitions, & Technical Services, 26*(4), 337-341.

Curtis, D. (2005). *E-journals: A how-to-do-it manual for building, managing, and supporting electronic journal collections.* New York: Neal-Schuman Publishers.

Curtis, D., Scheschy, V.M., & Tarango, A.R. (2000). *Developing and managing electronic journal collections: A how-to-do-it manual for librarians.* New York: Neal-Schuman Publishers.

Duranceau, E.F., & Hepfer, C. (2002). Staffing for electronic resource management: The results of a survey. *Serials Review, 28*(4), 316-320.

Fischer, K.S., & Barton, H. (2005). The landscape of e-journal management. *Journal of Electronic Resources in Medical Libraries, 2*(3), 57-63.

Fowler, D.C. (Ed.). (2004). *E-serials collection management: Transitions, trends, and technicalities.* New York: Haworth Information Press.

Ginanni, K. (2006). Talk about: E-resources librarian to the rescue? Creating the über librarian: Turning model job descriptions into practical positions. *The Serials Librarian, 50*(1/2), 173-177.

Graves, T., & Arthur, M.A. (2006). Developing a crystal clear future for the serials unit in an electronic environment: Results of a workflow analysis. *Serials Review, 32*(4), 238-246.

Gregory, Vicki L. (2006). *Selecting and managing electronic resources: A how-to-do-it manual for librarians* (Rev. ed.). New York: Neal-Schuman Publishers.

Harvell, T.A. (2005). Electronic resources management systems: The experience of beta testing and implementation. In G. Ives (Ed.), *Electronic journal management systems: Experiences from the field* (pp. 125-136). New York: Haworth Information Press.

Islam, M.S., & Chowdhury, M.A.K. (2006). Organisation and management issues for electronic journals: A Bangladesh perspective. *Malaysian Journal of Library & Information Science, 11*(1), 61-74.

Jasper, R.P., & Sheble, L. (2005). Evolutionary approach to managing e-resources. In G. Ives (Ed.), *Electronic journal management systems: Experiences from the field* (pp. 55-70). New York: Haworth Information Press.

Jewell, T.D., Anderson, I., Chandler, A., Farb, S.E., Parker, K., Riggio, A., et. al. (2004). *Electronic resource management: Report of the DLF ERM initiative.* Washington, D.C.: Digital Library Federation. http://www.diglib.org/pubs/dlf102/

Marshall, S.P., & Kawasaki, J.L. (2005). The master serial list at Montana State University: A simple, easy to use approach. In G. Ives (Ed.), *Electronic journal management systems: Experiences from the field* (pp. 3-15). New York: Haworth Information Press.

Mi, J., & Sullenger, P. (2006). Examining workflows and redefining roles: Auburn University and the College of New Jersey. *The Serials Librarian, 50*(3/4), 279-283.

Robbins, S., & Smith, M. (2004). Managing e-resources: A database-driven approach. In D. C. Fowler (Ed.), *E-serials collection management: Transitions, trends, and technicalities* (pp. 239-251). New York: Haworth Information Press.

Shorten, J. (2006). What do libraries really do with electronic resources? The practice in 2003. In A. Fenner (Ed.), *Integrating print and digital resources in library collections* (pp. 55-73). New York: Haworth Information Press.

Traill, S., & Huismann, M. (2004, September). *Beyond books: Blogs at the University of Minnesota.* Unpublished work; poster presentation at the 2004 OLAC Conference, Montréal, Canada.

White, H. (2005). Documentation in technical services. *The Serials Librarian*, *49*(3), 47-55.

White, J. (2005). Effecting change in periodicals service: Management models and a process. *Serials Review*, *32*(1), 22-25.

Wisniewski, J. (2006, March/April). Getting a handle on content. *Online*, 52-54.

Chapter III
Electronic Usage Statistics

Patricia Hults
Rensselaer Polytechnic Institute, USA

ABSTRACT

This chapter provides an overview of electronic usage statistics, including methods of defining, collecting, and using the data. A survey of some of the systems of estimating journal usage in the print environment is followed by a description of the development of electronic usage practices. The important contributions of the COUNTER and SUSHI projects are reviewed, along with issues in the management and use of electronic statistics. Examples of ways these statistics can assist in decision making throughout a product's life cycle are included, as well as other ways usage statistics can prove useful. The chapter concludes with a brief look at the use of statistics in the bibliomining process.

INTRODUCTION

Unless you have a mathematical bent or are one of those individuals who find satisfaction memorizing the major league baseball stats, the topic of user statistics is not immediately intriguing. In fact, it can be mind numbing and tedious, but user statistics are extremely useful, particularly now that we are able to get real, meaningful information—they cannot be ignored. This chapter will start with an examination of early, pre-electronic usage statistics. It will then look at the development of electronic statistics, including both the COUNTER and SUSHI standards. Management issues in collecting and using these statistics will be explored. Some of the applications of these data will be discussed, in the context of an electronic product's life cycle. The value of usage statistics beyond just product evaluation will also be covered.

Generations of librarians have struggled to find ways to practically measure usage of the material they so carefully select. The information on just how many times a book or journal was used is critical in both selection and retention decisions, and in broader collection development strategies. Without a sense of how many times something is used, it becomes impossible to evaluate its worth.

BACKGROUND

Books have always presented less of a problem. You could count the number of times a book was checked out, whether you were counting circulation cards or looking at automatically generated circulation statistics. There was still the bugaboo of in-house use, but there were significant amounts of real circulation data available. Journals presented a much larger challenge. Not only were many libraries organized so that journals were never checked out and sat on open shelves; journals came both bound and in single issues, so that the unit of count was unclear. Indexes, while officially in book format, generally never circulated and therefore their use was as hard to quantify as it was for journals.

Because librarians are an ingenious group, all sorts of methods were devised to estimate in-house use of journals and books and in general to evaluate the worth of a particular title. These efforts ranged from using photocopying requests (Cooper & McGregor, 1994), making correlations between check-outs and in-house use (Walter, 1996), counting journals left on study carrels and near photocopy machines (Bader & Thompson, 1989; Chen, 1972), sticking voluntary usage log sheets on journal protective covers (Konopasek & O'Brien, 1982), and more. Some librarians sent their work-study students skulking in the stacks, trying to measure the ratio of actual vs. recorded use.

Other efforts included using external criteria such as journal impact factors and citation analysis (McCain & Bobick, 1981; Rice, 1979). The journal impact factor is a measure of the number of times a journal is cited in published articles. Interestingly, at least one recent study examining electronic usage and impact factor found no correlation between impact factor and local use of the journals. Duy and Vaughan (2006) examined use of electronic journals from three major vendors; the American Chemical Society, Elsevier, and Wiley, and they found there was not a correlation between impact factor of a particular journal and actual use of that journal on their campus. What they did find more predictive was a local citation figure, calculated by determining how many times a specific journal was cited in articles by campus faculty.

DEVELOPMENT OF ELECTRONIC STATISTICS

Librarians continued the tradition of ingenuity when journals, books, and databases began to be available in electronic format, and they quickly began trying to extract more reliable statistics from the new medium. Before publishers began supplying usage information, librarians explored other sources including institutional Website logs, statistics supplied by A-Z list providers, and those generated by link resolvers. While each of these offered interesting insight into patterns of use, they fell far short of accurately and fully capturing the information librarians sought. Unless an institution had loaded the product on its own server, it was clear that publishers would be the primary suppliers of usage statistics. Initially this data varied widely in what was being measured, and many times, what was being measured was fairly meaningless. An example is the number of pages called up from anywhere within the publisher's site, including help pages, menu pages, and so forth. This type of count served only to create an inaccurate impression of use.

In response to pressures from librarians and for their own internal management needs, publishers began attempting to measure journal usage. Some began to supply pages that captured the number of downloaded files from a particular site. This was progress, but it was still very messy. Article and chapters were often divided into multiple files to reduce download time and each component of a single article might be counted as an individual use, greatly inflating overall usage rates. One publisher's response to statistics requests was to provide the raw data log (Table 1). At least one hapless librarian ended up manually parsing and counting the log files to come up with a reasonable statistic.

It was becoming clear that to realize the promise of electronic statistics, some sort of standardization was imperative. Professionals in both the library and the publishing world began to systematically approach the issue.

The JSTOR user group was an early participant in laying out the desired elements of e-statistics, beginning the work in 1997 (JSTOR, 1998). In 1998, that work was expanded when the International Coalition of Library Consortia (ICOLC, 1998) released "Guideline for Statistical Measures of Usage of Web-based Indexed, Abstracted, and Full Text Resources." Such recommendations started laying out just what elements would be needed to give meaningful information.

Even with these guidelines, information received from publishers continued to be highly variable. A count of article usage or number of database searches sounds straightforward, but

the way these were calculated could be very different. An article count might vary depending on how the article was segmented, whether links to graphics were a separate count, how printing and downloading the article was counted, how repeated use of an article within a short time was counted, whether articles linked to outside the publisher's Website were counted and how. Even what constitutes an article could be variable. Business resources tend to supply statistical graphs, company data, and other type of information that falls outside the standard definition of an article. In fact, at the time this chapter was written, business full-text information remains one of the most problematic subject areas for obtaining standardized user statistics.

Session and search counts also had their inconsistencies. How were repeated logins by the same user within a short time counted? How were searches that include more than one database counted—as one search or two or more? It gets even more complicated when federated searching is thrown into the mix. A single federated search

Table 1. Raw log file of downloads

SIADS	1	1	/SIADS/articles/40473PDF	Jul 13 14:36:28 2003
SIADS	1	1	/SIADS/articles/40473PDF	Jul 13 14:36:30 2003
SIADS	1	1	/SIADS/articles/40473PDF	Jul 13 14:36:38 2003
SIADS	1	1	/SIADS/articles/40473PDF	Jul 13 14:36:54 2003
SIADS	2	171	/SIADS/articles/39830PDF	Jul 14 15:20:06 2003
SIADS	2	171	/SIADS/articles/39830PDF	Jul 14 15:20:10 2003
SIAP	5	1604	/SIAP/articles/31271PDF	Jul 14 15:50:35 2003
SIAP	5	1604	/SIAP/articles/31271PDF	Jul 14 15:50:38 2003
SIAP	5	1604	/SIAP/articles/31271PDF	Jul 14 15:50:41 2003
SIAP	1	337	/SIAP/articles/30631PDF	Jul 14 15:57:00 2003
SIAP	1	337	/SIAP/articles/30631PDF	Jul 14 15:57:03 2003
SIAP	1	337	/SIAP/articles/30631PDF	Jul 14 15:57:06 2003
SIREV	4	761	/SIREV/articles/97006PDF	Jul 14 21:51:31 2003
SIREV	4	761	/SIREV/articles/97006PDF	Jul 14 21:51:34 2003
SIREV	4	761	/SIREV/articles/97006PDF	Jul 14 21:51:38 2003
SIREV	1	53	/SIREV/articles/38305PDF	Jul 15 18:39:24 2003

may generate 20 or more searches (Pesch, 2004). How do you count these?

Another problem was that the way a particular publisher produced its usage data might change, creating significantly different statistics as the method of count was revised. If your publisher changed the way statistics were calculated, the library may have to go back to reharvest data in order to get some consistency, if the older data was available in the new format at all. Another variable was the amount of retrospective data provided by the publisher, impacting how frequently statistics needed to be harvested. The reliability of the publisher providing the data also determined the frequency of pulling those statistics. While publisher statistics were evolving, it behooved an institution to harvest frequently to avoid losing data altogether.

The method of providing the statistics also varied widely, some publishers allowing user generated reports, others limited to requests sent to the publisher, some available only through the consortia manager. The format of the reports, even those containing comparable information, could differ widely, requiring significant intervention to be useful.

By 2000, less than half of publishers offering electronic journals provided usage statistics (Luther, 2000, p. 1), but the momentum was building. In 2000 and 2001 several significant studies and papers were released addressing the issue of standardized statistics for electronic products. 2000 saw Judy Luther's "White Paper on Electronic Journals Usage Statistics," and the initiation of the ARL (Association of Research Libraries) E-Metrics Project. In 2001 ARL released its phase II report (Shim, McClure, Fraser, Bertot, Dagli, & Leahy, 2001) and the IMLS (Institute of Museum and Library Services) published its report, "Developing National Public Library Statistics and Performance Measures for the Networked Environment," (Bertot, McClure, & Ryan, 2000). Other initiatives occurring during this time frame included those by the National

Commission on Libraries and Information Science and NISO's revision of the Z39.7 standard. These early efforts were the background in which the COUNTER Project (Counting Online Usage of NeTworked Electronic Resources) emerged out of work being done by PALS (Publishers and Librarian Solutions).

The PALS usage statistics working group began laying the framework COUNTER would codify. The group initially developed a code of practice including identification of data elements, definitions of these elements, report format recommendations and recommendations on delivery method (JISC, n.d.). This work evolved into the COUNTER Project, which received its own identity in 2002. Its remarkable success is due in large part to its collaborative nature, involving librarians, publishers, and professional societies. The first release of the code of practice appeared in January 2003. To insure long-term development of the standards, COUNTER was incorporated in the United Kingdom later in 2003. By 2006, due in large part to the COUNTER Project and the earlier work it stands upon, virtually all major, and many smaller publishers provided standardized reports—a phenomenal turn around.

The standards have elegance to them. They are not complicated statistics, although producing them can be challenging. They are based on the concept that it is better to have simple, useful statistics that can be provided by all publishers and understood by all users, than complicated reports beyond the scope of many publishers (Shepherd, 2004). This strategy has paid off producing a large number of COUNTER compliant publishers in a remarkably short time, 51 at the time of this writing.

Release 1 covered only journal and database reports. It answered the basic questions of how a search and an article download are defined, what a report should contain, in what format it should be available, and how frequently it should be produced. When publishers became compliant with these standards, it started to become possible to compare and evaluate across publisher platforms, although there is still work to be done to insure consistency across platforms (Davis & Price, 2006).

Release 2 of the code of practice for journals and databases did not expand on the set of data elements. Rather, it refined the content of reports, and most significantly, spelled out very carefully the steps necessary to prove compliance. For these standards to be widely accepted there needed to be a method to verify that any particular publisher was in fact, counting what COUNTER specifies as standard.

The auditing method includes very specific protocol to that end. First a vendor notifies COUNTER that it would like to be authenticated as compliant. The reports are then tested at an approved test library to verify the accuracy of the reports. Only when the test library is satisfied is the vendor certified compliant.

Once a vendor has achieved compliant status as verified by a test library, it has 18 months to complete an audit. This audit includes very specific instructions on the types of tests to be performed. These include specifications of the number of searches or downloads to be done, and the time intervals between searches and downloads, which are then matched against the usage report provided by the vendor. After the initial audit, annual audits are required to maintain compliant status. For Release 2, vendors must be initially audited by June 30, 2007, with annual audits required beginning in 2008 (COUNTER, n.d.).

Along with release 2 for journals and databases, release 1 for books and reference works appeared in 2006. Like the code of practice for journals and databases, the basic elements of the statistics were defined. Electronic book and encyclopedia statistics are even more challenging, since the basic unit of use is not as discrete or easily defined as a journal article. Along with defining these data elements, the necessary content of a report was also laid out, paralleling journal and database reports.

Although COUNTER has gone a long ways to standardize and make useful statistics provided by publishers, there are still some limitations. COUNTER does not addressed the problem of restricting statistics to those generated only by the subscription in question. At least one major publisher regularly includes uses of journals temporarily turned on for promotional use and downloads of titles generated within the institution's IP range, but not subscribed to by the institution. An institution can end up with usage figures for journals it does not subscribe to, but that are subscribed to by individuals within the IP range, such as researchers or professors. If there are multiple subscriptions to the same journal by both the library and individuals, all the usage figures go into the same report. Filtering out data for journals not subscribed to is tedious and becomes even more problematic as statistical gathering becomes automated.

COUNTER has decided that requiring publishers to indicate subscription status would complicate statistical compilation too much. Given the variety of ways institutions have access to journals, such as package deals, current subscriptions and archival subscriptions, and the increasing number of journals that are a combination of open access and fee based, it would be prohibitively complicated to try and sort these access methods out. (P. Shepherd, personal communication, Dec. 14, 2006).

Another problem identified by Davis and Price (2006) is the fact that the publisher platform design and functionality can change the usage count. They studied the ratio of HTML to PDF downloads within publisher platforms. The ratio was consistent from journal to journal, but changed from platform to platform. They also examined one journal mounted on two different platforms and confirmed that the platform varied the format ratio. Some platforms force users into the HTML version first, which then links to the PDF. Other platforms allow users to pick the full-text format from the citation or abstract level, thus reducing the number of HTML downloads and consequently total downloads.

Platforms also interface with URL resolvers and indexes differently. Some link directly to the PDF, others link to a higher level of the journal and force more downloads to navigate to the PDF. These varying methods influence the total number of downloads. Davis and Price suggest using a normalization factor when attempting to compare use across platforms.

Although usage statistics have improved significantly, you only have to go through the exercise of pulling the same statistics for a year you have already harvested once before to realize that there is still a lot of flux in the reliability and availability of the data. The author recently did just that, in preparation for this chapter, and found a disconcerting lack of consistency. One-half year of the data for one publisher was inexplicably missing. Most probably, the publisher would be able to recreate that data, if requested, but on occasion data is just lost. One or two other publishers had corrected errors in previously supplied statistics, a good thing, but which led to inconsistency with data gathered and used a year before. Other publishers had recently become COUNTER compliant and the format and count of data had changed accordingly. Experiences like these lend support to including other criteria in evaluation of electronic products.

Outside the scope of COUNTER is the problem of the sheer volume of statistics coming from multiple sources and in different packages. Library staff have began spending significant time pulling the reports from various sites and trying to merge them into a unified report covering statistics from all the electronic sources of the library. Bordeaux (Bordeaux, Kraemer, & Sullenger, 2005) reported spending 16 hours per month pulling and compiling data; the staff of the author's institution spends an average 14 hours per month. As library holdings migrate to electronic format, more and more electronic statistics will be available, requiring more staff time to process the data.

At the same time standards for electronic statistics were being developed, a parallel movement was occurring around electronic resource management elements. ERMI (the Digital Library Federation's Electronic Resource Management Initiative) began defining the elements necessary for an effective electronic resource management system. ERMI evolved into ERMI2 which included requirements for usage data intake and reporting. COUNTER had defined the statistical elements and reporting format; ERMI2 began looking at protocols to move that data into an ERM. While the data itself was now standardized, the way of moving it around was not.

In the summer of 2005 a small group met to start addressing this problem. The group included three librarians (Ivy Anderson, California Digital Library; Adam Chandler, Cornell University Library; and Tim Jewell, University of Washington Libraries) and representatives from four companies (Ted Fons, Innovative Interfaces, Inc.; Bill Hoffman, Swets Information Services; Ted Koppel, Ex Libris; and Oliver Pesch, EBSCO Information Systems) (Chandler & Jewell, 2006). Their efforts evolved into SUSHI (Standardized Usage Statistics Harvesting Initiative), soon operating under the wing of NISO. The initial group expanded to include additional publishers and automation system vendors. SUSHI began developing a protocol to allow automated harvesting of statistics from a variety of publishers, based on COUNTER standardization and using an XML envelope.

The basic concept of SUSHI is simple. An ERM system should be able to automatically request, receive, and integrate statistics provided by a site, without human intervention. XML was selected as the best, most flexible wrapper for this interchange. The ERM should be able to generate a request, identifying the institution requesting the data, specifying the date range needed, and the address to send the data. The ERM formulates the request, puts all the needed information into an XML file, and sends the file off to the site providing the statistics. The site should be able to receive this information, pull the requested COUNTER compliant data, pop it into an XML file and send it back to the originating ERM. If there is a problem, an error message should be sent. The ERM should then be able unwrap the report and load it into its databank. Finally, the ERM should be able to generate appropriate reports, although this final step is outside the SUSHI protocol, which only deals with the transfer of information to and from the ERM and the publisher. Currently SUSHI 1.0 protocol allows for the retrieval of any COUNTER report, including previous COUNTER releases. The XML schema developed was designed to be easily expanded to include additional COUNTER reports as they are developed.

In 2006 NISO and COUNTER came to a formal agreement, in a memorandum of understanding outlining which organization would take care of what. NISO, through SUSHI, will maintain the XML schema. COUNTER will maintain the COUNTER standards and will list SUSHI compliant publishers and vendors on its Website (SUSHI, 2006). NISO currently offers toolkits on its Website for publishers interested in participating in SUSHI.

Vendors are just beginning to move toward offering statistical harvesting features in their ERMs. A handful of vendors currently have released this feature, but the wave of the future is automated harvesting, as publishers offer both standardized reports and report transmission formats.

MANAGEMENT OF ELECTRONIC STATISTICS

There are some issues that need to be addressed for an institution to effectively manage the collection and analysis of user statistics. First, you must identify which products you want to track. Since electronic use is becoming a major component of most "gate counts," you want to collect as

many as practical, particularly with the growing inclusion of these statistics in national annual surveys. But, do you track each direct journal you subscribe to outside of your packages? Such tracking entails significant staff time. If you are looking at a major cancellation project, can you afford not to have them? Do you only collect statistics that are COUNTER compliant? This leaves you with a great deal of uncounted use. How do you count those products that provide statistics that are not COUNTER compliant, yet are evidence of significant use?

Second, staff must be assigned the task of collecting them. This requires training staff on how to get to the statistics and identifying what particular type of statistic to collect. COUNTER compliant sites are generally easier to navigate, but the exact location of the statistics you want to gather can reside several pages into a publisher's statistical interface, and may move around as publishers revise their Web pages. For nonCOUNTER sites, screen shots of selected data elements may be needed to ensure consistency of just what data is to be recorded. While the amount of time spent gathering statistics decreases as publishers move to providing them in COUNTER format, the overall time increases as more and more publishers provide them. Eventually, when all publishers provide statistics in both COUNTER and SUSHI compliant form, and all institutions have electronic resource management systems that can automatically harvest them, that effort will become much less onerous, but this future will not be quickly seen.

Even COUNTER compliant statistics profit from having an alert eye looking at them. One red flag is a sudden, very high peak in usage, which may be the result of automatic downloading software, usually constituting illegal use as spelled out in the product license. Publishers fairly frequently notify subscribers when there has been a problem with a certain segment of their user statistics and that they may be recalculated. When a publisher becomes COUNTER compliant, they often continue to provide the old format of statistics. Staff needs to monitor statistics and adjust to format changes. If a publisher includes statistics for titles not subscribed to by the institution, you may want those weeded out.

Once statistics are gathered, they need to be compiled in a meaningful way. Most institutions use spreadsheets at this point. The challenge is creating a spreadsheet that allows you to meaningfully present quite a range of statistics types, both COUNTER and nonCOUNTER. The author's institution currently uses a spreadsheet that divides statistics into searches, serial downloads, e-book downloads, other full-text, and other. Each product must be assigned a category and tracked. As the number of electronic products mount, this can be challenging. The annual ACRL statistical survey now asks for number of sessions, searches, and full-text article downloads, as defined by COUNTER. Since not all publishers provide COUNTER compliant statistics, you may want to indicate on your spreadsheet which ones are compliant.

Another decision to be made is how long you want to preserve these statistics. Ideally, you want to use them to look at use of both a particular product and overall use over time. How do you insure that the statistics from five years ago will be there when you want to do that analysis? Even with ERMs warehousing statistics, there are likely to be limitations on the number of years of storage.

USE OF ELECTRONIC STATISTICS

At this point user statistics are reasonably reliable and meaningful, at least compared to even two years ago. What we do with these statistics, what information they tell us and how we put them to work to improve different functions of the library is the next question. As Mercer (2000) states, "Important decisions about the nature of our individual libraries are made based on performance factors that often support what we intuitively believe to be true" (¶ 2). The metrics of electronic use may supplant, or will at least supplement, traditional library statistics such as door counts and circulation figures. It is obvious that physical visits to libraries are dropping dramatically as use of electronic materials increases. Proof that users, regardless of their method of access, are using library materials and using them heavily, will be important information for those who decide the fate of library budgets.

Subscriptions have a natural life cycle and statistics are helpful in each stage. It is not immediately obvious how statistics can be useful in the selection of a product. Since you do not have the product, you obviously do not have usage statistics. Hahn and Faulkner (2002), of the University of Maryland Libraries, have developed a method of using usage statistics, if the package or journal being considered has similarities to a subscription already held by the institution. First they evaluate an existing collection, developing three metrics: average cost per article, average cost per use, and content-adjusted use. They feel the quantity of articles published in a year, and the use of those articles, are helpful in evaluation. As shown in Table 2, they have a licensed collection with a known price, number of published articles, and number of downloads of those articles. From this they calculate the average cost per article (price divided by total number of articles), average cost per access (price divided by number of downloads), and content-adjusted use (number of accesses divided by number of articles.) Average cost per article can also be calculated for the candidate collection. In this instance, the candidate collection has a higher cost per article—a higher total cost and lower number of articles published.

The authors recognize this is not sufficient information for evaluating a collection and have developed three additional benchmarks: cost-based usage, content-based usage, and cost per access at the content-based usage (Table 3). The cost-based usage determines the number of yearly

Table 2. Comparison of candidate collection to licensed collection

	Licensed Collection	Candidate Collection
Price	$10,000	$25,000
Total number of online articles as of the end of the year	50,000	45,000
Total annual number of full-text accesses to the articles in the collection	25,000	Unknown
Average cost per article (cost/# articles)	$.20	$.55
Content-adjusted use (accesses/# articles)	0.50	Unknown
Average cost per access (price/accesses)	$.40	Unknown

Table 3. Use of benchmarks to compare candidate collection and licensed collection

	Licensed Collection	Candidate Collection	Benchmark
Price	$10,000	$25,000	
Total number of online articles as of the end of the year	50,000	45,000	
Total annual number of full-text accesses to the articles in the collection	25,000	Unknown	62,500 uses needed to match average cost per access (cost-based usage)
Average cost per article (cost/# articles)	$.20	$.55	
Content-adjusted use (accesses/# articles)	0.50	Unknown	22,500 uses needed to match content-adjusted use (content-based usage)
Average cost per access (price/accesses)	$.40	Unknown	$1.11 Cost if content-adjusted use met (cost per access at content-based usage level)

accesses, or downloads, the candidate collection will need in order to meet the same average cost per access as the licensed collection. This is calculated as the price of the candidate collection divided by the cost per access of the licensed collection, in this case $25,000 divided by $.40 = 62,500 accesses. Content-based usage is the number of articles in the candidate collection multiplied by the content-adjusted usage of the licensed collection. This gives the number of full-text accesses needed to match the content-adjusted use (number of accesses divided by number of articles). In this case it is 45,000 multiplied by 0.50 = 22,500 uses. The final benchmark is cost per access at the content-based usage level. This calculates the cost per access if the content-based usage is achieved. This is calculated using the candidate collection price divided by the content-based usage benchmark; $25,000 divided by 22,500 = $1.11.

Obviously other factors need to be included into the evaluation of a potential product. But this method allows an estimation of the quantity of use required for a product to match a similar product in cost effectiveness.

Another use for statistics when evaluating a potential purchase occurs when archives are being considered, particularly when used with other information such as that provided by Tenopir and King (2000, p.188). They analyzed the pattern of use of a journal broken down by article age. Scientists made up the demographic group they were studying and it is likely that discipline of the user would affect these patterns. However, a later examination of three studies on journal usage (King, Tenopir, Montgomery, & Aerni, 2003), which included nonscientific faculty, provided results that roughly approximated their original finding (Table 4). About 58.5% of the use of a journal involves articles that have been published within the last year.

If a library already subscribes to a journal, their data could be used to project usage of archives, particularly for a scientific or technical field. For example, let us look at Journal A. A subscription to Journal A includes the current 2 years, costs $2000.00, and generated 250 downloads within the last year. This represents a cost per article of $8.00 ($2000 divided by 250). These downloads represent about 70.8% of the total expected use of the publication (58.5% the first year and 12.3% the second year). If all years were available the projected use would be 353 downloads (250 divided by .708). The archives are priced at an annual fee of an additional $150.00. Use can be predicted to be 29.2% of the projected total use, for an estimated archival use of 103 articles per year. The cost per article is then calculated at $150.00 divided by 103, for a cost of $1.46 per article.

In another example, Publisher A offers an archival package that includes four journals, with coverage up to 1998. The institution's current subscription to those journals generated 1326 downloads in one year, covering a publication period of 8 years, and representing 90.3% of expected use, using Tenopir and King's chart, with a little extrapolation for the 6-10 year span. If all years were available, you can predict a total use of 1468 (1326 divided by .903). The cost of the current subscriptions is $8,752 (combined cost of the four journals) divided by 1326 uses results in a cost of $6.60 per article download. The archival package has an initial cost of $8,000 with an annual maintenance fee of $350. The projected annual use is 142 articles (1468 downloads times 9.7%). Using the average cost of $6.60 from the current subscription, it would take about 9 years before the initial cost is recovered (142 times $6.60 for an annual cost of $937.20, $8000 divided by the annual cost). But a comparison of document delivery costs should also be made. Assuming $30.00 per document requested, a ball-park document delivery charge, 142 documents requested a year would generate a total annual cost of $4,260. This makes that initial cost of $8000.00 begin to look much more cost effective.

Obviously, usage statistics can play a prominent role in the evaluation of an existing library's subscription. The literature frequently warns of relying too heavily on statistics, but truthfully, reliable statistics are taking some of the guess-work out of evaluation. Clearly, they are not the only criteria, factors such as the size of the program a

Table 4. Age and use of articles

Age of article	Percent of use
1	58.5
2	12.3
3	6.2
4-5	7.7
6-10	9.3
11-15	1.5
>15	4.6

journal supports, a journal's importance to its field, publishing patterns by the institution's faculty, membership on editorial boards by faculty, and so on, all need to be considered, but for the first time, we have some real data to frame decisions.

An emerging evaluation standard is the cost per article download. It is a relative figure and only has meaning in comparison to other cost per article calculations from the institution or in comparison to document delivery costs. Within that context, it is a very helpful metric. Kraemer reports creating an annual evaluation overview which includes a complete list of usage and cost per usage, a list of both high and low cost per use products, and a list of high demand titles generated from interlibrary loan requests (Bordeaux, Karmer, & Sullenger, 2005). Such analyses set a useful framework in which to place renewal decisions.

Cost per use is also helpful when evaluating a package subscription. A question that is often raised is whether it is better use of your money to subscribe to a package deal or to pick off the high use titles and subscribe to them individually. A straightforward examination of this question can be made.

The cost per use of the package is easily calculated. In the example represented in Table 5, the package deal comes with a requirement to maintain existing subscriptions to titles carried by the publisher. The total cost of the package is thus the package cost and the associated subscription costs. This figure, divided by the total usage, gives you the cost per use of the package. Looking at your individual title usage, arranged from high use to low, you could then calculate the point at which the total of individual title subscriptions would equal your package total. In this case, the cost of twenty journals with the highest use roughly matches the total package costs. These journals account for only 44.5% of the overall usage. Since use is not highly concentrated with a few journals, it clearly is more cost effective to subscribe to the whole package. With other packages, where use

is concentrated in fewer journals, it may turn out that picking off the high use journals is more cost effective. In either case your usage figures allow a methodical decision.

Occasionally, because of financial set backs, an institution may be required to conduct a cancellation project. Here too, user statistics can be of great assistance. In the following scenario, shown in Table 6, an institution has a projected electronic expenditure of $406,483. Unfortunately, the available allocation is $203,000. How can those funds be spent to maximize the return? There are several criteria that could be useful, such as total number of journals subscribed to, total number of article downloads, availability of articles through alternative sources such as document delivery, subject coverage of retained journals, and feedback from faculty.

Taking a methodical look at usage is helpful. Cost is projected for the next year as increasing 8%. In our example, direct subscriptions represent only 7.7% of the total number of titles, but account for 51.4% of article downloads. Perhaps we should save all direct titles, leaving just enough to also pay for package B. This option, option A, leaves us with 16.3% of our titles and 52.4% of article downloads.

How about concentrating on packages, which tend to give a broader depth of subject coverage? All packages exceed our limit; instead let us drop package B, option B. In this configuration we retain 83.7% of our titles but only 47.56% of the article downloads.

Then we can try dropping one of the pricier packages and picking up more direct titles. Option C, in which we drop package A, leaves us with 61.26% of journals and 74.21% of downloads, while option D, all packages except F, returns 70.51% of titles and 71.54% of downloads.

You can continue to calculate the percent of article downloads and the percent of titles saved for each combination of packages and direct titles. Table 7 summarizes the results of the four options above.

Table 5. Analysis of individual journal performance within a publisher's package

Title	Article down -loads	% total use	Direct cost	Cumulating Cost Total	Cumulating Use Total	% Total Use	Direct Cost/Use
Jrnl A	297	5.1%	$630.00	$630.00	297	5.1%	$2.12
Jrnl B	289	4.9%	$489.00	$1,119.00	586	10.0%	$1.69
Jrnl C	281	4.8%	$333.00	$1,452.00	867	14.8%	$1.19
Jrnl D	237	4.1%	$366.00	$1,818.00	1104	18.9%	$1.54
Jrnl E	187	3.2%	$3,540.00	$5,358.00	1291	22.1%	$18.93
Jrnl F	167	2.9%	$4,504.00	$9,862.00	1458	24.9%	$26.97
Jrnl G	134	2.3%	$3,137.00	$12,999.00	1592	27.2%	$23.41
Jrnl H	133	2.3%	$1,566.00	$14,565.00	1725	29.5%	$11.77
Jrnl I	99	1.7%	$1,246.00	$15,811.00	1824	31.2%	$12.59
Jrnl J	91	1.6%	$276.00	$16,087.00	1915	32.7%	$3.03
Jrnl K	87	1.5%	$2,858.00	$18,945.00	2002	34.2%	$32.85
Jrnl L	85	1.5%	$314.00	$19,259.00	2087	35.7%	$3.69
Jrnl M	85	1.5%	$1,200.00	$20,459.00	2172	37.1%	$14.12
Jrnl N	77	1.3%	$627.00	$21,086.00	2249	38.5%	$8.14
Jrnl O	67	1.1%	$2,456.00	$23,542.00	2316	39.6%	$36.66
Jrnl P	64	1.1%	$1,717.00	$25,259.00	2380	40.7%	$26.83
Jrnl Q	63	1.1%	$1,193.00	$26,452.00	2443	41.8%	$18.94
Jrnl R	60	1.0%	$1,561.00	$28,013.00	2503	42.8%	$26.02
Jrnl S	52	0.9%	$942.00	$28,955.00	2555	43.7%	$18.12
Jrnl T	50	0.9%	$5,522.00	$34,477.00	2605	44.5%	$110.44
Jrnl U	48						
Jrnl V	47						
Jrnl W	47						
Jrnl X	45						
Jrnl Y	44						
Jrnl Z	43						

Publisher A:

Total # of journals	*844*
Total article downloads in year	*5,848*
Package cost	*$8,765*
Required subscription cost	*$24,367*
Total cost	*$33,132*
Cost/use	*$5.67*

Table 6. Various characteristics of current subscriptions (Electronic Product allocation: $203,000)

Package	Available Ingenta?	Available ECO?	# Jrnls	% total Jrnl titles	Article Downloads 2005	% Total down loads	FY06 Cost	Cost/ Use 2006	Projected cost (8%<)
Package A	yes	yes	844	31.99%	5,848	6.71%	$33,132.00	$5.67	$35,782.56
Package B	no	coming	227	8.61%	905	1.04%	$6,322.00	$6.99	$6,827.76
Package C	partial	no	43	1.63%	6,720	7.71%	$15,820.00	$2.35	$17,085.60
Package D	yes	yes	123	4.66%	4,070	4.67%	$8,598.00	$2.11	$9,285.84
Package E	no	yes	528	20.02%	3,679	4.22%	$30,353.88	$8.25	$32,782.19
Package F	no	no	670	25.40%	21,148	24.26%	$100,599.40	$4.76	$108,647.35
Total packages			2,435	92.30%	42,370	48.60%	$194,825.28	$4.60	$210,411.30
Direct subscriptions			203	7.70%	44,813	51.40%	$181,548.35	$4.05	$196,072.22
Total packages & direct			2,638	100.00%	87,183		$376,373.63	$4.32	$406,483.52
Total number of Journal titles	2,638								
Total Number of Article Downloads 2005	87,183								

Option A: Package B, all direct journals

Package B	$6,827
Direct subs	$196,072
Total cost	**$202,899**
Total Number of titles saved	430
Total Number of Direct Titles	203
Total Number of articles downloaded	45,718
% of article downloaded	**52.44%**
% of direct titles saved	**100.00%**
% of total titles saved	**16.30%**

Option B: All packages, except B

All packages, except B	**$203,583**
Total Number of titles saved	2,208
Total Number of Direct Titles	0
Total Number of articles downloaded	41,465
% of article downloaded	**47.56%**
% of direct titles saved	**0.00%**
% of total titles saved	**83.70%**

Option C: All packages except Package A, as many direct journals as possible

All packages except A	$174,628
Direct subs w/ cost/use<$3.20 (25 titles and 28,175 downloads)	$26,435
Total cost	**$201,064**
Total Number of titles	1,616
Total Number of Direct Titles	25
Total Number of articles downloaded	64,697
% of article downloaded	**74.21%**
% of direct titles saved	**12.32%**
% of total titles saved	**61.26%**

Option D: all packages except F, as many directs as possible

All packages except F	$101,763
Direct subs w/ cost/use<$19.00 (95 titles and 41,148 downloads)	$100,546
Total cost	**$202,309**
Total Number of titles saved	1,860
Total Number of Direct Titles saved	95
Total Number of articles downloaded	62,370
% of article downloaded	**71.54%**
% of direct titles saved	**46.80%**
% of total titles saved	**70.51%**

Table 7. Summary of options

Option	Titles saved	% titles saved	article downloads	% article downloads saved
A	430	16.30%	45,718	52.44%
B	2,208	83.70%	41,465	47.56%
C	1,616	61.26%	64,697	74.21%
D	1,860	70.51%	62,370	71.54%

When you have two option with a close percent of article downloads saved, you need to remember that the count of article downloads still has a significant error factor. option C and option D, at 71.54% and 74.21% are essentially equal in number of downloads. You would then look at the total number of titles saved, the range of subject areas served, and the programs you are supporting.

A recent cancellation project at the author's institution included a review of proposed cancellations by faculty. Several of the faculty identified particular titles as critical to their field of study. The actual use of those titles was shockingly low; some of them fewer than 10 downloads per year. Perhaps the faculty had their own subscriptions, an argument against continuing an institutional subscription if it is redundant. Were those particular journals so significant that they were worth the high cost per article download, or was it an example of identifying what faculty think *should* be critical, rather than what is actually used?

Usage statistics can also be used in negotiating deals for publisher packages, both for individual institutions and consortia. A library or consortia that can demonstrate high use or low use enters bargaining from a knowledge base, always a good position when negotiating. Usage statistics can also be used to distribute cost, either across a consortium, or within a multicampus arrangement.

Besides being useful in evaluation of library materials during different parts of their life cycle, statistics can also be helpful in understanding how patrons use electronic material. They can provide insight on how to improve products, Web pages leading to those products, library training material, and how to most cost effectively buy those products.

Philip Davis (2002) conducted an interesting analysis of usage patterns within a consortium. He reported that title usage clustered by three types of institutions; large research, medical, and liberal arts. He suggested—based on usage patterns—consortia organized by institutional type rather than geography, may prove more effective purchasing agents. Studies such as these will help institutions to develop their buying models more thoughtfully.

Other studies are being done using deep log analysis, sometimes called data mining. Nicholas, Huntington, and Watkinson (2003) did an extensive study in which they examined log files of users accessing Emerald and Blackwell titles. These logs identified the IP address of each hit, recorded exactly which pages were hit, and how long a user stayed on a certain page. From this they reached several interesting conclusions. First, they discovered that the usage pattern of users coming from an institution that subscribed to the whole package differed from the pattern of use by users whose institution subscribe to only selected titles. There was a significant increase in the number of titles consulted from the package subscribers versus individual subscribers. They were also able to record the number of repeat visitors and the number of requests by one user in a particular session. The rate of hits on abstract pages, HTML and PDF pages, and printing requests pages were identified. Also, load data identifying use by day and time of day was captured. These statistics were useful to the authors in identifying patterns of use, looking at the preferred sequence of types of pages, preferences between HTML and PDF pages, and in identifying the end result sought by patrons, usually a printed PDF. The data would also be useful in looking at server and telecommunication capacity of the publisher.

Davis and Solla (2003) conducted another study using deep log analysis, this time examining behavior of patrons using chemical journals. These logs captured IP address and type of article downloaded, HTML or PDF. From the data collected, the authors were able to identify which campus departments were using the journals studied, and to what extent. They were also able to describe journal use patterns, by number of titles accessed and the number of articles downloaded by each user. From this the authors identified a correlation between the total number of downloads and the estimated user population. They were also able to examine the effect a few heavy users can have on overall usage rates.

FUTURE TRENDS

As usage statistics become more and more standardized and easier to obtain, increasing numbers of institutions will collect, analyze and undoubtedly give statistics greater weight in the evaluation process. There will be the expectation that all providers of library electronic products will make compliant statistics available. Indeed, the availability of such statistics is already becoming a selection criterion for new products.

New products are appearing on the market to facilitate the gathering and analysis of electronic product user statistics. Services such as EBSCO's *ScholarlyStats* and Thomson's *Journal Use Reports* collect, compile, and produce a variety of reports generated from the user statistics pulled from multiple sources specific to the particular library. The Thomson product further enriches these reports with journal citation and institutional publication data to provide more depth in the reports generated. These tools will undoubtedly prove useful for libraries coping with the challenges of managing user statistics from a variety of sources. It remains to be seen whether these products will continue to be viable in the long term as more and more institutions are able to automatically harvest their own data and become more versed in the use of the statistics.

But beyond the straightforward issues of obtaining and using statistics in the evaluation of products, user statistics will increasingly be utilized in more sophisticated analysis of library activity. This trend can already be seen in the deep log studies currently being conducted.

These techniques are beginning to extend into what Scott Nicholson (2006) and others call bibliomining. Similar to data analysis movements in other fields of study, strands of information from areas previously considered unrelated are being pulled together and new connections made. Bibliomining takes the results of deep log analysis, adds it to other data, such as user demographic information and library services information. The Penn Library Data Farm (Data Farm University of Pennsylvania Library, n.d.) is an example of bibliomining at work. The Data Farm makes available a variety of statistics, such as COUNTER data, gate counts, survey results, and Web log analysis, as well as providing some canned and customizable reports. Its stated goal is to be "a repository of quantitative information developed to aid the measurement and assessment of library resource use and organizational performance. In its design, this repository is multipurpose, providing space to assemble, process, integrate, analyze, and disseminate data" (¶ 1). Additional information on the developing field of bibliomining is available at the Bibliomining Information Center, maintained by Dr. Scott Nicholson (2005).

CONCLUSION

In summary, usage statistics have come a long way in reliability, standardization, and ease of collection, thanks to efforts by librarians, publishers, and library system vendors working in collaboration. The standards codified by both COUNTER and SUSHI will help insure the quality of statistics and lead to improvements in both the statistics themselves and the method of gathering them. Despite these advances, there are still issues of stability, consistency, and the influence of different publisher platforms on usage rates. The time required to gather and process these statistics will continue to be significant for the near term, but are well worth the effort. Statistical information improves evaluation and decision making throughout the life cycle of electronic products, including new purchases, renewals, and cancellation projects. More than just a product evaluation tool, they help us improve access to and use of electronic materials. Statistics enhance our ability to understand how and who uses our libraries, and how they use the products the libraries offer.

REFERENCES

Bader, S. A., & Thompson, L. L. (1989). Analyzing in-house journal utilization: An added dimension in decision making. *Bulletin of the Medical Library Association, 77*(2), 216-218.

Bertot, J. C., McClure, C. R., & Ryan, J. (2000). *Developing national public library statistics and performance measures for the networked environment: final report* (ERIC Document Reproduction Service No. ED447803). Washington, D.C.: Institute of Museum and Library Services.

Bordeaux, A., Kraemer, A. B., & Sullenger, P. (2005). Making the most of your usage statistics. *The Serials Librarian, 48*(3/4), 295-299.

Chandler, A., & Jewell, T. (2006). Standards – libraries, data providers, and SUSHI: The Standardized Usage Statistics Harvesting Initiative. *Against the Grain, 18(2)*, 1-2.

Chen, C. C. (1972). The use patterns of physics journals in a large academic research library. *Journal of the American Society for Information Science, 23*(4), 254-265.

Cooper, M. D., & McGregor, G. F. (1994). Using article photocopy data in bibliographic models for journal collection management. *Library Quarterly, 64*(4), 386-413.

COUNTER : Counting Online Usage of NeTworked Electronic Resources (n.d.). Retrieved November 11, 2007, from http://www.project-counter.org

Data Farm University of Pennsylvania Library (n.d.). Retrieved November 11, 2007, from http://metrics.library.upenn.edu/prototype/about/indexHTML

Davis, P. M. (2002). Patterns in electronic journal usage: Challenging the composition of geographic consortia. *College and Research Libraries, 63*(6), 484-497. http://www.ala.org/ala/acrl/acrlpubs/crljournal/backissues2002b/november02/davisPDF

Davis, P. M., & Price, J. S. (2006). eJournal interface can influence usage statistics: Implications for libraries, publishers, and Project COUNTER. *Journal of the American Society for Information Science and Technology, 57*(9), 1243-1248.

Davis, P. M., & Solla, L. R. (2003). An IP-level analysis of usage statistics for electronic journals in chemistry: Making inferences about user behavior. *Journal of the American Society for Information Science and Technology, 54*(11), 1062-1068.

Duy, J., & Vaughan, L. (2006). Can electronic journal usage data replace citation data as a measure of journal use? An empirical examination. *The Journal of Academic Librarianship, 32*(5), 512-517.

Hahn, K. L., & Faulkner, L. A. (2002). Evaluative usage-based metrics for the selection of e-journals. *College and Research Libraries, 63*(3), 215-227.

International Coalition of Library Consortia (ICOLC) (1998, November). Guidelines for statistical measures of usage of web-based indexed, abstracted, and full text resources. Retrieved November 11 2007, from http://www.library.yale.edu/consortia/webstatsHTML

JISC (n.d.). Usage statistics working group. About usage statistics working group. Retrieved November 11, 2007, from http://www.jisc.ac.uk/aboutus/committees/working_groups/working_groups_disbanded/usage_stats_group.aspx

JSTOR Web Statistics Task Force (1998, April). Guidelines for statistical measures of usage of web-based resources. Retrieved November 11, 2007, from http://www.library.yale.edu/~kparker/WebStatsHTML

King, D. W., Tenopir, C., Montgomery, C. H., & Aerni, S. E., (2003). *Patterns of journal use by faculty at three diverse universities. D-Lib Magazine, 9*(10).

Konopasek, K., & O'Brien, N. P. (1982). A survey of journal use within the undergraduate library at the University of Illinois at Urbana-Champaign. ED 225601.

Luther, J. (2000). *White paper on electronic journal usage statistics.* Washington, D.C.: Council on Library and Information Resources. http://www.clir.org/PUBS/reports/pub94/contentsHTML

McCain, K. W., & Bobick, J. E. (1981). Patterns of journal use in a departmental library: A citation analysis. *Journal of the American Society for Information Science, 32*(4), 257-267.

Mercer, L. S. (2000). Measuring the use and value of electronic journals and books. *Issues in Science and Technology Librarianship, 25.* http://www.istl.org/00-winter/article1HTML

Nicholas, D., Huntington, P., & Watkinson, A. (2003). Digital journals, big deals and online searching behaviour: A pilot study. *ASLIB Proceedings, 55*(1/2), 84-109.

Nicholson, S. (2006, May 15). *Balancing evidence-based librarianship and protecting patron privacy through the bibliomining process.* Paper presented at the Eastern New York ACRL Chapter 2006 Spring Conference. Retrieved November 11, 2007, from http://www.enyacrl.org/acrlkeynote.ppt

Nicholson, S. (2005). Bibliomining: Data mining for libraries. Retrieved November 11, 2007, from http://www.bibliomining.com/

NISO (n.d.). FAQ for the standardized usage statistics harvesting initiative (SUSHI) (Draft). Retrieved November 11, 2007, from http://docs.google.com/View.aspx?docid=d2dhjwd_63tk-kwf

NISO (n.d.). NISO standardized usage statistics harvesting initiative (SUSHI). National Information Standards Organization. Retrieved November 11, 2007, from http://www.niso.org/committees/SUSHI/SUSHI_comm.html

Pesch, O. (2004). Usage statistics: Taking e-metrics to the next level. *The Serials Librarian, 46*(1/2), 143-154.

Rice, B. A. (1979). Science periodicals use study. *Serials Librarian, 4*(1) 35-47.

Shepherd, P. T. (2004). COUNTER: Towards reliable vendor usage statistics. *VINE, 34*(4), 184-189.

Shim, W., McClure, C. R., Fraser, B. T., Bertot, J. C., Dagli, A., & Leahy, E. H. (2001). *Measures and statistics for research library networked services: Procedures and issues. ARL E-metrics phase II report.* Washington, D.C.: Association of Research Libraries. Retrieved November 11, 2007, from http://www.arl.org/stats/newmeas/emetrics/phasetwopreface.pdf

SUSHI for librarians and content providers. Recording of Webinar presented May 17, 2006. Retrived November 11, 2007, from https://niso. webex.com/niso/onstage/tool/record/viewrecording1.php?EventID=277481065

Tenopir, C., & King, D. W. (2000). *Towards electronic journals: Realities for scientists, librarians, and publishers.* Washington, D.C.: SLA Publishing.

Walter, P. L. (1996). A journal use study: Checkouts and in-house use. *Bulletin of the Medical Library Association, 84*(4), 461-467.

Section II
Workflow Management and Competencies of Electronic Resource Librarians

Chapter IV
Selecting, Acquiring, and Renewing Electronic Resources

Smita Joshipura
Arizona State University, USA

ABSTRACT

The purpose of this chapter is to provide in-depth and comprehensive coverage of the workflow for electronic resources (e-resources) from selection to acquisition. Along the way, it addresses major steps, processes, procedures, and issues in selecting and acquiring e-resources and acts as a teaching tool for librarians who would like to learn best practices for managing the life cycle of e-resources. This chapter covers various facets of the selection process, including tools, challenges, and criteria, and provides a checklist for collection development librarians for evaluating the resources. It also addresses acquisitions workflow from verification of a resource to ordering and acquiring the product and provides an additional checklist for acquisitions librarians for reviewing license agreements.

INTRODUCTION

In the last decade, there has been a sharp rise in the number and complexity of e-resources in library collections. Moreover, use patterns are shifting from print to electronic materials. Because of the proliferation of e-resources and user preferences for the electronic format, these resources are becoming essential mainstays of any library collection. Today's e-resources consist of wide varieties of materials including journals, books, indexes, abstracts, encyclopedias, reference books, aggregator databases, and full-text or partially full-text databases. As these resources change at a very rapid pace and as libraries continue to build larger collections of e-resources, finding ways to manage them effectively, from selection to licensing, is becoming a major challenge for librarians.

This chapter covers various aspects of the life cycle of e-resources and emphasizes major steps for the librarians involved in the workflow of selection and acquisition. The objective of this chapter is to include methods of handling these resources and to provide a practical and valuable tool for librarians in any library.

BACKGROUND

Selection of information sources is the core collection development function, and the primary objective of the selection decision for any format is fundamentally the same: satisfying user needs. With the advent of e-resources, job responsibilities of selectors have changed drastically. In the past, selectors recommended new titles on an individual basis using traditional selection criteria such as quality, relevance, use, and cost (Welch, 2002). Selectors analyzed faculty and user requests for new titles and made requests to add to the collection. But in the cyber world, the role of selectors has changed remarkably as e-resources have expanded and developed. Selectors must now address new issues as part of the selection and management processes, issues such as easy and quick accessibility for users, continuous content evaluation and technological and legal concerns.

Similarly, due to the overwhelming growth and availability of a variety of electronic products, the workflow of acquisitions has changed significantly, becoming more complex. Though the acquisitions process is closely connected to collection development in any type of library, it has distinct functions. The primary responsibility of the acquisitions department is getting the materials needed by the library's users in the most desired format and in the most efficient and economical manner. Thus, acquisition is defined as the technical process of ordering, receiving, and paying for an item after the intellectual decision to purchase an item has been made (Chapman, 2004). Even though the process of identifying, ordering, and paying for materials such as books, serials, and media is very similar to that of electronic formats, the life cycle of e-resources is more convoluted than that of print resources. It requires additional levels of details including tracking, recording, and reviewing the license and business terms, and investigating variable pricing ranges. Acquiring information for an electronic product is often much more time-consuming than for print resources. It requires more time for decision making at every step as well as higher levels of skills and knowledge among staff (Wilkinson & Lewis, 2003). Also, it can require additional budget allocations due to higher subscription costs than for print collections. Due to the increase in the number of electronic formats, acquisition librarians are no longer just an expert in acquiring materials, having knowledge about publishers and book vendors, and identifying incomplete citations as well as finding out-of-print materials. Now they are also responsible for solving more creative problems in the areas of collection development, licensing, cataloging, technology and other issues related to e-resources (Kennedy, 2004).

Finally, the renewal and cancellation of serial subscriptions are a systematic recurring process in any type of library. Due to high inflation rates for serial subscriptions in all formats, shrinkage of budgets or buying power, and the emergence of new products, selectors are required to assess their collections for potential cancellations during the renewal process. Several traditional criteria are considered for reviewing serial subscriptions, such as low usage data, significant inflation rates, cost per issue, type of publication, relevancy, quality, duplication in other formats, and coverage in index and abstracting services (Foudy & McManus, 2005). Evaluating e-resources is equally important, and similar criteria can be applied for such a process.

Even though some processes remain the same, the role of collection development and acquisitions librarians has been transformed by e-resources. Moreover, an electronic resources (ER) librarian/coordinator has emerged who may carry out various responsibilities of the acquisitions librarian.

SELECTION OF ELECTRONIC RESOURCES

Collection Development Policy

Selecting and adding e-resources for the collection becomes easier for the selectors when a collection development policy is in place. Such a policy provides a framework for decision-making and is a necessary planning tool, the use of which leads to consistent, informed decisions. It is a blueprint for the selectors and helps them to ensure uniformity in procedures and appropriate balance in the library collection. As more and more e-resources are acquired, it is wise to integrate these products into the library's overall policy. The three main purposes of a collection development policy include informing, directing, and protecting (Gregory & Hanson, 2006). The purpose of informing is to serve as a communications vehicle for the library's staff, administrators, and various constituencies. The purpose of directing is to serve as a guideline for the selectors to maintain balance in the collection for its users. It also serves as a training document for new collection development librarians. The purpose of protecting is to serve as a means of justifying the selection to the users. The policy serves as a supporting document for the library against challenges to its procedures and resources. To maintain currency, the policy should be reviewed and revised periodically.

There are various components to be considered in developing a collection development policy:

1. It should articulate the institutional mission of the library, the purpose of the policy, and the audience for whom it is developed.
2. It should describe the community served, including users, academic programs, off-campus users, and their needs.
3. It should provide criteria and guidelines for the selectors.
4. It should identify selection tools appropriate for the library.
5. It should address access versus ownership issues as to whether electronic access is sufficient to meet the user's needs or whether the library should add print subscriptions.
6. It should include guidelines for weeding, cancellation, retention, preservation and replacement of resources.
7. It should include cooperative collection development issues such as the role of consortia.
8. It should include general guidelines for licensing requirements for e-resources such as the number of authorized users at a time, remote access availability, and whether it allows for various library services such as interlibrary loans and digital reserves.
9. It should cover the process by which selection recommendations or decisions are made, that is whether selections are made by committee or by individuals.
10. It should include expectations from providers with regard to training, technical support, compatibility with existing platform, and so forth.

Examples of electronic collection development policies can be found at: http://www.ala.org/ala/rusa/rusaourassoc/rusasections/codes/codessection/codescomm/colldevpolicies/electroniccollectionpolicies/electronicpolicies.htm.

Selection Process

The selection of any e-resource is a three-step process, which includes identification/discovery, evaluation and finally the decision to select the product.

Identification of Electronic Resource

The discovery of e-resources is challenging due to a rapid increase in the availability of resources. A variety of tools can be used to make sound selection decisions. Examples of selection tools include trial offers and demonstrations from the publisher/vendor, faculty/patron suggestions, discussion lists, peer library Websites, and vendor exhibits at conferences. For trials of the product, vendors of e-resources allow users of the library, including library staff, faculty, and students, to use the resource and to examine and evaluate its content without cost for a limited period of time. Inviting vendors to demonstrate an e-resource in the library gives selectors an opportunity to ask questions and discover details about various features of the product. Another way to discover new resources is to ask librarians already subscribing to a product about their experiences. Various listserves such as COLLDV-L (listproc@usc.edu) and ERIL (http://www.joanconger.net/ERIL/aboutus.html) help in identifying new e-resources. The following are other selection tools that help the selectors during the identification process:

Publishers' catalogs received from various publishers/vendors.

Published reviews in various print and electronic sources such as *Library Journal, American Libraries,* and *Choice.*

Charleston Review (http://www.charlestonco.com/), which contains critical reviews of Web products.

Scout Report (www.scout.cs.wisc.edu/scout/report), which provides reviews of valuable resources on the Web.

NewJour (http://gort.ucsd.edu/newjour/), an electronic discussion list hosted by the University of California, San Diego, which helps to identify new electronic journals.

Electronic Journal Access (http://www.coalliance.org/ejournal), managed by the nonprofit Colorado Alliance of Research Libraries, which provides listings of electronic journals on the Web. These listings are available directly from publishers, professional societies, or smaller entities. Titles in aggregator databases are generally excluded.

WorldCat (http://oclc.org/worldcat) helps to find bibliographical details as well as availability in other libraries worldwide.

Ulrich's Periodicals Directory. Ulrich's is the world's premier periodicals reference source providing essential bibliographic, descriptive, and access information. It is available in print and online and is published by R. R. Bowker. http://www.bowker.com.

Serials Directory, which provides access to the most up-to-date and accurate bibliographical information as well as current pricing structures for popular serials. It is available in print and electronic format and is published by Ebsco. http://www-us.ebsco.com

Evaluation of Electronic Resources

Once the resource is identified, evaluation of the product is the second most critical step for selectors. Evaluation helps the selectors determine the cost, the reliability of the content provider, and most importantly the authoritativeness of the resource. A selection tool such as a trial or demonstration of the product by the provider, as well as reviews in print and electronic sources, helps in evaluating the product and leads to sound decisions. Traditionally with print resources, the selectors consider the credentials of the author, currency, intended audience, accuracy, ease of use, reputation of the publisher, the subject, cost and the curriculum or research needs of students/faculty/patrons. They also use methods such as citation analysis, user surveys, and so forth. However, with e-resources the selector must consider additional elements such as easy access to the content, coverage, search capability and functionality of the interface; quality of technical support; method of pricing; and provisions of licensing agreements. Thus, the typical evaluation process for e-resources has many facets, and following the various selection criteria is vital for selectors.

Evaluation Criteria

The evaluation criteria mentioned next should be considered:

Content: For content evaluation, the selector reviews the content of the electronic format and compares it with the print counterpart, if available, to find out about coverage in full text; availability of retrospective material; authoritativeness to determine the accuracy of the content, and completeness of content such as access to graphs, tables, illustrations, and advertisements. Also, it is important to check for duplication of the content in other e-resources, especially in the case of electronic journal packages.

Currency: It is important to find frequency of updates, archiving availability, and content embargos. Some providers impose one or two year embargos or moving walls on full-text access to journals. The moving wall represents the length of time between the last issues available in an electronic package with the most recent publication of the journal.

Reputation: Selectors should investigate the reputation of the provider before choosing a product. It is essential to investigate the business practices of the providers, their responsiveness to problems, and their reliability with peers.

Indexing: Selectors should consider whether or not the electronic product is well indexed.

Impact Factor: It can be important to consider the impact factor for evaluating journal titles using journal citation reports and local journal utilization reports, if available. Such sources provide systematic and objective data to evaluate the use and reputation of journals.

Ease of Access: Selectors should evaluate the functionality of the product, such as ease of access for users, by comparing the electronic to the print format, if available. Also selectors should evaluate the various interface features such as stability, possibility of customization, searching options such as Boolean and proximity operators, field-specific searching, availability of thesaurus, and downloading options such as e-mailing and printing, which add value for the users.

Cost: Cost considerations for e-resources can be confusing. Some products are monographic or serial in nature and the cost varies accordingly. The cost may also vary according to the number of simultaneous users/ports/passwords, remote access, and so forth. The pricing plans are not standardized between vendors, but may be standardized for individual vendors. Content providers may offer special deals for consortia members as a whole, and the pricing varies based on the number of full time students, materials budget, authentication of users, simultaneous use, and remote access for users.

Technical Support: E-resources are sometimes difficult and intimidating to use, unlike print resources, which do not require training. Thus, technical support is an important criterion to consider when selecting a resource. It is important to determine if the product is compatible with existing hardware and software, the flexibility of the software to accommodate users with disabilities or compliance with the Americans with Disability Act (ADA), the operating platform, and training availability for staff, online help, and detailed help pages for the users of the product.

Licensing Agreement: Though reviewing a license agreement is not considered a selector's job, it is important to carefully consider the general agreement such as various restrictions, access to archived information, definition of authorized users, use for distance education, off-campus access, and availability of usage statistics.

Challenges for Collection Development Librarians

The aforementioned evaluation criteria introduce new and unique challenges for the selectors. Moreover, the following factors would add more demands on the selectors during the selection process.

There are various types of e-resources such as electronic books, electronic journals, reference sources, and full text databases. Each one is unique and is considered differently during the selection process.

Many products are multidisciplinary in nature, which requires more than one selector in the selection decision process. In such incidences, selectors have to work collaboratively with selectors from other disciplines.

Selection of an e-resource requires more interaction between various library departmental staff, such as technical services for legal and access issues, technology for compatibility, and reference/public services for training and ease of use. Sometimes consortia deal with relatively low cost drives the selection process because the content provider offers special discounts on certain products. Many times, the consortia's special deal requires a quick response and supersedes the routine selection approach. Thus, selectors have to prepare themselves to work in teams and to cooperate with other libraries.

Another issue is lack of perpetual access to e-resources. A majority of e-resources is licensed for a limited time. Thus, at the end of the license period, if the selector decides to cancel the subscription, it results in a loss of access to the content. Thus, preserving and archiving e-resources adds different problems for selectors.

Moreover, the content of the resource may change over time and require periodic review by the selectors. It requires a continuous evaluation process by the selectors, which is a time consuming job. There can also be serious duplication of the content across databases, resulting in a waste of purchasing power. Duplication and availability of content from various sources add confusion to users as well as to the selectors. Therefore, selectors must consider very carefully the impact of these issues.

As more and more of a library's acquisitions budget is devoted to e-resources, selectors often have to curtail the purchase of monographs or cancel some print subscriptions. Due to an increase in the demand of users for e-resources, selection becomes more user-driven.

Finally, greater financial risk due to the high cost of e-resources requires extra care in selecting and handling. It is a financial liability to commit a large amount of money to a technology that may be outdated quickly or a product that may be replaced by better alternatives. Sometimes a content provider may not be reliable, which also increases the financial risk. As a result, the impact of a wrong selection decision can be far-reaching.

Selection Decision

All the evaluation criteria and challenges for e-resources must be considered while making the final selection decision. With the increase in costs and decrease in budgets, it is vital for the selectors to make sound purchasing decisions for e-resources. As e-resources continue to evolve and change, selection of these resources requires the selectors to consider the decision consciously for each resource by checking how each possible addition fits within the institutional vision. The selection process should be carefully carried out, ensuring that promotional promises made by the vendors, immediate appeal of a new product, or the selector's preferences do not affect the selection process.

Thus, the selection of an e-resource is a detailed process, and it is critical to develop a checklist of selection criteria, which assists the selectors in a sound selection process.

Figure 1 includes a checklist for the selection of e-resources and may help as a guideline for selectors before they submit their requests. It would ensure that the selectors do not overlook certain areas that need evaluation.

Selection Decision

Once the selector identifies a resource for the collection based on the institution's collection development policy, evaluates the resource against the check list, considers projected use,

and reviews budget and collection priorities, the decision regarding approval is made to the collection committee.

ACQUISITIONS OF ELECTRONIC RESOURCES

Though an acquisitions process for an e-resource resembles the process for a print resource, such

Figure 1. Check list for selection and recommendation of electronic resources for purchase

The following checklist should assist selectors in the decision-making process. Consider the following criteria while selecting e-resources for the collection.

Product Information

Title _____
URL _____
Description _____
Trial _____
Yes, date _____
No_____

Publisher/Vendor Information

Name of the Publisher _____
URL_____
Contact name _____
Telephone/E-mail_____

Audience

Primary users of the resource, such as students, faculty, researchers, general public, library staff

_____
Breadth of appeal across all types of library users_____
Relevance to programs such as degree programs, elective courses, faculty support, interdisciplinary use _____

continued on next page

Figure 1. (cont.)

Content

Type of product such as full text, index/abstract, statistical, graphics, reference source, electronic journal/package, electronic book, or other_____
Accuracy and currency of the product compared to print counterpart_____
The product is a primary or secondary source, peer-reviewed, scholarly, and so forth. _____
Current comprehensiveness of the product, for example for e-journal package, the number of titles

_____
Chronological coverage of the product, such as current, retrospective_____
Updates or frequency of the updates, such as daily, weekly, monthly _____
Duplication, such as equivalents in print or in other electronic products in the collection_____
Quality evaluation of the product. Check for reviews, demonstrations, a trial _____
Reliability of the vendor. Check for alternate vendors of same content or product _____
Stable access and coverage of the content for aggregator database_____

Cost

Cost based on yearly subscription, one-time purchase _____.
Initial cost, maintenance cost, cost based on full time equivalent (FTE), concurrent simultaneous use, consortia_____
Savings on cancellation of duplicate print of e-resource if available in the collection_____

Method of Access and Compatibility Issues

The resource resides on vendor's server, library's server_____
Access to backfiles/archives if available_____
Compatibility with current hardware/software, requirement of special plug-in_____
Authentication process, such as password, IP address, remote access _____

Interface Evaluation

Easy for novice users to access interface _____
Additional sophisticated features available for expert users_____
Screen layout, use of colors, browse functions_____
Response time for results_____
Allows Boolean, natural language, relevance search, truncation_____
Choice availability for display options, sort options_____
Ability to e-mail, download, print_____
Interaction with citation management system_____

continued on next page

Figure 1. (cont.)

Availability of online thesaurus_____

Availability of online help, such as tutorials_____

Space

Space-saving due to disposition of print resource_____

License

General agreement of the license, such as ability to provide interlibrary loan, copy, print, and download options_____

Technical Support

Training for staff, users, availability of online assistance_____

Special access for classroom instruction _____

Additional Information/Comments

as pre-order investigation and ordering, specific tasks vary between the two formats. Once the individual selector or selection committee has chosen a resource for the library's collection, the standard acquisition process of locating and acquiring the resource takes place.

The Acquisitions Process

The acquisition is a four-step process that begins after the selector discovers a new product. It includes verifying the bibliographic information for the product, identifying various pricing options, reviewing the license and business agreements, and finally, ordering and acquiring the product for the library collection.

Verification of Bibliographic Information

The verification of bibliographic information for an electronic product requires finding out

various details such as the content provider of the product, coverage, frequency of updates, and cost. Sometimes the same product may be available on multiple platforms or in more than one package. It is vital to understand various content providers' platforms and provide details to the selectors because they may have different content coverage; pricing; interface, search or retrieval capabilities; and user functions. Although acquisition librarians find various details from the publisher's Website, most of the time they have to work with a representative of content provider for clarification on various aspects of the product and for pricing and business negotiations. There are other tools that can be used for verification of bibliographic information, such as *WorldCat* (http://oclc.org/worldcat), *Ulrich's Periodicals Directory,* and *Serials Directory.*

Identification of Various Pricing Options

Content providers offer various pricing models. They may be based on the size of the library, the number of users, or the nature of the product. Unfortunately, there are no consistent standards for pricing, and acquisitions/ ER librarians need to negotiate a final price or pricing model. Some common pricing models are as follows:

Product Type: There are various types of products, for example, electronic journal packages, aggregator databases, and full-text databases. The pricing model may depend on the type of product, which may also be available through various options, such as yearly subscription or one-time purchase for archival products.

Institution Size: The size of the institution is another variable. The content provider may charge more when selling to large universities with multiple branches, locations, or sites compared to small sized universities or community colleges.

Number of Users: Price also varies with the number of potential users. Some content providers offer price based on full-time equivalents of students, while others include the total number of students, staff, and faculty members as potential users. Price may also be based on the number of simultaneous users or unlimited access including remote access, and so forth.

Consortia: Often content providers offer special pricing for consortia. In consortia deals, expensive electronic products can become affordable for small libraries because several libraries work together and share costs.

Journal Package Deals: Some providers offer bundled sets of titles in an electronic journal package. The library or consortium must acquire the entire list of journals with-out any individual selection. In such a deal, libraries may get relevant content at a lower price but may have to pay for titles with less or no relevance for the users; whereas, some providers of electronic journals packages offer pay-per-view options. In this option, libraries are not required to have subscriptions to all journal titles in the package, allowing users access to articles by paying the cost of an article from journals that are not subscribed to by the library. Sometimes, pricing models are based on a combination of print and electronic subscriptions. In such cases, publishers offer free electronic access or provide deep discounts for print plus electronic subscriptions.

Content Access: Sometimes pricing is based on the type of access to content. Some content providers require libraries to pay a large initial fee and then smaller annual fees for electronic packages where the annual fee is generally for continued access, which may or may not include additional content. Moreover, pricing depends upon the level of the content. Databases with full-text articles have higher prices compared to abstract and indexing databases.

Thus, each pricing model is unique and variations seemingly limitless. Acquisitions/ER librarians explore the above options with content providers and report their findings to the selectors. Most electronic journal packages are available directly from the publishers, while individual journal titles may be available directly from the publisher or through a subscription agent or another content provider. Electronic books can now often be purchased through a major book jobber as well as from the publisher or as a package deal through a third party, which may or may not be a consortium. Some expensive electronic databases or packages can be obtained directly from the publishers or by joining a larger consortium. Due to the high cost of e-resources, many libraries prefer a consortial approach in acquiring those resources. As a result, consortia play major roles in acquiring expensive e-resources. Purchasing through a consortium results in significant financial savings to individual libraries, which allows for wider access to materials for users.

Reviewing the License and Business Agreements

Once the source of acquiring the product is determined, the license agreement becomes the key part of the acquisition process. The license agreement includes description of the product, responsible parties that is, licensor and licensee who are signing the agreement, authorized users of the product, use of the product, and rights of the licensee and the licensor. Inquiring about the license agreement with a representative of the content provider before ordering the product is recommended. Many content providers make available their licensing agreements and terms of use on their Websites, while some licenses can be obtained through their representatives. Sometimes, publishers have "click-on" or "click-through" licenses on their Websites, where a user is required to click on a box to agree to the terms and agreements of the products. It is a normal tendency of the user to simply agree without reading the terms. In such scenarios, the acquisitions/ER librarians must review the agreement. If certain terms are not acceptable, then they should be negotiated with the publishers. It is most critical to get the contract reviewed and signed by both parties before the invoice of the product is paid. Licensing is becoming a day-to-day responsibility of an acquisitions/ER librarian and is the most important issue these days since it concerns a legally binding contract made on behalf of the institution. The challenges associated with the licensing agreement include understanding the content, determining the standard wording required by the institution, and identifying terms, which requires negotiation. Librarians who deal with licensing agreements should have negotiating skills and be required to work collaboratively with the institution's legal counsel. They should be familiar with the policies of their institution.

Librarians responsible for licenses should review each term and condition in the agreement very carefully. While reviewing the agreement, one should assure that each provision is clear. Librarians must work closely with content providers while reviewing the agreement and should make necessary changes to conform to the institution's policies. Almost all licenses are negotiable but require considerable time. Thus, librarians must be patient and persistent (Wilkinson & Lewis, 2003). If necessary, they should actively negotiate the terms, keep communication open and clarify the institution's service expectations.

The license agreement contains various clauses that define the rights of the libraries, users, and content providers. The following are some of the important clauses included in the license that can act as a checklist for the librarian who reviews the license agreement:

> **Content of Licensed Materials:** The license should clearly include the name of the product or the list of the titles that can be accessed.
>
> **Site:** It is important to include names of the sites/premises that have authorized access to the product. Sometimes access to the product is limited to a particular building or campus, and it is necessary to name them in this clause.
>
> **Authorized Users:** Definition of authorized users is an important clause in any license agreement. This clause defines authorized users such as students, faculty, and staff of an academic institution. Many public institution libraries require authorized access for public walk-in users who occasionally visit the library. This clause should be reviewed carefully and negotiated if necessary.

Copyright and Fair Use: Copyright and fair use laws of the United States allow libraries to make copies of some portions of the material and send them to other libraries for educational, research, and teaching purposes. The license agreement should allow users to view, download, or print a copy of the material. Some providers support library services such as interlibrary loan, electronic course reserve, and distance education. Librarians should carefully review this clause, identify the institutional needs, and include them in the agreement.

Confidentiality: Some agreements require libraries to keep the cost of the resource confidential. It is not possible for public institutions to accept such a clause. On the other end, libraries should protect the confidentiality of the users. Thus, this clause should be reviewed carefully.

Cost: This clause should clearly include the cost of the subscription.

Governing Law: Most of the time a publisher stipulates in the terms that the contract will be governed by the laws of the provider's particular state or country. Librarians should be very careful in reviewing this clause and should be aware of their institution's policy. It is important to negotiate this clause and change the governing law to the geographical location of the institution.

Perpetual Access: This clause allows the library to retain access to the materials for which payment has been made after cancellation of the product. Libraries should ask for archival access if it is not included in the contract.

Liabilities of Libraries: The agreement includes the responsibility of the library to monitor the use of the resource for unauthorized access by the user. Librarians should carefully review this clause and make sure to agree to a feasible level of monitoring, if any.

Terms of Payment and Termination: This clause includes payment of invoices within certain time frames as well as requirements for the renewal of the contract. It is important to review this clause and make necessary changes before signing the agreement. Termination includes reason and time of termination and notification from the provider.

Indemnification: This clause states that one or both parties will not be financially responsible for any monetary loss. This clause should be carefully reviewed and needs to have equal indemnification for both parties. Generally, the contract term also includes the phrase "hold harmless," which means that legal action will not be taken against the other party.

Usage Statistics: Under this clause, the content providers agree to provide usage statistics for e-resources. The data should be compliant with Counting Online Usage of NeTwork Electronic Resources (COUNTER), which helps libraries to compare usage statistics and make informed decisions for renewal or cancellation of e-resources.

Though librarians are becoming savvy in negotiating the terms and conditions of licenses and the content providers are becoming more familiar with libraries' needs, it is important to have consistent and transparent clauses. As of the time of this writing, there is no standardization in the agreements. Clarity and standardization in agreements would be beneficial for librarians as well as content providers. Some of the resources, guidelines, and models of the license agreement are listed as follows:

Yale University: http://www.library.yale.edu/ecollections/eresmanage.html. This site provides information for understanding various issues raised by licensing agreements. Various models can be found at http://www.library.yale.edu/~llicense/modlicintro.html.

Association of Research Libraries (http://mccoy.lib.siu.edu/arl/licensing/) provides an online course in licensing and negotiations.

The American Library Association, the Association of Research Libraries, and other associations have created principles for handling licensing agreements which can be found at http://www.arl.org/scomm/licensing/principles.html. Such principles can help librarians and providers to understand various problems involved in license agreements and how to resolve them successfully.

Columbia University Libraries' site (http://www.columbia.edu/cu/libraries/inside/ner/license-checklist.html) contains a checklist of important rights and provisions to look for in a licensing agreement.

Licensing Models Website at http://www.licensingmodels.com/ contains a standard license designed for the acquisition of electronic products. It includes four types of models, namely those for single academic institutions, academic consortia, public libraries, and corporate and special libraries.

University of Texas System at http://www.utsystem.edu/ogc/intellectualproperty/dbckfrm1.htm provides guidelines for librarians in the area of licensing.

The workflow of the licensing review process varies according to the type and size of a library. Some libraries have a team approach for license negotiation, while in some libraries legal counsel reviews the licenses. In some libraries, once the acquisitions/ER librarian reviews the license and negotiates the terms, it is sent to the institution's attorney for final review. Lately large subscription vendors have also started participating actively in the licensing process. They have started providing a new service for the library by interpreting the terms of a contract and negotiating on the library's behalf. It is also very important to keep copies of the signed agreement in the acquisitions department for future reference.

Ordering and Acquiring the Product

After the license is reviewed and signed, ordering and acquisition of the product begins. Acquisitions personnel communicate with the content provider about the resource that is being requested and provide technical information, such as Internet protocol (IP) addresses. The acquisitions department gets phone or e-mail notification from the provider's technical support staff once the access is set up based on the institution's request. The content provider also provides a stable URL for the product through which the resource can be accessed. Acquisitions or technology personnel verify access of the product and inform the rest of the organization of the availability of the new resource.

The acquisitions department must notify other library departments such as cataloging, technology, collection development, and public services once access to an e-resource is activated. It is essential to communicate with the cataloging department regarding access to the resource because they maintain the online public access catalog (OPAC). They also need all the details such as license restrictions, if any, content availability, mode of access, simultaneous use access, and so forth. The acquisitions department informs the technology or systems department because they maintain the technical access and local tracking of the database. The acquisitions department also informs the selector who requested the product and the public services staff who publicize the new resource to users. It is important to share details about contractual and legal terms such as acceptable and prohibited use of the resource and the number of authorized users. Timely communication between the acquisitions department and various library departments is vital to ensure rapid access to the product for the user.

Sometimes content providers offer training in the use of the resource once it is acquired by the library. In such a case, the acquisitions staff follows up with the provider's representative regarding training for public services staff. Periodically they also provide refresher training for the e-resource purchased by the library. The acquisitions librarian should take advantage of such offers to set up training for staff members.

After access is confirmed, the provider sends an invoice to the acquisitions department for payment. Acquisitions personnel review the invoice to make sure that the charges are as per the agreement and then process the payment.

The responsibility of the acquisitions department is not over as soon as the item is paid for. Maintaining access to the resource also becomes a part of this department's task. Sometimes, access is disrupted due to a delay in the renewal of the resource. In such a case, acquisitions personnel need to contact the provider immediately to resolve the issue. Frequently access is affected due to technical problems such as a change in the URL. Under such circumstances, acquisitions or systems personnel should follow up. It is important for acquisitions personnel to communicate with the provider whenever there is a change in the IP address so records can be amended and access provided to additional buildings or sites. Another ongoing responsibility of acquisitions personnel is to receive usage statistics from the provider and provide data to selectors so that they can review the usage and make informed decisions about renewing or cancelling the resource.

Challenges for Acquisitions Librarian

The work of acquisitions is constantly changing, and new challenges are added in the process. After the order for an e- resource is processed, it does not require traditional tasks such as physical check-in, shelving, and binding. Once access is verified, the title can be cataloged and added to link resolvers and electronic journal listings so that patrons have easy access. Thus the process is quick and simple compared to a print collection. However, it is critical to check access to the resource on a regular basis and follow up with

the provider in the case of loss of access, which requires special staff having technical skills and knowledge.

Another challenge concerns providing institutional details, such as data on full time equivalents, IP addresses, and proxy servers to the content provider. When processing an order for a new electronic subscription, acquisitions personnel should collaborate with technology staff in these matters. Similarly, the license agreement requires reviewing various terms and conditions with legal/licensing personnel, and thus collaboration with different departments is necessary.

Another issue, which does not exist in the print environment, is the need for multiple communication channels with a provider for a single order. Once the resource is acquired, various staff members from departments such as acquisitions, cataloging, and technology may need to contact the provider to obtain information which cannot be handled or understood by one person in the acquisitions department. Thus, from the acquisitions standpoint, e-resources require more follow-up than print resources.

Budget is yet another challenge, as most libraries do not systematically receive additional funding to maintain and develop electronic collections. It becomes difficult to add new resources within limited budgets.

Lastly, managing the necessary record keeping for e-resources, such as license records, advance notification before cancellation or renewal, access follow-up, and lists of various contacts for the same resource, is a major challenge. Manual control of e-resources is not practical, so libraries are trying to develop electronic resources management systems to resolve various problems associated with tracking of e-resource records in a systematic way.

Due to changes in user preference and technology, the acquisitions librarian has developed new skills such as business negotiation ability and knowledge about licensing terms and technology to manage the changes. Librarians should always consider their users and their institution's policies first. They should be unbiased when selecting content providers for a particular resource. Moreover, effective communication is required across library departments so that quick access can be provided to the user. AcqWeb http://www.acqweb.org/acqnet.html is a very useful Website for keeping abreast of what is happening in library acquisitions. It provides an excellent resource for pre-order searching; information about and from various publishers, suppliers, and vendors; lists of relevant associations and organizations; and a selected list of publications on library science in general and acquisitions in particular.

RENEWAL/CANCELLATION OF AN ELECTRONIC RESOURCE

Unlike most serial renewal subscriptions, which are based on a calendar year, the renewal for electronic subscriptions depends on the individual contracts. The majority of them are renewed every year, but sometimes contracts are signed for two or three years and are renewed accordingly. Usually, content providers send a reminder to the library's acquisitions department for renewal ahead of time with pricing and a copy of the contract. The core e-resources are most of the time automatically renewed unless there is a significant increase in the price or a change in the licensing terms. But noncore electronic subscriptions are reviewed by selectors based on various evaluation criteria before the renewal is processed by acquisitions. Once the invoice is paid, generally refunds are not available. Thus, evaluation of resources before the renewal process is critical.

During the evaluation process for renewing e-resources, selectors consider various criteria such as ranking based on quality and usage, access, cost-effectiveness, breadth, audience, and uniqueness of the resource:

> **Ranking:** The databases can be ranked by acquiring usage statistics.

Access: Access criteria are based on the technical reliability of the content provider, ease of use, remote access by users, and perpetual access. However, when the perpetual access/archive is not available or if a title is cancelled, the library loses access to current as well as retrospective material.

Cost-effectiveness: Cost-effectiveness is based on the number of searches per year, cost per search, and so forth. Usage data and especially cost per use helps in assigning the title for renewal or cancellation. The pricing for e-resources is very different compared to print resources. The price per title and the cost per use are extremely difficult to evaluate. Assessment of usage data from providers is extremely valuable for selectors during the renewal process, especially for evaluating expensive resources. Some content providers provide useful statistics such as number of queries per specific database, number of sessions, number of full-text articles or citations retrieved, and the number of times users were denied access. Such data can help selectors to increase the number of simultaneous users during the renewal process. There is still inconsistency in usage data received from the providers despite standards developed by COUNTER, and libraries should encourage the content providers to provide such data.

Breadth and Audience: The breadth and audience criteria include the relevance to research on campus and the curriculum, the potential number of users affected, the primary user group, and the number of searches per year.

Uniqueness: Uniqueness of the resource can be evaluated by comparing duplication in various formats or overlap in full-text resources. Individual titles in a publisher package generally cannot be cancelled. Sometimes, the titles are duplicated in aggregator databases, which do not provide stable access and hence require renewal of the subscription.

Budget: Finally, inadequate budget adds challenges for selectors in making decisions for renewal of e-resources.

Once a decision has been made, the acquisitions department is notified to renew or cancel the subscription. They process the invoice for payment or communicate with the provider for cancellation.

FUTURE TRENDS

With the increase in growth and demand for e-resources, libraries need to purchase and maintain significant e-resources in the collection. Due to high costs and the multidisciplinary subject coverage of e-resources, the final decision has become a team decision rather than an individual decision in many libraries. Such a team consists of members from various departments such as collection development, acquisitions, cataloging, technology, and public services. Bringing together differing expertise can be a very effective method for selection of e-resources. Such an approach helps selectors to be open-minded and flexible and leads to wise collection decisions. The creation of such teams helps in bringing together diverse skills needed to acquire a particular resource for the collection, but sometimes leads to delays in the decision process. Moreover, due to the rising cost of e-resources and shrinking budgets, the multilibrary consortia model will expand in the future.

Due to the complexity of tracking e-resources efficiently, libraries are at a crossroads in finding a complete system for electronic resources management. The Digital Library Federation (DLF) has defined requirements and suggests solutions for e-resources management. Various library system vendors have developed an automated electronic resources management (ERM) system for managing these resources in an efficient way. The ERM system helps to track the workflow from selection to acquisitions, license management to renewal and cancellation of the resource. This results in more systematic follow-up, and finally makes the overall management straightforward from resource selection to user support. Moreover, many institutions have hired electronic resources coordinator/librarians to oversee the electronic resources process and communicate with content providers about products and options.

CONCLUSION

In a nutshell, the revolution of e-resources has drastically changed the entire process of selection and acquisition of materials for collections and has added various challenges for librarians. E-resources have virtually transformed librarians into "cybrarians." In addition to possessing subject-matter knowledge, librarians are involved in the organization of resources so that users can have quick and easy access. Now, they also are required to possess technology expertise for selecting and evaluating resources. Similarly, acquisitions/ER librarians require legal and technological knowledge and business negotiations skills. Both selectors and acquisitions/ER librarians must work collaboratively with the technology, cataloging and public services departments.

It is very important for librarians to keep up-to-date on various changes and developments taking place in the areas of collection development and acquisitions. They should keep themselves current by reading relevant journals, searching the Internet, and attending meetings and conferences as well as subscribing to related discussion lists. Some important journals, conferences, and lists relevant to collection development and acquisitions are listed under the Appendix.

REFERENCES

Alford, L. (2000). *The impact of digital resources on organization and management of collection development and acquisitions.* Paper presented at the IFLA Conference Proceedings, Jerusalem, Israel. Retrieved November 12, 2007, from http://www.ifla.org/IV/ifla66/papers/168-180e.htm

Allison, D., & McNeil, B. (2000). Database selection: One size does not fit all. *College & Research Libraries, 61*(1), 56.

Bluh, P. M. (2001). *Managing electronic serials: Essays based on the ALCTS electronic serials institutes, 1997-1999.* Chicago: American Library Association.

Chapman, L. (2004). *Managing acquisitions in library and information services* (Rev. ed.). London: Facet.

Conger, J. E. (2004). *Collaborative electronic resource management: From acquisitions to assessment.* Westport, CT: Libraries Unlimited.

Ficher, K., & Barton, H. (2005). The landscape of E-journal management. *Journal of Electronic Resources in Medical Libraries, 2*(3), 57.

Foudy, G., & McManus, A. (2005). Using a decision grid process to build consensus in electronic resources cancellation decisions. *Journal of Academic Librarianship, 31*(6), 533-538.

Gerald, N. (2000). Collection development and organization of electronic resources. *Collection Management, 25*(1/2), 97-113.

Gorman, G. E., & Miller, R. H. (Eds.). (1997). *Collection management for the 21st century: A handbook for librarians.* Westport, CT: Greenwood Press.

Grahame, V., McAdam, T., & Association of Research Libraries. Office of Leadership and Management Services. (2004). *Managing electronic resources.* Washington, D.C.: Association of Research Libraries, Office of Leadership and Management Services.

Gregory, V. L., & Hanson, A. (2006). *Selecting and managing electronic resources: A how-to-do-it manual for librarians* (Rev. ed.). New York: Neal-Schuman Publishers.

Harvell, T. (2005). Electronic resources management systems: The experience of beta testing and implementation. *Serials Librarian, 47*(4).

Hawthorne, D. (2003/0). Administrative metadata to support the acquisition of continuing e-resources. *Serials Review, 29*(4), 276-281.

Holleman, C. (2000). Electronic resources: Are basic criteria for the selection of materials changing? *Library Trends, 48*(4), 694.

Icolc guidelines and preferred practices for selection and purchase of electronic resources (2001). *Online Libraries & Microcomputers, 19*(12), 1.

Jaguszewski, J. M., & Probst, L. K. (2000). The impact of electronic resources on serial cancellations and remote storage decisions in academic research libraries. *Library Trends, 48*(4), 799.

Kennedy, M. R. (2004). Dreams of perfect programs: Managing the acquisition of electronic resources. *Library Collections, Acquisitions, & Technical Services, 28*(4), 449-458.

Kovacs, D. (2000). *Building electronic library collections: The essential guide to selection criteria and core subject collections.* New York: Neal-Schuman Publishers.

Lugg, R., & Fischer, R. (2005). Acquisitions' next step. *Library Journal, 130*(12), 30-32.

Managing electronic resources at Yale University library (2006). Retrieved November 12, 2007, from http://www.library.yale.edu/ecollections/eresmanage.html

McGinnis, S. D. (2000). *Electronic collection management.* Binghamton, NY: Haworth Information Press.

McGinnis, S., & Kemp, J. H. (1998/0). The electronic resources group: Using the cross-functional team approach to the challenge of acquiring electronic resources. *Library Acquisitions: Practice & Theory, 22*(3), 295-301.

Metz, P. (2000). Principles of selection for electronic resources. *Library Trends, 48*(4), 711.

Miller, R. G. (2002). Shaping digital library content. *Journal of Academic Librarianship, 28*(3), 97.

Miller, R. H. (2000). Electronic resources and academic libraries, 1980-2000: A historical perspective. *Library Trends, 48*(4), 645.

Newman, G. (2000). Collection development and organization of electronic resources. *Collection Management, 25*(1/2), 97-113.

Pattie, L. W., & Cox, B. J. (1996). *Electronic resources: Selection and bibliographic control.* Binghamton, NY: Haworth Press.

Sadeh, T., & Ellingsen, M. (2005). Electronic resource management systems: The need and the realization. [Electronic version]. *New Library World, 106*(5/6).

Welch, J. M. (2002/0). Hey! what about us?! Changing roles of subject specialists and reference librarians in the age of electronic resources. *Serials Review, 28*(4), 283-286.

Wilkinson, F. C., & Lewis, L. K. (2003). *The complete guide to acquisitions management.* London: Libraries Unlimited.

KEY TERMS

Consortium: A group of libraries or other entities that work together for a common goal of interest. Many libraries are becoming a part of consortium for ordering expensive e-resources to get better pricing deals and wider access for users.

Discussion List: An electronic mailing list for sharing information and problems to or among those who subscribe to the list. Usually devoted to a particular topic or subject area (e.g., ACQNET). Any message sent to the list will be sent to everyone in the group either automatically or through a moderator.

Embargo: The period during which articles in a periodical are not available in full-text online, usually for 3, 6 or 12 most recent months.

IP (Internet Protocol) Address: A unique identifier used by computers to communicate with each other over the Internet.

Impact Factor: It is a measure of the citations to science and social science journals which helps in evaluating the importance of the journal.

Licensing Agreement: A legal agreement between the library or institution and the content provider clearly stating the requirements and specifications of the agreement.

Packages They are grouping or bundling of publication titles, generally all of the same format (i.e., either journals or books).

Perpetual Access: It is a permanent right to the library from the publisher to have access to paid licensed materials.

Site: Description of locations of the institution served by the license.

Trial: A request by the library to the content provider to supply free access to an e-resource for a limited time. The library uses such a trial to decide whether to add an e-resource to its collection.

APPENDIX

The List of Journals, Electronic Discussion Lists, Organization, and Conference/Seminars

Journals

Many library science journals publish information related to collections development and acquisitions:

Acquisitions Librarian. Articles related to acquisitions. ISSN: 0896-3576. Haworth Press. http://www.haworthpressinc.com

Advances in Librarianship. Articles about issues in librarianship. ISSN: 0065-2850. Academic Press. http://www.elsevier.com

Advances in Serials Management. Research articles about serials issues. JAI Press. http://www.elsevier.com

Against the Grain. Articles related to acquisitions and publishing. ISSN: 1043-2094. Katrina Strauch. http://www.against-the-grain.com/

ALCTA Newsletter Online. The newsletter of the American Library Association's Association for Library Collections and Technical services. ISSN. 1523-018X. http://www.ala.org.

American Libraries. It contains articles and news about libraries. ISSN: 0002-9769. American Library Association. http://www.ala.org/alonline.

ARL Newsletter. Newsletter of the Association of Research Libraries. It contains news about publishing and member libraries. ISSN: 1050-6098. http://www.arl.org/newsltr/index.html.

Book Collector. Articles about collecting and collectors. ISSN: 0006-7237. Collector, Ltd.

Booklist. Reviews of new materials. ISSN: 0006-7385. American Library Association. http://www.ala.org/booklist/index.html.

Bookseller. Articles about U.K. bookselling and publishing. ISSN: 0006-7539. http://www.thebookseller.com.

Bowker Annual: Library and Book Trade Almanac. Information about libraries and publishing. ISSN: 0068-0540. http://www.infotoday.com.

Charleston Advisor. News and critical reviews concerning electronic resources and publishing. ISSN: 1525-4011. Charleston Company. http://www.charlestonco.com.

Choice. Reviews of books for college and research libraries, published by the American Library Association's Association of College and research Libraries. ISSN: 0009-4978. http://www.ala.org.

Collection Building. Articles about collection management issues. http://emeraldinsight.com.

Collection Management. Articles about collection management issues. http://www.haworthpressinc. com.

College and Research Libraries. Articles about trends and issues in academic and research libraries. American Library Association's College and Research Libraries Division. ISSN: 0010-0870. http://ala. org.

College and Research Libraries News. News about trends and issues in academic and research libraries, published by the American Library Associations College and Research Libraries Division. ISSN: 0099-0086. http://www.ala.org.

Free Online Scholarship Newsletter. News and discussion about the migration of print scholarship to the Internet and efforts to make information available free of charge. http://earlham.edu/~peters/fos/.

Journal of Academic Libraries. Articles about academic librarianship and scholarly publishing. ISSN: 0099-1333. Elsevier Science Inc. http://www/elsevier.com.

Journal of Electronic Publishing. Articles about electronic publishing. ISSN: 1080-2711. University of Michigan Press. http://www.press.umich.edu/jep/.

Journal of Librarianship and Information Science. Articles about librarianship. ISSN: 0961-0006. R.R.Bowker. http://www.bowker.com.

Journal of Scholarly Publishing. Articles about scholarly publishing and publishers. ISSN: 1198-9742. University of Toronto Press. http://www.utpjournals.com.

Learned Publishing. The journal of the Association of learned and Professional Society Publishers. News and articles concerning all aspects of academic and professional publishing. ISSN: 0953-1513. http://www.alpsp.org/journal.htm.

Librarian's eBook Newsletter. News about electronic books. <http://www.lib.rochester.edu/main/eb-ooks/.

Library Collections, Acquisitions, and technical Services. Articles and conference reports related to collection management, acquisitions, and technical services. ISSN: 1464-9055. Elsevier Science, Inc. http://www.elsevier.com.

Library Journal. News, articles, and reviews. ISSN: 0363-0277. Library Journal. http://libraryjournal. reviesnews.com/.

Library Resources and Technical Services. Articles about technical services issues and trends, published by the Association for Library Collections and technical Services. ISSN: 0024-2527. http://www.ala. org.

Library Trends. Articles about all aspects of libraries and library science. ISSN: 0024-2594. University of Illinois Press. http://www.lis.uiuc.edu/puboff/catalog/trends/.

NASIG Newsletter. News about NASIG activities and membership. ISSN: 0892-1733. http://www.nasig. org.

Publishers Weekly. News about publishing and reviews. ISSN: 0000-0019. Publishers Weekly. http:// publishersweekly.reviewsnews.com/.

Publishing Research Quarterly. Articles about publishing and scholarly communication. ISSN: 1053-8801. Transaction Periodicals Consortium. http://www.transactionpub.com/.

Serials: The Journal for the Serials Community. Articles about serials. ISSN: 0953-0460. United Kingdom serials Group. Full text online. http://www.uksg.org.

Serials Librarian. Articles about serials. ISSN: 0361-526x. Haworth Press. Table of contents and abstracts online. http://www.haworthpressinc.com.

Serials Review. Articles about serials. ISSN: 0098-7913. Elsevier Science, Inc. Full text online. http://www.elsevier.com.

Electronic Discussion Lists

The purpose of the discussion lists are to facilitate informative discussion about topics and provide quick distribution of news. The following are some of the discussion lists in the field of collections development and acquisitions:

ACQNET-L. For those interested in acquisitions work. listproc@listproc.appstate.edu.

ARL-Ejournal. For discussion of all aspects of the management of electronic journals. ARL-EJOURNAL@ARL.ORG.

Backserv. For exchanging and replacing back issues of serials. http://lists.swetsblackwell.com/mailman/listinfo/backserv.

COLLDV-L. For those librarians who are interested in collection development issues. listproc@usc.edu.

ERIL. For discussion of practical aspects related to electronic resources. http://listserv.binghamton.edu/cgi-bin/wa.exe?SUBED1=eril-l&A=1.

ExLibris. For discussion of issues related to rare books and special collections. Listproc@library.berkeley.edu.

GIFTEX-L. For discussion of gifts and exchanges. Listserv@lsv.uky.edu.

LIBLICENSE-L. For issues related to licensing electronic resources. Listproc@lists.yale.edu.

MEDIA-L. For information about media literacy. Listserv@listserv.binghamton.edu.

Newjour. For new journals announcements. Listproc@ccat.sas.upenn.edu.

SERIALST-L. For discussion of issues related to serials. Listserv@list.uvm.edu.

VIDEOLIB. For discussion of the acquisition and use of video materials in libraries. http://library.berkeley.edu/MRC.

Organizations

The following are some of the major organizations and associations in the areas related to collections development and acquisitions:

American Association of University Presses (AAUP). An association of nonprofit scholarly publishers. http://aaupnet.org.

American Library Association. (ALA). An organization which provides leadership for the development, promotion, and improvement of library services and librarianship. http://www.ala.org.

Antiquarian Booksellers' Association of America. An association of rare and antiquarian booksellers. http://abaa.org.

Association of American Publishers (AAP). An association of American publishers. http://www.publishers.org.

Association of Learned and Professional Society Publishers (ALPSP). An association which represents not-for-profit publishers. http://www.alpsp.org.

Association of Research Libraries (ARL). An association of major North American research libraries. http://www.ala.org.

Association of Subscription Agents and Intermediaries. (ASA). The purpose of this association is to provide high standards of service for libraries and publishers. http://www.subscription-agents.org.

Book Industry Communication (BIC). This organization promotes and develops standards for electronic commerce and communication in the book and serials industry. http://www.bic.org.uk.

Book Industry Study Group. This organization gathers, analyzes, and disseminates information about publishing industry. http://www.bisg.org.

Canadian Library Association. (CLA). It provides services to librarians in Canada. http://www.xla.ca

International Coalition of Library Consortia (ICOLC). A group of library consortia, mainly higher education institutes, that discusses issues of common interest. http://www.library.yale.edu/consortia.

Conferences and Seminars

The American Library Association (www.ala.org), The Special Libraries Association (http://www.sla.org/), The Public Library Association (http://www.pla.org/ala/pla/pla.htm), and the Medical Library Association (http://www.mlanet.org/about/contact_mla.html) are the primary conferences of interest to librarians in all areas including collections development and acquisitions. At the ALA conferences, the meetings related to acquisitions are sponsored by the Association for Library Collections and Technical Services (ALCTS) or the Library and Information Technology Association (LITA). Some other conferences of interest are:

Association of College and Research Libraries (ACRL) National Conference. The conference is held every year in the spring. http://www.ala.org/acrl/.

Charleston Acquisitions Conference. This conference is related to book and serials acquisitions. The conference is held annually in the fall. http://www.cofc.edu/cdconference/.

Electronic Resources & Libraries Conference. A new conference established in 2006 for information professionals to explore ideas, trends, and technologies related to electronic resources and digital services. http://www.electroniclibrarian.org/moodle/.

International Federation of Library Associations (IFLA). The conference is held every year in summer. http://www.ifla.org.

North American Serials Interest Group (NASIG). The conference is held annually in early summer. http://www.nasig.org.

Timberline Lodge Acquisitions Institute. Discussion of acquisitions and collection development issues for librarians, vendors, and publishers. The conference is held in early summer. http://libweb.uoregon. edu/acqdept/institute/home.html.

Chapter V
Sharing the Albatross of E–Resources Management Workflow

Jodi Poe
Jacksonville State University, USA

Mary Bevis
Jacksonville State University, USA

John-Bauer Graham
Jacksonville State University, USA

Bethany Latham
Jacksonville State University, USA

Kimberly W. Stevens
Jacksonville State University, USA

ABSTRACT

Management of electronic resources is a time-consuming and, at times, a difficult process. Although the management of electronic resources is often seen as a strictly technical services endeavor, it should be considered a multifaceted process requiring all areas of the library. This chapter will provide a detailed account of how one library handles the electronic resources management workflow in a collaborative effort. It will be especially helpful for libraries working with a limited staff and resources and libraries trying to foster a more collaborative relationship between technical services and public services. The objective and mission of the chapter is to present successful library electronic resources workflow concepts in a straightforward and realistic approach. It aims to provide useful information on current workflow applications, procedures, and ideas from practicing library professionals at Jacksonville State University (JSU) that will contribute to the literature and area of electronic resources management. This chapter will provide considerations for workflow enhancements and detail the advantages of centralized workflows and collaboration between units.

INTRODUCTION

"Water, water every where
And all the boards did shrink;
Water, water every where,
Nor any drop to drink" (Coleridge, 1798).

Nowhere in the library world do these famous words from "The Rime of the Ancient Mariner" ring through clearer than in the management of electronic resources. As more and more of our resources move to an electronic environment, the deeper we get into trying to manage them. They are indeed all around us, and a lot of the time, we even begin to drown in them. However, if a library uses a collaborative effort, these resources will not take over the staff.

Fundamental changes in workflows for library technical services procedures were set in motion with the introduction of integrated library systems in the 1980's. At that time, a rethinking of traditional workflows was needed in order to take advantage of the tracking mechanisms offered by automation. For instance, moving tasks traditionally assigned to the cataloging and processing units such as the identification of bibliographic records, to the initial site of order in the acquisitions department allowed for better tracking. In a 1994 survey, Bevis and McAbee found that, "Sixty-nine percent of the responding libraries stated that there had been or was a planned reorganization of nonprofessional staff because of ... integration, and 81% reported that there had been a shift in nonprofessional tasks" (p. 36).

As workflows and process analysis evolved to accommodate new technologies, the resources that these technologies were tracking were also evolving. E-resources, which in the not so distant past were anomalies are now commonplace purchases, and have easily been incorporated into established workflow procedures. Moreover, the increasing number of resources moving to an electronic format, whether completely or partially forced librarianship to create an entirely new job:

the electronic resources librarian. JSU is aware of the need to fill this position, which can be seen in the fact that two of the authors of this chapter have electronic resources in their titles. The two electronic resources positions at JSU are classified in technical services due to other elements of the job. However, according to Fisher (2003), a majority of electronic resources librarian job descriptions include public service characteristics. Fisher (2003) conducted a study of job postings for electronic resources librarians which appeared in *American Libraries* during a 17 year period. The main component centered on reference services, instead of management. Of the 23 most cited characteristics, management/coordination was ninth on the list. However, Bednarek-Michalska (2002) developed a job description for electronic resources librarians that calls for this position to be located in the acquisitions department and notes the responsibilities of acquiring and managing electronic resources. The varying job descriptions and requirements attest that managing electronic resources should be more of a collaborative effort between technical services and public services librarians.

The time requirements for managing electronic resources forces workflow changes. Some of the tasks involved in the process may very well be the responsibility of the paraprofessional staff. Duranceau and Hepfer (2002) discovered this trend in their survey related to staffing issues and electronic resource management. JSU's Houston Cole Library (HCL) distributes some of the managerial tasks to the paraprofessional staff as well. This frees up the time for the librarians to complete other requirements in the process.

LITERATURE REVIEW

While there are a number of articles available regarding managing electronic resources, the majority of these articles deal with specific maintenance procedures for databases, e-journals, e-books, and so forth. Additionally, there are several articles that provide insight into how specific departments (acquisitions, cataloging, etc.) in libraries manage these resources. Unfortunately, there are few publications detailing the entire workflow process from start to finish. Joan Conger (2004) produced an article that illustrates the importance of collaboration throughout the entire electronic resource management process from management to customer service. Beginning with management, she details how a library should employ a collaborative decision-making process that includes input from key personnel, including the administration, in order to have the decisions more widely accepted and have the staff buy into the decisions. This type of environment will lead to more trust between the staff and the decision-makers. Conger ends with the need to use a collaborative effort with customer service, or public services librarians, to ensure the users have a good experience with the library and its resources. Richard Jasper (2002) has also produced an article that touches on the collaborative efforts by one academic library in managing electronic publications. This effort involves a number of librarians from various areas and departments in the library. The author sums up the basic necessity for the collaborative effort by stating: "A collaborative, team-approach to managing electronic publications helps ensure that the necessary skills are brought to bear on the tasks at hand" (p. 356). He provides details for what each person does in the process and concludes with a poignant statement:

Now that libraries are providing access to literally thousands of electronic resources, the likelihood of a single librarian or a single library department being able to manage the entire process of managing online resources available seems very small. The key to successfully managing electronic resources is to identify a collaborative process in which key players know their respective roles and responsibilities, have some idea of how to back each other up, and

know where to turn when the "next question" that needs to be addressed in solving an access problem touches on an area outside of his or her expertise (p. 360).

There are a number of publications that discuss specific workflows and processes. Ellen Finnie Duranceau (1998) details the differences in the workflows for print and electronic journals at the MIT libraries. She provides insights into the collaborative approach the library staff undertook and the position they created to cover all of the requirements of electronic journals. Although the article primarily deals with acquisitions-related workflow, the ideas expressed can be easily translated to other areas of the library. Duranceau states: "Web-based serials require an entirely new workflow, one that is no longer a series of linear and standardized steps, but is rather a complex, cyclical, labor-intensive, variable, and team-based process (p. 83)." This is true for the workflow involved with all electronic resources and is the principle behind the workflow incorporated at HCL. Another author, Kristin Gerhand (1998), continues this thread by providing insights into Iowa State University's process of managing electronic resources. Iowa State created an electronic resources coordinator position that is responsible for all aspects of electronic resource management. While the process is managed by one person, this person collaborates with all other areas of the library to ensure a quality collection with optimum access and constant communications of all things related to electronic resources. The author states, "The unpredictability of ERs [electronic resources] also prevents us from writing a simple, one-size-fits-all procedure for handling them" (p. 282). HCL believes that is true as well, which is the reason there is constant communication between all parties involved. Gerhard (1998) also states: "The fact that ER [electronic resource] management crosses not only departmental but divisional lines complicates the situation… " (p. 282).

Since the management of electronic resources begins with acquisitions, crosses over to cataloging, and trickles down to the public services librarians, this one statement clearly identifies why a collaborative effort must be used when dealing with these resources. Furthermore, Peggy Johnson (2004) discusses the selection process and suggests that it should not be "… as linear as a form or checklist implies. Decisions require continuing interaction" (p. 211). She suggests that a collaborative effort should be incorporated during the review process. Conger (2004) also agrees with this type of collaboration. Johnson expands on this idea by providing an example of a committee consisting of people from each area of the library. This committee would allow each person to present their expertise from the various areas of the library, which will help the library select the best resources. Duranceau (1998) discusses this type of committee at MIT. The Networked Electronic Resources Discussion Group (NERD) was established to assist with purchasing decisions. While Duranceau does not indicate any negatives with this group effort, Johnson does not imply that this collaboration will work without problems. Instead, she describes some possible drawbacks: "bureaucratization" (p. 212) of the selection process, cumbersome work due to the size of the committee, complicated issues over consortium deals, and issues of individuals feeling left out of the process or that their opinions do not matter. It is important to note some of these since they may appear in other areas of collaborative workflows. Carol Montgomery (2004) demonstrates the necessary workflow changes for each department in the library when the W. W. Hagerty Library at Drexel University converted to an electronic journal collection. Although her article does not discuss a collaborative approach, it does illustrate how workflows are changing and reiterates how Drexel, like most universities, created a position specifically for electronic resources.

There are some articles that discuss specific collaboration efforts but not the entire management process. John Dupuis and Patti Ryan (2002) provide insight into the collaborative efforts of two public services librarians in managing electronic resources. These efforts involve putting aside their own subject specialties and compromising to develop the best collection for the library. Even though this article does not discuss the entire process for managing these resources, it provides good suggestions on how a small staff can work together to produce excellent results. The authors present methods used at York University to overcome the challenges of both limited staff and time and detail how the collaborative effort yielded positive results. Jeannette Ho (2005) describes how one academic library uses an integrated, Web-based form to encourage a collaborative environment for electronic resource maintenance. The integrated library system in place at Texas A&M University Libraries includes the form as part of the Web-based catalog, which is accessible to all users. Users, including the public services librarians, can submit requests that are routed to the technical services librarians indicating corrections or enhancements for the library's catalog and Website. While this article does not specifically discuss collaboration starting at the beginning of the process, it does offer a good suggestion on beginning the collaborative effort.

There are a number of articles that do not address the management of electronic resources, but do discuss collaborative efforts. Naomi R. Sutherland and Valarie P. Adams (2004) produced such an article in which they provide good examples and reasons for cooperation between public services and technical services librarians by detailing their experiences at the University of Tennessee-Chattanooga. The authors discuss how the cooperation between the two areas led to a better understanding of each area: public services librarians understood the reasons for following the cataloging rules and the technical services librarians understood why there was a need to be flexible with some of the local cataloging practices. The cooperation that they detail will ensure a quality catalog that will also be easy to use and understand. In the end, Sutherland and

Adams (2004) summarize the cooperation concept with one statement: "the key lies in regular communication and in interaction with colleagues in a variety of settings" (p. 14).

BACKGROUND

JSU is a medium-sized, public comprehensive university offering both undergraduate and graduate programs. It was founded in 1883 as Jacksonville State Normal School. Its purpose in 1883 was to provide a preparatory education for citizens of a rural Alabama county and the surrounding areas. The mission and the student population of the university have changed over time. The current enrollment is approximately 9,000 students. The university hosts students from all over the United States and from almost every corner of the globe. Its institutional borders have expanded. It is no longer bound to the twelve acres of land it originally sat on—it has grown beyond actual physical space.

This is also true for HCL. The library's collection has grown beyond its physical space, too. It has expanded from books, journals, newspapers, and microforms to include electronic resources such as CD-ROMs, databases, Websites, e-journals, and e-books.

ORGANIZATION

The library is staffed with fourteen professional and nineteen paraprofessional employees and has a collection of over 650,000 titles. The library's organizational chart is illustrated in Figure 1.

Library public services are scattered throughout the library, a thirteen-story building divided into eight subject divisions managed by subject specialist librarians. Each public service librarian is responsible for reference, collection maintenance and development, supervision of student employees, departmental liaison activities, and instruction for the respective subjects on their floor. User services (i.e., circulation, ILL, and reserves) are centralized in the lobby of the building. A centralized reference desk is found on the second floor.

Library technical services are centralized in the basement of the library. Technical Services consist of six librarians and seven paraprofessionals. Technical service librarians are responsible for acquisitions, collection development, government documents, cataloging, and processing. In addition to the aforementioned professional duties, all librarians are required to participate in scholarly and service activities.

Figure 1. Houston Cole Library organizational chart

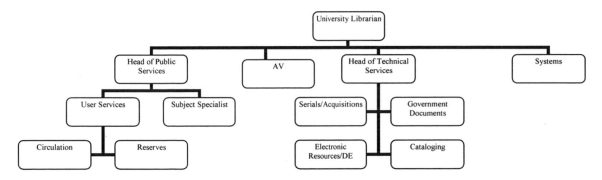

Sharing the Albatross of E-Resources Management Workflow

PUBLIC SERVICES/TECHNICAL SERVICES COLLABORATION

This explosion of electronic resources has created a new workload requirement: management. Management of electronic resources is a time-consuming and, at times, a difficult process. Although the management of electronic resources is often seen as a strictly technical services endeavor, it should been considered a multi-faceted process requiring all areas of the library. Bergman (2005) found that the workflow surrounding managing electronic resources does not fit into a neat package belonging entirely to the realm of technical services librarians or public services librarians. The workflow currently in place at JSU is just such a practice. The management of electronic resource workflow is a collaborative effort between public service and technical service librarians. At JSU, the public services librarians collaborate with the technical services librarians in order to provide a substantial collection of electronic resources and to make this collection available to the users as quickly as possible. It is this collaboration that makes the workflow inimitable. The collaborative effort begins with the review process, both trial reviews of databases, e-journals, and so forth and reviews of freely accessible materials such as Websites, extends through the acquisitions, administration, cataloging/bibliographic control, marketing, training, and ends with the assessment of the resources. No matter what workflow a library uses for electronic resources, good communication at each stage in the process is paramount since there is no physical trail of where the item is in the workflow until it gets to the bibliographic control stage (Mitchell & Surratt, 2005).

Despite the physical division between "technical" and "public" services in the library, managing electronic resources is one of many shared responsibilities. The mission of the HCL is to provide information services and bibliographic resources to support the scholarly and informa-tional needs of the university community. To meet user expectations better, the public service librarians' responsibilities at JSU have evolved to include four major professional areas. All areas are both interchangeable with and interconnected to one another. For example, effective reference is impossible without a sound collection and vice versa. The four areas are: (1) reference, (2) collection management and development of their respective subject areas, (3) instruction, and (4) liaison activities. Liaison activities include a structured liaison partnership between university teaching faculty and library faculty which includes appointment letters, a list serve, and formal communications between librarians and departmental liaisons. An informal relationship between librarians and teaching faculty is also encouraged and expected as part of their liaison activities job responsibilities.

Additionally, these four professional areas for the public service librarians are dependent on and mirror the four technical services professional responsibilities to: (1) Provide the correct bibliographic data and access points; (2) order, pay, and process the materials requested; (3) deliver or notify the public services librarians of new information sources; and (4) process non-library faculty request and inform them of new information sources. (Figure 2)

IDENTIFICATION OF RESOURCES

The initial process in any library materials acquisition procedure begins with the identification of resources. All resources, regardless of format, are discovered through similar means: professional review selection tools such as *Choice* or *Library Journal*, print or electronic advertisements, faculty requests, telephone marketers, professional recommendations, and sales visits. Although the usual selection criteria that are applied to print materials such as scope, relevancy, price, and so forth, should also be applied to the selection of

Figure 2. Library collaboration

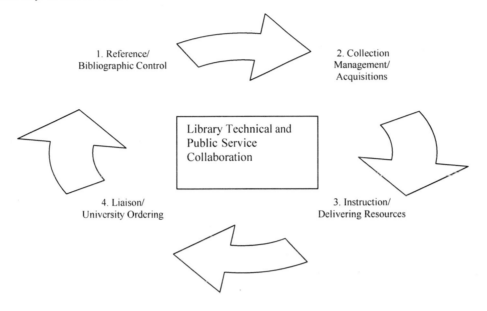

electronic books, journals, and databases, there are additional factors that should be considered due to the nature of the electronic format. Some, but not all of these are: the level of ownership (is the resource a subscription purchase with renewal obligations or will the library have perpetual access rights); annual maintenance fees, platform or access fees; licensing agreements; levels of publisher technical support; levels of in-house technical support; vendor reliability for content integrity; and possible subscription cancellation opportunities for print resources.

REVIEWING ELECTRONIC RESOURCES

At HCL, the management of electronic resources begins in the technical services area; specifically, acquisitions, where the majority of the resources in the collection begin their journey. A trial review of an electronic resource generally begins the workflow process. For more costly products that may require multiyear fiscal commitments, such

as publisher or aggregator database, or publisher journal packages, it is highly recommended that a preview or trial be requested from the vendor. In some instances, the vendor will initiate the trial themselves. An in-house review of an electronic resource is a relatively simple process to accommodate, without the consideration of the physical items to track and return if the product is not accepted. Whether the HCL staff requested a trial or the vendor initiated the trail, the review process normally takes a month, but sometimes it can be longer.

Coordination of the responsibilities for monitoring current database trials is essential for efficiency and organization. A well-established workflow pattern for this procedure will ensure that all trials are given equal attention. If the library has an individual specifically responsible for maintaining electronic resources in the library's catalog, active coordination between this person and the acquisitions unit is an effective way to maintain reliable trial information. At HCL, the distance education/electronic resources manager (DEERM) is responsible for this part of the workflow.

Once a resource is available for trial, the DEERM adds the trial information to a secured, restricted page. This page requires a username and password for access, so the information is limited to a specific group of people. This specific group of people includes all of the librarians at HCL and the departmental faculty liaisons at JSU. After the information is added to the Web page, the DEERM retrieves the page to make sure the layout is correct and also verifies the URL opens the correct page and the username/password are accurate and working accordingly. Once the information has been added to the site and verified, the trial information, including any username and password, is e-mailed to the librarians and faculty liaisons through listservs created for these groups. HCL has created an online evaluation form for these databases. There is a link to this form on the secured, restricted Web page and in the e-mail message. The form includes some open-ended questions about the content, the interface, and the accessibility of the resource. The form is available at http://www.jsu.edu/depart/library/graphic/temp/dbform.htm. This form is not the only method of evaluating the resources. The librarians and faculty liaisons are informed that they can submit evaluations by using the form, e-mailing comments directly to the serials/acquisitions librarian, and/or calling the serials/acquisitions librarian with their comments. However, using the online form to submit a review is the ideal method, because the online form or e-mail responses that are routed to the serials/acquisitions librarian and the DEERM are the simplest ways to collect database reviews.

During the trial period, all reviews should be centrally gathered and archived for future reference. The previously mentioned online form and e-mails allow for a simple means of filing them electronically in an organized fashion. If the product is favorably reviewed, but funds aren't available for immediate purchase, then later consideration is facilitated by having reviews readily available. If trials are extended or altered

in any way, all reviewers should be notified. The secured Web page is updated with any extensions or alterations of the trials. In addition, the links and log in information about the trials are removed at the end of the trial period in order to avoid dead links and confusion.

The public services librarians and the faculty liaisons are charged with evaluating all of the databases that are available through a trial, but the liaisons normally only review the resources in their academic areas. An online form is provided for the librarians and nonlibrary faculty to evaluate the electronic resources. This provides valuable information when a decision is needed with regards to the acquisition of a product. This is especially true in times of limited budgets. In addition to purchased products, the public services librarians also review freely available products, such as Websites, to determine if records should be added to our Web-based catalog.

Along with trial access to the product, many database vendors offer onsite demonstrations. Encouraging interested faculty to attend demonstrations and participate in trial reviews is indispensable in getting informative feedback. A good liaison system between subject specialist librarians and departmental faculty is an excellent way to encourage involvement. Trial periods and demonstrations should be set for times when teaching faculty and librarians are available for participation, avoiding summers and holiday times when faculty involvement would be minimal. A typical review period is one month, but depending on vendor policy, may be extended upon request. The level of trial access can vary from full database access to sample usage only. It is always best to have full access so that a review can be as complete as possible.

Evaluations and recommendations from the public services librarians regarding electronic resource subscriptions are routed to the serials/acquisitions librarian, while evaluations and recommendations regarding freely accessible resources are routed to the DEERM or the electronic resources/documents librarian. The serials/acquisitions librarian begins the acquisitions process by determining if the product is available through a consortium deal or if JSU will have to purchase it separately. Orders are placed and an initial record is entered into the Web-based catalog. This record allows the JSU librarians to track the progress of the resource. The DEERM handles general electronic resources, while the electronic resources/documents librarian handles any government related resources. No matter what type, a record is added to the Web-based catalog.

ACQUISITIONS WORKFLOW

The acquisitions of all library materials, regardless of format should follow similar paths according to established library policies and procedures, whether it's through a collection development committee, an acquisitions unit, or other centralized entity. If the library is collecting in multiple formats, the consistency of procedures ensures that acquisition decisions, and statistical applications for reporting and assessment purposes, are not biased depending on material format. This is not to say that electronic resources do not have added considerations during their journey through the collection development process, but rather that they should be viewed equally within the boundaries of institutional collection development policies to satisfy stated goals.

Generally acquisitions decisions for moderately priced e-materials such as individual books or single journal subscriptions can be made simply by set procedures through committees, subject specialists, or collection development librarians. Decisions to transfer established print journal subscriptions to electronic only subscriptions could be made at annual renewal times, and easily transferred by the institution's subscription agent. The process of updating bibliographic records indicating these format changes and establish-

ing access with the publisher should follow set procedures between the acquisitions department and the staff member responsible for maintaining electronic resources in the catalog. This will ensure that nothing is overlooked.

Pricing models vary widely among products and vendors. Vendor pricing policies are based on an array of factors including individual FTE (with any combination of faculty, graduate or undergraduate enrollment), tier group FTE, highest institutional degree offered, levels of database access (full database or product/title specific), multiyear discounts, print plus online package pricing for individual journals, and archival rights. Database vendors frequently offer discounts for group subscriptions. Participation in a state or regional consortium is an excellent way to be eligible to receive these discounts. Product choices, trial periods, license agreements, and cost divisions are determined at the consortium level, while review processes and decisions to purchase are determined at the institutional level. Discounts are applied according to number of participants; the more participants, the better the discount, usually. Licensing and invoice decisions vary according to vendor policy and can usually be negotiated centrally at the consortium level. To avoid duplication of effort, consortium offerings should follow as closely as possible the same acquisitions route for trials and purchasing decisions as the individual in-house institutional electronic resource purchases, and coordinated by the same staff.

In Alabama, a consortium has been established for the academic libraries. The consortium is called the Network of Alabama Academic Libraries (NAAL). "The purpose of the Network of Alabama Academic Libraries (NAAL) is to coordinate academic library resource sharing to enhance education and research. NAAL is an unincorporated consortium of the Alabama Commission on Higher Education and Alabama's eligible public and private four-year colleges and universities. In addition, other research libraries not affiliated with educational institutions may join as nonvoting cooperative members" (NAAL, 2006, para. 1). JSU is a member of NAAL. In addition to establishing trial reviews of resources, NAAL also provides workshops for the members on various library-related issues. Some of the recent workshops NAAL has conducted have been related to marketing your library, making decisions on resource cancellations, emerging technology showcases, using LibQual, and database training sessions.

The value of an outstanding consortium administrator cannot be over appreciated, and is essential for consortium acquisitions to succeed. Fortunately, NAAL has such an administrator. Coordination of all the disparate facets of electronic resources purchasing, along with various institutional fiscal abilities and personalities is not easy. A commitment to state and regional goals for the group is fundamental in achieving successful consortium purchasing. If there is a formal consortium committee in place, full participation is recommended to keep abreast of group activities. Centralization of all communications through one library designee prevents duplication of effort within the institution, and aids in better management.

License Agreements

One of the most intimidating aspects of electronic resources acquisitions is dealing with the license agreements. A license agreement can vary from a simple one-page paper to an extended multipage document of legal jargon. If there are any questions regarding the implication of statements within the agreement, they should be addressed with the vendor before purchase. Any ambiguities that may conflict with the institution's state laws should be resolved, and seeking input from the institution's legal representative to assist with unresolved issues can be helpful. Libraries committed to walk-in and interlibrary loan patrons must be very careful that agreements allow for

this usage. Vendors are usually willing to modify agreements to allow for individual library policies such as this if access is guaranteed on a secure site for authorized users.

Some vendors may allow for multiyear contracts with stated price increase limits, eliminating the need to sign annual contracts. Commitment to renew for the life of the license is generally not required, and the stated price increases can facilitate the budgeting process. If the vendor does not ask for two signed copies to be returned (one for the vendor to keep, one to be returned to library with vendor signature), a photocopy should be made and kept on file for the extent of the contract.

Once a decision is made to acquire a subscription-based resource, the serials/acquisitions librarian downloads a record for that resource into the library's Web-based catalog. The record is attached to a purchase requisition in the integrated library system, Voyager. The requisition contains the purchasing information, such as subscription costs, subscription period, and the vendor/provider of the resource. When the record is added to the catalog, the serials/acquisitions librarian forwards the access information to the DEERM.

ACCESS

HCL prefers to have IP authentication instead of username and password. Unfortunately, not every vendor/provider allows for this means of authentication. So, the initial step in the access process is to review the registration information and determine if the authentication is through IP or username/password. The next step is to submit the registration with any required information, including the IP ranges used at JSU. It is very important to make sure the IP addresses have been entered correctly on the vendor/provider side. Next, the resource's access point must be added to the library's campus proxy information. Proxy updates also includes the EZproxy server, which

HCL uses for remote authentication for authorized users. Once these issues have been handled, the DEERM continues the access process by ensuring the entry points are accurate and accessible.

Once the access information has been verified, the catalog record is updated with the appropriate link. Furthermore, the Library maintains several Web pages for electronic resources, such as Web pages for databases and the e-journal portal through serials solutions for journals. These access points are also updated with new resources. Once the library catalog, Web pages, and serials solutions profile are updated, listservs are used once again to "announce" the resource to the JSU community. This message includes a brief description of the product along with the URL for access. Also included in this message are the pages and links to those pages on which that the resources appears. Although this is a time-consuming method of announcing the new product, it provides enough detail about the resource and its location to be useful. Unfortunately, that is not the end of the cataloging process for an electronic resource. More work must be completed.

CATALOGING WORKFLOW

HCL began cataloging electronic resources in the mid-1980's with the purchase of *The Magazine Collection* and *The Business Collection*. The process of cataloging electronic resources continued to expand with the subscription of various databases. With each resource that was added, new local cataloging procedures were created (Bevis & Graham, 2003). The workflow has evolved into the streamline process outlined below. Even from the very beginning of the cataloging process, the librarians at HCL have tried to "keep it simple for the users and give them access to everything" (Munson & Frisque, 2004, p. 11). Skaggs, Poe, and Stevens (2006) provide detailed information about the cataloging process for specific electronic resources, such as e-books, government documents, journals, e-reserves, and Websites.

Once an electronic resource item has a record in a library's Web-based catalog, it is made available to the end user. It is at this step in the electronic resources workflow that full cataloging and bibliographic control begins. Taylor defines bibliographic control as "the process of creating, arranging, and maintaining systems for bibliographic information retrieval" (Taylor, 2004, p. 501). The two components of bibliographic control are record creation, which can be original cataloging or copy cataloging, and record maintenance.

Most libraries create bibliographic records for electronic resources by both copy and original cataloging. Like other types of library resources, it is often easier and faster to modify an existing electronic resource record from a copy cataloging source than it is to create an original record. Thus, in most cases, the majority of electronic resource records are copy cataloging records, and these records can be obtained from a number of sources. Most libraries purchase them from vendors or subscription services, and OCLC is the bibliographic utility most often utilized to search and export these records. There are also subscription services by vendors which offer batch sets of records for a specific class of resources (e.g., Marcive for government documents). Most of the major database and e-book vendors (e.g., EBSCO, Gale, NetLibrary) also offer free catalog records with the purchase of their electronic resources. These records often contain only minimal information, so even when free records are offered, many libraries still use copy cataloging from a source such as OCLC. For libraries which cannot afford OCLC or similar bibliographic utilities, Z39.50 sites (i.e., other libraries' catalogs) are a good alternative for finding and exporting records.

If there is not a record to be found in the sources the library traditionally uses to export bibliographic records, original cataloging must be employed. The cataloger must access the electronic resource and construct a record from scratch or use a locally developed template. Electronic resource records can be more difficult to create than records for tangible resources, and much has been written about the limitations of the MARC format when it comes to electronic resources. Additional fields and format designations (e.g., "electronic resource") for MARC records and the modification of already existing fields (such as the 300 descriptive field), have moved the MARC format towards more efficient representation of intangible resources. Another modification that many libraries employ as a local practice is to add specific uniform access points, or "hooks," for pulling electronic resource records when searching. These hooks can range from a code in an extra 246 field to a designation of "e-book" in a 655 or the name of the vendor in a 710 field. These access points allow libraries to quickly search and retrieve specific sets of electronic resources. This retrieval can prove useful when updating records as it allows for batch updating which is vastly more efficient than manipulating records individually.

When adding records to a library's catalog, there are two major approaches: single and multiple records. The multiple record approach involves inputting a separate bibliographic record for each format iteration of the same resource. For instance, a title may be received as a book, a microform, and have a link to an online PDF version; with the multiple record approach, this one title would have three separate catalog records. Most libraries find that this clutters the catalog and confuses the end user, so they prefer the single record approach. This method of cataloging allows for inclusion of all iterations of a resource on a single record, albeit with multiple holdings records attached. In this case, the title mentioned above would have one bibliographic record in the catalog with two separate holdings records attached for the tangible formats (i.e., the print and microform). The electronic resource appears as a masked hyperlink in an 856 field on the bibliographic record and in both holdings records.

Because most libraries utilize the single record approach, when adding batches of electronic resource records from vendors, the library must de-dupe the records to ensure that it is not adding a new record for a resource already owned and represented in the catalog. Most library automation software has the capability to de-dupe on a number of bibliographic record fields, including, but not limited to, the 020 (ISBN), the 035 (OCLC accession number), and the 245/246 (title/alternate title). De-duping is not the only problem to be addressed when adding batch vendor records to a library's catalog—batch imports also often involve a massive upsurge in authority work. For example, dumping a batch import of approximately 10,000 NetLibrary e-book titles into the library system can result in a massive authority maintenance project for technical services staff. "Unauthorized headings" can range in the hundreds of thousands for this single batch import. Reports can be used to clean up existing authority headings or add authority headings that are not currently in the catalog, but the influx of thousands of new records yields hundreds of pages of unauthorized name, subject, and title headings in the library system, resulting in months of work for technical services staff in order to clean up these headings.

Authority file issues are not the only maintenance which must be done on electronic resource records. From a record maintenance standpoint, electronic resources are some of the most labor-intensive records to maintain in a library's catalog, and the most time-consuming aspects of electronic resources bibliographic control includes URL changes, title changes, and dropped titles. These are all ongoing maintenance issues which must be addressed on a regular basis.

Libraries often receive information about upcoming changes from content providers. Open lines of communication between the person receiving this advance notice, usually the person responsible for licensing or someone involved with acquisitions, and the cataloging department are important so that resulting changes to the catalog can be incorporated into the workflow (Mitchell & Surratt, 2005, p. 49).

ADMINISTRATION

Electronic Resource Management Systems

An electronic resource management system (ERMS) can streamline the entire process of managing electronic resources. There are a number of ERMS available, such as Endeavor's Meridian, Ex Libris' Verde, Innovative Interfaces, Inc.'s Electronic Resource Management, Serials Solutions' ERMS (E-Resource Management System), SirsiDynix's ERM Module, and VTLS, Inc.'s Verify. There are several articles that provide detailed information about these systems (Collins, 2005; Duranceau, 2004; Meyer, 2005; Sadeh & Ellingsen, 2005), so this chapter will not go into detail about them.

These systems are designed to track an electronic resource through its' entire life cycle: discovery, review, evaluation, purchase, access, administration, renewal, and so forth. While these systems would be extremely helpful in the process, it will still take people to manage the resources as Medeiros (2005) found: "electronic resource management systems are just one step in helping libraries manage e-resources" (p. 94). For example, a library has to have an individual that will maintain the ERMS. Again, this would have to be a collaborative effort in order to get all of the parts in the system.

Unfortunately, these products come at a cost, which is out of the HCL budget. Because of the cost factor, HCL decided to forgo using an ERMS and instead rely on the expertise of the technical services and public services librarians for the administration and management of electronic resources.

Database Administration

Once a resource is acquired, the library must decide how much control the staff wants to have over that resource. There are a couple of options: (1) take the interface as is straight "out of the box," (2) make small changes by contacting the vendor/provider and having them do it, or (3) receive access to the administrative module, which most major resources have, and completely customize the resource.

The simplest management style is to keep the "out of the box" appearance. While this is the method that requires no work at all, it is also the method of least service to the users. Without customizing the resource to any extent, the user may not realize that the library has paid for this resource. With the "everything is free on the Internet" attitude, it would be to the library's benefit to indicate that this resource is free to them through their library's purchase; meaning it is not actually free!

Another easy management style is to submit your changes to the vendor's technical support staff and have them make the necessary changes. While this provides some level of customization, it can be time consuming in that the library has to wait for the request to be process. In some cases, it can take weeks for the customizations to appear in the interface.

The most time consuming method is to gain access to the administrative module because someone has to learn the module and actually do the work. This is also the most effective way of delivering the resources to the users, because it is customized in order to facilitate their use. Most of the major database vendors provide this level of management and provide documentation and/or training on the administration of the resource.

To facilitate the use of electronic resources, the HCL decided to use the administration modules to add specific customization to the resources and tailor the interfaces to meet the user's needs. This allowed the databases to have some level of similarity, such as opening to the advanced search, having the same text for links, having the same links to the catalog and serials solutions, and having the same branding options. All of these customizations increase the awareness of the users that these resources are part of the HCL collection. Hopefully, it will also increase the users' ability to use the resources.

E-Journals Administration

Once a library acquires an electronic journal, that title must be activated. Activation can be processed directly at the publisher's site or through a subscription agent such as EBSCO. The simplest way to activate e-journals is through the subscription agent. The agent will submit the subscription to the publisher with the library's registration information. Once the publisher receives this information, the library's contact person is notified. Unfortunately, this is not always the method the publisher allows or the library has a direct order through the publisher.

If the publisher requires the library to activate their individual subscriptions directly, the library must contact the publisher for activation directions including the required information for activation. Most publishers require the subscription number that appears on the mailing labels. This is easy to find unless the publishers mails the journal in a shrink wrap package. If a journal is delivered in a shrink wrap package, the person responsible for opening the mail must be made aware of the need for the mailing label. This can be time consuming due to the fact that the library has to wait for the next issue to arrive in order to activate the title. If a journal is quarterly, that may take a while. However, in most cases, the library can contact the publisher and obtain this information.

Online activation is normally a simple process. The DEERM opens that publisher's activation page and enters the required information including, but not limited to, contact information (mailing address, telephone number, fax number, e-mail

address), registration/subscription identifier, and then, if allowed, IP ranges. If IP authentication is not allowed, a username and password must be obtained. If a username and password are required, the HCL staff has decided to create a way to distribute this information without violating the license agreements. The DEERM creates a Web page with the URL, the username, and the password for those journals. These pages are placed on a secure and restricted page in the course reserve system, ERES. Authorized users can gain access to these resources by authenticating through the reserve system.

Serials Solutions

HCL subscribes to Serials Solutions' AMS, Access and Management Suite, product. This product is used to provide access to all journals that the Library has available to the users in electronic format. "AMS helps you simplify e-journal access and management at your library:

- Provide easy access to your entire electronic journal collection
- Reduce time spent searching for specific journals
- Reveal what's in your aggregated databases
- Link your abstract and indexing databases to your full-text resources
- Simplify your e-journal management
- Quickly evaluate the contribution of individual databases to your collection" (Serials Solutions, 2006, para. 3)

AMS does eliminate some of the management process, but not all. Serials Solutions makes it very easy to add journals to the collection. When HCL subscribed to this product, all of the aggregated databases were added. What followed next was an onslaught of electronic journals. Individual publisher packages were added, then individual journals, and then free accessible journals. Now,

Serials Solutions even allows their users to submit titles to be tracked. Any and all electronic journals can now be tracked through this product. The Client Center, Serials Solutions administrative module, is the tool that must be used in order to add journals to the profile. Administrators can also obtain overlap analysis reports and usage statistics from the Client Center. These tools assist the library in determining if a resource should be considered for adding/cancelling through both of these reports. Finally, Serials Solutions now allows the library administrator to receive a report of all of the titles tracked in the profile. Previously, this report was delivered through e-mail by Serials Solutions. So, once again Serials Solutions is making improvements to the way a library manages their electronic resources.

Maintenance

Dead links in a library's catalog are frustrating for the end user and detrimental to the credibility of the library. Automated link checking is the most effective way to ferret out problematic links in the catalog, and a link checking script can be useful for detecting broken URLs in records. One that runs a portion of the library catalog each week so that over the course of a month the entire catalog is checked is a manageable way to go. Some link checkers will provide detailed reports of the types of problems encountered with the URLs. Such reports may tell whether the page has been moved, where it has been moved, or if it has been removed altogether. One caveat is that automated link checkers are often not able to distinguish broken links from links that time-out during the check. Sometimes batch updates of aggregated database links can be done when a vendor changes its domain name, saving much tedious record manipulation.

E-journals are a particular maintenance quandary. Tracking changes to titles can be problematic and may require wearisome manipulation of vendor-supplied reports to obtain useful results.

For example, rather than provide a report of titles added and titles removed from the databases, Serials Solutions only provides a report of all the titles in the databases. Customers can generate their own Excel reports of every title in their profile; however, if a title appears in four databases, the title will appear four times in the report. By converting these reports to a Microsoft Access report, an application can be devised which removes duplicate titles. Each month a report can be run, comparing it to the previous month's report to see where titles differ. These reports can then be run against the library's catalog to see which titles are already in the catalog. Further reports must be run to see which of these titles are new and which titles have been removed. Serials Solutions does not currently provide a list of title changes, either, so these kinds of changes must be tracked manually.

Usage Statistics

Monitoring and collecting usage statistics is an especially important part of the process in determining renewal decisions for electronic resources. The level of formality for keeping statistics depends on individual institutional needs, and can range anywhere from complete monthly detailed analysis to a simple annual review at renewal time. No matter what the level of record keeping is involved, the review of these statistics should be an integral part of the acquisitions workflow for determining renewal decisions. Because of the time-consuming nature of collecting this data, vendors now offer commercial products that will collect and organize usage statistics for institutional subscribers. Pricing levels for these products are dependent on the number of databases monitored.

MARKETING

If you buy it will they come? Once the process for acquiring, cataloging, and providing access to an electronic resource has been completed, all of the library staff works together to promote and market that resource. Without this collaboration, a resource that may be a huge part of the budget may not be used. If it is not used, then that money was not spent wisely.

This collaborative effort can extend outside of the library as well (or straight to the source so to speak). Occasionally, once items have been selected or purchased, database or electronic resource vendors and/or sales representatives offer training sessions to introduce their product. Along with these introductory sessions, vendors often provide training and promotional material. It is a good idea to ask what promotional or training materials are available. These vendor led showcases or vendor sponsored "freebies" are a great way to get others interested in the product and to introduce the new resources to your library and university as a whole. If any promotional materials are sent to the library it is suggested that the library staff display them at public service points or student commons. Nobody can sell or market a product better than a library vendor so take advantage of all the materials and training or marketing support they have to offer.

Another marketing method is to distribute an e-mail message using the preestablished listservs. This message includes a brief description of the product along with the URL for access. Also included in this message are the pages and links to those pages on which that the resources appears. Another marketing method is to add information about the new resources to the library's Web page on the "What's New" page at http://www.jsu.edu/depart/library/graphic/whatsnew.htm. This page provides the same information that is included in the e-mail message: brief description, a link to the resource, and where the resource has been added to the Web pages. The public services librarians are charged with maintaining communications between themselves and their departmental faculty liaisons. Part of this communication should include announcements about new resources and

updates on other resources. Finally, new resources are discussed with students in library instruction sessions.

TRAINING

The next step in the electronic resource management workflow belongs to the public services librarians. This step takes place when the public services librarians begin instructing the users about the electronic resource and how to use it. Again, if the resource is not being used, the money was wasted. Library patrons are "trained" on the new electronic resources in a number of ways. Through in person reference interactions with librarians, through e-mail, phone, or other contact with librarians, and through the numerous formal library instruction sessions conducted by librarians throughout the academic year.

All subject specialist librarians are expected to teach library instruction sessions. The library instruction program is coordinated from the Head of Public Services Office. Currently there is no credit bearing information literacy course at JSU. Most, if not all of the library instruction sessions come in the typical "one shot" variety where the library is asked to conduct a session for a class during their regularly scheduled time. The pros and cons of the "one shot" course are endlessly debated, however the instruction program and system at the HCL is both vibrant and successful. The library faculty typically teaches over 400 sessions, reaching over 5,000 students, in the fall and spring semesters. Because of the strong liaison activity, university faculty are very supportive of the library's instruction efforts and do not hesitate to schedule an instruction session or to bring their classes over to the library.

Additionally, the library's instruction program is available to distance students who are less likely to sit in a face to face instruction session or come to the library for help, but yet are perhaps more dependent on electronic resources for their research and library needs. To assist our patrons who are not actually in the library, the library provides a virtual tour, a "what's new" section on it's home page, an online tutorial, a tutorial and instruction session online and available in CD-ROM, and just recently the library has been busy embedding itself (or a librarian) in the online course management systems at the university. The student taking a class online through Blackboard or WebCT can have access to the library resources and librarians without leaving the online course. Librarians can embed themselves in a course and be available at prescribed times for chat reference, e-mail reference, or can simply post a power point or handout with pertinent information regarding resources that available to help with assignments for the class. The embedding feature also provides the librarians with a vehicle to deliver a tutorial or to gather feedback about library services offered to the distance education student.

Because the librarians are actively teaching the library's resources throughout the year, it is very important that they keep abreast of all the new electronic resources as well. Often the latest and greatest electronic resource is exactly what the student's need to complete an assignment, and although the electronic resources can be overwhelming, the librarians assure the students that it is our job to keep up with them so they do not have to. Because these electronic resources can be added once a semester, once a month, mid month, or even day to day, the librarian's ability to "keep up" is vital to the user's success with, and ultimately acceptance of, any new electronic resource.

ASSESMENT

And finally the process ends where it began—with the public services librarians. The final step of the electronic resource management workflow takes place when the public services librarians re-evaluate the resource to determine if the library needs to continue providing the resource or to cancel it. During the assessment process, usage statistics from Serials Solutions and/or the individual vendors/providers should be reviewed. No matter how "good" the resource is, if the users are not accessing it, it is not of value to the collection. Usage statistics are not the only deciding factor. The overlap analysis report will aid in the determination of an electronic resource. For example, if the library owns two resources that have the exact same materials and coverage but one is not being used, that one resource would be a good candidate for cancellation.

The subject specialists (public service librarians) are asked to assess their collections on a regular basis. The library assesses its collection by doing a detailed qualitative and quantitative report on call number ranges and subject areas. The librarians report on the number of items in the collection and provide a narrative about the strengths and weaknesses of each area found after the assessment is completed. The library follows the guidelines established by the OCLC/WLN collection assessment service. Part of the assessment process is to evaluate the "defined access" or electronic resources that are available in each of the respective subject areas. Defined access can include Websites, electronic books, electronic journals, and databases. The electronic resources are assessed, just like the physical collection, and decisions are made as to the advantages or disadvantages of such resources.

In addition to the aforementioned assessment techniques, word of mouth and user reaction are great indicators of how well an electronic resource is working in or for your library. Librarians at the reference desk or on their floors should pay attention to which resources are being used more heavily or more regularly than others.

CONCLUSION

The management of electronic resources is an enormously involved process best handled by a coordinated group. Since there is a huge amount of work involved in the managerial process, it can overwhelm a single person. This multifaceted process requires the cooperation of all areas of a library from public services to technical services. This cooperation can lead to an even more effective method of managing electronic resources: collaboration. The collaboration between technical services and public services librarians will not only ease the workload and streamline the workflow; it will lead to a quality collection of electronic resources that the users know about and use. It will also provide an added benefit of allowing each service area to see what the other does and provide a way for each group to see the whole process, which will lead to workforce that concentrates on the "team" instead of the "individual" and provide insight into the "big picture."

"And from my neck so free
The Albatross fell off, and sank
Like lead into the sea"

So, let the albatross fall off the neck of one person and have it be distributed to a group of people. The entire process will become easier and much more efficient.

REFERENCES

Alabama Commission on Higher Education (2006, December 12). NAAL index. Retrieved November 12, 2007, from http://www.ache.state.al.us/NAAL/

Bednarek-Michalska, B. (2002). Creating a job description for an electronic resources librarian. *Library Management, 23*(8/9), 378-383.

Bergman, B. (2005). Looking at electronic resources librarians: Is there gender equity within this emerging specialty? *New Library World, 106*(1210/1211), 116-127.

Bevis, M. D., & Graham, J. B. (2003). The evolution of an integrated electronic journals collection. *The Journal of Academic Librarianship, 24*(2), 115-119.

Bevis, M. D., & McAbee, S. L. (1994). NOTIS as an impetus for change in technical services departmental staffing. *Technical Services Quarterly, 12*(2), 29-43.

Coleridge, S. T. (1798). The rime of the ancient mariner. Retrieved November 12, 2007, from LitFINDER database.

Collins, M. (2005). Electronic resource management systems: Understanding the players and how to make the right choice for your library. *Serials Review, 31*(2), 125-40.

Conger, J. E. (2004). *Collaborative electronic resource management: From acquisitions to assessment.* Englewood, CO: Libraries Unlimited.

Duranceau, E. F. (1998). Beyond print: Revisioning serials acquisitions for the digital age. *The Serials Librarian, 33*(1/2), 83-106.

Duranceau, E. F. (2004). Electronic resource management systems from ILS vendors. *Against the Grain, 16*(4), 91-94.

Dureanceau, E. F., & Hepfer, C. (2002). Electronic journal forum: Staffing for electronic resource management: The results of a survey (Column). *Serials Review, 28*(4), 316-320.

Dupuis, J. & Ryan, P. (2002). Bridging the two cultures: A collaborative approach to managing electronic resources. *Issues in Science and Technology Librarianship, 34.* Retrieved November 12, 2007, from http://www.istl.org/02-spring/article1.html

Fisher, W. (2003). The electronic resources librarian position: A public services phenomenon? *Library Collections, Acquisitions, & Technical Services, 27*(1), 3-17.

Gerhand, K. (1998). Coordination and collaboration: A model for electronic resources management. *The Serials Librarian, 33*(3/4), 279-286.

Ho, J. (2005). Enhancing access to resources through the online catalog and the library website: A collaboration between public and technical services at Texas A&M University Libraries. *Technical Services Quarterly, 22*(4), 19-37.

Jasper, R. P. (2002). Collaborative roles in managing electronic publications. *Library Collections, Acquisitions, & Technical Services, 26,* 355-361.

Johnson, P. (2004). *Fundamentals of collection development & management.* Chicago: American Library Association.

Medeiros, N. (2005). Electronic resources management: An update. *OCLC Systems & Services, 21*(2), 92-94.

Meyer, S. (2005). Helping you buy: Electronic resource management systems. *Computers In Libraries, 25*(10), 19-24.

Mitchell, A. M., & Surratt, B. E. (2005). *Cataloging and organizing digital resources.* New York: Neal Schuman.

Montgomery, C.H. (2000). "Fast track" transition to an electronic collection: A case study. *New Library World,* 101(1159), 294-302.

Munson, K. I., & Frisque, M. (2004). How we treated our clients' need for remote access through a single interface. *Computers In Libraries, 24*(9), 10-15.

Sadeh, T. & Ellingsen, M. (2005). Electronic resource management systems: The need and the realization. *New Library World, 106*(1212/1213), 208-218.

Serials Solutions (2006, December 12). *Products – Access and management suite.* Retrieved November 12, 2007, from http://serialssolutions.com/ams.asp

Skaggs, B. L., Poe, J. W., & Stevens, K. W. (2006). One-stop shopping: A perspective on the evolution of electronic resources management. *OCLC Systems & Services, 22*(3), 192-206.

Sutherland, N. R., & Adams, V. P. (2004). Territorial invasion or symbiotic relationship? Technical services and reference cooperation. *College & Research Libraries News, 65*(1), 12-15.

Taylor, A. G. (2004). *Wynar's introduction to cataloging and classification.* Englewood, CO: Libraries Unlimited.

Chapter VI
Process Mapping for Electronic Resources:
A Lesson from Business Models

Marianne Afifi
California State University, Northridge, USA

ABSTRACT

The number of electronic resources is continually growing and the processes associated with managing them are ever more complex. Consequently, completely new ways of managing these resources efficiently and effectively must be invented or borrowed from industries that also must manage complex processes. This chapter describes how a method generally employed in business and industry can be applied in managing electronic resource-related processes in libraries. Specifically, a technique called process mapping and its potential application to electronic resource management in libraries is described. Existing electronic resource management guidelines are conceptually linked to actual management situations. A case study is presented which is intended to illustrate the process.

INTRODUCTION

Electronic resource management differs from long-established collection development and technical services operations in that the latter have largely dealt with physical items. Over time, libraries and other information organizations have had a wealth of experience in how to select, acquire, and make accessible physical materials. With the emergence of virtual and electronic resources, the types of processes that libraries have traditionally employed do no adequately serve these new formats. Moreover, there is no clear consensus on how to manage these virtual materials efficiently and effectively within the information organization. Efforts to standardize how to manage electronic resources from a technical perspective were originally begun at the Digital Library Federation (DLF) and the National Information Standards Organization (NISO) and are still ongoing. Because of the delays inherent in organizational work, these efforts are moving along slowly and are not yet widely adopted. Vendors offer a variety of solutions based on early standardization efforts but the systems are not yet mature. In the meanwhile, libraries that must process these resources are confronted with questions about how to respond both technically and organizationally to the continuous change in the acquisition, management and delivery of electronic resources. Specifically, it is often not clear what types of skills are needed for different aspects of electronic resource management and who in the information organization should be responsible for the work. In this chapter, process mapping is presented as a mechanism to systematically manage the people and processes involved in electronic resource management in libraries.

BACKGROUND

Over the last 10 years the number and variety of electronic resources have been continually growing and the processes associated with managing them appear to be ever more complex. In a review of the serials literature, Corbett (2006) concludes that the literature reflects a rapidly changing environment. Although she found a good variety of articles relating to collection management of electronic resources, she found only a few articles in the areas of management and archiving of electronic serials products. The way libraries and other information organizations are handling this type of management differs from place to place. Breeding (2004) divides electronic resource management functions into back-end operations and user delivery. This chapter is concerned with how the back-end delivery can be accomplished in a changing library environment.

While some organizations integrate electronic resource management into technical services processing, others rely on a variety of options in different parts of the organization to accomplish these tasks. In all these models, staffing for managing electronic resources has been challenging because a diversity of new skills are necessary. These skills are not always easily defined and typically are learned by experimentation and self-training and not by means of formal training. In a survey of staffing for electronic resources management, Duranceau (2002) found that the libraries surveyed felt that they were understaffed and unprepared for the many facets of electronic resource management. Since then, Srivastava and Taglienti (2005) have observed in a larger survey of mostly smaller and midsized libraries that close to 50% of respondents identified as "Other" the job titles of the employees who managed electronic resources. A scan of job postings for electronic resource librarians during the last year, for example, finds a variety of position responsibilities and skill requirements. Furthermore, staffing levels have not kept up with the explosion of the number and diversity of electronic resources. Specifically, either existing personnel must be retrained or new personnel with appropriate skills must be hired to accommodate the management of electronic resources.

DLF's Electronic Resource Management Initiative (ERMI) has provided recommendations for the management of electronic resource collection development, acquisition, access and delivery from a technology and systems perspective. The workflow chart from *Electronic Resource Management Workflow Flowchart* Appendix B, pages B4-B7, shows a template for such processes but is too extensive to reproduce here.

Their overview flowchart, reproduced in Figure 1, shows the differences between physical and electronic resource management. While the ERMI addresses issues of license, metadata, and technical management, organizations must implement these processes with the appropriate staffing and budgeting. From a library management perspective, it is apparent that managing electronic resources cuts across departments and units within library organizations, requires

Figure 1. Workflow flowchart

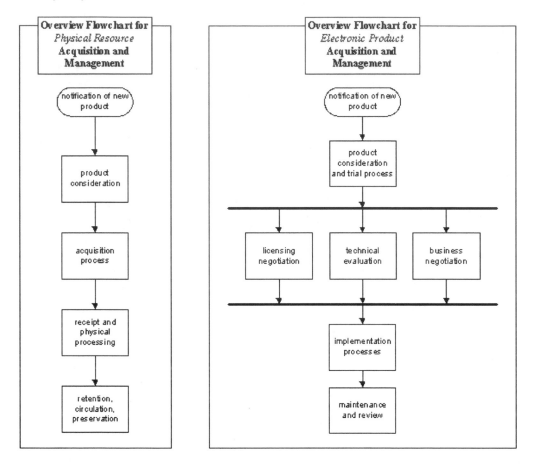

a variety of new skills as well as training and professional development, and calls for new ways of approaching tasks related to electronic resource management.

PROCESS MAPPING

A business method, called process mapping, is used in systems development and in managing large and complex projects. It presents a promising approach to the management of electronic resources from an organizational and staffing perspective. Process mapping is often synonymous with business process reengineering (BPR) and has its roots in the total quality manage-

ment (TQM) movement first championed by W. Edwards Deming (1986). Following his lead, a wave of reengineering business and organizational processes began in the 1990's. The idea, promoted by Hammer and Champy (1993), was to create flexible organizations by continually re-evaluating business processes. In turn, the newly reengineered processes would improve performance and productivity as well as deliver the best quality products and services to the customer. In a more recent article, Champy (2006) discusses the fact that in the new global economy it is getting more difficult to execute BPR well. As organizations become more complex because of technology, outsourcing, and rapid change, they must also adapt their reengineering processes accordingly. De Jong (2006) gives some practical examples of workflow systems and new ways of thinking about business process modeling as they relate to the organization's goals. Wang (2006) traces TQM applications in academic libraries from their beginnings in the 1990's where they occurred alongside efforts in the business world to more recent BPR efforts that address such issues as customer service and improvement of operations. While Wang addressed technology issues only briefly, it is evident that libraries continually need to manage the changes caused by rapid technological developments using TQM principles and BPR techniques.

Process mapping itself is a way of breaking down a process into distinct steps with beginning and end points, somewhat similar to a flowchart:

Process maps are used to help analyse and understand a process and to aid its improvement or, ultimately, its replacement. The process map can show what controls a process, what it produces, what areas it covers and which elements make up the process. It shows the sequence of activities, flow of information, decision points and the range of possible process outcomes... (JISC infoNet, ¶1 n.d.)

Process maps can help businesses understand and control how their companies function, what actions are involved and who is performing the necessary steps to manufacture a product or manage a service. Although most libraries are not businesses in the profit sense, they are complex organizations that purchase and process resources and provide services related to these resources. Thus library tasks and workflows lend themselves easily to process mapping even though the published literature does not present many examples of redesigning organizational processes using process mapping. For example, Maharana and Chandra Panda (2001) discuss BPR in academic libraries and conclude that in

response to radical changes in the information environment, libraries must use techniques such as process mapping to keep their organizations viable. Hayes and Sullivan (2003) discuss a project that addressed work redesign in libraries using process mapping. Their emphasis was on involving staff to re-examine organizational workflow using process mapping. In addition, an outside consultant provided perspectives and guidance that most likely would have been more difficult to generate from within the organization. Zuidema (1999) describes a process-reengineering project in library technical services in the late nineties where the changes brought by rethinking manual processes and creating automated ones benefited the library by making everyone more open to change than they were before. Graves and Arthur (2006) describe a workflow analysis in their serials unit that uses variations of process mapping to successfully restructure the unit and positions. These examples all show different approaches to process mapping but with similar goals, that is, rethinking how the organization works.

In general, process maps have a beginning and an end point or show an input and an output. A process' output often becomes the input for another process, thus showing the handoffs and linkages from one process to another. The inputs and outputs can be very specific or very general. For example, a library could process-map an activity such as "cataloging monographs." The goal would be to first create a big-picture map that breaks the activity down into a number of manageable steps. These higher-level tasks are then further broken down into more detail in additional process maps. The end result should be a map that shows distinct single steps such as, for example, "save record and upload to the system."

While there are many ways to graphically create a process map, one effective path is to begin with the inputs on the left side of the page and end up with the outputs on the right side of the page. In the middle of the page, between the inputs and outputs, are the tasks that need to be accomplished. Similar to flowcharting, tasks are designated by geometric figures of a certain shape such as rectangles indicating a task or action or diamonds indicating a decision point. Decision points then are split into their own sub-tasks. Across the page one draws so-called swim lanes that indicate who is involved in a particular task, so that in one picture it is clear who is responsible for which task. The task box reaches across as many swim lanes as necessary depending on who is involved. The map can also be represented in text format.

Figure 2 shows a possible process map for selecting, acquiring, delivering, and managing electronic resources, which is the highest-level process for ERM. Each of the subprocesses, for example, "acquire/deliver electronic resources" is represented by its own process map. Subsequently, any processes that need more detailing can be the subjects of further process maps. Figure 3 shows the textual version of a process map, entitled Process Definitions. Here, the processes are clearly outlined and reflect the drawing in figure 2. Both these types of maps should be used in tandem but can also be used separately.

Process maps ideally begin by assessing the current or "as is" flow of activities. This process may be time-consuming and may be met with skepticism on the part of employees because there is an implication of something not working properly. Working through process maps can shed light on existing processes that work very well and those that do not as well as allow the process manager to make adjustments. After the "as is" map is drawn, a "should be" map is constructed. This map can be based on the "as is" map and usually is, but does not have to be if there are substantially new steps or a complete redesign of a process due to technological or organizational changes. For electronic resource management, many processes are completely new or change frequently, thus an "as is" map may be sketchy or nonexistent in some cases.

To illustrate the construction of a process map, we can use the following example, which can serve as a model for a "should be" trial procedure. A vendor/publisher contacts a collection development librarian at a university about a new resource and suggests that the institution order a trial. To manage the potential acquisition of the new resource, a process map is drawn depicting the necessary steps toward acquisition. First the inputs and outputs of this particular map, the anchors, must be considered. The input might be the call from the vendor; the output might be a campus-wide trial of the resource. The activity in between, that is, what it takes to get from the input to the output, is the main content of the process map. In this example, the collection development librarian may next call a subject bibliographer to determine whether this is a good idea. Next, the bibliographer may call several faculty members, other librarians, or contact students about their interest in the resource. She may also consider such resources as the content descriptions, reviews, and the user interface to determine whether the resource is suitable. Without describing all steps in this particular process map here, we can assume that there is considerable interest in the resource and that there is a decision to ask for a trial.

The subsequent steps for the bibliographer in this example may be to inform the electronic resources librarian about this trial. She then would communicate with the vendor on what technical issues need to be worked out. Again, all the transactions involved would be broken into separate steps. Other steps could be to put a link on the library's Web page and send out an announcement. The last step or output would be the completion of the trial and a survey of the faculty and students about the new resource. If, for example, the institution decides that the trial was successful, and that the resource will be licensed, then another process map should be created to document the process where the completion of the trial would then be the input for the next process

Figure 2. Process flow chart

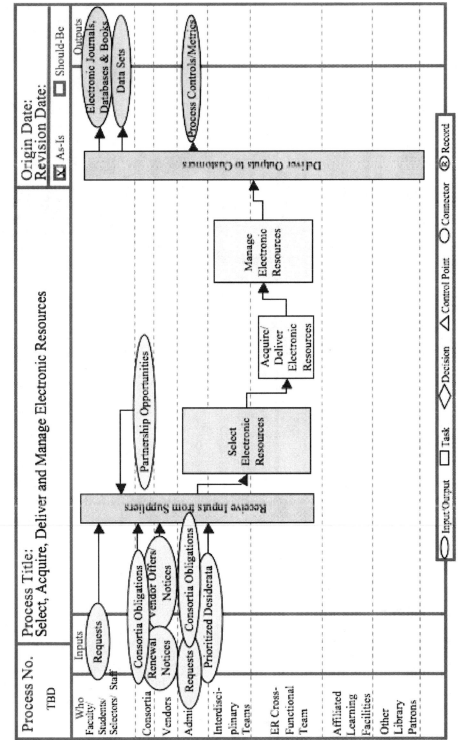

Figure 3. Process definition chart

Process Definition

Process No.	Process Title:	Origin Date:
TBD	**Select, Acquire, Deliver and Manage Electronic Resources**	Revision Date:

Higher Level Process: TBD

Process Objective: Provide seamless access to Electronic Resources in an effective and efficient manner

Inputs
- Requests
- Renewal Notices
- Vendor Offers/Notices
- Consortia Obligations
- Prioritized Desiderata
- Partnership Opportunities

Suppliers
- Faculty/Students/Selectors/Staff/Consortia
- Publishers/Vendors
- Administration
- Interdisciplinary Teams

Process Requirement Sources:
- Strategic Plan
- Strategic Pathways
- Policies/Procedures
- Mission and Values
- Operational Goals
- Publishers/Vendors' Help Screens/IS

Process Tasks

Beginning Boundary Task:
- Receive Inputs from Suppliers

.01 Select Electronic Resources

.02 Acquire/Deliver Electronic Resources

.03 Manage Electronic Resources

Ending Boundary Task:
- Deliver Outputs to Customers

Info Systems:
ILS, ER Database, OCLC, RLIN, Publishers/Vendors, IS, Internet

Outputs
- Electronic Journals
- Electronic Databases
- Electronic Books
- Alpha-Numeric Data Sets
- Process Controls/Metrics

Customers/Patrons
- Faculty/Students/Selectors/Staff
- Affiliated Learning Facilities
- Consortia
- Other Library Patrons

Process Owner(s):
Director
Process Customer(s)/Patron(s): TBD

map, possibly the acquisitions process. In our example, each of the participants in the activities, such as the collection development librarian, the electronic resources librarian, an acquisitions assistant, or a technologist, would have a swim lane indicating in which of the steps she is involved. Furthermore, the people guiding the input and the ones receiving the output are also identified. In this example, in addition to mapping out who does what when, we can also look at what type of work is involved, what skill set is needed for each employee and then derive a possibly more detailed workflow from the process map.

The *Electronic Resource Management Workflow Flowchart* presented by Jewell, Anderson, Chandler, Farb, Parker, Riggio, et al. (2004) charts the major processes in electronic resource management, but it is not a process map. It was not the intention of the authors of the flowchart to create one, but organizations can take the example of this flowchart as a "jumping-off" point and begin to create their organization-specific process maps, breaking down steps even further, adding swim lanes and defining the type of personnel who will be working on the individual steps. The ERMI flowchart also can uncover what functions libraries are currently not fully performing or only partially performing. For example, licensing information is often not tracked systematically. The flowchart also intentionally leaves out the details of a category called "routine product maintenance," which includes troubleshooting and resolving problems. The activities involved here can and should be very easily be detailed in process maps.

The construction of process maps can be accomplished by using a variety of software. Microsoft Visio, for example, provides templates that can easily be used to create process maps. Word-processing, presentation, or drawing software are others, but possibly more cumbersome alternatives. Other commercial software packages specifically designed for flowcharting or process mapping are also available. Initially, it may be easier to use whiteboards or large flip charts to sketch out the maps since it is preferable to construct them in a group process where changes are generally made frequently before arriving at a robust solution. A designated person who has expertise in using the software and drawing skills can then transfer the hand-drawn maps to electronic format.

As with every organizational change, it is imperative that the process maps be created using a mechanism in which employees of the library have a stake and participate actively. This type of work can be accomplished by setting up a variety of groups of different stakeholders. For instance, a wide variety of library employees should be involved in ERM. This is not to say that the group must be large, but it should include the major stakeholders in the ERM. For example, it should include an electronic resources librarian or someone with a similar job description; at least one but preferably more members of a technical services operation, including acquisitions and cataloging; one member from public services; a person with automation, database, and technology skills; and a person with at least a basic understanding of licensing. The group must be given a charge, a time line, basic training in mapping processes, access to software, and a meeting room, preferably with a projector as well as supplies to accomplish the tasks. Time must be allocated for the team members and others to work on the project. A project manager should be named who can manage the group, the timeline and the process. Other stakeholders in the library should be available for consultation and feedback.

The communications process for such an undertaking should also be carefully considered. Personnel working with electronic resources are likely very familiar with many of the steps in the process, although others in the library may only be familiar with one aspect of ERM. Therefore, the mapping project must be well communicated to the rest of the library. The project manager may be put in charge of this aspect of the project, but library management and others must also be involved in reporting the accomplishments and progress of the project. The project manager also must use a process numbering system that makes clear which are the higher level processes and which ones are subordinated to others. A hierarchical numbering system is recommended.

Once the mapping process is complete and a "should be" process map is created, the next step is the implementation of the process. In general, if communication throughout the process was good and reached the appropriate personnel, the implementation should not come as a surprise to the staff. Nevertheless, some training and restructuring might be needed to assure that the proper steps and sequences are being followed. Since a large part of ERM consists of parallel processes, care must be taken to assure that those processes are truly carried out in a parallel fashion and that there are no delays so that a process that depends on the completion of another does not hold up the overall flow. Managers and unit heads must ensure that the new or enhanced processes are being followed. They also should take note of flaws and hold-ups in the process. These problems should be corrected right away and the process maps adjusted accordingly. Since ERM is operating in a rapidly changing environment, the process maps should be revisited periodically. How often will depend on the size of the institution and experience level with electronic resources. Changes in vendor packages, licenses, systems, library practices, storage, and archival needs among others, may necessitate a review of the process maps and subsequent changes. Process maps in libraries, but especially in ERM are dynamic documents that have to adjust as the environment changes. That said, care should also be taken that the process mapping process is followed not for its own sake but because it is supposed to facilitate ERM in the organization.

One of the more difficult issues in ERM process mapping is the assignment of time to the processes that are being mapped. Taking into account individual differences, an average time for a step in the map should be calculated after carefully watching and trying out the "should be" process maps. From experience in managing electronic resources, we know that for some transactions estimating an average time is almost impossible. This dilemma is mostly due to interactions with outside constituencies, such as vendors or consortia, where a time estimate of a resolution of issues is often highly unlikely. Also, if a library's information technology operation is not within the library's organization, delays may occur, especially regarding maintenance and troubleshooting issues. Perhaps establishing a median time rather than an average time for determining the lengths of process steps may be more useful for a manager than using an average. This way, if a process consistently takes more time than planned, it may be necessary to make adjustments.

CASE STUDY

A large, multilibrary research library undertook a comprehensive process-mapping project to improve operations and processes in all areas of the library. With the help of a business process consultant, the library's faculty and staff mapped a variety of processes including selection, book acquisition, cataloging, and interlibrary loan. The consultant, an expert from industry who was not familiar with library processes, provided training in process mapping to all faculty and staff involved. A steering team managed the overall project. Area teams were formed with each team leader being responsible for guiding the teams through the process and reporting back to the steering team. The consultant met with the teams along the way to help guide the work and then translate the results of the teams' work into a template format that would later aid in a visual representation of the processes and their relationships to other processes.

As the teams began their work, they first mapped existing processes with the goal of depicting accurately the flow of an existing operational process step by step. This mapping activity included a definition of the inputs and outputs of the process, the people or groups involved, the steps and substeps that were taken for each process, and the handoffs to other processes. Once this "as is" process map was completed, the goal was to then improve the processes, if necessary, and to construct a "should be" process map. The maps were extensively publicized, and others in the organization provided feedback on the accuracy and logic of both the "as is" and the "should be" processes. Based on this feedback, process maps were reevaluated and changed as needed. An interesting outcome of this mapping was that some units depicted some processes in an idealistic fashion, which were then challenged by the "customers" or recipients of this process as not realistic. Although this type of interaction was sometimes quite unpleasant, it provided an opportunity to find out what was really occurring and where changes were necessary. It is important to remember that some processes in organizations become entrenched because there is no impetus for change either from inside or from outside the organization. The mapping process provided a good picture of where there were communications breakdowns, where individual work practices had not kept up with overall organizational goals, and where a complete review and restructuring of a process was necessary.

Because of the complex nature of electronic resource management (ERM) and a lack of awareness of the behind-the-scenes issues librarians and staff were confronting in managing the various aspects of handling electronic resources, an electronic resources (ER) team was formed to create process maps for the selection, acquisition, delivery, and management of electronic resources in the organization. The team consisted of a member of the library administration in charge of public services and collections, the collection development coordinator, an electronic resources acquisition staff member who handled all electronic resource acquisitions, and the two librarians who were working closely with electronic resources, one of whom became the team leader. Neither of these librarians' time was fully assigned to electronic resource management. The consultant attended most of the meetings of the team, assisted with drawing the draft process maps and then entered the information into a template. In addition, an organizational consultant who was a member of the steering team and was assisting in shepherding the process mapping effort for the library administration, also occasionally attended the meetings of the group. Unlike the other teams, after a short time of "as is" mapping, the team realized that the differences between "as is" and "should be" were small and that it would take less time to concentrate on the "should be" processes to arrive at a process map that would successfully map ERM.

The team set an ambitious meeting schedule that took away considerable time from other projects and operations, but was necessary to fully discuss the complexity and Web-like structure of ERM. The meetings alternated between everyone on the team meeting and only the people who were actually working on ERM meeting. The meetings of the whole team often became quite animated because the discussions about the complexity and iterative nature of some of the processes in ERM were little understood and often seen as too detailed. The ER team was encouraged by the others in the group to think about the public service implications of some of its assumptions and actions. The ER team was also encouraged to think about the handoffs to other areas that they previously had not considered. In its own sessions, the ER team considered detailed workflow issues but then presented summarized versions to the larger group, in order to speed up the process and save the time of the team members who were not involved in the minutiae of everyday ERM.

Along the way, the team called on subject experts in public services, serials cataloging, government documents, and digital libraries to get feedback and clarification about existing processes and handoffs, as well as suggestions about their possible improvement. The subject experts were presented with draft "should be" process maps for ERM and were invited to a face-to-face discussion for feedback. In those sessions, the maps were altered based on the subject experts' feedback when necessary. A final set of process maps was created and the project leader then presented the result of the process to the steering team. The team identified three major processes to map. These were process 01 entitled "select electronic resources," process 02 entitled "acquire/deliver electronic resources," and process 03 entitled "manage electronic resources." Process 01 consisted of four subprocesses, process 02 of six, and process 03 of four. Some subprocesses needed more detail and were broken down into further sub-processes. For example, Figure 4 shows process 02—acquire/ deliver electronic resources and Figure 5 shows subprocess 02.05—activate access. In process 02 the decision to acquire a resource was made. The actors are the university administrators (in this case legal counsel), a collection development group (CDC) and the acquisitions staff. The actions begin with a preliminary license review and end with delivering access to the resource in a linear fashion. In sub-process 02.05, one activity, namely the activation of access, is broken down into more detail. Here, only the acquisitions staff is involved. We can see that this process includes some yes-no decision points and also refers to the next subprocess 02.06.

A few loose ends that depended on the completion of other processes were listed in a so-called "parking lot issues" document to be revisited at a later date (i.e., "parked" somewhere until later). Overall, the mapping process achieved its goal of questioning existing processes, rethinking them, mapping them and tying them to other processes in the library. Most importantly, the mapping pro-

cess served to clarify ERM processes to library staff who were not familiar with them. The mapping provided a cross section of the personnel, departments and activities that were involved and provided points of intersections with other processes in the library.

FUTURE TRENDS

ERM implementation became easier after the creation of ERM systems by companies that recognized a dire need for them. Most of these systems were based on the original work created under the auspices of the DLF and are in use today by many libraries. Even though these systems integrate and make easier the work of managing electronic resources, there are still questions in a library manager's mind about how these systems can help libraries accomplish their goals. For example, where does an ERM system fit into the electronic resources and the acquisitions workflow; who will be using the system and populating it with data; what skills are necessary to do these tasks; how long will the tasks take; and how does this work affect and tie into other, existing systems? All these questions need to be answered regardless of the sophistication of the ERM system.

One aspect of ERM, licensing management, has generally been dealt with minimally by a majority of libraries. As publishers struggle to find business models that are acceptable to their shareholders as well as the library community, we must expect that the legal landscape will be continually changing for the foreseeable future. There are efforts in the ERM community to make sense of this landscape and to codify it for the benefit of libraries (Farb (2006). Yet, in terms of process management and staffing there are many questions about licenses and legal issues that library managers must resolve now. For example, do libraries need their own legal experts in managing licenses, or are institutional

Figure 4. Process flow chart 02: Acquire/deliver electronic resources

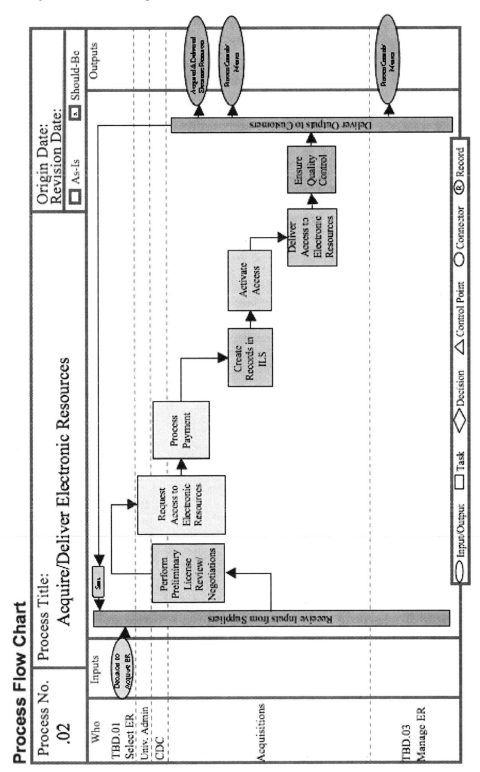

Figure 5. Process flow chart 02.05: Activate access

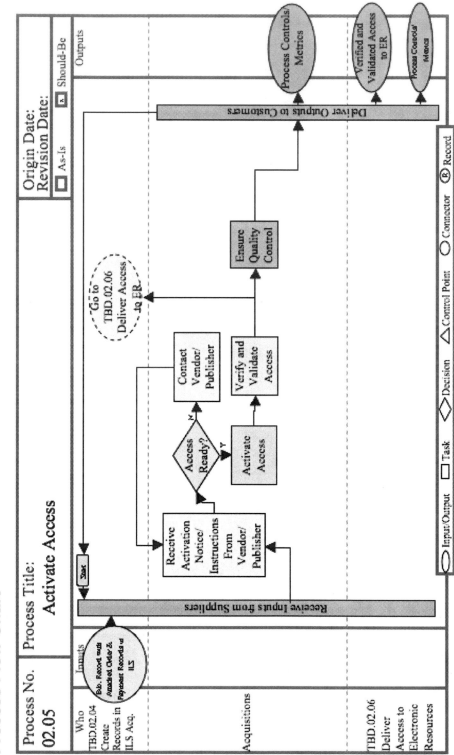

legal services sufficient? How would one or the other affect the process of ERM? Libraries will need to find solutions to these questions sooner rather than later before they can potentially get caught up in legal disputes with publishers and aggregators.

As libraries are experiencing profound changes in terms of digital content and delivery, managers must understand what is going on in their organizations and how to best staff them. They are increasingly turning to proven business practices that allow them to evaluate and design new methods of delivery of resources and services. Process mapping has a future in libraries, especially since it allows library staff to handle complex processes such as ERM. Publication of other case studies and discussions of process mapping within the library community may lead to increased adoption of these models and methods. Future research will be increasingly concerned with various implementations of ERM and comparing workflows in terms of tasks, time, efficiency, automation and required competencies.

CONCLUSION

In this chapter, a method of setting up an organizational process that allows for making ERM an integral part of a library organization has been described. Process mapping at its best can help this very important, but fragmented and ever-changing area, fit into the already existing organizational processes of a library. Furthermore, it can clarify exactly what must be done to get the complex tasks of ERM segmented and analyzed as to their necessity, validity, and connection to other library processes. Process mapping is flexible enough to fit into any size organization and should not become an end into itself, but a tool for library staff and library managers alike providing better resource access and services to library patrons.

REFERENCES

Breeding, M. (2004). The many facets of managing electronic resources. *Computers in libraries.* Retrieved February 2, 2007, from http://www.infotoday.com/cilmag/jan04/breeding.shtml

Corbett, L. (2006). Serials: Review of the literature 2000-2003. *Library Resources & Technical Services, 50*(1), 16-30.

Champy, J. (2006). People and process. *Queue, 4*(2), 34-38. Retrieved May 1, 2007, from http://doi.acm.org/10.1145/1122674.1122687

De Jong, P. (2006). Going with the flow. *Queue, 4*(2), 24-32, Retrieved May 1, 2007, from http://doi.acm.org/10.1145/1122674.1122686

Deming, W. E. (1986). *Out of the crisis.* Cambridge: Massachusetts Institute of Technology, Center for Advanced Engineering Study.

Digital Library Federation (2004). *DLF electronic resources management initiative.* Retrieved February 1, 2007, from http://www.diglib.org/standards/dlf-erm02.htm

Duranceau, E. F. (2002). Staffing for electronic resource management: The results of a survey. *Serials Review, 28*(4), 316-320.

Farb, S. (2006). Libraries, licensing and the challenge of stewardship. *First Monday, 11*(7). Retrieved May 1, 2007, from http://www.firstmonday.org/

Graves, T., & Arthur, M. A. (2006). Developing a crystal clear future for the serials unit in an electronic environment: Results of a workflow analysis. *Serials Review, 32*(4), 238-246.

Hammer, M., & Champy, J. (1993). *Reengineering the corporation: A manifesto for business revolution.* New York: HarperBusiness.

Hayes, J., & Sullivan, M. (2003). Mapping the process: Engaging staff in work redesign. *Library Administration & Management, 17*(2), 87-93.

Jewell, T., Anderson, I., Chandler, A., Farb, S. E., Parker, K., Riggio, A., et al. (2004). *Electronic resource management. Report of the DLF ERM Initiative*. Washington, DC. Digital Library Federation. Retrieved January 13, 2007, from http://www.diglib.org/pubs/dlf102/

JISC infoNet. infoKits (n.d.). Process mapping. Retrieved January 13, 2007, from http://www.jiscinfonet.ac.uk/InfoKits/process-review/process-review-9.4

Maharana, B., & Chandra Panda, K. (2001). Planning business process reengineering (BPR) in academic libraries. *Malaysian Journal of Library and Information Science, 6*(1), 105-111.

Srivastava, S., & Taglienti, P. (2005). E-journal management: An online survey evaluation. *Serials Review, 31*(1), 28-38.

Wang, H. (2006). From "user" to "customer": TQM in academic libraries? *Library Management, 27*(9)

Zuidema, K. (1999). Reengineering technical services processes. *Library Resources & Technical Services*, 43(1), 37-52.

Chapter VII
Evolving Roles for Electronic Resources Librarians

Debra Engel
University of Oklahoma, USA

Sarah Robbins
University of Oklahoma, USA

ABSTRACT

This chapter examines the evolution of the electronic resources librarian position within academic libraries as a result of increasing demands for electronic resources and the need for librarians devoted to planning, selecting, implementing, and evaluating electronic resources. The authors discuss the core competencies of electronic resources librarians and analyze the content of job advertisements for electronic resources librarian positions published in the College & Research Libraries News and The Chronicle of Higher Education between July 2001 and June 2006. The analysis reveals that electronic resources librarians are expected to be skillful communicators and collaborators as well as experienced with technology and versed in the issues surrounding electronic resources. Implications of these findings on the organizational structure are discussed.

INTRODUCTION

For the past several decades, new information technologies have dramatically changed the way academic libraries provide information and services to their patrons. The profession has become adept at adapting new technologies to best meet the needs of users. The impact of the digital environment on library collections, providing access to electronic resources, and the need to manage hybrid collections of print and electronic resources are ongoing challenges. The increasing demand for electronic resources has resulted in the need for more librarians and library staff devoted to job functions related to planning, selecting, implementing, and evaluating electronic resources. In the 1990s, as a response to the increasing and differing workload introduced by electronic resources and online services, electronic resources positions were created that specialized in these areas (Fisher, 2003).

While the specific job titles, job responsibilities, and job qualifications vary by institution, a holistic study of the evolution of the electronic resources librarian position and the role they currently play within academic libraries can provide guidance to administrators seeking to create similar positions within their institutions, to library and information studies educators developing curriculum, and to graduate students interested in pursing similar positions upon graduation. In addition, an examination of core competencies for electronic resources librarians can be useful for recruitment, professional development, and training.

This study analyzes job advertisements and position announcements for electronic resources librarians as they appeared in the *College & Research Libraries News* and *The Chronicle of Higher Education* from July 2001 to June 2006. It explores already published literature discussing the job titles, duties and qualifications required for electronic resources librarians and shows how core competencies have evolved since the electronic resources librarian position was introduced in the early 1990s. This study will examine the following questions:

1. How are core competencies defined?
2. What are the core competencies of electronic resources librarians?
3. How have electronic resources librarian positions evolved?

A qualitative analysis of job advertisements for electronic resources librarians allowed the researchers to trace job responsibilities and job qualifications and identify patterns of change through the five-year time period studied.

BACKGROUND

Core Competencies

Core competencies within librarianship have been discussed since the early 1990s (Corbin, 1993; Dole, Hurych, & Liebst, 2005; Fisher, 2001; Nofsinger, 1999; Ojala, 1993). The trend within academic libraries to identify and to use core competencies in performance evaluations gained momentum in the mid- to late-1990s. (McNeil, 2002). The discussion of core competencies has been approached in a number of ways for different purposes including identification of needs for professional education programs as well as continuing education programs identified by library associations, state libraries, and library organizations. References to core competencies have generally included discussions of skills, knowledge, and abilities.

Murphy (1991) defines competencies as "knowledges, skills and attitudes required to perform a job effectively" (p. v). Fisher (2001) echoes this sentiment and asserts that, "work-related competencies are a combination of knowledge, skills, and attitudes needed to be successful at a certain job and into the future" (pp. 180-181). The Association of Research Libraries (ARL) Systems and Procedures Exchange Center (SPEC) Kit #270 on core competencies similarly defines core competencies as "skills, knowledge, abilities, and attributes that employees across an organization are expected to have to contribute successfully within a particular organizational context" (McNeil, 2002, p. 7). Competencies are a framework used to identify expected levels of performance for and desirable traits of employees and can be generalized to the profession as a whole, created for specific specializations within the profession, or developed by local institutions as a way to measure their employees. A variety of library associations have created lists of core competencies for their memberships (e.g., American Library Association, 2005; American Association of Law Libraries, 2001; Reference and User Services Association, 2003; Special Libraries Association, 2003).

Corbin (1993) suggests "a competency is defined as a personal characteristic or trait, or what one should know or what one should be able to do in order to achieve a desirable objective or outcome. Fundamentally, competencies are not aspects of jobs in electronic information service, but rather characteristics of those who do the jobs best" (p. 7). Corbin divides competencies into the categories of personal characteristics, basic skills, general knowledge, and specialized knowledge. Within each of these categories, he lists the types of competencies required. Personal characteristics are defined as a service attitude, or effective interpersonal communication ability. Basic skills are defined as the use of one's knowledge and abilities effectively such as information analysis and evaluation skills or computer skills (p. 10). General knowledge is defined as the understanding of general facts or principles such as information transfer or information networks (pp.7-8). Specialized knowledge is defined as the knowledge expected for specific electronic information services being offered such as the discipline, relevant literature and what electronic resources are offered in that discipline (p. 16). Although Corbin does not report the findings of a research study, his work is beneficial for documenting the competencies needed by electronic resources librarians before the profession saw many job advertisements in this specialization. His article provides a foundation for further studies on this topic.

Fisher (2001) identifies three types of competencies including professional competencies, personal competencies, and educational competencies. Professional competencies are those that are "occupation-related knowledge and skills that make one technically proficient at the tasks that comprise one's job and are needed for success in a particular work setting" (p. 180). According to Fisher, these competencies evolve with the job. Fisher defines personal competencies as "individual traits, attitudes, and behaviors needed for success in almost any venue" (p. 180). The third competency area, educational competencies, is related to "those skills, traits, and attitudes that result from studying a body of knowledge on a given topic as one learns how to learn" (p. 180). Fisher's types of competencies are closely aligned with those identified by Corbin (1993) and are useful for developing an organizational schema for the current study.

Job Advertisement Content Analyses

Analyzing job advertisements to identify trends related to job skills and responsibilities within librarianship is a well-established practice (e.g., Albitz, 2002; Beile & Adams, 2000; Copeland, 1997; Deeken & Thomas, 2006; Fisher, 2001, 2003; Foote, 1997; Lynch & Smith, 2001; Nofsinger, 1999; Osorio, 1999; Reser & Schuneman, 1992; Sproles & Ratledge, 2004; White, 1999, 2000; Xu, 1996; Zhou, 1996). The literature discussing position announcements for librarians is extensive and covers a variety of positions within libraries. White (2000) suggests that studying position announcements offers "important insights not only into the characteristics desired in the job but into the changes and developments taking place in the field as well" (p. 265). These studies not only document changes to the job market in librarianship but also position qualifications required for specific types of library positions. A review of the literature reveals the various methodologies that have been used by researchers examining job descriptions and qualifications through content analysis of job advertisements. In recent years, the impact of technology and automation on job requirements and types of responsibilities has been well documented through this type of research.

Xu (1996) uses job advertisement analyses to examine the impact of automation on job qualifications and requirements of catalogers and reference librarians. He uses advertisements that appeared in *American Libraries* between 1971 and 1990, with two issues per year being randomly drawn. Xu groups data into five year spans and compares and contrasts specialized subject knowledge, work experience, computer skills, administrative duties and other skills. The author concludes that the requirement of computer skills and previous work experience were similar for both positions although there were still differences in major responsibilities and knowledge and skills required for the position (p. 29).

Zhou (1996) performs a study similar to Xu (1996) and examines the demand for computer-related skills for 2,500 academic librarians from job announcements in *American Libraries* between 1974 and 1994. Zhou concludes that, "possession of computer-related skills has changed from an incidental issue to a major qualification for all types of academic library positions" (p.270). Sproles and Ratledge (2004) examined 1,441 entry-level librarian position announcements published in *American Libraries* from 1982 through 2002. They conclude that employers were requiring more knowledge and experience gained from outside the classroom and increasing required job-related experience, such as computer experience.

Foote (1997) surveys systems librarian job requirements through an analysis of 107 job announcements in *College & Research Libraries News* from 1990 through 1994. She concludes that systems librarian positions require two essential qualifications: knowledge of computers and the ability to work effectively with others (p. 524). In addition, Foote notes that 38.4 % of the systems librarian positions analyzed require a degree *other* than the ALA-accredited MLS degree (p. 524).

White (1999, 2000) researched two articles concerning position announcements—one on academic subject specialists and one on head of reference positions. In the 1999 study on academic subject specialists, he analyzes academic library position announcements appearing from 1990 through 1998 in *American Libraries, College & Research Libraries News*, and *The Chronicle of Higher Education*. White finds that, "there was a somewhat steady growth in the percentage of announcements listing electronic resources as a job responsibility" (p. 379). In 2000, White studied the head of reference position descriptions from 1990 through 1999 from *American Libraries, College & Research Libraries News* and *The Chronicle of Higher Education*. He concludes that the most often cited position requirements for heads of reference positions were communication or interpersonal skills and the MLS. degree. He also notes that almost 60% of the position announcements for head of reference positions contain language related to electronic resources.

Beile and Adams (2000) examined 900 unique job announcements for public services and technical services librarians published in *American Libraries, The Chronicle of Higher Education, College & Research Libraries News*, and *Library Journal* during 1996. Similar to Xu (1996) and Zhou (1996), Beile and Adams conclude that the position requirement for computer skills was growing (p. 345). They identify a significant number of position announcements that relate to electronic services and do not fit into the public services or technical services areas. Beile and Adams note, "Academic library positions appear to be becoming more specialized, and many requisite skills of these positions are changing rapidly and dramatically" (p.346).

Electronic Resources Librarians

Albitz (2002) studies the electronic resources librarian in academic libraries by analyzing the position announcements as they appear in the *College & Research Libraries News* from January 1996 through December 2001. She explores where the electronic resources librarian position falls within the organizational structure, the requirements and responsibilities of the position, and the experience required. Through examination of 101 electronic resources librarian position descriptions from 1996-2001, Albitz finds that electronic resources librarians are expected to perform a wide variety of tasks (pp. 597-598). Albitz concludes that "electronic resources librarians tend to be jacks and jills-of-all trades" and are typically expected to perform public service duties such as reference and instruction as well as manage electronic resources, maintain Web sites, and provide technical support (p. 598). Albitz concurs with White (1999) and confirms that electronic resources librarians, similar to subject specialists, tend to be new to the profession with three years or less of experience.

Croneis and Henderson (2002) published a study similar to that published by Albitz (2002) that examines job announcements published between 1990 and 2000 in *College & Research Libraries News.* Their study includes all position announcements that contain either "electronic" or "digital" in the position title and compare the similarities and differences between positions with electronic in the position title versus those positions with digital in the position title. Position announcements were analyzed by position title, by function area, by institution and by year the advertisement first appeared. Croneis and Henderson conclude that both "electronic" and "digital" types of positions "use technology to enhance access to information" but that "electronic" positions often include public service responsibilities while "digital" positions focus more on project management and administration (p. 235). They also find that there was a dramatic increase in the number of positions from 1990 through 2000 and that the electronic and digital positions were reflected in the areas of public services, technical services, systems and digital projects. Croneis and Henderson write:

Initially public service librarians were the only professionals involved in work with electronic resources because those resources were few in number and available only on stand-alone workstations in reference departments. Networking capabilities, the development of the Web, and the explosion in the number of resources required the involvement of librarians with technical expertise. In addition, a wider variety of departments became involved in such activities as negotiating licenses, establishing authorization mechanisms, and providing access via online catalogs and Web pages. (p. 235)

This illustrates the far-reaching impact of electronic resources into all aspects of librarianship.

Fisher (2003) traces the development of the electronic resources librarian position from January 1985 through December 2001 by examining job advertisements in *American Libraries.* Fisher chose the year 1985 as the start date for his study in order to encompass position descriptions long before they were common in the profession. He discovered that the position title "electronic resources librarian" was first used in July/August 1992 (p. 4). Through examination of 298 electronic resources librarian position descriptions over the 17-year time period, Fisher identifies 74 skills or attributes for these positions and analyzes each position announcement by title and by content. In addition, he groups the characteristics into public service attributes, personal attributes, and technology attributes. Fisher finds that public services duties ranked highest in responsibilities for electronic resources librarians and that the technological specializations first appear fifth on the list of characteristics most cited by position announcements. He writes, "Knowledge of public service functions and process, regardless of the environment, clearly is fundamental" (p.11). In addition, knowledge of technology available and communication skills are necessary. Surprisingly

Fisher notes, "Acquisitions and related duties (like vendor relations and dealing with licensing agreements) were found in some of the positions announcements, but to a much lesser extent than anticipated" (p. 4). Fisher raises an interesting question when he writes, "Does the electronic resources librarian position represent something new and revolutionary or does it represent the current iteration along an evolutionary continuum of public services in libraries?" (p.11).

METHODOLOGY

For the purposes of this study, the authors performed a content analysis of job advertisements for electronic resources librarian positions published in the *College & Research Libraries News* and *The Chronicle of Higher Education* between July 2001 and June 2006. These publications were chosen because of their focus on higher education and academic libraries which is the focus of the study. *The Chronicle of Higher Education* is published weekly with a wide range of job announcements for a variety of different academic institutions; *College & Research Libraries News* is a monthly publication which includes job advertisements of library positions within a host of academic institutions. Announcements selected were for full-time positions in academic libraries including university and college libraries, special libraries within the academic community such as medical or law libraries, and community college libraries. Both the Albitz (2002) and Fisher (2003) studies ceased gathering data in 2001 which made 2001 a logical starting point for the current study.

Because of the diversity of possible job titles for this type of position, the authors read all advertisements that included the words "electronic," "digital," "virtual," and "online" in the position title. Only the advertisements for jobs dealing specifically with the management, maintenance, and/or organization of electronic resources in some way were collected for further analysis.

Advertisements for those positions dealing exclusively with electronic services, virtual reference, digital projects, or systems were excluded from this, which differs from the studies by Albitz (2002) and Fisher (2003). Duplicate job advertisements were also removed so that each advertisement was studied only once per year. It is possible that a job advertisement was included twice if the advertisement appeared over a series of months that spanned two different years. The job advertisement would then be included in both years, though only once per year even if it appeared several times each year. The researchers chose not to eliminate duplication between years because it is possible that the position was filled and vacated within the time period.

The authors did an initial content analysis of select advertisements from each year. During the initial analysis, the authors identified recurring job responsibilities and qualifications. From these responsibilities and qualifications, broad category classifications were developed for the coding of all advertisements. Twenty-six different job duties were also identified for study. These were broadly grouped under the headings of materials, services, technology, management/administration, interpersonal, and other job responsibilities such as professional involvement and scholarly activity (see Appendix A). Thirty-two different qualifications were identified for analysis; these include specific experience requirements, abilities, skills, knowledge, education, evidence of research, publication, and/or creative activity, and professional involvement (see Appendix B). There was some overlap between the identified job responsibilities and job qualifications, and the researchers based the coding of the item on how it was presented in the job advertisement.

All data was recorded dichotomously in an Excel workbook—either the item was present in the job advertisement or it was not (yes=1, no=0). Each year of data was recorded in a separate spreadsheet so that the authors could look at possible changes in qualifications or duties throughout the period of the study. To ensure consistency in coding between authors, each job advertisement was coded by each author. If there were discrepancies, the authors discussed their rationale for their particular coding and an agreement was reached for the final coding of the advertisement. For example, one area of discussion was whether to code particular items as job responsibilities or job qualifications because of overlap in the coding categories. It was decided to use the organization of the advertisement to guide the researchers' coding. The researchers utilized Fisher's (2003) tabulation method for the current study.

In some cases the full position description and qualifications were not available because the complete position announcement was on a Web site and not included in the printed announcement. In those instances, as much information as could be discerned from the printed job advertisement was coded and included on the Excel spreadsheet, but a note was made that a Web address was provided for a complete job description.

FINDINGS

Job Advertisements

The authors analyzed a total of 183 electronic resources librarian position advertisements that were published in *College & Research Libraries News* and *The Chronicle of Higher Education* between July 2001 and June 2006 and that met the criteria specified in the methodology. Table 1 illustrates the number of job announcements analyzed by year; it should be noted that within both 2001 and 2006 only six months worth of data were compiled.

Job Responsibilities

Table 2 illustrates the 12 most cited job responsibilities of electronic resources librarians and the percentage of job advertisements listing each job responsibility.

The most frequently listed job responsibility included in two-thirds of the job announcements was "acquire/evaluate/license electronic resources." Half of the job advertisements analyzed list "manage/maintain/troubleshoot electronic resources" as a primary job responsibility, and almost half included "organize electronic resources, through cataloging, electronic resource management system or, on Web sites." Other frequently cited job responsibilities included performing reference services, teamwork/collaboration, performing library instruction, and Web-authoring or Web-management. Each of these appeared in at least one-third of the job advertisements studied.

Required Qualifications

The authors coded the required qualifications cited by each job announcement. Table 3 summarizes the 12 most cited required qualifications and provides the percentage of the total that required each qualification.

Electronic resources librarian positions consistently require a Master's degree in library and information studies (MLIS) with 72% of the ads studied requiring this degree. Beyond the required

Table 1. Number of advertisements used by year (July 2001-June 2006)

Year	Number of Advertisements
2001 (July-December)	26
2002	52
2003	31
2004	32
2005	25
2006 (January - June)	17
Total	**183**

Data source: College & Research Libraries News and The Chronicle of Higher Education

Table 2. Top 12 job responsibilities for electronic resources librarians

Job Responsibilities	% of Total Job Announcements
Acquire/evaluate/license electronic resources	66%
Manage/maintain/troubleshoot electronic resources	50%
Organize electronic resources, through cataloging, electronic resource management system or, on Web site	46%
Perform reference service	42%
Teamwork/collaboration	36%
Perform library instruction	33%
Web authoring/Web management	32%
Training	26%
Collection development of print resources	25%
Committee work	23%
Responsibilities for serials, both electronic and print	19%
Supervision	18%

MLIS, the most frequently listed requirement for the electronic resources librarian position is "demonstrated oral and written communication skills" which is listed in 44% of the advertisements. This is closely followed by "experience with, or knowledge of, electronic resources" which is required in 43% of the positions. Another frequently cited job requirement is the "ability to collaborate or work in a team environment" which is included in 38% of the advertisements. "Experience with, or knowledge of, computer software" was listed as a job requirement in 29% of the studied ads. It is interesting to note that of the top five requirements for electronic resources librarians two of the requirements are related to technological skills and two are related to interpersonal skills.

Preferred Qualifications

The researchers analyzed each position announcement's preferred job qualifications, though more than 50% of the position announcements did not include them. The most often cited preferred qualifications include: training experience; experience with a particular library system such as an ILS or bibliographic utility; experience with, or knowledge of, electronic resources; experience with, or knowledge of acquisitions and/or business practices; familiarity with licensing and contract negotiation; experience with, or knowledge of, computer software; and experience with computer programming languages. Some of the preferred qualifications were specific to an institution such as an institution's specific ILS. Often the specific needs of an organization will override whatever previous experience may have taught, though a familiarity with the principles and concepts certainly guides a person new to a position.

DISCUSSION

Perhaps Albitz (2002) said it best when she describes electronic resources librarians as tending to be "jacks- and jills-of-all-trades" (p. 598). As evidenced in previous studies (Albitz 2002; Fisher, 2003) as well as the current study, electronic resources librarians are expected to perform a

Table 3. Top 12 required job qualifications for electronic resources librarians

Top 12 Required Job Qualifications	% of Total Job Announcements
Masters degree in library and information studies	72%
Demonstrated oral and written communication skills	44%
Experience with, or knowledge of, electronic resources	43%
Ability to collaborate or work in a team environment	38%
Experience with, or knowledge of, computer software	29%
Experience with, or knowledge of, computer hardware	25%
Awareness of trends in electronic resources	24%
Academic/professional library experience	21%
Experience with, or knowledge of, Web development/ Web site management	21%
Experience with, or knowledge of, cataloging	20%
Experience with, or knowledge of, metadata standards	19%
Experience with a particular library system, such as an ILS or bibliographic utility	18%

wide range of job duties and are responsible for an assortment of tasks. Albitz notes, "Librarians who chose to enter the field of electronic resources management could find themselves required to perform almost any function one might typically find in an academic library, from Web design to circulation to bibliographic instruction" (p. 595). What was no doubt true in 2001 is still true five years later. While the current study narrowed the focus and included only those positions dealing with electronic resources such as databases, e-journals, and/or e-books specifically, it still appears that electronic resources librarians may be expected to have experiences in public services and technical services as well as a clear grasp of technology.

Fisher (2003) divided the 74 characteristics he identified (through an analysis of a combination of position descriptions and qualifications statements) into three categories (1) traditional public services functions, (2) technology-related functions, and (3) interpersonal functions (p.10). Despite the current study's focus solely on those electronic resources librarian positions that had responsibility for acquiring, maintaining, or organizing electronic resources in some fashion, the study confirms Fisher's findings of the electronic resources librarians being heavily involved in public services. Acquiring, maintaining, and organizing electronic resources by the very nature of the work fits within the realm of technical services, and while all job advertisements included in the current study involve one or more of those duties, almost half (42%) of the advertisements included providing reference services as a part of the job, and approximately one-third listed performing library instruction as a job duty. Fisher found communication skills to be a highly cited job characteristic for electronic resources librarians; this study found the same to be true with demonstrated oral and written communication skills, which appeared as a required qualification in 44% of the job advertisements, and the ability to collaborate or work in a team environment, which was required in 38% of the job advertisements.

This study confirmed the findings of Lynch and Smith (2001) who wrote, "Most academic library jobs require a degree from an ALA-accredited program" (p. 416). Electronic resources librarian positions consistently require a Master's degree in library science with 72% of the ads studied requiring this degree. This also concurs with Albitz (2002) and White (2000). It is possible that many of the remaining 28% of the ads actually do require the degree; however, due to a large proportion of the ads providing a Web address for more information rather than a full position advertisement, it is uncertain as to whether the Web site listed an MLIS as a requirement.

One limitation of the current study is the growing trend of posting full job advertisements on the Web rather than publishing the full advertisement in national publications. Of the 183 position announcements included in the study, 58 (32%) of the announcements referred readers to a Web address where a complete position description could be found. Deeken and Thomas (2006) estimated that 10% of the job ads they reviewed were excluded from the final study because the ads listed URLs rather than complete information (p. 138). Albitz (2002) also noted that sometimes only a "skeletal" job announcement was listed in *College & Research Libraries News* and that a Web address was provided where candidates could locate complete information (p. 594). Since information on the Web is transitory, this type of research study is likely to prove more problematic in the future. Researchers wishing to analyze job advertisements may need to conduct the study in real time and gather data from Web sites rather than rely solely on what has been published in trade journals.

FUTURE TRENDS

Computers and technology are a way of life in libraries. In their 2006 study, Deeken and Thomas found that "collecting data on computer skills was meaningless" because it is now assumed that applicants will possess computer skills (p. 143). In her 1997 article, Foote notes, "the systems librarian must accept change as a characteristic of the position responsibilities" (p. 524). While electronic resources librarians are not typically characterized as systems librarians, change is just as much a way of life for them as it is for systems librarians. The landscape for managing electronic resources is changing, and those responsible for managing electronic resources will have to adapt with each new technology and procedure.

The nature of electronic resources management and changes in technology as a resource delivery mechanism has strongly influenced the evolution of electronic resources librarian positions. One of the results of a fast-changing landscape within electronic resources management is seen in the position responsibilities concerning teamwork and collaboration within the organizational structure, as well as in the job requirements that indicate skills and abilities in interpersonal communication and working in a team environment. Electronic resources librarians are required to be collaborative, and job advertisements often indicate that the applicants must have skills and abilities in teamwork combined with excellent oral and written communication skills. In a discussion of the role of electronic resources librarians at Washington State University, Felt (1999) writes:

As part of their official job descriptions, electronic resources librarians teach both librarians and library patrons how to use new electronic resources. They are also positioned to have regular, official and unofficial, conversations with others in non-public service departments where decisions about technology are sometimes made. Because electronic resources librarians deal regularly with new technologies, talk technology with patrons and colleagues, and keep current with pertinent manuals and articles, they can understand the unique language that accompanies this specialized field. It is important for a reference department to have individuals who can talk and understand that language. (p. 85)

Translating technical jargon into words of meaning for public services librarians and other nontechnically minded librarians can be a vital role of electronic resources librarians within the organization and will likely continue to be part of the communication role for this position in the future. While librarians in all sectors of the profession are increasingly expected to have a functioning level of computer literacy, it is unreasonable to expect each and every librarian to stay abreast of the latest technology trends and the myriad issues surrounding electronic resources, as well as to monitor the trends in their own area of specialization. This is why it is important that electronic resources librarians are able to filter information related to their area of specialization, electronic resources, and repackage it in a succinct and meaningful way to keep their colleagues up-to-date in what they must know to best serve their patrons and perform their own job duties.

Lynch and Smith (2001) discuss the presence of behavioral skills in the job advertisements they analyzed and indicate that, while observers are deeming these skills essential for successful library work, it has not been determined "who should teach these skills" (p. 418). They comment that in library and information studies educational programs "[p]ractice in doing such activities [team projects, oral presentations, instruction] might be included in courses, but instruction in how to do it is not" (p. 418). It is important as a profession that new professionals are properly trained with the skills they will need to succeed; if oral and written communication skills, collaboration, and teamwork are being listed as qualifications in job advertisements, library schools should provide students with opportunities for developing these skills in a demonstrable way.

Corbin (1993) identifies six methods of acquiring proficiency in competencies related to electronic resources and services; these include: formal education and training programs, on-the-job training, self-education, apprenticeship, experience, and continuing education (pp. 19-21). Of these, experience is probably the best training ground for developing communication and collaboration skills (p. 21). Some of these experiences may start in a formal education setting, but it is hoped that as new librarians enter professional positions, they will have opportunities to fine-tune and develop their personal communication styles and to learn to create collaborative environments around them. Those in electronic resources librarian positions will have no choice but to continue to develop their skills in this area if they wish to thrive.

However, will the electronic resources librarian position be needed in the future or will it go the way of the microform librarian? Will job responsibilities within electronic resources librarian positions become standard for other library positions? Perhaps it is too soon to tell. The current research indicates that communication among diverse library constituencies is a key role of the electronic resources librarian. At some point, it is possible that discussing IP authentication, terms of licensing agreements, and long-term preservation of digital formats will be a standard part of every library studies curriculum just as interpreting a MARC record and conducting a reference interview are. However, until that time, someone with knowledge of these issues that can effectively communicate these issues to colleagues will be needed in most organizations. Future research studies could examine how job responsibilities from electronic resources librarians have been incorporated into other library positions, especially in institutions without an electronic resources librarian.

CONCLUSION

The increasing number, variety, and complexity of electronic resources available to academic libraries have increased tremendously since the first job announcement for an electronic resources librarian was listed in 1992 (Fisher, 2003, p.4). Managing electronic resources is an "ever-evolving process" (Skaggs, Poe, & Stevens, 2006, p. 194). Not surprisingly the position of electronic resources librarian must change as the nature of the work evolves. When electronic resources librarian positions were first listed often the electronic resources management job responsibilities and job requirements were simply "added to" an existing position, and Fisher (2003) found that the foundation of the electronic resources librarian was based strongly in public services (p.7). Building upon the work of Albitz (2002) and Fisher (2003), this study reinforces that the electronic resources librarian position represents a position that evolves as the technological and environmental landscape changes.

While academic librarians have often been bridge builders within their academic communities, electronic resources librarians are expected to be bridge builders within their library organizations. They often bring together administrators, technical services librarians, public services librarians, and systems librarians to focus on the current challenges of "any time, any place" delivery of library resources and services. The emphasis on communication and collaborative skills for these positions is an indication of the strong role electronic resources librarians play in fostering a team environment within their organizations. Electronic resources librarians are expected to be skilled communicators with an in-depth expertise of technology and the issues surrounding the acquisition, management, and organization of electronic resources. Bergman (2005) notes, "The one thing that is clear is that the specialty [electronic resources librarian] has arisen because of the ever increasing need for librarians to have information technology skills in addition to—not instead of—people skills" (p. 116). Just as a reference librarian or bibliographer develops expertise in a particular discipline or subject area, the electronic resources librarian develops expertise in managing people, relationships, and technology in a fast-paced, ever-changing library and information environment.

REFERENCES

Albitz, R. S. (2002). Electronic resource librarians in academic libraries: A position announcement analysis, 1996-2001. *Portal: Libraries and the Academy, 2*(4), 589-600.

American Association of Law Libraries (2001). Competencies of law librarianship. Retrieved November 17, 2007, from http://www.aallnet.org/prodev/competencies.asp

American Library Association (2005). Draft core competencies. Retrieved November 17, 2007, from http://www.ala.org/ala/accreditationb/Draft_Core_Competencies_07_05.pdf

Beile, P. M., & Adams, M. M. (2000). Other duties as assigned: Emerging trends in the academic library job market. *College & Research Libraries, 61*(4), 336-347.

Bergman, B. J. (2005). Looking at electronic resources librarians: Is there gender equity within this emerging specialty? *New Library World, 106*(3/4), 116-127.

Copeland, A. W. (1997). The demand for serials catalogers: An analysis of job advertisements, 1980-1995. *The Serials Librarian, 32*(1/2), 27-37.

Corbin, J. (1993). Competencies for electronic information services. *Public-Access Computer Systems Review, 4*(6), 5-22. Retrieved November 17, 2007, from http://epress.lib.uh.edu/pr/v4/n6/corbin.4n6

Croneis, K. S. & Henderson, P. (2002). Electronic and digital librarian positions: A content analysis of announcements from 1990 through 2000. *Journal of Academic Librarianship, 28*(4), 232-237.

Deeken, J., & Thomas, D. (2006). Technical services job ads: Changes since 1995. *College & Research Libraries, 67*(2), 136-145.

Dole, W. V., Hurych, J. M., & Liebst, A. (2005). Assessment: A core competency for library leaders. *Library Administration & Management, 19*(3), 125-132.

Felt, E. C. (1999). Holland library's electronic resource librarians: A profile of these positions. *The Reference Librarian, 64*, 75-113.

Fisher, W. (2001). Core competencies for the acquisitions librarian: Analysis of position announcements. *Library Collections, Acquisitions, & Technical Services, 25*(2), 179- 190.

Fisher, W. (2003). The electronic resources librarian position: A public services phenomenon? *Library Collections, Acquisitions, & Technical Services*, 27, (1), 3-17.

Foote, M. (1997). The systems librarian in U.S. academic libraries: A survey of announcements from *College & Research Libraries News*, 1990 1994. *College & Research Libraries, 58*, 517-26.

Lynch, B., & Smith, K. R. (2001). The changing nature of work in academic libraries. *College & Research Libraries, 62*(5), 407-420.

McNeil, B. (Comp). (2002). *SPEC kit #270: Core competencies*. Washington, D.C.: Association of Research Libraries.

Murphy, M. (1991). Preface. *Future Competencies of the Information Professional* (pp. v-vi). Washington, D.C.: Special Libraries Association.

Nofsinger, M. M. (1999). Training and retraining reference professionals: Core competencies for the 21st century. *The Reference Librarian, 64*, 9-19.

Ojala, M. (1993). Core competencies for special library managers of the future. *Special Libraries, 84*, 230-234.

Osorio, N. L. (1999). An analysis of science-engineering academic library positions in the last three decades. *Issues in Science and Technology Librarianship*. Retrieved November 17, 2007, from http://www.istl.org/99-fall/article2.html

Reference and User Services Association (RUSA), American Library Association (2003). Professional competencies for reference and user services librarians. Retrieved November 17, 2007 from, http://www.ala.org/ala/rusa/rusaprotools/referenceguide/professional.htm

Reser. D. W., & Schuneman, A. P. (1992). The academic library job market: A content analysis comparing public and technical services. *College & Research Libraries, 53*, 49-59.

Skaggs, B., Poe, J. W., & Stevens, K. W. (2006). One-stop shopping: A perspective on the evolution of electronic resources management. *OCLC Systems and Services: International Digital Library Perspective, 22*(3), 192-206.

Special Libraries Association (2003). Competencies for information professionals of the 21st century. Retrieved November 17, 2007 from, http://www.sla.org/content/learn/comp2003/index.cfm

Sproles, C., & Ratledge, D. (2004). An analysis of entry-level librarian ads published in *American Libraries*, 1982-2002. *Electronic Journal of Academic and Special Librarianship, 5* (2-3). Retrieved November 17, 2007, from http://southernlibrarianship.icaap.org/content/v05n02/sprolesc01.htm

White, G. (1999). Academic subject specialist positions in the United States: A content analysis of announcements from 1990 through 1998. *The Journal of Academic Librarianship, 25*(5), 372-382.

White, G. (2000). Head of reference positions in academic libraries: A survey of job announcements from 1990 through 1999. *Reference & User Services Quarterly, 39*(3), 265-272.

Xu, H. (1996). The impact of automation on job requirements and qualifications for catalogers and reference librarians in academic libraries. *Library Resources and Technical Services, 40*(1), 9-31.

Zhou, Y. (1996). Analysis of trends in demand for computer-related skills for academic librarians from 1974 to 1994. *College & Research Libraries, 57,* 259-272.

APPENDIX A
Job Responsibilities for Electronic Resources Librarians

Materials
- Acquire/evaluate/license electronic resources
- Organize electronic resources, through cataloging, electronic resource management system or on Web sites
- Manage/maintain/troubleshoot electronic resources
- Collection development of print resources
- Responsibility for serials, both electronic and print
- Catalog, print resources or special formats
- Monitor trends in electronic resources

Services
- Perform library instruction
- Provide reference service
- Provide virtual reference specifically
- Act as a liaison or perform outreach to an external department
- Web authoring/Web management

Technology
- Maintain computer hardware and software
- Coordinate/supervise computing in library
- Monitor trends in technology
- Act as a liaison with the campus information technology department

Management/Administration
- Supervision
- Training
- Committee work
- Project management
- Teamwork/collaboration
- Policies and procedures/documentation

Interpersonal
- Facilitate communication between departments
- Demonstrate a commitment to customer service

Other Job Responsibilities
- Involvement in professional associations and activities
- Scholarly activity

APPENDIX B
Qualifications for Electronic Resources Librarians Positions

Experience, Abilities, Skills, Knowledge
- Experience with, or knowledge of, electronic resources
- Academic/ professional library experience
- Experience with, or knowledge of, acquisitions and/or business practices
- Experience with, or knowledge of, cataloging
- Experience with, or knowledge of, collection development
- Experience with, or knowledge of, library instruction or teaching
- Experience with, or knowledge of, reference and public services
- Experience with, or knowledge of, serials
- Supervisory or management experience
- Experience with a particular library system such as an ILS or bibliographic utility
- Training experience
- Experience with, or knowledge of, Web development/Web site management
- Familiarity with licensing and contract negotiation
- Ability to collaborate/work in a team environment
- Demonstrated oral and written communication skills
- Customer or public service orientation
- Experience with, or knowledge of, computer hardware
- Experience with, or knowledge of, computer software
- Experience with, or knowledge of, instructional technologies
- Leadership ability
- Experience with policy and procedure documentation
- Demonstrated project management, organizational, and/or problem-solving skills
- Experience with computer programming languages
- Experience with, or knowledge of, metadata standards
- Awareness of trends in electronic resources
- Ability to work independently/self-motivated

Education
- MLIS
- Advanced degree, additional masters or PhD
- Associates degree
- BA in a specific discipline

Other
- Evidence of research, publication, and/or creative activity
- Evidence of professional involvement

Section III
Copyright and Licensing

Chapter VIII
The Evolution of License Content

Trisha L. Davis
The Ohio State University, USA

Celeste Feather
The Ohio State University, USA

ABSTRACT

The terms of licenses for electronic resources have changed in the past decade as librarians and publishers strived to reach common ground. A review and analysis of thirty-five licenses in effect prior to 2000 and their 2006 counterparts reveals how licenses evolved to meet the licensing principles set forth in recent years by the American Association of Law Libraries, the International Federation of Library Associations, and the NorthEast Research Libraries. Thirteen aspects of licenses were analyzed in the study. Eight aspects have evolved in the spirit of the principles, and four have not. The remaining aspect has not evolved as part of a license, but has emerged as a preferred business practice outside the license agreement that is in keeping with the practice the licensing principles encourage. The results of the analysis indicate that efforts in the library community to encourage the development of licenses that meet the needs of most libraries are having a positive impact.

INTRODUCTION

The need for licenses for electronic resources that are acceptable to publishers, vendors, and librarians is substantial. As the number of licensed electronic products increased in the 1990's, librarians began to gain expertise in understanding license terms, legal requirements, and appropriate procedures for entering into a legal contract between a publisher and the library or its parent organization. Library associations began to create lists of licensing principles in order to educate their members and take a formal position on many of the common issues encountered in the licensing negotiations. The three most recent sets of licensing principles from the library community have a great deal in common. Have the principles and the support they have garnered within the library community had an impact on the way licenses have changed over time? This study reviews 35 licenses in existence prior to 2000 and their counterparts in 2006 in an effort to answer the question.

BACKGROUND

The negotiation of licenses for the acquisition of or access to electronic content has been challenging the academic library community for over a decade. Various professional associations and individual universities have developed documents to state the needs and requirements for licenses that are acceptable by individual research institutions and library consortia. These documents have been revised over time to reflect the changing understanding and requirements of the community.

In the United States, work in the library community regarding licensing principles for electronic resources first came to fruition in June, 1995 by the Electronic Publishing Licensing Agreements Subcommittee of the Publisher/Vendor-Library Relations Committee of the Association for Library Collections and Technical Services, a division of the American Library Association. The Massachusetts Institute of Technology developed its "Licensing Principles for Electronic Materials" in December of 1995, followed quickly by the University of California's "Principles for Acquiring and Licensing Information in Digital Formats" in May of 1996, the University of New Mexico's "Guidelines for Licensing E-Products" in November of 1996, and California State University's "Principles for Acquisition of Electronic Information Resources" in December of 1996. In 1997 the Association of Research Libraries led a joint effort with the American Association of Law Libraries, the American Library Association, the Association of Academic Health Sciences Libraries, the Medical Library Association, and the Special Libraries Association to develop a

set of national principles (Schottlaender, 1998). These principles were known as the "Principles for Licensing Electronic Resources" (Association of Research Libraries [ARL], 1997).

Similar work was in process in Europe and elsewhere during the same time period. In 1997, the Dutch Association of University Libraries and the German Association of Research and University Libraries in North and Middle Germany drafted a set of licensing principles that provided a basis for the International Coalition of Library Consortia to develop a "Statement of Current Perspective and Preferred Practices for the Selection and Purchase of Electronic Information" in the spring of 1998 (International Coalition of Library Consortia [ICOLC], 1998). More than 80 consortia worldwide had adopted the ICOLC document by May, 2000. The European Association of Research Libraries, known as LIBER, drafted its own set of principles in July, 1998 (Klughist, 2000). This document is known as the LIBER "Licensing Principles" (Ligue des Bibliothèques Européennes de Recherche [LIBER], 1998).

More recently, the International Federation of Library Associations prepared a set of "Licensing Principles" in 2001 (International Federation of Library Associations [IFLA], 2001). The American Association of Law Libraries (AALL) developed a set of "Principles for Licensing Electronic Resources" in 2004 that was built upon the earlier collaborative work that the AALL had performed in 1997 with other U.S. library associations (American Association of Law Libraries [AALL], 2004). The NorthEast Research Libraries (NERL) consortium in the northeastern United States maintains a current set of "licensing guidelines" that the group uses to provide guidelines for vendors and NERL members as they negotiate licenses for electronic content (NorthEast Research Libraries [NERL], 2006). The California Digital Library of the University of California system has created a "Checklist of Points to be Addressed in a CDL License Agreement" that calls attention to areas of licensing that are of special concern and provides guidance and background information for these areas (California Digital Library [CDL], 2006). The University of California Libraries has a set of "Principles for Acquiring and Licensing Information in Digital Formats" that mainly addresses broader issues in scholarly communication (University of California Libraries, 2006). Together, these two California documents address many of the same issues previously mentioned in other documents that were developed since 2000.

METHODOLOGY

The authors of this study focused on the three documents from IFLA, AALL, and NERL that have been developed since 2000 and directly address the content that the library community desires in licenses for electronic resources. They selected primary areas of overlap in the principles documents on which licenses could be evaluated objectively, and gathered a selection of 35 licenses for review for which there were pre-2000 versions and counterparts in use in 2006. The licenses were gathered from the files of the libraries at The Ohio State University, the University of Akron, the University of Minnesota, the University of North Carolina at Chapel Hill, and the University of Washington. The analysis in the study examined how the licenses in the review set evolved over time, and how the changes did or did not correspond to the current principles established by the library community for licenses governing the acquisition of electronic content.

The authors acknowledge that the review set of licenses may be skewed because it was drawn only from academic libraries and contains more licenses from nonprofit than from for-profit providers. The bias toward nonprofits occurred because many nonprofit societies were among the first to offer online access to their resources and because those societies still exist in the form that they existed in the previous decade. In the for-profit

sector, mergers and acquisitions among publishers frequently have left no current counterpart for a pre-2000 license for a given product. The review set of licenses contained examples from eight for-profit licensors and 25 nonprofit licensors. This analysis, albeit with a limited sample, revealed no significant differences in the ways that licenses have changed over time based on the profit status of the licensor. The results of the analysis may be specific to licenses for products of interest to the scholarly community.

The licensors represented in the review set are listed below. The dates of the pre-2000 licenses examined from each licensor appear after the licensor's name:

- ABC-CLIO (1998)
- American Association for the Advancement of Science (1999)
- American Chemical Society (1997)
- American Institute of Physics (1997)
- American Mathematical Society (1997)
- American Physical Society (1999)
- American Society of Civil Engineers (1999)
- Association for Asian Studies (1998)
- Association for Computing Machinery (1999)
- Bloomberg (1994)
- Cambridge Scientific Abstracts (1997)
- Cambridge University Press (1998)
- Columbia University Press (1999)
- Company of Biologists (1998)
- Commonwealth Scientific and Industrial Research Organisation (CSIRO) (1998)
- EDP Sciences (1999)
- Elsevier (1999)
- Evolutionary Ecology Ltd. (1999)
- Federation of American Societies for Experimental Biology (1999)
- HAPI (1998)
- Heron Publishing (1998)
- Institute of Electrical and Electronics Engineers (1999)

- Institute of Physics (1997)
- Iter, Inc. (1998)
- JSTOR (1997)
- National Academy of Sciences (1998)
- NISC (1998)
- NRC Research Press (1998)
- Optical Society of America (1998)
- Oxford University Press (1998)
- Project Muse (1997)
- ProQuest (1995)
- Royal Society (1998)
- Society for Industrial and Applied Mathematics (1996)
- University of Chicago Press (1999)

The 13 aspects selected for objective analysis from the three principles documents follow:

- Authorized site definition
- Authorized user definition
- Breach cure period
- Confidentiality of business terms
- Dispute resolution and governing law
- Electronic reserves and coursepacks
- Indemnification
- Interlibrary lending and scholarly sharing
- Licensee's responsibility for actions of authorized users
- Modification of license terms
- Perpetual use/archival rights
- Remote access
- Usage statistics

ANALYSIS AND DISCUSSION

The analysis of the licenses in the review set follows the quoted language related to each aspect from the principles documents.

Authorized Site

Authorized site definitions, if present in a license, are generally based on one of two qualities. The first is the geographic contiguity of the site; the second is the nature of the administration of the institution. Licenses require either that the authorized site exist in one physical location, or that a group of geographically disconnected sites be united under a central administration. The three principles documents are concurrent in their inclusion of all sites administered as part of a single organization, regardless of location. They describe an authorized site as follows: "A license agreement should recognize the affiliation of users with a given library or institution, regardless of users' physical location and should allow for routine remote access to licensed electronic information resources" (AALL).

"A license should provide access for geographically remote sites if they are part of the licensee's organization" (NERL).

"The license should provide access for geographically remote sites if they are part of the licensee's organization" (IFLA).

An example of language in a current license that follows the principles regarding an authorized site is:

If the subscriber has one or more remote sites or campuses which do not have their own central administrative staff, but instead are administered by the subscriber's site or campus, persons affiliated with those remote sites or campuses will also be considered authorized users.

An example of current language that does not follow the principles of the authorized site definition is:

For the purposes of this license, an "authorized site" is a localized site (one geographical location) that is under a single administration. For an organization with locations in more than one city, each city is considered to be a different site. For an organization that has multiple locations in the same city that are administered independently, each location is considered to be a different site. No access from remote campuses or remote sites,

Table 1.

2006 Licenses	Site Limited to Single Geographic Location	Site Based on Administration Pattern	Silent
35 (100%)	18 (51.4%)	8 (22.9%)	9 (25.7%)

Pre-2000 to 2006 Changes	
Did Not Change	**27 (77.1%)**
Single Geographic Location	13 (37.1%)
Silent	8 (22.9%)
Administration Pattern	6 (17.1%)
Changed	**8 (22.9%)**
Silent to Single Geographic Location	4 (11.4%)
Single Geographic Location to Administration Pattern	2 (5.7%)
Administration Pattern to Single Geographic Location	1 (2.9%)
Single Geographic Location to Silent	1 (2.9%)

and no consortia or other forms of subscription sharing are allowed under this license.

Table 1 provides the data regarding the definition of authorized site that was gathered from the license review set. The majority of licenses prior to 2000 and in 2006 define an authorized site by geographic contiguity. Half of the changes in the licenses over time were to move to a site definition that focused on geographic contiguity.

In an academic environment it can be difficult to define site purely by location, yet this concept of geographical contiguity persists. Several 2006 licenses provided university names and locations as examples of sites that were not contiguous. In some states with large university systems spanning the state under a common name this is a reasonable differentiation, for example California, Pennsylvania, and New York. In other systems, this approach requires even the smallest branch or research institute of a large university to be defined as a separate location requiring a unique site license. Not only is it costly to negotiate two licenses for the same institution, but also frequently the accompanying base fees for a single site are beyond the resources available to the smaller entity.

Little progress has been made toward meeting the definitions outlined by the license principles documents. Only half of the 2006 licenses agree with the principles' definitions and the greatest change occurred in the shift toward geographic limitation. Differential pricing based on geographic location seems to be continuing as an evolving trend.

Authorized Users

Given the academic nature of the license review set, faculty, staff, and students are included in all of the definitions present in these licenses. The question for analysis centered on whether persons who are not officially affiliated with the licensee are permitted to use the resource when they are physically present within a library facility. These users are commonly known as "walk-in" users and normally include the general public accessing a resource via a public workstation in a library building. The three principles documents are concurrent in their inclusion of all users, regardless of affiliation or location. The NERL and IFLA principles specifically include walk-in users at public workstations in library facilities. They define authorized users as follows: "A license agreement should recognize the affiliation of users with a given library or institution, regardless of users' physical location and should allow for routine remote access to licensed electronic information resources" (AALL).

"A license agreement should define authorized users to include students, faculty, researchers, and staff of the NERL member institutions, as well as walk-in users of the institutions' library facilities. It should permit remote access by authorized users, except walk-in users, and include students enrolled in official distance education programs" (NERL).

"The license should provide access for all of the users affiliated with a licensee, whether institution or consortium, regardless of whether they are on the licensee's premises or away from them" (IFLA).

"The license should provide access to individual, unaffiliated users when on the licensee's premises" (IFLA).

An example of language in a current license that follows the principles regarding authorized users is:

Authorized users must be employees, faculty, staff, or students officially affiliated with the subscriber, or authorized on-site patrons of the subscriber's library facilities.

An example of language in a current license that does not follow the principles of the authorized site definition is:

"Authorized users" refers to the staff, faculty, and students of the customer, the membership of the customer, or the employees of the customer.

Table 2 shows the data found in the license set related to the inclusion of walk-in users in the definition of authorized users. There is substantial agreement among the current licenses that walk-in users should be included, and all of the changes to authorized user definitions in the review set from pre-2000 to the present have been to include walk-in users.

The fact that 91.4% of 2006 licenses, as compared to 57.1% of 1990's licenses, include walk-in users is encouraging for public institutions which by law must allow access to such products. For many academic libraries, this is a make-or-break issue that must be addressed before public funds

Table 2.

2006 Licenses	Authorized Users Include Walk-ins	Authorized Users Do Not Include Walk-ins	Silent
35 (100%)	32 (91.4%)	1 (2.9%)	2 (5.7%)

Pre-2000 to 2006 Changes	
Did Not Change	**23 (65.7%)**
Included Walk-ins	20 (57.1%)
Silent	2 (5.7%)
Did Not Include Walk-ins	1 (2.9%)
Changed	**12 (34.3%)**
Silent to Include Walk-ins	12 (34.3%)

may be spent. It is reassuring to see that licensors are acknowledging this more frequently.

Breach Cure Period

Many licenses describe and define the steps that will be taken when a suspected breach or violation of the license terms occurs. Some licensors choose to terminate access immediately upon suspicion of a breach, while others establish a certain time period within which the licensee must investigate the problem and take corrective action. Some licenses remain silent on the issue. The AALL and NERL principles are concurrent in their requirement of notification of a suspected breach; all three principles documents agree that a breach cure period should be provided for the licensee to investigate and resolve any true breach. They define such activities as follows: "A license agreement should require the licensor to give the licensee notice of any suspected or alleged license violations that come to the attention of the licensor and allow a reasonable time for the licensee to investigate and take corrective action, if appropriate" (AALL).

"A license agreement should require the licensor to give NERL member institutions notice of any suspected or alleged license violations that come to the attention of the licensor and allow a reasonable time for the institution to investigate and take corrective action, if appropriate" (NERL).

"The license should provide for remedy periods and other modes of resolution before either cancellation or litigation is contemplated" (IFLA).

An example of language in a current license that follows the principles regarding breach cure periods is:

If either party breaches any term of this agreement, the other may send written notice of the breach including a description of all unacceptable actions. If the breach is not corrected within 30 days, the nonbreaching party may terminate the agreement upon written notice.

An example of language in a current license that does not follow the principles regarding breach cure periods is:

Table 3.

2006 Licenses	Include Breach Cure Period	Explicitly Deny Breach Cure Period	Silent
35 (100%)	13 (37.1%)	6 (17.1%)	16 (45.7%)

Pre-2000 to 2006 Changes	
Did Not Change	**28 (80%)**
Silent	15 (42.9%)
Included Breach Cure Period	8 (22.9%)
Denied Breach Cure Period	5 (14.3%)
Changed	**7 (20%)**
Denied Breach Cure Period to Include Breach Cure Period	5 (14.3%)
Denied Breach Cure Period to Silent	1 (2.9%)
Silent to Include Breach Period	1 (2.9%)

This agreement will terminate immediately if any term or condition of this agreement is violated for any reason.

Table 3 reveals that there are many differing opinions and practices about breach cure periods. There is no clear trend toward either including a breach period or remaining silent on the matter.

While there was a surprising lack of change over the decade, the few revisions that did occur recognized the need for a breach cure period. The practice of explicitly denying a cure period appears to be diminishing. This change may indicate that licensors are becoming more receptive to the concept and may be more willing to negotiate these terms with a library.

Confidentiality of Business Terms

The practice of keeping business terms confidential as part of a license agreement is not common, but occasionally occurs. Many publicly supported institutions cannot legally agree to not disclose these terms and still abide by the laws of their state. The three principles documents are concurrent in their prohibition of such confidentiality clauses. They describe the issue as follows: "A confidentiality or nondisclosure agreement should not be a prerequisite to a license agreement" (AALL).

"A license agreement should not require nondisclosure of licensing terms or prices" (NERL).

"Requirements for nondisclosure of license terms are generally inappropriate" (IFLA).

Current licenses that follow the principles regarding confidentiality of business terms simply are silent on the matter. An example of language in a current license that does not follow the principles is:

Confidential information shall include, but not be limited to, the terms and existence of this agreement, including pricing, site locations, population counts, and proprietary information relating to products or services of the parties disclosed for the purposes of providing price quotes.

Table 4 shows the stability in licenses regarding confidentiality over the past decade. Confidentiality clauses were not common prior to 2000, and remain that way. This principle appears to be one of the few receiving widespread support from all parties in the licensing community.

Dispute Resolution and Governing Law

Governing law in licenses is used to help define procedures and legal arguments in the event of

Table 4.

2006 Licenses	Require Confidentiality	Silent
35 (100%)	1 (2.9%)	34 (97.1%)

Pre-2000 to 2006 Changes	
Did Not Change	**33 (94.3%)**
Silent	33 (94.3%)
Changed	**2 (5.7%)**
Silent to Required Confidentiality	1 (2.9%)
Required Confidentiality to Silent	1 (2.9%)

a dispute between the parties. Licenses either mention a specific jurisdiction, which is usually the state of the licensor if the licensor's place of business is within the United States, or remain silent on the matter. Licenses originating outside the United States generally state the law of their country. This section is critical for state-supported institutions that must abide by state law and cannot agree to a governing law outside that state.

The three principles documents each discuss this issue from a different perspective. The AALL principles suggest the option of using alternative dispute resolution, such as binding arbitration, in place of legal proceedings. While this may be a preferable alternative, such options are frequently not permitted by state law or institutional policy. NERL principles are silent on the matter. AALL principles recommend a choice of law and venue, and provisions for resolving disputes outside the courtroom. The IFLA principles recommend that the applicable law be acceptable to both licensor and licensee, but favor the licensee. They describe the issue as follows: "A license agreement should allow for the use of alternative dispute resolution to resolve any conflicts that may arise in relationship to the agreement" (AALL).

"A license agreement should state the choice of law and choice of venue by which the parties will be governed in the event of a dispute" (AALL).

"The choice of applicable law should be acceptable for both parties. Preferably it should be the national or state law of the licensee" (IFLA).

Language in current licenses regarding dispute resolution is not common, but one example was found:

All claims, disputes and causes of action arising from or related to this agreement shall be subject to binding arbitration to occur in [City, State]. Arbitration shall be by single arbitrator either agreed upon by each of the parties, or by each party appointing a representative who shall meet with the other party's representative and those two parties shall appoint the arbitrator.

Governing law statements in current licenses are generally stated in the following manner:

This agreement will be governed by and construed in accordance with the laws of the state of [State Name], applicable to contracts entered into and fully performed in the State of [State Name].

Table 5 provides the data from the license review set related to the mention of governing law. The 2006 sample is almost evenly split (48.6%-51.4%) on this issue. Changes made since the 1990's significantly favor the elimination of

Table 5.

2006 Licenses	Specify Governing Law	Silent
35 (100%)	18 (51.4%)	17 (48.6%)

Pre-2000 to 2006 Changes	
Did Not Change	**28 (80%)**
Specified Governing Law	17 (22.9%)
Silent	11 (31.4%)
Changed	**7 (20%)**
Specified Governing Law to Silent	6 (17.1%)
Silent to Specified Governing Law	1 (2.9%)

a specific governing law. When terms are unacceptable, this is usually one of the easier sections to alter or remove in a license negotiation.

Electronic Reserves and Coursepacks

Mention of coursepacks, printed copies of material for sale and distribution to authorized users in a course, involves either permitting or prohibiting the practice through license language. Many licenses are silent on the matter. In a similar manner, digital content may be stored on an access-controlled server for access only by students registered for the specific course. Because this practice frequently replaces the control of materials in a physical reserves collection, the practice often is referred to as electronic reserves.

Although students are considered authorized users and thus automatically have access to licensed materials through the library catalog or indexing tools, instructors often want all materials available at a single site. The three principles documents are concurrent in their consideration of coursepacks and electronic reserves as a standard practice and inclusion as a desired license term.

They describe these terms as follows: "A license agreement should clearly state the permitted uses of the electronic resource. The licensee should make clear to the licensor those uses critical to its particular users including, but not limited to, printing, downloading, copying, electronic reserves, and the development of course packs" (AALL).

"A license agreement should recognize and not restrict or abrogate the fair use rights of a NERL member institution's user community permitted under copyright law. The license agreement should define the purposes for use of the resource as education and research, and should allow for the printing, downloading, and copying that are inherent in scholarly work. The license should also specifically provide for instructional use in the form of electronic reserves and coursepacks" (NERL).

"Licenses should support local teaching and learning efforts, from elementary through university level, by permitting links to, or copies of, specific course-related information to appear in online course-support activities such as electronic reserve" (IFLA).

Table 6.

2006 Licenses	Allow Coursepacks	Prohibit Coursepacks	Silent
35 (100%)	6 (17.1%)	7 (20%)	22 (62.9%)

Pre-2000 to 2006 Changes	
Did Not Change	**26 (74.3%)**
Silent	18 (51.4%)
Prohibited Coursepacks	7 (20%)
Allowed Coursepacks	1 (2.9%)
Changed	**9 (25.7%)**
Silent to Allowed	4 (11.4%)
Allowed to Silent	4 (11.4%)
Prohibited to Allowed	1 (2.9%)

An example of language in a current license that follows the principles regarding electronic reserves and coursepacks is:

The licensee may include copies (print or electronic) of items from the online database in: (a) coursepacks in print or digital form for distribution to the authorized users for use in classroom instruction; (b) in reserves or offprints collections set up by the licensee's libraries for access by authorized users in connection with specific courses offered by the institutions. Copies of items in digital form which are included in online coursepacks, reserves, or offprints collections must be deleted by the licensee's libraries at the end of the terms in which the related course concludes.

An example of current license language that is counter to the principles is:

Institutional subscribers or licensees many not make multiple copies of materials from [the product] for the purpose of classroom use or place materials from [the product] on electronic reserve without prior written permission.

Table 6 shows the data gathered from the license review set related to coursepacks. Silence on the matter prevails in 2006.

Data gathered from the review set provides similar insights into license trends related specifically to electronic reserves. As shown in Table 7, silence prevails to an even greater degree in the 2006 licenses regarding electronic reserves.

The trend shown by this data is a movement away from prohibiting the use of licensed material in coursepacks. However, as the movement towards digital content progresses, more content is available via deep linking, and course management systems encompass traditional electronic reserves, the printed coursepack probably does not have a sustainable future. The need for permission to make digital copies of licensed material and temporarily deposit them on a local server for electronic reserves also will diminish.

Indemnification

The legal issue of indemnification appears in licenses in several ways. The verb "indemnify" means (1) to secure against hurt, loss, or damage, or (2) to compensate or reimburse for incurred hurt, loss, or damage (Merriam-Webster's Dictionary

Table 7.

2006 Licenses	Allow Electronic Reserves	Prohibit Electronic Reserves	Silent
35 (100%)	5 (14.3%)	3 (8.6%)	27 (77.1%)

Pre-2000 to 2006 Changes	
Did Not Change	**29 (82.9%)**
Silent	27 (77.1%)
Prohibited Electronic Reserves	1 (2.9%)
Allowed Electronic Reserves	1 (2.9%)
Changed	**6 (17.1%)**
Silent to Allowed	4 (11.4%)
Silent to Prohibited	2 (5.7%)

of Law, 1996). Sometimes the licenses require both parties to indemnify the other. Sometimes one party is required to indemnify the other, and sometimes the licenses are silent on the matter. The two principles documents from United States library associations are concurrent in their requirement that the licensor indemnify the licensee. They suggest the following approach to indemnification: "A license agreement should require the licensor to defend, indemnify, and hold the licensee harmless from any action based on a claim that use of the resource in accordance with the license infringes any patent, copyright, trademark, or trade secret of any third party" (AALL).

"A license agreement should require the licensor to defend, indemnify, and hold NERL and NERL member institutions harmless from any action based on a claim that use of the resource in accordance with the license infringes any patent, copyright, trademark, or trade secret of any third party" (NERL).

An example of current license language that follows the principles of indemnification is:

The licensor shall indemnify, defend, and hold harmless the subscriber and its authorized users from and against any loss, damage, costs, liability and expenses arising from or out of any third-party action or claim that use of the licensed products in accordance with the terms and conditions herein infringes the intellectual property rights of such third party.

An example of current license language sets forth the opposite scenario from the principles' direction is:

The institution assumes the sole responsibility for all use of the service through its IP addresses and hereby indemnifies and agrees to hold the licensor indemnified from any liability or claim of any person arising from such use.

Table 8 provides the data for the analysis of indemnification in the license review set. This area is often a point of negotiation in licensing due to state laws. The principles have not had the desired impact on licenses regarding indemnification.

Table 8.

2006 Licenses	Licensee Indemnifies Licensor	Licensor Indemnifies Licensee	Mutual Indemnification	Silent
35 (100%)	10 (28.6%)	1 (2.9%)	2 (5.7%)	22 (62.9%)

Pre-2000 to 2006 Changes	
Did Not Change	**27 (77.1%)**
Silent	20 (57.14%)
Licensee Indemnified Licensor	6 (17.1%)
Licensor Indemnified Licensee	1 (2.9%)
Changed	**8 (22.9%)**
Silent to Licensee Indemnified Licensor	3 (8.6%)
Mutual Indemnification to Silent	2 (5.7%)
Mutual Indemnification to Licensee Indemnified Licensor	1 (2.9%)
Silent to Mutual Indemnification	1 (2.9%)
Licensor Indemnified Licensee to Mutual Indemnification	1 (2.9%)

The preference prior to 2000 and now is to remain silent about indemnification, but mutual indemnification sometimes is an acceptable alternative. The analysis demonstrated that indemnification by licensor of licensee only and mutual indemnification are rare. In fact, 28.6% of 2006 licenses require indemnification of licensor by licensee. This is an area of obvious disagreement between libraries and publishers and perhaps should be left silent.

Interlibrary Lending and Scholarly Sharing

Rights for interlibrary lending (ILL) to individuals outside the licensee's authorized user community vary considerably. The most common definitions fall into three general concepts: ILL may be prohibited explicitly, allowed if the material is first reduced to print, or allowed via electronic transmission of the digital file. This review found that when electronic transmission of the digital is permitted, then transmission of the print is generally also permitted. The three principles documents are concurrent in their requirement of interlibrary loan rights as established by the interlibrary loan provisions of Section 108 of the U.S. Copyright Act (17 U.S.C. 108). They define these rights as follows: "A license agreement should recognize and not restrict, abrogate or circumvent the rights of the licensee or its user community permitted under copyright law, including but not limited to the fair use provisions of Section 107 of the U.S. Copyright Act (17 U.S.C. 107) and the interlibrary loan provisions of Section 108 of the U.S. Copyright Act (17 U.S.C. 108)" (AALL).

"A license agreement should permit library-to-library lending of full-text, within limited conditions analogous to those provided by the CONTU guidelines for print materials" (NERL).

"Licenses (contracts) for information should not exclude or negatively impact for users of the information any statutory rights that may be granted by applicable copyright law" (IFLA).

"Provisions for interlibrary loan or equivalent services should be included" (IFLA).

An example of current license language that follows the interlibrary lending principles is:

Institutional subscribers and licensees may use hard or electronic copies derived directly or indirectly from the electronic edition of the journals for the purpose of interlibrary loan with the same limitations that apply to paper copies for that purpose made from the print edition of the journals. Specifically, copies must be made in accordance with Section 108 of the Copyright Act of the U.S. and with guidelines developed by the National Commission on New Technological Uses of Copyrighted Works (CONTU Guidelines).

An example of current license language that does not follow the interlibrary lending principles is:

The systematic making of print or electronic copies for transmission to nonsubscribers or non-subscribing institutions (such as in "interlibrary loan") is prohibited.

Table 9 provides information regarding the interlibrary loan rights that are present in the license review set. There has been a great deal of change over the decade, but this area remains a persistent issue in negotiations.

In the licenses in effect prior to 2000, 19 (54.3%) either prohibited ILL or were silent. In the 2006 set, only 12 (34.3%) prohibited ILL or were silent. Eight of the licenses (22.9%) were for products that can be described as databases, which may or may not have full text worth sharing, so this change is a valid improvement. The trend to explicitly allow ILL is encouraging. For many academic libraries, ILL rights for electronic journals remain an important issue. For some, this can be a make-or-break issue, regardless of format. It is reassuring to see that licensors are acknowledging this more frequently.

Table 9.

2006 Licenses	ILL Via Print Only	ILL Via Print and Electronic	ILL Prohibited	Silent
35 (100%)	16 (45.7%)	7 (20%)	9 (25.7%)	3 (8.6%)

Pre-2000 to 2006 Changes	
Did Not Change	**23 (65.7%)**
ILL Via Print Only	10 (28.6%)
ILL Prohibited	9 (25.7%)
ILL Via Print and Electronic	2 (5.7%)
Silent	2 (5.7%)
Changed	**12 (34.3%)**
Silent to ILL Via Print Only	3 (8.6%)
ILL Prohibited to ILL Via Print Only	3 (8.6%)
Silent to ILL Via Print and Electronic	2 (5.7%)
ILL Via Print Only to ILL Via Print and Electronic	2 (5.7%)
ILL Prohibited to Silent	1 (2.9%)
ILL Prohibited to ILL Via Print and Electronic	1 (2.9%)

Scholarly sharing, the right of an authorized user to occasionally provide a copy of a limited amount of material to an unauthorized user for educational or research purposes, appears in licenses in the form of permitting the right or denying the right. Many licenses remain silent on the matter. None of the three principles documents address the issue, but the presence of this additional type of sharing right in the license review set warrants discussion.

An example of current license language that explicitly permits scholarly sharing is:

An authorized user may transmit a hard copy or electronic copy of any article to any individual who is not an authorized user provided such transmission is (1) not for compensation, (2) for purposes of scholarly exchange of ideas, and (3) not part of any systematic provision of content to such user or any third party.

An example of current license language that is counter to the principles and denies the right of scholarly sharing is:

Users are not permitted to transmit any part of the materials by any means to any unauthorized user.

Table 10 indicates the status of scholarly sharing in the license review set. The analysis does not reveal any significant trends toward a common goal.

Over the decade, changes in licenses related to scholarly communication were quite varied. The identified changes were almost evenly divided among change to permit, change to deny, and change to remain silent on the matter. Significantly more licenses (48.6%) specifically prohibit the practice as specifically permit it (28.6%). Silence is a significant portion of sample (22.9%). Licensors seem to be moving toward interlibrary lending, but at the same time seem to be reluctant to allow scholarly sharing. The intermediation effort by

Table 10.

2006 Licenses	Prohibit Scholarly Sharing	Permit Scholarly Sharing	Silent
35 (100%)	17 (48.6%)	10 (28.6%)	8 (22.9%)

Pre-2000 to 2006 Changes	
Did Not Change	**24 (68.6%)**
Prohibited Scholarly Sharing	13 (37.1%)
Permitted Scholarly Sharing	6 (17.1%)
Silent	5 (14.3%)
Changed	**11 (31.4%)**
Prohibited Scholarly Sharing to Silent	3 (8.6%)
Silent to Prohibited Scholarly Sharing	3 (8.6%)
Prohibited Scholarly Sharing to Permitted Scholarly Sharing	3 (8.6%)
Silent to Permitted Scholarly Sharing	1 (2.9%)
Permitted Scholarly Sharing to Prohibited Scholarly Sharing	1 (2.9%)

the library staff for interlibrary lending is a more trusted method of sharing than from one authorized user directly to a scholarly colleague.

Licensee's Responsibility for Actions of Authorized Users

Licenses vary in the degree that they require licensees to assume responsibility for the actions of individual users. Some licenses require licensees to take total responsibility for all user actions, while others require the licensee to assist the licensor in the event of suspected misuse of the product and investigate and take corrective action. Many licenses are silent on the matter, which is the preferred approach for libraries. The three principles documents are concurrent in their recommendation that the licensee should not be held responsible for the actions of end users. However, they also emphasize the library's responsibility to make reasonable efforts to notify end users of any use restrictions. They present these terms as follows: "A license agreement should not hold the licensee liable for unauthorized uses of the licensed resource by its users, as long

as the licensee has implemented reasonable and appropriate methods to notify its user community of use restrictions" (AALL).

"A license agreement should not hold NERL or a NERL member institution liable for actions of users, except to require the institution to make reasonable efforts to notify its user community of use restrictions" (NERL).

"Libraries should work with users to educate them about proper use of electronic resources and take reasonable measures to prevent unlawful use, as well as with providers to halt infringing activities if such become known. Nonetheless, the library should not incur legal liability for actions of individual users" (IFLA).

An example of current license language that follows the principles regarding the responsibility of the licensee for the actions of authorized users is:

The subscriber shall use reasonable efforts to ensure that all authorized users are notified of and comply with the usage restrictions set forth in this agreement. The subscriber shall not be liable for breach of any of the terms of this agreement by any authorized users provided that the subscriber did not intentionally assist in or encourage such breach or permit such breach to continue after having actual notice thereof and provided that the subscriber reasonably cooperates with the licensor to prevent misuse.

An example of current license language that does not follow the principles of licensee responsibility for the actions of authorized users is:

The subscriber assumes sole responsibility for all use of [the product] by the subscriber and by each authorized user.

Table 11 shows the data from the license review set related to licensee responsibility for the actions of end users. In every case, even though a license may explicitly state that the licensee is not held responsible for end user behavior, a requirement exists that the licensee help investigate suspected breaches by an end user.

The evolutionary trend regarding responsibility for user actions has been to stop requiring the licensee to assume all responsibility for all users. No license changed to require such total

responsibility for user actions and behavior. This evolution is in keeping with the directions set forth by the principles.

Modification of License Terms

Licenses set forth mechanisms that enable licensors to modify the terms of the agreement in a number of ways. Sometimes both parties must agree in writing to any change in terms. Sometimes the licensor will give the licensee advance notification of a change in terms, and if the licensee does not agree to those terms then further negotiation must occur. In yet other licenses, if the licensor does not receive a response from the licensee regarding the changed terms, then continued use of the product is deemed to be an acceptance of the changed terms. Some licensors now are simply posting changed terms to their Web sites without notification to licensees.

The IFLA principles do not address the issue of license modification. The other two sets of principles concur that license terms should not change without advance notification and that there should be an opportunity for the licensee to terminate the agreement if the changes are not acceptable.

Table 11.

2006 Licenses	Licensee Not Responsible for User Actions	Licensee Responsible for User Actions	Silent
35 (100%)	10 (28.6%)	6 (17.1%)	19 (54.3%)

Pre-2000 to 2006 Changes	
Did Not Change	**30 (85.7%)**
Silent	19 (54.3%)
Licensee Not Responsible for User Actions	6 (17.1%)
Licensee Responsible for User Actions	5 (14.3%)
Changed	**5 (14.3%)**
Silent to Licensee Not Responsible for User Actions	3 (8.6%)
Licensee Responsible for User Actions to Silent	1 (2.9%)
Licensee Responsible for User Actions to Licensee Not Responsible for User Actions	1 (2.9%)

The relevant principles are as follows: "The terms of the license should be considered fixed at the time the license is signed by both parties. If the terms are subject to change (for example, scope of coverage or method of access), the agreement should require the licensor or licensee to notify the other party in writing in a timely and reasonable fashion of any such changes before they are implemented, and permit either party to terminate the agreement if the changes are not acceptable" (AALL).

"If the terms of a license are subject to change, an agreement should require the licensor to notify NERL member institutions at least 90 days in advance of implementation and permit institutions to terminate the agreement with a prorated refund. Likewise, an agreement should specify that NERL institutions will be given 30 days notice and the option of terminating the agreement with a prorated refund if the product is to be subject to substantive change (other than normal updating)" (NERL).

An example of current license language that follows the principles regarding the way in which license terms may be modified is:

The terms and conditions of this agreement may be changed from time to time and the subscriber will be notified of all revisions that impact authorized user rights to access including concurrent user restrictions, copyright and protection conditions, subscription cycles and payment terms. If subscriber does not agree to the revised license terms, it may terminate its subscription within thirty days after receiving such revised license terms. A failure to terminate the subscription shall constitute acceptance of the revised license terms. A subscriber shall be entitled to a prorated refund for the remainder of the subscription cycle for a subscription cancelled in accordance with the terms and conditions of [this section].

This type of language is unusual among the licenses in the review set. Prorated refunds are generally only offered in conjunction with a reduction of product content. A common approach to the matter is to only permit modifications to a license if both parties agree in writing, but there usually is no mention of a prorated refund if a license is terminated.

An example of language that clearly is not in alignment with the principles is as follows:

Licensor reserves rights to amend, remove, or add to the terms of service at any time. Such modifications shall be effective immediately. Accordingly, please continue to review the terms of service whenever accessing or using this site. Your access or use of the site after the posting of modifications to the terms of service will constitute your acceptance of the terms of service, as modified. If at any time you do not wish to accept the terms of service, you may not access or use the site. Any terms and conditions proposed by you which are in addition to or which conflict with these terms of service are expressly rejected by the licensor and shall be of no force or effect.

The data in Table 12 provides evidence from the license review set that there is no best practice or standard emerging on the issue of terms modification. Silence is still largest category for license terms modification, but over the course of the decade there was change in all directions. The pattern of avoiding further negotiation on a license by posting changed terms on a Web site and expecting licensees to abide by them (with or without prior notification) has been adopted slightly more than change to require new negotiations if there are modifications to a license. License terms need to change as new situations arise, and licenses should allow for this flexibility to benefit both parties. No clear pattern exists for the evolution of licenses in this category.

Perpetual Use/Archival Rights

Some licenses include continuing rights to access content that was licensed during a certain time period but for which there exists no current license. The type of rights and the steps that need to be taken in order to take advantage of such rights vary. The licenses grant some archival rights explicitly, explicitly state that no archival rights exist, or remain silent on the matter. The three principles documents concur that perpetual access and archival rights should be addressed specifically in a license. They elaborate on the issue as follows: "When permanent use of a resource has been licensed, licensor should provide a usable archival copy of the licensed content, including any necessary interface. The license should specify the conditions under which the licensee may access or refer users to the archival copy" (AALL).

"When subscription-based or renewable use of a resource has been licensed, a license agreement should specify what, if any, access to the licensed material would continue to be available after the subscription period lapses" (AALL).

"A license agreement should state clearly what access rights are being acquired by NERL or NERL member institutions' permanent use of the content or access rights only for a defined period of time. If the license provides for permanent use, specific detail should be provided regarding extent of backfile, method of access to backfiles, and assurance that access to backfiles will continue even if the institution or the consortium cancels its agreement for ongoing access" (NERL).

"A license should include provision for affordable, perpetual access to the licensed information by some appropriate and workable means" (IFLA).

"A license should address provisions for long-term access and archiving of the electronic information resource(s) under consideration and should identify responsibilities for these" (IFLA).

An example of archival and perpetual rights language found in a current license in the review set that follows the principles is:

Table 12.

2006 Licenses	Requires Renegotiation to Change Terms	Failure to Respond to Notification of Changed Terms Equals Acceptance	Changed Terms Posted to Web Site Without Notification	Silent
35 (100%)	9 (25.7%)	8 (22.9%)	3 (8.6%)	15 (42.9%)

Pre-2000 to 2006 Changes	
Did Not Change	**22 (62.9%)**
Silent	12 (34.3%)
Required Renegotiation to Change Terms	6 (17.1%)
Changed Terms Posted to Web Site Without Notification	4 (11.4%)
Changed	**13 (37.1%)**
Silent, to Failure to Respond to Notification Equals Acceptance	4 (11.4%)
Required Renegotiation to Silent	2 (5.7%)
Silent, to Required Renegotiation	2 (5.7%)
Silent, to Changed Terms Posted Without Notification	2 (5.7%)
Required Negotiation, to Changed Terms Posted Without Notification	1 (2.9%)
Failure to Respond to Notification Equals Acceptance, to Required Negotiation	1 (2.9%)
Failure to Respond to Notification Equals Acceptance, to Silent	1 (2.9%)

If a subscription lapses, licensor will provide customers with access to material for the years in which they held an online subscription. The material will be accessed either from the licensor's server or from a third party server or by downloading electronic files to the institution's server.

An example of current license language for a package of electronic journals that explicitly denies any archival rights or perpetual access is:

Upon termination of this agreement all online access to the product by the licensee and authorized users shall be terminated.

Table 13 shows data gathered from the license review set that indicates that the majority of licenses today remain silent regarding archival or perpetual use rights. Of the seven licenses that changed over the decade, only one removed archival rights altogether. The other six moved either from explicit denial or from no mention of archival rights to including them. While this change is positive, the largest percentage of licenses continues to ignore the issue with a deafening silence. Finally, the type of archival

rights granted varies widely across the licenses reviewed. Some licenses commit to providing a copy of the content on CD for those years that the library held a subscription granting permanent online access. Other licenses allow archival rights only if the library is willing to purchase such a CD at an extra cost. The cost presumably would be at a discounted rate, but nothing is confirmed at the time of signing the agreement. The technological and financial challenges inherent in providing perpetual access and archival rights are likely causes of the reluctance on the part of licensors to include language of this nature in licenses.

Remote Access

Remote access is access by authentication for authorized users when they are not physically located on the licensee's premises. Licenses explicitly permit such access, remain silent, or explicitly prohibit it. The three principles documents are clear in their direction to permit remote authenticated access to electronic content. Their statements are as follows: "A license agreement should recognize the affiliation of users with a given library or institution, regardless of users'

Table 13.

2006 Licenses	Grant Perpetual Use/Archival Rights	Deny Perpetual Use/Archival Rights	Silent
35 (100%)	8 (22.9%)	2 (5.7%)	25 (71.4%)

Pre-2000 to 2006 Changes	
Did Not Change	**28 (80%)**
Silent	25 (71.4%)
Grant Perpetual Use/Archival Rights	2 (5.7%)
Deny Perpetual Use/Archival Rights	1 (2.9%)
Changed	**7 (20%)**
Silent to Grant Perpetual Use/Archival Rights	4 (11.4%)
Deny Perpetual Use/Archival Rights to Grant Perpetual Use/Archival Rights	2 (5.7%)
Grant Perpetual Use/Archival Rights to Silent	1 (2.9%)

physical location and should allow for routine remote access to licensed electronic information resources" (AALL).

"A license agreement should define authorized users to include students, faculty, researchers, and staff of the NERL member institutions, as well as walk-in users of the institutions' library facilities. It should permit remote access by authorized users, except walk-in users, and include students enrolled in official distance education programs" (NERL).

"The license should provide access for all of the users affiliated with a licensee, whether institution or consortium, regardless of whether they are on the licensee's premises or away from them" (IFLA).

An example of the type of language in a current license that follows the principles is:

Authorized users may access the service from terminals or work stations from which they undertake work for the institution and from remote sites or campuses.

The data gathered from the license review set about remote access is presented in Table 14. The issue largely has become noncontroversial. The practice of denying remote access has vanished from this pool of licenses. The practice was not

common even before pre-2000. All three-model licenses explicitly permit remote access. Trust in maturing authentication technology has helped to make the question of remote access less challenging at the point of negotiation.

Usage Statistics

As libraries increased their expenditures for licensed resources, the need to monitor usage became essential. In 2003 Project COUNTER (Counting Online Usage of NeTworked Electronic Resources) was established by a group of publishers and libraries to build a code of practice for reporting usage statistics for electronic journals. The number of publishers providing COUNTER-compliant statistics has been growing steadily, even though requirements to do so are not routinely part of licenses. The three principles documents are concurrent in their recommendations for inclusion of usage statistics provisions in licenses. They address the issue as follows: "A license agreement should describe the usage statistics collected or generated by the licensor or any third parties, and the means available for the licensee to access those statistics" (AALL).

"A license agreement should require the licensor to provide basic use data on a timely and regular basis. In addition, the agreement should

Table 14.

2006 Licenses	Explicitly Allow Remote Access	Silent
35 (100%)	23 (65.7%)	12 (34.3%)

Pre-2000 to 2006 Changes	
Did Not Change	**26 (74.3%)**
Explicitly Allowed Remote Access	14 (40%)
Silent	12 (34.3%)
Changed	**9 (25.7%)**
Silent to Explicitly Allowed Remote Access	7 (20%)
Explicitly Prohibited Remote Access to Explicitly Allowed Remote Access	2 (5.7%)

provide NERL member institutions the right and opportunity to gather use and management data independently at local sites" (NERL).

"The networked information provider should offer usage (as opposed to user) data so that the library licensee may assess the effectiveness of the use of the resource" (IFLA).

An example of current license language that addresses usage statistics is:

Licensor shall provide the subscriber with COUNTER-compliant usage data on the articles downloaded, by journal title, on a monthly basis for private internal use by the licensor and the subscriber only.

Table 15 reveals the data from the license review set, and provide evidence that very few licenses include a commitment from licensors to provide usage data to licensees. Usage statistics often are provided by licensors in 2006. The trend has perhaps become so common that libraries are no longer feeling the need to press publishers to include the provision of usage data in a license.

FUTURE TRENDS

Of the 13 areas of licenses examined in this study, eight of them showed movement toward the spirit of the licensing principles or are firmly in keeping with the principles already. In these eight areas, the impact is that fewer and fewer negotiations of these terms will be necessary as licenses will usually include language that is acceptable to libraries. Publishers have heard the library community's message in these areas. These are all welcome trends.

One area, usage statistics, does not show movement toward the licensing principles that encourage discussion of the matter in licenses. However, the practice of providing usage statistics in a standardized way is becoming much more common, particularly with the advent of COUNTER standards. In this regard, the licensing principles helped encourage the entire community to address the issue, but neither the licensor nor the licensee community seems to regard the presence of a usage statistics section in a license as essential as time marches on.

The remaining four areas, which are authorized site, electronic reserves and coursepacks, indemnification, and modification of license terms, showed movement away from the spirit of the principles or unchanging disagreement with principles. The challenges presented by these areas differ. Some may disappear as technologies evolve, while others may continue to require negotiation for a long time to come.

Table 15.

2006 Licenses	Explicitly Commit to Providing Usage Statistics	Silent
35 (100%)	5 (14.3%)	30 (85.7%)

Pre-2000 to 2006 Changes	
Did Not Change	**29 (82.9%)**
Silent	29 (82.9%)
Changed	**6 (17.1%)**
Silent, to Committed to Providing Usage Statistics	5 (14.3%)
Committed to Providing Usage Statistics, to Silent	1 (2.9%)

The definition of authorized site is particularly challenging to some because of the wide variation of organizational structures among library parent organizations. A large "branch" campus of one university with an enrollment of 10,000 students and graduate degree programs is not the same as a small "branch" campus of another university with 400 students that basically offers undergraduate classes for two years and then sends the students to the main campus to finish a degree. The unfortunate result from a license that bases an authorized site on geographic contiguity is that smaller branch campuses are denied access to resources as they cannot afford to license many products just for their small community. Publishers are moving away from the definition of an authorized site based on central administration that the principles encourage. Many academic libraries oppose authorized site definitions based on geographic contiguity for the reasons given above, and a continuing struggle in this area is likely.

The purpose and function of electronic reserves and coursepacks are merging; just as electronic reserves and online course management systems are merging. A list of items developed for use in a course preferably is housed within a course management system so that it can be fully integrated with assignments, online discussion, quizzes, and so forth. Integrated library systems have developed electronic reserve modules, but unless those can be integrated into the workflow or the online course management system in some way, they will not be as useful and as used in the future. The future of the printed coursepack is growing dimmer, as students are increasingly resistant to paying large sums of money for printed textbooks and coursepack material. The concept of electronic reserve provisions in licenses relies on the notion that a copy of a digital file will be placed on a server within the institution for a temporary period of time. Linking technology now has made it possible to simply provide a list of links to electronic documents stored on a vendor's server within a course management system, and for this, no explicit permission in a license is needed. No significant movement toward the inclusion of language that explicitly permits electronic reserves and coursepacks is apparent, as the principles encourage. Perhaps, though, the need for such language is decreasing due to evolving technologies.

Indemnification by the licensor of the licensee as encouraged by the principles is almost nonexistent. The trend seems to be silence on this matter, which could be regarded as in keeping with the principles' spirit of not requiring the licensee to indemnify the licensor. This area of obvious disagreement may continue to be resolved at the point of negotiation by eliminating indemnification provisions from licenses entirely. From a legal perspective including language that requires the licensee to indemnify the licensor is beneficial to the licensor, but since such language often is unacceptable due to the legal requirements within the state of the licensee, licensors generally are willing to eliminate the clause. The presence of such clauses in licenses may remain, with the burden falling on the licensee to request removal.

Modification of license terms is a complex process. License negotiation requires a great deal of effort for all parties. Understandably, once a license is negotiated neither party wants to reopen negotiations unless a critical change is needed. However, requiring the licensee to abide by any changes to the license over time without formal acceptance is not acceptable according to the principles. Some publishers are moving away from requiring signed licenses to a statement of terms and conditions on a Web site that is changed as needed and requires no signature. Since there is no discernible trend among the license review set in this study, the future of this issue remains unknown. What is clear is that there is considerable disagreement and uncertainty. A study of trends and issues regarding the use of signed licenses versus an online statement of terms and conditions, and the reasons for choosing one over the other, would be interesting.

CONCLUSION

Efforts in the library community to encourage the development of licenses that meet the needs of most libraries have had a positive impact over the past decade. License language indeed has evolved in ways that are in keeping with principles established by librarians. Areas of concern and fluctuation still exist, but in general the licenses of 2006 have language that is more acceptable to libraries than licenses in effect prior to 2000.

REFERENCES

American Association of Law Libraries (2004). Principles for licensing electronic resources. Retrieved November 17, 2007, from http://www. aallnet.org/committee/reports/LicensingPrinciplesElecResources.pdf

Association of Research Libraries (1997). Principles for licensing electronic resources, final draft, July 15, 1997, by the American Association of Law Libraries, the American Library Association, the Association of Academic Health Sciences Libraries, the Association of Research Libraries, the Medical Library Association, and the Special Libraries Association. Retrieved November 17, 2007, from http://www.arl.org/scomm/licensing/principles.html

California Digital Library (n.d.). Checklist of points to be addressed in a CDL License Agreement. Retrieved November 17, 2007, from http://www.cdlib.org/vendors/checklist.html

International Coalition of Library Consortia (1998). Statement of current perspective and preferred practices for the selection and purchase of electronic information. Retrieved November 17, 2007, from http://www.library.yale.edu/consortia/statement.html

International Federation of Library Association Committee on Copyright and Other Legal Matters (2001). Licensing principles. Retrieved November 17, 2007, from http://www.ifla.org/V/ebpb/copy.htm

Klughist, A. C. (2000). LIBER licensing principles for electronic information. *Journal of Academic Librarianship, 26(3),* 199-201.

Ligue des Bibliothèques Européennes de Recherche (1998). Licensing principles. Retrieved November 17, 2007, from http://www.kb.dk/liber/currentinitiatives/licensing.htm

NorthEast Research Libraries (n.d.). Licensing guidelines. Retrieved November 17, 2007, from http://www.library.yale.edu/NERLpublic/licensingprinciples.html

Merriam-Webster's Dictionary of Law (1996). Springfield, MA: Merriam-Webster.

Schottlaender, B. (1998). The development of national principles to guide librarians in licensing electronic resources. *Library Acquisitions: Practice and Theory, 22(1),* 49-54.

University of California Libraries (n.d.). Principles for acquiring and licensing information in digital formats. Retrieved November 17, 2007, from http://libraries.universityofcalifornia.edu/cdc/principlesforacquiring.html

Chapter IX
Copyright Implications for Electronic Resources

Aline Soules
California State University, East Bay, USA

Donna L. Ferullo
Purdue University, USA

ABSTRACT

The chapter begins with an examination of the sections of copyright law that impact electronic resource management, and reviews the various laws that have been enacted in recent years to attempt to delineate appropriate uses of information in the electronic environment. In section two, the impact of copyright is discussed in relation to particular types of electronic resources. The unique characteristics and chal lenges inherent in both access and format are discussed. Section three reports on responses to a series of interview questions the authors posed to librarians working in a wide variety and type of libraries. The goal was to elicit information about how librarians are managing to implement copyright law in the daily reality of their increasingly electronic environments.

INTRODUCTION AND BACKGROUND: COPYRIGHT AND THE LAW

An understanding of the nuances of copyright law and its relationship with other areas of library law is critical for anyone whose responsibilities include electronic resource management, which today encompasses almost everyone. There are basic elements of copyright that apply to all information resources, regardless of format, but the emergence of electronic resources and their characteristics have brought particular concerns into bold view. New laws have subsequently been enacted to try to deal with these concerns and the cycle continues as new concerns arise and new bills are introduced to deal with them.

For a long time, people knew that copyright existed. If they were employed in the library, they took certain steps to inform the public of various limitations, for example, by posting official notices on copying machines (U.S. Copyright Office, Circular 21, 1998) or by using the guidelines set forth in such documents as the revised *Guidelines for Classroom Copying of Books and Periodicals* (2001), agreed to by the Association of American Publishers and the Author's League of America. However, copyright was, in large measure, disconnected from the daily work or something that was dealt with if a problem occasionally arose. Now that various types of electronic resources are becoming a primary method of delivering information, copyright is becoming an integral part of daily work and the "gray" areas that were laid aside for so long are now being considered. In some ways, these laws have been with us and are just now coming under intense scrutiny. In other ways, there are new considerations to incorporate.

A Review of the Basics

Copyright law is about balance. It weighs the public's right to use copyrighted works with the rights of the copyright holder (not necessarily the author). United States copyright law is based on English copyright law, as first enacted by the British Parliament in the Statute of Anne in 1710. The Statute provided copyright protection for authors for 14 years and was renewable for another 14 years if the author was still alive. This new law was in response to a monopoly by publishers, in particular the Crown of England, which was very restrictive in what could be published. Authors wanted more control over their works and the Statute theoretically provided that. However, in reality, the authors needed the publishers to print their works, so there remained an unequal balance of power. Nonetheless, the principle of balance was established and remains a fundamental goal to this day.

Our forefathers recognized the importance of copyright to the future success of our new country, believing that the dissemination of knowledge was the key to an informed democracy. When they drafted the constitution, they created copyright law and gave authority over that law to Congress through the Constitution:

Congress shall have the power ... to promote the Progress of Science and useful Arts, by securing for limited Times to Authors and Inventors exclusive Right to their respective Writings and Discoveries. (United States, 1787)

The founding fathers wanted to encourage citizens to create new works and the incentive was to give them control over their work for a limited period of time, but not so long as to create a sinecure. This was the beginning of the struggle to balance the rights of users and authors (or owners) of copyrighted works, a struggle that is increasingly raging today.

Within the federal government, the three major players who have a role in different aspects of copyright are Congress, the federal courts, and the United States Copyright Office.

Congress is responsible for drafting legislation for new laws and amending existing laws. The first copyright law was enacted by Congress in 1790. Since then, the most comprehensive updates to the law were enacted in 1909 and 1976, the latter being our current fundamental law. There have been many amendments to the law over the years, but there is only one copyright law—Title 17 of the United States code. The amendments are merely changes to different sections within that law.

To handle the functions associated with copyright law, the United States Copyright Office was founded and eventually became a separate department within the Library of Congress. Its role is to administer and sustain the national copyright system.

As copyright is a federal law, disputes are settled in federal courts, which interpret the law. Trials are held in federal district courts. If the parties are dissatisfied with the outcome of the trial, they can file an appeal in the Circuit court for their district (there are 12). Appeals from those courts are filed in the Supreme Court, which may or may not choose to hear those cases.

In copyright, as in other areas of law, there is statutory law and case law. Congress passes the laws (statutory). Case law is the result of judicial opinions in the courts. Even though they may research what has been decided in each others' courts, different Circuit courts can interpret the law differently and their rulings are only binding in their respective regions. While all courts must begin in the same place—interpreting the current law—some courts are known to be more sympathetic to one group over another. For example, the Second Circuit Court of Appeals, which includes New York, is perceived to favor publishers while the Ninth Circuit, which includes California, is perceived to favor the author or creator of a work. As a result, litigants will go "forum shopping" to file suit in the Circuit that may give them the best chance to win their case. It might appear at first glance that understanding the distinction among courts and the different arenas of law is only for lawyers, but it is equally important to anyone who is trying to understand why some legal decisions hold or maybe only appear to hold more weight than others.

The Law and Electronic Resources

Under our current law (1976) and its amendments, there is automatic copyright protection for works that are original and are "fixed in a tangible medium of expression" (17 U.S.C. §101). To be fixed, the work must be in a form that is not merely transitory. If it can be perceived by a person, machine, or device, then it is fixed. In the 1976 law, works eligible for copyright protection had to fall into these eight categories:

1. Literary works
2. Musical works, including any accompanying works

3. Dramatic works, including any accompanying music
4. Pantomimes and choreographic works
5. Pictorial, graphic, and sculptural works
6. Motion pictures and other audiovisual works
7. Sound recordings
8. Architectural works (17 U.S.C. §102a).

Over the years, many specific types of works have been added to the categories, for example, computer programs (which are considered literary works) and Web sites. It should be noted, however, that computer programs are sometimes also protected by patents, another area of intellectual property law. As new electronic resources are developed, if there is doubt about whether copyright or patent applies, rights of ownership may be sought via both avenues.

A work has to be original, but the originality only has to be minimal in order to receive protection. In the early 1990's, the court ruled in *Feist Publications Inc. vs. Rural Telephone Service Co* (1991) that an alphabetical listing in a white pages telephone book did not have sufficient originality while in the *Bellsouth Advertising & Publishing Corp. vs. Donnelley Information Publishing, Inc* (1993) case, the court decided that a yellow pages arrangement of listings by subject might have sufficient originality to be protected. This is an example of an early form of electronic database, as the data was stored electronically for purposes of easy updating prior to printing. It is also an example of a variation in ruling from one case to another.

Automatic protection means that the copyright holder does not have to register the work with the United States Copyright Office nor place a copyright symbol (©) on the work. Many copyright formalities were rescinded to bring United States copyright law into harmony with international copyright treaties; however, to move forward with any litigation through the United States courts, the work must first be registered.

Not all works qualify for copyright protection. Ideas are exempted; only the expression of ideas is protected. Other unprotected areas include facts, titles, names, short phrases, and slogans, although some of these are protected through other intellectual property laws such as patents or trademarks. Also unprotected are works by employees of the United States federal government whose work is a direct result of their jobs; works whose copyrights have expired; and works not fixed in a tangible medium of expression, for example, an extemporaneous speech that remains unrecorded. These works are now in the public domain, free to be used.

Rights of Copyright Holders

Copyright holders (not necessarily the authors or creators) have the exclusive right to:

1. Reproduce the copyrighted work in copies or phonorecords
2. Prepare derivative works based upon the copyrighted work
3. Distribute copies or phonorecords of the copyrighted work to the public by sale or other transfer of ownership, or by rental, lease, or lending
4. In the case of literary, musical, dramatic, and choreographic works, pantomimes, and motion pictures and other audiovisual works, to perform the copyrighted work publicly
5. In the case of literary, musical, dramatic, and choreographic works, pantomimes, and pictorial, graphic, or sculptural works, including the individual images of a motion picture or other audiovisual work, to display the copyrighted work publicly
6. In the case of sound recordings, to perform the copyrighted work publicly by means of a digital audio transmission (17 U.S.C. §106).

With electronic resources, those rights extend to reproduction in electronic form.

The Right of First Sale

In the print world, copyright holders knew that when their works were published to the world, users would be able to resell the physical copies they held, whether at garage sales, used bookstores, or online via ebay or some other venue (17 U.S.C. §109). In addition, it also permitted libraries to loan these materials and to engage in interlibrary loan transactions. When information is provided digitally, this right is far less clear. In principle, many believe that this right should continue; however, without having purchased the information in a tangible form, it is difficult to argue that this right continues to be transferred to the user. In fact, often, the information is not even purchased, but licensed or "rented" and there have been discussions about this right for a number of years.

Exemptions

Copyright holders' rights have limitations, commonly called exemptions. One is the time limit during which those rights apply. The latest extension, the Sonny Bono Copyright Term Extension Act, was enacted in 1998 and extended the rights to the life of the author plus 70 years. In cases of corporate creations, works for hire, and anonymous or pseudonymous works, the limit is 95 years from the date of first publication or 120 from the date of creation, whichever is the first to expire. Due to the many changes in this area, determining the exact expiration can be difficult, but works published in the United States prior to 1923 can safely be considered in the public domain. The 1998 act was challenged in the supreme court case, Eldred vs. Ashcroft (Berkman Center, 2003). The Supreme Court ruled that as long as the time was not unlimited, Congress could establish the duration of the copyright term. As more profitable works near the timeline, it is likely that further extensions will be sought.

Given the length of copyright protection, it becomes even more critical for the public to understand and use the exemptions as appropriate, such as fair use, library copying, and educational use in classroom and distance learning. These exemptions are not mutually exclusive and must be applied to a situation wholly to ensure that all rights under the copyright law are exercised.

Fair Use

Fair use is probably one of the most highly used exemptions in education and possibly the most confusing. Congress purposely built in flexibility through the four-factor test that applies whether the information is presented as a traditional or an electronic resource. The first is the purpose and character of the use to be made of the work. If the use is for educational purposes rather than commercial purposes, then it weighs in favor of fair use. The second factor, nature of the work, protects factual works less than creative works. The amount of the work being used is the third factor, with less being preferred over more. In spite of guidelines that suggest specific amounts, for example, the Conference on Fair Use (CONFU) and multimedia, they are not the law and can be misleading (University of Texas System, 1997, 2004).

The fourth and most contentious factor assesses market effect. If there is an impact on the market for the work, then it generally weighs against fair use. In terms of electronic resources, a key consideration is Web exposure. If the use is on a restricted access Web site, then there is less impact on the market than if the work is made available via the World Wide Web, creating the potential for a great deal of harm to the market.

After the four factors have been applied to the use of the work, a determination is made as to the likelihood that the use is fair. Often, the determination is unclear. At that point, users must decide how much risk to assume, whether individually, as a group, or as an institution. This often presents another challenge, as institutions are often more concerned about potential liability than individuals. It is also an area that has received heightened awareness and caused increased tension in recent years.

An important example of this occurred at Cornell University. In a press release issued by Cornell University's Press Relations Office, the following statement was made:

As part of ongoing discussions over the manner in which Cornell University provides copyrighted course content to students in digital formats, the Association of American Publishers (AAP) and Cornell recently announced a new set of copyright guidelines to govern the use of electronic course materials on the library's electronic course reserves system, on faculty and departmental Web pages, and through the various 'course management' Web sites used at Cornell. The guidelines affirm that the use of such content is governed by the same legal principles that apply to printed materials (2006).

These new guidelines make it clear that parallels are being confirmed between traditional and electronic formats. Also recommended are methods to restrict access and the need to de-link or take down information at the end of courses in order to prevent wholesale distribution without appropriate permission.

The Libraries Exemption

Section 108 of the copyright law is known as the "libraries exemption," which permits copying for preservation, interlibrary loan, and private study by users (17 U.S.C. §108). Each category has its own requirements, but the overall section is not digital-friendly. As of this writing, a Section 108 study group has been convened by the Library of Congress to examine the changes to libraries and archives as a result of the digital explosion. Their charge is to determine what part of Section 108 might need to be amended in order to provide the public, including copyright owners and users, the rights to which they are entitled under the Constitution. The group is to submit their recommendations to the Librarian of Congress in 2007 and is currently in the process of conducting roundtable discussions around the country to hear opinions from the field. The group maintains a Web site that provides details about the group, its roundtables, and the public comments it has gathered to date (Library of Congress, 2006).

Educational Exemptions

There are two exemptions for education both included under Section 110 of the copyright law (17 U.S.C. §110). Section 110(1) delineates the use of copyrighted works for the classroom or face-to-face teaching. Basically, teachers and students can display or perform any work legally made in any format in the classroom provided the work has some relation to the course content. On the other hand, mounting that work or the performance of that on a course Web site is a different matter, as the Cornell guidelines make clear.

Section 110(2) specifies the use of works for distance learning. This section is known as the TEACH Act, that is, the Technology, Education, and Copyright Harmonization Act (21st Century Department of Justice Appropriations Authorization Act, 2002). This was an instance where the law was lagging behind the technology and severely limiting what and how educators could use digital resources. It is an improvement over its predecessor, but it falls far short of embracing the diverse educational opportunities offered in the digital world. It expands the exemption that allows dramatic literary or musical works to be used in distance education by adding the ability to use dramatic works and audiovisuals, but only in "limited and reasonable portions." In addition, before that exemption can be claimed, many

requirements must be met. Institutions must be accredited and nonprofit; must have a copyright policy in place; and must distribute copyright information to their faculty, students, and staff. There are also technological restrictions and restrictions as to the type of material that qualifies under this exemption. Throughout this amendment, there is the persistent restriction that the use of digital works in a distance environment is to be comparable to what takes place in a live classroom. It is evident that vendors were quite concerned that their revenue stream would be negatively impacted if broad use of digital works was allowed.

Digital Millennium Copyright Act

The year 1998 saw more than one amendment to the copyright law. In addition to the Sonny Bono Copyright Term Extension Act, Congress passed the Digital Millennium Copyright Act (DMCA) (United States Copyright Office, 1998). The DMCA is quite complex and controversial. It offers immunity from liability for online service providers under certain circumstances, which immunity is helpful to educational institutions that generally qualify as online service providers. There is also an anticircumvention provision of technological protection systems that is quite confusing and a bone of contention among many players. When drafting this legislation, the intent was to stop widespread piracy of digital works. While this was well meant, the reality is of grave concern to libraries and educational institutions who foresee far greater restricted access to copyrighted works, as well as an erosion of fair use rights. After all, if the material is digitally locked up and circumventing the copy protection technology is a violation of the DMCA, how can a fair use analysis even be applied in such situations? Further, what happens to the right of first sale? There have been several cases, both criminal and civil, brought under the DMCA, but the concern remains that it is far more harmful than beneficial to the general public and users of copyright protected works. In essence, it forces individuals and institutions into negotiating contracts for the use of materials and determining the rights of each party to the contract. The DMCA is constantly being reviewed and legislation introduced to clarify and refine the statute. One aspect of the DMCA is that every three years, the United States Copyright Office is required to hold hearings on the possible need for exemptions. On November 22, 2006, the librarian of Congress issued a statement regarding six exemptions that would apply for the next three years. The exemption of most interest to this discussion is as follows:

Audiovisual works included in the educational library of a college or university's film or media studies department, when circumvention is accomplished for the purpose of making compilations of portions of those works for educational use in the classroom by media studies or film professors. (United States Copyright Office, Statement, 2006)

While this can be viewed as a small step towards redressing the copyright balance, it should be remembered that it is very limited (to media studies or film professors) and only in effect for the next three years, at which time a determination will be made as to whether to continue this exemption or expunge it. However, it is the first time that any exemption of this type has been introduced.

Orphan Works

Another pending legislative issue, as of this writing, is the orphan works issue. Orphan works are works which are still protected by copyright but where it is difficult, if not impossible, to identify or locate the copyright owner to seek permission to use the work. As the duration of copyright becomes increasingly longer, more works are falling into this no man's land. The United States Copyright

Office held roundtable discussions to determine the issues and concerns of all parties. In January 2006, they submitted to Congress their report which was based on the discussion. A house bill on orphan works was introduced in May 2006 and subsequently incorporated into H.R.6052 entitled the "Copyright Modernization Act of 2006" (Public Knowledge, 2006). Unfortunately, this bill died due to the fact that additional unrelated restrictions were added regarding music licensing. The intent of the orphan works section of this legislation was to reduce the liability of users of orphan works should the copyright owner come forward. Should similar legislation be introduced and passed at some future time, it would allow for unknown numbers of orphan works to be used in numerous ways which would benefit the public. Further, as information proliferates on the Web, inadvertent digitization of an orphan work would result in less harsh consequences than might currently be the case.

The International Scene

The United States is part of the international community in harmonizing copyright laws around the world, something that is increasingly critical with the growth of the World Wide Web and electronic resources generally. It is in our best interest on many fronts to work with other countries in having uniform copyright laws, especially given the digital nature of many works and the international exchange and collaboration on multi-authored works. The challenge is that it is difficult to keep up with the national scene, let alone the international one. It would be impossible to cover the international scene fully in this chapter; however, a couple of highlights should be considered.

In 1989, the United States became a signatory to the Berne Convention, an international copyright treaty. In order to be a party to the treaty, the United States had to remove some of the formalities associated with U.S. copyright law, such as the registration and copyright notice requirement (see previous section). Unfortunately, that placed many items formerly in the public domain back under copyright, but this is all part of an effort to promote globalization of copyright laws.

Another major player on the international copyright scene is the World Intellectual Property Organization (WIPO), an agency of the United Nations. They are responsible for promoting and protecting intellectual property throughout the world. This organization, however, focuses more on protecting owners' rights than promoting users' rights to intellectual property (World Intellectual Property Organization, 2006). One example of this is WIPO's support of database protection legislation coming out of the European Commission (2006). This type of protection is more in favor of owners than the protection currently afforded by United States legislation. This legislation has been under consideration and discussion for almost ten years, but no final determination has yet been made.

Legislation that is closer to home, but still international, is the North American Free Trade Agreement (NAFTA) (1992). This agreement among Canada, the United States, and Mexico deals with trade regulations, but copyright is impacted because these three countries have different copyright laws and as electronic information travels back and forth as a "commodity," different regulations apply in each of the three countries.

The intricacies of both international and United States copyright laws can potentially impact the use of electronic resources, but copyright is not the only regulator. Many electronic resources are governed by contract, not copyright law. Contracts set the terms of use for the product. When managing electronic resources, contracts must be reviewed to ensure that the use of these resources complies with contract terms. An analysis of copyright law and its exemptions is the next step in the process. For details about

contracting for electronic resources, please see the chapter on licensing.

COPYRIGHT, THE NATURE OF ELECTRONIC INFORMATION, AND ITS DELIVERY

The law is slowly evolving to accommodate electronic resources and to try to address the principle of balance that has been the foundation of United States copyright law from its beginning. It is useful to look at the particular characteristics and nature of electronic resources to understand the challenges this represents.

When the book was invented, the world of information underwent a revolution. Prior to that, the oral tradition was the vehicle by which information was conveyed from one person to another. Print was a major change. Today, we are experiencing another revolution, in this case involving far more than a single transfer from oral to print. The nature of information itself is not that different from the past, although there is a great deal more of it—facts, opinions, fiction, the human mind made manifest through prose and poetry, sharing discoveries. The change is really in the packages in which that information comes. To understand the relationship of copyright laws and electronic resource management, it is useful to look briefly at some of the ways information is delivered.

To do this, we have organized this section to discuss access, that is, platforms and other ways to reach information—the Internet and World Wide Web, course management systems, electronic reserves, institutional repositories, and interlibrary loan—and formats, also including new and emerging formats—electronic databases, electronic journals and articles, electronic books, digitized print material, and media and streaming media. We end the section with a brief discussion of the blurring of information among creators and users, the possibilities of future formats, and the importance of thoughtful copyright decisions as these developments evolve.

Access: The Internet and World Wide Web

The Internet granddaddy that enables electronic information to be delivered has been around for longer than many people realize. The foundations of the Internet were developed in the 1960's and the Internet itself was first introduced to the public in 1972 (Berners-Lee, 1996). After being used by the Department of Defense for a number of years, it expanded from being a network used by the government and scholars to an open environment, available to anyone who could afford a domain name and server space, and had the ability to create or pay for code to make information available (Leiner et al., 2005).

The current World Wide Web content, which travels over the Internet, includes material that appears only in electronic form, material that appears both in electronic and print form, material that is copyright-controlled, material in the public domain, material that copyright owners permit users to use freely or with credit or with other restrictions—in other words, every type of copyright condition imaginable. What is clear, however, is that the moment the content is issued, there is a copyright condition attached. If it is not in the public domain by virtue of its being issued by the federal government or being taken from content that is older than the current length of copyright, then the copyright belongs to someone (individual, author, group, association, etc.), whether that copyright holder provides a statement permitting use in full or in part or whether no statement appears.

It is possible for the copyright holder to place the information on the Web "as is" or, if the holder wishes to restrict its use, to introduce some sort of technological device that prevents copying or downloading (protected by the DMCA). When

issuing information without such a technological restriction, the copyright holder should be aware that it is easy for users to copy, print, or cut and paste the information regardless of what printed restrictions may be listed on the site. Even with a technological restriction in place, if a user chooses to circumvent it, in violation of the DMCA, the holder has no recourse unless the offender is caught—a serendipitous event at best.

Access: Learning (or Course) Management Systems

An institution's learning management system is another access route to the library's electronic information; however, in this case, the environment is controlled because authentication is required both on campus and for remote use, and is restricted to class enrollees. In spite of this control, it is possible for the professor to allow "guest" access to a course site. That guest access can be set up to exclude information sources, as is generally requested by the institution, but it is controlled by the professor, who should be educated in the reasons for that requirement. In addition, there are sometimes issues with the URLs that link the user from the learning management system to the full text in electronic databases, particularly in the case of remote use, and the professor must ensure that the links "work" from noncampus sites on a "persistent" basis. The technical challenges involved in that process make it tempting to download full text documents from the electronic database to remount in PDF format, which is making a digital copy. While there are advantages, such as making user access more reliable (particularly when users have a variety of computer capabilities to receive information) or setting up the PDF file to prevent copying, downloading, and so forth. (although that is optional on the part of the person mounting the file), it is not appropriate. It is easily assumed that because copyright is already paid, there is "no harm done," but making such a copy requires permission and, when required, the payment of copyright fees. This issue is specifically addressed in the Cornell guidelines, which will provide library staff with additional support as they work to educate their users. If links prove too difficult to establish, it is possible to provide faculty with templates that provide descriptions for users on how to access information items for themselves.

In the case of courses that are fully part of distance learning, the TEACH Act eases some restrictions. The information does not change, but the conditions do. Details of the act are covered in the previous section.

As a result of these various issues, while the contract may be clear, some user knowledge of copyright guidelines is needed to promote an understanding of what is and is not appropriate, whether information is accessed directly from the electronic database or through a learning/course management system.

Another access mechanism for electronic database information is for a commercial provider to enable searching through sites such as Google, Yahoo, and so forth. In this case, the user may get a list of search results that includes links to indexed or even abstracted information, but to retrieve the full text, the user will be asked to pay-per-access. This method of access is fully controlled and the information is paid for in the same way as a widget. In this scenario, the model is structured on an industrial rather than an intellectual property basis.

In addition, there is Google Scholar, which enables users to set preferences for the institution to which they are affiliated and to search databases through Google in the same way as they would search the open Web on regular Google. The advantage is that copyright protections are fully in place; the disadvantage is that users, particularly novice users, are frequently unaware of what they are actually searching and when back on the open Web or Google, they are confronted

with requests for payment that they do not fully understand. This too requires education.

Access: Electronic Reserve Systems

A consideration when it comes to digitized articles and books is electronic reserve systems, generally administered by libraries. Under copyright, fair use is one option when it comes to e-reserve content. Which of the following determinations will be made? Will library staff apply fair use one time then seek permission for subsequent uses, will they require permission for every use, or will they apply fair use each time that the library owns or has rights to a copy of work in print or electronic form? In the case of electronic content, are there contractual obligations that will dictate uses for electronic reserves?

As electronic reserves are a dominant resource in higher education at this point in time, these questions are critical and the decisions libraries make are gathering attention. Publishers express escalating concern about the use and/or digitization of materials without appropriate permissions or payment and there is controversy over whether the library continues to have special rights, as they do with print reserves, or whether these pieces of information are similar to course packs or course readers, subject to full requirements for copyright permissions with or without fair use. While the Cornell guidelines address the issue of what is provided in a learning/course management system, they are equally applicable to electronic reserves. In fact, the Cornell guidelines may prove to be a watershed in the evolution of electronic resource management from a copyright perspective.

It should be noted, however, that errors in copyright do work in two ways. In licensing databases, libraries pay copyright fees for the appropriate use of those materials, whether for class or research purposes. Faculty, however, may not be fully aware that the item they want is available in these resources and may seek permission unnecessarily. If they ask that an item be put on electronic reserves, however, library staff will generally check to see if that item is available in a licensed database as a first step in their procedures and will pursue permissions only if it is not.

If it is determined that an item is in a licensed database, either the library staff or the faculty member can provide a link (hopefully persistent) through an electronic reserves system or a learning/course management system with confidence that copyright requirements are met. In the case of faculty, it is possible to provide a link through a personal Web site, but then it is necessary to ensure that authentication is required at some point before the user can access the item.

These methods generally take care of articles; however, book chapters and whole books are another matter. Whole books are generally still placed on traditional reserves (unless they come in electronic form), but book chapters are another matter. To make a book chapter available electronically, either purchase of an electronic form or the digitization of a chapter from a print book is needed. From the publisher perspective, either condition requires seeking copyright permission and this is not always granted. From the library perspective, fair use analysis is an option that should be applied. This is currently a source of tension.

In fact, it is impossible to know what is permissible until that permission is sought. In the Taylor & Francis license, for example, the following statements are included:

- "For the avoidance of doubt, the Licensee may not incorporate all or any part of the Licensed Materials in Course Packs and Electronic Reserve collections without the prior written permission of the Publisher or the Publisher's Representative, which may set out further terms and conditions for such usage."
- "A link to the Licensed Material may be incorporated in Electronic Reserve collec-

tions" (Taylor & Francis Group Journals, 2006).

On the other hand, an e-mail on the SerialSt listserv provided the following information regarding the practices of Haworth Press: "Right now, Haworth Press allows the preparing of coursepaks [sic] from journal articles at no charge, if the library subscribes to our journals. It is our way of expressing appreciation to the library" (Cohen, 2006).

While it should be said that the first scenario is the more likely condition, it is clear that publisher practices vary.

The challenges in the permission-seeking process include the murkiness of fair use analysis, as described above, the cost of permissions, and the pressure of time, as faculty often make decisions about materials close to the time they wish to use them, and that time is not sufficient to secure that permission. Thus, both the cost of permissions and also the time to secure them are not necessarily built into the infrastructure. Publishers are responding more quickly to permissions requests; however, there are occasions when the publisher's time frame is impractically long and other occasions when the requestor comes to realize that no answer is an answer. The budget issue, however, is the requestor's to manage.

Access: Institutional Repositories

This relatively new effort, primarily in academic or research libraries, is an attempt to make information available without the expenses incurred through established publishing routes for electronic information. Copyright discussions take place over the rights of creators, users, and the institution that supports the repository. Authors who allow their creations to be made available in an institutional repository are generally not expecting that information to garner them income in a commercial sense. They are primarily interested in sharing their work; however, they do want to retain their full rights to that information, to be cited appropriately, to gain recognition, and to be rewarded financially through the indirect route of tenure and promotion. As long as they remain connected to the institution where the repository resides, matters generally lie fallow. If they choose to change their affiliation to a different institution and wish to switch that information from one repository to another, it is best for some contractual agreement to be in place prior to the original mounting of the information.

Another concern is institutional repositories that present students' work, for example, theses or dissertations. Students have long been subject to graduation requirements that involve the submission of their material to a commercial source for these types of materials; however, with the institutional repository, there may either be requirements for submission to both or the submission requirement may be switched from the commercial source to the institutional repository. When this practice of mounting student dissertations on the Web began, there was some question about whether the material had already been "published," and some newly-minted engineering PhDs who pursued academic careers found that they were unable to rework their research into publishable articles for tenure. This issue seems to have abated as the practice becomes more commonly considered and more familiar.

The establishing of institutional repositories brings into play not only user rights, but also creator rights. Faculty, students, or anyone who submits material for inclusion in an institutional repository may have the same rights as any other creator, per copyright law, but the open nature of institutional repositories is such that there is a need to clarify the boundaries of these rights in advance. One attempt to deal with these still-gray areas is the Creative Commons license (2006). This and similar types of licenses are focused on the importance of sharing and crediting information and not concerned with monetary recompense. As is stated on the Creative Commons Web site,

"Creative Commons provides free tools that let authors, scientists, artists, and educators easily mark their creative work with the freedoms they want it to carry. You can use CC to change your copyright terms from 'All Rights Reserved' to 'Some Rights Reserved.'" They continue by saying, "We're a nonprofit organization. Everything we do—including the software we create—is free" (Creative Commons, 2007). The development of the Creative Commons has become a grass roots groundswell, but still depends on user good will. It does provide templates, however, which express the general principles of appropriate sharing and provide a framework within which to work.

There are also established networks, such as the social science research network, that act very much like institutional repositories, housing working papers that may or may not appear eventually in more traditional journals. While the same copyright conditions apply, those who submit papers are seeking dissemination, feedback, and credit, not direct monetary recompense, and they have no expectations that their work will be subject to the same copyright restrictions as is the case with commercial enterprises. They do, however, rely on user goodwill in the same way as those who invoke Creative Commons license options.

Access: Interlibrary Loan

This area has now evolved into an almost solely electronically based service. Exceptions include whole books and those articles that are restricted from electronic transfer by publishers. The availability of systems such as Ariel has made it possible for libraries to "loan" articles and book chapters through electronic means. Electronic versions are made available for limited periods of time (generally 30 days) and users must authenticate to gain access to the electronic item that has been "loaned." Once that access is gained, they may print or download the items from a Web site behind the authentication. This reduces the time it takes for articles and book chapters to be made available, but the system hinges on user ethics. If a document is downloaded, the user can share it with others. If users have the full Adobe Acrobat program, not just the free reader, they could even choose to alter the document before distributing it to colleagues, and so forth. It is useful here to remember that it is Section 108 of the U.S. copyright law that permits copying for interlibrary loan, and that this section is now being reviewed (see Section 1). What changes will result are still unknown.

Format: Electronic Databases

The most common electronic databases are integrated electronic information sources that are highly controlled by their commercial providers. Access requires subscription because commercial information providers have a great deal invested in this information. They contract with publishers to include information sources (articles, news, book chapters, conference proceedings, journals, etc.) in their databases. They create indexes, which are not merely a list (like the telephone book), but involve complex algorithms and programming and, in some cases, human intervention to ensure that the information is retrievable through multiple search strategies. Abstracts may be taken directly from the original content or written by staff members who work for or are contracted by the company. Some databases include only indexes; some include indexes and abstracts, yet others also include full text. That full text may be available in html or PDF format or both. Information is updated on a continual basis, in this case by the addition of new pieces of information or by the withdrawal of information for various reasons, for example, a change in a contract with a publisher or a copyright case, such as New York Times Co., Inc., et al. v. Tasini et al. (FindLaw for Legal Professionals, 2001). In this case, freelance authors filed a lawsuit alleging that their copyrights were infringed when some of their articles were placed in electronic databases by their publishers and without their permission. Their contract with the publishers was silent on the issue of electronic rights and only specifically cited print. The authors won their case, but in many ways, it was a Pyrrhic victory. Their articles were pulled from the databases and future contracts with authors were amended to include electronic rights for publishers.

In addition to text databases, there are numeric databases with data sets. There are differences in indexing, but the search and retrieval process for the user is similar. Some numeric or numeric and text databases are time-delayed, for example, information from the stock market, but some offer real-time, streaming data. Protection on these databases is particularly critical, and costs for real-time data are higher than for time-delayed information. Corporations, particularly financial ones, will pay significant money for real-time data; educational institutions generally operate with time-delayed information. Both, however, are copyright-protected.

Users generally sign contracts for electronic database information and when contracts are signed, the conditions of the contract prevail over copyright law if the contract signs away such rights. The language in the contract should include a provision that preserves the rights permitted by copyright law. Users essentially divide into two groups—corporate and educational. Corporate contracts are expensive and restricted to corporate employees or third party contractors, who may be asked to sign nondisclosure or other agreements prior to being given access. In the case of educational users, the cost is generally cheaper. The information may also be slightly different in terms of what's included. For an educational institution, the general rule of thumb is that the information is available to their primary clientele (students, faculty, and staff) and, in the case of the libraries affiliated with public institutions, "walk-ins," that is, those who physically walk into the library building. For administrative units in the institution, however, there may be more restrictive conditions and those units may pay a different fee from the fee paid by the library, depending on the database and its intended use. What is important from a copyright perspective is the definition of "educational use." It does not mean any use that takes place in an educational institution, but is restricted to uses that are educational in nature.

For public libraries, the issue is more complicated because their user base is not as easily defined. They have struggled to meet the vendor need for a definition by trying to limit remote access to the residents of their jurisdiction's geographical boundaries, but there have been difficulties in implementing that definition.

In terms of remote use, generally only the primary clientele is granted access and authentication is required. The libraries are responsible for putting these conditions in place; however, if a primary user chooses to share access with family or friends, for example, there is little the database provider or the libraries can do in the way of prevention, other than providing education about the appropriate use of commercial electronic database information and taking action if such violations come to light.

Over time, however, as vendors find more and more ways of tracking activity, a number of loopholes will undoubtedly be filled. It is also one of the reasons that tension has increased over the last few years—vendors now have more ways of monitoring copyright restrictions than was the case in the print world.

Format: Electronic Journals and Articles

The focus in these cases is full-text access. While a journal run is often available through an electronic database that provides indexing and abstracting, it cannot be browsed in quite the same way as a print run. There are electronic databases, such as JSTOR, which began as a way to digitize, archive, and make available the full text of the journals,

but which also offer ever-growing sophistication in their search capability. Contracts again prevail and the conditions of use are the same as for electronic databases; however, these sources have a slightly different orientation, as the first focus was on journal content and search capability was added later, whereas electronic databases began with indexing and abstracting and added full text access later. Some journal archives still require an indexing electronic database so that users can conduct a subject search for a particular article (either in electronic or print format), unless the user knows the exact article wanted or simply wants to browse a particular title. There are many efforts to digitize journals and there are embargos, both in electronic databases and also in electronic journal sources, in order to protect copyright and ensure that institutions continue to purchase current issues, whether in print or electronic format. This is driven by the desire to protect copyright in order to preserve income streams, essentially a protection for the fourth fair use factor of "effect on the market."

There are also electronic-only journals. They can be contracted like electronic journals available through a database or they can be available over the World Wide Web. If on the Web, the same challenges apply when it comes to protecting copyright as apply to other information provided over the Internet, unless some technological restriction is in place. In most cases, however, the goal is dissemination rather than income, in which case, asking users to credit the journal is more important than whether they use or re-use the information.

Format: Electronic Books

Electronic books are a more recent development in electronic information resources. There are commercial providers that contract with publishers to provide certain books in their electronic book databases. These are much like electronic databases for journal articles because these vendors provide packages of books, for example, ebrary, netLibrary. Fortunately, it is possible to download individual records for these items, enabling faculty and students to retrieve them in searches. Electronic books that are most used in academic libraries are those chosen by faculty as class textbooks or as supplementary reading (generally a particular chapter). Electronic books are also very popular in public libraries.

The advantages of electronic books include such features as increased search capability within the book and the ability to highlight, dog-ear, and so forth without "damaging" the book for the next person. One disadvantage is that reading an entire book online is not an easy prospect, although some books are good candidates for this format when users need only subsets of pages—a chapter or an extract of some sort. Another challenge comes either with the number of simultaneous copies available (usually at test or exam time), an issue that is license-based; however, in spite of the "parallel" to the print book that may be checked out, users tend not to understand why they cannot access the electronic book. This may be due to technical problems, which is the most common reason in academic libraries, or because the electronic book disappears after a certain number of viewings, a condition that occurs primarily in public libraries. Another disadvantage is copyright-based. Generally printing is restricted to one page or just a few pages at a time. It is presumed that the inconvenience will deter extensive copying of large amounts of the book. The vendor's statistics may reveal whether that is true or not. Most users complain about the disadvantages or work around them. If they understand why they are not gaining access, they wait and try to access the book later. As for printing, this is the feature users find most irritating. They can resort to online reading, which is feasible, but not popular. They generally try to print in small batches. If they are in the library when they are trying to work with electronic books, they will come to a service desk, offering

an opportunity to provide a brief explanation of how these resources work.

Some electronic books are now purchased individually from commercial sources with the entire attendant licensing conditions attached, making them more complex to purchase than is the case with books in print. Some electronic books are made available over the Internet by individuals or groups. These books are either digitized versions of public domain titles or of original works created by the person mounting them. These materials may provide useful access, particularly to remote users, but all of these titles are subject to the same copyright "dos and don'ts" as any print book or as any agreed-upon contract requires, whether negotiated or click-through.

Another feature that affects copyright is beaming. It is possible to beam an item from PDA to PDA or to computer. Presumably publishers will find a way to control or track that through technological means.

The future is likely to provide continuously improving technology, whether through electronic book readers or through the increasingly multipurpose PDA (who does not have a public domain title like *The Last of the Mohicans* on a PDA?), but, in the meantime, electronic books offer a key feature that users want—anywhere availability anytime.

Format: Digitized Print Material

The amount of electronic information is increasing daily, both in terms of new material and also because of the intervention of individuals and groups to digitize print formats.

JSTOR is an example of the mass digitization of journal issues and a further example of an operation that works comfortably within the law and with the consent of publishers. To achieve this, they make agreements with publishers to restrict digitization of current issues for a certain length of time, three to five years being most common, and to "move the wall" each year as issues become older than the embargo period and they are then permitted to update the title with another year's worth of issues. Certain titles, however, are entirely excluded if JSTOR is unable to reach an agreement with a publisher. As a result, JSTOR is able to digitize retrospective material within the confines set by publishers and can be secure in the knowledge that they have met copyright requirements as set by publishers.

The scenario for the digitization of books, however, is a very different story and, unlike the quiet efforts of JSTOR, a very public one. Google's grand vision is "to organize the world's information and make it universally accessible and useful" (Quint, 2004). To that end, they have developed the Google Scholar project and have contracted with major research libraries (originally Harvard, Oxford, Stanford, the University of Michigan and New York Public Library) to digitize their collections. This digitization includes works in the public domain and works that are still protected by copyright. Since Google's first announcement, work has progressed, but not without objections from copyright holders.

Lawsuits have been filed by publishers against Google and the Scholar project, but as of this writing the cases have yet to be heard in court. If the cases do reach the courts, one theory is that Google will claim fair use as its defense. Google will more than likely argue that, under fair use, their use of the copyrighted works is a transformative one. In essence, in order to make a new or transformative work, they must use the entire original work. On the other side, publishers will more than likely claim that all Google is doing is making a copy and that the only change is in the format, thus not rising to the level of a new creative or transformative work. In the publishers' view, it is quite simply a derivative work without any transformative value. Not surprisingly, courts in the various circuits have different views on what constitutes transformative use (see Section 1 for an explanation of this disparity). It remains to be seen as to whether the courts' analyses and

decisions will favor Google and its Scholar project or the publishers. Many in the library community and beyond are closely monitoring the legal developments for this initiative, understanding that much is at stake not only for Google, but also for all other mass digitization projects.

Format: Media and Streaming Media

Media has generally been subject to more restrictive copyright use guidelines than has text. Streaming media is no different, whether in audio, video, or some learning object format. The advent of the MP3 player and the iPod resulted in a greater effort to provide downloadable information with clear statements as to whether the information is free or fee. Various music sources now provide easy download capability and have set prices for such downloads at an individually affordable level. This encourages copyright-appropriate use, although there is great vigilance on the part of groups such as the Recording Industry Association of America. There have been regular references to RIAA activity in such publications as *Edupage*, Educause's electronic newsletter that provides short news briefs on information technology issues and IT news related to higher education. Podcasting and vodcasting are developing trends that will no doubt push the copyright boundaries once again.

There is also more integration of media with text, for example, encyclopedias with audio pronunciation, video clips illustrating motion, and so forth. Off-air taping, a copyright challenge in the preelectronic information world, is not copyright-legal to stream without permission. Prevention is however still not technically possible, but requires education.

Video information sources can be categorized. Commercial movies are restricted from a copyright perspective; however, educational media are purposely less controlled. Annenberg, for example, offers teachers professional development, resources, and activities on a free basis and it is possible to make arrangements to stream media selections through a learning/course management system as well as directly. A third category is the individual use category, whether an item is rented or purchased. It is illegal to make a duplicate copy; an additional copy should be rented or purchased. A word should also be said about international availability. There have been cases where an individual has purchased a movie in one country and found that it cannot be viewed in another. These types of restrictions are built into the products. Objections have been made in certain cases, but, as yet, these limitations continue to be part of the technology.

This is an area which includes multiple library types. Academic and public libraries have offered audio and visual media for some time in the formats of the day—LPs, CDs, videos, DVDs. For some time, they just purchased a standard copy or copies and loaned them to users. In some cases, this may still continue; however, for many libraries, the contract world has entered into the picture. Libraries may pay extra for what are called "educational" media in order to be able to show them in classrooms or at free public library events in their meeting rooms. For commercial media in the form of the latest movie, public libraries can now license through Swank, the nontheatrical distributor of motion pictures (Swank, 2006). Some libraries contract through a service such as Netflix to get titles on a one-time basis periodically. In some cases, however, the fact that Netflix does not provide invoicing acceptable to various regulatory bodies prohibits such contracts. In those cases, libraries are reduced to negotiating with individual distributors or sending individual users to services such as Netflix and Blockbuster to pursue individual rentals. This limits the renter to "home use," however, as that is the copyright restriction in these cases. For some libraries, providing commercial films is particularly difficult in light of copyright and other considerations; however, the cost of the copyright permissions is generally the biggest hurdle.

Blurring Information and Future Formats

Wikis, blogs, MySpace, Facebook, instant messaging, and what is generally known as social software are recent developments that blur the information lines between creator and user. Wikipedia is an excellent example of how creators and users essentially forego copyright in the interests of putting information "out there." An article in the *New Yorker* on the 25th anniversary of Wikipedia's existence elaborated on the challenges of the reliability, maintenance, upkeep, and management of this information source (Schiff, 2006). While the moment the information is supplied, it is under copyright, the creators are not known and Wikipedia disclaims ownership. In fact, they invoke a principle known as copyleft, "the practice which removes restrictions on the distribution of copies and modified versions of a work for others and requires the same freedoms be preserved in modified versions"(GNU, 2006). Wikipedia states: "The Wikimedia Foundation does not own copyright on Wikipedia article texts and illustrations. It is therefore useless to e-mail our contact addresses asking for permission to reproduce content." (Wikipedia, 2006). Copyright cannot apply, as the creators should be aware that their words are unassignable. This brings the discussion of the nature of information full circle—back to the Internet and the endless stream of information that it can now provide.

The constantly shifting information on the Web is very easily manipulated. Copyright is essentially disclaimed by Wikipedia because its information can literally change daily. Other Web sites, however, may not issue such disclaimers and if nothing is said by the content owners to relax the conditions under which they are willing to let their information be used, copyright law applies in full. The ease with which users can download and save, even change, Web information does not change the application of copyright law. If a user saves a page, which later disappears from the Web, that saved page is still protected by copyright law, even if it no longer appears anywhere else.

A reference should be made to the new forms of scholarly communication that are emerging in response to the challenges presented by the traditional publisher model of providing information. It is impossible in this chapter to address the many experiments in scholarly communication, whether they involve licensing (e.g., Creative Commons) or prepublication (e.g., social science research network) or other methods by which authors are attempting to develop new models for publishing information that is less about making money and more about sharing content, but it is important to note that the same copyright principles apply. Often, conditions for the use of the information are included on the Web site or in an electronic appendix to the information. The information provider relies on the ethical perspective of the user to follow those conditions. If no conditions are provided, standard copyright law applies and permission should be sought for any use beyond that of fair use or other copyright exemptions.

What the future will bring is unknown, but it is likely that new forms of providing information will shift the nature of information, new technologies will enable more effective tracking of what is actually being used and printed, new inventions will continue to challenge copyright laws, and all of the above will require significant thought by creators and users of information as well as by those who create the laws by which copyright is governed.

IMPLEMENTING COPYRIGHT

How are library staff managing this complex combination of copyright law and evolving electronic resources? We began by examining a variety of copyright policies available on the Web (see appendix I) to get a sense of the approaches taken by various library types and sizes. Next, we queried various libraries, both with and without

Web-mounted policies (see appendix II). These libraries included a wide range of types and sizes, including academic, public, and school libraries (we omitted corporate libraries that function under a very different rubric); large, medium, and small libraries; and public and private libraries. Anonymity was promised to the respondents in order to elicit the most open comments. As expected, answers varied significantly from place to place and came from a variety of parts of the institution, not necessarily always the library.

This section addresses how respondents interpreted the term "electronic resources," fundamental library philosophy and focus, policies, education (libraries' main method of addressing copyright issues with users), and budget.

Interpreting the Term "Electronic Resources"

When asking the questions outlined in appendix II, we intended the term "electronic resources" to encompass the broad range of platforms and electronic information discussed in this chapter. Our respondents, however, did not necessarily share that interpretation. Some respondents interpreted the term to mean simply commercial electronic databases or resources provided by vendors, and one suggested that, "all those copyright issues are handled by them," (i.e., the vendor). Presumably, negotiation about who can use these resources takes place, but the respondents rely on the vendor to handle copyright clearances, relieving them of that responsibility, and they see no other copyright concern.

Another respondent interpreted "electronic resources" to mean only electronic reserves, indicating, perhaps, that this is a primary work responsibility or that this is an area of particular importance in that library at this time.

Clearly, academic libraries are most concerned about copyright as it relates to electronic resources and the bulk of the policies in appendix I are from those types of library, even if the interpretation of "electronic resources" is just commercial electronic databases or electronic reserves. Certainly, these are major concerns at the moment. A growing area of concern, however, is distance learning, which was referenced by some academic respondents. One expressed an effort to interest the institution in drafting a copyright policy, but was unable to succeed until the TEACH Act, when instructional technology began to develop more and more online courses and the issue of copyright became a concern to those beyond the library.

None of the respondents made specific reference to any special copyright-related issues in regard to the Internet or the World Wide Web, which we had expected from public libraries in particular. In fact, while some public libraries have policies, many do not have a specific person responsible for copyright and some of their responses reflected that they are still thinking and working in the pre-electronic world. For example, when asked about educating users, one response was to say that the official copyright notice is posted at all photocopy machines. It is not clear how long it will take before that perspective expands to include electronic resources. Public libraries are far less involved with electronic databases, but the expansion of the electronic book may come into play. Media are still in tangible formats, such as CDs and DVDs, but if streaming comes to the public library, that too, will trigger a different response.

When it comes to school libraries, little concern was expressed. Some school boards have policies (see appendix I), but what happens in the classroom or in the library is limited because of budget. In California, for example, there was an effort in 2006 to pass legislation to provide money for all K-12 schools to purchase online database subscriptions (AB 2540), but it did not come to fruition. In 2007, the database proposal will be reintroduced (California School Library Association, 2006). This and other efforts will create greater awareness and drive concerns about copyright.

Policies

Policies are generally the first step in implementation. Sometimes these policies are developed by the libraries; sometimes, they are developed by the larger organizations of which the libraries are a part. In some cases, libraries are the prime resource for copyright in their organizations; sometimes, they are not. Sometimes, libraries are included in the development of institutional policies; sometimes, they are not. The level of involvement of the libraries is on a sliding scale. The reasons for this extreme variation are not entirely clear, but possibilities include the level of expertise of individuals in the library and/or information technology areas, the presence or absence of legal counsel somewhere in the organization, the level and location of knowledge about intellectual property and copyright in particular, and, to some degree, the type of library/institution involved. It became clear in reviewing responses that institutions and libraries of higher education are much more likely to have policies and be focused on managing copyright and electronic resources than institutions or libraries of other types.

As will be seen from a look at the list of web policies in appendix I, there is everything from the elaborate to the general. On one end are highly detailed policies that delve into user expectations, ownership rights, technology transfer, and include statements that try to spell out the specifics of the application of laws to a particular environment. In some institutions, there are multiple policies. There might be a policy from a central office plus policies from various sub-units on the campus or in the system. On the other end of the policy spectrum, as the questions subsequently elicited, there are places with no policy at all. One respondent even thanked the authors for bringing the lack of a policy to his attention. Frequently, policies range somewhere in between, offering more general statements to clarify the institution's intent, but relying on ever-changing laws to direct from day to day what is intended. The approach to the creation of these policies is driven by individual and institutional philosophy, dictating whether the approach will be detailed or general, but a typical approach is to write something general or relatively general and include the specifics in the procedures so that revisions are easier to implement. The purpose of the policies is to provide a philosophy and a broad set of parameters, but also to meet legal requirements and ensure that the institution and/or the library have a foundation on which to build an infrastructure, create specific guidelines, implement some strategies, and help if and when contentious issues arise.

One interesting element that emerged from the responses was an indication of the degree to which politics can play a role in policy-making. There is no doubt that the growth of electronic resources has made copyright policy-making and implementation more complex. As a result, there are more stakeholders and copyright has assumed more prominence. One respondent indicated that it took eighteen months to create a copyright policy and reach approval, which supports the idea of a general policy that requires infrequent revision. Another respondent indicated that after eighteen months, the committee and stakeholders could not reach agreement and that they still did not have a policy. In these days of elaborate consortia, which have often evolved to take advantage of such things as the licensing of electronic resources, copyright policies can require the approval of boards or state governments. With such varied stakeholders and interests, there is frequently disagreement as to the extent of the parameters of such elements as fair use. Even lawyers do not necessarily agree among themselves. Further, if these matters end up in an office such as that of a state attorney general, there can be tension between the fear of a lawsuit and the right to exercise fair use. Further, some lawyers are not intellectual property specialists and may not fully understand or necessarily care about this arm of the law, particularly if their workload is heavy in other areas. Tensions between the library and the legal offices can result. In other cases, the presence of legal counsel works in the opposite way, affording an opportunity for collaboration. The library then works together with legal counsel on the policy, but works independently in implementing that policy and attending to the daily details. Legal counsel is there to assist with issues and problems. All of these scenarios were represented in the responses we received.

Regardless, once a policy is written, regardless of which part of the organization is responsible for its creation, the library is usually the implementer because library staff are the front line for the user.

Education

To achieve their goals with copyright, library staff must be vigilant, exercising fair use rights, complying when the use exceeds fair use limits, communicating with constituents to ensure that they stay as up-to-date as possible, and being active in the political arena. While there may be disagreements as to where the line falls between fair use and the need for permission, respondents express the desire to behave ethically and to encourage their users to do likewise.

However, the issue of education is one area where there is a gap. When asked if he thought there was a gap between policy and behavior, one respondent replied "always." The problem is that copyright compliance is still not enforceable by the library. The library cannot be "big brother," watching every screen and every download for copyright violations, particularly when users are not in the library, but accessing information remotely. If they cannot be tracked electronically, it will not happen. This, in turn, raises the question of ethics and privacy, and what should be watched and what should not.

The library relies on education, which has usually been its preferred method of dealing with issues. Education efforts include any or all of the following: a copyright office or specialist who answers copyright questions through various means (telephone, e-mail, in person), copyright Web pages, publicity materials, copyright workshops, and even DMCA copyright classes for users caught using excess bandwidth or in response to DMCA claims. It is not clear how many are reached through these methods and it is not clear whether the lessons stick or whether, in moments of time crunch or laziness, users violate copyright even when they know better.

The significant differences between print and electronic resources in the realm of copyright center around these key elements—the technological ability to track the use of electronic resources by the publisher or the broker (library, in this case); the technological inability to allow fair use, yet restrict the ability to copy or print beyond what fair use would permit (assuming a clear definition is possible); the lack of ability to control distribution; and the continuing legal struggle over what should be permitted. This is the environment in which library respondents attempt to educate their users.

In the print world, the fact that some users were, as one respondent described, "complacent or illiterate" regarding the understanding and observation of copyright law was suspected, but not easily proved. What happened at a copy machine was unobserved and up to individual conscience. Now, however, publishers and distributors can track the number of prints or downloads that are made and know which pages were reproduced. This enables them to present arguments about the effect on their market, the fourth fair use factor. "Professors get 'F' in copyright protection knowledge," an article in the *Seattle Post-Intelligencer*, emphasizes the need to deal with the "complacent or illiterate" user (O'Neill, 2006). The end result is that the pressures on licit copying are now greater than ever; assuming that what is licit can be defined in a more absolute way.

In the electronic realm, fair use has been under threat. It is certainly possible for someone to copy, either by hand or by retyping, a small portion of an electronic text; or to print or download a page and later incorporate a portion of that into another document for criticism, a research paper, or other appropriate use. Publishers, however, argue that allowing electronic reproduction, particularly by download, gives users too much latitude because, while it is now possible to limit printing to a single or a few pages or to control downloading technologically at the original site, it is not possible, once the capability has been given, to prevent users from printing more than is reasonable or distributing multiple copies at a single keystroke. This issue has still not been addressed, but if and when technological means are in place to track an item beyond the first download, users may see a change in what they are able to do. Alternately, they may experience consequences, such as receiving a bill from the provider, for taking more than a publisher thinks is reasonable. If a user cannot be identified (e.g., anonymous access through a public terminal), the library may get the bill. On the other hand, in the matter of fair use vs. seeking and paying for permissions, one respondent encourages faculty to practice fair use "because if educators don't, or if we seek permission for things we don't need to based on fair use … we will lose it."

Respondents frequently handle copyright questions when individuals call with specific issues. In their environments, they become known as copyright experts or persons with an interest in copyright, whether they think they are experts or not. Handling copyright is not necessarily in their job descriptions, but they do what they can.

Some provide print or online materials about copyright; however, as one respondent pointed out, there is the question of finding a person to write it, when the person handling copyright may not consider him or herself to be an expert, and a further question of finding a unit to absorb the costs for staff time, coding information on to the Web, or printing a brochure. Other educational methods include workshops, and/or required classes for students who are caught violating the DMCA. Many respondents are seeking ideas for promoting copyright to users, particularly faculty. One respondent said "We warn. We do not educate. Education would be better." This implies that in that library, staff takes responsibility for some sort of policing. The amount of education possible is clearly dependent on staff levels, staff expertise, and resources of time and money.

Budget

Touched upon in the last section, this proved to be a particularly interesting issue. One respondent, in a richer library environment, commented "While it [copyright] is certainly expensive, we consider it the cost of doing business and budget for it accordingly."

Other respondents, however, said that the budget was not impacted "to any significant degree." Interestingly, these responses came from institutions where there was an expressed concern about who would pay for educational materials on copyright. There also seemed to be a separation in thinking between the cost of such things as electronic databases and the budget for copyright. Perhaps it is the lack of understanding about how much of a database cost is for copyright permissions and how much is related to other elements. The respondents seemed to think of budget impact in terms of specific line items, rather than inherently built into other services.

In fact, in many institutions, the financial infrastructure has largely been left out of the copyright equation, unless it is a formal part of licensing a database or a previously established budget line for interlibrary loan. Electronic reserves introduce a whole new level of financial obligation, which some institutions are prepared to absorb and some are not. These financial obligations may well increase with streaming media and with new formats that have yet to be invented. The new publishing models, however, may mitigate some of that.

Respondents clearly fight for the retention of fair use, as in the example of the person who encourages faculty to exercise those rights or the respondent who does battle with the Attorney General's Office in his state, but it would be naïve to end this chapter without acknowledging that there are users who violate copyright laws, abuse fair use limits, and generally ignore copyright law, whether through ignorance, situational ethics ("just this once"), or willfully. To reference the *Seattle Post-Intelligencer* article once again, publishers claim they "must protect $3.35 billion in annual U.S. college textbook sales" (O'Neill, 2006). Publishers are taking a tip from the music and film industries and growing more aggressive about the impact of materials use on their markets. Continuous education is one approach to address this; further technological developments are another. Both impact budget. If fair use rights are further reduced or eliminated, institutions or individuals will have to pay significant fees for resources, incurring costs that current budgets cannot handle.

While budget affordability is not a reason for sanctioning these behaviors, it does raise the question of how the system is going to adapt either to the increased need for financial resources or to another way of doing business.

FUTURE TRENDS AND CONCLUSION

There will continue to be changes to the laws. Currently, the Section 108 study group is examining portions of the 1976 law to update it for the electronic age. This process includes a series of roundtable discussions for public comment. The DMCA exemption process has already sanctioned exemptions and will continue to hold open hearings every three years. Other laws will also change. The harmonization of law internationally will likely become more important.

Meanwhile, there are grass roots movements to ensure the availability of documents. Digital rights management now includes alternatives to the standard publishing process. There are open access publications and public access is also being addressed in the contractual process through the efforts of groups such as SPARC (Scholarly Publishing and Academic Resources Coalition), ARL (Association of Research Libraries), and ACRL (Association of College and Research Libraries). On the SPARC Web site (2006), three major initiatives are described. The organization "creates and develops competitive alternatives to current high-priced commercial journals and digital aggregations," "promotes fundamental changes in the system and the culture of scholarly communication," and "develops campaigns aimed at enhancing awareness of scholarly communication issues and supports expanded institutional and community participation in and control over the scholarly communication process." Their goal is to "reclaim" scholarly communication and output. These efforts bring copyright law back into balance.

Institutional repositories are another effort to change how business is done. While they are highly work-intensive, they are another alternative to enable authors to share their scholarly work and ideas. In those situations, copyright law provides a reasonable balance that supports the creative process while allowing users to make reasonable and cited use.

The complexity of copyright and its implementation continues to grow, as does the intensity of attention the subject receives. Core to concept of copyright are these important ideas: the original intent of copyright as expressed in the Constitution, something that is unique to this country and which has fostered invention, knowledge, and dynamism; the all-important need to continue the balance between the rights of the author or owner

with the rights of the user; and the translation of these concepts to electronic resources. Then, and only then, will copyright be able to work as it is supposed to work, whether in a traditional or an electronic environment. There is constant concern that the struggle to maintain balance will continue to be difficult. To achieve the full transformation of copyright to the electronic environment, therefore, requires continued effort by library staff and others in the legislative and educational arenas.

REFERENCES

21st Century Department of Justice Appropriations Authorization Act. (2002). Retrieved November 17, 2007, from http://www.copyright.gov/legislation/pl107-273.html

Bellsouth Advertising & Publishing Corp. vs. Donnelley Information Publishing, Inc. 999 F.2d 1436 (11th Cir.). (1993). Retrieved November 17, 2007, from http://www.coolcopyright.com/cases/chp4/bellsouthdonnelley.htm

Berkman Center for Internet and Society, Harvard Law School. (2003, January 15). Openlaw site: Eldred v. Ashcroft. Retrieved November 17, 2007, from http://cyber.law.harvard.edu/eldredvreno/

Berners-Lee, T. (1996). The world wide web: Past, present and future. Retrieved November 17, 2007, from http://www.w3.org/People/Berners-Lee/1996/ppf.html

California School Library Association. (2006). Legislation and advocacy. Retrieved November 17, 2007, from http://www.schoolibrary.org/leg/

Cohen, B. (2006). E-reserve use of e-journal content. Email on SERIALST listserv. Retrieved November 17, 2007.

Cornell University. (2006, September 19). Cornell University and publishers announce new copyright guidelines governing use of digital course materials. Retrieved November 17, 2007, from http://www.news.cornell.edu/pressoffice/Sept06/AAPCopyright.shtml

Creative Commons. (2007). Main page. Retrieved November 17, 2007, from http://creativecommons.org/license

Creative Commons. (2006). License your work. Retrieved November 17, 2007, from http://creativecommons.org/license/

European Commission. (2006). About this site. Retrieved November 17, 2007, from http://ec.europa.eu/about_en.htm

Feist Publications, Inc. vs. Rural Telephone Service Co., 499 U.S. 340. (1991). Retrieved November 17, 2007, from http://www.coolcopyright.com/cases/chp2/feistrural.htm

FindLaw for Legal Professionals. (2001, June 25). New York Times Co., Inc. et al. v. Tasini et al. Retrieved November 17, 2007, from http://caselaw.lp.findlaw.com/scripts/getcase.pl?court=US&vol=000&invol=00-201

GNU. (2006, August 3). What is copyleft? Retrieved November 17, 2007, from http://www.gnu.org/copyleft/copyleft.html

Guidelines for classroom copying of books and periodicals. (2001, August 9). Retrieved November 17, 2007, from http://www.utsystem.edu/OGC/INTELLECTUALPROPERTY/clasguid.htm

Leiner, B. M. et al. (2005, October 31). *A brief history of the internet.* Reston, VA: Internet Society. Retrieved November 17, 2007, from http://www.isoc.org/internet/history/brief.shtml

Library of Congress. (2006). The section 108 study group. Retrieved November 17, 2007, from http://www.loc.gov/section108/

North American Free Trade Agreement. (1992). Office of NAFTA and inter-American affairs: Intellectual property rights. Retrieved November 17, 2007, from http://www.sice.oas.org/TRADE/NAFTA/naftatce.asp

O'Neill, J. M. (2006, November 20). Professors get "F" in copyright protection knowledge. *Seattle Post-Intelligencer.* Retrieved November 17, 2007, from http://www.google.com/search?sourceid=navclient&ie=UTF-8&rls=RNWE,RNWE:2004-50,RNWE:en&q=professors+get+f

Public Knowledge. (2006, September 11). H.R. 6052: Copyright modernization act of 2006. Retrieved November 17, 2007, from http://www.publicknowledge.org/node/621

Quint, B. (2004, December 20). Google and research libraries launch massive digitization project. *Information Today.* Retrieved November 17, 2007, from http://www.infotoday.com/newsbreaks/nb041220-2.shtml

Schiff, S. (2006, July 31). Know it all. *The New Yorker, 82,* 36-43.

Scholarly Publishing and Academic Resources Coalition. (2006). About SPARC. Retrieved November 17, 2007, from http://www.arl.org/sparc/about/index.html

Swank Motion Pictures, Inc. (2006). Home page. Retrieved November 17, 2007, from http://www.swank.com

Taylor & Francis Group Journals. (2006, January). Terms and conditions of access. Retrieved November 17, 2007, from http://www.tandf.co.uk/journals/pdf/terms.pdf

United States. (1787, September 17). Constitution Article 1, Section 8. Retrieved November 17, 2007, from http://www.law.emory.edu/cms/site/index.php?id=3080

U.S. Copyright Act. 17 U.S.C. §101 et seq.

United States Copyright Office. (1998). *Circular 21: Reproduction of copyrighted works by educators and librarians.* Washington, D.C: Library of Congress, Copyright Office.

United States Copyright Office. (1998, December). The digital millennium copyright act of 1998:

A U.S. copyright office summary. Retrieved November 17, 2007, from http://www.copyright.gov/legislation/dmca.pdf

United States Copyright Office. (2006, November 22). Statement of the librarian of congress relating to section 1201 rulemaking. Retrieved November 17, 2007, from http://www.copyright.gov/1201/docs/2006_statement.html

University of Texas System. (1997). CONFU: The conference on fair use. Retrieved November 17, 2007, from http://www.utsystem.edu/ogc/INTELLECTUALPROPERTY/confu.htm

University of Texas System. (2004, November 22). Offsite: Fair use. Retrieved November 17, 2007, from http://www.utsystem.edu/ogc/INTELLECTUALPROPERTY/offsite.htm#fair

Wikipedia. (2006, December 31). Retrieved November 17, 2007, from http://en.wikipedia.org/wiki/Wikipedia:Copyrights

World Intellectual Property Organization. (2006). Home page. Retrieved November 17, 2007, from http://www.wipo.int/portal/index.html.en

APPENDIX I

Policy Sites

Retrieved July, 2006

- American Association of Law Librarians, Model Law Firm Copyright Policy. http://www.aallnet. org/about/model_law.asp

- Association of Research Libraries, Ownership of Faculty Works and University Copyright Policy. http://www.arl.org/pp/ppcopyright/author-rights-resources.shtml

- Bates College, Requirements of Faculty for Reserves. http://abacus.bates.edu/Library/aboutladd/ departments/circulation/reserve.shtml

- Carnegie Mellon University. http://www.cmu.edu/policies/documents/Copyright.html

- Columbia University. http://www.columbia.edu/cu/provost/docs/copyright.html

- Columbia University, Computing, Network, and Information Policies. http://www.columbia.edu/ cu/policy/copyright-info.html

- Dartmouth University. http://www.dartmouth.edu/copyright/

- Drexel University. http://www.drexel.edu/provost/policies/copyright.asp

- George Mason University. http://www.gmu.edu/facstaff/policy/ae.html

- Grand Valley State University. http://www.gvsu.edu/library/services/index.cfm?id=9FDBEF4E-9317-B72F-9106BCDE2DF76CE3

- Greenville County Schools Online. http://www.greenville.k12.sc.us/district/web/policy/webcopy. asp

- K12, Inc. http://www.k12.com/copyright.html

- Kansas Board of Regents, DMCA policy. http://www.kansasregents.org/copyrightDMCA.html

- Northwestern University. http://www.research.northwestern.edu/research/ori/copyright/copyright-policy.html

- Portland Community College. http://www.pcc.edu/about/policy/copyright/

- Public Schools of North Carolina. http://www.ncpublicschools.org/legalnotices/

- Rochester Institute of Technology, Digital Media Library. https://ritdml.rit.edu/dspace/simple-search?query=copyright&submit.x=0&submit.y=0&submit=Go

- Stanford University. http://www.stanford.edu/dept/DoR/rph/5-2.html

- Syracuse University. http://library.syr.edu/copyright/

- University of California, Irvine, Network and Academic Computing Services. http://www.nacs.uci.edu/policy/copyright.html

- University of California, Los Angeles. http://www2.library.ucla.edu/copyright/index.cfm

- University of California Los Angeles, Civil Rights Project. http://www.civilrightsproject.ucla.edu/copyright.php

- University of California Office of the President. http://www.ucop.edu/ott/faculty/crprimr.html

- University of Florida, Software Copyright Policy, Guidelines, and Training Materials. http://www.it.ufl.edu/resources/copyright/TRAINING.HTM

- University of Georgia. http://www.libs.uga.edu/staff/copyright_policy.pdf

- Univ. of Missouri. http://www.umsystem.edu/ums/departments/gc/rules/business/100/030.shtml

- University of North Carolina. http://www.unc.edu/campus/policies/copyright.html

- University of North Carolina, Patent and Copyright Policy. http://intranet.northcarolina.edu/docs/legal/policymanual/500.2.pdf

- University of North Carolina – Chapel Hill, Computing Policy. http://www.unc.edu/policy/copy-infringe.html

- University of Texas System. http://www.utsystem.edu/OGC/intellectualProperty/cprtpol.htm

- University of Virginia, Acquisitions Department. http://www.lib.virginia.edu/acquisitions/copyright/

- University of Wisconsin System, Copyrightable Instructions Materials, Ownership, Use and Control (G27). http://www.uwsa.edu/fadmin/gapp/gapp27.htm

- University of Wisconsin-Extension. http://www.uwex.edu/ces/copyright/

- Washington State University. http://www.wsu.edu/Copyright.html

- Wellesley University. http://www.wellesley.edu/Library/copyright_ToC.html

- Yale Office of Cooperative Research. http://www.yale.edu/ocr/pfg/policies/index.html

APPENDIX II

Interview Questions

1. Do you have a copyright policy? What areas of copyright does your policy address? Are there specific references to electronic resources? If so, what?

2. What department/area is in charge of your copyright policy? Why was that area chosen/selected?

3. If there are legal questions on the application of the policy, who responds to that?

4. If so, will you share it?

5. Why did you draft a policy? What was the intent? Were electronic resources a factor in your decision?

6. How easy/difficult is the policy to implement? What are the issues in implementing it?

7. Does copyright impact your management of electronic resources and, if so, how?

8. How often do you update your policy and what is the focus of the updates? Are electronic resources a factor?

9. What is your procedure for updating your policy? Does the procedure hinder the completion of the update?

10. How successful/unsuccessful is your library in implementing the policy? How do you measure success? We are particularly interested in the implementation and success of your policy as regards electronic resources.

11. How do you promote your policy?

12. How do you educate your community on copyright issues?

13. If you think there is a "gap" between your policy and the behavior of your users, are you trying to address this? If not, why not? (cost, time, view it as impossible, other) If so, how?

14. How do you envision the future of copyright? Do you see it tightening to the point where copyright permission/payment will be required for everything? Or do you see it undergoing a change in the other direction because users, such as young people, will simply by-pass it and just do what they want? What impact do you envision the increase in electronic resources having on the future of copyright?

15. What advice would you give to a library which is just starting to draft a copyright policy?

16. What are the absolute "must haves" in a copyright policy?

17. What advice would you give in regards to implementation? Education? The ongoing process of coping with copyright?

18. What impact has copyright had on your budget? How has it affected your ability to purchase or contract for information sources and to provide users with access to materials?

19. How knowledgeable do you think you are as regards national copyright policy? How well do you keep up? How much do you think changes in laws affect your copyright policies and daily implementation of those policies?

20. How knowledgeable do you think you are as regards international copyright policy? How well do you keep up? How much do you think changes in those laws affect your copyright policies and daily implementation of those policies?

21. Is there any other information you would like to share with us?

Chapter X
Tactics and Terms in the Negotiation of Electronic Resource Licenses

Kincaid C. Brown
University of Michigan, USA

ABSTRACT

This chapter introduces the reader to the realm of electronic resource license agreements. It provides the reader with an overview of basic contract law as it relates to electronic resource licensing. The chapter then discusses the electronic resource license negotiation process as well as license agreement term clauses. The aim of this chapter is to provide librarians with an understanding of basic licensing concepts and language in order to aid librarians in the review and negotiation of their own license agreements. The author hopes to impart lessons and tips he has learned in reviewing and negotiating license agreements with a number of publishers to further the awareness and understanding of licensing in the library community.

INTRODUCTION

Almost every electronic resource to which a library will subscribe requires either a signed license or an acceptance of a vendor's terms and conditions via a click-through license. Every signed license or clicked-through acceptance of a vendor's terms is a legal contract that provides rights and protections (mostly) to a vendor, but also to a library. Some vendors allow for interlibrary loan and off-campus access while other vendors want to limit usage to individual computers and have limits on printing or downloading. It is important for librarians to understand what a license is, what its terms mean, and to be able to get a vendor to agree to terms more aligned with a library's interests through negotiation. This is especially important, as many librarians are uncomfortable with the licensing process, not just because of the opaque legal language but also due to the prospect of trying to get, often monolithic, corporations to agree to our terms.

BACKGROUND

The increase in the use of license agreements is fueled by content owners' beliefs that the fair use, interlibrary loan, and other library principles and practices that have served well in the print era are sure to cause rampant copyright infringement in the digital era. License agreements are, in fact, the publishers' tool of choice for protecting their intellectual property (Okerson, 1997) by specifically counteracting the "first sale doctrine" (Rice, 2002). The "first sale doctrine" transfers ownership of a title with the initial sale of a copy and is what has historically allowed libraries to lend and interlibrary loan materials or permitted a bookstore to resell used books. Because licensing grants a mere permission instead of ownership to a user or library, there has been no "first sale" and the publisher can tightly control the uses of its digital copies via the license agreement terms.

From the library point-of-view, it is important that licenses be negotiated to allow libraries to continue their mission of promoting access to information. This is especially important as electronic resources have continued to be more expensive than their print counterparts despite the consensus among librarians that electronic format materials should be less expensive than the print because of the elimination of printing, binding, and shipping costs (Alford 2002; Okerson, 1997). Due to the cost of digital resources, which is further exacerbated by the present economic climate, libraries are finding that they have to choose between digital resources and materials in other formats. In order to best serve patrons and steward a library's budgetary resources, libraries will have to carefully monitor their license agreements and try to negotiate terms that are favorable to libraries. Most licenses are written by publishers to protect their interest and as such can rarely be signed without at least some minor amendments (Okerson, 1996).

THE LAW GOVERNING LICENSE AGREEMENTS

A license agreement is a contract between a user/ subscriber (licensee) and a content owner/vendor (licensor). In the library realm, a subscription for an electronic resource will generally entail the signing of a written license agreement or the acceptance of a slate of terms and/or conditions. The contract determines the rights and obligations of the parties, including the services that the licensor will provide and the conditions the licensee must adhere to in order to use the electronic content. In the library setting where most electronic resources are subscriptions, the license provides the library and its patrons permission to use the vendor's electronic resource and/or content pursuant to the agreed upon terms for the time period specified.

According to Murray (2001) a valid contract is formed when its formation is comprised of the following components:

- A promise, offer and acceptance that are "sufficiently definite" (see below)
- Consideration (value such as payment or performance of a service),
- The parties have the legal capacity to make a contract (for example, no party is a minor or mentally ill)
- There is no legal barrier to the formation of the contract (for example, a contract entered into through fraud or duress)

A promise is one party's intention to act or not act in a particular manner, (American Law Institute, 1981-2006) for example by providing certain goods or services to another party. Breaking a contractual promise is where a party opens itself up to liability for damages or penalties for the harm caused to the other party. An offer is one party's willingness to make an agreement regarding such a promise and an acceptance is another party's willingness to so agree.

The promise, offer, and acceptance also need to be definite enough to be enforceable. This means that if the contract ends up in litigation the court must be able to precisely decide what the party at fault must do to make the other party whole. This may be to perform the service or provide the goods contracted for or pay monetary damages as a remedy (Farnsworth, 1999).

The offer, acceptance, and consideration are the three main elements of an enforceable or valid contract (Bielefield & Cheeseman, 1999; Harris, 2002). These elements are controlled by state law (Richards, 2001), but because all of the states have passed some form of the uniform commercial code there are relevant similarities in the contract law across the country (Bielefield & Cheeseman, 1999).

Many electronic resource license agreements take the form of end user license agreements (hereinafter EULAs) which are sometimes called browse-wrap, shrink-wrap, or click-through licenses. EULAs are a list of terms or conditions that generally take two forms (Kutten, 2003-2006). The first version is where the licensee must agree to the terms prior to using the resource by clicking a button often labeled "accept" or "agree" at the end of the list of terms. The second form is where the licensee is told that by using the resource he or she accepts the terms and conditions that are then referred to on a separate Web page (Kutten, 2003-2006).

EULAs are not covered by the uniform commercial code but are specifically endorsed by the Uniform Computer Information Transaction Act (hereinafter, UCITA) (UCITA, 2002-2006) which is an outgrowth of the failed attempt to cover EULAs within the uniform commercial code (Kutten, 2003-2006). UCITA has only been passed in Maryland and Virginia (American Library Association [State], 2006; Harris, 2002; Kutten, 2003-2006) and has been strongly criticized by the library community because it shifts the middle ground of license negotiations toward the vendor to the detriment of the licensing library

community. The library community aversion to UCITA is because UCITA:

- Accepts EULAs (UCITA §209, 2002-2006) which generally undercut a library's ability to negotiate a license
- Allows publishers to change contractual terms unilaterally
- Eliminates the historical contract law standard where limitations in contracts need to be stated in the contract itself and favors the publisher when construing the scope of use of licensed materials (UCITA §307(a), 2002-2006)
- Specifically undermines the copyright fair use protections, including the "first sale doctrine" (UCITA states that transfer of title as a digital copy does not transfer ownership (UCITA §501-502, 2002-2006) of the title), on which libraries rely

(Alford, 2002; American Library Association [Impact], 2006). Because only Maryland and Virginia have passed UCITA and because of the conflict between historical contract negotiation requirements the state courts deciding EULA contract cases have come down on either side of the issue with some affirming the use of these click-through or browse-wrap licenses and others refusing to accept such licenses as valid (Kutten, 2003-2006).

THE LICENSE NEGOTIATION PROCESS

A license negotiation begins when the library starts to consider a subscription to or purchase of an electronic resource. This is important to remember that the utility of an electronic resource is dependent in part on the license because the license agreement sets the cost, access method, uses, and users of an electronic resource. When the library begins to look at an electronic resource it is important to ask for a copy of the license agreement because the negotiation of the license may take some time to complete. As noted previously, these licenses will take the form of either a formal written contract or an EULA. Both types of license agreements are negotiable although vendors often loathe negotiating changes to EULAs. Indeed some commentators note that most publishers are of the opinion that license agreements are not negotiable except for price because the publisher generally is the party who drafted the license and is accordingly favored (Alford, 2002).

However, at the University of Michigan Law Library we have had success negotiating changes to EULAs by altering the EULA so that signature is necessary or via an e-mail agreement. When we have amended a EULA via e-mail we indicate that our amended terms and the vendor's return message accepting the amendments become part of the EULA. When amending a EULA, regardless of the other terms that are changed, it is important to amend the notice and/or amendment clauses so that changes to the EULA on the vendor's Web site do not bind the library to those provisions without the requisite notice or agreement. Bielefield and Cheeseman (1999) state that EULAs may be negotiated on a clause-by-clause basis. Note that the Blackwell-Synergy (2006) EULA states that if an institution has signed a written license agreement, that contract will take precedence over the EULA.

Before negotiating a license with a vendor it is best for the library to have already made some decisions regarding negotiation policies and specific license terms the library may find acceptable, unacceptable, or mandatory. It is also important to have an understanding of license agreement language, especially if there is not a licensed attorney on staff to review licenses (Bielefield & Cheeseman, 1999). Library group licensing Web sites as well as workshops, library or legal literature, and other resources will aid in the understanding of license terms and will provide examples of licensing language. The library itself should also have

an archive of license agreements already in force that can be referred to for licensing language and examples of what the library was able to negotiate as amendments. It is often a good idea to have a side-file or database of license clauses that the library prefers that can be consistently used in negotiations with vendors.

When negotiating the license for an electronic resource, it is important to remember there should be some middle ground between the library and the licensor, as both parties ultimately want to reach an agreement. The library wants to gain an appropriate amount of access to the electronic resource for a reasonable price while meeting the needs of its patrons. The licensor wants the library to subscribe to its content while protecting its property rights (Bielefield & Cheeseman, 1999). Harris (2002) notes that a license negotiation should not be considered a zero sum affair with a winner and loser. Okerson (1996) states that it is rare that a publisher and library are unable to agree on an acceptable middle ground. Of the libraries answering the question in Tashbook's (2004) survey, 85% indicated that publishers met library demands at least half of the time.

Harris (2002) notes that to start a license negotiation the library must know what it needs, wants, and can afford. If a library cannot negotiate a license to meet its basic needs or a price that it can afford then the time comes when the library must walk away from that electronic resource and spend its time exploring alternative avenues to gain access to that or similar digital information. Because licenses for electronic resources begin with the vendor's standard license the negotiation can be entirely about which amendments the vendor is willing to make. But, it is also important for the library to be flexible—although the vendor may be unwilling to change a license clause to the library's preferred language a middle ground may be acceptable. Harris (2002) states that it is important to give up items in a negotiation as long as you get something in return. In the case of a license agreement, these items may be extra protections the library may be willing to forego or specific language that may be generalized or cut back. Harris (2002) also asserts the importance of not making assumptions; a licensor may be willing to meet all of your licensing needs, but you will never know until you ask.

In a negotiation, we have often found it useful to be able to refer a licensing issue further up the library hierarchy. This is because the library administration may be able to negotiate some favorable terms by agreeing to some less than favorable terms from their position as the final arbiter of library policies or finances. We have also made use of the university's general counsel's office to refer difficult license negotiations and to get guidance on particular licensing terms.

Statistics are a bargaining chip that can be used to bolster the library's position in regard to price. This is especially true when the cost for a particular electronic resource is noticeably more expensive than what the library understands the going rate for that sort of resource is. Libraries can often gauge the amount of use that a particular resource will generate based on past experience. If a resource under license negotiation is priced too steeply, especially in the case of a price increase for an electronic resource renewal, then the ability to refer to statistics to state a case for a lesser price is important. For a first time license for an electronic resource, if a vendor does not provide statistics and you believe the cost is higher than ordinary for like resources, it is important to ask what the price is based on, if not actual usage.

Access to a similar resource or the ability to subscribe to the same material from another vendor can also help in negotiating a better price. If it is possible to subscribe or purchase the same or substantially similar digital content at a lower price then use that as a negotiating tool. A threat to rely on a competing product may be enough for the vendor to lower the price in order to get a library's business. Of course, many electronic resources may be offered by vendors with a monopoly on the content so such a threat will not be available as a negotiation tool. But, even though the content may be unique, the resource will be similar in type (e.g., a single electronic journal, a full-text document archive, or a journal index) to other resources where a library does have pre-existing subscriptions. Based on past experience, the library should have a good idea of a reasonable price range where the price for a resource should fall. In cases where a unique resource is more costly, the library should approach the vendor with a counter-offer of a reasonable price range along the lines of other resources of the same type and size. However, if the library and the vendor cannot reach a middle ground the library will need to do without that resource if the money is not available and/or the library does not want to set a high priced precedent that the budget will have to meet in future fiscal years. Additionally, libraries caving into exorbitant pricing schemes reinforce the vendor's immobility in regard to the cost.

In one negotiation we had, a vendor did not provide usage statistics and we thought that the price that was being asked was exorbitant. We looked at some of our existing subscriptions on those subjects and made some calculations for cost per use based on the statistics provided by those vendors. We then assumed similar use and calculated cost per use for the electronic resources under negotiation. Our existing subscriptions averaged out to between $5 and $40 per session. The same amount of usage for the resources under negotiation was going to be between $100 and $800 per session. And, this was for resources that that we felt were each much less complete than the resources to which we already subscribed—while much of the commentary material that comprised the resource being negotiated was unique, commentary as well as primary legal materials themselves (i.e., laws, regulations, caselaw) were also included in our pre-existing subscriptions. This cost discrepancy combined with the resource's lesser scope and inclusiveness relative to our existing subscriptions steadied our resolve not to pay the asking price. In this case we ended up not subscribing to the resources because of the exorbitant pricing, but bolstered with our statistical analysis we were able to defend our decision to the faculty who supported us in our refusal to subscribe to those resources.

LICENSE TERMS

It is important for the license agreement to reflect the terms that have been negotiated between the library and the publisher. Otherwise, the time and effort spent during negotiation will have been wasted. A license is all about the terms and as such the terms need to accurately portray the agreement that is being struck. For example, once we had negotiated to subscribe to electronic resources via IP (Internet protocol) access only to be given a license to sign that described the access method as a password system administered by the library. The vendor in this case said that it did not matter—it was merely a license for a different client group that they had all libraries sign because there was no other. We revised the access method terms in order to ensure that the license we were signing reflected the subscription that we were getting (and wanted) to protect the library from future hardship, in this case having to manage a password system to provide access to the resource.

Some of the most common license terms that require negotiation are discussed below.

Access Versus Ownership

An issue that will make a large difference in the make-up of the rest of the license is whether you are purchasing or leasing the electronic content. A purchase of the content will provide ownership of content to the library generally with a large down payment and modest annual maintenance fee. A lease of the content will take the form of access to content via an annual subscription.

This access versus ownership dilemma is new for libraries with the advent of electronic resources. Libraries are paying large sums of money for information that they will lose access to at the end of a subscription, if a vendor disappears, or if the product is sold or discontinued. This practice is a direct contrast to the past when a purchased book would be on the shelf and the library would possess the information itself. Pace (2003) comments that in the past libraries would have been unlikely to spend vast amounts of money on materials where access would be lost at the end of a subscription period. Because of the amount of money at issue and its impact on the future strength of a library's collection, the access versus ownership issue is an important area within license negotiations. For many resources, such as finding aids, indexes and citators, access alone makes sense; it is for full-text materials where ownership or perpetual access is more important. Okerson (1996) maintains that an acceptable license should provide for either perpetual access to the digital materials that were published during the license term or provide an option for archival access.

The purchase of content can take many forms including the deliverance of digital backfiles of an entire database's content to the library once the license is signed (usually combined with access to the same content via the vendor's interface), perpetual access to content via a vendor's Web interface, or access to the materials published during the time of the agreement either via perpetual access or backfile but no access to materials published after the expiration of the license. For materials where the license only provides access to materials, the access will cease at the expiration of the license agreement.

Access versus ownership is something that will often be open for negotiation. The major issue will be cost, as ownership of the content will cost a premium. Note also that ownership in this context generally will refer only to the housing or perpetual access to the content for research purposes. This ownership will not provide ownership to the intellectual property contained in the databases and will still be governed by other terms negotiated in the license (e.g., copyright or fair use provisions). Some vendors will only be willing to license for access on a subscription basis but ownership, even if it just to a partial backfile of a single journal title, may be negotiable from others.

Vendors will often license ownership of content for large digitization projects of historical materials and sometimes may not be willing to go the subscription route. For large digitization projects where licensing options may be limited to purchasing the entire backfile and paying an annual maintenance, it is often a good idea to include an "opt out" clause in the license. This clause would typically be enforceable after a negotiated term of years, after whish the library could "opt out" of paying the maintenance fee if the charge became too onerous and load the digital files on its own servers. Of course, in this case the library would also need to provide a search mechanism or other access method to get to the electronic content since access would no longer be available via the vendor's interface.

Amendment of License Terms or Services

It is always best to include language in the license that requires both parties to agree in writing to any amendments to the terms of the license or the services covered by the license. In a fall back position for end user license agreements (EULA), the license should at least indicate that the licensor give written notice to the licensee when the terms are amended. Alford (2002) asserts that prior written notice and the option to terminate the license if the amendment constitutes a material change in terms is the least to which a library should agree. It is never in the best interests of the licensee library to accede to terms that allow the vendor to alter the terms of the license at any time without notice. Okerson, Stenlake, and Harper (Amendment, 2006) maintain that any amendment or modification to the license should be finalized in the same manner as was the original license agreement.

One negotiation we had concerned a license that not only included a provision that allowed the vendor to alter the terms of the license without notice but also allowed the vendor to change the product without notice. This provision would have left us in a difficult legal position should the vendor amend the license or product in a way that is detrimental to a library's use of the product. When we were in the process of negotiating this license, the vendor was surprised when we balked at signing it, saying in essence that they would never eliminate the database we were interested in and not return our money. Whether that is true or not is of course irrelevant from a licensing rights perspective as it could be possible under the terms of the license for the vendor to take such actions. In the principle of managing the library's resources in the best possible way it is imperative that a licensee library not negotiate away future rights or abilities by allowing a licensor unfettered ability to amend the terms of the license. A case-in-point of a license that contains such problematic language is the CQ Press EULA (2006).

Authorized Users

The authorized users section limits who is able to access the electronic resource in question. Because of the ease of access to digital information, license agreements for digital content must contain a definition for "users" (Alford, 2002) in a way that was not necessary for print materials where copyright law defined that term (Richards, 2001). If your library provides services to walk-in patrons outside of your primary patron group (e.g., public patrons in an academic library or nonresidents in a public library) this section will need to include language that allows "walk-ins" to access the electronic resource. In academic settings, licensors may want to limit access to a resource to the school's faculty, students, and staff, so it is important to make sure that the license includes provisions that will allow the library's diverse patron base access to the resource. If the college or university has a distance education program then those faculty students should fit within the authorized user definition, but it may be best to include that in the definition or verify that point with the vendor. The same would be true of a corporate library where the resource could be used in teleconferencing or other distance communications. Some vendors will want to limit access to a resource to a school within a larger university (e.g., law, medicine, business). In this case, agreeing to such a limitation would be a point where a library can try to negotiate a lower price, in essence agreeing to less access for less money, especially when limiting a resource to a single school is not uncommon on a given campus. It is also sometimes possible to pay more in order to provide access to an additional patron group (e.g., alumni). In Tashbook's (2004) survey 15 percent of libraries indicated that the definition of authorized users was the easiest issue to get publishers to accommodate.

The authorized user section is also often where language-allowing access to patrons from outside of the library buildings should be included. If this language is not included in the "authorized users" section the license may include an "authorized site" section. Off-site access is generally provided via a proxy server which requires users to authenticate when out of the library or off-campus before using a resource. We have had success getting wary vendors to agree to allowing access via a proxy server, in an academic setting, by including license terms that acknowledge that the library is responsible for setting up the authentication system and making sure that only its primary patrons (e.g., faculty, students, and staff) will be able to access the electronic resource from off campus. Note that in Tashbook's (2004) survey,

15% of libraries indicated that use of a proxy server was the easiest issue to get publishers to agree to. Because many vendors prefer to license content in an on-campus environment only, it is imperative to make sure that the license includes language allowing off-site usage if the library wants to provide such access to patrons (Harris, 2002).

The University of Chicago Press Journals Division (2006) license for astronomy journals includes an authorized user provision that is very well suited to an academic library's needs. It allows access for faculty, students, staff, and on-site patrons as well as allows the institution the ability to use a proxy server via the university network provided that the institution take measure to prevent unauthorized users from accessing the content.

Authorized Uses

The authorized uses section is sometimes named "rights granted" or "permissions" and is one of the most important sections of a license agreement. For academic institutions it would be generally reasonable to agree not to use the resource for commercial purposes, but in a corporation or business setting a commercial purpose, as defined in the license, may be the reason for subscribing to the resource (Alford, 2002). Authorized use language may contain key digital information practices like viewing, downloading, printing, and displaying. These are really basic rights of using electronic information and a library should really consider how a product is going to be used before agreeing to the limitation of such electronic rights. Uses contained in authorized use sections that more commonly are negotiated between the library and the vendor are end-use in nature. These uses include interlibrary loan, electronic reserves, coursepacks, distance education, backup copies, inclusion in an intranet, and linking. The authorized use provisions of license agreements are where the content owner aims to protect its rights pursuant to copyright law by limiting the rights that it is licensing.

Vendor-created use license provisions will generally limit how a licensee may use the electronic content that is the subject of the license even though these uses may otherwise be protected under United States copyright law via the "fair use" provisions (17 U.S.C. §107-122, 2001-2005). The fair use provisions are rights granted to an owner of a copy of a copyright protected work by United States copyright law (Richards, 2001). Under the fair use doctrine, a use may be determined to not violate copyright law after looking at:

- "The purpose and character of the use"
- "The nature of the copyrighted work"
- "The amount and substantiality of the portion used"
- "The effect of the use upon the potential market for or value of the copyrighted work" (17 U.S.C. §107, 2001-2005)

Authorized uses are very important provisions to look at and understand because it is in the vendor licensor's interest to limit the library licensee's authorized uses as much as possible. Harris (2002) notes that libraries should be aware that many licenses allow or prohibit uses with general or expansive phrasing. It is important to pay attention to such language as it will have an effect on the bundle of rights that a license allows. The fair use doctrine provides users with a wide array of permissions but these permissions can be waived or negotiated away (Okerson, Stenlake, & Harper [Authorized Use], 2006; Okerson, 1997). When a license reduces the rights that a library holds in relation to a copyrighted work, the library and its users are restrained by the terms of the license and are no longer protected by United States copyright law (Richards, 2001). Needless to say, a library should think very hard before negotiating away its fair use rights. Also, note that a library licensee cannot generally negotiate away the rights of its patrons but a licensor may

try to hold a library responsible for its patron's actions through cancellation of service or litigation (Okerson, Stenlake, & Harper (Authorized Use), 2006).

As noted, when a library signs a license that includes more restrictive authorized uses than provided for pursuant to fair use, it is those terms that will govern. In the early days of electronic content and license agreements, many libraries signed licenses without contemplating the fair use issues and these contracts have minimized or eliminated fair use rights (Pace, 2003). For this reason the licensee should be sure to include language acknowledging its fair use rights and/or specifically delineating particular rights that it wants to reserve because of their importance to a library's patrons (e.g., course packs and electronic reserves for an academic library or electronic document delivery and use in teleconferencing for a corporate library). Alford (2002) asserts that it is important for a patron to have the same permitted uses for print and digital materials and that the license should accordingly contain an explicit statement that fair use applies to the electronic resource content. When a license specifically mentions fair use rights or does not include restrictions on authorized uses, fair use will govern (Okerson, Stenlake & Harper [Authorized Use], 2006; Richards, 2001). For this reason, it is a good idea to negotiate license terms that include fair use rights (Okerson, 1996; Richards, 2001).

The ability of a library licensee to negotiate fair use rights will vary depending on the vendor, but it is common for a vendor to balk at the inclusion of a long list of rights that the library would like to reserve. When we have tried to include the authorized use terms from LIBLICENSE (Okerson, Stenlake, & Harper [Authorized Use], 2006, section 2) one vendor licensor refused to agree to modify any of its terms to meet ours and we spent a great deal of time and energy at an impasse. We have had greater success where we have asked vendors to eliminate specific authorized use provisions (on the licensee side) and restrictions (on the licensor side) and rely on a general fair use statement declaring that nothing in the agreement is intended to limit the library licensor's fair use rights. Because this is a simple statement it may not merit a drawn-out negotiation between the library and the licensor and will still fully protect a library's abilities to provide interlibrary loan and other services. Note that Haworth Press (2006) specifically allows for coursepacks as pursuant to fair use.

Okerson, Stenlake, and Harper (Authorized Use, 2006) note that the interlibrary loan system that has worked well for academic and public library print material lending worries publishers when it comes to electronic publications. Accordingly, the right to interlibrary loan is a relatively difficult term to negotiate with a vendor in a license agreement for an electronic resource even though interlibrary loan is expressly permitted by the federal copyright law (17 U.S.C. §108, 2001-2005) and libraries voluntarily adhere to the CONTU (1979) guidelines that place limitations on library interlibrary loans practices in an effort to protect publishers' copyrights.

Alford (2002) states that although a vendor may not agree to the interlibrary loan of digital materials via e-mail, they should at least accede to a license where a library can interlibrary loan a printed copy of an electronic resource. Note that this is not permitted under the JSTOR (2006) or Cambridge Journals Online (2006) licenses. However, some vendors do expressly allow for interlibrary loan rights for digital materials equal to the rights available for print materials in their licenses. For example, the University of Chicago Journals Division (2006) license for astronomy journals specifically allows for interlibrary loan pursuant to United States copyright law and the CONTU guidelines.

Cancellation

This provision specifies if and when a party to the license may end an agreement and what the repercussions for that action would be. Often cancellation of a license by the licensee before its term has run will result in a forfeiture of the already paid annual subscription cost or a payment penalty in the case of a multiyear agreement. If a library's budget fluctuates year to year—for instance a court or public library whose budget is controlled by the state—it is a good idea to include language in this section that would allow the library to cancel a multi-year agreement, without penalty, if the library's financial situation changes such that continued subscription and payment for an electronic resource becomes an impossibility.

Choice of Law and Venue

The choice of law section is where the license designates which state's law will govern a contract dispute as contracts are governed by state and not federal law (First Options of Chicago, Inc. v. Kaplan, 1995). In which court the contract litigation takes place is controlled by the venue or choice of forum section. Venue as specified by the license terms need only be a jurisdiction where a lawsuit can proceed often due to a connection with one of the parties. Jurisdiction in this sense (as a locale) should not be confused with the legal concept of jurisdiction which is the court's power to hear a case and is often specifically authorized by statute. See Wright (1994) for more detail on the jurisdiction/venue dichotomy.

Public institutions, whether school, government or public library, may be forbidden by statute from signing a license in which the institution surrenders to the law of another state and may hold special defenses or rights under the law of its home state (Okerson, Stenlake, & Harper [Governing Law], 2006). It is especially important to amend a governing law section that specifies the law of Maryland or Virginia for the contract as these are the two states that have passed UCITA, licensing law which is unfavorable to libraries. Accordingly, if other states pass UCITA it would be best for a library to avoid signing license agreements that specify those additional states' laws as governing law as well. If a library's home state has passed UCITA, then the library should specify in the license that it opts out of UCITA (allowed by UCITA (§104, 2002-2006). As for the venue section, a library should not agree to a distant venue in the license. In the event of litigation, short of a granted change of venue motion, the trial will take place in that distant court, adding to the cost of the litigation.

In our experience, the choices of law and venue sections are the easiest sections to negotiate with a vendor. Because we are not able to sign a license that designates anything other than Michigan law and venue, vendors have been willing to accommodate us in order to get our business. We have had a couple of license negotiations with foreign-based companies in England and Hong Kong in which the vendors were not willing to designate Michigan law in the contract terms. In these cases we eliminated the sections entirely and both parties were able to move on.

Confidentiality of License Terms

Some vendors include a provision in their licenses that would prohibit the discussion of the terms of the license by the licensee. Vendors will generally include this in a license when they want to keep the licensee from sharing terms with other parties and libraries. This is most often an issue when a vendor is in the practice of varying its pricing, access, or authorized uses for a product on a license-by-license basis. These terms are problematic in that they allow vendors to control the information available to libraries as they try to negotiate their own licenses and generally ensure that the library has a weaker bargaining position because of this lack of information.

It is always good practice to eliminate this clause if a vendor is willing to do so or to negotiate a clause that only prohibits the sharing of specifically identified information (Okerson,

Stenlake, & Harper [Confidentiality], 2006). At the very least, public institutions will often need to modify such a confidentiality section to comply with state "Freedom of Information Acts" (a.k.a. FOIA, generally modeled on the federal Freedom of Information Act, 2001-2005) as contracts signed by a public institution are records that can be requested pursuant to many state FOIA statutes such as Michigan's Freedom of Information Act (2004-2006).

Cost

The price of a resource can be a major issue in a license negotiation and sometimes will be the main issue. Many resources will have a standard list price on a take it or leave it basis. This is especially the case when a license is for a single electronic journal where the price is set for print only, electronic only, or print plus electronic subscriptions, but is also true for larger packages. Indeed, half of the libraries surveyed by Tashbook (2004) that answered the question indicated that price was the issue on which publishers were least likely to make accommodations to a library. It is for the larger databases and digital archives where the price may be negotiable although it may always be the case that a library will have to go without a resource because funds are not available for the one-time purchase or the encumbrance of an expensive annual subscription. Regardless of the payment model, it is important that the contract prohibits the vendor from unilaterally changing the pricing (Okerson, Stenlake, & Harper [Fees], 2006).

One model for negotiating down the price of a resource is to agree to restrict access to the resource. It is possible to reach a consensus point with a vendor by limiting access to an electronic resource to a particular campus (for a state-wide institution), affiliates of a single or few schools on a campus, eliminating alumni or walk-in patron access, or restricting access to on-campus use only. In a public library options include restricting access to in-building use only, limiting access to one or more dedicated terminals, or requiring a patron to login (thereby limiting access to residents for many public libraries). Obviously, the palatability of these options will depend on the nature of the resource, the perceived usage of a resource by the groups to be excluded under a license, the degree of hardship the exclusion would cause those groups (e.g., is it unreasonable to make students on a campus go to the business school to use a resource on the stock market if is will halve the price?), and the mission of the library. A less onerous way to restrict access to a resource would be to negotiate down the number of simultaneous users that may access a resource. Often simultaneous user limits will be tiered and each tier will have a standard price affixed to them. When a resource is available with various simultaneous user price tiers, statistics are an important tool in understanding how much access a library needs to negotiate and pay for. The statistics for total number of uses are important, but when negotiating a level of simultaneous usage the statistics for peak simultaneous logons and turnaways will let a library know whether the current level of usage is too little or too much.

Another way to easily reduce the annual cost of an electronic resource subscription is to license a multiyear subscription to the resource. A multiyear license can cut 5 to 20% from the annual price for a resource. Additionally, if a resource is available from multiple vendors you will often be able to get vendors to match or beat the subscription cost offered by another vendor. If multiple libraries on a university campus are interested in the same electronic resource then it may also be possible to share the cost so that no one library has to pay for access to a resource where usage would be largely spread across a campus. A further way to cut costs is for a library to cancel print subscriptions to material that it is also subscribing to electronically. If this is a real possibility or definite plan it is imperative to negotiate the ability to cancel print into the license agreements

as some licenses have language prohibiting print cancellations.

Some resources will have alternative pricing models that may be less expensive. These models can be flat-fee, package, or pay-per-view. A flat-fee model is similar to a monthly or annual subscription cost. Usage, but more usually downloading, can be capped at a certain amount in any given month or annually. A package plan, which is often a pricing model for electronic journals, will provide access to an array of journals for a single cost rather than licensing each journal separately. Richards (2001) notes that package plans often do not meet librarian expectations because usually a small percentage of the journal titles in a package get the large majority of usage, in essence meaning that libraries are paying for electronic access to additional journals that may not be necessary for their patrons' research needs. Package plans will often allow for the cancellations of print subscriptions, but allowed cancellations may be capped at a certain percentage per year. A pay-per-view plan would limit the cost to the library to the actual searches and downloads performed. This plan is most appropriate for an electronic resource that will not receive much use and is costly on a subscription basis. For a resource that is highly used, a pay-per-view model will generally be more expensive than a subscription.

A library's membership in a consortium is another way for a library to get more electronic resources for less money. As Kohl and Sanville (2006) note, this should not be confused with getting electronic resources more cheaply via a consortia membership (i.e., a library can increase its access to electronic resource titles, usually e-journals or e-books, for a percentage more money than it currently pays for the titles it holds in print). While the relatively cheap additional expenditure for access to a large number of new titles can be a tantalizing incentive, consortial deals can have other costs including high administrative costs (Stange, 2006), a movement away from a patron-focused collection to a more general collection due to the aggregate nature of multilibrary packages (Scigliano, 2002), and a lesser ability to re-negotiate deals at renewal. Other positives to consortial packages include the ability to cancel print subscriptions to rely on the electronic version (this needs to be negotiated at the outset as many consortial packages have print cancellation limitations) and the ability of the member libraries to withdraw print collections in reliance on the electronic for access and a particular member library for archival purposes.

Other factors that can be used to positively negotiate the price of a resource are having previously purchased the same material in another format or a library having purchased another electronic resource in the same series from the vendor. Additionally, some vendors may be willing to extend pricing deals similar to consortium pricing to university libraries that have historically purchased a large number of that vendor's electronic resources either themselves or in conjunction with other libraries on campus.

We have had the most difficulty in negotiating the cost of resources where the vendor bases the price of the resource on FTE enrollment (full time equivalent, i.e., the number of full-time students enrolled where two half-time students would be combined as 1 FTE). The difficulty we have had in negotiating down such prices is due to the fact that FTE price quotes are more set in stone from the vendor's point-of-view than other electronic resource pricing. FTE cost is based on the theory that a school with a 1000 FTE will use a resource twice as much as a school with a 500 FTE. While this may be the case for some resources, we feel that for many resources, especially those on a particular subject (e.g., tax law), this is not an accurate theory as larger institutions may have more resources available thereby reducing the usage of any specific resource. It is for these types of resources that we have tried to negotiate FTE quoted prices. We have had some, but not universal, success in getting out of the FTE price track by agreeing to restrict access to dedicated

terminals or by purchasing passwords instead of IP access (we prefer not to use passwords because of their administrative hassle). There have also been resources that we have chosen not to subscribe because of a nonnegotiable FTE-based price when we have felt that the usage based on FTE theory was not an accurate predictor of the usage from our institution.

Definitions

Some license agreements will have a separate definitions section while others will include definitions of terms in the individual sections of the license where they arise. Generally, a good contract or license agreement is clear to the parties who sign it and that means that the terms at issue in the license should be clearly and specifically defined, especially if the usage varies from common dictionary meaning (Harris, 2002; Kutten, 2003-2006). Harris (2002) notes the importance of deciding whether a license term is being used in its common manner. The definitions of the terms of the license are where a great deal of the negotiation may take place. A definition of "authorized users" may not include alumni and if the library wants alumni to have access to a resource, the library will need to negotiate that change to the definition. The same is true of a definition of "library network" that omits access from off-campus in an academic setting or to a public library's patrons from home. Note that Taylor and Francis (2003) include a set of definitions including "authorized users," "course packs," "library premises," and "subscription period" at the beginning of their EULA.

Reimbursement

The license agreement contract will generally cover continual access to digital content for a subscription period. There are times where access to an electronic resource is not available due to Internet or network problems at the library but also due to network problems on the vendor side. In the latter case it is important that a library be able to receive a pro rata refund for the resource downtime if the electronic content is unavailable for a sufficient period of time. Downtime of an hour or even a couple of days may not be worth the effort of getting a refund, but if a resource is unavailable for weeks, then continual access as licensed was unavailable and the library should be allowed a refund for that time under the terms of the license agreement. Sometimes the agreement will provide for the refund by extending the license term by the same amount of time as the downtime.

Subject Matter

This section deals with the content covered by the license. It is important that the license clearly and accurately details the content to which the library is subscribing. The subject matter is often included in another section of the license such as the preamble or definitions section instead of standing on its own. It is important to note that the preamble and definitions sections are not legally binding parts of a contract but are used by courts to discern the intent of parties

Termination

The termination of a license will most often be due to the expiration of the term set by the license agreement. The termination section of the license delineates when one of the parties to the license can terminate the agreement for another reason. It is important that a library make sure that the termination clause allows the library to terminate the agreement for a material breach, such as the disappearance of important content, and not allow only the licensor to terminate the agreement. Murray (2001) notes that a material breach is a failure to perform the contract so substantial that a party does not receive the benefits of the contract; thereby making termination of the contract an

appropriate remedy for the aggrieved party. The termination section is where a library should indicate that a termination based on a default by the publisher mandates a pro rata refund of the prepaid subscription cost (Harris, 2002). In our experience, vendors are generally willing to agree to a pro rata refund.

The termination section is also the appropriate place to include language allowing a library to not renew a multiyear subscription that is paid on an annual basis because of funding shortfalls. This may most often be a problem in governmental libraries but can touch other types of libraries as well. This language would allow a library to terminate its subscription in the event of a budget shortfall or cut without penalty.

Harris (2002) cautions that libraries should make sure that a license agreement not allow vendors to terminate an agreement due to the actions of library patrons. The library should have a role in educating its patrons about the use of electronic resources and will generally be responsible for mediating access to an electronic resource (via passwords, the set-up of library terminals, or a proxy server) but should be wary of agreeing to allow a vendor the right of termination due to patron misuse.

Warranty & Indemnity

The warranty and indemnity clauses will often be combined in a license agreement. A warranty is a promise or guarantee regarding the electronic resource at issue. In the warranty portion the licensor will generally promise that the vendor is the content owner and has the right to license the electronic content. Warranty sections will often also state that the license is for the electronic resource "as is" and that the vendor cannot be held liable for any errors in the product or damages caused by reliance on such erroneous information although the warranty should at least indicate that the product is free from defects. Warranty and indemnity terms will often be boilerplate clauses that may be difficult to get vendors to amend. Harris (2002) suggests that it is not necessary to negotiate these sections in minute detail, as a general warranty and indemnity section will be appropriate for most licenses for library electronic resources.

Alford (2002) asserts that an important warranty for a library to negotiate is a warranty against copyright infringement where the publisher would maintain that the digital materials included in the electronic resource in question do not infringe the intellectual property rights of another party. This is especially important because a library may be liable for copyright infringement under law even if the fault in not obtaining permissions lies with the publisher (Alford, 2002). The LexisNexis (1996) terms include such a guarantee.

The indemnity section provides for compensation should there be a contractual breach resulting in damages to a party. From a library perspective, an indemnity clause should provide at a minimum that any problem with the electronic resource making it unusable must be fixed in a prompt manner or the library would be able to cancel the agreement and ask for a refund. Alford (2002) states that the library should not agree to indemnify the publisher for anything and especially not for misuses of electronic content by library patrons as the library has no real control over how patrons will use the materials. Alford (2002) continues that is would be acceptable for a library to agree to make efforts of a reasonable nature to remedy a situation of misuse once the library has knowledge of such a situation. Okerson, Stenlake, and Harper [Warranties] (2006) state that indemnity clauses should impose equal burdens on each party.

Other Common License Terms

Alternative Dispute Resolution (ADR): This clause allows for resolution of a dispute between the parties outside of a court of law. ADR processes often include mediation,

negotiation, and arbitration as a final step. Arbitration may be binding or non-binding where nonbinding arbitration allows for the parties to go to court after the arbitration stage. Arbitration may be expensive as arbitrators in the United States are generally chosen through the American Arbitration Association (Harris, 2002). When reviewing an ADR clause a library will generally want to ensure that both parties equally pay the costs.

Assignment: This clause may prohibit the assignment of the license to another party. Corporate libraries especially will want to be sure that the assignment clause details how an assignment may be made in the case of a corporate purchase or takeover.

Complete or Entire Agreement: This clause stipulates that the negotiated agreement is enforceable on its own and any other written communication between the parties is irrelevant. Accordingly, a library will want to make sure that the provisions it wants are indicated in the negotiated license and not agreed on verbally or via e-mail.

Force Majeure: Literally a superior force and generally refers to an act of God, act of war, or another condition outside of the control of either party. This clause will apply provided that the act was not foreseeable enough that due care on the part of a party would have avoided the failure to meet the terms of the contract (Harris, 2002). The *force majeure* section should apply equally to both parties and common technical issues (e.g., server failure) are generally not covered.

Severability: This clause ensures that if any provision of a contract is deemed illegal or unenforceable the remainder of the contract still stands.

Support: This clause indicates what kind of technical support the library may rely on under the contract. The library may want to try to negotiate for free-of-charge support if the vendor does not typically provide that and the library believes that such support may be necessary.

Waiver: This clause prevents the failure to enforce a particular provision in the contract from constituting a waiver of that or any other part of the license. It is good practice to include language that states that amending the contract in writing is the only way that provisions may be waived.

WHAT NEXT?

What will the future bring? It is probably safe to say "more license agreements." A license agreement will likely arrive hand-in-hand with each new electronic resource as it becomes available and as the number of electronic resources increases so will the licenses to sign.

The real question will probably be whether publishers and libraries will be able to find a more universal middle consensus on some important issues like fair use, cost, ownership, and amendment of licensing terms. Libraries will certainly need to continue to argue their case regarding the use of materials and patron rights, but it will be difficult to make sweeping changes considering both the current political and publishing climate as well as the large number of publishers creating these electronic resources. It seems unlikely that Congress will reverse course against the interests of contributors and shorten the term of copyright or add material to the public domain so libraries will still need use licenses to gain permission to content. At present, publishers have no reason to start license negotiations anywhere other than a strictly curtailed list of authorized uses in order to both protect their rights in the content as well as to allow for the possibility of increased payment in compensation for looser use restrictions. This does not seem likely to change but movement toward the middle may be possible if libraries are able

to intelligently negotiate licenses and are willing to step away from a resource with unfavorable licensing language. The more libraries that are willing to take this step the more likely it is that publishers will amend their practices.

A licensing area that libraries will want to watch will be increased use of Creative Commons licenses (2007b) and their effect on electronic resources. Creative Commons' goal is to provide a middle "reasonable" level of copyright protection between no protection and the national and international legal regimes (Creative Commons, 2007a). Note that there is some dissent about the advantageousness of the Creative Commons scheme as a way to get around the use problems of traditional copyright (see e.g., Dusollier, 2006; Elkin-Koren, 2005; Katz, 2006). Creative Commons licenses are attached to a work by the creator and in addition to requiring attribution may also restrict commercial use, restrict derivative works, or require derivative works to carry the same license as the original work (Creative Commons, 2007b). What does this mean for a library licensing resources from a vendor? Currently, it does not mean much. Resources that are currently being licensed from vendors may include works that the creator has attached a creative commons license to - probably these would be only the "Attribution" or "Attribution No Derivates" licenses (Creative Commons, 2007b) because of the commercial nature of the larger electronic database—but it would presently be a daunting task to try to ferret out any Creative Commons licensed materials on a work-by-work basis in a large database (Dusollier, 2006). At present, there are two areas where libraries may want to focus their licensing energies regarding creative commons. First, libraries may want to add a clause to license agreements that specifically protects the libraries ability to use works attached to Creative Commons licenses as allowed by those licenses. Second, libraries may want to negotiate with the vendor terms that mandate that the vendor indicate whether a Creative Commons license (and which one) is applicable to a particular work in the work's metadata. This second area is going may be the more difficult term to negotiate, as it would require work on the vendor's part to add metadata indicating Creative Commons licensing to the existing database as well as to materials added in the future.

CONCLUSION

As electronic resources become a larger proportion of library collection budget expenditures, the importance of being able to negotiate favorable terms for a library become more imperative. License agreements are contracts and as such use rights given to libraries pursuant to United States copyright law can be negotiated away. In order to protect a library's interest as well as the interests of a library's patrons, librarians must become more knowledgeable concerning electronic resource license agreements and the licensing language and terms included in them.

REFERENCES

17 U.S.C. §107-122 (2001 & Supp. 2005).

Alford, D. E. (2002). Negotiating and analyzing electronic license agreements. *Law Library Journal, 94*(4), 621-644.

American Law Institute (1981-2006). *Restatement of the law second, Contracts 2d: As adopted and promulgated by the American Law Institute at Washington, D.C.* St. Paul, MN: American Law Institute Publishers.

American Library Association (2006). UCITA: Impact on libraries. Retrieved November 18, 2007, from http://www.ala.org/ala/washoff/WOissues/copyrightb/ucita/impact.htm

American Library Association (2006). UCITA: UCITA & related legislation in your state. Retrieved November 18, 2007, from http://www.ala.org/ala/washoff/WOissues/copyrightb/ucita/states.htm

Bielefield, A., & Cheeseman, L. (1999). *Interpreting and negotiating licensing agreements: A guidebook for the library, research, and teaching professions.* New York: Neal-Schuman Publishers, Inc.

Blackwell-Synergy (2006). Terms and conditions. Retrieved November 18, 2007, from http://www.blackwell-synergy.com/help?context=terms_and_conditions

Cambridge Journals Online (2006). Online terms of use. Retrieved November 17, 2007, from http://journals.cambridge.org/action/terms

CONTU (National Commission on New Technological Uses of Copyright Works) (1979). *Final report of the national commission on new technological uses of copyright works.* Washington, D.C.: Library of Congress.

CQ Press. (2006). Terms of service for the online services at cqpress.com. Retrieved November 18, 2007, from http://www.cqpress.com/TermsOfUse/general.htm

Creative Commons (2007a). About us. Retrieved November 18, 2007, from http://creativecommons.org/about/history

Creative Commons (2007b). Creative commons licenses. Retrieved November 18, 2007, from http://creativecommons.org/about/licenses/meet-the-licenses

Dusollier, S. (2006). The master's tools v. the master's house: Creative commons v. copyright. *Columbia Journal of Law & the Arts, 29*(3), 271-293.

Elkin-Koren, N. (2005). What contracts cannot do: The limits of private ordering in facilitating a creative commons. *Fordham Law Review, 74*(2), 375-422.

Farnsworth, E. A. (1999). *United States contract law* (Rev. ed.). Huntington, NY: Juris Publishing.

First Options of Chicago, Inc. v. Kaplan, 514 U.S. 938 (1995).

Freedom of Information Act, 5 U.S.C. § 552 (2001 & Supp. 2005).

Freedom of Information Act (Michigan), Mich. Comp. Laws Ann. § 15.231 *et seq.* (West 2004 & Supp. 2006).

Harris, L. E. (2002). *Licensing digital content: A practical guide for librarians.* Chicago: American Library Association.

Haworth Press (2006). The Haworth Press multi-site online terms. Retrieved November 18, 2007, from http://www.haworthpress.com/pdfs/Multi-SiteLicense.pdf

JSTOR (2006). Terms and conditions of use. Retrieved November 18, 2007, from http://www.jstor.org/about/terms.html

Katz, Z. (2006). Pitfalls of open licensing: An analysis of creative commons licensing. *IDEA, 46*(3), 391-413.

Kohl, D. F., & Sanville, T. (2006). More bang for the buck: Increasing the effectiveness of library expenditures through cooperation. *Library Trends, 54*(3), 394-410.

Kutten, L. J. (2003-2006). *Computer software: Protection/liability/law/forms* (2003 Recompiled ed.). St. Paul, MN: Thomson/West.

LexisNexis (1996). Terms & conditions of use for the LexisNexis services. Retrieved November 18, 2007, from http://www.lexisnexis.com/terms/general/

Murray, J. E., Jr. (2001). *Murray on contracts* (4th ed.) New York: LexisNexis.

Okerson, A. (1996). What academic libraries need in electronic content licenses. Retrieved November 18, 2007, from http://www.library.yale.edu/~okerson/stm.html

Okerson, A. (1997). Copyright or contract? *Library Journal, 122*(14), 136-139.

Okerson, A. S., Stenlake, R., & Harper, G. (2006). LIBLICENSE: Amendment. Retrieved November 18, 2007, from http://www.library.yale.edu/~llicense/amendgen.shtml

Okerson, A. S., Stenlake, R. & Harper, G. (2006). LIBLICENSE: Authorized use of license materials. Retrieved November 18, 2007, from http://www.library.yale.edu/~llicense/usecls.shtml

Okerson, A. S., Stenlake, R., & Harper, G. (2006). LIBLICENSE: Confidentiality. Retrieved November 18, 2007, from http://www.library.yale.edu/~llicense/confgen.shtml

Okerson, A. S., Stenlake, R., & Harper, G. (2006). LIBLICENSE: Fees. Retrieved November 18, 2007, from http://www.library.yale.edu/~llicense/paygen.shtml

Okerson, A. S., Stenlake, R., & Harper, G. (2006). LIBLICENSE: Governing law; Dispute resolution. Retrieved November 18, 2007, from http://www.library.yale.edu/~llicense/remgen.shtml

Okerson, A. S., Stenlake, R., & Harper, G. (2006). LIBLICENSE: Warranties; Indemnities; Limitations on warranties. Retrieved November 17, 2007, from http://www.library.yale.edu/~llicense/warrgen.shtml

Pace, A. K. (2003). *The ultimate digital library: Where the new information players meet.* Chicago: American Library Association.

Rice, D. A. (2002). Legal-technological regulation of information access. In T. A. Lipinski (Ed.), *Libraries, museums, and archives: Legal issues and ethical challenges in the new information era* (pp. 275-294). Lanham, MD: Scarecrow Press.

Richards, R. (2001). Licensing agreements: Contracts, the eclipse of copyright, and the promise of cooperation. *Acquisitions Librarian, 13*(26), 89-107.

Scigliano, M. (2002). Consortium purchases: Case study for a cost-benefit analysis. *The Journal of Academic Librarianship, 28*(6), 393-399.

Stange, K. (2006). Caught between print and electronic. *IFLA Journal, 32*(3), 237-239.

Tashbook, L. (2004). *Survey on licensing.* Buffalo, NY: Williams S. Hein & Co., Inc.

Taylor & Francis (2003). Terms and conditions of access. Retrieved November 18, 2007, from http://public.metapress.com/download/profiles/taylorandfrancis/terms-and-conditions-of-access.pdf

Uniform Computer Information Transactions Act (2002-2006). *Uniform laws annotated* (Vol. 7, Part II). Minneapolis, MN: Thomson/West.

University of Chicago Press Journals Division (2006). Electronic access to astronomy journals. Retrieved November 18, 2007, from http://www.journals.uchicago.edu/sitedocs.pdf

Wright, C. A. (1994). *The law of federal courts* (5th ed.). St. Paul, MN: West.

Section IV
Working with Electronic Resources

Chapter XI
Working with Database and E–Journal Vendors to Ensure Quality for End Users

Heather Christenson
California Digital Library, USA

Sherry Willhite
California Digital Library, USA

ABSTRACT

This chapter describes how the California Digital Library (CDL) supports the thousands of electronic journals, databases, collections and reference works that are licensed by CDL on behalf of the ten campuses of the University of California (UC). Three key components are vital to the success of this activity: the involvement of librarians at all the campuses to monitor and evaluate UC's electronic resources; CDL's internal processes for working with vendors; and CDL's requirements documents which emphasize both technical standards and best practices. By sharing these processes and documents, the authors hope to provide a foundation for developing practices to work successfully with vendors and ensure quality for library patrons.

INTRODUCTION

The California Digital Library (CDL) licenses thousands of electronic journals, databases, collections and reference works on behalf of the ten campuses of the University of California (UC), which are located across the state of California from San Diego in the south to Davis in the north.

The CDL is an all-digital library and is located at the UC Office of the President, rather than on a campus. The CDL's responsibilities include monitoring UC's systemwide electronic resources for access, performance, features, functionality, completeness of content and usage. Within this large consortium, the relationships are complex, and the range of digital content provided to end users takes many forms and covers many subjects. Since the CDL is not directly connected to the users of the electronic resources we license, we have created a process to gather and share information about electronic resource use, monitor and evaluate the resources, prioritize issues and problems, and work with vendors to improve the resources.

This chapter describes three key components of the CDL's electronic resources program: the involvement of librarians at all the campuses to monitor and evaluate UC's electronic resources; CDL's internal processes for working with vendors; and CDL's requirements documents which emphasize both technical standards and best practices. The authors hope these processes and documents will provide a foundation for librarians who wish to develop practices for working successfully with vendors and ensuring quality for end users, regardless of the size of their organization and numbers of staff.

BACKGROUND

Today's libraries license and provide access to an ever-increasing array of digital content from a wide variety of vendors. The vendors, and associated publishers and platforms, can range from small scholarly organizations to large corporations, and have varying levels of technical expertise and engagement with librarians.

UC makes a sizable investment in licensing electronic resources from these vendors, and we must ensure that our investment results in useful content and services for our end users. The electronic resources licensed by the CDL on behalf of the campuses fall into two categories: resources licensed for all ten UC campuses, which we call "tier 1" resources, and resources that are championed by one UC campus and may include other campuses in the license, called "tier 2" resources. The ten campuses license electronic resources for the use of their individual campus locally, but these are currently out of the scope of our programs. However, some of the principles we describe could indeed be adapted to an individual campus or library.

Everything we do is for the purposes of ensuring a quality research experience for the students, faculty and staff of our university. The quality of their experience is critical for their pursuits of teaching, research and knowledge. Because the CDL centrally licenses electronic resources for all ten campuses, we are well positioned to advocate for quality. But this effort also involves our campus librarians, since it is they who work with the end users and are the subject experts.

The two primary groups whose work we will discuss are the CDL Resource Liaisons (CDL, 2005b), a campus-based, consortium-wide group, and a team of six staff at CDL called the Resource Wranglers. The beginnings of our current processes date back to 1999, when CDL formed the Resource Liaisons group to monitor UC-wide licensed electronic resources.

The CDL's electronic resources program, which includes the Resource Liaisons and the Resource Wranglers, demonstrates that a successful program does not have to be centralized to provide maximum benefit and that it can be achieved without requiring an enormous amount of time from any one staff member. Investing the time to identify the services critical to users, the technologies necessary to support these services, and the requirements that brings these together is necessary for a successful program. In addition, these activities provide vendors with a clear picture of the user community and can aid them in their process of product development.

THE CDL RESOURCE LIAISON PROGRAM

Central to CDL's "watchdog" efforts is a group called the CDL Resource Liaisons. Resource liaisons are campus librarians who volunteer to take responsibility for monitoring a licensed resource or set of resources in their areas of expertise on behalf of all ten campuses and the CDL. This group is centrally administered from CDL by a resource liaison coordinator, but it "lives" on the campuses, where more than 100 UC librarians have been appointed to carry out the charge:

It is important to monitor bibliographic and full-text content licensed by the University of California and hosted at external sites. In some cases, the features and functionality of a resource could be improved and, as a single large customer, we would like to influence product development. In others, the performance of a producer (server availability, completeness and currency of content, etc.) must be monitored. In both cases, there may be issues that should be brought to bear upon renewal.

Subject experts who regularly use these resources are in the best position to monitor functional progress, completeness of content, and performance and may be the most interested in the use data. They also are the most appropriate people to gather input from colleagues and users, and recommend enhancements to the resources. (CDL, 2005b)

Monitoring the Resource

Each resource liaison serves as the central communications point in a process that involves colleagues at their own library, colleagues at other libraries on their campus, colleagues at other campuses, database and e-journal vendors, and the CDL. From this central position, the resource liaisons monitor and share information about their assigned resource in a number of ways. Most immediately, they actively use their assigned resource, help patrons use it, and solicit feedback from their colleagues to learn how others are using the resource.

As the central point of contact for their assigned resource, the resource liaison is often involved when access or content problems are discovered. Colleagues across UC may refer problems to them, or contact them for information regarding the resource. Resource liaisons explain problems to the vendor; suggest the ideal outcome for resolution of a problem and follow up until the problem is satisfactorily resolved. This information is shared with the CDL via a listserv.

Each year in January and in July as contracts come up for renewal, there is often a flurry of access problems, and it is especially effective to have the resource liaisons' help. Also, when there are changes to a resource such as removal or addition of features or content, the resource liaisons notify the UC campus community via systemwide listservs, CDL's e-mail newsletter, and campus Web site sites, blogs or newsletters. Much-awaited database platform upgrades, books added to book collections, and backfiles added to journal collections are examples of the type of improvements which need to be announced and placed into context. The resource liaisons are in the best position to do this. The CDL provides centralized problem reporting mechanisms, including a telephone helpline, a Web-based helpline database application, and several listservs which can be used to report problems.

When resource liaisons take on their assignment, the CDL provides them with initial vendor contacts and background information. Most of the resource liaisons get to know their vendor representatives, and subscribe to vendor newsletters, listservs, or RSS feeds. Resource liaisons are encouraged to participate in vendor advisory groups, if possible. At conferences, the resource liaisons attend user group meetings meet with vendors in person to smooth the way for working relationships. The CDL staff works alongside the resource liaisons when there are especially difficult or ongoing problems to work through with vendors. In addition, the CDL serves as a conduit for addressing issues that affect multiple resources licensed from an individual vendor.

Reports

In addition to the ongoing monitoring of resources, the Resource Liaison group's major evaluation activity is an annual report, known as the "vendor report card," which is sent to the CDL resource liaison coordinator. The report provides a means to evaluate key aspects of each resource: content, user interface, technical functionality and robustness, technical support and support in general. The report includes a request for updated instructional materials, either vendor or librarian-created to be included in the Instructional Materials section of the CDL Web site. Finally, the report includes a few open-ended questions which allow the resource liaison to do a full overall evaluation of the vendor's strengths and weaknesses and identify issues not covered in the rest of the report. A sample of the report form is included as Appendix I.

This reporting activity has evolved over the years, and has been iteratively informed by feedback from the Resource Liaisons group. When the group meets each year, both the outcome of the reports and the reporting process is discussed, and in the past the group has voted on whether to make adjustments to the process. Originally, the evaluation of vendors was separate from the evaluation of resources, and the resource liaisons reported quarterly. As vendor offerings seemed to gradually stabilize, the scope of the reports merged and was narrowed down to one report per year. The CDL's assessment team (CDL, 2005a) assisted in distilling our needs into a set of six questions. Having one report seems to balance the workload of the campus librarians with what CDL really needs to know about the systemwide resources. However, if the situation changes, a process is in place to consider new or varied ways of reporting.

Surveys

In addition to the annual report, the CDL will occasionally survey the resource liaisons about functional aspects of the resources, or current trends in vendor offerings. For example, the resource liaisons who are assigned to databases were asked to report on whether their particular database incorporated openURL support, durable links, and other services. Resource liaisons who are assigned to e-journal collections were asked to find out which version of a journal article the vendor considered to be the "copy of record." Other survey topics have included vendor support for metasearch standards, whether RSS feeds are offered, and whether "paid for by library" branding is available. The CDL has also asked the resource liaisons to weigh in on the success of our own services such as our helpline and reporting mechanisms. In the future, the CDL will likely survey the group on issues surrounding vendor strategies for digital preservation.

Statistics

Another key element in the evaluation of licensed resources is usage statistics. This area had fallen under the scope of the Resource Liaison program, but activities have evolved over time as the CDL has continued to seek greater efficiency and consistency across vendors. A number of years ago, the resource liaisons collected systemwide statistics from the vendors. Although now there are vestiges of this activity with a few vendors, the data is now centrally collected by CDL, with assistance from individual resource liaisons when needed.

The resource liaisons still provide important expertise in the interpretation of usage statistics. At annual report time, and informally at renewal time, the resource liaisons are asked to review the statistics and make sure the numbers match the perception of usage on that particular liaison's campus. Given their expert understanding of their assigned resource, the resource liaisons can identify factors that may contribute to the amount the resource is used. For example, low usage may reflect barriers to access such as port limits, a need for publicity, or an inherently small user community. Although port limits are becoming a thing of the past, resource liaisons are still charged with notifying CDL when users complain of frequent turnaways. High usage may be attributed to the cancellation of a competing database or a recent transition to a more usable interface.

In addition, the resource liaisons are a strong voice in encouraging database and e-journal vendors to support standards for reporting usage statistics. In the past, the group has successfully lobbied vendors to conform to the ICOLC statistics guidelines (ICOLC, 2006) With the coming of the COUNTER initiative (COUNTER, n.d.), the group now advocates for the latest version of the COUNTER guidelines (COUNTER, 2005). The draft standard, "NISO Standardized Usage Statistics Harvesting Initiative (SUSHI)" (NISO, 2006) is the next logical step in this progression, for it will enable harvesting and local manipulation of COUNTER statistics. In the future the CDL and the resource liaisons will most likely encourage vendors to become SUSHI-compliant.

Being Proactive

In light of a strong user service perspective, the CDL encourages resource liaisons to be proactive in identifying improvements that they and their colleagues would like the vendor to make to their products. In the recent past, these improvements have often been enhancements to the user interface. CDL's user interface principles document (CDL, 2003) is a high-level encapsulation of the knowledge gained from years of articulation of many user interface issues to vendors. The user interface principles address consistency and clarity, context and navigation, search, ease of learning, flexibility and personalization. The resource liaisons use this document as a starting point for conversations with colleagues and vendors. Key issues can be easily pointed out in relation to the principles, with ready examples of the reasoning behind each item. As user interface design

continues to evolve, so will the user interface principles document. In the near future, principles for integrated discovery interfaces and mobile search interfaces will most likely be added.

The CDL works with the resource liaisons to gather and prioritize requests for enhancements and changes before sending them to a vendor. The resource liaisons are then invited to participate in vendor meetings where the issues are discussed. This is especially effective in situations where we have multiple products from a vendor and more than one resource liaison. In a recent vendor meeting that included such diverse topics as consistent presentation of linking services, problems with pop-ups, browser compatibility issues and schedules for adding content, the vendor was riveted by the first person accounts given by the resource liaisons of end users grappling with these aspects of the vendor's product. The CDL will work with the vendor to implement resulting enhancements and provide feedback to resource liaisons on the status of requests for changes and enhancements. This process is discussed in detail later in this chapter.

Instructional Materials

The CDL provides a central location for instructional materials covering systemwide-licensed resources as a service to librarians on all of the UC campuses (CDL, 2006c). Although the vendor-supplied embedded help is usually the first resort of the end user, librarians on all of our campuses need to reference the tutorials, help and other instructional materials for a given resource, especially when they are teaching classes of students or instructing faculty. Resource liaisons provide links to vendor-supplied materials in their annual report. In addition, whenever there is a significant change to a resource, the CDL asks the resource liaison to supply updated instructional materials once new features have been incorporated. Often the most helpful and engaging instructional materials are those created by UC librarians. UC-created materials can be especially useful since they place the resource in the context of specific use in the campus environment. Materials from one campus can be modified for use on another campus. Most instructional materials tend to be documents, but they may also be interactive tutorials, "tours," Web-conference recordings, videos, podcasts, or guidance in other formats.

Because the resource liaisons contribute the instructional materials, it is not an onerous task for a central entity such as CDL to maintain a simple Web page listing the materials. There may be more dynamic methods for sharing this sort of information (e.g., wikis, blogs) across an institution or consortium, but the CDL has found this low-barrier solution to be effective.

Vendors appreciate the fact that these instructional materials are surfaced to a wide audience of librarians, so this arrangement benefits everyone. By periodically turning their attention to instructional materials, resource liaisons may also surface unmet training originating from the campuses, which can then be passed along to the vendors for attention.

The Value of the Resource Liaison Program

Power of the Group

Resource liaisons make sure that ensure that UC's faculty and students realize the value of licensed resources. The oversight that the resource liaisons provide regarding the performance of each licensed resource is particularly important at renewal time, when it provides great leverage to understand the strengths and shortcomings of a given resource. Examples of issues that resource liaisons might bring to CDL's attention are user interface problems, missing content, or lack of conformance to technical requirements. The technical requirements are essential to this process, and will be discussed in more detail later in the chapter.

In addition, the Resource Liaison program saves time both for CDL and individual campuses in responding to all kinds of problems and changes to resources. When resource liaisons report upcoming user interface changes, administrative changes, and content changes, the CDL can be proactive in taking the appropriate action to ensure the best possible outcome for end users. The Resource Liaison program provides UC with a powerful group voice in discussions with vendors. This effort gives us a great platform for making sure the needs of UC's staff and scholars are taken into account by our licensed resource vendors and incorporated into vendor offerings.

The CDL serves generally as a central point where UC creates efficiencies in our systemwide licensed resources activities. The Resource Liaison program specifically adds to these efficiencies in a number of ways. The group gives CDL access to subject expertise and depth of knowledge about particular resources that the CDL does not have in-house. The campuses have, for example, music librarians who understand the limitations of "Beethoven" as a search term within music collections, life sciences librarians who understand the intricacies of each layer of biological taxonomies in depth, government documents librarians who have a sense of how licensed content dovetails with documents available on the Web, and chemistry librarians who understand the challenges of the search and presentation of chemical formulas and models. This type of specific expertise is essential for evaluating completeness of content and appropriate search mechanisms, as well as for understanding user needs. In addition, the participation of many resource liaisons who talk to the vendors creates a vital channel for informal "heads up" reports. The CDL could not possibly know about the sheer scope of content changes, platform changes, details of user interface updates, and other changes that the resource liaisons report directly from our libraries. Because the resource liaisons are on the front lines and see user behavior, including how databases and e-journals are really used, they can best identify problems and give the CDL a clear picture of what goes on at our constituent campuses.

Common Technology Standards

The resource liaisons advocate for UC-preferred technology standards and services that benefit the entire university. The CDL provides technical expertise, and having consistent advocates on all the campuses keeps UC's name and CDL-recommended technical requirements in front of database and e-journal vendors. This tactic has resulted in great success with vendors implementing our recommended technical solutions. For example, link resolver services are very important to end-users. UC relies on our openURL-based link resolver service to get users to the appropriate copy of electronic text, to link to campus OPAC records, and to link to our interlibrary loan and document delivery service. The resource liaisons and the CDL have worked together to raise the awareness level of the vendors in this area and work to convince vendors of the need to support this critical function. The CDL technical staff worked closely with our database and full content vendors to help them implement openURL services and to improve both the quality and the amount of the metadata sent in the openURL.

Connection and Enrichment

The Resource Liaison program also enriches UC systemwide relationships, and provides professional development opportunities to librarians. The program forges connections between UC libraries and librarians at the systemwide level, since resource liaisons are charged with communicating with their colleagues among the various bibliographer groups and campuses. A good example of this is when a transition of a database from one vendor to another is made; an evaluative process is lead by the resource liaison and involves colleagues across the university. The

program also connects CDL to the campuses, and gives the CDL an opportunity to inform campus librarians via the Resource Liaison program about CDL activities and practices.

In addition, the Resource Liaison program is a good channel for propagating skills such as user interface evaluation, understanding of linking technology, licensing and more. This experience is a form of professional development for the resource liaisons, which also benefits their campus libraries. Most importantly, the work that the Resource Liaisons group does with CDL aims towards happy end users—UC's scholars.

Value to Our Vendors

Not only do the resource liaisons gather opinions and information from their colleagues across the university to present to vendors, they also can serve as a point for vendors to disseminate information, conduct user testing and gather feedback that supports the vendors' goals for product enhancement and development. The CDL and the resource liaisons provide vendors with examples of how their products are being used, and the relative popularity and/or success of a given functionality. Currently, vendor usability testing is taking place on several of UC campuses, facilitated by the resource liaisons. Some resource liaisons have served on advisory groups to recommend content additions to vendor products; the resource liaisons based their feedback on content recommendations from their colleagues across UC.

In addition, the CDL advocates for standards, as laid out in technical requirements and as monitored by the resource liaisons. Because of this advocacy, vendors have brought in high-level technical staff to meet with CDL about such subjects as authentication protocols, creation of current awareness and citation export services, interface design and metadata for linking. The CDL aims for two-way communication which can benefit both sides.

Value to the Participants

Although librarians who participate as resource liaisons have varying levels of engagement, by participating they all are taking a visible role among their colleagues. Serving in the volunteer role of resource liaison is a plus for campus librarians at performance review time. If they have been actively engaged in this role, the CDL will support them with letters of recommendation for their service to the university. By actively participating in the program, campus librarians gain a systemwide view and develop contacts with the CDL, with vendors, and across UC. Resource liaisons are empowered to work with the CDL and vendors on improving our resources. Some have been motivated to volunteer for resource liaison duties in order to address problems from a UC-wide position. The CDL hosts an annual meeting of the resource liaisons (CDL, 2006a), during which the group is updated on CDL and UC-wide activities that have an impact on their work in the resource liaison role. Each year the meeting includes panel discussions, where members of the group discuss aspects of their experience. Past panels have focused on working with vendors and managing transitions of databases from one vendor to another. The panels have surfaced lively anecdotes of how each person's personal style (gentle and congenial, direct and energetic) can be adapted to the role using the framework the CDL provides.

THE CDL RESOURCE WRANGLERS

Although a network of librarians across the campuses communicate between vendors and the CDL, the CDL must still monitor vendor issues internally. The Resource Wranglers is an internal CDL group that monitors issues regarding the CDL licensed databases and e-journals. The wranglers have a depth of technical expertise that many of the resource liaisons do not have, and a deeper understanding of the issues concerning all of all of the CDL licensed resources, and can serve as a guide for the resource liaisons. The group works with the resource liaisons to proactively communicate UC's needs to vendors, track vendor issues, and follow up on these issues until they are resolved.

This group was inspired by the CDL's transition from loading A&I databases in-house to accessing the databases via vendor interfaces. The range of primary job responsibilities of the staff involved in the transition-working group ensured that issues were evaluated and addressed from a number of perspectives, and meeting as a group facilitated the process. The need for an ongoing oversight group for licensed content became obvious during the transition process, and the Resource Wranglers group was created.

The Resource Wranglers members have a range of job responsibilities within CDL, and include the resource liaison coordinator, the helpline and user feedback coordinator, the information services manager responsible for instruction, education and communication, a member from the Business and Licensing group, the technical lead for our link resolver service, and the Resource Wranglers group convener who is responsible for monitoring database and e-journal specific issues, services issues and tracking these to resolution.

The Resource Wranglers group takes the input from the resource liaisons and carries it further by aggregating and prioritizing the needs and issues. Vendor issues lists are prepared, based on what is reported by the resource liaisons. The resource wranglers then set up vendor meetings, create vendor status reports based on these issues, and distributes the reports to the campuses. The issues lists and status reports are used to track the progress UC makes and to hold vendors accountable for resolving these issues.

The Resource Wranglers also create and maintain key documentation and information such as the resource selection criteria (CDL, 2006e), and other database evaluation and transition documentation used by the resource liaisons and campus bibliographer groups when changing vendors, information about CDL-licensed resources on the CDL Web site (CDL, 2006b), and the Technical Requirements for Vendors documents made available on the CDL's Vendors and Content Providers Web page (CDL, 2006h).

The group focuses on the following areas for licensed resources:

1. User interfaces for licensed databases and e-journals
2. Access (includes proxy/VPN support, searches conducted outside of the vendor interface, for example, via EndNote's Z39.50 function, etc.)
3. Database and e-journal specific issues as reported by the resource liaisons, other UC campus groups, and end-users
4. Linking issues such as getting vendors to support the openURL standard and other items of this nature as suggested by the CDL's UC-eLinks team
5. Multi-item services, for example, the CDL's use of the PubMed order function to allow users to send a list of citations to the CDL UC-eList service that provides inline links to electronic full text, and access to CDL's Request service to ask for a group of items via campus document delivery service or interlibrary loan
6. Usage statistics

The wranglers develop an annual work plan based on the responses to the resource liaisons' annual reports, any additional issues raised via the CDL Helpline or feedback links and any areas where the vendors does not meet UC's expectations as detailed in our technical requirements for vendors document, and any business issues that need to be addressed, for example port limits. The work plan is divided into sections based on the type and extent of issues reported.

In the highest priority category are vendors needing full review by the Resource Liaisons and Wranglers groups. To be included in this category, a vendor's products must have triggered overwhelming user dissatisfaction. A full review begins with the creation or updating of the list of vendor issues causing problems for UC users. The list is then sent to resource liaisons for additions, deletions and prioritization. The next step is a conference call with resource liaisons, the resource liaison coordinator, and wranglers convener to review "final list." A letter is sent to the vendor asking that the vendor review and reply to the prioritized issues list. This letter includes a link to the technical requirements. If there are complex issues to be addressed, the letter asks for a face-to-face meeting or a conference call to discuss the issues. The vendor responses are reviewed; any areas requiring follow-up are identified and the group drafts UC's response.

In the second priority category are the vendors that need to respond to each section of the appropriate technical requirements document. In this case, there are too many problems reported to focus on a single issue, but not enough issues to warrant a full review.

In the third category are single-issue problems. In this group the resource liaison sends specific letters requesting vendor response and timeline for any planned changes. The two major issues that fall into this category are support for UC's openURL requirements and support for UC's statistics requirements.

Any other issues with individual resources, for example, a specific database within a vendor site or business issues, are handled case-by-case by the resource liaison.

CDL'S TECHNICAL REQUIREMENTS FOR VENDORS

How and Why the Requirements Were Developed

In 2001, the CDL began a transition from loading several core A&I vendor databases on-site and providing Z39.50 access to other A&I databases via our OPAC interface, to providing access to these databases via the vendor's native interfaces. A vital part of the transition was ensuring that the services and functions that were available in our internal system were also available in the vendor's native interface. Some of the key services were provided by software that was internal to the OPAC and developed by UC, and the vendor solutions for these services were in some cases new to the general marketplace, for example, linking from a citation directly to the content of the item. The CDL needed a consistent way to communicate UC's needs and expectations to the potential vendors. To fill this need we created a set of technical requirements describing the key components that users needed, and listing our expectations of how these requirements would be met. At the core of these requirements was a commitment to using recognized national and international standards as the preferred solution.

Principles Used for Drafting the Requirements

In general, quality and consistency of electronic resources across the university is the primary goal expressed in the technical requirements. The following principles were agreed upon and endorsed by the campus libraries, and were used in developing the technical requirements documents:

1. Proprietary vendor solutions should be discouraged in favor of methods based on standards or solutions that can work with multiple vendors
2. Existing linking to catalog holdings, to full content from all publishers licensed by the CDL and to the interlibrary loan and document delivery service should be preserved and extended
3. The level and consistency of services should be improved for *all* databases licensed by the CDL (and by individual campuses)
4. UC should be proactive in developing expertise and mechanisms for influencing the quality of vendor user interfaces and services

The Technical Requirements Overview section, included next, sets expectations in context for the vendor.

When selecting vendors for abstracting and indexing databases, CDL aims not only to maintain existing standards for access and service, but also to improve, whenever possible, on existing arrangements. Moreover, by choosing our technologies and vendor relationships carefully now, we hope to lay the groundwork for future improvements. To that end, the following document sums up the major technical issues of our decision-making process, and offers vendors insight into our preferred solutions, why they're important to UC, and what their implications are for prospective vendors.

Preferred vendors will provide the CDL opportunities for input on development priorities. CDL sets a high standard for vendors that ultimately benefits all academic customers and leads to more competitive products for the publisher or vendor. CDL is willing to work closely in the development and implementation of new features and functionality for existing products as well as codevelopment on new, cutting edge products that fit CDL's own strategic plans. These opportunities could take place via a users group, focus groups, working with the vendor's director of development, or discussions with the development planning team. (CDL, 2006f; CDL, 2006g)

A preference for standards-based solutions over proprietary solutions is a major point of emphasis in the technical requirements documents. Although compliance with standards and interpretation of them will never approach 100% agreement, at the very least the standards provide a common language that enables service integration at a baseline level.

Two versions of the requirements document are referenced, one for database vendors and one for e-journal vendors. Although there is quite a bit of overlap between the two, there are enough differences to make the two versions necessary.

How the Requirements Are Applied

The technical requirements provide the vendor with a comprehensive view of UC's expectations. When CDL is considering licensing databases, e-journals or other electronic content on behalf of UC, vendor representatives are asked to have their technical staff review the technical requirements document and respond item-by-item. This provides a clear view of the vendor's baseline functionality, and of how well the vendor system meets our user's needs. The vendor's response also highlights any gaps in a common understanding of the issues and is used as the basis for further discussions and negotiations. When the CDL updates the technical requirements documents, the CDL or the resource liaison sends an updated version to the vendor and asks for another section-by-section response. The CDL asks the resource liaisons to be familiar with the technical requirements, and to encourage vendors to comply. For example, the resource liaisons encouraged their vendors to attend NISO's May 2003 meeting,

NISO Metasearch Strategy Workshop: May 7-8, 2003 in Denver Colorado and the NISO workshop on *OpenURL and Metasearch: New Standards, Current Innovations, and Future Directions* in Washington, D.C. on September 19-21, 2005. As the UC libraries move forward with metasearch implementation, the resource liaisons will work with their vendors to reinforce the need for standards-based search API's in support of UC's metasearch implementation. In the current version of our *Technical Requirements for Database Vendors,* we list the following methods (in order of preference) of accessing a vendor site from CDL's metasearch application: Z39.50; SRU (preferred) or SRW; NISO metasearch XML gateway (MXG) protocol (NISO, n.d. a) based on the NISO-registered SRU protocol (NISO, n.d. b); and lastly via a proprietary XML gateway.

Which Requirements are Most Essential Now, and Why?

The key requirements—access control, clean, comprehensive metadata for linking to content, and quality data—focus on getting end users to what they want when they want it.

Access

Users need access from where they are—from home, a conference, or a sabbatical location. Access should be designed to allow UC's user community to get to the resource from anywhere with a minimum of effort on the part of UC or that of the user, and with minimal disclosure of identity information. The legacy method of authentication uses IP addresses. Because the IP method is labor intensive, error-prone, and often frustrating for end users, the CDL is actively seeking new solutions; particularly those that stress federated identity management and privacy protection. UC is seeking to implement access control mechanisms that simplify the authentication protocols.

Linking

Clean metadata in openURLs is needed, in order to provide end users with viable links to electronic content that they can access immediately online, or links that contain enough information to get to the item on their home campus or via interlibrary loan. The CDL has a specification for the items that must appear in an openURL. UC requires more metadata than many of the vendor's other customers, since in our environment the metadata is used to send requests for interlibrary loan direct to lender. This situation appears to be changing, as other institutions are now also asking for a more robust set of metadata. The CDL's Metadata Requirements for OpenURLs (CDL, 2006d) may be useful as a model for other institutions.

Data quality

Scholarship requires high quality data. Sloppy scanning, black and white scans of color graphics, and intrusive watermarking can result in unusable data. Indexing schemes designed for print indexes do not make the cut in the online world.

End users' needs evolve over time, and so should the vendor services. In 2002 when the CDL transitioned from loading key A&I databases in-house to using these databases via vendor Web sites, one of the core services our users had on our system and wanted on the vendor system was a "passive" current awareness service, based on an existing search strategy, that automatically provided a list of relevant items via e-mail each time the data was updated. This allowed end users to do a search once and get new relevant citations via e-mail every time items were added. Thus, one of our top requests in 2002 for features to be added to vendor systems was for current awareness service. Now our users want their updates to be provided via RSS feeds, and we are asking vendors to provide this service.

The value of the technical requirements is their focus on what is needed now and what is expected for the future. We are doing things now as a matter of course that were not even on the table ten years ago. Many of the items in the first version of our requirements addressed emerging technologies and required a significant amount of descriptive text highlighting the advantages to the end-user and to the vendor. Lengthy explanations of the benefits of some services, such as openURL, were necessary in the original version of the requirements when most vendors had not yet set-up this type of service, but are now no longer necessary. The requirements for statistics support have changed over time from ICOLC to COUNTER to COUNTER2 and SUSHI. Recent revisions were made to add or update sections on user privacy, perpetual access and preservation responsibility.

In the future, a number of emerging areas will need to be addressed in the technical requirements. Use of mobile applications must be addressed by the academic community. Texting and podcasting are the norm for our incoming students (the next decade's faculty) and we need to keep pace with their needs. We have ample evidence of how quickly changes happen in the online environment, such as the transition from line-mode interfaces to Web interfaces, moving the copy of record from print to electronic, and changing the way metadata is delimited to focus on online retrieval rather than the more limited number of access points used to create print indexes. Vendors need to think about keeping their metadata "nimble" and be able to move forward as technology moves forward. Our requirements will also need to address image services providing access to images and their associated metadata. Integration of UC services with open access journals, and freely available discovery platforms such as Google Scholar and Windows Live Academic will also eventually need to be taken into account.

BEST PRACTICES AND RECOMMENDATIONS

Given the CDL's experience working with these processes and requirements, we can offer the following words of wisdom to librarians working in consortia, on campuses, or in individual libraries of any size.

It is all about your end users. The end user's needs are the focus of all interactions with the vendor. Make sure that your vendor supports your users' needs and, most importantly, supports them in a way that they can take full advantage of the vendor's product. The best return on the investment in online resources is high use.

Vendors spend time, effort and expense on focus groups to determine features and functions for their products. Your end users provide that type of data every time they ask you a question about how to find an article or how to use a vendor product, or send a complaint via e-mail, or talk with their colleagues. With the advent of Google Scholar and other services piggybacking on commonly used free services, the A&I vendors will need to offer better features to keep their user base. Even then, this may not be enough to retain some end users that are more focused on "one-stop" searching, than on the search tool. The library community is looking to metasearch systems that will offer one stop searching for licensed materials as well as freely available scholarly materials. To be successful across vendors, the query process for these systems needs to leverage the strength of standards based search mechanisms; API's such as Z39.50, SRU/SRW, or the NISO metasearch XML gateway (MXG) protocol that is based on SRU instead of relying vendor specific API's or "screen scraping" techniques.

Items that are not easily accessible are not attractive to end users and do not meet their needs—even if the resource is, in fact, the best resource for their topic. Simultaneous user limits are becoming an anachronism. End users that are told to go away because of system limits, will go away, and will not come back.

End users will often be content with an answer, even if it is not the best answer. Vendors must provide easy access and keep the learning curve low. Look at the success of PubMed. One of the greatest services that NLM/NCBI has provided is to remove the need for intensive user training on how to search for appropriate MeSH terms, and to provide behind-the-scenes subject term mapping. The system is easier to use and the users get better results. This is the type of effort we must encourage the A&I vendors to make in order to retain users.

Vendor interactions are based on the five "B's:"

- Be proactive
- Be specific
- Be realistic
- Be persistent
- Be part of the solution

Be proactive. If something is not working for your end users, it probably is not working for other end users at other institutions. Talk to your vendor about the issue as soon as it becomes apparent that there is a problem. If end users cannot figure out how to download their list of articles, let the vendor know. The sooner you raise the issue, the sooner it can be resolved. The interaction should not be adversarial. You and the vendor have the same goal in mind: getting the maximum number of users to the resource and actively using it.

Go to the source of the problem. This requires knowledge of the data producer/database vendor relationship. If the issue is with the data, go to the data producer first. The interface vendor cannot easily index the volume number if it is sent a part of a larger field, for example, as part of the source field, and it does not have consistent labeling. This is a data producer issue. Keep in mind that the majority of the items online began in the print world and the data divisions useful for a print index do not always translate well to an online index. It may be that the backfiles cannot be altered but that a change can be made going forward. When the problem is partly from the producer and partly the vendor, establish a three-way dialogue.

Be specific. The CDL has had the most success when we include screen shots that show the problem, or examples of how other vendors handle the same function in a way that works for end users. We try to frame each of our problem reports in the same way:

1. This is what happens now (Provide screen shots, include a narrative description.)
2. This is the impact on the users (Provide narrative description.)
3. This is what we would like to happen instead

Provide narrative description; if useful include a mock-up showing desired action; if the problem situation is handled well by other vendors provide examples from other vendor systems. Suggest solutions for both the short term and the long term. Short-term solutions mitigate the impact of the problem, but the problem still occurs. These often rely on interface messages and are relatively simple to implement. Long-term solutions fix the problem so that it no longer occurs, but generally take more time since the vendor has to make infrastructure or indexing changes. These take time and may need to be integrated with other changes in the works or wait for the development team to have an opening.

Example from one of our vendor communiqués used as the starting point for discussion:

The thesaurus could be a very useful tool; instead it is confusing. In the example below the user is given the message that the search for architecture competitions retrieved no results, and then first suggested heading is architecture/ competitions which contains the same words in the same order but has a slash instead of a space. Users find this response quite confusing:

Your search for architecture competitions returned no results. Perhaps one of these other terms will help you:

- *Architecture/Competitions, awards, etc.*
- *Houses/Competitions, awards, etc.*
- *City planning/Competitions, awards, etc.*

In this case it seems that the punctuation is being indexed. Users do not really see the difference and it looks like the system is having problems. The punctuation should not be indexed. An interim option would be to change the message from "Your search for <term(s)> returned no results. Perhaps one of these other terms will help you:" to "Your search for < term(s)> did not exactly match a subject heading. Perhaps one of these other terms will help you."

Be realistic. Manage your expectations as well as the user's expectations. Some times there is a simple change the vendor can make to mitigate the problem, such as adding an example to a search screen. This type of change is usually simple to make and you can see results relatively quickly. In other cases, the resolution requires a change in the way the data is indexed or loaded, these changes take time to implement. If this is the case, work with the producer and the vendor to resolve the problem. When the vendor/producer agrees to make the change, ask for a time frame. It is easier to manage expectations if you have a date; even a ballpark figure of late next year is helpful.

Be persistent. Do not take no for an answer on the first pass. If the vendor does not agree to make the change your users need, ask again. Use more/different examples of the negative impact. Let the vendor know if they are the "trailing edge" and that all of your other vendors are using the solution you have proposed. There have been times that it has taken the vendor several years to make the changes we have requested. The key here is to be persistent, not pesky.

Be part of the solution. It is not helpful to say, "This feature is abysmal," and stop. If you stop there, it is a complaint and not a constructive comment. Offer one or more alternatives that the vendor could apply to fix the "abysmal" feature. Once the vendor makes the change, be willing to participate in testing the change.

The two things the CDL hears most frequently from our vendors when working on interface issues are the following. Before the vendor makes the change: "Nobody else has asked for this." After the change is made and released: "We are getting a lot of good feedback; this is a very popular feature."

FUTURE TRENDS

From the point of view of the CDL's electronic resources program we see a number of trends that we'll need to adapt to address. The CDL will need to refine our practices to better enable working with data providers and service providers in situations where we do not have a license or contract (for example, open access journals, Google Scholar). We'll also need to adapt to the increasingly blurry boundaries of scholarly information and find the economies of scale for the support and evaluation of new types of resources and delivery mechanisms (e.g., comprehensive access and service for mobile devices, "real time" data sources). In addition, libraries and vendors will likely evolve services towards tighter integration with the end user environment. We will need to encompass next generation linking, personalization and transactional situations into our requirements and evaluative processes. As our virtual library collections become predominate and our in-person interactions with end users become an anomaly, we'll need to adjust accordingly.

In terms of our process, a promising area of exploration may be the translation of our best practices model into new forms via Web-based collaborative technology. Our years of experience have lead us to a certain scale of activities, but collaboration at more or less granular levels, both institution-wise, and practice-wise, is now easily possible and may be more fruitful for a wider community. There is potential in homegrown tools that could emulate rating, evaluation and informational aspects of services as the Charleston Advisor (The Charleston Advisor, 2007); projects such as SHERPA RoMEO (SHERPA, 2006), or the University of California report on Bibliographic Services (Riemer, Declerck, Kautzman, Martin,& Ryan 2005); and in collaborative efforts such as the American Society for Engineering Education's best practices work (American Society for Engineering Education, 2006).

In addition, library ERM systems show promise in tying evaluative information more closely to electronic resources, and thus making this information more readily available to librarians managing electronic resources across an entire user group (in UC's case, the entire consortium). ERM systems may provide rich, detailed comparisons between resources and vendors, and also may enable a more precise communication of these details to our vendors. Furthermore, the workflow adjustments that are made when a library adopts an ERM system may enable the librarians to more efficiently incorporate evaluative activities into their workflow. If we establish common checkpoints within an ERM system for the many different activities in an electronic resources workflow, it may result in a shared understanding of where the handoffs are, across both the internal user group and the points where external vendors are involved.

CONCLUSION

The need for access to quality (good, complete, and authoritative) information in a way that makes sense in the end user's workflow will always exist.

How we understand that needs change over time, so our practices will always be evolving. Communications methods have changed and will keep changing, but the need for good communications, evaluation of end user needs, and clear requirements will always be relevant.

The process and documents described in this chapter are intended to be living processes and living documents. As the environment within which we work evolves, we will continue to reassess, change and improve. Our current materials and processes are not final—they reflect where we are now.

Certainly not many institutions are structured to include a central entity such as the CDL, or are large enough for the same efficiencies to be realized. However, the key ideas presented here can be applied to any library consortium or individual library. Defining what your end users need, creating a system for evaluating how well a vendor meets those needs, systematically performing a check on the quality of individual electronic resources before they are up for a renewal payment, tracking problems in a central place, encouraging librarians to be the "eyes and ears" of the organization, advocating for standards, and maintaining communication with vendors are all worth doing.

We encourage you to adapt and build upon our practices as appropriate to your needs. In the rapidly changing world of licensed, and now openly available content, librarians will need to continue to play the role as advocates for quality. Our voices are more likely to be heard if we view working with vendors and content providers as a positive, and if we advocate for common, reasonable standards.

REFERENCES

California Digital Library (2005a). Assessment. Retrieved November 18, 2007, from the California Digital Library Web site: http://www.cdlib.org/inside/assess/

California Digital Library (2005b). CDL resource liaison charge. Retrieved November 18, 2007, from the California Digital Library Web site: http://www.cdlib.org/inside/groups/Resource liaison/charge.html

California Digital Library (2006a). CDL resource liaison meetings. Retrieved November 18, 2007, from the California Digital Library Web site: http://www.cdlib.org/inside/groups/rl/meetings.html

California Digital Library (2006b). Information About CDL-Licensed Resources. Retrieved November 18, 2007, from the California Digital Library Web site: http://www.cdlib.org/inside/resources/licensed/index.html

California Digital Library (2006c). Instructional materials. Retrieved November 18, 2007, from the California Digital Library Web site: http://www.cdlib.org/inside/instruct/

California Digital Library (2006d). Metadata requirements for OpenURLs. Retrieved November 18, 2007, from the California Digital Library Web site: http://www.cdlib.org/vendors/Metadata_requirements.pdf

California Digital Library (2006e). Resource selection criteria. Retrieved November 18, 2007, from the California Digital Library Web site: http://www.cdlib.org/inside/resources/licensed/resource_selection_criteria.rtf

California Digital Library (2006f). California digital library technical requirements for database vendors. Retrieved November 18, 2007, from the California Digital Library Web site: http://www.cdlib.org/vendors/CDL_ejournal_Vendor_Req.rtf

California Digital Library (2006g). California digital library technical requirements for e-journal vendors. Retrieved November 18, 2007, from the

California Digital Library Web site: http://www. cdlib.org/vendors/CDL_DB_Vendor_Req.rtf

California Digital Library. (2003). User Interface Principles. Retrieved November 18, 2007, from the California Digital Library Web site: http://www. cdlib.org/vendors/Interface_Principles.rtf

California Digital Library (2006h). Vendors and content providers. Retrieved November 18, 2007, from the California Digital Library Web site: http://www.cdlib.org/vendors/

The Charleston Advisor (2007). TCA review scorecard. Retrieved November 18, 2007, from the Charleston Advisor Web site: http://www. charlestonco.com/scorecard.cfm

COUNTER (n.d.). About. Retrieved November 18, 2007 from the Project COUNTER Web site: http://www.projectcounter.org/about.html

COUNTER (2005, April). Release 2 of the COUNTER code of practice for journals and databases. Retrieved November 18, 2007, from the Project COUNTER Web site: http://www.projectcounter. org/code_practice.html

Engineering Libraries Division, American Society for Engineering Education (2005, May). Punch list of best practices for electronic resources. Retrieved November 18, 2007, from the Engineering Libraries Division of American Society for Engineering Education Web site: http://eld.lib.ucdavis. edu/punchlist/PunchlistRevision2005.pdf

ICOLC (2006, October). Revised guidelines for statistical measures of usage of web-based information resources. Retrieved November 18, 2007, from the ICOLC Web site: http://www.library. yale.edu/consortia/webstats06.htm

NISO (2006). NISO standardized usage statistics harvesting initiative. Retrieved November 18, 2007, from the NISO Web site: http://www.niso. org/committees/SUSHI/SUSHI_comm.html

NISO (n.d. a). NISO RP-2006-02, NISO Metasearch XML Gateway implementers guide. Retrieved November 18, 2007, from http://www.niso. org/standards/resources/RP-2006-02.pdf

NISO (n.d. b). *NISO Z39.92-200X.* Information retrieval service description specification DRAFT STANDARD FOR TRIAL USE. Period: November 1, 2005 – October 31, 2006

Riemer, J., Declerck, L., Kautzman, A., Martin, P., & Ryan, T. (2005). Bibliographic services task force final report. Retrieved November 18, 2007, from the University of California Libraries Web site: http://libraries.universityofcalifornia. edu/sopag/BSTF/Final.pdf

SHERPA (2006). SHERPA RoMEO publisher copyright policies and self-archiving. Retrieved November 18, 2007, from the SHERPA Web site: http://www.sherpa.ac.uk/romeo.php

APPENDIX I

Vendor Evaluation Report

Use this form to give an overall ranking for your vendor. There is no length limit for comments. Please be specific in your comments and use examples whenever possible.

1. The content of this information resource meets UC standards and users needs. This should include complete content, good quality, links from citations to full-text, and so forth. For more information see: http://www.cdlib.org/vendors/CDL_DB_Vendor_Req.rtf; http://www.cdlib.org/vendors/CDL_ejournal_Vendor_Req.rtf

    Check one:

    | ☐ Always Agree | ☐ Agree | ☐ Disagree | ☐ Always Disagree |

    Comments:

2. The user interface of this information resource meets CDL standards of quality, as outlined in the CDL User Interface Principles, for example, consistent terminology, easy to navigate, clear search screens, and so forth. For more information see: http://www.cdlib.org/vendors/Interface_Principles.rtf

    Check one:

    | ☐ Always Agree | ☐ Agree | ☐ Disagree | ☐ Always Disagree |

    Comments:

3. This information resource meets the standards outlined in the technical requirements established by CDL, including remote authentication, usage statistics, and so forth. For more information see: http://www.cdlib.org/vendors/CDL_DB_Vendor_Req.rtf; http://www.cdlib.org/vendors/CDL_ejournal_Vendor_Req.rtf

Check one:

☐ Always Agree   ☐ Agree   ☐ Disagree   ☐ Always Disagree

Comments:

4. Technical and customer support for this resource meets UC standards. The vendor is responsive and prompt in responding to problem reports, provides training materials, usage data, and is fair and reasonable to work with.

Check one:

☐ Always Agree   ☐ Agree   ☐ Disagree   ☐ Always Disagree

Comments:

Please provide links to the *most up-to-date* version of vendor-provided and/or to campus-created training materials:

5. What should this vendor do better? What about this resource should be improved? Are there any issues, big or small, that you would like to see addressed?

6. What does this vendor do well? Are there things that this vendor does or aspects of this resource that can be used as a model for other vendors?

Chapter XII
One–Stop Shopping
for Journal Holdings

Janet A. Crum
Oregon Health & Science University, USA

ABSTRACT

In this chapter, the author advocates providing a unified, seamless interface—one-stop shopping—for the full range of journal literature available and of interest to library patrons. After outlining the reasons why libraries should provide this access, the chapter reviews the tools available for making journal collections accessible, then analyzes the categories of journal literature to which a library could provide access—print and individual electronic titles, aggregated collections and big deals, free titles, free articles, and articles available for purchase. The chapter discusses the challenges associated with each category, as well as tools available to overcome these challenges. It closes with a brief look at future trends that will affect the ability of libraries to provide coherent, seamless access to journal literature.

INTRODUCTION

A patron stops at the reference desk and asks the librarian, "Do you have this journal?" This scene is played out in libraries across the world every day, yet the answer is no longer a straightforward yes or no. Where does one look to answer the question? The catalog? A Web-based list of journals? Both? Somewhere else? There is a disconnect between what the patron wants to know—"How do I get this article?"—and what library catalogs and other bibliographic control tools are designed

to answer —"Does the library own this item?" This disconnect did not exist when journals were available only in print. Either the desired item was in the library's collection, or it was not. But now the range of possibilities is much greater:

- The library may own the item in print and/or microform
- The library may have purchased electronic access to the item, in addition to or instead of the print

- The library may have purchased access to an aggregated database that includes the full text of the journal the patron wants
- The journal (or only the specific article) may be freely available online, either on the publisher's site or as part of an open access resource (e.g., an institutional repository or PubMed Central)
- The article may be available for a fee from the publisher/vendor site or a document delivery service
- The article may only be available via inter-library loan.

Answering the patron's seemingly simple question may require searching several sources—online catalog, Web list, aggregated database, publisher Web site, internet search engine, and so forth—and considerable knowledge of electronic journals. So much for the simple, known-item search.

This chapter will explore these issues in depth, focusing on the patron's experience in searching for journal literature. The specific objectives of this chapter are as follows:

- Convince the reader that one-stop shopping for journal literature is a worthy goal, with an emphasis on how it meets user needs
- Demonstrate the extent to which this goal can be achieved with current tools and standards
- Explain the challenges and limitations that prevent a library from achieving true one-stop shopping
- Explore what would be needed to bring us closer to this ideal

BACKGROUND: HISTORY AND LITERATURE REVIEW

While this chapter will primarily focus on electronic journals, it is useful to briefly review challenges associated with serials, regardless of format. Serials caused problems in library catalogs before the advent of electronic journals, and these problems continue today, whether or not the serial in question is received in print or electronically. In order to have a serial in a library catalog, one must catalog it, which can be a daunting prospect. Osmus (1996), Cole and Williams (1992) and Williams (1997) provide an overview of serials cataloging issues through the advent of electronic journals in the early 1990's. Once in the catalog, serial records can be difficult for users to find and interpret. Snavely and Clark (1996) provide a clear, readable, and all too accurate view of the pain a library user must endure when using journals in academic libraries. They address a variety of problems with searching for journals in online catalogs, as well as the difficulties users experience when attempting to interpret holdings and locate actual articles. Fescemyer (2005) analyzes both the difficulty finding journals with one-word titles and the complexity of many catalog records for serials, concluding with a plea for single records, shorter displays, consolidated holdings, and consistency across catalogs. According to Shadle (2006), the Functional Requirements for Bibliographic Records (FRBR) standard may provide a way to make it easier for users to find and interpret serial records in library catalogs. Finally, Black (2006) provides an excellent overview of bibliographic control of serials, both print and electronic. As these resources demonstrate, serials are by nature complicated—complicated to catalog, complicated to manage, and complicated to use. The advent of electronic journals has increased the complexity significantly, as explained in the introduction to this chapter.

The management of electronic journals has followed a fairly consistent pattern in most libraries, a pattern that is well documented in the literature. The remainder of this section will provide a brief overview of the history of electronic journal management in libraries, based on a review of the literature and the author's experience. A more detailed literature review covering the early years of electronic journal management, up to the late 1990's, is provided by Copeland (2002), while Jones (2003) provides an exceptionally readable history of e-journal cataloging practices. Several case studies are also available which illustrate the stages of electronic journal management as played out in specific libraries, for example Tobia (2001) and Ferguson, Collins, and Grogg (2006).

When e-journals first became common, libraries typically provided access to them in two ways: via static Web pages and the library catalog. Libraries created one or more Web pages which included links, holdings information, and notes on access. Electronic journals were incorporated into the library catalog, either by adding information about the online version to the bibliographic record for the print version or by creating a new bibliographic record for the online version. As the number of electronic journals grew, however, these two access methods became more time-consuming. They became positively unsustainable upon the advent of two new models for purchasing full text: the Big Deal and aggregated databases. The Big Deal is defined by Frazier (2001) as, "an online aggregation of journals that publishers offer as a one-price, one size fits all package." An aggregated database is defined by Martin and Hoffman as, "A collection of electronic resources (usually full text) from separately issued publications, assembled as a convenience to libraries and other subscribing institutions. JSTOR and LexisNexis are examples of such databases" (2002, p. 64). Around the same time, more publishers began offering selected content free of charge as the open access movement grew. Suddenly libraries had access to many thousands of electronic journals, and, in the case of aggregated databases, with holdings that changed frequently and unpredictably. Static Web pages gave way to Web-enabled databases, which could handle larger numbers of titles more gracefully, and traditional cataloging went by the wayside. Since libraries could no longer provide full cataloging for their electronic

journals, they began limiting the scope of their cataloging in various ways, such as: (1) cataloging only electronic journals for which the library had archival or perpetual access rights (Sennema, 2004); (2) providing only a link to full text with no information on holdings (Ferguson et al., 2006); (3) cataloging only purchased electronic journals, excluding all free titles; (4) excluding titles outside the library's collecting scope; and (5) excluding all titles in aggregated databases. Instead of including these vast numbers of titles in their catalogs, libraries relied increasingly on their Web lists to provide access, or, as Anderson writes, "It was the thousands of constantly fluctuating journal titles available through aggregator databases that caused catalogers to cry 'Uncle!' and yield to the keepers of the lists" (1999, p. 313). Some libraries used electronic journal gateways from their subscription agents to provide access to their electronic journals (Ferguson et al., 2006). In either case, library users now had to look in two places to determine whether or not the library had access to a desired journal: the catalog (for print and some electronic journals) and a Web list (for the full range of electronic offerings).

Libraries were overwhelmed with the effort of managing all these holdings and clearly needed help. In response, a new type of vendor entered the library market—the publication access management service, or PAMS. PAMS are "companies who take on the messy responsibility of figuring out what titles are contained in which aggregator packages, and produce reports for libraries on which titles (and which dates ranges) they therefore have access to" (Jones, 2003, p. 23). Libraries told the PAMS which packages and individual titles they purchased, and the PAMS provided a Web-based database, often offering more advanced features than libraries could implement on their own, for example browsing by subject. But users still had to check in two places to see if the library had access to a desired journal, and the catalog remained incomplete. Chen, et al. summed up the problem well, writing, "Libraries almost universally present some portion of their electronic holdings on Web lists instead of, or in addition to, their catalogs. This trend sets a dubious precedent of dividing the library's holdings between two different sources and possibly complicating matters for its users. To make matters more chaotic, there existed no common agreement among libraries concerning which categories of resources should be listed in the catalog, which in the Web list, and which in both. Conversely, all libraries did list at least some of their electronic resources in their catalogs. No libraries, however, cataloged all of the electronic resources that they hold, with even the most thorough institutions resorting to a collection-level record for databases such as LexisNexis [™]" (Chen, Colgan, Greene, Lowe, & Winke, 2004, p. 175).

Since that article was published, new tools have become available that make it easier for librarians to unify their journal holdings in one source. The first electronic resources management module from an integrated library system vendor debuted in 2004, when Innovative Interfaces released their Electronic Resources Management™ (ERM) product. Since then, other integrated library system vendors have followed suit, providing tools that allow libraries to integrate their electronic resources—including electronic journals—into their integrated library systems and, by extension, into their catalogs. For a behind-the-scenes look at the development of Innovative's ERM product, see Grover and Fons (2004). Tull, Crum, Davis, and Strader (2005) provide a detailed overview of the product itself and how it fits into a library's workflow for managing electronic resources. *Computers in Libraries* offers a buyers guide to these systems that provides an overview of the major products in this category (Meyer, 2005). Meanwhile, PAMS vendors began offering MARC records for electronic journal holdings, allowing libraries to load electronic journal information into their catalogs without cataloging each title individually, and some libraries developed in-house systems to generate MARC records from

their Web lists or from publisher data (Johnson & Manoff, 2003; Mitchell & Surratt, 2005).

What, then, is the status of electronic journal management now, in early 2007? Electronic resource management systems, whether part of an integrated library system or standalone, are being implemented widely, though the cost of these systems is still prohibitive for some libraries. Large aggregated databases and packages of titles from publishers are still being purchased. But new, potentially disruptive changes are occurring that will require yet another shift in the way libraries manage electronic journals. Journal publishing practices are changing as open access becomes more widespread, articles are posted in institutional repositories and other freely accessible systems, and the article rather than the journal becomes the least publishable unit. At the same time, user expectations are heavily conditioned by nonlibrary Web sites such as Amazon™ and Google™. User demand for simpler, more seamless systems is causing libraries to rethink how they deliver resources and services. The remainder of this chapter will explore the extent to which libraries can provide simple, seamless access—one-stop shopping—for their journal collections, analyzing the tools available and the challenges that remain to be addressed.

ONE-STOP SHOPPING: WHY

What is One-Stop Shopping?

The concept of one-stop shopping as used in this chapter refers to a single place for users to look to determine whether or not they have access to a desired article. It does not necessarily mean that all accessible journal holdings are in a single database. Rather, it means that a patron can start looking in a single place and be led seamlessly to all available holdings. After several years of putting electronic holdings in separate Web lists, more and more librarians are recognizing the need for unified access to all serial holdings, regardless of format (paper, electronic) or source (aggregated database, individual subscription, etc.). As Jones writes, "Libraries need a gateway. Or, perhaps more accurately, library users need that gateway, that one entry point into the increasing wealth of information in e-serials (and all things "e") which their library can provide for them. They should not have to fritter away their time trying to figure out which catalog/Website/listing to consult" (2003, p. 24). McCracken emphasizes the importance of including electronic journals from aggregated databases in the library catalog, even though the content is leased rather than owned and changes rapidly. He argues, "What about the customers who lose out if they do not know that a journal is available in a specific database? How many patrons go away empty-handed, when the library is actually already paying for access to the journal? Money—and the patron's time—is regularly wasted in interlibrary loan requests for journals the library does not know it can access electronically" (2004, p. 32).

Why Should Libraries Provide One-Stop Shopping for Journal Information?

Offering one-stop shopping for journal holdings is key to making a library's journal collection user-centered and user-friendly. Dempsey's writings on the role of the library in a network age provide some relevant arguments to support the one-stop shopping concept. According to Dempsey, libraries can make life easier for their users by aggregating supply and demand. One aggregates supply through consolidation, combining lots of materials into one central source. That large central source (Google™, NetFlix™, or a database of journals) then attracts more users than would be attracted by several smaller sources, thereby aggregating demand and making it more likely that each item in the collection will be found by an interested user—or in Ranganathan's words,

"Every book its reader" (Dempsey, 2006; Five laws of library science, 2006). Dempsey then points out that failure to aggregate supply and demand through integrating systems and resources results in higher transaction costs for the user—not necessarily financial costs, but costs in time and effort required to use a complex, poorly-integrated system (2006). If libraries integrate their resources, including information on journal holdings, they help to satisfy another one of Ranganathan's five laws of library science, "Save the time of the user" (Five laws of library science, 2006; Dempsey, 2006). Dempsey further notes that large Web entities such as Google and Amazon further aggregate demand by going out to where their users are, that is, where demand already exists (2006). This argument suggests that the one-stop shopping concept can include making journal holdings accessible to users at the point of need, for example from citation databases. That concept is especially relevant to the role of link resolvers, discussed later in this chapter. Finally, Dempsey reminds librarians that libraries are no longer the only—or even primary—source of information for users, writing, "In our current network environment, libraries compete for scarce attention. This suggests that if the 'library long tail' is to be effectively prospected then the 'cost' of discovering and using library collections and services needs to be as low as possible" (2006).

This notion of competing for scarce attention is supported by current principles of Web usability and the behavior of library users. Steve Krug sums up Web usability principles nicely in the title of his seminal work on usability, *Don't Make Me Think* (2006). Krug emphasizes that users will not devote large amounts of time and effort to learning how systems work. In his words, "If something requires a large investment of time—or looks like it will—it's less likely to be used" (2006, p. 6). He argues that users "don't figure out how things work. We muddle through," because, "It's not important to us" to figure out how the system works (2006, pp. 26-27). Instead, users are conditioned by popular commercial Web sites, especially Google™, which can be used—often effectively—without any instruction at all. Novotny found, "Library catalog users are heavily influenced by trends in Web searching… Both experienced and novice users adopted search strategies more appropriate to Google than to a library catalog" (2004, p. 533). Novotny also found that extensive experience using the Web convinced users that they knew how to search: "A new disincentive to learning is the fact that many searchers believe they are already proficient information seekers. As experienced Web searchers, many new students enter college confident in their own ability to locate information" (2004, p. 530). Similarly, users' experience online fosters a desire for self-sufficiency. According to the 2003 OCLC Environmental Scan, "People of all age groups are spending more time online doing things for themselves" (De Rosa, Dempsey, & Wilson, 2004, p. 5). If users want to be self-sufficient and perceive themselves as proficient searchers, they are unlikely to read instructions or attend bibliographic instruction sessions. Krug's work on Web usability supports this assertion. He explains, "When we're creating sites, we act as though people are going to pore over each page, reading our finely crafted text, figuring out how we've organized things, and weighing their options before deciding which link to click. What they actually do most of the time (if we're lucky) is *glance* at each new page, scan *some* of the text, and click on the first link that catches their interest or vaguely resembles the thing they're looking for. There are usually large parts of the page that they do not even look at" (2006, p. 21).

Yet we know that, at least where journals are concerned, library users do not know enough to use our journal collections to the fullest extent. According to Giles, "Studies have shown that users are really confused, and library catalogs and policies are the culprit. Users do not know the difference between e-journals and aggregator databases (why should they?), and as such will

not understand why some titles available at the library have direct links from the catalog while others don't even appear in the catalog" (2003, p. 41). Usability testing at the Oregon Health & Science University Library suggests that users—even experienced, motivated researchers—will give up quickly if they have difficulty finding a journal (Zeigen, personal communication, October 2006). Librarians may be disheartened by the lack of effort exerted by library users, but "Librarians cannot change user behavior and so need to meet the user" (De Rosa et al., 2004, p. 77).

To sum up the situation with respect to usability and user behavior: Users will not work too hard to learn how to use library systems effectively. They expect them to be self-explanatory and seamless. So, if libraries build complicated systems for their journal collections, with holdings located in multiple places without distinctions that are obvious to the user, users will either not use the collection at all or, more likely, will use only one part of it, potentially missing many useful items. It seems clear, then, that librarians need to provide users with a single source for journals to which they have access, that is, one-stop shopping. But what should that single source be—the catalog, a Web list, or something else? Or can libraries integrate several tools into a seamless system for guiding users to relevant journal literature? The next section examines two common tools—Web lists and the library catalog—to help libraries determine how to provide access to their journal collections. It also discusses the role of the link resolver in providing seamless access to journal holdings from citation databases and other resources not managed by the library.

ONE-STOP SHOPPING: WEB LISTS, THE CATALOG, AND BEYOND

Today libraries have several tools that can facilitate one-stop shopping for journal literature – the catalog, integrated electronic resources management modules, link resolvers, and federated search tools. With these tools, libraries can—and should—provide access to print and electronic holdings, including holdings from aggregated databases and selected free titles, from a single source. The first question to answer, then, is what should this source be—the catalog or a Web list of journal holdings?

As Web lists have gained popularity, the catalog is no longer as prominent as it once was. As Primich and Richardson note, "The ILS is now 'a' resource instead of 'the' resource" (2006, p. 125). The catalog-versus-Web-list debate centers on several issues: usability, staff time, local control, standards and interoperability, and flexibility.

Many libraries have found that users prefer browsing a list of journals to searching the catalog, for example Chrzastojwski (1999); Ferguson, Collins, and Grogg (2006); Zeter, Thunell, and Maguire (2003). Users often prefer the cleaner results provided by a Web list to the complex, often cluttered results one gets from a journal search in most library catalogs. Catalog searches generally produce more results than a similar search in a Web list, and many of those results may be irrelevant, especially if the library catalog does not offer a separate search for journals only. Plus, without a separate search for journals, it becomes extremely difficult to find records for journals with short titles consisting of common words (e.g., *Science* or *Time*). Even with a journals-only search, previous and succeeding titles, alternative or uniform titles that differ only slightly from the main title, and separate records for the same title in different formats (e.g., print, electronic, microform) all produce cluttered lists of results through which a user must wade to find the desired record. Once the user does find the right record, s/he may find that record difficult to interpret. Serial records tend to be long and complex, and the information explaining the details of electronic access is typically buried in notes fields that users rarely see. In fact, Giles found that even an experienced library school student had difficulty interpreting

complicated serial records (2003). These problems with catalog access to serials are not new. Long before electronic journals came along, many libraries maintained printed lists of their serial holdings to make access simpler for users. But the problems have been exacerbated as electronic access has increased the number of journals to which libraries have access, as well as the demand for journal literature, thereby increasing use of the catalog for journals and exposing these problems to wider audiences.

Despite these problems, the catalog offers some significant advantages over Web lists when searching for journals. First, most catalogs offer powerful, sophisticated search interfaces that Web lists cannot match. With the catalog, one can search for journals by subject or corporate author or limit a search in various ways. Plus, catalogs offer much richer data as a target for these searches. For example, "The alphabetical list greatly limits the accessibility that MARC records provide. The 'least effort' way is satisfactory for quick reference, but it allows for no additional access point other than title entry and provides no cross-linking features. It also limits in-house reporting capabilities that can be coded into MARC records" (Bevis & Graham, 2003, p. 116). Michigan State University's browse list includes "no standard cross references," and "the title search capability is limited because the user must enter the exact title" (Zeter et al., 2003, p. 203). According to McCracken, the title list "misses critical access points, from title variations to series names; from publishers to subject headings; from foreign titles to ISSN; and so on. The process for using and searching by all of these access points has already been incorporated into the OPAC, and current A-to-Z title lists do not, unfortunately, take advantage of these access points" (McCracken, 2003, p. 104). Cole offers a detailed explanation of the advantages of catalogs over Web lists for journal searching (2003).

Staff time and effort are also a major concern when considering whether to use a catalog or a

Web list for access to a library's journal collection. As libraries buy more and more big aggregated databases and vendor packages, it is no longer possible to provide individual, full MARC cataloging for every electronic journal the library purchases, let alone relevant free titles. For the titles that do receive individual, full cataloging, expertise in serials cataloging is required. Serials cataloging is a complicated specialty, and many libraries may not have adequate staff skilled in this area. Then there is the need to develop and harmonize local practices for cataloging serials; cataloging and electronic resources staff need to work together to develop procedures for managing electronic titles in the catalog. Conflicts may arise over the scope of the catalog, with some staff wanting to include a broad range of materials, including many free titles, while others wish to limit the number of titles included. Similarly, cataloging rules and practices may conflict with the way that electronic journal providers present their wares, for example regarding whether supplements should be cataloged separately or tacked onto the record for the parent publication. Significant staff time may be required to work through these differences and find workable compromises.

These problems illustrate another weakness of catalogs as tools for managing electronic journals—lack of flexibility. Libraries that use Web lists are not bound by either national or local cataloging policies and practices or by a vendor's product development plans. The design of the Web list can be changed as needs change. The library does not have to lobby a vendor to make needed changes—but of course the library must have adequate technical staff to make changes in-house. Procedures can be changed as needs change (Briscoe, Selden, & Nyberg, 2003). With a Web list, journals can be entered the way providers offer them, independent of how they are offered in print; if a provider offers a supplement under a separate URL, it can receive a separate entry in a Web list, regardless of whether the cataloging rules indicate that it should have one. Web lists,

if well designed, also allow libraries to enter or remove large numbers of titles easily. If they purchase data from a PAMS provider, libraries can easily update holdings information in their Web lists. But as Chrzastowski argues, the catalog is not nimble enough to cope with resources that change so frequently, and "Updating records often becomes secondary to new cataloging pressures" (Chrzastojwski, 1999, p. 318). Similarly, Ferguson, Collins & Grogg argue, "The MARC record lacks the flexibility to adjust to a format as fluid and constantly changing as the e-journal" (2006, p. 32).

On the other hand, MARC records conform to an international standard that is widely supported in the library world. Having records that conform to such this standard supports interoperability and allows libraries to integrate disparate systems more easily. MARC records can be exported, imported into other systems, or converted into XML or Dublin Core with free tools. If the library's integrated library system supports the MARC format for holdings data, serial holdings can be exported and used to populate other systems, for example local holdings records for union listing on OCLC. Conforming to standards, then, limits flexibility while enhancing interoperability.

Despite its many weaknesses, the catalog is the best long-term option for providing access to journal collections. Using the catalog allows libraries to integrate their journal collection with other resources, which can be an advantage to users if the interface is designed to minimize clutter and complexity. When the library uses a separate retrieval system for journals, users have to remember to look in a different place for journals—and they have to know that what they seek is actually a journal. Similarly, the library has to decide what gets included in the journals database—journals, of course, but what about annuals or monographic series that are sometimes cited as journals? Using the catalog as the primary retrieval system for all materials allows the library to avoid making these kinds of distinctions. It also represents a more sustainable choice and a better use of library resources over the long term than does maintaining individual, in-house systems. Staff time and energy are better invested in partnering with vendors to improve the way catalogs manage journals, as the benefits of these partnerships are available to all of a given vendor's customers. In fact, the library catalog seems to have reached a turning point in the last few years. Librarians and vendors are beginning to rethink catalog interfaces in exciting ways. New interfaces are being designed or implemented; see Antelman, Lynema, and Pace for one example (2006). If libraries use their catalogs to manage their entire journal collections, these exciting enhancements should improve access to journal literature considerably. Finally, electronic journals are no longer new, unusual formats that require special treatment. As Anderson notes, libraries used to provide,

Separate lists of new videorecordings or compact discs or computer software as these media were being introduced into library collections. When these were the new 'cutting edge' resources and their numbers were relatively few, public services librarians were eager to promote their use and legitimately concerned that they would be lost in the jungle of the online catalog... As the complexity of maintaining the lists increased, and the glamour of the 'new' media wore off, library staff began to find ways to leverage the online catalog search options. Eventually, the lists were abandoned, and the catalog become the sole method of access for these and other library material. (1999, p. 312)

The time has come for libraries to leverage the catalog to manage electronic journals, and many efforts to do so are already well underway.

Making Catalogs Work for Journal Collections

Libraries have several options for making their catalogs more flexible and user-friendly for journal collections: they can load batches of records, either brief records generated in-house or records obtained from vendors; use electronic resources management systems that integrate with their catalogs; conduct usability studies related to retrieving journal information from their catalogs and use this information to partner with vendors to improve catalog interfaces to journal literature; and use catalog data to create Web lists and other interfaces desired by users.

When individual, full cataloging is not practical, libraries can load batches of records, either brief records generated in-house or records obtained from a vendor. Brief records can be generated from data provided by publishers, aggregators, or PAMS using various software programs (Mitchell & Surratt, 2005). Judicious use of brief records represents a compromise approach, balancing the labor required to create and maintain full catalog records with the need to provide one-stop shopping in the catalog for as many journals as possible. Using brief records allows a library to enter title and holdings information, a level of access similar to that provided by a Web list. Unfortunately, brief records share many of the drawbacks of Web lists, lacking alternate titles, subject headings, and classification information. Because they also lack standard control numbers, for example OCLC numbers, brief records may be problematic in union catalogs which rely on these numbers for matching and overlay. They may also cause problems in other projects that rely on control numbers, for example batch updating union list information. An alternative to brief records is the vendor record. Vendor records can often be obtained from PAMS, integrated library system vendors, or producers of aggregated databases. They usually contain more complete data than brief records, as they are often generated from CONSER records. Many libraries use a "hybrid approach," using records from one or more vendors and/or brief records for some packages and full cataloging for others (Collins, 2005). Decisions are typically based on the nature of the collection (e.g., how rapidly the contents change), selection priority, usage, and so forth.

Another tool to help libraries manage large numbers of electronic titles in the catalog is the electronic resources management system (ERMS). ERM systems are primarily designed to help library staff manage information about electronic resources, but many of them, especially those produced by integrated library system vendors, integrate with library catalogs and provide options for batch loading holdings. For example, using the Electronic Resources Management ™ product from Innovative Interfaces has allowed the Oregon Health & Science University Library to batch load holdings for thousands of journals into its catalog. The library can load delimited text files from publishers, aggregators, and/or PAMS. The load process matches holdings information to existing bibliographic records, or creates new, brief bibliographic records if desired, and it also creates MARC holdings records. Updating holdings is also a batch process. This level of integration allows the library to offer seamless access

Figure 1. Patron view of journal holdings, Oregon Health & Science University Library

LOCATION	CALL #	STATUS
OHSU MAIN--PRINT JOURNALS	V.337-344 1991-94 INDEX	AVAILABLE
OHSU MAIN--PRINT JOURNALS	V.339 APR-JUN 1992	AVAILABLE
OHSU MAIN--PRINT JOURNALS	V.339 JAN-MAR 1992	AVAILABLE
OHSU MAIN--PRINT JOURNALS	V.340 JUL-SEP 1992	AVAILABLE
OHSU MAIN--PRINT JOURNALS	V.340 OCT-DEC 1992	AVAILABLE
OHSU MAIN--PRINT JOURNALS	V.341 APR-JUN 1993	AVAILABLE
OHSU MAIN--PRINT JOURNALS	V.341 JAN-MAR 1993	AVAILABLE
OHSU MAIN--PRINT JOURNALS	V.342 JUL-SEP 1993	AVAILABLE
OHSU MAIN--PRINT JOURNALS	V.342 OCT-DEC 1993	AVAILABLE
OHSU MAIN--PRINT JOURNALS	V.343 APR-JUN 1994	AVAILABLE

via its catalog to many journals without requiring excessive staff time. See Figure 1 for a patron view of holdings from Oregon Health & Science University's integrated ERM module.

The primary drawback of ERM systems is cost. Even though managing electronic resources is now a core function in libraries, adding this functionality to an integrated library system costs extra. As Breeding notes, "The typical library automation environment today, especially for a medium-sized to large academic library, would require an ILS to manage traditional content and a suite of additional products to lend support for electronic content" (2006, p. 28). For more infor-

mation, including a feature-by-feature comparison of nine of these tools, see Meyer (2005).

Batch loading, with or without an ERM system, can help a library to get large numbers of titles into the catalog. But loading holdings into the catalog does not address usability problems associated with library catalogs. Searching for journals in library catalogs remains a frustrating experience for users. What can libraries do to improve this situation? First, libraries can and should do regular usability tests on their catalogs, including journal searches. In some cases, problems can be corrected or ameliorated by changing wording, indexing, or other aspects of the system that are under the

Figure 2. Web list from Oregon Health & Science University Library

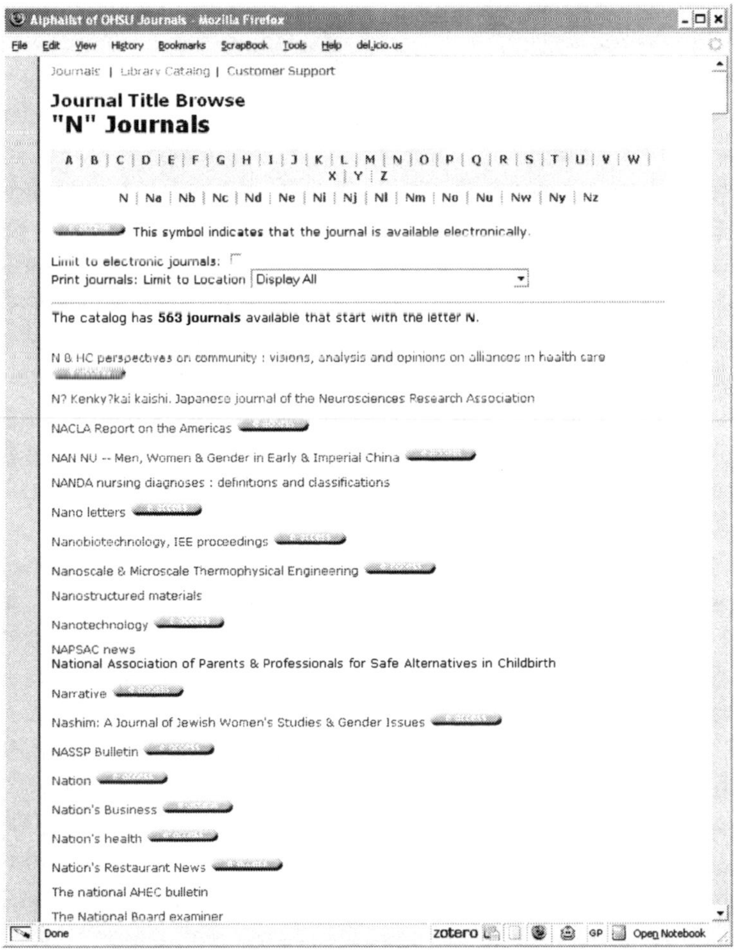

library's control. For example, when the Oregon Health & Science University Library retired its Web list of journals in favor of the catalog, users complained that title searches produced long lists of results with lots of irrelevant entries. Library staff were able to improve the lists of results by changing indexing parameters and adjusting cataloging practices to reduce redundant or unnecessary title added entries in the title index. Other problems will prove to be more intractable. For those, libraries should share the results of usability testing with their catalog vendors, lobby for improvements, beta test new interfaces, and otherwise partner with their vendors to ensure the best access for their users. Many vendors are redesigning their catalog interfaces in response to a spate of criticism—for example Schneider (2006a; 2006b; 2006c) and Tennant (2005)—providing an opportunity for libraries to lobby for changes on behalf of their users.

No matter how much libraries improve their catalogs, some users will likely want to browse rather than search for journal holdings. So, the optimal solution for many libraries is not the catalog *or* a Web list but the catalog *and* a Web list. The key point is to maintain the data in a single place and serve it out in multiple ways. MARC records can be generated from a local database of holdings, and Web lists can be generated from catalog records (Briscoe et al., 2003). The latter option is dependent, of course, on the catalog vendor allowing catalog data to be accessed outside of the standard catalog interface. For an example of a Web list that is generated from and links to catalog data, see Figure 2.

Link Resolvers: One-Stop Shopping Outside of the Catalog?

Having journal holdings integrated in one source—the catalog—is extremely helpful for users searching for journals. But many users begin their searches in article databases, using the catalog or a Web list afterwards to find out which of their desired articles the library can provide. To provide those users with seamless access to these articles—one-stop shopping from article databases—the library needs another tool, the link resolver. The link resolver matches metadata from a citation against a database of the library's holdings, often called a knowledge base, and offers the user a menu of links to full text and/or other services (e.g., a document delivery request form). The link resolver, then, can link the user directly to the desired article or journal from a citation, without requiring the user to visit the library catalog. If all of the library's journal holdings, including those from aggregated databases as well as some free titles, are loaded into the resolver, it can provide another form of one-stop shopping. The situation is complicated, however, by the fact that users are starting their searches in resources the library did not purchase and over which the library has very little, if any, ability to customize—for example Google Scholar™, Windows Live Academic™, and CiteULike™. Further, users may not realize where the library stops and the rest of the online world begins (Manoff, 2000). How can libraries guide a user seamlessly between these non-library sites and the library's resources, without the user having to know how to get to the library's information space? Recent developments with link resolvers may provide an answer. Latent openURLs (Apps & MacIntyre, 2006; Chudnov, Cameron, Frumkin, Singer, & Yee, 2005) are openURLs embedded in Web pages, invisible to human readers but accessible to software applications. A recent example is the COinS specification (Hellman, 2005), which embeds bibliographic metadata in a Web page so that software programs such as browser extensions, for example OpenURL Referrer (2006), can generate openURLs. The user configures the browser extension to point to the desired link resolver and is then directed to library resources to fulfill an information need.

ONE-STOP SHOPPING: WHAT AND HOW

One-stop shopping represents a return to the model libraries have used for decades—library holdings represented in one place (for the most part). But as one looks at the current state of journal literature, one must ask, "What is a library holding?" To which materials should libraries attempt to direct users, and which materials are outside the library's responsibility? To some degree, the answers to these questions will be different for each library, just as collecting scope is different for each library. Then, once one has decided what should be included in the collection, one must figure out how to provide access to those materials, taking into account issues related to bibliographic control, workload, and more. This section will examine the universe of journal literature in detail, discussing both the philosophical and practical issues related to including various categories of journal literature in library collections.

Individual Print and Electronic Journals

Figure 3 attempts to capture the universe of journal literature to which a library may wish to direct users. As one moves from left to right, one moves from materials to which libraries have traditionally provided access, and for which current tools work well, to materials that are new to the library's purview and more difficult to manage. Print journals, then, are at the far left, along with their direct electronic counterparts, individual electronic journals with archival rights. The term "individual e-journals" refers to electronic journals that are selected and purchased in ways similar to print journals, that is individually or in small packages, and which are essentially electronic copies of their print counterparts. If the library has perpetual access and/or archival rights, the library retains access to subscribed materials even after the subscription has ended; in essence, the library "owns" these titles. By contrast, if the library does not hold archival rights, as in the next oval in Figure 3, access to all volumes is lost when the subscription is canceled. Current integrated library systems can handle individual print and electronic titles fairly well, and the effort required to provide access to these materials is usually manageable.

"Big Deals," Aggregated Databases, and Free Titles

Beginning with the next level, big deals and aggregated databases, managing journal holdings becomes more challenging. Both "big deals" and aggregated databases often include large numbers of titles, including some that the library would not have selected individually. Likewise, as the open access movement has grown, many publishers offer at least some journal content free of charge.

Figure 3. The universe of journal literature (graphic by Laura Zeigen; used with permission)

Sometimes entire journals are free (e.g., titles in Biomed Central). In other cases, publishers restrict access to the most current content but offer older content free, or they offer certain journals free for a limited time. According to Hood and Howard, "The best way to add value to open access journals is by cataloging and maintaining open access bibliographic records in our catalogs... Adding these records increases the currency and relevance of the catalog, encourages access to e-resources through the OPAC rather than separately maintained utilities, and legitimizes 'freely available' resources" (2006, p. 250). With batch loading via an ERM system, vendor records, or other means, aggregated databases and other large packages can be managed in the catalog, but libraries must overcome significant challenges and make compromises to manage these titles successfully.

There are several barriers to managing aggregated databases and groups of free titles in the catalog. First, it can be challenging to get current, reliable, usable data about availability and holdings and to keep this data current and accurate. As McCracken explains,

Most aggregators have devoted the majority of their efforts to improving access, database management, marketing, usability, and other important issues. Relatively little attention has been paid to the quality of the title lists most aggregators generate, and this is a shame. Title lists are rife with invalid ISSNs. Notes of title changes, when they appear, rarely include a changed ISSN. Title changes are often absorbed into holdings notes for the new title, leaving little or no indication of holdings under the previous title. Though librarians catalog serials using a standard of successive entry—with a separate entry for each significant version of the title—aggregators often tend to list their journals using a modified form of latest entry, usually citing just the most recent version of the title. (2003, p. 106)

Free titles also can be difficult to track unless the library relies on sites or services that aggregate free titles, for example the Directory of Open Access Journals or a PAMS vendor. With free titles, then, the library is often dealing with what are essentially aggregated collections. Holdings information for the titles in these collections also must be kept up-to-date with whatever mechanisms the library employs for loading and maintaining electronic holdings data. Aggregated databases tend to have volatile contents, with titles appearing and disappearing and years of coverage changing frequently. Similarly, some free titles may be unstable, for example titles offered free for a limited time, yet may be of great value to library users. The library must determine whether or not it can get reliable information about these titles and manage them efficiently enough to make the benefit to users worth the staff time required.

Large packages of electronic holdings—whether purchased or free—often include titles peripheral to the library's collection. Manoff writes,

The more we purchase databases of electronic journals or compilations of electronic text or data, the fewer choices we have about the specific documents or information we acquire. We buy the whole package or none of it. The larger the package, the more likely it is that it will contain a considerable amount of material that we would not otherwise have chosen. It is also more likely that it will duplicate some material that we receive from other sources. (2000, pp. 859-860)

For both aggregated databases and collections of free titles, the library must consider whether to provide access to selected titles in these packages or all of them. To do so, the library must weigh several challenging philosophical issues, as well as significant practical constraints. Libraries often use a variety of criteria to decide which of these titles to include in their collections, including the scope of the collection and user demand.

Some libraries choose to catalog only those titles for which they hold archival rights (Sennema, 2004), whether the titles are part of a package or purchased individually. Carstens and Buchanan argue for a traditional model of selection based on user needs, taking a very broad view of the types of materials to include:

The concept of collection has always included the physical items held by the library. Most librarians now include online subscription databases and paid electronic journals within their concept of the collection. However, the definition should be extended to include the free Web sites included in the catalog, information available through a consortium, and perhaps even those resources available through the library's document delivery services. What will make any of these information resources 'part of the collection' is the fact that the library specifically selects them because of their value to the library's clientele and the fact that the library is prepared to make them available. (2004, p. 40)

Their argument suggests that resources should be made accessible to users if they fit into the library's collecting scope, whether or not those resources are purchased. Another possible criterion is usage: titles that are heavily used, whether in print or via interlibrary loan requests, are good candidates for inclusion. Interestingly, however, the Oregon Health & Science University Library has found that titles considered in-scope are not necessarily the most heavily used. For example, in the 2005-2006 academic year, the ninth-most-popular title in Oregon Health & Science University's EBSCOHost databases—out of over 11,000—was *People*™ magazine. Yet it would be difficult to argue that *People*™ fits in the collecting scope of a biomedical library. Further, there is a relationship between usage and representation in the library's catalog or other systems. Many users do not request articles via interlibrary loan. If those users do not know that a title is available

to them, free or otherwise, they will not use it.

Though these philosophical issues can produce interesting discussions, it is often the practical considerations—specifically, workload constraints—that determine how libraries manage these large collections of electronic holdings. With batch loading tools, it is much easier to load records for an entire package than it is to pick and choose specific titles. Also, since aggregated databases and collections of free titles are quite volatile, any selection done initially would have to be repeated each time an updated list of titles and holdings was received. So, libraries that purchase big packages have little choice but to acquire materials that are out of scope or that duplicate material already in the collection. Yet loading large numbers of out-of-scope titles clutters the catalog, thereby decreasing usability.

Articles: Free and Pay-Per-Download

The outermost two categories of material, free articles and articles available for a fee, present significant challenges for libraries, because the unit to be controlled is not the journal but the article. Free articles are distinguished from free journals in that with free articles, one cannot assume that a whole journal, or even a whole issue, is freely available. Free articles are becoming more and more common. Some publishers allow authors to pay a fee to allow an article to be available free to all users, while other publishers allow authors to deposit copies of their work in institutional or other repositories such as PubMed Central. Individual articles often are also available for paid download from journal Web sites or document delivery services. In some cases, libraries are granted a set number of free downloads from a certain publisher as part of a package purchase. All of these possibilities present useful options for library users. The article a user wants may be available free of charge, but the user (or the library) may pay for an interlibrary loan, because the library lacks systems that can easily locate these free articles.

Historically libraries have not cataloged articles, leaving that activity to indexing and abstracting databases, but libraries may no longer be able to avoid providing bibliographic control at the article level. The 2003 OCLC Environmental Scan notes a trend toward disaggregation, with articles replacing journals as the least publishable unit, and microcontent becoming a desired commodity. "Increasingly, the information seeker doesn't care what the original container looked like, and wants to be able to use this microcontent immediately… Content is disaggregated from its original container" (De Rosa et al., 2004, p. 100). Because current library systems are designed to manage journals, not articles, however, directing users to these articles seamlessly is extremely difficult, if not impossible. If libraries include records in their catalogs for every journal for which some free content is available, they will have to manage many, many more titles. Constructing detailed, accurate holdings statements would not be possible, making it difficult to communicate to users which articles they could expect to access. Link resolvers also do not handle these materials gracefully. Since holdings are not consistent, they cannot be loaded into the resolver's knowledge base. No centralized database of article metadata exists for free articles in various repositories. Hence the link resolver could only offer links to individual repositories. The list of links could get quite long and confusing, and the user could potentially click on each one, only to find out that the article is not available free anywhere. Federated search tools could also provide access to this material, especially if metadata from many repositories could be harvested or otherwise consolidated.

Articles that can be downloaded for a fee also present challenges for libraries. Large document delivery services offer articles from many different journals. Users could be directed to these services via a link resolver, with either the user or the library's document delivery department paying for the service. But in some cases, the library may have a number of free downloads (sometimes called tokens) available as part of a package deal with a publisher. How can these free downloads be presented to the user? The University of Tennessee Libraries created brief bibliographic records for journals available to their users only through paid download or with tokens. They found that use of these titles, as well as those they actually subscribed to, doubled when they were represented in the catalog (Johnson & Manoff, 2003). The Oregon Health & Science University Library used a different tool to provide access to some of this material. As part of its contract with a large publisher, the library received a set number of tokens, each one allowing a download from a title offered by that publisher but to which the library did not subscribe. The library loaded holdings data for these titles into its link resolver; once all the tokens had been used, the titles were deactivated in the link resolver.

ONE-STOP SHOPPING: ONE LIBRARY'S EXPERIENCE

While previous sections have mentioned the Oregon Health & Science University's efforts to provide one-stop shopping for journal literature, this section will briefly summarize that experience. OHSU's implementation should be viewed not as a model to follow but rather as a real-life, imperfect example illustrating the concepts presented in this chapter.

Like many libraries, OHSU began with a Web-based list of electronic journals in the late 1990s. When a journal was added to the page, a link was also added to the catalog record for the title. As the number of electronic journals grew, the Web pages became unmanageably long. When the library purchased a suite of full-text databases from EBSCOHost™—thereby gaining about 11,000 new electronic journals—the static Web pages were retired in favor of a Web-based database. Aggregated and free titles were not added to the catalog, so patrons and staff now had to look in two places to see if they had access to a given article. Both users and staff began to complain, so library staff looked for ways to restore one-stop shopping for journal holdings.

In 2003, the library agreed to beta-test the new Electronic Resources Management™ (ERM) product from Innovative Interfaces, Inc., in the hope that all journal holdings could be included in the catalog once again. This module provides the ability to load delimited text or XML files of journal holdings in batches, creating MARC holdings records and attaching them to existing bibliographic records or creating brief bibliographic records as needed. In addition, the ERM module populates a database of holdings, which is also used by the library's link resolver (Web-Bridge™ from Innovative Interfaces, Inc.) as a knowledge base. With these new capabilities, the library was able to load holdings from aggregated collections into the catalog, along with holdings for some free titles. The OHSU Library purchases holdings data for collections of free titles (e.g., Directory of Open Access Journals, PubMed Central) from EBSCO A to Z™. Some of these holdings have been loaded into the catalog, with others to follow later in 2007. The OHSU Library is also considering creating brief catalog records for selected journals with articles available for a fee, as well as offering access to these articles via the library's link resolver. The OHSU Library has not yet found a way to provide seamless access to free articles.

Using the catalog plus Innovative's ERM module, the OHSU Library is able to provide one-stop shopping for print journal holdings, individual electronic journals, some journals from aggregated collections, and some free journals. Holdings for all versions of a journal, print and electronic, are consolidated on a single bibliographic record, as shown in Figure 1. Because all of this data is stored in the catalog, which uses an Oracle database, the library is able to provide browsing by title, as shown in Figure 2, by using SQL to query the database and Cold Fusion™

to display the query results. The library had to make some compromises, however, to manage workload. Titles from aggregated databases are loaded into the catalog only if they have an ISSN. The ERM module will match incoming holdings to existing bibliographic records based on title as well as ISSN, but title matches often result in holdings attached to the wrong bibliographic record. Rather than clean up mismatches from every load, library staff remove all titles lacking an ISSN from the file of holdings data prior to load. Library staff rarely add free titles to the catalog, unless they are included in a package of data provided by EBSCO A to Z™. It simply takes too much time to maintain accurate holdings data for individual free titles. The library also does not provide full cataloging for all journals in its catalog. Instead, the library relies on brief bibliographic records, created by the ERM module, for two categories of titles: free titles and titles from aggregated databases, unless a record for the title already exists in the catalog. These brief records provide limited access, as they can be retrieved by title, ISSN, or keyword searches only. See Figure 4 for an example of a brief record created by the ERM module.

Despite these compromises, consolidating journal information in the catalog has simplified access to journal literature for patrons and staff alike.

FUTURE TRENDS

Several emerging trends bode well for seamless access to journal literature. First, in recent years library catalogs have come under heavy criticism for being old-fashioned, difficult to use, and vastly inferior to commercial retrieval systems such as Google™ and Amazon™. New discovery platforms with faceted searching, relevance ranking, and other features borrowed from the commercial Web should make all library resources—including journals—easier to find. These new features

Figure 4. Brief bibliographic record from Oregon Health & Science University Library

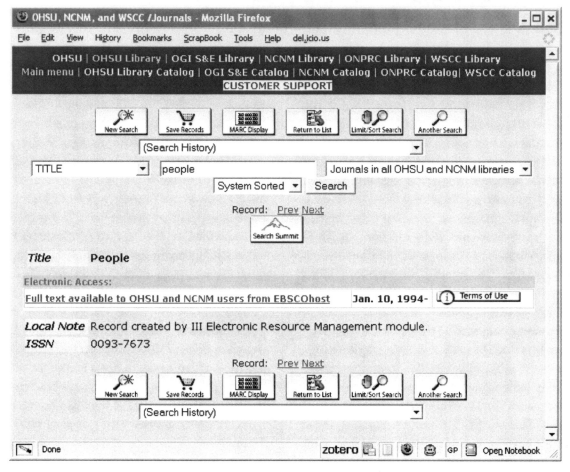

will likely rely heavily on the richness of MARC data to function well, however, which may mean that journals represented only by brief records will not be found as easily by users. Some of the proposed discovery layers (e.g., Encore from Innovative Interfaces, Inc.) incorporate federated searching to enhance results from the library catalog. The NISO MetaSearch Initiative (*NISO MetaSearch initiative,* 2005) should make this technology more effective with a broader range of resources, helping to bridge the gap between what is generally included in a library catalog and what is not (e.g., articles). This notion of a discovery layer is part of a larger movement to bury system complexity behind the scenes, rec-

ognizing the "don't make me think" principle of Web usability discussed earlier in this chapter. Researchers such as Dempsey advocate moving a user seamlessly from discovery to delivery, providing information at the point of need to allow the user to make choices without having to understand much of anything about how library systems work (Dempsey, 2006). Some proposed models include revamping document delivery to include a variety of options, including purchases from commercial services such as Amazon™ (Dempsey, 2006). If that can be done gracefully, users can be linked seamlessly to articles, regardless of whether or not they are part of the library's collection.

If this model of seamless document delivery is to include free articles—as it certainly should—metadata about these articles needs to be harvested and consolidated into centralized repositories that can be queried by federated search tools and link resolvers. Existing standards for metadata harvesting should be adequate to support this type of centralization, which would allow libraries and their users to benefit greatly from the growing open access movement. In order for link resolvers to fit the "don't make me think" model of Web usability, however, they need to be able to query various data sources automatically, behind the scenes, and offer the user a menu of links based on what is actually available. Otherwise, users will remain frustrated with what they see as the resolver's failure, when in fact the desired material is not available in a given location. This functionality is currently available for querying knowledge bases of library holdings, but it does not yet exist for querying data repositories outside the purview of the library.

Emerging standards such as COinS can also help bridge the gap between library systems and the rest of the online world. In order for a standard such as COinS to be truly effective, however, users will have to be connected seamlessly to the appropriate link resolver. They cannot be expected to know the address of their library's link resolver at the point of need. The OCLC OpenURL Resolver Registry (2006), designed to direct users to an appropriate link resolver based on IP address, should address this issue. In the future, one would hope that the process would be handled automatically by the software that processes the COinS.

CONCLUSION

The world of journal literature has changed dramatically in the last decade and continues to change rapidly. To respond to these changes effectively, libraries should focus on the needs of users and find ways to make journal literature more easily accessible. A key component in that vision is providing one-stop shopping for as many relevant journals as possible, both via the library catalog and at the point of need via a link resolver. Currently libraries can provide one-stop shopping for print and electronic journals, including titles from aggregated databases, as well as some free titles. But this vision often must be compromised as libraries weigh benefits to users against staff time and resources required to deliver all relevant journal information to their users. Meanwhile, providing access to individual articles, whether free or available for paid download, remains the most challenging aspect of the one-stop-shopping ideal. So, libraries cannot provide complete one-stop shopping for all journal literature of interest to their users. But they can provide simplified access to some of it and work with vendors and standards organizations to facilitate access to the rest. Library users deserve nothing less.

REFERENCES

Anderson, B. (1999). Web lists or OPACs: Can we have our cake and eat it, too? *Library Computing, 18*(4), 312-316.

Antelman, K., Lynema, E., & Pace, A. K. (2006). Toward a twenty-first century library catalog. *Information Technology and Libraries, 25*(3), 128-139.

Apps, A., & MacIntyre, R. (2006, November 9). Why OpenURL? *D-Lib Magazine, 12*(5).

Bevis, M. D., & Graham, J. B. (2003). The evolution of an integrated electronic journals collection. *Journal of Academic Librarianship, 24*(2), 115-119.

Black, S. (2006). Bibliographic control of serials. *Serials in libraries: Issues and practices* (pp. 83-102). Westport, CT: Libraries Unlimited.

Breeding, M. (2006). Musings on the state of the ILS in 2006. *Computers in Libraries, 26*(3), 26-28.

Briscoe, G., Selden, K., & Nyberg, C. R. (2003). The catalog vs. the home page? Best practices in connecting to online resources. *Law Library Journal, 95*(2), 151-174.

Carstens, T., & Buchanan, H. (2004). The future of the catalog: A user-friendly academic search engine. *Technical Services Quarterly, 22*(2), 37-47.

Chen, X., Colgan, L., Greene, C., Lowe, E., & Winke, C. (2004). E-resource cataloging practices: A survey of academic libraries and consortia. *Serials Librarian, 47*(1/2), 153-179.

Chrzastojwski, T. E. (1999). E-journal access: The online catalog (856 field), web lists, and "the principle of least effort". *Library Computing, 18*(4), 317-322.

Chudnov, D., Cameron, R., Frumkin, J., Singer, R., & Yee, R. (2005, May 24). Opening up OpenURLs with autodiscovery. *Ariadne* (43). Retrieved November 18, 2007, from http://www.ariadne.ac.uk/issue43/chudnov/

Cole, J. (2003). Impacts of the abandonment of catalog records for electronic serials. *The Serials Librarian, 45*(1), 27-33.

Cole, Jim E. & Williams, J. W. (1992). *Serials cataloging: Modern perspectives and international developments.* New York: Haworth Press.

Collins, M. (2005). The effects of e-journal management tools and services on serials cataloging. *Serials Review, 31*(4), 291-297.

Copeland, A. W. (2002). E-serials cataloging in the 1990s: A review of the literature. *The Serials Librarian, 41*(3/4), 7-29.

De Rosa, C., Dempsey, L., & Wilson, A. (2004). *The 2003 OCLC environmental scan: Pattern recognition: A report to the OCLC membership.*

Dublin, OH: OCLC Online Computer Library Center. Retrieved November 18, 2007, from http://www.oclc.org/reports/escan/

Dempsey, L. (2006). Libraries and the long tail: Some thoughts about libraries in a network age. *D-Lib Magazine, 12*(4). Retrieved November 18, 2007, from http://www.dlib.org/dlib/april06/dempsey/04dempsey.html

Ferguson, C. L., Collins, M. D. D., & Grogg, J. E. (2006). Finding the perfect e-journal access solution... the hard way. *Technical Services Quarterly, 23*(4), 27-50.

Fescemyer, K. (2005). Serials clutter in online catalogs. *Serials Review, 31*(1), 14-19.

Frazier, K. (2001). The librarians' dilemma: Contemplating the costs of the "big deal". *D-Lib Magazine, 7*(3). Retrieved November 18, 2007, from http://www.dlib.org/dlib/march01/frazier/03frazier.html

Giles, V. (2003). Single or multiple records for print and electronic serials titles: When less is more (more or less). *The Serials Librarian, 45*(1), 35-45.

Grover, D., & Fons, T. (2004). The innovative electronic resource management system: A development partnership. *Serials Review, 30*(2), 110-116.

Hellman, E. (2005). OpenURL COinS: A convention to embed bibliographic metadata in HTML. Retrieved November 18, 2007, from http://ocoins.info/

Hood, A., & Howard, M. (2006). Adding value to the catalog in an open access world. *The Serials Librarian, 50*(3/4), 249-252.

Johnson, K., & Manoff, M. (2003). Report of the death of the catalog is greatly exaggerated: The E-journal access journey at the University of Tennessee. *The Serials Librarian, 44*(3/4), 285-292.

Jones, W. (2003). A personal mini-history of e-serials cataloging. *The Serials Librarian, 43*(3), 21-24.

Krug, S. (2006). *Don't make me think: A common sense approach to web usability* (2nd ed.). Berkeley, CA: New Riders.

Manoff, M. (2000). Hybridity, mutability, multiplicity: Theorizing electronic library collections. *Library Trends, 49*(1), 857-876.

Martin, C. K., & Hoffman, P. S. (2002). Do we catalog or not? How research libraries provide bibliographic access to electronic journals in aggregated databases. *The Serials Librarian, 43*(1), 61-77.

McCracken, P. (2003). Beyond title lists: Incorporating ejournals into the OPAC. *The Serials Librarian, 45*(3), 101-108.

McCracken, P. (2004). The OPAC reborn. *Library Journal NetConnect, 129*, 32.

Meyer, S. (2005). Helping you buy: Electronic resource management systems. *Computers in Libraries, 25*(10), 19-23.

Mitchell, A. M., & Surratt, B. E. (2005). *Cataloging and organizing digital resources : A how-to-do-it manual for librarians.* New York: Neal-Schuman Publishers.

NISO MetaSearch initiative (2005). Retrieved November 18, 2007, from http://www.niso.org/committees/MS_initiative.html

Novotny, E. (2004). I don't think I click: A protocol analysis study of use of a library online catalog in the internet age. *College & Research Libraries, 65*(6), 525-537.

OCLC OpenURL resolver registry (2006). Retrieved November 18, 2007, from http://www.oclc.org/productworks/urlresolver.htm

OpenURL referrer (2006). Dublin, OH: OCLC Openly Informatics. Retrieved November 18, 2007, from http://www.openly.com/openurlref/

Osmus, L. L. (1996). The transformation of serials cataloging 1965-1990. *Technical services management, 1965-1990.* (pp. 171-190). Haworth Press.

Primich, T., & Richardson, C. (2006). The integrated library system: From innovation to relegation to innovation again. In A. Fenner (Ed.), *Integrating print and digital resources in library collections* (pp. 119-133). New York: Haworth Press.

Schneider, K. G. (2006a). How OPACs suck, Part 1: Relevance rank (or the lack of it). Retrieved November 18, 2007, from http://www.techsource.ala.org/blog/2006/03/how-opacs-suck-part-1-relevance-rank-or-the-lack-of-it.html

Schneider, K. G. (2006b). How OPACs suck, Part 2: The checklist of shame. Retrieved November 18, 2007, from http://www.techsource.ala.org/blog/2006/04/how-opacs-suck-part-2-the-checklist-of-shame.html

Schneider, K. G. (2006c). How OPACs suck, Part 3: The big picture. Retrieved November 18, 2007, from http://www.techsource.ala.org/blog/2006/05/how-opacs-suck-part-3-the-big-picture.html

Sennema, G. (2004). Our e-journal journey: Where to next? *Serials Librarian, 47*(3), 35-43.

Shadle, S. (2006). FRBR and serials: An overview and analysis. *The Serials Librarian, 50*(1/2), 83-103.

Snavely, L., & Clark, K. (1996). What users really think: How they see and find serials in the arts and sciences. *Library Resources & Technical Services 40*, 49-51.

Tennant, R. (2005). Lipstick on a pig. *Library Journal, 130*(7), 34.

Tobia, R. C. (2001). Electronic journals: Experiences of an academic health sciences library. *Serials Review, 27*(1), 3-17.

Tull, L., Crum, J., Davis, T., & Strader, C. R. (2005). Integrating and streamlining electronic resources workflows via innovative's electronic resource management. *Serials Librarian, 47*(4), 103-124.

Wikipedia. (2006). Five laws of library science. Retrieved November 18, 2007, from http://en.wikipedia.org/wiki/Five_laws_of_library_science

Williams, J. W. (1997). Serials cataloging, 1991-1996: A review. *The Serials Librarian, 32*(1-2), 3-26.

Zeter, M. J., Thunell, A., & Maguire, J. (2003). Success in searching for serials: What is the MAGIC solution? *Serials Librarian, 44*(3/4), 201-207.

Chapter XIII
Beyond OpenURL:
Technologies for Linking Library Resources

George Boston
Western Michigan University, USA

Randle J. Gedeon
Western Michigan University, USA

ABSTRACT

This chapter provides a general overview of the development and implementation of existing techniques for the reference linking of scholarly research materials, additionally, some of the new techniques designed for advanced linking are described. Also presented are several new technologies currently under development, with an eye toward enhancing resource discovery and the interlinking of resources. The progress of computer technology, the adoption of those technologies by the information consumer, and the implementation of Web 2.0 and Library 2.0 tools to existing resources have combined in opening up new avenues of linking previously isolated resources together. Information professionals must come to appreciate and apply these new techniques and in doing so will provide library patrons with a more user friendly and thorough research experience.

INTRODUCTION

The ready availability of Internet resources has revolutionized the research process, richly enhancing resource discovery and being presented with links to related subject matter, with the major benefit coming from the convenience of performing research in a virtual environment. Initially, Internet based resources were located at static URLs on servers, with established links pointing toward these addresses. When the addresses of these resources changed through relocation to a new server or site redesign these connections were broken, necessitating frequent verification and updating, highlighting the need for more reliable forms of linking these resources together. Several techniques have been introduced in a search to resolve this dilemma, culminating in the digital object identifier protocol and the present openURL standard.

The continuing introduction of new computer technology, an increasing quantity of information, and the availability and use of new multimedia formats further illustrate the need for the continuing improvement of linking technologies. This chapter explores the development and implementation of linking standards, examines the practices of today and reviews some of the enhanced linking technologies currently under development with a design for meeting future challenges (Frick, Duncan, & Walsh, 2005).

EARLY LINKING PROTOCOLS AND THE APPROPRIATE COPY PROBLEM

A central concern for all types of linking initiatives focuses on directing users to accessible and licensed material. In order to address the problem of linking to the "appropriate copy," several proprietary and provider specific linking programs were initiated. In these instances, a subscriber indicates to a database vendor the accessible resources for that given institution. The vendor then applies that information using proprietary programming providing outbound links to the appropriate copy. These technologies present the user with reliable context sensitive links from abstracting and indexing databases to an institution's subscribed resources.

Examples of vendor supplied context sensitive linking products include: Ebsco's SmartLinks, the Institute of Physics' HyperCite, BioMednet's Bundled Link, OVID's OpenLinks and Silverplatter's SilverLinker products. Also, several publishers provide proprietary "link-to-services" such as Academic Press, the American Physical Society, Elsevier, and UMI's sitebuilder. Applying these services allows for context sensitive linking to the appropriate copy. The appropriate copy problem can be addressed by using the linking to a

library holding by means of a publisher service, like Silverlinker, or a link resolver, such as SFX, based on technology developed by Herbert Van De Sompel. (Grogg & Tenopir, 2000) However, with the increasing number of electronic resources available, maintaining these systems increasingly have become problematic.

At the same time, publishers and providers were working on providing bidirectional-linking services. Beginning in 1997, one of the first efforts for providing outbound linking to related resources began with the Chemical Abstracts Service's Chemport Connection http://www.chemport.org/. Several publishers and content providers followed by offering inbound links to CAS under the name "ChemPort Reference Linking Service" (Grogg, 2004). The Web of Science aggregator from the Institute for Scientific Information offers both bidirectional linking between web of science records and content from selected publishers. Openly Informatics also provides an interpublisher linking solution called "Scholarly Link Specification Framework."

While not providing the standards based linking protocol the openURL would later become, these services were a precursor of the openURL and basically solved the appropriate copy problem.

OPENURL AND DOI: THE PRESENT STANDARDS

Two technologies widely recognized today for solving the problems associated with reference linking are the openURL and the digital object identifier (DOI), with both of these technologies providing a means for dynamically linking electronic resources.

The earliest proprietary linking systems required extensive maintenance and formal inter-publisher agreements. These particular problems were remedied by the Publishers International Linking Association in 2000 through the work of the CrossRef Initiative. The CrossRef system uses digital object identifiers (DOIs), which are unique identifiers tagged to the specific article's metadata. The DOI of an Internet resource is permanent, so that the content can always be located, even if the URL changes. The DOI is governed by the International DOI Foundation and managed by CrossRef organization which operates a citation linking system requiring providers to deposit DOIs and associated citation metadata. This system allows a researcher to click on a reference citation on one publisher's platform and then directly link to the cited content on another publisher's platform. Implementation of the DOI ensures permanent interpublisher links (Grogg & Tenopir, 2000). In 2005, the syntax for the digital object identifier was standardized by the National Information Standards Organization as ANSI standard Z39.84.

However, this reliance upon DOI linking potentially presented drawbacks for the user. When a user clicks on a link in a reference list of a journal published by a participating publisher, he or she goes to the publisher's Web site, where access is determined by subscription. In some instances, full text access may not be available directly from the publisher but through another route (an aggregator, secondary provider, or an institutional repository). Currently, the CrossRef link only takes the user to the publisher-supplied full text, not necessarily to the "appropriate copy." The DOI reliably identifies where a resource is located, however it may not identify whether the user has full text rights or not. CrossRef's ability to link the user to the full text is extremely limited in that it can only direct the user to the URLs supplied by CrossRef members. CrossRef alone cannot identify those resources to which the library subscribes (Grogg, 2005).

Beginning in the late 1990's, research was conducted examining the possibility of using journal metadata in creating a dynamic link to the resource. Beit-Arie, Oren, Caplan, Priscilla, et al., (2001) Herbert Van de Sompel, and oth-

ers developed the ideas behind the openURL. This open source means of reference linking depended on a link resolver to retrieve resources. The resolver could then be populated with those resources where full text rights exist. For example, when an article search is conducted within an openURL enabled database, the search results will display outgoing links to the relevant openURL resolver. Thus, in this case the database is acting as an "openURL source." Conversely, an "openURL target" refers to the incoming request to a specific electronic resource. Then, when an incoming request to the openURL link resolver arrives it takes into account access rights and directs users to the appropriate full text source. The openURL protocol is now standardized by the National Information Standards Organization as ANSI standard Z39.88. OpenURL version 0.1 has been superseded by version 1.0 furthering the development of context-sensitive linking (Grogg, Development, 2006).

Increasingly, the openURL framework is being marketed by providers. Taking advantage of this opportunity link resolving software from Ex-Libris (SFX), Endeavor (LinkFinder) and others become more available and are being widely adopted. Both of these standards are widely used to provide context sensitive linking in a cross-publisher setting, as well as from libraries to content providers. In addition to linking users with the appropriate full text resource, these systems can also provide information about related resources such as the availability of print resources or perhaps directing users to interlibrary loan services if the resource is not available. The simplicity and transparency in access offered by openURL resolvers helps keep patrons happy and helps keep them coming back (McElfresh, 2005).

THE NEED FOR BETTER LINKING PROCEDURES

The use of the openURL standard combined with the added features of link resolving technology simplifies and improves context sensitive linking between resources. As a result, various link-resolving technologies have been adopted in academic libraries (see Figure 1 for a comparison of the request flow for various linking services).

The development of these advanced tools facilitates linking between resources, creating a more personalized and user-friendly approach enhancing interoperability and resource discovery in a scholarly environment. However, as the advantages of these new linking tools have become apparent these new technologies have been adopted by a growing number of libraries and scholarly research providers as well as commercial enterprises.

LINKING INFORMATION TO USERS

The process of scholarly research and resource discovery continues to evolve. The combination of link resolving technology and the openURL standard have substantively solved the problems arising from linking to nonauthenticated versions of the material. The combination of these elements makes it possible to provide access to the appropriate copy of the material requested, as well as providing links to related resources. Secondly, the DOI has solved problems associated with interpublisher linking by providing a standard protocol linking to a publisher's content.

While the techniques of recalling information have been addressed, the process of resource

Figure 1. Request flow comparison of linking services

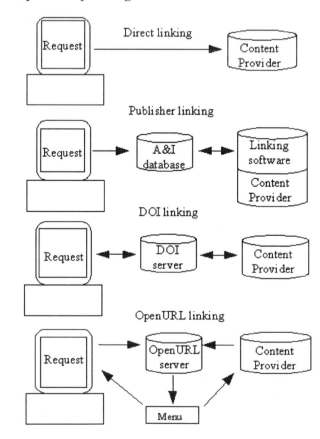

discovery also involves recognizing the existence of other information sources and providing the user with appropriate links to these resources. In accomplishing this, new techniques need to be created and applied to existing research tools; thereby providing links to related content and also providing users with means to access and utilize these materials. This is accomplished with the combination of advanced linking procedures along with the innovative use of computer software technology and programming.

Current Linking Applications

Vendors offer similar functionality regarding linking to external and internal content, with generally only minor variations. Researchers are often presented with multiple linking options within an article or citation that may include: (1) links to the full-text through a cited reference or the reference list; (2) links to other proprietary services such as CrossRef or Scopus; and (3) possibly navigational links within an article or citation taking the researcher to appendices, charts and tables, or possibly an outline of the article presented as a series of links allowing the researcher to quickly move through an article.

Innovative forms of linking designed to address these linking problems to related materials have been introduced by content providers, with some examples including: forward, citation, dynamic, and conceptual or associative linking.

Forward linking, or "cited-by" links provide researchers with links to articles citing the retrieved article and linking users to more recent articles on the same topic. This concept was first introduced in 2004 by CrossRef and Atypon and requires that publisher participants deposit citation metadata with CrossRef, allowing them to construct the appropriate links. This kind of linking has been accepted and adopted by several providers including: the American Physical Society, BioOne, Blackwell's Synergy, the Institute of Physics, and others.

The article *Five Futures for Academic Medicine* in the journal PloS Medicine (DOI http://dx.doi.org/10.1371/journal.pmed.0020207) illustrates an example of forward linking. In this instance, a link is provided to a list of seven other articles citing this particular article (Awasthi, Beardmore, Clark et al., 2005).

Conversely, citation or "backward" linking provides the user with links to items containing material cited by a particular article. Examples of forward and citation linking are illustrated by Blackwell's Synergy product. Articles within that product provide both forward and citation links to the "appropriate copy" via an openURL link resolver.

Another form of linking gaining adoption is dynamic linking, a method employing a computer algorithm to generate links to related resources. Applying this algorithm is a basic concept of various link resolver technologies. In this case, when the link resolver receives a request the metadata is analyzed and links are constructed in a dynamic environment providing the user with access to the material as well as links to relevant research resources such as: local resources, dictionary or thesauri entries, or possibly subject encyclopedias. Using the article listed above as an example, we can see that it provides a link to associated PubMed and the Google Scholar records.

Conceptual or associative linking has also been introduced. This linking procedure uses thesauri data for providing links to further information on related subjects, thus going one step further than dynamic linking. This type of "more like this" form of linking often are used in online bookstores and other commercial Web sites and have seen application to scholarly research as well. In fact, it is being adopted by providers like Blackwell's Synergy for offering links to related resources. By using customized tagging a "conceptual tree" can be built for directing users to materials from broader or narrower subject categories (Miles-Board, Carr, & Hall, 2002).

For example, the Emerald Library presents users with full-text articles that link out to cited references when available within their database and also links to companion/affiliated services, such as JSTOR and Google Scholar. When available, researchers using Emerald will find links to JSTOR articles citing the current item and other articles written by the author. Alternatively, links into Google Scholar may lead the researcher to articles citing the author, other articles written by the author, and related articles.

Researchers searching ScienceDirect are presented with citations that may contain options linking to the full-text and links within the article, a PDF of the article and what is termed the summary plus of that article. This extended summary includes an abstract, a linked article outline, possibly tables and graphs, along with linked references where available. Accessed articles allow the user to link within that article's outline, link to references within the body of the text along with links to all the contained tables, charts and appendices. ScienceDirect affords users the option to link out into their companion product Scopus to find "cited by" references and material cited in the article's references.

A combination of these innovative linking strategies provides the user with a more useful and user-centric method of research and resource discovery while coincidently providing links to a wide variety of related information sources. These linking methods allow the user to navigate from resource to related resource through multiple databases, all the while expanding or narrowing the subject as desired.

The introduction of advanced Web technologies further refines the process of scholarly research providing the user with a more convenient and complete research experience.

Google Scholar and Windows Live Academic

Recently, the commercial search services Google Scholar and Windows Live Academic also have adopted in the openURL standard. When conducting a search on these services, links are presented to the user which allows for a connection from the search results to local openURL resolvers. In the case of Google Scholar, a file containing an institution's subscribed resources is scanned. When a search on Google Scholar is conducted, the search results are compared with an institutions' metadata which are then used to create links to relevant content. Originally, when Google Scholar was introduced the search results linked directly to the publisher's site. However, this did not take institutional subscription rights into account. In response to requests for providing links to the appropriate copy within their search results, Google Scholar was redesigned to act as a openURL source providing links to an institution's openURL link resolver. In 2005, this function became available, providing Google users with links to the appropriate fulltext copy. Google Scholar requires that an institution register its openURL resolver and provide metadata on the institution's subscribed resources (Grogg, Innovative, 2006).

In 2006, Windows Live Academic was introduced; like Google Scholar it provides links to an institution's openURL link resolver from search results. However, Windows Live Academic works in a different fashion from Google Scholar. It relies on IP authentication to determine when to display links to the appropriate openURL resolver. However, the adoption of the openURL standard by Google and Microsoft illustrate that this information retrieval method is gaining popularity and is being adopted by nonlibrary systems.

The introduction of Library 2.0 tools provides new methods of delivering existing library resources making scholarly research and resource discovery easier and more intuitive.

The integration of links to relevant wikis, blogs, blikis, and twikis provide users with current research, opinions, and relevant discussions of topical information. By combining these tools with appropriate commercial search engines, podcasting, vodcasting, RSS feeds and SMS these resources can provide users with more complete access to research materials.

The use of these Web 2.0 tools also provides a more personalized approach to research and resource discovery than is possible with standard reference linking. Their introduction and use is determined to a large extent by the development of these new tools. "…There's still a huge amount of disagreement about just what Web 2.0 means, with some people decrying it as a meaningless marketing buzzword, and other accepting it as the new conventional wisdom" (Notess, 2006, p. 40).

Library 2.0 Tools

While the innovative use of the DOI and openURL standards, combined with advanced linking procedures provide links to related content; new tools are developing to further enhance authentication, personalization, and related content linking for the user. These new tools are developed by utilizing new programming techniques and creating browser based applications, delivering an interactive research experience while also providing links to subscribed materials and other related content to the user.

The increasing availability of collaborative and social networking represented by interactive applications, such as: Blogs, wikis, social networking and bookmarking, chat services, multimedia, RSS feeds, commercial search services, and other Web 2.0 tools, illustrate the move toward new venues for scholarly research; providing links from traditional resources to these new sources and providing a new challenge in the use of openURL linking services. The integration of these new tools with link resolving technologies and traditional library software has now become generally known as Library 2.0. Library 2.0 is an evolving concept that will no doubt see ongoing revisions as new technologies become available.

Browser Tools

Modern Web browsers also provide tools designed to improve the browsing experience that also can be used in providing links to research resources. For example using the JavaScript scripting language to execute applets embedded in Web pages provides enhancements to Web content accomplishing this. In addition, with the introduction of small JavaScript applications called bookmarklets, applications can be created and added into the "favorites" or bookmarks of a Web browser interacting with user input or even embedded metadata within the Web page to provide linking with various related resources. This technology can be utilized in several ways to an enhance library linking, specifically, a bookmarklet can be constructed to automatically add the authentication proxy prefix in front of a link. Also, bookmarklets can be used in directing users to a local or remote resource, or perhaps searching for a highlighted word in a dictionary, resolving a DOI, or to searching the local catalog.

Another Web service available from within the browser are based on Context Objects in Spans (CoinS, http://ocoins.info/). In this instance, a specialized bookmarklet is constructed to interact with metadata embedded within a Web page. In this way, a COinS bookmarklet application is constructed displaying links to a local openURL resolver, providing the user with links to fulltext content and related resources. In his article "Innovative uses of the openURL" Grogg states that COinS allow Web developers to embed bibliographic metadata within their Web pages providing access to appropriate copy information (Grogg, Linking, 2006). Currently only a few databases, including CiteBase and OpenWorldCat, employ the correct metadata format required to interact with COinS. The usefulness of this service will increase as more databases adopt this technique. For a list on databases supporting COinS see: http://ocoins.info/#id3205609424).

Ajax is another one of these new technologies used in creating interactive Web pages and is an acronym standing for asynchronous JavaScript and XML. Ajax is not a stand-alone programming language, rather it is the term used for grouping a number of complimentary Web technologies together, with examples including: JavaScript, style sheets, the XMLHttpRequest object, and the document object model (DOM) in developing Web services.

When employing Ajax, Web applications are constructed allowing the user to update part or all of a Web page without having to communicate with the Web server and refreshing the entire page, thus increasing the Web page's usability and speed. The use of Ajax in delivering Web content can rival the responsiveness of desktops applications (Wusteman & O'hlceadha, 2006). There are some drawbacks to using Ajax Web services though, most notably being the fact that only modern, graphical browsers current support all of the features of Ajax, raising issues about compatibility with the Section 508 Compliance Standards.

Other Web application support services are available and capable of providing linking enhancements, such as: JAVA, .NET, Python, PHP, and Ruby, all of which may be used in developing other Web services. Web applications can be constructed in several different programming languages (Lerner, 2006). Each one of these programming environments offers one or more Web application frameworks and is meant to provide an environment for developing applications. There are also applications called widgets that are used for accessing the API (application programming interface) of a Web service, an example being Google Maps or Amazon.com. As the number of accessible APIs increase, the concept of providing users with direct links to relevant Web services will become an increasingly important part of scholarly research.

Recently, several JavaScript frameworks like Dojo, Bindows, Prototype, and others have been developed. These are client-side JavaScript libraries providing for easy and quick construction of interactive Web applications. A more complete list of these frameworks can be found at: http://ajaxpatterns.org/Javascript_Multipurpose_Frameworks.

There are a number of ways of delivering and integrating these various resource discovery tools. A common way this is accomplished is by including links to resources and Web applications in a toolbar integrated within the user's browser.

Toolbars provide links to online catalogs, search services, and bookmarks to useful links. Several libraries provide customized toolbars linking to various local and remote resources such as George Mason, Penn State, and the University of Illinois. These and other examples of library toolbars and other useful library related browser tools can be found at: http://www.libsuccess.org/index.php?title=Web_Browser_Extensions.

Recently, Virginia Tech University Libraries and the Department of Computer Science at Virginia Tech developed the LibX FireFox extension. A LibX toolbar can be designed to provide links to the Library's OPAC, an institutions openURL resolver, a DOI resolver, and several other resources, thereby delivering several of the new Library 2.0 tools. Some examples of toolbars made with LibX can be found at: http://libx.org/editions.php.

Currently LibX, as a FireFox extension only works with that browser, as does the HALbar toolbar (http://www.asl.edu/library/halbar/) from the Appalachian School of Law. FastJack (http://www.gsb.stanford.edu/library/toolbar/index.html) from the Stanford School of Business provides an example of a toolbar capable of working with Internet Explorer, as well as Firefox, providing more versatility.

Web Applications and Services

Web logs or blogs have the image of being a social Website or a gathering space, similar to MySpace or an issue discussion site like Insta-

Pundit. However, blogs are also being used to exchange scholarly information and provide a forum for the dissemination of links to relevant Web pages, as well as other media related topics. Blogs are also used to announce and market library resources. The information contained in a blog is arranged chronologically, enabling readers to easily identify recent or updated information. Blogging has been shown to be a useful tool for broadcasting information to users. (Bhatt, 2005; Conhaim, 2006)

Recently, we have seen a variety of blogs established for the purpose of scholarly communication. BlogScholar, located at http://www.blogscholar. com/, provides news related to academic blog sites, as well as a directory of scholarly blogs. Notably, blogs were introduced at the University of Illinois at Urbana-Champaign providing a place to discuss the impact of new technologies in scholarly communication, it can be located at: http://www. library.uiuc.edu/blog/scholcomm/, as well as the Transforming Scholarly Communications blog located at: http://info.lib.uh.edu/scomm/transforming.htm.

The increasing popularity of blogs for transmitting scholarly information highlights the need and desirability of providing users with links to appropriate Web log resources. Blogs, along with RSS feeds are examples of "Push" technologies offering users the capacity to review current information without being deluged and inconvenienced with email messages.

A number of blogs use real simple syndication or rich site summary feeds to push information contained in individual blog entries to users in a more targeted fashion than what e-mail provides. Using this method, a user subscribes to the RSS feed which is actually a selection of links generated by software at the host site providing the user with the ability to review updated information at that particular site.

Listservs and email notifications can serve the same purpose, however the use of RSS feeds provides the user additional flexibility to review information in a more targeted fashion. Specifically, RSS can be used to disseminate news, events or summary information on a particular topic. Additionally, several electronic journals and databases use RSS feeds to distribute table of contents information and current awareness information, such as Project MUSE, http://feeds. muse.jhu.edu/latest_issues.html, the American Institute of Physics, http://www.aip.org/rss.html, and Blackwell's Synergy. "Using a variety of methods, content providers create an RSS document, or feed, and make it available for subscription so that users can access content when it is added to the feed" (Cohen, 2005, p. 14).

To read an RSS feed, a reader is required to transform the actual data, which is delivered in an XML file into a readable format. Several commercial and free stand-alone RSS readers are available like FeedReader, Newsgator and others. Additionally, modern browsers like FireFox, Safari, or the latest versions of Netscape and Internet Explorer have RSS readers already integrated into them. The number of RSS feeds is increasing rapidly. Directories of these RSS feeds are available at www.sydic8.com and www.rssfeeds.com.

Ward Cunningham developed the WIKI concept in 1995. Wikis are a collaborative means of authoring Web pages and exchanging content; providing a quick and easy method of sharing information between users, linking to relevant content, and commenting on particular research points. Individual entries within a wiki can be easily modified and updated by the user. As a result, developing a wiki on a particular topic often leads to a spontaneous and shared discussion of issues and may provide the added benefit of increased collaboration on projects. Traditional wikis allow anyone to write and edit online documents raising concerns about the reliability of the information. (Fichter, 2005)

Initially, wikis were used primarily for software documentation and other technical uses, but as the concept gained acceptance and software became more readily available wikis have been seen cropping up in other disciplines. Recently, the authoritative nature of wikis has come under some question. The open and editable nature of wikis has lead to erroneous entries, resulting in changes to the basic wiki design in order to address this problem. Illustrating this problem, in a New York Times article the Wikipedia biography for John Seigenthaler, Sr. was erroneously edited by a prankster to imply that Mr. Seigenthaler was involved in the assassination of the Kennedys. (Seelye, 2005) There are now several wikis oriented toward scholarly communications, such as the LISauthor wiki and the JISC Depository Research wiki. The number of wikis continues to grow, for those interested parties an expanding directory is available at http://www.wikiindex. com.

Wikis and blogs share similar characteristics in that they are both are quick and easy ways of posting information on a particular topic, but there are in fact some differences in their informational structure. Blogs tend to be more organized and chronological in their approach, while wikis have a topical orientation. A hybrid, known as a bliki, has recently been introduced, with bliki software taking a middle of the road approach. A bliki is a blog with wiki characteristics in which blog posts can be converted into a regular wiki article. The primary benefit of a bliki is that the originating blog posting cannot be edited, thereby increasing the authoritative nature of the bliki over a conventional wiki (Fichter, 2005).

Another modification of the wiki format is the twiki. Twikis are structured wikis that have been extended with the addition of various plugins, providing users with the ability to create and use several types of media content. The structured aspect of a twiki means easier user input and its ability to accommodate hundreds of plugins means that the information stored in a twiki can be made available in a wide variety of formats. Twikis can also be used to develop Web applications, thereby offering the possibility of creating dynamic content and can be used to centrally

manage documents (Guenther, 2005). Twikis are presently in use at the Free Library of Philadelphia and Pace University Law Library.

The introduction of small audio and video playback machines and their "cool" factor have made the iPod and related players a common feature on university campuses. While used primarily for music they can be used to conveniently deliver lectures, introductions to scholarly subjects, providing guidance on research strategies, or informing users on how to use research resources or even deliver complete audio books. Ipoddler (www.ipoddler.org) and iTunes can be used to download audio content to a portable audio device (Notess, 2005). Creating a MP3 file or other type of audio file and loading it onto the device accomplishes this process. The user can then play the file at their leisure. The provision of these audio files is called podcasting. Podcasting is the method of distributing multimedia files, such as audio programs over the Internet using RSS feeds. Although designed primarily for personal mobile devices, a desktop or laptop computer can also be used to review podcasts. "Individual librarians who have been contributing to professional discourse through blogging are turning to podcasts as another means of distributing content" (Balas, 2005, p. 31).

Recently, the capability to add video has been integrated into podcasting, adding an extra dimension to an already useful tool. The combination of video and audio is called vodcasting. Like podcasting, this can be played on a small mobile device or a desktop or laptop PC.

Another available tool is SMS or short messaging service. As the name implies these are very short text messages gaining popularity as a peer-to-peer messaging technique. Originally, these were sent between cell phones, but now they can also be transmitted from PC's allowing for broadcasting of SMS messages to a larger number of recipients.

SMS can be used to inform users of new resources becoming available, provide quick notes, reminders, short directional or "how to" messages which can be sent to user's mobile device on research strategies or important topics. They can also be used to transmit database search results to a user's cell phone or other mobile device, acting as a method to temporarily store and retrieve search results (Reidy, 2004). Utilizing SMS services to deliver selected content to patrons provides another way for libraries to improve research services.

Providing seamless links from traditional information resources to these new tools provide the user with an "added value" research experience. Using innovative programming and existing openURL link resolving products, new applications can be developed that link to these new Web services, directing our users to the "appropriate copy" of the desired resource and allowing our users the ability to fully use these devices to assist in their research.

Software Tools

Several software tools are developing and are being adopted which present and organize information in various forms. Utilizing openURL link resolvers and other software tools are important to establish appropriate resource linking resources that provide the user seamless access to content.

Learning management systems like Moodle or Blackboard are invaluable tools for presenting scholarly materials in a teaching environment. Presenting links to users that direct them to appropriate content is a major challenge.

One tool finding wide acceptance and adoption is the federated search engine. In the past, commercial Internet search engines were designed around the metasearch concept. However, with the advent of Metalib, WebFeet, Encompass and other library-oriented metasearch utilities we now see this application becoming available for use in scholarly research.

Before the advent of federated search systems, a user needed to select a specific database, search that database, collect and evaluate results, then potentially repeat the procedure with another database; a time consuming and inefficient process requiring the user to select the "right" database, conduct the search, then evaluate the results. Here we see that each step is to a lesser or greater extent different for each database. The various database interfaces offer different search features and options that the user must learn before being able to accurately and reliably execute the search. Also, each database might provide different formatting features and the consequent results list might also offer differing information. The advent of federated searching has greatly assisted library researchers as illustrated by (Boss & Nelson, 2005; Curtis, 2005).

Federated searching systems simplify the search procedure by allowing the user to perform their search once using a common interface and then harvesting the results from several different databases all at once. Search results are then collated and presented to the user in a clustered format, eliminating duplicates and organizing them for evaluation, thus providing a more thorough search. With the inclusion of an institution's OPAC, digital repository, local and remote resources, a federated search creates a more comprehensive and complete search, including not only online resources, but potentially adding an institution's print materials and other resources like multimedia or digitized objects. As we see, federated searching vastly simplifies the research process and consequently, the number of federated search engines now being marketed has grown rapidly. The Library of Congress maintains a list of these systems that is found at http://www.loc.gov/catdir/lcpaig/portalproducts.html. Although most of these search engines are sold commercially, several are available as open source applications including: DbWiz: http://dbwiz.lib.sfu.ca/dbwiz/, KeyStone DLS: http://www.indexdata.dk/keystone/, and ARC: http://oaiarc.sourceforge.net/)

Federated search systems do have a potential drawback. The search syntax and field structure of every database is not identical, especially across providers. Given the general nature of a federated search, searches conducted on obscure or specialized topics within a federated search environment may not find all relevant materials.

Another software method improving resource discovery of scholarly resources are expert systems. These applications present the user with a series of questions or a group of menus relating to their research topic. Responses are analyzed and presented to the user in the form of a dynamically produced set of links to appropriate information sources (Ma & Cole, 2000).

Expert systems are typically designed using artificial intelligence software in creating a dynamic question and answer session. A related technique is known as the "Wizard," where we see questions manually created and users are instructed to follow a path or a set of rules directing them to the appropriate resources.

A third major type of software tool available is the portal or "My Library" kind of service. This type of service provides a list of research resources which can be customized by the user to reflect his or her personal research needs and in some instances by applying specialized software an individualized profile is constructed reflecting the individual's specific research interests. This profile can be stored, recalled and executed providing the user with links to material reflecting the person's specific interests. It may also be later reexecuted, modifying and updating the results reflecting ongoing research. "...many libraries of all types (academic, medical, public, school) and sizes (small to large) are implementing "my library" services, eager to join their peers in offering their users a "personalized library experience" (Ghaphery & Watstein, 2001, p. 276).

The advent of these new software tools provides the user with additional resource discovery tools. However, as in all research, presenting the user with links to the appropriate copy is critical.

Integrating local openURL resolvers, as well as innovative browser tools can meet this need.

Local Resources and Linking

Locally mounted research digital resources are becoming an increasing part of the research experience. Providing users with links to these materials, as well as to remotely located digital archives is an important service. To this end, the Open Archives Initiative (OAI) was initiated to build a framework for digital archives. The Open Archives Initiative Protocol for Metadata Harvesting (OAI-PMH) provides a standard for defining metadata to materials contained within the archive. This standard allows the remote harvesting of metadata, thus providing the ability to present the researcher with links from various local or remote digital repositories. Then, by utilizing mashups, XML programming, and other technologies to interlink these materials with related resources they can then be fully integrated into a libraries' collection providing users with the capability to utilize these materials in context with other resources.

Advanced Linking Mechanisms

One of the principal types of research in the area of resource linking under investigation is the ability to present users with information gleaned from related Web pages found in differing locations. This process is called a "mashup," using RSS feeds, JavaScript, or an API, content originating from different locations is integrated directly onto a Web page providing the user with seamless access to these various Web services. For example, a Web page of openURL links could use the metadata to display links from a bibliographic service or a page of geographic data might be combined with a mapping service API to display a dynamically generated map. Utilizing mashups provides a method of extending library services by using additional Web services from other locations to enhance content and provide users with a more complete and satisfying research experience. Three factors have been identified in constructing mashups, the "right to remix," creativity, and technical know-how (Fichter, 2006). John Musser provides a growing list of mashups, APIs, and related information at: http://www.programmableweb.com/.

Another application that will have an impact on resource linking are "tag clouds." Tag clouds are groups of dynamically generated links to various Internet sources that are weighted according to their metadata with the link text to the content being displayed in a larger or smaller font depending upon the frequency that that particular link is accessed. Created in a variety of methods, often by using Java, Perl, or Ruby, tag clouds can indicate which links previous searchers have found useful. Also, tag clouds can be designed to emphasize links based on other criteria, for example journals having a higher citation rating would receive greater emphasis. Properly designed, a tag cloud presents the user with visual representations in the form of a clear and unambiguous set of links to useful materials.

Another factor in designing future linking technologies will be a tagging protocol using various taxonomies and folksonomies. Taxonomies are structured forms of organized data and their description, for example, the Library of Congress classification schedules or the Dewey Decimal System are considered taxonomies. Alternatively, folksonomies are unstructured and can be defined by the particular user, responding to how individuals categorize content. Tag clouds from informal folksonomies are as messy as you would expect (Notess, 2006). While folksonomies might not follow the formal structured organization offered by taxonomies, they do allow users the ability to link out to content that others have deemed useful, thereby opening up a more collaborative research methodology. Integrating tag clouds that use various taxonomies or folksonomies in their construction present researchers with links

to various resources providing them with a more intuitive research experience.

The "Long Tail" and Linking

One of the problems inherent in designing linking mechanisms is that of the "long tail."

This concept is based on the statistical distribution of various objects. For example, in the area of research linking popular items would get the majority of use, with the less popular getting proportionately fewer. However, it is these less popular items that are often considered to be the most important by our users. As a result it is extremely important that these less used materials remain accessible. Although popular items are accessed frequently, the large amount of library materials accessed infrequently is nonetheless important to our users and maintaining access to that infrequently used material is equally important (Notess, 2006). Ensuring access to this "long tail" information will be a major challenge for information professionals.

CONCLUSION

In the previous sections some of the existing tools and those soon available for enhancing resource linking and research were described. The implementation of these new tools will, to a large extent, be driven by available technology. One of the founders of Intel, Gordon Moore projected that the density of transistors that could be applied to a computer chip roughly doubled every 24 months. This is now referred to as Moore's Law which states that the computing power doubles every two years. Past projections saw this ending as computer hardware reached the limits of miniaturization. However, the introduction of new technologies and software still makes this a reasonable assumption.

Among the factors effecting the implementation of these new technologies are the storage capacity of devices, the ease of transmitting information, and above all whether or not new and better techniques become available. The capability and interoperability of various devices will also play a major role in the practicality, as well as in the design of the services to enhance resource linking (Balas, 2006; Schmidt, 2005).

Computer hardware advances present new challenges, however the development of appropriate software applications to fully utilize the introduction of these new devices present information professionals with new challenges and opportunities. Programming resources and the availability of public APIs will allow the creation of these applications providing library users to a wealth of context sensitive links and resources.

REFERENCES

Awasthi, S., Beardmore, J., Clark, J., Hadridge, P., Madani, H., & Marusic, A., et al. (2005). Five futures for academic medicine. *PLoS Medicine, 2*(7), e207 OP.

Balas, J. L. (2005). Blogging is so last year-now podcasting is hot. *Computers in Libraries, 25*(10), 29.

Balas, J. L. (2006). The "magic" of wireless access in the library. *Computers in Libraries, 26*(3), 32.

Balas, J. L. (2006). What's in their pockets? Mobile electronics. *Computers in Libraries, 26*(4), 32.

Beit-Arie, & Oren, Caplan, Priscilla, et al. (2001). Linking to the appropriate copy: Report of a DOI-based prototype [Electronic version]. *D-Lib Magazine, 7*(9).

Bhatt, J. (2005). Blogging as a tool: Innovative approaches to information access. *Library Hi Tech News Incorporating Online and CD Notes, 22*(9), 28(5).

Boss, S. C., & Nelson, M. L. (2005). Federated SearchTools: The next step in the quest for one-stop-shopping. *The Reference Librarian, (91/92),* 139-160.

Cohen, L. B. (2005). Finding scholarly content on the web: From google scholar to RSS feeds. *CHOICE: Current Reviews for Academic Libraries, 42*(SPECIAL), 7-17.

Conhaim, W. W. (2006). Blogging: A modern tool for an age-old quest. *Information Today, 23*(2), 27-29.

Curtis, A. (2005). Why federated search? *Knowledge Quest, 33*(3), 35-37.

Fichter, D. (2006). Doing the monster mashup. *Online, 30*(4), 48.

Fichter, D. (2005). Intranet librarian - intranets, wikis, blikis, and collaborative working. *Online, 29*(5), 47.

Frick, R., Duncan, C. J., & Walsh, W. D. (2005). Nuts and bolts of linking: Understanding context sensitive linking services and implementation. *The Serials Librarian, 48*(3/4), 257-264.

Ghaphery, J., Kesselman, M., & Watstein, S. B. (2001). Personalized information clients: Short answers to simple questions about "my library" services. *Reference Services Review, 29*(4), 276.

Grogg, J. E. (2004). Linking in the traditional online world. *Searcher, 12*(6), 34.

Grogg, J. E. (2005). Land of linking. *The Serials Librarian, 49*(3), 177.

Grogg, J. E. (2006). The development of context-sensitive linking. *Library Technology Reports, 42*(1), 14.

Grogg, J. E. (2006). Innovative uses of the openURL. *Library Technology Reports, 42*(1), 35.

Grogg, J. E. (2006). Other linking issues. *Library Technology Reports, 42*(1), 38.

Grogg, J. E., & Tenopir, C. (2000, Nov/Dec). Linking to full text in scholarly journals: Here a link, there a link, everywhere a link. *Searcher, 8*(10),

Guenther, K. (2005). Socializing your web site with wikis, twikis, and blogs. (web site management methods using webcasting). *Online, 29*(6), 51(3).

Lerner, R. M. (2006). At the forge: Extending web services using other web services. *Linux Journal, 2006*(144), 9.

Ma, W., & Cole, T. W. (2000). Genesis of an electronic database expert system. *Reference Services Review, 28*(3), 207.

McElfresh, L. K. (2005). Accessing E-journals through link resolvers. *Technicalities, 25*(6), 3.

Miles-Board, T., Carr, L., & Hall, W. (2002). Looking for linking: Associative links on the web. In *Proceedings of the Thirteenth ACM Conference on Hypertext and Hypermedia,* College Park, Maryland (pp. 76-77).

Notess, G. R. (2005). Casting the net: Podcasting and screencasting. *Online, 29*(6), 43-45.

Notess, G. R. (2006). On the net - the terrible twos: Web 2.0, library 2.0, and more. *Online, 30*(3), 40.

Reidy, K. (2004). Succesful messaging services: SMS [& MMS] 4 biz 2day. *EContent, 27*(9), 30.

Schmidt, A. (2005). The young & the wireless. *School Library Journal, 51*(10), 44.

Seelye, K. Q. (2005). Snared in the web of a wikipedia liar. (Week in review desk)(rewriting history). *The New York Times,* WK1(L).

Wusteman, J., & O'hlceadha, P. (2006). Using Ajax to empower dynamic searching. *Information Technology and Libraries, 25*(2), 57.

Zhu, Q. (2006). The nuts and bolts of delivering new technical reports via database-generated RSS FEEDS. *Computers in Libraries, 26*(2), 24.

Chapter XIV
Authentication and Access Management of Electronic Resources

Juan Carlos Rodriguez
California State University, Sacramento, USA

Bin Zhang
California State University, Sacramento, USA

ABSTRACT

This chapter opens with a discussion of the varying needs of libraries to provide their users with both local and remote access to electronic resources within the context of the various legal and technical issues surrounding them. An overview of the various types of authentication and authorization mechanisms currently in use by libraries, their parent organizations and electronic resource providers is presented. Further discussion follows on the unique needs and requirements of consortia licensed electronic resources and metasearch applications. The chapter concludes with a look at future considerations and directions libraries and e-resource providers may take with regard to secure and seamless access to electronic resources.

INTRODUCTION

As late as the early 1990's, the library's primary method of access management to its collections was either performed at the library's entrance or through the use of publicly inaccessible collections or "closed stacks" that required some form of permission or authorization to access them.

Additional access management was introduced when it came time to borrow the library materials from the library. Typically this was done by requiring the library patron to present a valid and current library card that was issued to them as a member of the community, a faculty member, or student of the university. Also, most libraries were not concerned with providing remote access to their collections since they still existed primarily in physical form and all access was limited to in person. With the introduction of online electronic resources such as electronic journals and online databases, these traditional methods of access management became no longer sufficient. It was no longer possible just to control access through physical methods, additional methods were needed.

Over the past ten years, the amount of licensed electronic resources purchased by libraries has increased dramatically. During the period from 1995 through 2005 the average Association of Research Libraries (ARL) library's allocations of financial resources devoted to electronic resources (e-resources) had increased from a little more than 6% to almost 38% of the library's entire collections budget (Kyrillidou & Young, 2006). The bulk of these resources have been electronic journals and index and abstracting databases. Included in most, if not all, of the license agreements is the need to restrict access only to those that are members of the library community. For academic and special libraries this community generally consists of its faculty, staff and students. However, it's much more difficult to identify a public library's community considering most members of the community served by a public library, and often residents of the state, are potential members of this community. For this reason access to electronic resources is typically restricted to computers that are physically in the library while remote access is generally provided to those that posses a valid library card.

Initially the use of passwords that were given to libraries from e-resource vendors to distribute to its users was the primary mechanism for providing access to e-resources licensed by the library. However as the amount of e-resources and vendors grew, so did the workload in managing passwords. This method quickly became a growing concern and problem for libraries. As a result, the ability to restrict access to a particular physical network location through the use of IP address filtering

soon became the de facto standard on how access was managed. An IP (Internet protocol) address is a unique string of four numbers separated by periods (such as 216.230.155.100) that is assigned to a device, such as a computer, connected to the Internet. Typically computers in a library or university have IP addresses that fall into a common range. For example, a public library may have five Internet-connected computer workstations that have the following IP addresses: 216.239.255.101; 216.239.255.102; 216.239.255.103; 216.239.255.104 and 216.239.255.105. In this example, all five workstations share the same first three strings (i.e. 216.239.255) of numbers. IP address filtering is a method where the vendor only accepts requests that originate from registered networked computers that fall within the range of IP addresses that the library has supplied the vendor. Again, this method quickly became restrictive as more and more users began requesting access to these resources remotely. Thus there became an increasingly important need to implement mechanisms that addressed licensed restrictions while at the same time meeting the needs of both local and remote users.

This chapter will explore the various mechanisms that are currently in place that provide both authentication and authorization for the variety of library licensed electronic resources. It will address issues related to the legal, technical and privacy issues associated with providing local and remote access to licensed resources.

BACKGROUND

When a library decides to purchase an e-resource it must also consider the methods that it will use to provide access to these resources. Typically, most e-resources are available for access from the vendor. Since many pricing models for electronic resources factor in the size of the user base, the vendor of the electronic resource requires that access to the electronic resource be restricted only to authorized users of the library. Most license agreements clearly outline the need to control access only to those specified during the license process. The responsibility to enforce these restrictions generally falls on the library.

The mechanisms to provide access to these resources have changed over the years. Initially these resources were accessed through the library's Web site via A to Z pages or subject-based pages of databases and e-journals. As the amount of e-resources grew it became increasingly difficult to maintain these pages. Many libraries began cataloging e-resources and provided access to them via the library's Web-based catalog. More recently, libraries have been using openURL link resolvers, such as SFX from Ex Libris, as the linking mechanism that provides access to these resources.

As the demand and expectation to provide anytime, anywhere access to the library's licensed e-resources grows, so does the need to provide access management mechanisms that extend beyond IP address filtering. For this reason, a variety of methods and technologies that provide improved identity and access management are being evaluated and implemented by both libraries and their parent organizations. Libraries generally have been in a good position to take an active role in developing new authentication mechanisms considering most libraries already have a good idea of who their users are through the use of patron databases. However, few libraries have used their patron databases as a source for their authentication system. In a survey of ARL libraries, Plum and Bleiler (2001) found that 98% of the libraries are using some form of authentication. However, only about 20% of them were using patron databases as their authentication source.

Identity and access management is becoming more and more important for libraries and their parent organizations. Identity management is of critical importance to the provision of controlled access to the library's e-resources and services. It defines which users exist and what roles they have (which access and to what degree of functionality). It comprises creating and defining the list of users with access to the various e-resources and assigning access rights in the form of roles. Access management also defines the roles and enforces authorization roles—what should a faculty member have access to, or the undergraduate student? Access management needs a valid identification of the user by the authentication system and the information about which users are assigned to which groups. The roles defined here will be used within identity management to permit library users what they need to be allowed access to specific e-resources. Clifford Lynch (1998) provided an excellent introduction to issues in cross-organizational authentication and access management in the late 1990's that has provided the foundation for future discussion on this important topic.

The next several sections will discuss the evolution of the various authentication methods that have been in place for the past ten years and look at future methods that are currently under development. The current authentication methods will be discussed with their strengths and weaknesses as well as the issues surrounding the management and maintenance. It will also explore the relationships that will need to be established with library's parent organizations to ensure that issues related to privacy are resolved and seamless access is provided. However, before these methods are discussed, it's important to understand the various legal issues associated with providing access to licensed e-resources.

LEGAL CONSIDERATIONS

In the electronic environment where the traditional print practice of ownership through purchase is being replaced by access through license, libraries need to be aware that licensing arrangements may restrict their legal rights and those of their users. Providers of electronic information resources are employing licenses as a legal means of controlling the use of their products. As responsible agents for an institution, librarians must negotiate licenses that address the institution's needs and recognize its obligations to the licensor (American Association of Law Libraries, American Library Association, Association of Academic Health Sciences Libraries, Association of Research Libraries, Medical Library Association, Special Libraries Association, 1997).

Components of most license agreements generally identify the authorized users, state of jurisdiction, and the site location; address issues of remote access, fair use, interlibrary loan, and indemnity; and contain information relating to the vendor notification of Web downtime and any changes in product software (Wolverton, 2003, pp. 153-154). Moreover, before the license agreement is signed, careful consideration should be taken to ensure that the library has the necessary technical resources in place to provide the mechanisms that will provide appropriate access defined in the license.

Probably two of the most important elements of any e-resource license agreement are the determination and definition of the authorized users and how the e-resource will be accessed. Librarians need to pay very close attention to how "users" are defined in the e-resource license agreement. Unlike printed materials where users typically were taken for granted because the general law of copyright defined the user, e-resources and who is eligible to access them needs to be clearly defined in the license agreement (Richards, 2001, p. 91). As Okerson stated, librarians must carefully consider who should fall within the definition of "users" within their particular library community. "Users" should at least include the current faculty, staff, and students of the university. Distance education students, temporary researchers, and patrons walking into the library on campus likely should fall within the definition of "users." There may be additional groups of users who should be included, for instance, retired faculty if they

retain their university network identification numbers for a period of time (as cited in Alford, 2002, p.635-636).

It is also recommended that the library make every effort to ensure that the definition of "user" is consistently applied, whenever possible, for all licensed e-resources. Otherwise, it will be very difficult to implement the various authentication and access management mechanisms that will be discussed in this chapter if the definition of "user" varies from licensed e-resource to licensed e-resource.

Many licensing principles developed by library organizations such as the International Federation of Library Associations and Institutions' "Licensing Principles" (2001); the "Principles for Licensing Electronic Resources" (1997) jointly written by six library associations including the American Library Association and the Association of Research Libraries; and the "Statement of Current Perspective and Preferred Practices for the Selection and Purchase of Electronic Information" by the Libraries and International Coalition of Library Consortia (1997) recommended that the definition of "user" be carefully defined and if possible as broadest as possible. These principles also recommend that access to the e-resource should be permitted regardless of the users' physical location. Librarians must consider how users will access the e-resource. Since, most e-resources are available over the Internet from the vendor's Web site, authentication methods will need to be determined as well as whether remote access will be permitted. The mode of access to the e-resources is closely related to the definition of users and should be carefully considered prior to entering into an electronic licensing agreement (Alford, 2002).

AUTHENTICATION AND ACCESS MANAGEMENT

In order to satisfy the contract terms with electronic resource vendors, libraries need to make sure that only authorized users (i.e., faculty, staff, and students in an academic setting, and library patrons for public libraries) have access to these resources. To accomplish this, a form of access control needs to happen. Access control is normally a two-step process: authentication and authorization.

Authentication is the process of validating the identity of someone. In other words, it addresses the question of "Are you who you say you are?" It uses information provided by the authentication source to determine whether the user is really who s/he claims to be. Authentication is normally performed by checking against identity credentials that are usually based on unique factors that only the user would know (e.g., student/employee ID number, barcode number, user name, password, a PIN that is assigned by the integrated library systems [ILS], etc.).

Authorization is the process to determine if an identified user is authorized to perform a function that the user has requested. Authorization answers the question of "We already know who you are, but are you permitted to access this?" Successful authentication is often the prerequisite for authorization. Authentication and authorization are two processes that are closely related. For this reason, the term "authentication" is sometimes used to refer to both authentication and authorization. However, it's very important to recognize that even though someone's identity can be verified through the authentication process, it does not necessarily imply that they are able to gain access to the requested e-resource. For example, alumni and currently registered students of a university may have access to quite a different set of e-resources.

It should also be noted that authentication does not necessarily prove that a particular individual is who he or she claims to be; instead authentication is more about obtaining a level of confidence in this claim.

ELEMENTS OF AN AUTHENTICATION SYSTEM

The authentication process consists of five separate elements. The first element is the particular person or group of people to be authenticated. The person or group-seeking authentication typically consists of library patrons or group of patrons such as students and faculty from a university. As individuals they must present valid credentials and as a group they must present the authentication source evidence that any member of this group is authorized to access the e-resource based on a trust model.

The second element consists of a distinguishing characteristic that differentiates that particular person or group of people from others. Distinguishing characteristics typically include something you know such as your username, password or library card barcode. It can also include your location such as a computer workstation in the library. Additional factors can also include: something you have such as an ID card and what you are such as a fingerprint or voiceprint.

The third element, and probably one of the most important elements a library needs to consider when implementing an authentication system, is the authenticator. The authenticator is responsible for providing the mechanisms that will be used to distinguish authorized users from nonauthorized users. The authenticator's primary responsibility is to positively identify the user's identity and indicate whether he or she is authorized to access the e-resource. Typically this is done by asking the person for user credentials when the authentication request is issued. The source of the user's identity is the source of authentication. Authenticators are generally managed either by the library or its parent organization. In the case of an academic library the parent organization would be the university's computing center. Examples of authenticators, or authentication sources, include: Patron database in ILSs (patron barcode number, patron type, PIN, etc.); institutional directories; student information systems; institutional information systems (e-mail server, ftp server, file servers, etc.); and user data stored at vendors' systems. Regardless of what authenticator is used, an authentication process must be performed that will result in some outcome value that will be used to determine information about the person at a later time. The authenticator then collects the information and passes it on to the authentication mechanism.

The fourth element is the authentication mechanism that is used to verify the presence of the distinguishing characteristics. The authentication mechanism consists of three parts that work together to verify the presence of authenticating characteristics provided by the person. The three parts are: input, the transportation system and the verifier. The input is generally a computer keyboard but can be any other device that accepts the user credentials such as card reader or voice recognition system. The transportation system is responsible for passing data between the input device and the element that confirms the person's identity. Typically this is done over a secure and private network protected by security protocols such as Kerberos or secure socket layer (SSL). The third part is the verification component which is the access control mechanism.

The fifth element is the access control mechanism that will grant access to the e-resource when the authentication succeeds or deny access if the authentication fails. User identification and authentication information is passed to access control over the network and validated against the information in its database. The access control mechanism then determines whether the information matches. If a match is detected, the access control system then issues temporary credentials authorizing the person to access the e-resource.

As stated earlier, the authenticator or source of authentication is one of the most important elements a library needs to consider when implementing an authentication system. For this reason, it's worth providing additional information about commonly used authentication sources.

Almost all libraries maintain a patron database as part of their ILS. An ILS performs its own authentication for resources included in its own collection. The ILS patron database can also be used by external authentication systems via application programming interface (API) or Web services. An API is a set of definitions of the ways one piece of computer software communicates with another. Web services are generally XML-based information exchange systems that interact with other Web-based applications for the purposes of exchanging data. Such external systems could include document delivery systems, proxy servers, metasearch systems, and so forth. Some ILS vendors provide their patron API as part of the ILS; others sell it as an additional product or module. As an authentication source, ILS provides some unique data about library users that may not be available elsewhere: patron type defined by the library, patron status (how many books are checked out to the patron, how much money the patron owes the library, etc.).

Another common authentication source available to most academic libraries are institutional directories that contain student registration data and employee information. This data is typically populated to other systems, for example, enterprise portals, networked file systems, e-mail systems. Many institutions use a LDAP directory as the central repository for basic user information, so other system can use it for authentication purposes. LDAP, which stands for lightweight directory access protocol, is a well-established protocol for accessing personal data in a directory. LDAP APIs are available in all major programming languages. It is very easy for other information systems, such as ILSs, metasearch systems, proxy servers, e-mail systems, and so forth, to authenticate against its user base. Therefore, if such infrastructure exists in the organization, it would be the ideal single source of authentication, not only for library systems, but also for all other information systems.

Patron databases and institutional directories are usually not used by resource vendors for various reasons. Most vendors accept IP ranges alone as an acceptable authentication mechanism, while some require individual library users to be identified. Some vendors assign user IDs and passwords and require library users to login using these vendor-created passwords, the same way as individual subscribers. This presents a challenge for libraries, especially those libraries that have to maintain large number of passwords. Many libraries put IP authentication as a requirement in the contract, so they do not have to deal with individual passwords. In addition to IP filtering and user ID/password, some vendors also allow libraries to upload their patron data into their system, so library users will be able to use the same credentials to access the resource. However keeping patron data updated on all vendors' systems is a real challenge, and may not be a realistic solution for large libraries.

ACCESS POINTS

Libraries provide their users with different ways of accessing its electronic information resources, such as the ILS, a library developed Web site that include listings of available e-resources and a metasearch system (sometimes referred to as federated search). Library users may start an e-resource research session from any of these systems. Many libraries also provide access through other nonlibrary systems, such as the Learning Management System (LMS), an enterprise portal, and so forth. Many of these systems perform authentication. Depending on how the user starts the research, the user may have different experiences in terms of authentication. These access points are briefly discussed in the next section.

Integrated Library Systems (ILSs)

Usually, when a patron tries to access a resource that is part of the library's local collection and restricted, such as an item in an electronic reserves collection, the ILS itself will authenticate the patron. In other words, the ILS will use its own internal authentication mechanism to authenticate the user.

However, if the resource resides outside the ILS, such as an electronic journal, the ILS will simply redirect the user to the resource itself, or to another authenticator, such as a proxy server, which in turn authenticates the user. In this case, the ILS delegates the authentication to another authenticator. Some ILS vendors provide a proxy server as an add-on module that is integrated to the ILS (e.g., Web Access Management from Innovative Interfaces, Inc.). These modules authenticate patrons using the ILS's internal patron database.

Metasearch Applications

Metasearch applications such as MetaLib from Ex Libris are becoming increasingly popular in libraries, especially academic libraries. It allows users to simultaneously search multiple resources, and provide alert, saving search history and other personalization features. Because of these and other features, metasearch systems are likely to become the primary access point of electronic resources by library users. Metasearch systems provide their own user database, and some systems can also authenticate against external sources, such as LDAP directories, ILS patron databases, and so forth. For licensed resources, most metasearch systems can also be configured to selectively link to a URL-rewriting proxy server. As we can see here, a metasearch system actually performs three types of authentication: (1) authenticate internally using its own user database; (2) authenticate against an external source (e.g., LDAP directory, ILS patron database, etc.); and (3) authenticate against the users' computer IP and redirect off-site users to a URL-rewriting proxy server.

Link Resolvers

A link resolver allows a patron to find an appropriate copy of the resource (a fulltext article, an e-book, etc.) that the library and the parent organization owns or has access to, and redirects the user to that resource. Most link resolvers do not perform their own authentication, but they can be configured to selectively redirect a user to a proxy server, or directly to the resource itself based on the IP address of the users' computer and on the status of the resource (whether it's free or licensed). Users do not normally start with the link resolver. Rather, a user will start from somewhere else (e.g., ILS, a citation database, an e-journal list Web site, a metasearch system, etc.). Common types of link resolvers used by libraries rely on the openURL framework. Examples include SFX from Ex Libris and WebBridge from Innovative Interfaces, Inc.

Library Web Pages

Many libraries provide Web pages that list available electronic resources (e.g., A-Z list of databases, e-journals and e-books, etc.) These pages generally serve as the starting point for library users to access e-resources. These pages normally do not perform authentication.

Campus/Organizational Portals

An increasing number of institutions, especially large academic institutions, are making e-resources accessible through their institutional portals, LMSs and student information systems. In these cases, these systems have become the starting access point to e-resources. These systems all have their own authentication mechanisms, using institutional user databases, such as the student registration system, employee directory, and so forth. While these systems provide a convenient "one-stop shopping" environment for users to access all the resources (not only the resources libraries can provide, but all other e-resources), it also presents a challenge. Users may have to be authenticated multiple times, with different usernames and passwords. One way to solve this problem is to use the same source for authentication (such as an institutional LDAP directory). This method will at least provide the user with only one username and password to remember. However, a user may still have to login multiple times. To eliminate the need for multiple-logins, a single sign-on (SSO) system may be implemented, so the user will only have to login once. More details will be discussed in the SSO section later in this chapter.

Library Computer Workstations

Computers in libraries are usually set up to allow easy access to e-resources by the library. This not only includes all Web-based resources, but also includes nonWeb resources, such as those only accessible by special client software such as SciFinder Scholar, a chemistry bibliographic and reference research tool, from the American Chemistry Society. These computers are also where libraries provide access to e-resources which are not IP-authenticated, or those with only limited number of IP addresses, rather than a whole range. Libraries may also set up Web-based OPACs to authenticate users using vendor-supplied cookies.

Resource Vendor Systems

Vendor systems always perform authentication. The most common form of authentication at vendor sites is IP filtering, although some vendors only use username/password authentication. Vendors also provide other alternatives, such as patron ID matching, cookie-based authentication, referring URL, and so forth. Some vendors also support external authentication. In this case, when a user tries to access the vendor's resource, the user will be redirected to the library's authentication site. This authentication method is sometimes referred to as "CGI" by vendors (common gateway interface or CGI is an interface that allows applications/scripts to interact with browsers through the Web server. As new technologies develop, CGI no longer is the only way server-side applications interact with user browsers). "CGI" here refer to any external authentication mechanisms, whether CGI-based or not. If any of these authentications fail, vendors' systems revert back to the username/password authentication mechanism.

If possible, libraries should use the vendors' authentication as the last point of authentication. This will give the library and the institution more flexibility, and will be able to provide its patrons a unified interface.

AUTHENTICATION METHODS IN USE

As we discussed earlier, there are five elements in the authentication process. The fourth element or authentication mechanism used in the process is where the "real action" happens. When the user starts a session by requesting a specific e-resource from an access point, the authentication mechanism kicks in. At this time, more than one authentication method may be involved, depending on the particular situation. For example, in a typical academic library environment, an IP authentication is first performed. If the authentication mechanism detects that the user is from an "on-site" computer, the user gets a "green light," and the authentication is complete, so the user is sent directly to the resource requested. On the other hand, if the authentication mechanism detects the user is coming from an nonregistered IP,

then an additional authentication methods needs to be involved to identify the user as authorized user to access the resource. If the user is unable to successfully be authenticated, then the user is denied access to the resource. The most common authentication methods currently supported by vendors and in use by libraries are: IP address filtering; credential-based; referring URL and cookies-based.

IP Address Filtering

Authentication based on the IP address of the user's computer is the most commonly used authentication mechanism. IP authentication is also generally used as the first method of authentication. If IP authentication fails, other methods will be used to identify the user. If the user has been identified as being "on-site," the library system would send the user directly to the resource on the appropriate vendor's site, which will perform its own IP authentication. IP filtering is and should be performed by both library and vendor systems. To make vendor-side IP filtering work properly, a library would provide the vendor with a range of IP addresses of the network of the library or the parent organization (e.g., the university that the library is part of).

An IP range can be expressed in one of the forms:

216.239.0.0 - 216.239.255.255
216.239.*.*
216.239.0.0/16

All three lines have the same meaning: this covers all IP addresses within this range (i.e., any IP that is between 216.239.0.0 and 216.239.255.255). Some vendors (e.g., small journal publishers) only allow a limited number of IP addresses for each customer. In this case, you would have to identify a few workstations, and provide the IP addresses to the vendor.

IP ranges can be obtained from the network support personnel at the library or the parent organization, or from the Internet service provider (ISP), if the library's Internet access is provided by an ISP.

IP-based authentication is a good choice if the library's user base is physically close and can be covered by a single network. Situations might include: access to e-resources is only provided to users who are physically in the library building; access is provided only to on-campus users, and so forth. The assumption is that everyone who is in the IP range is permitted to access the resource. If the library or its parent organization shares an IP range with other users, or the library patron population is spread out in different areas, IP filtering does not work. Some vendor contracts specify that users have to be individually identified. If this is the case in your library, IP filtering alone is not sufficient to satisfy the contract terms. In this case, an additional credential-based authentication method needs to be used in addition to IP-filtering.

Credential-Based

Credential-based authentication methods refer to those that ask and verify identities of individual library users. The individual's identity can consist of a user name and password, library card barcode number, or other types of identifiers that would uniquely identify an individual user. Credential-based authentication is one of the most common methods in use. They are supported by most information content management systems, as well as e-resource vendor sites. Common examples of credential-based systems include: ILS, proxy server, metasearch systems, e-resource vendor, and locally created systems.

An ILS normally authenticates users against its own patron database. Authentication occurs when a user tries to access personal account-related functions (e.g., renew books, check fines, place holds, save search history, set personal

preferences, etc.) or restricted resources such as electronic reserve materials or restricted e-resources that are locally mounted to the ILS. The ILS itself cannot provide direct authentication for resources that it does not manage, but it can perform authentication on behalf of an external system via patron APIs. For example, a proxy server can be set up to authenticate users against the library's patron database. One advantage of using the ILS patron data as the authentication source is the ability to filter users based on patron status or category (e.g., does the patron owe money?) or other information that only exists in the ILS patron database. Most major ILS vendors provide an API to access patron records (some may provide it as an additional product or enhancement).

Proxy servers provide remote access to e-resources by first performing an IP-based authentication, so only true remote users are being served, then it performs a credential-based authentication against one or more of the supported sources, including its own user base to determine if the user should be granted access to the resource. Different proxy server software may support different external authentication sources. For additional information on proxy servers, please refer to the Remote Access section later in this chapter.

Similar to proxy servers, metasearch systems also have their own authentication mechanism that can authenticate users against various external sources as well as their own user base.

As noted earlier in this chapter, most vendors perform IP-based authentication. In addition, most major vendors also provide several other forms of authentication. For example, libraries may provide the vendor with a list of library card numbers (bar code numbers in most cases). Some vendors also support an ID pattern, in which case the library does not have to upload all the individual bar code numbers into vendor's management system. Instead, the library would provide a pattern of the patron IDs. For example, if the pattern is: "a 9-digit barcode that begin with 933," a patron enters a library card number 9339823480 is allowed to access the resource, but 398123403 is not considered a valid user. Another example of a patron ID pattern could be "Letters DZP followed by a nine-digit number."

Another form of authentication that most (if not all) vendors support is user ID and password pairs. In this scenario, the vendor sets up a user ID and password for each institutional account. Vendors also typically assign individual subscribers a unique username and password to access its resources. Although this method may be sufficient for individual subscribers, it represents problems for institutional users, such as libraries. It is very difficult for libraries to maintain such password lists for each vendor the library deals with. One possible solution would be to embed the various passwords on the library's Web site. However, this method poses several security risks and would make it very easy to have these passwords sent to unauthorized users. For these reasons, some libraries keep the passwords at the reference desk and require library users to come to the reference desk to receive the passwords. Of course, this method is very inconvenient for patrons and would not work for off-site users.

Locally created systems refer to an authentication system that is developed locally by libraries or their parent organizations using user data from institutional data sources, such as student registration system, human resources systems, and so forth. This type of authentication system is usually specifically developed to meet the need of the institution. Many large institutions use LDAP-based servers as the central repository of user base and as the authenticator, so all other applications that need to have access to the user base are able to authenticate against the repository using a standard communication protocol. This approach makes it very easy for different parts of the organization and for applications to share the same user data set. It also makes it easy for end users to access different services on campus with a single user name and password. The LDAP

protocol is understood and supported by most commercial content management systems.

It should also be noted that an increasing number of institutions have started to implement a single sign-on (SSO) system among all applications. A SSO system would eliminate the need for users to login multiple times. SSO systems will be discussed in greater detail later in this chapter.

Referring URL

In this scenario, the library is responsible for setting up a secure Web page that only authorized library users have access to. Authorized users are directed to the vendor's site. Vendor's system automatically grants access if the user comes straight from that secure Web site. In order for this to work, the library would already have an internal authentication mechanism in place, so only authorized users can get to the protected page.

If the library or the parent organization already has a protected site in place, this can be a very easy way to provide access to electronic resources. There is nothing else the library needs to do to implement this authorization. Keep in mind, though this form of authentication/authorization is not as widely supported by vendors as the IP filtering method.

Cookie-Based Authentication

The way it works in this scenario is that the library obtains a special cookie from the vendor, and stores the cookie on each of the library's public access computers. Cookies are small text files that can contain information about a Web site and its visitor's actions. These files usually are sent from a visited Web site and stored on the computer. The next time you visit that Web site, the information contained in the cookie is sent to the Web site. A common use of cookies is to store personal information or preference that will be used to remember you the next time you visit the Web site. Once the cookies have been installed, library users will be able to access the resources from that particular vendor without the need to login. This authentication approach is useful if there are only a handful of vendors, and the number of public workstations is small. The process is relatively straight forward, but library staff would have to go through the same process on every single computer that needs to access the resource. Also, the cookie is only for one single vendor, library staff would have to go through the same process with each vendor on every workstation. If the library supports multiple browsers, then the cookies need to be installed on all of the browsers. This method would also not work for users who need to access the resources remotely.

Please note that the term "cookie-based authentication" here only refers to vendor-supplied cookies. Many other authentication mechanisms (e.g., single sign-on systems, etc.) use cookies to store session data, but they do not belong to the cookie-based authentication we are discussing here.

SINGLE SIGN-ON (SSO)

As was discussed earlier in the chapter, in an enterprise-type environment (a university, a large organization, etc.) where multiple access points for e-resources exist, a user has to be authenticated multiple times, even with a consolidated source of authentication (authenticator). The situation gets worse when each one of these systems uses its own authentication mechanism and authenticator. One way to address this problem is to implement a so-called single sign-on system.

Single sign-on (SSO, sometimes more accurately referred to as RSO, reduced sign-on) refers to a type of authentication system where a user only has to be authenticated once, and is able to gain access to multiple software systems where he has access permission, without having to enter

his password again (Wikipedia, December 30, 2007). If there is an infrastructure that allows users to login once, and be able to access other e-resource systems without being asked to login again during the session, then we effectively have a SSO system, regardless of the method or technologies used to accomplish it. SSO not only provides a more convenient user experience, but because of the reduced number of authentication systems used, it makes the systems involved more secure.

How SSO works depends on the implementation (Mencik, 2001). Examples of SSO implementations that are being used include Central Authentication Service (CAS), Shibboleth, Athens (mainly in European countries), and various "WebAuth" systems. It should be noted that SSO itself is not a standard or protocol.

CAS, initially developed by Yale University, is now part of the Java Architectures Special Interest Group (JA-SIG) project. JA-SIG is global consortium of educational institutions and commercial affiliates supporting open source software development and promoting open computing architectures for higher education. CAS is a SSO implementation system that includes its own protocol (also named CAS). In a "CASified" environment, when a user reaches an application system (e.g., a campus portal), the system redirects the user to the CAS server. CAS then authenticates the user via a secure database (an active directory, LDAP, etc.). If the authentication is successful, the CAS server sends the user back to the application with a ticket (a randomly-generated number), and a ticket-granting cookie is set on the user's browser. The application then sends the service ticket along with the service identifier (i.e., the URL to the application server) back to the CAS server. CAS validates the ticket and the service identifier. If the validation is successful, CAS sends the user ID back to the application. At this point the authentication is complete. The application server never sees the user's password in the whole process. CAS can also communicate with a non-Web service that has its own authentication mechanism and has Web front-end, such as an ILS, e-mail server, and so forth, via proxy authentication. In this situation a trust relationship is established between the nonWeb application and the CAS (Java Architectures Special Interest Group, n.d.).

As of this writing, CAS has been adopted by over 60 institutions worldwide, most of which are universities. CAS is also supported by some ILS (e.g., Innovative Interfaces, Inc.), proxy servers (e.g., EZProxy), and enterprise portals (uPortal, PeopleSoft and some other content management systems). Unfortunately very few resource vendors support CAS at this time, but institutions can still provide SSO for remote users by establishing a SSO between a proxy server and the CAS. More details about how CAS works can be found at the CAS site (http://www.ja-sig.org/products/cas/overview/).

Shibboleth is a project of the Internet2 Middleware Architecture Committee for Education. According to its official Web site, "Shibboleth is standards-based, open source middleware software which provides Web single sign-on (SSO) across or within organizational boundaries. It allows sites to make informed authorization decisions for individual access of protected online resources in a privacy-preserving manner" (Internet2, n.d.). Shibboleth takes a different approach than CAS. In Shibboleth, multilateral relationships are established among different identity providers (IdP) and resource service providers (SP) by joining a Shibboleth federation. The IdP is the authentication source that provides verification of users attempting to access restricted resources. The SP is the resource that is protected by the Shibboleth architecture. A Shibboleth federation provides part of the underlying trust relationships among IdPs and SPs that are required for the Shibboleth architecture to function. Members of the federation (i.e., universities, organizations, e-resource providers) agree to exchange information using an agreed upon set of protocols, policies and practices.

When a user of a member university (the IdP) tries to access a resource at a vendor (a member SP within the same federation) site, the SP redirects the user back to the user's home campus authentication system to be authenticated. This redirection is referred to as the where are you from (WAYF) service that is part of the Shibboleth architecture. Once authenticated, the SP can ask the IdP to provide information about the user so it can make decisions on whether the user is authorized to access the resource. When the user later tries to access another resource from a different vendor (also a member SP within the federation), he/she does not have to login again. IdPs can decide how much information is released to a SP. User's credentials are never passed on to an IdP.

Because both vendors and libraries (or their parent institution) can be members of the same Shibboleth federation, authorized users at participating libraries will be able to access e-resources either from a participating member library or from the vendor. Access to the e-resource can be obtained either locally or remotely, without involving a remote access solution, such as a proxy server or virtual private network (VPN).

Shibboleth is still relatively new. As of this writing, the number of vendors that have joined one of the Shibboleth federations is still limited. Although it has great potential, implementation of Shibboleth is not an easy task. More information about the Shibboleth project can be found at its Web site (http://shibboleth.internet2.edu/).

Athens was developed by Eduserv Technologies Ltd. of the United Kingdom, and has been used primarily in Europe, especially in the UK. Athens stores all of the user's information, including username and passwords and what resources each user is permitted to access in a central repository. Domain administrators at each participating institution can load and update its own user information. Athens has recently added the capability to allow institutions to integrate existing local authentication system into Athens (Eduserv Technologies Limited [Eduserv], Local Access section, n.d.). Gateways between Athens and Shibboleth have also been developed (Eduserv, n.d.; Federal Access section, n.d.). These gateways allow "Shibbolized" users to access resources registered in Athens, and registered Athens users to access "Shibbolized" resources. When a user at a participating institution accesses a resource, Athens authenticates the user. If the authentication is successful, the user is able to access all the resources from all vendors that the user is permitted to access. Access can be obtained either locally at the library or remotely, without the need to login again.

Athens is a well-established system in Europe, especially in the UK, and is supported by most major resource vendors. It also works well for off-site users. More information about Athens can be found at the Athens Web site (http://www.athens.ac.uk/).

The term WebAuth is used by many institutions to refer to their institution-wide authentication system. Some of these are SSO implementation using an existing system, such as CAS, Shibboleth, while others are developed locally, even though they are all called WebAuth. Some of them are SSO implementations, other are not. All these systems are primarily used as enterprise-wide authentication systems. It may be difficult to make them work smoothly with commercial information resource management systems, such as ILSs, metasearch tools, and so forth, depending on how they are developed and whether they supports well-established standards. These systems do not necessarily address off-campus access issues, either. To overcome the remote access issue, a proxy server or VPN can supplement these systems.

Stanford University (http://www.stanford.edu/services/webauth/) and Duke University (https://webauth.duke.edu/) both developed their own WebAuth SSO systems, and have made them available for downloading. Both systems are based on Kerberos 5 for authentication. Stanford WebAuth can also work with Shibboleth as an IdP.

REMOTE ACCESS

Most of the authentication and authorization methods discussed so far (IP filtering, referring URL, cookies, etc.) work well with on-site users. However, they do not address the issue of users accessing resources from off-site locations such as a user's home, work place, or out of town. Libraries are currently using several methods to provide remote access to their e-resources. Proxy servers and virtual private networks are two of the most common methods currently in use by libraries. Some of the SSO methods, such as Shibboleth, can also be used to provide remote access.

Proxy Servers

Proxy servers process requests on behalf of another application or system. Typically, the proxy server sits between a library user's browser and the e-resource vendor's site. When a library user tries to access a licensed resource, the Web browser sends the request to the proxy server. The proxy server then checks the IP address of the end-user's computer. If the IP matches the IP ranges registered with the proxy server, it simply redirects the user to the resource itself. If there is no match, which means the user is coming from off-site, the proxy server performs an authentication. Most proxy servers are able to authenticate against various types of sources, such as an ILS patron database, LDAP directory, e-mail server, and so forth, in addition to its own user database. Libraries can also import basic user information (user ID and password) into the proxy servers' internal user database from other sources. Some proxy servers also support external authentication mechanisms, such as a customized authentication system developed in house by the library or its parent institution.

Upon successful authentication and/or authorization, the proxy server sends the request to the vendor site, on behalf of the library user. The vendor's site sees the IP address of the proxy server, rather than that of the library user's computer. Because the proxy server's IP address is within the range of what the library has registered with the vendor, the vendor authorizes the access, and the result is sent to the proxy server, which in turn sends it back to the end user browser.

Most proxy servers that are currently in use can only proxy Web sites. This means you won't be able to proxy any resource that is based-on Z39.50 or other nonWeb-based resources such as *SciFinder Scholar*. This also means that off-site users will not be able to access resources using reference management systems, such as *EndNote*, *ProCite*, and so forth. For these resources, libraries have to find other ways to provide remote access, such as using a virtual private network (VPN).

For the purpose of this chapter, we will group proxy servers into two categories: Traditional proxy servers and URL rewriting proxy servers. Traditional proxy servers are typically used to:

- Improve local users' access to the Internet
- Provide shared Internet access
- Provide content filtering for local users
- Provide access to protected sites for remotely authenticated users.

Traditional Proxy Servers

Traditional proxy servers store the content it retrieves the first time. When the same content is requested again, the proxy server compares the stored content with the remote server. If the content is the same, the proxy server sends the stored copy to the user's browser.

To implement this type of proxy server, the user's browser has to be told to use the proxy server. The user can manually configure the browser to use a particular proxy server or use a library created autoconfig file that redirects the user's requests (via the browser) to the right proxy server for the resources. This script can be hosted on a library owned Web server. In this case users do not have to manually configure the browser

for all the sites he/she need to access through proxy server(s). All the user has to do is to tell the browser to use the autoconfig file.

To provide remote access to licensed resources, libraries need to add vendors' domain names or URLs into the autoconfig file, so when a user requests a licensed resource, the request is sent to the proxy server, instead of the target URL directly. The following script uses the syntax specified in the proxy auto-config file format (Netscape, 1996):

```
1: function FindProxyForURL(url, host)
2: {
3: var ip = myIpAddress();
4: var proxyserver = "PROXY proxy.library.
yourorg.org:3128"
5: var noproxy = "DIRECT";
6: if (isInNet(ip, 192.168.0.0, 255.255.0.0))
{ return noproxy; }
7: if (shExpmatch(url, "http://melvyl.cdlib.
org/*")) { return noproxy; }
8: if (dnsDomainIs(host, ".ebscohost.com"))
{
9:    return proxyserver;
10: }
11: return noproxy;
12: }
```

In the script, line 3 defines a variable called "ip", which refers to the IP address of the end-user's computer as seen by the script; line 4 defines a proxy server, and line 5 defines a variable for "no proxy."

Line 6 tells us when the user is accessing the script from within the institution (IP 192.168.*.*), the user will be redirected straight to the resource. No proxy is needed for on-site users.

Line 7 says if a user is trying to access MELVYL, no proxy server will be involved and user is sent to the catalog site directly.

Line 8-10 says if a user is requesting any sites at EbscoHost domain (*.ebscohost.com), the session will be proxy'ed.

Line 11 says for all the other requests, proxy server is not involved and user is sent straight to the resource.

In this script, Line 7 is not necessary, because Line 11 would have covered it. Line 8 is the most important part of this script. It specifies the site that needs to be proxy'ed. We can repeat line 8-10 to include all licensed resources that need to be proxy'ed; or we can include all the resources in one statement by connecting the conditions with a Boolean OR operator. We can rewrite lines 8-10 as follows:

```
if (dnsDomainIs(host, ".ebscohost.com") ||
  dnsDomainIs(host, ".gale.com") ||
  dnsDomainIs(host, ".galegroup.com") ||
  dnsDomainIs(host, ".galenet.com") ||
  dnsDomainIs(host, ".galenet.gale.com")) {
  return proxyserver;
}
```

In addition to the autoconfig file as shown, all the e-resource sites need to be added to the proxy server configuration. Squid, one of the most popular traditional proxy servers, allows a separate text file that contains list of URLs to be attached to the configuration file. Squid supports Web sites (HTTP), FTP and Gopher protocols. More information can be found at the Squid project Web site (http://www.squid-cache.org/).

URL Rewriting Proxy Servers

Unlike traditional proxy servers, rewriting proxy servers do not store the content. Instead, they rewrite the URLs of the request. URL re-writing proxy servers do not require end users to configure their browsers to implement proxy servers. All the end user has to do is to point the browser to a proxy'ed version of the requested Web site's URL. Libraries can implement proxy'ed URLs in their Websites, including the list of databases, A-Z list of e-journals, subject guides, and so forth. Other tools, such as link resolvers and federated search portals, Learning management systems (LMS) can also be configured to use proxy'ed URLs for remote users.

For example, Academic Search Elite from EbscoHost URL is: http://search.epnet.com/login.asp?profile=ehost&defaultdb=afh.

A "proxy'ed" version of this URL would be: http://proxy.library.yourorg.org/login?url=http://search.epnet.com/login.asp?profile=ehost&defaultdb=afh.

When a user clicks on a proxy'ed URL, the proxy server checks to see if the target URL (the part after url=) is registered with the proxy server. If the URL is not registered in its profile/configuration, it simply rejects the access (proxy server can usually be configured to either generate an error message, or redirects the user to the target URL without proxying). Once a match is found, the proxy server will check the IP of the user's computer. If the user is from an on-site computer, the proxy server simply redirects the user to the target URL; if the IP is a remote IP, the proxy server will make the request to the remote server on behalf of the user (i.e., "proxy" the user's request). The vendor's server sees the request as coming from the IP address of the proxy server, not that of the end user. Because the proxy server's IP has already been registered with the vendor, the vendor system grants access and starts the access session, sends the response back to the proxy server, which in turn sends the request back to the end user's computer. The proxy server rewrites all the URLs received from vendor so throughout the session, all the subsequence requests and responses will go through the proxy server and be proxy'ed. This not only includes the URL the server sends back, but also all the URLs embedded in the Web pages. However, because vendor systems use various ways to present the content, such as JavaScript, the proxy server cannot always detect and rewrite them correctly (Zagar, 2000). Proxy servers are usually able to apply some special configuration parameters to address special needs for specific vendor systems. Examples of what these database-specific configurations might look like in EZProxy, a commonly used URL rewrite proxy server, can be found at the vendor's support site (http://www.usefulutilities. com/support/db/). Database-specific issues are also a constant discussion topic on the EZProxy mailing list (http://www.usefulutilities.com/support/list.html).

URL-rewrite proxy servers can re-write URLs by using different port numbers, or using distinct host names.

In a "proxy by port number" proxy server, each resource's URL is assigned a different port by the proxy server, and the rest of the URL remains the same. For example, if your library's proxy server's domain name is proxy.library.org and port 2050 has been assigned to EbscoHost. EbscoHost's URL (http://search.ebscohost.com/login.aspx) would be become: http://proxy.library.org:2050/login.aspx.

Similarly, http://metalib.calstate.edu:8331/V may be re-written as http://proxy.library.org:2051/V.

This strategy works well in most cases, but it does have some problems, especially when it comes to firewalls. Most enterprise firewalls do not allow users to access external Web sites that use these "nonstandard" ports. Only port 80 (nonsecured) and 443 (secured) are permitted. Also, if the proxy server is behind a firewall, the firewall has to be configured to open all possible ports to the outside world (Zagar, 2007).

When a proxy server rewrites URLs using host names, instead of assigning each target URL a different port number, it assigns a unique host name for each combination of host name and port number. The two resources would be rewritten as:

- http://search.ebscohost.com/login.aspx -> http://search.ebscohost.com.proxy.library.org/login.aspx

- http://metalib.calstate.edu:8331/V -> http://p8331-metalib.calstate.edu.proxy.library.org/V

With this method, users behind enterprise firewalls will be able to access resources through the proxy server the same way as other users.

There is one catch, however. For this method to work, the domain name service (DNS) server that manages the proxy server has to be configured to handle this new change. In other words, the DNS has to be able to resolve any host names ending with .proxy.library.org (including search.ebscohost.com.proxy.library.org and p8331-metalib.calstate.edu.proxy.library.org) to proxy.library.org. To accomplish this, the DNS administrator needs to set up a "wildcard" entry in the DNS (assuming the IP address for the proxy server is 192.168.10.15):

```
proxy.library.org. IN A 192.168.10.15
*.proxy.library.org. IN A 192.168.10.15
```

The EZProxy support sites has more detailed explanations about wildcard DNS (Zagar, 2007).

Examples of URL-rewrite proxy servers include: EZProxy (http://www.usefulutilities.com/) and Web Access Management (WAM) from Innovative Interfaces, Inc.

EZProxy, developed by Chris Zagar at Useful Utilities, was specifically designed for libraries and has a large customer base. EZProxy supports a wide variety of authentication sources, including various ILS patron APIs, FTP, LDAP, referring URL, CAS, Shibboleth, Athens, and so forth. Earlier versions of EZProxy rewrote URLs using different port numbers. Recent versions have added a "new strategy," which rewrites URLs using distinct host names for each target host/port combination (Zagar, 2007). There is also an active mailing list hosted by State University of New

York. More information about the list and subscription information can be found at http://www.usefulutilities.com/support/list.html.

WAM from Innovative Interfaces, Inc (http://www.iii.com/) is an add-on module for Millennium, III's ILS. It uses Millennium's authentication mechanism to authenticate users. Like EZProxy's "new strategy," it rewrites URLs by host names.

There are several advantages to implementing a traditional proxy server instead of a URL-rewrite proxy server. Since most traditional proxy server can cache or store sites, performance is usually enhanced when a user requests a full text article that has been previously requested before. The proxy server would send the user the stored copy without requesting it again from vendor's server. Many e-resource systems use javascripts to direct user to the full text content. Because the URL is not directly embedded in the Web page itself, some URL-rewrite proxy servers may not be able to detect and rewrite them, causing these URLs not to be proxy'ed. Unlike URL-rewrite proxy servers, traditional proxy servers do not use special URLs, so libraries only need to maintain a single URL for each resource, rather than two URLs as with a rewrite proxy server.

One major drawback of traditional proxy servers is that each user browser has to be configured to use the proxy server or to use an autoconfig file, which in turn determines when to use a proxy server (Zagar, 2000). This additional step required by the user could cause problems, especially for users with little or no experience configuring their browser.

Virtual Private Network (VPN)

Virtual private network is a private communication network over a public network (e.g., the Internet) using tunneling technologies. Wikipedia defines tunneling as "the transmission of data through a public network in such a way that routing nodes in the public network are unaware

that the transmission is part of a private network ... Tunneling allows the use of public networks (e.g., the Internet), to carry data on behalf of users as though they had access to a 'private network,' hence the name."

Unlike proxy servers, VPN is a client-server environment, which means users will have to install a VPN client software on the user's computer, in order to connect to the VPN network. Once connected, a new IP address will be assigned to the user's computer. VPN can be set up to only let identified resources (by checking the IP of the requested destination) go through the private tunnel. The end result is: when a user connects to a resource vendor's site that is identified by the VPN server configuration, vendor's server sees the IP address assigned by the VPN server as the user's IP. Since the VPN IP range has been previously registered with vendor, the user is recognized as a valid request.

VPNs are normally set up at the institutional level by network personnel of the library's parent organization to provide authorized users (employees and students) access to networked resources behind the institutional firewall (e.g., shared folders on networked file servers, restricted applications and internal Websites, etc.) securely. Libraries can provide access to licensed e-resources through VPN by adding vendor IP addresses to the VPN profile, so resources at these vendor sites can be routed through the VPN. This practice, however, introduces an additional workload for the VPN administrator. A list of valid IP addresses needs to be up to date. Also, as vendors expand or change their network infrastructure, IP addresses could change on a regular basis. Vendors may not always inform libraries about these changes which could result in IP addresses included in the VPN profile to become out of date. If an IP is not in the VPN profile, all routing requests to this IP address is blocked causing the end-users IP address to be revealed to the vendor's server. The vendor's server would see the request coming from an unrecognized IP address and would either deny access or prompt the user to enter a password. One way to resolve this problem is to tell the VPN server to route any requests regardless the destination IP. This will makes library's job easier and will make library users happy. But this may add overhead to the institutional network traffic. If this is not an option at your organization, you can instruct users that when a particular resource does not work, disconnect from the VPN server, and retry (this will activate the proxy server if one is set up), and inform the library about the resource, so librarians can investigate and inform the VPN administrator about the IP discrepancy and make adjustment to the VPN profile.

A Web-based VPN (WebVPN) service has recently been developed that eliminates the need for client software. It uses secure socket layer (SSL) as the encryption mechanism. Users establish a VPN connection by logging in to the WebVPN Website. Once connected to the Web-based VPN service, a separate WebVPN tunnel area within the browser window is created along with a special floating toolbar. You must use this area to gain access to all licensed e-resources. The toolbar allows you to enter URLs or end the VPN session. If you open a bookmark or type a Web page address in the browser window, the visited page will not be accessed through the WebVPN server. Since this method is still relatively new, not all e-resources are supported. Many libraries that have implemented a Web-based VPN inform users that not all e-resources are supported and recommend that they install and use the VPN client software for resources that do not support WebVPN. WebVPN also does not currently support nonWeb-based applications. As more e-resource vendors support this new technology, the ability to provide remote access to e-resources without the need to install additional software will become an attractive alternative.

The advantages of using VPN compared with proxy servers is that the transmission is secure, and it also provides access to other resources available on the VPN supported network such as other university network resources, and nonWeb-based e-resources.

Other Remote Access Solutions

Federated identity management systems, such as Shibboleth and Athens, have been used to address remote access issues. In these systems, because a users' institutional affiliation is known to service providers (i.e., e-resource vendors), the vendor site will easily identify authorized users upon successful authentication, whether on-site or off-site.

This kind of systems has eliminated the need of a proxy server or VPN, and users do not need to login again. One drawback to these systems is that both the library's parent institution and all the vendors have to join the same federation for this approach to work.

PRIVACY AND SECURITY

Libraries have historically protected their user's privacy. Although many authentication systems require some user identity information, it is possible through the use of anonymous authentication to provide access to these resources without requiring the user to submit personal information to the authentication system. Some systems provide guest accounts with minimal privileges. For example the patron that walks into the library can sit down at a library public computer and access its resources without the need to identify themselves. A guest account would not provide membership attributes but could have entitlement values allowing access to e-resources that permit walk-in or campus users. The American Library Association policy concerning Confidentiality of Personally Identifiable Information about Library Users (2004) states that,

The ethical responsibilities of librarians, as well as statutes in most states and the District of

Columbia, protect the privacy of library users. Confidentiality extends to 'information sought or received and resources consulted, borrowed, acquired or transmitted' and includes, but is not limited to, database search records, reference interviews, circulation records, interlibrary loan records and other personally identifiable uses of library materials, facilities, or services.

Many authentication systems provide mechanisms that keep their personal identities secret and instead only identify the user as belonging to an authorized group of users such an undergraduate of the university. Although authentication's implications for privacy do not necessarily equate violations of privacy, understanding the distinctions requires being aware of how privacy can be affected by the process of authentication. However, this awareness is usually absent since authentication usually is connected more with security than with privacy (Kent & Millett, 2003, p. 1).

The International Coalition of Library Consortia (2002) has established its privacy guidelines for electronic resources vendors. According to the guidelines, libraries should require that vendors, at a minimum, meet these guidelines. The guidelines include:

- **Privacy of users:** PUBLISHER respects the privacy of the users of its products. Accordingly, PUBLISHER will not disclose information about any individual user of its products (hereinafter referred to as "personal information"), including information about the specific content of a user's searches, to a third party without the permission of that individual user, except as required by law.
- **Authorized use protected:** PUBLISHER will not deny an authorized user access to its product on account of that user's election not to permit distribution of personal information to a third party.
- **Privacy policy statement:** The PUBLISHER will post a privacy policy statement on

its online site. The privacy policy statement should be easy to find, easy to use and comprehensible.
- **Responsibility:** PUBLISHER will maintain full control over its site to prevent any violation of the privacy policy by a third party, such as an advertiser or ISP.
- **Monitoring:** PUBLISHER will review regularly the functioning of its Web site to insure that its privacy policy is enforced and effective.
- **Control of authorized use of products:** Nothing in these guidelines is intended to interfere with a PUBLISHER's right to enforce license terms concerning which users are authorized to use its products. It is understood and accepted that owners of licensed Web products may need to transmit information such as an ip address or a user id to a third party as part of the mechanism by which the owner limits use of its product to authorized users. These guidelines do not prohibit such transmission.

Libraries should be involved in the planning and decision making process of any authentication or digital credential system. According to the Digital Library Authentication and Authorization Architecture (Gargano, Glenn, Graham, Gurnani, Houser, Millman, 2000) the development of any authentication architecture should have the following functional requirements: The individual requesting access to an e-resource should be able to choose whether to use a persistent identity or an anonymous identity for a given transaction; the library or institution should not reveal information that could be used to identify the particular individual in order to allow access the request e-resource; and the information contained in the certificate payload should be minimized to ensure that only information strictly necessary to determine the institutional affiliation of an individual and to locate externally stored access control information.

SPECIAL CONSIDERATION

During the last 20 years, the price of e-resources has increased significantly. These increases have occurred at the same time that the library has increasingly shifted from print to electronic versions while continuing to grapple with shrinking acquisitions budgets. To address these changes, libraries have been relying more and more on consortia purchases as way to reduce their costs and still provide access to an increasingly larger percentage of e-resources. Although, consortia purchases have great benefits in terms of price negotiation, they do present some challenges in providing access to licensed e-resources.

Generally, one contract is written for all participating members of the consortium and is usually a prerequisite for obtaining a consortial discount. As in regular license agreements between one library and the vendor, the definition of "user" must be carefully defined to include all possible users of the consortium. Careful consideration must be made to ensure that all participating libraries are able to have their unique definition of "user" be part of the consortium definition of "user." Also, as additional libraries join the consortium, their needs and "user" definitions must also be factored into any new license or renewal of an existing license.

Additional factors that will need to be considered include licenses that restrict access to a limited number of simultaneous users or access ports. This limitation could be resolved if the vendors allow alternatives for access during specified periods or possibly special locations such as instruction labs when used for training or instructional purposes. Other alternatives could be the use of special training or instructional passwords or a temporary increase in the number of simultaneous users for a specified site.

Most consortia licenses address the "user" definition by using an aggregate of all the participating library's "users." Typically access is provided to consortial members via IP address filtering. IP addresses of all consortia members should be included in the license agreement and allow for changes as the need arises. Since it is very unlikely that there exists a comprehensive authentication source for all the consortia member's users, the responsibility of providing remote access will typically fall on the participating library. However, some larger consortia may have additional technical resources that could assist a member library in implementing authentication mechanisms. This may be especially useful for smaller member libraries without sufficient technical staff. Other mechanisms can be implemented such as digital certificates or federated authentication mechanisms such as Shibboleth.

As the interest and use of metasearch applications increases, so will the need to establish a widely supported set of standards and best practices in the use and development of these metasearch applications. To begin these discussions and to address these issues, the National Information Standards Organization (NISO) sponsored a MetaSearch Initiative in 2003. One of the three groups chartered by NISO was the Access Management Task Force. As Teets and Murray (2006) mentioned, the focus of this group was on gathering requirements for metasearch authentication and access needs, inventorying existing processes, developing best practices given today's processes, and recommending and pursuing changes to current solutions to better support metasearch applications. The task force's report identified eleven environmental factors that were viewed as critical success factors in metasearching. The report (NISO Metasearch Initiative Task Group 1, 2005) also stated that these environmental factors must also be applied within three different contexts: the metasearch service provider, the information service provider, and the licensing organization and its users. The eleven environmental factors include: Suitability/effectiveness; ease of implementation, licensing cost, implementation cost, software expertise required, security, maintainability, robustness, scalability, simplicity of understanding, and market acceptance/preexisting implementations.

CONCLUSION

As more and more people find their place in this increasingly online world of information, many users will come to the library already possessing several online accounts to other personal Web-based resources such as social networking Web-sites, online commerce and banking sites among others. Users are already becoming increasingly frustrated with the need to learn yet another authentication mechanism to access library e-resources. Librarians, publishers and vendors of electronic resources must participate in the dialogue to develop and implement new identity and access management systems. The need to establish a universal authentication and authorization infrastructure will become increasingly important as the desired expectation to integrate the educational and research environments with the commercial environment increases.

Work is currently underway to establish federated digital rights management systems as well as other digital identity management frameworks such as the Liberty Alliance Project (http://www.projectliberty.org/) and OpenID (http://openid.net/). The management of digital identities is a core issue that everyone who uses the Internet for research, recreation, communication or commerce will need to be aware of. Many individuals may possess multiple identities based on multiple underlying technologies. Although it's very unlikely that a centralized or single identity system will be implemented, it's more probable that an interoperable system of systems will be developed. A system that will allow individuals to own and manage their own identities instead of having them managed by others is also a possible alternative that will need to be addressed. Libraries will need to be aware of these new developments and, if possible, be involved in these discussions.

Of course, much of the success of these new methods will require the adoption of these new technologies by the e-resource vendors.

As was evident in the April 1998 workshop on access management, the five key properties for the design and adoption of systems that would enable access for users and libraries while respecting the rights and interests of authors and publishers are still very much true in 2007. These properties include:

1. **Simplicity.** The less complex a system of access management, the more readily it can be adopted technologically and organizationally, and the more acceptable it is to all involved in its implementation.
2. **Privacy.** Systems that manage access to the cultural record must protect the privacy of users from detailed tracking and disclosure of use. User privacy must not be compromised.
3. **Good faith.** Agreements on access to scholarly information rely on trust among the parties involved. Users and providers would each prefer to depend, in an access management system that implements these agreements, on reasonable barriers against abuse rather than complex restrictions that inhibit use.
4. **Trusted intermediaries.** Intermediaries play an essential role in providing access to the cultural record as parties trusted by both users and providers and as efficient aggregators of distribution and usage. System design must take the role of intermediaries into account.
5. **Reasonable terms.** Access management systems and license agreements must recognize the distinction between access and use. Overly tight control of access to a resource may impose inappropriate constraints on its use, especially in teaching and research contexts. The most useful system will not limit access to specific user groups known

in advance to be interested in a resource but will be reasonably open to serving unlikely users whose curiosity and research interests may lead them in directions not predicted by those responsible for making the agreements or designing the systems (Arms, 1999).

Although it is very difficult to predict the future, it is becoming evident that the bulk of resources that libraries will be providing in the next five to ten years will be increasingly available online. Providing easy and seamless access to these resources will become one of the more important challenges that libraries will be facing. How this is done will need to be discussed not only among librarians, but also with universities, public institutions, government agencies, policy groups and of course the commercial vendors that provide the e-resources. As more and more information moves to the Internet so will the need to securely and effortlessly provide the appropriate access to this information. The current methods based on IP-filtering and proxy servers have been in use for many years and will probably, for the foreseeable future, continue to serve as the primary method of authentication for local and remote access to e-resources. However, these mechanisms should eventually be replaced by systems that provide improved usability, interoperability and security. A technology that has had a great deal of potential for replacing both IP-based and traditional username and password is the use of digital certificates. However, despite the benefits of using digital certificates, they have yet to be widely adopted among the library community. Regardless of the identity and access management (IAM) system used by libraries to provide access to their e-resources, it is important to remember that the goal of any IAM system should be for it to be seamless, secure, private, simple-to-use and relatively easy to deploy and manage.

REFERENCES

Alford, D. E. (2002). Negotiating and analyzing electronic license agreements. *Law Library Journal, 94*, 621-644.

American Library Association (2004). Policy concerning confidentiality of personally identifiable information about library users. Retrieved November 21, 2007, from http://www.ala.org/alaorg/oif/pol_user.html

American Association of Law Libraries, American Library Association, Association of Academic Health Sciences Libraries, Association of Research Libraries, Medical Library Association, Special Libraries Association (1997). Principles for licensing electronic resources. Retrieved November 21, 2007, from http://www.arl.org/sc/licensing/licprinciples.shtml

Arms, C. (1999). Enabling access in digital libraries: A report on a workshop on access management. Retrieved November 21, 2007, from http://www.clir.org/pubs/reports/arms-79/contents.html

Eduserv Technologies Limited (n.d.). Eduserv athens. Retrieved November 21, 2007, from http://www.athensams.net/

Gargano, J., Glenn A., Graham, R., Gurnani, S., Houser, L., Millman, D., et al. (2000). A digital library authentication and authorization architecture. Retrieved November 21, 2007, from http://www.cdlib.org/inside/groups/stas/links.html

International Coalition of Library Consortia (1997). Statement of current perspective and preferred practices for the selection and purchase of electronic information. Retrieved November 21, 2007, from http://www.library.yale.edu/consortia/statement.html

International Coalition of Library Consortia (2002). Privacy guidelines for electronic resources vendors. Retrieved November 21, 2007 from http://www.library.yale.edu/consortia/2002privacyguidelines.html

International Federation of Library Associations and Institutions (2001). Licensing principles. Retrieved November 21, 2007, from http://www.ifla.org/V/ebpb/copy.htm

Internet2 (n.d.). Shibboleth - Internet2 middleware. Retrieved November 21, 2007, from http://shibboleth.internet2.edu/

Java Architectures Special Interest Group (n.d.). CAS overview. Retrieved November 21, 2007, from http://www.ja-sig.org/products/cas/overview/index.html

Kent, S. T., & Millett L. I. (Eds.) (2003). *Who goes there?: Authentication through the lens of privacy.* Washington, D.C.: National Academy Press.

Kyrillidou, M., & Young, M. (2006). ARL statistics 2004-05: A compilation of the statistics from the one hundred and twenty-three members of the Association of Research Libraries. Retrieved November 21, 2007, from http://www.arl.org/stats/annualsurveys/arlstats/index.shtml

Lynch, C. (1998). A white paper on authentication and access management issues in cross-organizational use of networked information resources. Retrieved November 21, 2007, from http://www.cni.org/projects/authentication/authentication-wp.html

Mencik, S. (2001). How single sign-on work. Retrieved November 21, 2007, from shttp://searchsecurity.techtarget.com/ateQuestionNResponse/0,289625,sid14_cid391596_tax285453,00.html

Netscape (1996). Navigator proxy auto-config file format. Retrieved November 21, 2007, from http://wp.netscape.com/eng/mozilla/2.0/relnotes/demo/proxy-live.html

NISO Metasearch Initiative Task Group 1 (2005). Ranking of authentication and access methods available to the metasearch environment. Retrieved November 21, 2007, from http://www.niso.org/standards/resources/MI-Access_Management.pdf

Plum, T., & Bleiler, R. (2001). *User authentication. SPEC Kit. 267.* Washington, D.C.: Association of Research Libraries.

Richards, R. (2001). Licensing agreements: Contracts, the eclipse of copyright, and the promise of cooperation. *The Acquisitions Librarian, 26,* 89-107.

Ragouzis, N., Hughes, J., Philpott, R., & Maler, E. (Eds.) (2006). Security assertion markup language (SAML) V2.0 technical overview. Working Draft 10. Retrieved November 21, 2007, from http://www.oasis-open.org/committees/security/docs/draft-sstc-saml-01.pdf

Teets, M., & Murray, P. (n.d.). Metasearch authentication and access management. *D-Lib Magazine.* Retrieved November 21, 2007, from http://www.dlib.org/dlib/june06/teets/06teets.html

University of California, Berkeley Library (2007). *Proxy server setup instructions.* Retrieved November 21, 2007, from http://proxy.lib.berkeley.edu/instructions.html

Wikipedia, the free encyclopedia. (2006, December 27). Central Authentication Service. Retrieved November 21, 2007, from http://en.wikipedia.org/wiki/Central_Authentication_Service

Wikipedia, the free encyclopedia. (2007, January 18). Shibboleth. Retrieved November 21, 2007, from http://en.wikipedia.org/wiki/Shibboleth

Wikipedia, the free encyclopedia. (2007, January 30). Single sign-on. Retrieved November 21, 2007, from http://en.wikipedia.org/wiki/Single_sign-on

Wolverton, R. E. (2003). E-journal licensing and legal issues: A panel report. *The Serials Librarian, 45*(2), 153-156.

Zagar, C. (2000, January 24). Proxy server vs. URL rewriter for authentication. Message posted to Web4lib listserv. Retrieved November 21, 2007, from http://lists.webjunction.org/wjlists/web4lib/2000-January/030233.html

Zagar, C. (2007). URL rewrting. Retrieved November 21, 2007, from http://www.usefulutilities.com/support/rewrite.html

Chapter XV
Using Consistent Naming Conventions for Library Electronic Resources

Diana Kichuk
University of Saskatchewan, Canada

ABSTRACT

There are no accepted standards governing naming electronic resources in A to Z lists or electronic resource management (ERM) systems. Current practice superficially resembles cataloging standards and guidelines, but is substantially ad hoc, and reliant on local adaptation and innovation. A little more predictability is needed to make finding and using electronic resources easier. This chapter describes issues related to naming electronic resources and concludes with a draft set of principles and conventions for designating names or titles in the context of A to Z lists and ERM systems. It will also examine the unique issue of electronic resource volatility and its impact on maintenance. The focus will be on integrated or continuously updated electronic resources, such as bibliographic and full text databases, and reference works.

INTRODUCTION

"What is the title?" "What is it called?" Variations of these questions are asked countless times a day in library physical and electronic spaces. The success of online information retrieval is not dependent on correct search strategies and query syntax alone. In addition to formulating a topic and keywords, a researcher must also know which electronic information resources to use from prior experience or advice, or know how to go about finding them. As Mary E. Brown puts it, "to find the right information, the *right* name is needed" (1995, p. 347). Identification and recall depend in part on effective naming practices of publishers and vendors, but ease of access and use of electronic collections also depend on how effective a library's finding aids and systems are. Successful library naming practices play an important role in determining that effectiveness.

If the name used in a library finding tool, such as the catalog or database A to Z list, does not correspond with the name or title cited, recalled, or viewable on the resource itself or some other name perception, then the researcher's quest becomes more difficult, if not doomed to fail.

Although naming electronic resources is a surprisingly complex task, the problems associated with it are not widely discussed in the literature. In an intense search using expected keywords, the author failed to locate articles that focused specifically on naming problems in the context of electronic resource management. This gap is difficult to explain given the centrality of electronic resources in library collections today. The relatively small electronic resources librarian (ERL) community has not taken the time to articulate the problems from their perspective; their reluctance is due perhaps to a potential conflict with their standard-bound cataloging colleagues. Or, a fear that by drawing attention to the problem in their practice, formal guidelines or rules will be implemented that interfere with their management of the dynamic world of electronic resources? The literature includes sources on naming related to information retrieval, including how humans name things or concepts, and how names are recalled. Guides for cataloging electronic resources, especially serials, are a good source for deriving the language and description of good naming practice.

There are no accepted standards governing naming electronic resources in A to Z lists or electronic resource management (ERM) systems. Current practice superficially resembles cataloging standards and guidelines, but is substantially ad hoc, and reliant on local adaptation and innovation. Each library adopts a practice that changes over time often resulting in a hodgepodge of naming applications in its systems, even in a single A to Z list. Assuming it is desirable to compile a draft set of general principles and conventions, what should be included? While the hard and fast rules of the kind found in cataloging standards are not applicable, there is a need for universal guidelines or harmonization, or at the very least, internal consistency within a library's A to Z lists and ERM systems. In the same way that bibliographic citations follow sanctioned styles and are convertible, electronic resource naming practices should follow a consistent, rational style within an institution, and be convertible across institutions. Less ad hoc treatment and a little more predictability is needed to make finding and using electronic resources easier for the researcher and for interoperability within and across institutions, for example for peer collection comparison and analyses, or consortia acquisition. How can a consortium recognize common resources if each member names a resource differently?

This chapter describes issues related to naming electronic resources, proposes a set of principles and conventions for designating names or titles in the context of A to Z lists and ERM systems, and briefly considers future trends. It will also examine the unique issue of electronic resource volatility and its impact on maintenance. The words *name* and *title* are used interchangeably to refer to the word or set of words by which an electronic resource is known. In addition to a primary title, or "title proper" in the language of catalogers, a resource may be known by alternate or variant titles. That complex of primary and alternate titles forms what the Digital Library Initiative (DLI) calls a "title group" (Parker, Anderson, Chandler, Farb, Jewell, Riggio, & Robertson, 2004, p. 15). For the purposes of this chapter, an electronic resource is defined very broadly, as any work published in electronic form, either on CD-ROM, DVD, or online. The focus will be on integrated or continuously updated electronic resources, such as bibliographic and full text databases, and reference works.

BACKGROUND

In Libraries, Everything is a Naming Problem

When Gordon Irlam stated that "In computing, it is rumoured: Everything is a naming problem" (1995), he might as well have been referring to libraries. In libraries, everything, in one way or another, is a naming problem. Naming objects in library collections is an ongoing and time-consuming technical services and systems activity. Every object in a library's physical or electronic collections has one or more names or titles assigned to it. Cataloging, subject classification, indexing, document classification, serials management and openURL linking services, A to Z lists, ERM, reference interview and keyword or topic searching, all involve naming exercises. The utility of an online collection is dependent on the effectiveness of resource naming in library systems.

The problem of naming electronic resources in A to Z lists and ERM systems starts with the decision about which page level to default to for access—the vendor's splash or product home page, the basic or advanced search page, or some other page? The decision may depend on local practice; a decision of a reference or subject liaison librarian, or it may be dictated by the internal logic of the resource. The choice will vary from one resource to the next. Publishers and vendors themselves may not reference a resource consistently from one page to another on the resource site or in their information pages. If they differ, which source should prevail to derive the primary name or title? Title identification in the access page itself is often difficult. Even the typical title banner across the top of the page may display competing information such as the publisher, vendor, or interface name. Because of conflicting source information or vagueness, an ERL may assign a hybrid or constructed name to suit a perceived local patron need. This practice may not be consistent with any known naming standard, but it is a common

across library sectors as any random review of electronic resource A to Z lists can attest.

Library Standards and Electronic Resources

Libraries are standard-bound institutions, applying rigorous rules to cataloging, classification, coding, indexing, and authority work. The international descriptive cataloging standard, the *Anglo-American Cataloging Rules*, 2nd edition, (*AACR2*) (2002), for example, includes rules governing naming library print, audiovisual, and electronic media in the title statement. Even when no title exists, there are rules for compiling one. But standards are never comprehensive, nor can they be. There are always exceptions that do not fit the rule. *AACR2* uses language of sufficient generality and vagueness to leave catalogers with considerable interpretive or subjective latitude. This flexibility works fairly well for print and microfilm, since these "old" media are relatively stable in their presentation, making exceptions finite. This flexibility becomes a liability in the case of electronic resources, where presentation is far from stable and where name changes occur frequently. The standard makers cannot keep up with the evolving nature of "new" media in libraries. As a result, a small cottage industry of additional guidelines and interpretations flourish between standards editions. The continually updated, *Library of Congress Rule Interpretations (LCRI)* (Office of Descriptive Cataloging Policy, Library of Congress, 1989), for example, amplifies and explains existing rules and adds new ones for areas not covered in *AACR2*. CONSER (Cooperative Online Serials) is an international online serials cataloging program run by the Library of Congress. Module 31 of the *CONSER Cataloging Manual* (2006) is a supplemental standard specifically geared to deal with the complexities of cataloging online serials. Module 31 only applies to individual electronic journals and newsletters, that is, to serials in the narrow sense, and not to databases. While such guides assist catalogers in interpreting standards, they also sanction subjective interpretation and make exceptional applications quasi-standards. When it comes to the ever-changing field of electronic resources with their multiple sources for description information, the cataloger is often at sea, and must extrapolate from standards applicable to print media or invent totally new approaches for emerging realities. Since its first appearance, *AACR2* has gone through a series of revisions and updates. Yet it still lags behind the real world of electronic resources. A so-called third edition, AACR3, is now under development. This potentially new backward-compatible standard is intended to address some of the most awkward problems *AACR2* has in application to electronic resources (Weiss, 2006).

Library systems in general become corrupted over time. Standards are applied differently from institution to institution, from one individual to another, and over the life of a system. As new standards and local administrative policies are implemented and displace old standards and policies, catalogs demonstrate a hodgepodge of different standards and policy applications. This is true even in the relatively short time that electronic resources have been widely accessible in libraries A spot check of library catalogs reveals that in many, electronic resource titles receive different treatment, for example, for capitalization, that is only explainable as a change in policy or interpretation. The inconsistency remains embedded in the catalog record unchanged perhaps for the life of the catalog.

Cataloging standards and guidelines cannot be systematically applied in the creation of metadata for electronic resource A to Z lists or ERM records, where their weaknesses in relation to electronic resources are even more apparent than in the catalog.

The Rise and Fall, and Rise Again of the Catalog

Some may argue that the traditional catalog is still the premier library access tool—a comprehensive index and finding aid to all of the library's holdings. The only significant content universally excluded from the catalog is journal articles. They continue to be covered separately in index and full text journal databases. Catalog records may however, include book tables of contents, reviews, and even book cover images. In theory, catalogs encompass the full range of library collections—print, microform, kits, and digital or electronic media. In practice, the traditional catalog does not work very well as the primary retrieval source for electronic resources. Early on, libraries identified the need to distinguish their valuable databases that would otherwise languish in the catalog and created additional access systems—alphabetical and subject lists, also known as A to Z lists. Lists by resource type, such as electronic journal lists, are commonplace. Federated search portals, such as MetaLib (Ex Libris), provide a uniform search platform with cross-database search functionality, and integrate distributed library access systems. Portals vie with the catalog as the central library retrieval tool.

But the prediction of the demise of the catalog is premature. The pendulum appears to be swinging back, and an improved or enhanced catalog is on the ascendant. The proliferation of separately maintained library lists for emerging electronic resource types appears to have abated. Instead, the database list has become all-inclusive, including a full range of resource types, excluding electronic journals and books. The former are still usually maintained in separate in-house systems or in serials management or openURL linking services. Electronic reference works are often included in electronic resource A to Z lists, perhaps because their numbers initially did not warrant separate lists, but more likely because they share seriality and quick look-up functionality with the bibliographic databases that still make up the bulk of such lists. Other resource types such as image collections, data resources and streaming audio also fit easily into a single "database" list. As the potential for their numbers became clear, it was not a viable option to have electronic books appear in separate lists in addition to the catalog. Libraries routinely catalog individual electronic book collection titles; but after expending so much time and energy first creating then maintaining A to Z lists for electronic journals and databases, creating yet another segregated list for books seemed impracticable. The need for a more integrated solution becomes apparent as the range of resource types expands and their numbers grow. In-house spreadsheets and systems cannot practically keep up with the growth and complexity of electronic collections. They are also inadequate for tracking license information and usage statistics, or administrator information. ERM systems have the potential to integrate the various in-house library applications into a single system and enhance the catalog. The result is a kind of super catalog with multiple access points generated from a single set of records. ERM systems can output A to Z lists similar to those generated in the past and more. License information can be integrated and publicly accessible for the first time. Current usage statistics harvested from vendor sites can be viewed by staff without the necessity to maintain a separate library system. Secondary outputs, such as resource information pages, can also be generated. Instead of navigating distributed systems, the patron can navigate freely from the macro electronic resource or database level, to the micro electronic journal or book level in a single integrated system. The one-stop, super catalog is easier to use, with fewer "clicks" to desired content than traditional catalogs (Bracke, 2001, p.7). ERM systems have the potential to return the catalog to the center of the library's information retrieval service.

Part of the advantage of ERM systems is their capacity to capture all the relevant names or titles of an electronic resource so that patrons can find them. That capacity depends on moving beyond naming principles applied in the discipline of cataloging, including its inclination to catalog an electronic resource once, then, forget about it. ERM systems combine the nonstandard, even unorthodox naming practice applied in A to Z list creation with the formal standards applied in cataloging. In addition to the primary and alternative titles in the catalog's bibliographic record, there is the potential for a differently derived primary title and alternative titles. For example, the public name used by a library's openURL linking service, the subscription package name, the often cryptic name cited on an invoice, and spelling variants are all potential alternate titles. Both the A to Z list and the ERM system from which it is ideally derived, are potentially very current. Catalog records for electronic resources are either not updated at all or updated only when major name changes occur, and only after a significant passage of time. Once created, catalog records are rarely revisited by the cataloger. In contrast, ERM records, like the ERL maintained spreadsheets on which they are often based, are works in progress. In an effort to keep up to date with ongoing changes as they are reported or discovered in their role as primary acquisitions and technical contact, the ERL is constantly updating details of the A to Z list or the ERM record. It is their currency, in part, that makes these tools so central to electronic resources retrieval.

Seriality and Electronic Resources

Library electronic collections are currently comprised of a broad range of resources—from the now familiar bibliographic abstract and indexing databases, full text aggregator databases, and book, document and journal collections, to new kinds of content delivered in new media, including: digital images, streaming audio, data, newspapers, news services, and multimedia reference works. *AACR2* considers electronic resources to be of two types: finite (that is, monographic in nature or continuing with a limited duration), and continuing—either serial or integrating. Integrating resources incorporate updates into the whole. Databases and loose-leaf publications are integrating resources. Electronic resources can also exhibit both monographic and serial characteristics (Program for Cooperative Cataloging, 2005). But despite the evidence of monographic electronic resources, electronic resources are fundamentally serial in nature, or have the potential to be. Obvious exceptions are life-of-edition reference works or electronic books. But even they demonstrate seriality; for example, life-of-edition reference works are periodically superseded by a new edition. Even finite monographic works, such as electronic books and documents, may be delivered as part of a subscription collection on a periodically upgraded platform. There is the potential at least for multiple versions and editions of monographs, with publicized or unannounced updates or revisions of the original by the publisher or the author.

In a conference presentation, T. Scott Plutchak, a medical library director, guessed that information technology people "would consider all of this electronic information a database." Databases conjure up visions of constant revision. Plutchak proposed that the concept of what is a serial is outdated when applied to electronic resources, where the line drawn between a journal, book, and database is fading if not being eliminated altogether (reported in Tonkery, 2006). Melissa Beck (1995), who prepared the first draft of module 31 of the *CONSER Cataloging Manual*, "Remote Access Computer File Serials," raised the issue of the problem of defining serials in *AACR2* and *LCRI*, as early as 1995, but an expanded definition has yet to be formalized. Whether or not an electronic resource is even a publication was settled early on in order to avoid cataloging them under the rules for manuscripts. However there are continuing problems with the notion of seriality applied to electronic resources (Anderson

& Hawkins, 1996). When is a work complete? Licenses often include clauses that permit the publisher to remove or revise content at their discretion. In the online environment, the user has few assurances regarding the completeness of a work. Has it been abridged or revised? Is the accessed version, the latest version?

A serial in the narrow sense represented by print and electronic journals is related to the database and other electronic resources. The latter are serials in a broad sense. Conventions for their description, including naming, can draw on robust serials cataloging standards; but those standards, closely associated with print serial standards do not have the flexibility and range to cover electronic resources, especially outside of the traditional catalog, in A to Z lists and ERM systems.

DISCUSSION

The Art of Naming Electronic Resources

The title or name of a library object is what it is called or known as. The Oxford English Dictionary (OED Online) defines "title" as "an inscription placed on or over an object, giving its *name* or describing it," "a descriptive or distinctive appellation; a *name*…" and as "the *name* of a book, a poem, or other (written) composition; an inscription at the beginning of a book, describing or indicating its subject, contents, or nature…" (italics added by author). Simply stated, a title is a name. A "name" is "a word or phrase constituting the individual designation by which a particular person or thing is known, referred to, or addressed." The verb "naming," means, "to mention or specify (a person, place, or personified thing) by its proper name; to call by the right name." Naming electronic resources in library systems is the act of designating a resource by its proper or right name or names, or title or titles. Effective library naming practice ensures that an object is designated by all the titles by which a patron may know it. An incorrectly or incompletely named resource cannot be found readily or not at all. If it cannot be found, it effectively does not exist, even though the library has expended substantial time and money on it.

Unless using the time-honored methods of browsing and serendipity, retrieval—of print, microform, or electronic journals, books, articles, or documents, digitized facsimiles and databases—begins with a name or title. The source of the title might be a citation in hand, a recalled title, a subject guide, an A to Z list, a catalog record, or a bibliographic database search result. While titles in the catalog or a bibliographic database are derived using rigorous cataloging or citation standards, there are no formal standards for naming electronic resources in A to Z lists, order records, or ERM resource records. Naming electronic resources may take some ideas from cataloging models and other object description systems, but in reality it follows its own independent and idiosyncratic practice—more art than science at this juncture in the development of electronic resources management.

AACR2 Naming Conventions

AACR2 is based on an edition first compiled in 1967, before electronic resources even existed and when print was the dominant medium in libraries. Even microform did not become a familiar library storage format until later, in the 1970's (Kichuk, 2000). *AACR* "remained bound by card catalog concepts and practices that have no relevancy in the online world" (Larkin, 2006, p. 287).

Two clauses in *AACR2* illustrate the divisions between traditional cataloging naming practice and the naming practice in A to Z lists and ERM systems. Clause 9.0B1, designates the resource itself as the chief source of information for electronic resources, including the "title proper," or primary title. Clause 9.0B2 requires that a "Source of Title" note, identifying the source of evidence,

must appear in all electronic resource records. The note is an important tool for tracking a cataloger's practice when naming a resource. Unfortunately, the clause is silent on what should go into the note and gives only a few inconsistent examples. It does not articulate standards for what evidence is or how to describe it. Catalogers have attempted to compile recommended best practices. A general guide compiled by Online Audiovisual Catalogers, Inc., for example, tries to clarify evidence sources and best descriptive practices. It advises that the title should come from formally presented evidence, for example, the "title screen(s), main menus, program statements, initial display(s) of information, home page(s), the file header(s) …" (Subcommittee on the Source of Title Note for Internet Resources, Online Audiovisual Catalogers, Cataloging Policy Committee, 2005). Clause 12.0B1 recommends that integrating resources (that is, continuously updated electronic resources) should be described using the current iteration of the resource.

Clause 9.0B1 has some application to naming in A to Z lists and in ERM systems; but the title or home page does not consistently serve as the primary title source. Additional and sometimes crucial sources may, for example, be found in the order or license information exchanged between the library and the vendor, the invoice, or the vendor's subscription information pages. What did the library actually subscribe to or buy? What is the accessible content? While the resource might link by default to the resource portal, access may be restricted to a subscription package within it. The latter may be the source for the primary title, not the home page. Such details are not normally available to the cataloger. The ERL, as the acquisition, administration, and technical contact for electronic resources, will have key acquisition and access details firsthand.

Clause 12.0B1 ensures that the resource iteration active at the time of acquisition is catalogued. However electronic resources are not static entities. A to Z lists and ERM systems on which they are based, endeavor to keep up with these dynamic changes. Cataloging is geared to working with entities that do not change. The latest iteration at the time of acquisition and cataloging may be superseded soon after the catalog record is saved. There is an endemic lag time before catalog records are updated to reflect major changes, even when the standards permit it. A to Z lists and ERM systems are mandated to keep up with the name and description changes in the last iteration viewable by the patron. While a gap between the change and their records may exist, these systems are agile and flexible enough to include vendor announced changes and through systematic review and serendipity, discover small and large changes that vendors may never announce formally.

Electronic Resource Name Volatility

The frequency of name changes complicates the already complex work of naming electronic resources. Major and minor title and interface changes are now launched on a routine basis as publishers or vendors, driven by marketing or design reasons, try to perfect their product presentation. When resources merge or undergo major transformations, as they often do, a new name may emerge. Products from some fields, like business and commerce, are particularly prone to rapid name and content structure transformation. Titles that have recently migrated from print to online may initially assume the original print title, with or without the modest addition of a word like "online" to distinguish it from its print equivalent. But there is a trend away from this close association with print titles, to titles with Web credentials. Shorter, more graphic titles, including the use of abbreviations, acronyms, and other Web-friendly phrasing, are now distinguishing the online version from the print.

Resources with an established print predecessor, such as the MLA International Bibliography, have strong name identification in their discipline, and may demonstrate greater name stability

when migrating online. An example of a volatile name change over the span of only a few years is Springer's online journal collection. In 2001 it was called Link. It changed to SpringerLink a couple of years later (and for a brief time its primary title could be transcribed as [SpringerLink]) marking its evolution into a portal to all of its electronic content: electronic journals, books, book series, and databases.

Tracking name changes is an important issue across library systems. While authority work in this area is practically nonexistent, each library tries at least to track the history of a resource title in its own collection. Consortia also benefit from title tracking and title currency for such needs as the identification of common holdings.

Different Perspectives on Electronic Resource Names

What the title of an electronic resource is may differ depending on your point of view—whether you are a patron, acquisitions or reference staff, or the resource administrator. In addition to the various ways in which an electronic resource presents itself, there are the various, sometimes contrary, ways in which everyone, the ERL, reference staff and patron alike, appropriates the name and refers to it—by its interface name, for example. When the library creates an artificial name to suit a unique and often time-limited need—for example, to distinguish a resource available via more than one interface—the resulting artifact assumes a life of its own within an institution:

- **The patron.** Library patrons have their own unique strategies for appropriating library object names. For physical objects they may recall the color, size, spine design, or the position on a shelf, or they may remember the title from the title page or the binding spine. In the online environment, identification and recall may include physical and relational clues. For example, a patron may track the number of clicks from a start point or recall a prominently named interface, or a persistent icon. How the user knows the resource, depends primarily on the resource as perceived in the act of information retrieval. The "stimulus-as-received is given a name by the user" (Collantes, 1995, p. 117). Collantes concluded that part of the problem of naming electronic resources could be resolved by not only including more primary and secondary evidence based alternate names but also popular names. Those designated titles play a significant role in how the user will try to access a resource. By anticipating potential titles in library systems, such as an ERM enhanced catalog, patrons have the potential to find a resource no matter by what name or names they know a resource as.

- **The selector.** The selector views the electronic resource as primarily an information source or research tool. She may refer to it by its print equivalent title or by some other name such as the name of the subscription package, rather than by the title from the current home page of the electronic resource. The ERL must identify what the selector is actually selecting. That is, what will the library subscribe to or license? Once acquired, the primary title is posted in the A to Z list, or the ERM system on which it is based. If it differs from the primary title, the subscription name can be added to the ERM system record as one of several alternative titles. The electronic resource known as Microbiology Abstracts is actually a set of three abstract and index databases the vendor CSA promotes as the Microbiology Collection. Microbiology Abstracts is actually the long established print equivalent title. The CSA Illumina menu of databases does not list Microbiology Abstracts[1]. Yet some libraries may choose to continue to refer to the three databases as Microbiology Abstracts, or by

their promotional name, Microbiology Collection, in their A to Z list, believing that the databases will be found more readily by this descriptive title rather than the actual long and difficult to remember titles of the databases.

- **The cataloger.** The cataloger is restricted by the practice of cataloging with item in hand or on view at the time of acquisition. Thereafter only when major title changes occur is the record revised. Since the cataloger is not cognizant of most of the details related to acquisition or access, the cataloger is often unaware of major and minor title changes to electronic resources. Rigorous cataloging standards of transcription are often contrary to the ERL's primary principle of representing the resource as perceived currently by the user. For example, the cataloger may not transcribe the title with capitalization, instead imposing a standard catalog record syntax for titles, capitalizing the first letter only of a title regardless of how it is spelled in the evidence, for example, "Academic search premier," instead of "Academic Search Premier."

- **The electronic resources librarian.** The ERL regards resource names or titles as multifaceted and changeable and recognizes every change, large or small, as significant. From the moment a price quote or trial is requested, to the establishment of a new license and its ongoing renewal, the ERL communicates using a variety of names or titles, depending on who the audience is—collections librarian or selector, systems or acquisitions staff, students or faculty, and the publisher or vendor, and what the context is—the subscription package, the license, the serials management and openURL services, or the invoice, resource home page or sub-pages and product descriptions. All are correct. All are relevant, depending on the context. The familiar name of the print equivalent may be appropriate when communicating with faculty. The public name used by the openURL service may be appropriate when assisting a patron to read the menu of links to full text targets. The name of the subscription package is the appropriate name when communicating with a vendor sales representative.

- **The publisher or aggregating vendor.** The publisher or vendor may have one or more ways of referring to the same product at various levels within the resource itself or information pages. Constantly tweaking or radically changing the title in pursuit of a new "it" name, even they have trouble keeping up with the name changes they have generated. The sometimes archaic and cryptic names itemized in invoices are evidence of the disconnection between vendor marketing and accounts payable staff.
- **The third-party vendor.** Because vendors may package and therefore name their third-party resources differently, especially if they add value, when libraries migrate from one platform to another, the resource name may change even though the content is identical. Ovid Technologies, Inc. for example, names

its enhanced version of Medline, Ovid Medline®.

PROPOSED NAMING CONVENTIONS

A to Z Lists

Currently most electronic resource A to Z lists (see Table 1) are dynamically derived from updated in-house databases or, more rarely, they are continuously updated static HTML lists. Federated search portal services, such as MetaLib (Ex Libris), which enable searching across a library's electronic collections, may also have an A to Z list output functionality. A growing number of libraries now have A to Z lists output from recently implemented ERM systems. Naming practices for library in-house systems are an odd mix of adaptations of cataloging practice and ad hoc innovations to suit local needs and the dynamic reality of electronic resources. The following proposed general principles and conventions are not intended to be definitive or prescriptive. This is a first attempt to describe models of good practice in naming electronic resources[2]. It is recognized that as electronic resources evolve, so must

Table 1. A sample research databases A to Z list derived from an in-house library system

Research Databases A to Z List
Algology, Mycology & Protozoology Abstracts (Microbiology C) SEE **Microbiology Abstracts**
Bacteriology Abstracts (Microbiology B) SEE **Microbiology Abstracts**
CINAHL Plus with Full Text: Cumulative Index to Nursing and Allied Health Literature
Industrial and Applied Microbiology Abstracts (Microbiology A) SEE **Microbiology Abstracts**
Medline (CSA)
Medline (OCLC)
Medline (OVID)
Microbiology Abstracts
PreCINAHL™ SEE **CINAHL Plus with Full Text**

conventions or practice. The use of cataloging standards as a source of models for language and description for naming conventions is based on the circumstantial identity of the title and description fields in an A to Z list and catalog records. But that identity is somewhat misleading, since these applications are usually so different in their outcome and use. The following principles and conventions apply specifically to A to Z lists derived from in-house database systems rather than portal or ERM systems. ERM systems differ, for example, by permitting a repeatable alternate title field, making added primary title qualifiers and *see* references redundant. As a result, the output may be a more streamlined and longer, but have equal or even greater effectiveness over the in-house A to Z list, while adding the considerable benefit of an integrated system.

General Principles

- Normally, only one entry per resource—the primary title
- A linked *see* reference from an alternate title to the primary title is used if needed for clarity or ease of use, for example, a former title. However, *see* references are used sparingly and deleted after usefulness ends.
- The chief source for the title and description information is the resource itself
- The title is based on the last iteration of the resource
- Formally presented evidence in primary sources is used first. Only when it fails to provide a title are secondary sources consulted. If further evidence is required, other library sites can be consulted for consensus or to discover alternative treatments.
- Naming strives to designate what the user perceives as the title on the default screen and subsequent screens of a resource
- The typography and form of a name has significance. The title is transcribed exactly

as presented according to wording, symbols, capitalization, and punctuation.
- Overall consistency in syntax and treatment is sought for the whole list
- When deriving a title unconventionally, consistency and internal logic are strived for. However, unconventional titles are an exception in the list.
- The title is updated when major or minor changes are reported or discovered. While major changes are the most important, all changes to the title as viewed by the user are significant.

Conventions

- Primary evidence or the chief source for an electronic resource title or name are the:
  o Title screen
  o Home page
  o Initial display of information
  o Prominently displayed title banner graphics and text
  o In the absence of a prominent title banner, self-evident title graphics and text in the primary source
- Secondary or supporting evidence for an electronic resource title include:
  o "About" information pages
  o Frequently Asked Questions (FAQ) pages
  o Running titles on secondary pages
  o The HTML header title field coded in the document and viewable in the Web browser title bar along the bottom of the screen
  o Encoded metadata
  o Labeled buttons in navigation bars or embedded text links to the resource
  o Track-back labeling in resource subsidiary pages
  o "Librarian" or "Libraries" information pages on vendor or publisher sites

- o Subscription information pages on vendor or publisher sites
- o Vendor or publisher product information or description pages
- o Vendor or publisher communiqués or newsletters about current or forthcoming changes to a resource
- o Electronic resource details or information pages from other library Web sites
- o News items about the product posted in news services and blogs
- The exact transcription of a name may require the use of lowercase and uppercase letters. Exceptions may be necessary if a library system cannot alphabetize the transcribed name properly.
- A title is not italicized unless it is italicized in the primary or secondary evidence.
- Nonessential content in the source is excluded from the primary title or subtitle, including:
  - o Introductory words obviously not intended to be part of the title or subtitle, for example "Welcome to"
  - o Splash page linked content, for example: "English|French," "Enter"
  - o Tagline phrases that are not meaningful subtitles, for example "The world's best science and medicine on your desktop"
- A publisher or vendor name is included if it is an integral part of the presented title
- Parallel titles, such as English and French language equivalents, may both be transcribed as a compound title or as separate primary titles
- A meaningful title may be constructed for a resource with a generic title by the addition of a corporate name or resource scope (NRC Research Press Journals)
- The title is updated to reflect major changes announced by the vendor or on discovery. Major changes may also require catalog

revisions. Minor changes are changed on discovery:

- o A major change to a title implies a substantial transformation that will change the alphabetical order or the recognition value of the title, for example, when:
  - ➢ The first three words (except initial articles, prepositions or conjunctions) are deleted, changed, or reordered
  - ➢ A part or all of the title changes from the full form to an acronym or initialism, or *vice versa*
  - ➢ Changes occur after the first three words that change the meaning, subject or scope of the title, including geographic, frequency, or coverage scope (CRSP 1925 US Stock Database)
  - ➢ There is an addition or deletion at the end of a title of a word or words that indicates the type or scope of the resource, such as "Journals," "Online," "Collection," or "Full Text"
  - ➢ There is an addition, deletion, rearrangement, or name change of a corporate body name where it is an integral part of the title
  - ➢ A substantially different or new name is launched. The resource itself may be unchanged or have undergone a major revision. Either way, the newly named resource is regarded as new. A *superseded by* statement may be considered for a brief period to transition patrons to the new resource.
- o A minor change to a title represents a small revision that is not major, for example, when:
  - ➢ An abbreviated word or symbol is spelled out, or *vice versa* (&, and)

- ➤ Numbers or dates are spelled out, or *vice versa*
- ➤ Capitalization is changed to lowercase, or *vice versa*
- ➤ Hyphenated words are unhyphenated, or *vice versa*
- ➤ Two-word compounds are joined into one-word compounds, or *vice versa*
- ➤ A singular term is changed to a plural form, or *vice versa*
- ➤ A spelling is changed
- ➤ Articles, prepositions, or conjunctions are changed
- ➤ A trademark is added or deleted at the end of the name or title (®, ™)
- ➤ There are changes in punctuation

- An electronic resource has several hierarchical or derivative layers, only one of which is designated as the opening or default page. The library may bypass the publisher or vendor-designated default and select a page that conforms to local policies or needs. The default may be, for example:
  - o The resource home page—the prevalent default
  - o A portal home page—a framing device or gateway to multiple resources usually with added value, for example cross-searching functionality
  - o A splash page—a welcoming page that may include high-impact visuals about the resource or present language of platform choices. For example, Canadian academic libraries may choose to default to the English and French splash page for Government of Canada online resources
  - o Either a basic or advance search screen
  - o A page presenting a segregated hyperlinked list of a library's electronic book or journal title subscriptions in a collection

- Selected qualifiers are added to the title consistently or occasionally. The qualifiers may be quasi subtitles added to the primary title as a string of words. The latter may appear in parentheses, after a colon, or on a separate line. Qualifiers are often used to distinguish a nondescriptive primary title, or a duplicate name. The syntax may be determined by technical limitations in the system. For example, a familiar acronym may be added to the primary title in order for the acronym to be searchable from the Web browser "Find" function. Some examples of common qualifiers are:
  - o Acronym (Oxford English Dictionary [OED])
  - o Aka or popular name (UNSTATS)
  - o The full form of an acronym in the primary title (CINAHL: Cumulative Index to Nursing and Allied Health)
  - o Publisher or vendor name (Medline [CSA])
  - o Interface or platform name (Academic Search Premier [EBSCOhost])
  - o Scope, such as "Journals," "e-Books," or "Annual" (AACR Journals)

- Subtitles are transcribed to expand meaning and context, and to add significant keywords. Subtitles are separated from the primary title by a colon or dash, or appear on a separate line. Subtitles resemble qualifiers, but they appear alongside the title in the primary evidence. They include:
  - o Meaningful subtitles or tag lines
  - o A statement of responsibility or issuing body presented as an integral part of a sub-title (Digital Engineering Library: McGraw-Hill Engineering Online)

- To avoid frequent updates, rolling coverage dates or edition statements are avoided unless the resource is finite, or if the information is essential for identification.

- If a resource splits into two or more re-sources, separate entries are created for each one and a *see* reference from the former title may be used, at least temporarily.
- Separate entries for different access levels may be considered, for example, for the:
  - Portal
  - Interface
  - Vendor
  - Collection
  - Sub-databases or resources

ERM Systems

ERM systems (see Table 2) are a recent library management solution for electronic resources. It is still early days, but ERM applications have already distinguished themselves as a base library system. An ERM system integrates order record information, provides access to standardized usage statistics, and exposes license information.

It consolidates the array of desktop and library spreadsheets and in-house applications that proliferate in libraries grappling with the problem of managing their electronic collections. It enhances the traditional catalog through the addition of a broad range of potential alternate titles or access points derived in the broadest and noncatalog standard sense impractical in spreadsheets or in-house A to Z lists. The addition of alternate names normally excluded by standard cataloging practice increases the probability of successful search outcomes and effective library systems. Similarly for A to Z lists presented above, the following proposed principles and conventions are not comprehensive or unassailable. Indeed, since ERM systems are so new and our experience with them so shallow, whatever is suggested here may turn out to have a very short half-life.

Table 2. Sample ERM records for research databases

ERM Resource Records		
Resource Name:	**Algology, Mycology & Protozoology Abstracts (Microbiology C)**	Primary name
Alternate Names:	**Biological Sciences**	CSA database collection name
	Microbiology Abstracts	Print equivalent name
	Microbiology Collection	Subscription package name
Interface:	**CSA Illumina**	Interface/platform name
Vendor:	**CSA**	Vendor name
Resource Name:	**Microbiology Abstracts**	Primary name
Alternate Names:	**Algology, Mycology & Protozoology Abstracts (Microbiology C)**	Database part
	Bacteriology Abstracts (Microbiology B)	Database part
	Biological Sciences	CSA database collection name
	Industrial and Applied Microbiology Abstracts (Microbiology A)	Database part
	Microbiology Collection	Subscription package name
Interface:	**CSA Illumina**	Interface/platform name
Vendor:	**CSA**	Vendor name

General Principles

The general principles applied to naming in A to Z lists, also apply to ERM systems, with some exceptions and additions:

- Multiple names or titles are permitted. In addition to a primary title, all relevant alternate titles may be added. A library decision to index alternate titles with the primary title makes all of the titles equally accessible through the ERM enhanced catalog.
- The use of alternate titles makes *see* references and qualifiers redundant. By their addition related records are automatically cross-linked.
- Alternate titles are based on the same primary and secondary resource-specific evidence that is used to identify primary titles. However, they are not limited to these sources.
- There is greater latitude in designating alternate names than permitted in cataloging, including the potential for:
  - Surrogate titles that suit local needs (Russian Newspapers)
  - Titles originating in external systems, such as serials management and openURL linking services. They typically assign a unique public title that appears as the resource title in the library's linking service menu. For example, CINAHL Plus with Full Text is cited as EBSCOHOST CINAHL Plus with full text, in the SFX openURL linking service menu presented to patrons when they click on the library linking service link embedded in database citations.

Conventions

Many of the naming conventions for A to Z lists also apply to ERM systems. But there are several differences:

- Alternate or variant resource names or titles, may be added. The range of possibilities include:
  - Acronyms or initialisms (WOS)
  - Full form of a resource or a corporate name known by its acronym or initialism (National Research Council)
  - Full form of an acronym in the primary title (Cumulative Index to Nursing and Allied Health)
  - Commonly known as name (Grove Dictionary of Art)
  - Parallel title in another language
  - Alternative spellings
  - Alternative syntax, including spaces (ABI Inform)
  - Print antecedent name (Excerpta Medica)
  - Subscription package name (IEEE/IEE All Society Periodical Package)
  - A superseded title
  - Portal name (ISI Web of Knowledge)
  - Serial management or openURL service public title (GaleGroup InfoTrac Academic Index)
- Publisher or vendor names and interface or platform names may be included as separate fields in a resource record, giving them greater prominence in descriptions, and readily searchable by patron and staff.

FUTURE TRENDS AND NAMING CONVENTIONS

ERM Systems and Naming

Despite the importance of names and naming in library systems, there are no applicable regional or international standards on the horizon to deal with the problem of naming electronic resources in noncatalog library systems. There is even some indication that naming practices for electronic resources are becoming more inconsistent with the passage of time. As electronic resources proliferate, grow more diverse, and sever close ties with print, and as publishers launch names based more on Internet design principles than on print antecedents, confusion abounds about electronic resource names in library systems. The evolution of noncatalog library systems for electronic resources, such as A to Z lists, grew out of the necessity to expose essential and costly resources that would otherwise languish within the restrictive confines of the library catalog. As electronic collections grow, A to Z lists are becoming longer and more complex, using added value, such as brief descriptions and indicator icons to assist users with identification and access. The isolated, manually created and managed A to Z list is now happily superseded by dynamically generated lists based on databases. ERM systems represent a new development, integrating the advantages of electronic resource segregation and special treatment with the library's monolithic integrated library system (ILS). This integration has the additional advantage of potentially avoiding, or at least substantially reducing, redundancy. ERM system development and application has not yet matured sufficiently to judge whether it can potentially resolve all naming issues related to electronic resources and library systems.

Name Hierarchies

ERM systems expose "also known as" names that encompass a much broader range than permitted by international cataloging standards. For example, unconventional name sources, such as openURL linking services or acquisitions packages and invoices. Currently, prominent ERM systems differentiate the full range of names in only two levels: primary and secondary. But this may change in the future. Instead of the current practice of lumping names together alphabetically in two fields, ERM records could include a hierarchy of names, with some of the following categories:

1. Primary name or names:
   a. The principle name (see previous suggested conventions). For example, *CSA Neurosciences Abstracts*
   b. One or more principle "also known as" name or names intended to appear in an A to Z list in addition to the principle name. The utility is similar to a "see" reference:
      i. Name segment by which a resource could reasonably be identified. For example, *Neurosciences Abstracts* for *CSA Neurosciences Abstracts.*
      ii. Third-party publisher's name for a resource differing from the name assigned by a vendor. For example, *MEDLINE®* for *Ovid MEDLINE®.*
      iii. Secondary name or names elevated to primary name status for the purpose of populating an A to Z list with appropriate access points for continuing or temporary reasons internal to the library.
2. Secondary name or names:
   a. Secondary "also known as" names:
      i. Alternate spellings
      ii. Acronyms
      iii. Interface name
      iv. Vendor name
      v. Popular name
      vi. Name of print equivalent
   b. Superseded names
   c. Names of collection parts or sub-databases
   d. Name of the collection of which a resource is a part
   e. OpenURL service knowledgebase resource name, for example, SFX target name
   f. Name used in library ILS acquisitions module:

i. Subscription name
ii. Package name
iii. Invoice line item name

g. Ad hoc names, created to improve access locally

International Unique Identifiers

Most electronic books and journals are assigned international unique identifiers: electronic international standard book number (eISBN) or electronic international standard serial number (eISSN). However, research databases and many electronic reference works are not. The lack of a standard identifier that remains constant through name revisions and renaming poses a problem for identification and synchronicity across bibliographic, ERM and order records for a resource. An international standard identifier is needed for all electronic resources. Ideally part or all of the standard identifier would migrate with an electronic resource from one vendor or platform to another. This is not however how eISBNs and eISSNs work. They are modeled after print ISBNs and ISSNs and are assigned by publishers. The unique distribution model for electronic resources may require a different approach for assigning unique identifiers than for print. Given that a vendor may host various third-party resources and through its proprietary platform and delivery in various formats transform the presentation of the resource and to some extent its content, it would be worthwhile to consider identifiers that are constant across various platforms for the same resource.

International standards agents such as the Digital Library Federation's Electronic Management Initiative (DLF ERMI) are actively creating important standards for ERM, for example, for electronic resource license expression and usage statistics collection. Resource names are treated in a very general way in DLF's ERM resource field descriptions. Both DLF standards and ERM applications, such as Innovative's, have

not moved beyond this initial development stage. More progress is being made towards a unique identifier for research databases, where the topic has been raised by such leaders in the field as Ted Koppel, Ex Libris' Verde (its ERM service) Product Manager (Koppel, 2006, p. 8).

Database and Electronic Reference Work Name Authority Control

The library community is familiar with the concept of authority control applied to author names in catalogs. Could the same concept of authority work be applied to the changeable electronic resources and be utilized within ERM systems? Currently, deriving names is a local application. Copy cataloging might benefit part of the process, but catalog copy arrives too late in the process for ERM record creation. Consulting a name authority database would make the work of assigning names significantly easier for electronic resources staff. It would reduce the duplication of effort across libraries and ensure the use of common name across libraries. Publishers and vendors are already considering delivering skeletal ERM records, including names, to subscribing libraries that could be loaded into an ERM system much like MARC records into a catalog.

CONCLUSION

Libraries have adopted new naming practices for their electronic resource A to Z lists and ERM systems. These practices are currently inconsistently applied across institutions and even within an institution or individual system. Just as patrons become confused about what databases are called, staff lose track of resources with their constant name changes, and libraries are unable to recognize identical holdings in peer libraries or within consortia. There is an immediate need for internationally recognized naming conventions that will bring improved recognition and findability to electronic resources in library systems. ERM systems, with their wide latitude for naming, appear to make naming a nonissue by permitting users and staff to access a resource by whatever name they know a resource as, at least potentially. In practice, the application of names in ERM systems requires conventions to establish the range of names and their hierarchy. The implementation of A to Z lists and early ERM systems exposed the fundamental problems related to naming electronic resources. It is hoped that further ERM system development and application, and the involvement of international standards bodies will soon bring electronic resources naming issues closer to resolution.

REFERENCES

Anderson, B., & Hawkins, L. (1996). Development of CONSER cataloguing policies for remote access computer file serials. *The Public-Access Computer Systems Review, 7*(1). Retrieved November 21, 2007, from http://epress.lib.uh.edu/pr/v7/n1/adne7n1.html

Anglo-American cataloguing rules (2nd ed.) (2002). Ottawa: Canadian Library Association, the Chartered Institute of Library and Information Professionals, and the American Library Association.

Beck, M. (1995). *CONSER cataloging manual: Module 31, Remote access computer file serials.* Washington, D.C.: Library of Congress.

Bracke, P. J. (2001). Access to remote electronic resources at the University of Arizona. *Science & Technology Libraries, 20*(2/3), 5-14.

Brown, M. E. (1995). By any other name: Accounting for failure in the naming of subject categories. *Library and Information Science Research, 17*(4), 347-385.

Collantes, L. (1995). Degree of agreement in naming objects and concepts for information retrieval. *Journal of the American Society for Information Science, 46*(2), 116-132.

CONSER (2006). *CONSER cataloging manual: Module 31, Remote access electronic serials (online serials).* Washington, D.C.: Library of Congress. Retrieved November 21, 2007, from http://www.loc.gov/acq/conser/module31.html

Irlam, G. (1995). Naming. Retrieved November 21, 2007, from http://www.gordoni.com/web/naming.html

Joint Steering Committee for Revision of AACR (1999). *Revising AACR2 to accommodate seriality.* Ottawa: Library and Archives Canada. Retrieved November 21, 2007, from http://www.collectionscanada.ca/jsc/ser-rep6.html

Kichuk, D. (2000). *Library space study.* Unpublished internal report, University of Saskatchewan Library, Saskatoon.

Koppel, T. (2006). *An Introduction to the rapidly changing world of ERM standards.* Ex Libris White Paper. Retrieved November 21, 2007, from http://www.exlibrisgroup.com/resources/various/Koppel_ERM_Standards.doc

Larkin, M. R. T. (2006). AACR3 is coming—what is it? [Report on a presentation by P. J. Weiss] *Serials Librarian, 50*(3/4), 285-294.

Nicklen, J. E. (2003). *Serials cataloguing and harmonisation. A briefing session paper.* UKSG Conference, April 7-9, 2003, Edinburgh. Retrieved November 21, 2007, from http://www.uksg.org.uk/presentations3/nicklen.pdf

Office of Descriptive Cataloging Policy, Library of Congress (1989). *Library of Congress rule interpretations.* Washington, D.C.: Cataloging Distribution Service, Library of Congress.

Parker, K., Anderson, I., Chandler, A., Farb, S. E., Jewell, T., Riggio, A., & Robertson, N. D. M.

(2004). *Electronic resource management: Report of the DLF ERM Initiative, Appendix E: Electronic resource management system data structure.* Washington, D.C.: Digital Library Federation. Retrieved November 21, 2007, from http://www.diglib.org/pubs/dlf102/

Program for Cooperative Cataloging / BIBCO (Revision) (2005). *Integrating resources: A cataloging manual. Appendix A to the BIBCO participants' manual and Module 35 of the CONSER cataloging manual.* Washington, D.C.: PCC/BIBCO. Retrieved November 21, 2007, from http://www.loc.gov/catdir/pcc/bibco/irman.pdf

Riggio, A. et al. (n.d.). Report of the DLF electronic resource management initiative, Appendix D: Data element dictionary. Retrieved November 21, 2007, from http://www.library.cornell.edu/cts/elicensestudy/dlfdeliverables/DLF-ERMI-AppendixD.pdf

Subcommittee on the Source of Title Note for Internet Resources, Cataloging Policy Committee (CAPC) (2005). *Source of title note for internet resources (3rd ed).* Online Audiovisual Catalogers, Inc. (OLAC). Retrieved November 21, 2007, from http://ublib.buffalo.edu/libraries/units/cts/olac/capc/stnir.html

Tonkery, D. (2006, May 8). Best of show—what's a serial when you are running on internet time. *Liveserials* [blog]. Retrieved November 21, 2007, from http://liveserials.blogspot.com/2006/05/best-of-show-whats-serial-when-you-are.html

ENDNOTES

[1] CSA's Microbiology Collection includes: *Algology, Mycology & Protozoology Abstracts (Microbiology A), Industrial and Applied Microbiology Abstracts (Microbiology B), and Bacteriology Abstracts (Microbiology C).*

[2] Several resources were consulted for appropriate wording and structure for the following naming conventions, especially resources related to cataloging serials (Riggio et al., 2006) (OLAC CAPC, 2005) (Nicklen, 2003) (Joint Steering Committee for Revision of AACR, 1999).

Section V
Electronic Resource Management Systems (ERMS)

Chapter XVI
Standards, the Structural Underpinnings of Electronic Resource Management Systems

Ted Koppel
Ex Libris, USA

ABSTRACT

Electronic resource management (ERM) software is in the spotlight as a new management tool within libraries. Built to manage all steps in the lifecycle of an electronic product, ERM systems must interoperate with existing Integrated Library System (ILS), public service, and financial software already in use within the library. Although ERM software leverages and expands earlier standards work (MARC, Onix for Serials, openURL, metasearch, etc.), most contemporary ERM systems are built using the DLF-ERMI specification as the underlying guide for data element and functional requirements. Recent efforts, such as SUSHI and the License Expression Work Group, are defining new standards and protocols to address new ERM issues. Further, experience in the era of electronic resource management has pointed out the need for additional standards and protocols, which are discussed in this chapter.

INTRODUCTION

Standards—particularly those approved by national or international standards bodies—are the core of almost all recent development in the library automation industry. From the early days of library systems (arbitrarily assigning the starting date of library automation as we know it to the development of the MARC communications format by the Library of Congress in the mid-1960's), the use of industry-developed and industry-accepted standards has made interoperability and the sharing of bibliographic data possible. As an outcome of the widely accepted MARC platform various derivatives and related standards and protocols evolved. For example, the Z39.50 search protocol, the Bath Profile, the U.S. National Profile, and several others have their roots in early work done with the MARC record.

Electronic resource management (ERM) is now moving into the spotlight as a crucial management tool in the world of library management. Delivery of information using electronic products has been part of library service for several decades, beginning in the mid-1970's with SDC Orbit databases, NASA RECON, Lockheed Dialog, and (a bit later) BRS, all of whom delivered abstracting and indexing data through idiosyncratic retrieval mechanisms. Most of these early systems were built by large R&D corporations not in the library arena that were searching for ways to handle a large and growing number of technical and research reports. (Bourne & Bellardo-Hahn, 2003)

The "modern" era of electronic resource management began around 1999 or 2000, with the confluence of several different trends. First, technology was such that large collections of full-text material—e-journal, e-book, or other types of electronic materials —could be stored and retrieved rapidly. High-density magnetic and optical storage hardware costs dropped markedly. Second, the cost of delivery plummeted. Broadband Internet service, delivered over high-speed access lines, and the ubiquitous availability of the Internet meant than any library, and, indeed, any person, could download large chunks of data in seconds. Third, user needs and user behavior changed. As end users (to distinguish them from library-based or institutional users) came to depend on the Internet for all of their information needs, they expected immediate information delivery. Finally—and no less important than the first three factors—economics in the information industry changed. The cost of library resources (paper and electronic subscriptions) skyrocketed and caused libraries to closely examine their needs. Recession and economic malaise kept acquisitions money tight and put many libraries into contraction, rather than collection, mode. Rather than searching for new services to provide, libraries had to make decisions about which services to cut.

[Why did e-resource pricing take such a huge jump? That is a topic for another chapter. The author of this chapter suggests reviewing various publications from the Association for Research Libraries (ARL), North American Serials Interest Group (NASIG), the United Kingdom Serials Group (UKSG), and industry journals such as *Serials Librarian, Against the Grain,* and so forth, for background and ongoing evidence of the tremendous rise in the cost of serials over the last decade.]

We see the result of these four factors today. In many large university libraries electronic resources constitute 50% or more of the library's acquisitions budget. (Kyrillidou & Young, 2006) Some special libraries, particularly in the medical and pharmaceutical industries, spend 90% or more of their materials budget on electronic resources. The shift from paper-based resources to electronic resources has meant that old, paper-centric management tools have become inadequate. The ERM industry is reacting by developing and integrating new tools, developed specifically for the complex world of electronic resource management.

This chapter discusses standards and protocols that are the foundation of current ERM applications. It describes existing standards and how they are being adapted and changed in an ERM world. Finally, it introduces several new and developing standards and makes suggestions for new ERM-based protocols for the future.

THE EARLY DAYS OF ERM STANDARDS

Electronic resource use began to rise in the late 1990's due to the confluence of factors described earlier. For fiscal, legal, management, and other reasons, libraries felt they had to track contracts, licenses, and similar data elements related to the electronic resources they were purchasing. Some libraries developed their own local ERM systems—MIT's VERA, Harvard University's Harvard ERM, and Boston College's ERMdb, for example. Many libraries used spreadsheets or

Microsoft® Access (or other database) software to organize and maintain their records. A few libraries developed multiple hybrid systems—one to handle contracts, another to handle statistics, and a third to handle processing workflow and acquisitions steps. Of course, some libraries based their record keeping (and still do!) on large collections of photocopies kept in ever growing file folders. Each of these different electronic resource record-keeping systems was idiosyncratic and local to the institution; each followed its own rules, stored and maintained locally relevant data elements, and interoperated with nothing else.

DLF-ERMI

Libraries began to consider the burden of managing their electronic resources in the late 1990's. Tim Jewell's *Selection and Presentation of Commercially Available Electronic Resources: Issues and Practices* (Council for Library and Information Resources, 2001) was an early examination of the issues facing libraries in the areas of electronic resource acquisition, licensing, and management.

By late 2001, staff at large academic libraries recognized that a standard approach to electronic resource management would benefit them all, and provide leadership to the library community as well. Library staff from Harvard, Yale, MIT, UCLA, Johns Hopkins, Cornell, the University of Washington, and others organized the Electronic Resource Management Initiative under the auspices of the Digital Library Federation (DLF ERMI) and began to design a specification for an electronic resource management system. This small group worked with a larger "reactor panel" to ensure that there would be widespread understanding and acceptance of the work being done. In late 2004, this group published, on the Web, a document called "Electronic Resource Management: The Report of the DLF Initiative." It was subsequently released in paper in mid-2005. This report, along with its six substantial appendices, has come to be known as the "DLF spec." In particular, Appendices A, D, and E (covering ERM function, ERM data elements, and ERM data structure) are the bases of most of the commercial electronic resource management systems on the market today.

It is important to note that the DLF-ERMI specification is not an official standard in the sense of having been approved and registered by a standards-issuing agency such as the US National Information Standards Organization (NISO), the International Standards Organization (ISO) or similar. It has, however, become a de-facto standard because of its adoption (at one degree of adherence or another) by all of the ERM systems currently on the market.

COUNTER

Parallel with the DLF ERMI project was the creation of COUNTER (Counting Online Usage of NeTworked Electronic Resources). The COUNTER group defined sets of data elements, several electronic resource usage reports, and the delivery format for those usage reports. COUNTER's goal was to ensure that statistics released from any publisher would be delivered in the same standard XML format and therefore would be easier for any system working with them to ingest and manipulate. COUNTER puts weight to its effort through the use of its *Code of Practice,* which outlines the minimum levels of data presentation that qualify as COUNTER compliant. Release 2 of the COUNTER code of Practice for Journals and Databases (published April 2005) and release 1 of the COUNTER Code of Practice for Books and Reference Works (published March 2006) each details a set of auditing requirements and tests to ensure the completeness and consistency of statistical data being delivered by publishers, if they want to be considered COUNTER compliant.

ONIX for Serials

Another relevant standards effort that took place during the early 2000s was ONIX for Serials. ONIX (standing for Online Information Exchange) for Books is an initiative of the publishing industry, largely in the UK, to enable different players in the publishing supply chain to share information about books being published. Most of the ONIX work has been done by, or under contract to, EDItEUR, a group based Great Britain promoting standards for electronic commerce in the book and serials industry sectors. ONIX for Books is a highly granular, descriptive XML structure that carries not only tightly defined bibliographic elements, but also data about a book's color and weight, advertising plans and vendor participation, and extending even to the number of cartons of that book that could be shipped on a freight pallet.

The serials publishing industry saw the potential for defining and using a similar granular group of data elements for a number of purposes, and ONIX for Serials was started. Participating in this project was the U.S. National Information Standards Organization (NISO), and EDItEUR. Together NISO and EDItEUR created the Joint Working Party for the Exchange of Serials Subscription Information. The Joint Working Party has three subgroups, each working with a different area of serials information exchange:

- Serials online holdings (SOH), an XML format for communicating serials holdings in electronic form. SOH is most useful in transmitting serials holdings information between different systems that need reflect identical holdings information.
- Serials release notification (SRN), an XML format for the announcement of a new serials issue or article. This SRN message might be sent by the publisher or subscription agent to announce the release of an issue or article, and thereby forestall a cacophony of claims should that issue be late in shipping. If the

SRN notification refers to an en electronic publication, it can act as a trigger for various e-journal retrieval mechanisms to retrieve the new issue. As ERM systems mature and pay-per-use models become common in the ERM world, article-level SRN data will become useful both to openURL and ERM systems.

- Serials products and subscriptions (SPS), an XML format for communicating serials catalog data (from vendor to customer, for example) or details of existing subscriptions

The Joint Working Party and its three subgroups are, at the time of this writing, finishing their work and publishing the three XML formats for trial and use by the library and publishing communities. The SRN group is expanding its 2006 draft (which concerned itself with issue releases) to include article notifications. The final SRN document is expected some time in 2007.

In addition to the standards efforts mentioned earlier, various other developments relating to electronic resources were taking place. Although these may not be specifically relevant to the development of a current electronic resource management system, each of them dealt with some aspect of electronic resource service delivery, and therefore contribute to the requirements of an ERM system.

OpenURL and Link Resolution

Link resolution (using Z39.88, the openURL standard) began commercially with the Ex Libris SFX® link server and has grown to be a necessity for libraries that want to deliver full text to users efficiently. It was based on Herbert von de Sompel's research on citation linking at Ghent University (Belgium) in the late 1990's. The path that openURL took from concept (Von de Sompel & Beit Arie, 2001) to NISO standard is an interesting one, because it speaks both to the advantages and disadvantages of a collaborative standards development effort.

Link resolution is usually made available on the article citation level in an abstracting and indexing database (or sometimes a footnote) which is marked with an openURL icon. Clicking on that icon begins a process in which the article citation is turned into a URL-anchored metadata string (known as the openURL) which is transmitted to a link resolver. The link resolver receives the incoming string, parses it, and presents the data elements (which may include some or all of the following: title, author, ISSN, journal name, volume, page, date) to the link resolver.

Central to the concept of link resolution is a database (or knowledge base) that holds information about which full text journals are delivered by which electronic products. Depending on the sophistication of the link resolver, pointers to additional sources of information about the item desired may be provided. For instance, a link resolver may point to several sources for the full text of an article, but also provide links to the publisher's Web site, the library catalog, an interlibrary loan or document delivery service, and other relevant sources of information.

Key to the success of openURL use is localization—that is, the knowledge base described above must be made aware of what a specific library holds. This is known as "providing access to the appropriate copy." Otherwise the link resolution is generic and inexact. Vendors in the openURL category have taken different approaches to localizing electronic resource data, but the goal of all link resolver products is to provide locally relevant results.

The specific functions of a link resolver are the decision and responsibility of the vendor that has developed that specific resolver software. In all cases, however, the Z39.88 openURL standard is used as the underlying communications mechanism between the article database (or source of citation data) and the openURL link resolver.

Metasearch

Known by a number of different names—metasearch, aggregated search, parallel search, federated search, broadcast search, cross-database search—metasearch describes the ability of a software product to search multiple databases, often from multiple and different suppliers, and report the results back to the end user as an collected set of uniformly presented result citations. To the end user, metasearching means filling in a single search box, selecting (or not selecting) several resources in which to search, and having all of the result citations displayed in a single stream.

Metasearch services require a high degree of sophistication on the part of the software that does the actual searching, because the target database from one vendor may be accessed differently from another vendor's data. Therefore, any metasearch system must be flexible enough to perform searches using Z39.50, proprietary APIs, SRW/SRU, screen scraping, and dozens of variants of each of these methods.

Early metasearch programs—largely based on screen scraping—placed a heavy processing load on the information providers whose resources were being taxed much harder than before by the large number of automated searches being sent to their sites as a result of metasearch software. In order to address that issue, and several related metasearch challenges, NISO convened a group in 2004 which was named the Metasearch Initiative.

Three major issues were identified as crucial to solve for metasearch to flourish:

a. Authentication and authorization of users when an intermediary (metasearch agent) is used to search
b. Discovery and collection description (so that a metasearch user can be aware of all relevant data collections)

c. Search and retrieval: What metadata can a search contain (for use by the resource in the search process) and what metadata can the content provider return with the data to make presentation of results more sensible?

Under the Metasearch Initiative umbrella, three standards committees were formed. Each had the goal of examining all relevant information and making recommendations about best practices or standards that would be useful. Their results are contained in Table 1.

As these reports, standards, and documents have only recently been published, metasearch system developers and content providers are only now (January 2007) beginning to modify their software to use these directives.

Summary

In 2007, four years after these seminal developments in the library automation industry, the following trends appear to be continuing:

- Electronic resource adoption continues to grow at double-digit rates
- Sophisticated management tools are entering the ERM market
- Libraries (customers) increasingly realize that paper-resource management tools do not work for electronic resources
- Current e-resource management applications *still* require tedious effort to collect statistics, enter license data, and perform many other tasks

EMERGING STANDARDS IN THE ERM INDUSTRY

All electronic resources management systems have certain characteristics in common. Among them, ERMs all promise to organize, retain, store, and report on licensing information and the permissions granted to the library by the publisher or publisher's agent. They all promise to collect,

Table 1.

Committee	Charter	Product
BA – Access management	Ranking of Authentication and Access Methods Available to the Metasearch Environment	Best Practices document that suggested that IP authentication, imperfect as it is, was best approach for Metasearch authentication
BB1 – Collection Description Specification	Collection & Service Descriptions	Z39.91 - Draft standard (2007) : means of describing collections, where a collection is defined as an aggregation of items. Uses Dublin Core Application Profile. Vote expected 2007.
BB2 – Information Retrieval	Information Retrieval Service Description Specification	Z39.92 - method of describing Information Retrieval oriented electronic services, including but not limited to those services made available via the Z39.50, SRU/SRW, and OAI protocols. Uses ZeeRex standard
BC1	Search/Retrieve	NISO RP-2006-02, NISO Metasearch XML Gateway Implementers Guide
BC2	Search/Retrieve	NISO RP-2005-02, Results Set Metadata
BC3	Search Retrieve	NISO RP-2005-03, Citation Level Data Elements

manipulate, and calculate user statistics from all the different vendors and publishers that are supplying electronic resources. Current software requires library staff to collect these data elements by themselves and then upload or manually enter the data into their ERM—tasks that are tedious and time consuming. ERM software, which brings central management to electronic resources, relies on the library's entry of complete and accurate data to be truly useful as a management tool. The following two standards—both in development—will ameliorate this burden.

SUSHI

SUSHI—Standardized Usage Statistics Harvesting Initiative) is a protocol that will allow an ERM system to request from a publisher, through a Web service request, the delivery of an XML file (in COUNTER format) of usage statistics for a particular customer during a particular month. SUSHI, if and when adopted by the publisher community, has the potential to practically eliminate the need for libraries to chase down and retrieve statistical data from hundreds of different electronic resource suppliers. As of this writing (January 2007), SUSHI is a "draft standard for trial use," a status that allows developers to work with the standard and report problems (and give the standards committee time to fix the problems) before submitting the draft standard to a final vote.

Original SUSHI participants were Ex Libris, Innovative Interfaces, Swets, and EBSCO. Ex Libris and Innovative developers wrote proof-of-concept client applications and Swets and EBSCO wrote proof-of-concept server software. Early success was achieved in November 2005 when both client applications were able to retrieve message payloads (that is, COUNTER statistics files) from each of the test servers. Early in 2006, ISI-Thomson Scientific joined the group and is working on software that would let its product act as both a server and a client. In addition, a number of other companies in the library automation and content provider industries have signed on as observers and are experimenting with the draft SUSHI standard.

SUSHI is a Web service, meaning that data is passed between parties using "normal" Web protocols and ports (80 and 443). With a Web service, as opposed to another telecommunications approach, problems with security and firewalls are minimized. The library's ERM (or other) software initiates the Web service conversation by sending a request message to the content provider. This request contains information about the requester—what library, the library's customer number, a username and password, and the name(s) and chronological period of the report(s) being requested. The responder (that is, the content provider) responds with a message acknowledging the request, and includes a "payload"—that is, a COUNTER-XML formatted data file containing the statistical data that was requested.

The use of COUNTER files means that the structure of the "payload" being shared between parties is XML, a well known and easily parsed data structure.

As of this writing, SUSHI testing among parties continues. Innovative Interfaces has released a version of its ERM with SUSHI support. The Verde product from Ex Libris will include a SUSHI protocol data collector in version 3.0, to be released in 2007. Other ILS systems are preparing their SUSHI harvesting software. The SUSHI steering group is encouraging publishers and content suppliers to provide SUSHI servers and services as quickly as possible. Since vendor participation is crucial to the success of this protocol and to widespread automated statistical data harvesting, anything that can be done to reduce technological hurdles to implementation is beneficial. Several SUSHI webinars took place in late 2006 and were primarily aimed at publishers and vendors, to promote the adoption and use of this standard across the industry.

SUSHI planners are looking at several additional protocol enhancements as the protocol begins to be used and accepted. Some areas of future development include the issuing of a "claim ticket" when a server is too busy to provide the report at the time of a request, and the expansion of the menu of reports available. Currently SUSHI handles COUNTER Journal Report-1 [JR1]; COUNTER has defined several other reports which will also be retrievable.

License Expression Delivery

A major role for any ERM software is to store and make accessible information that relates to license terms—that is, the rights and responsibilities that a library has with relation to the resource being used.

Current practice is for libraries and vendors (or agents) to negotiate a license, which is memorialized on paper and stored in some piece of furniture. License and permission data for end users is offered inconsistently, if at all. If a library happens to be using an ERM system, completing entries in the licensing section is usually an onerous manual task, involving marking up a version of the paper license. This method of license data entry is not only slow and inefficient but is also prone to error (both typographical and substantial, based on the legal verbiage and skill level of the staff member doing data entry.)

The publishing world and the library world (and its ERM systems) both recognize the benefit of license terms exchange in a machine-readable, structured format that would be easily parsed and loaded. Replacing the manual entry process, an XML loader would immediately fill in an ERM's licensing module with whatever data had been sent by the publisher. Then, as updates are required based on negotiations between the parties, the draft license would be archived and replaced by data from more recent downloads. In principle, machine updating of complicated fields would be a huge benefit to all parties—from publishers and vendors, to the libraries that are covered by the licenses and to other consumers of the resource's data.

For a license exchange protocol to be effective, there must first be agreement on what terms are to be included in the XML structure and how they are to be represented. The original DLF ERMI group defined about 160 licensing terms as part of the original specifications. EDItEUR also prepared a similar, but not identical, approach to licensing in its draft document, *ONIX for Licensing Expressions.*

Rather than work at cross-purposes, these two groups decided to combine efforts and explore whether a single standard for the exchange of license information between libraries and publishers was possible. This combined effort, called the License Expression Working Group (LEWG), began its work in January 2006. Support for the group comes from the DLF, EDItEUR, and the Publishers Licensing Society (UK). Membership as of mid-February 2006 was 59 institutions, including ILS and ERM vendors, publishers, universities, digital rights management organizations (such as the Copyright Clearance Center in the U.S.), and several national libraries. LEWG bases its work on a draft *ONIX for Licensing* document released in August 2005, along with several sample publisher licenses made available by large publishers with an interest in the outcome of this group.

As might be expected with a committee of this size, a smaller working group emerged. The working group has done some work over e-mail, but a face-to-face meeting in December 2006 led to significant progress in the License Expression project. Prior to December 2006, a wide gap separated the DLF-ERMI approach to license terms from the ONIX approach, which can be described as multi-dimensional and highly granular. Among the decisions taken in December 2006 was a new approach where the ONIX for License Expression creators would create a subset of their data in an ERMI "dialect" for ease of exchange and mapping.

Work of the LEWG is sensitive, because the results of this effort may have weighty consequences for stakeholders in this group. Publishers and agents are interested in asserting their content ownership and unambiguously describing the rights that they are granting to licensees. Libraries, on the other hand, want to respect the rights of publishers while at the same time providing the greatest access and service to their user populations. A final draft of the License Expression standard should be available in mid-to-late 2007, at which point the "draft standard" status will begin. A final license expression standard format can be anticipated in mid-2008.

FUTURE OPPORTUNITIES FOR STANDARDIZATION

The ERM industry is in its infancy. Existing systems have begun to meet the needs of libraries in 2006. Still, by the end of 2006, ERM system sales in the United States numbered no more than 500—meaning that thousands of U.S. libraries have yet to discover the efficiencies that an ERM system can deliver. As libraries integrate ERM functionality into their processing, they will have higher expectations of functionality and interoperability, and increased standardization possibilities will begin to emerge. The author sees the following areas as emerging opportunities for standardization in the next several years:

a. **IP address communication and a standardized protocol for communicating IP address changes:** Despite the tendency of IP addresses to change as networks expand and network topology at user sites is improved, IP address authentication is still the most used method of user authentication for electronic resources. (In fact, the NISO Metasearch Initiative (Standards Committee BA – Access Management, see above) in 2005 noted in its recommendations that, at present, IP authentication and password authentication were the two best practices for authentication for electronic resources use.) Communication of IP address changes from libraries to vendors could be made far easier through the use of a communications protocol that would pass IP address information updates and acknowledgments electronically. Note that some early discussions on this issue—as part of a clearinghouse—took place in late 2005, but no further progress has been made.

b. **Communication of incidents and breaches from ERM to vendor:** Almost all ERM systems track performance and service interruptions on the part of the vendor. A system of automatically reporting service glitches, through a communications protocol, would capitalize on an ERM's tracking logs and directly report problems with a vendor's system. Among the benefits of this approach: immediate notification of problems to the vendor, and a large reduction in telephone call handling of problems, because notification would be automatic.

c. **Similar to (b):** A vendor-initiated protocol to advise customers of service interruptions.

d. **ERM-to-ERM data sharing protocol:** Each ERM system vendor wishes, of course, to keep and satisfy their own customers. Nevertheless, there are times when the sharing of information between ERM systems will be a requirement. Intraconsortium sharing of data is an example of this need for sharing. Currently, almost all ERM systems use the DLF ERMI specification as the core set of data elements in their ERM. Sharing those elements is a logical next step.

e. **An international unique identifier assigned to collections (including packages and interfaces):** As of this time, MARC records and unique identifiers exist for e-journals and e-books, but not for the collections (often packages and interfaces) in which they are delivered. As a result, there is no consistent way of referring to collections. Titles are sometimes used for this purpose, and artificial, temporary identifiers are sometimes assigned, but no system that has international acceptance or recognition has been devised. The ERM industry would rapidly take advantage of such an identifier, when created.

f. **Acquisitions record and transaction sharing data elements:** Related to (d). Libraries may use an ILS from one vendor and an ERM system from a different automation vendor. Both systems need to share data related to materials acquisitions, invoices, funding, and payment amounts. An acquisitions record-sharing format would enable libraries, vendors, consortia, payment agencies, and other interested parties to easily transfer data from one automation platform to another.

The Digital Library Federation chartered a subcommittee led by Norm Medeiros to look into the need for such a standard in November 2006; the subcommittee published a white paper in January 2007 (Medeiros, Miller, Adam et al., 2007) which surveyed several libraries and ERM vendors. It is unclear whether that white paper will trigger further standards activity.

ERM STANDARDS AND THE FUTURE

ERM systems sit in the center of a number of interactions—some internal to the library (such as interoperability with an OPAC, a link resolver, and a metasearch engine) and some calling for interoperability with external sources of data. Interoperation across an industry is far easier and more efficient if shared, negotiated, and accepted standards exist. Lacking standards, time and effort are wasted on idiosyncratic solutions to individual library problems.

Therefore, by working with vendors and publishers to deliver ERM data efficiently through standards-based mechanisms, the ERM industry can enhance the value of its products as a core component in delivering library management solutions.

REFERENCES

Bourne, C. P., & Bellardo Hahn, T. (2003). *A history of online information services, 1963-1976.* Boston: MIT Press.

Kyrillidou, M., & Young, M. (2003). ARL library trends 2003-04. Retrieved November 21, 2007, from www.arl.org/stats/arlstat/04pub/04intro.html.

Medeiros, N., Miller, L., Adam, C., et al. (2007). White paper on interoperability between acquisitions modules of integrated library systems and electronic resource management systems: A draft for comment. Retrieved November 21, 2007, from www.haverford.edu/library/DLF_ERMI2/ACQ_ERMS_white_paper.pdf

Van de Sompel, H., & Beit-Arie, O. (2001). Open linking in the scholarly information environment using the OpenURL framework. *D-Lib Magazine, 7*(3). Retrieved November 21, 2007, from http://www.dlib.org/dlib/march01/vandesompel/03vandesompel.html

KEY TERMS

Standards: Industry-accepted description or definition relating to expected behavior, quality, or function

Protocols: A standard set of industry-created and approved instructions for communication and data exchange

Electronic Resource Management: Broadly, activities and tools used by a library to manage their investment in electronic products. More finely, electronic resources management refers to several specific management areas (acquisitions, access, workflow, trial, statistics, costs, etc.) that have been defined by the Digital Library Federation.

Metasearch: A process where one or more data sources are searched simultaneously and results are collected and presented to the end user as a single set.

Link Resolution: A process used by the openURL standard to parse an incoming openURL string, determine its data elements, compare the data elements to a resolver's data store, and return relevant referral information to the end user

License Expression: The significant terms of a publisher's license (referring to the customer's privileges when using that publisher's content). Generally, the expression refers to a format or structure of license terms that is different from the (prose) text of the license

Harvesting: An automated service used to collect (or harvest) data of a particular type for indexing, retrieval, and use by another computer system

Integrated Library System (ILS): An older model of delivering library automation services to libraries. Provided by a single software vendor, an ILS generally provided an OPAC, circulation system, acquisitions and serials control, and sometimes other modules, all based on the same data model and designed to work together.

Chapter XVII
Challenges and Potentials of Electronic Resource Management

Yvonne Wei Zhang
California State Polytechnic University, Pomona, USA

ABSTRACT

This chapter will focus on two ERM services, ExLibris' SFX and III's ERM. ExLibris' SFX is an example of a link resolver, whereas III ERM is an example of an ERM system. The discussion of these ERM services will focus on key issues encountered during ERM implementation at Cal Poly Pomona. The main objective of this chapter is to make the readers aware of the challenges and potentials ERM services offer, distilled from the experiences gained at Cal Poly Pomona.

INTRODUCTION

During the past decade, there has been phenomenal growth in the number of electronic resources including electronic journal packages and full text aggregations acquired by libraries. Cornell University Libraries projected that by 2005 their holdings will become mostly digital (Cornell Libraries, 2000). Though this prediction has yet to come to pass, the Association of Research Libraries (ARL) expenditure trend data (Association of Research Libraries, 2002) showed that academic libraries are "in the midst of a profound shift toward reliance on electronic resources, and this reliance seems to have deepened just within the last year or two as libraries have shed

paper journal subscriptions to help pay for online access." Since providing access to electronic resources have become such a major part of the library services, it was crucial for libraries to tackle these new challenges head on.

As early as 2000, librarians began to search for a working tool to help manage electronic resources. Some of the in-house solutions included home grown A-Z list, paper files, spreadsheets, and stand-alone databases (i.e., using Microsoft Access). Virtual Electronic Access (VERA) developed at MIT and Digital Acquisitions Database developed at UCLA were two of the most well-known in-house examples. In July 2000, Digital Library Federation (DLF) Electronic Resource Management Initiative (ERMI) was formed to create standards such as functional require-ments, workflow diagrams, and data dictionary (Digital Library Federation, 2004). Based upon these standards, commercial electronic resource management (ERM) services began to appear in two major categories: Link resolver and ERM systems. Link resolver is a linking function based upon openURL that works with a majority of the electronic resources and ties together information about the cited resource, the user, and the library's online subscriptions. An ERM system can either be stand-alone software or a module within the integrated library system (ILS).

This chapter will focus on two ERM services, ExLibris' SFX and III's (i.e., Innovative Interfaces Inc.) ERM. ExLibris' SFX is an example of a link resolver, whereas III ERM is an example of an ERM system. The discussion of these ERM ser-vices will focus on key issues encountered during ERM implementation at Cal Poly Pomona. The main objective of this chapter is to make the read-ers aware of the challenges and potentials ERM services present, distilled from the experiences gained at Cal Poly Pomona.

BACKGROUND

California State University (CSU) purchased ExLibris' SFX in the summer of 2002. SFX implementation among all 23 CSU campuses was subsequently carried out in phases during a span of four years. The CSU's main SFX server resides at the chancellor's office, managed by the system SFX coordinator. Each library of the 23 CSU campuses is an instance managed by the individual library's SFX Team. Cal Poly Pomona, an instance of CSU/SFX main server, was one of the first CSU campuses to roll out SFX to the public in Sept. 2002. From that experience, knowledge was gained in areas such as consortia specific tasks, workload and staff support, and implementation strategies.

In addition, Cal Poly Pomona purchased III ERM as a "natural" extension of the library's

ILS system right after the product was publicly released in Oct. 2004. As the implementation of III ERM occurred at a time when there was limited guidance and proven "best practices" available, the lessons learned revolved around defining code, record creation, batch load troubleshooting, and constantly improving the current practices for better ERM utilization in the future.

SFX CHALLENGES AND POTENTIALS

ExLibris' SFX is a context-sensitive linking ser-vice commercially available since 2001. Based upon the openURL standard approved by the National Information Standards Organization (NISO), SFX provides links from one information resource to another, such as e-journal databases and full text aggregations, in a transparent manner to the public (Lagace, 2003). Using SFX allows the library to offer a consistent menu/user inter-face which promises direct links not only to the full text, if it is available, but also to alternative resources, customized at the library's discretion. In addition, SFX not only generates a customizable and updatable journal title list for the library's Web site but also provides on the same list pertinent coverage data as well as print holdings. Although the success and the usefulness of SFX depend upon many factors such as the source database metadata, the construction of the openURL string, the resulting target database structure, and the lo-cal libraries' collection development (Wakimoto, 2006), a link resolver such as SFX is considered by both the library users and the librarians as a significant step forward for full text search and delivery across multiple databases.

The key issues encountered during SFX implementation at Cal Poly Pomona included staff qualifications and support, SFX menu set up, target activation and update, and teamwork in a consortium environment.

Workload and Staff Support

Ex-Libris gives the clients two options for SFX service. Option one sets up the SFX server at the local library site. This requires higher technical level and expertise (i.e., Unix server related knowledge) for the staff, but allows for a considerable saving in cost. The other option sets up the SFX server at the Ex Libris site. As a result, high-level technical skills are not required for the staff, but the cost is considerably higher. Which option is better depends upon not only the financial solvency of the library but also upon local staff qualifications and staff support availability. If the library has the necessary staff with the proper qualifications, running its own SFX server makes more sense. It is less expensive and it offers local libraries more control and flexibility. Once established, a relatively high level of independence and stability can be achieved with respect to SFX, except for the ongoing updates and maintenance. If help is needed, SFX listserv (i.e., SFX-METALIB-DIS-CUSS-L@listserv.nd.edu) and Ex Libris help desk are readily available to provide a good support system. For libraries where staffing and technical support are insufficient, SFX service via SFX main server at Ex-Libris site is the reasonable choice. These libraries will still have to handle library-specific content and databases that are different from the default SFX knowledge base (KB).

Obviously, staff deployment will differ in libraries running their own SFX server from those that rely on Ex Libris to run the SFX server. In this case, as CSU maintains its own SFX server at the Chancellor's Office site, it is vital that the consortium has at least one full time position dedicated as the system SFX coordinator, preferably librarians with system related knowledge and experience. In June 2002, CSU hired a system coordinator/librarian with substantial technical background including instructional technical consulting, database development and management using SQL (i.e., structured query language) databases, library catalog Web server maintenance, and visual basic programming. In addition, clearly defined SFX responsibilities and staff deployment at both the chancellor's office and the local instance levels needed to be worked out. The system SFX coordinator at the chancellor's office has complete overall administrative responsibility over the SFX main server and its KB. If needed, this person can override what has been previously modified at the instance level. At the individual library instance level, each SFX team has discretionary control over its own instance's admin. The team is responsible for managing the unique set of electronic resources that are different from those in the SFX KB (i.e., once a local change is made it will stay intact with every new system update) and for managing SFX menu set up, source and target activation, statistics, and monthly report review.

SFX-specific work can be divided into two categories, the initial implementation and the regular maintenance over the long haul. Thus, staff deployment for both the short term and the long term needs to be considered and planned. During the initial implementation of SFX, the staff needs to have qualifications in the areas of: (1) basic knowledge in Unix and HTML in order to navigate SFX server environment, moving around directories, opening, copying, and altering files; (2) basic cataloging experience in order to resolve bibliographic problems; (3) basic understanding of proxy, CrossRef, DOI, and openURL in order to select proper criteria for SFX target, based upon related specifications; (4) basic knowledge of aggregated databases content and structure in order to perform SFX menu customization and logic design. To support ongoing maintenance of SFX, the staff needs to have qualifications in the following areas: (1) competence with Excel and/or Word in order to create proper SFX DataLoader feed files; (2) basic understanding of SFX structure and functions in order to perform maintenance at different layers/levels of a specific target, i.e., the SFX hierarchical structure of "targets → services → portfolios → threshold" (similar to "packages → services → journal titles → coverage data"); (3) basic knowledge of cataloging in order to facilitate the updating of changes made in the library catalog to SFX.

At Cal Poly Pomona, the SFX team initially consisted of two people, the systems librarian and the assistant university librarian (AUL) for technical services (both have cataloging background). Since neither could devote full attention to SFX because of other responsibilities, it was decided to divide the SFX work into two portions. The systems librarian took care of SFX menu set up, in close consultation with reference librarians and SFX sources (i.e., databases where users start their search), and SFX A-Z list generation for the library catalog on a monthly basis. The AUL for technical services took care of SFX targets (i.e., databases where users retrieve their search results) including portfolio and threshold editing, troubleshooting, and SFX monthly report review. During the initial implementation stage, if there were a batch of portfolios needing to be edited for SFX, additional staff assistance was occasionally required to produce proper SFX DataLoader feed files. Between the two librarians, around 30-40% each of their time was spent on SFX implementation during June – Aug. 2002. Since then, about 10% each of their time has been spent on SFX related maintenance and troubleshooting. In 2005, Cal Poly Pomona's SFX team expanded to include five people. The original two librarians continue to oversee troubleshooting; one library assistant (LA) IV and one LA III in technical services support routine maintenance; one systems specialist supports SFX source, A-Z list, and statistics. Currently, on average, each person spends about 5-10% of his/her time on a regular basis.

Merged Target

One of the benefits of SFX in the CSU consortia environment is the ability to identify common databases across all campuses for centralized control by the system SFX coordinator, instead of separate controls at the local library level. These identified common databases are called "merged targets." In addition, each individual campus may select and submit local databases as another type of merged targets controlled by the system SFX coordinator. To become a merged target, a database must fulfill one of the following conditions: (1) the library subscribes to the entire package as a whole (i.e., American Chemical Society [ACS] journals consists of 51 journal titles in the SFX KB. This entire package matches exactly both in title as well as in coverage with Cal Poly Pomona's subscribed ACS package.); (2) the database must be an A&I database such as Ebsco Academic Search Elite (ASE); (3) the database must be an online search engine or service such as Google Scholar. Conversely, the following conditions will preclude a database becoming a merged target: (1) the library only subscribes to part of the package (i.e., Chicago University Press package has 43 e-journal titles in the SFX KB and Cal Poly Pomona subscribes to only 15 titles of the package), therefore, local maintenance is required; (2) the library's online access coverage is different from the default coverage provided in the SFX KB, therefore, local maintenance is required; (3) the database is acquired on a temporary basis (i.e., Latino literature by Alexander Street Press was purchased by a grant).

Although the merged target option can save substantial time and effort for the local libraries, maintaining an accurate and updated library specific merged target list at both the main server and the local instance levels is by no means an easy task, due to the dynamic nature of the merged target list. Although most of the SFX work can be carried out separately and independently at both local instance and main server levels, some work has to be done in synch. For example, merged targets need to be deactivated completely at the local level to ensure they are properly controlled at the main server level. Also, if the library's A-Z list needs to be directed/populated into a different system, such as Google Scholar, in a manner such that Cal Poly Pomona's SFX full text icon will appear next to the proper citation, the appropriate action needs to be carried out at the CSU SFX main server. In situations like these, close communication and judicious follow ups between the two parties is a must.

SFX Menu

How to set up the SFX menu best to meet the individual library's needs can also be a challenge. In addition to modifying or customizing the "look and feel" of the SFX menu, applying the appropriate "display logic" will allow the menu to display the most pertinent information and to avoid a cluttered and confusing interface for the users. What should be displayed on the SFX menu, how should the services be ordered, whether and when links should be suppressed are some menu related questions that should be considered.

Based upon reference staff input and preference, Cal Poly Pomona uses the following display logic for the SFX menu: (1) if "Get full text" is available, do not display "Get TOC" or "Get abstract;" (2) if "Get full text" is available, do not display "Get document delivery." Otherwise, do display; (3) if "Get full text" is available, do not display the statement/label "No full text available," and so forth. As a result, when there is no full text, SFX is able to direct users to related abstract and/or table of content as well as to library delivery services such as document delivery and consortia services such as LINK+ (i.e., LINK+ is a union catalog of contributed holdings from the participating 46 libraries in California and Nevada). When full text does exist, the menu will suppress all options except the linking to the library's online public access catalog (OPAC) and related/expanded Web resources via Google Scholar and Web search engines like Alta Vista, Yahoo. To facilitate proper SFX menu display, especially in cases where duplicated titles are covered by multiple databases, Cal Poly Pomona developed its own criteria to select and activate

the "best suitable" database(s) (i.e., it will be discussed later in the article).

Since SFX has become an important and usually the preferred method for full text search for students, the SFX menu has the potential to be, and in Cal Poly Pomona's case has been, utilized as a "marketing tool" to publicize important library services. For example, under a category called "Research Questions? Ask a Librarian," users can click and connect instantly to services such as E-Z Workshop, AskNow (i.e., a chat service staffed by local librarians and across the United States 24x7), and In Person Help, and so forth.

Database Activation

Usually, the databases requiring the most maintenance are those that the library has only partial subscription and those that have online coverage different from the SFX KB. There are three levels of activating a particular portfolio (i.e., journal) in these databases: target level, services level (i.e., including full text, abstract, and table of content service choices among others), and the portfolio level (i.e., where the proper journal title and associated coverage data need to be reviewed and activated). Portfolio activation tends to be the most complicated due to issues such as target name differences, multiple providers, and multiple subdatabases, and so forth. For example, the database name "AIP" at Cal Poly Pomona may not be the exact database name used by SFX (i.e., it is called AIP_SCITATION in SFX). Also, the journal title "National Civic Review" is provided by multiple databases such as Ebsco ASE and Wiley Interscience in SFX. Some targets/packages have dozens of subdatabases such as Proquest which has 83 subdatabases in the SFX KB. Thus, locating a specific Proquest title/portfolio among all those subdatabases takes time and effort. When dealing with the multiple providers situation in SFX, the following criteria are used: (1) activate based upon the level of full text access, such as journal title level, issue level, or direct full text level linking.

Choose direct full text level linking if available; (2) activate target with the most complete coverage for the specific portfolio; (3) activate target with full text in both PDF and HTML formats over those with only one format; and (4) activate all if in doubt. Combining these local activation criteria with the SFX menu display logic, Cal Poly Pomona's SFX menu reduces clutter by linking only to the most complete and updated databases. To deal with the multiple subdatabases situation in SFX, a good approach seems to be manually locating the proper subdatabase for a particular portfolio via the "Search Object" function prior to portfolio editing.

Depending upon the amount of portfolios to be activated in SFX, the staff has at its disposal two options. The first option is to update manually when the amount is manageable. Using "Search Object" in SFX admin, one can quickly identify the title in its proper target for editing by ISSN, EISSN, and titles, and so forth. After each update, it is good practice to save the change and then verify the result using the "tester" icon next to the portfolio to confirm the intended change. The second option is to update SFX via the DataLoader when there are batches of titles. Although creating a proper feed file for the DataLoader requires work and attention, the DataLoader (see Figure 1) is the preferred vehicle for SFX updates at Cal Poly

Figure 1. SFX DataLoader

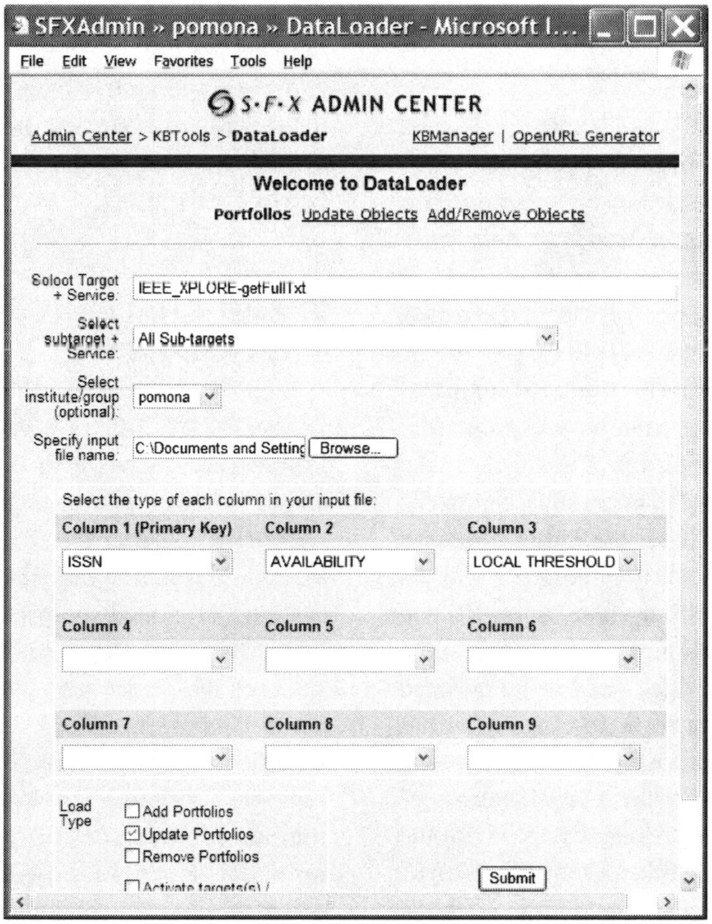

Pomona. When creating a feed file, experience has shown SFX seems to handle simple text files such as the ones created by Notebook better. Files created in Microsoft Word or Excel sometimes do not work well, because there are hidden tags that cause loading problems. For portfolio update, the feed file usually contains three columns: one for ISSN (i.e., SFX prefers print ISSN over EISSN), one for availability such as the status "ACTIVE" or "DEACTIVE," and one for the specific coverage data (i.e., threshold in SFX terms with a formula like "$obj->parsedDate(">=",1997,undef, undef)"). In addition to manually creating the feed file, the library's ILS III is sometimes used to extract and export related ISSN of a particular package for a feed file. The DataLoader always produces a load report at the end of each load, thus, the staff will be able to trace a problem easily if necessary.

A-Z List

Currently, most of the SFX A-Z lists (i.e., e-journal title list) and the local library catalog serve different functions. Although they complement each other to meet user needs, neither is yet able to deliver all the information users demand by itself. At Cal Poly Pomona, there is in fact a large difference between the SFX A-Z list and the library's catalog, because the library has only cataloged e-journal packages (i.e., no full text database cataloged) in the past. Cal Poly Pomona's SFX A-Z list, on the other hand, covers all the accessible electronic resources regardless of the cataloging status. In spite of the differences, it is imperative that the SFX A-Z list and the library catalog match one another for all of the e-journals cataloged in the library catalog. These titles need to be updated in SFX in a timely fashion for the following reasons: (1) to ensure proper online access to the full texts; (2) to avoid "blind hit/error message" when e-journal titles are no longer acquired by the library; and (3) to avoid "blind hit/error message" if the e-journal title's coverage data is different

from the SFX KB. In other words, while what is in SFX may not exist in OPAC, what is in OPAC has to be accurately reflected/activated in SFX. To carry out this process, the appropriate SFX admin rights and permissions need to be assigned to the staff responsible for cataloging e-journal titles. Once a new title is cataloged, a staff member will investigate and activate the title in SFX as part of the cataloging process, after making sure it is not part of a package or not part of a merged target. The staff will follow the same procedure and deactivate the title in SFX in the event the online access is cancelled or terminated.

Because Cal Poly Pomona's SFX A-Z list serves different functions when compared to the library catalog, the library has taken advantage of that fact and selected certain types of electronic resources to be covered only in SFX. HighWire Press publications and DOAJ (i.e., directory of open access journals), for example, do not warrant cataloging treatment based upon content and coverage restrictions. However, these two databases are activated in SFX to make them available, as they present potential full text access values for the users.

III ERM CHALLENGES AND POTENTIALS

In the fall of 2002, University of Washington Libraries partnered with III to develop an electronic resource management module based on DLF ERMI. Being the first vendor to integrate electronic resource management into its library system, III named the product/module "ERM" (Tull, 2005). III ERM enables libraries to keep track of their e-journal licensing and purchasing details using a single system, to streamline workflows, and to eliminate the need to maintain separate databases (Innovative, Inc., 2006). It introduced new types of records, the electronic resource (ER) record and its satellite/associated records including the contact and the license records.

The ER record describes the resource and allows the staff to keep track of important data such as statistics, change history, and access notes, and so forth. The license record provides contractual details, while the contact record contains relevant contact information mainly for system and access support. In addition to MARC record loading, ERM enables libraries to create coverage-holding records (i.e., e-check in records) and to link them to bibliographic records automatically via batch load. It also enables linking between holding records and their parent ER records as part of the loading process (Tull, 2005). The end result of this two-layer linking provides direct full text access with updated coverage data to a bibliographic record in OPAC. In addition, the automated loading process improves the library's cataloging efficiency to an extent not previously possible.

The key issues encountered during III ERM implementation and maintenance at Cal Poly Pomona include staff support, data provider selection and profile creation, record setup, and batch load tasks.

Workload and Staff Support

At Cal Poly Pomona, ERM staff qualifications are similar to library technical services staff qualifications including knowledge and experience in acquisition and cataloging. In addition, an in-depth knowledge of a library system such as III Millennium (especially competence in creating list/query functions) is crucial, because III ERM is closely integrated with III ILS. Familiarity with database management and a basic understanding of license terms and regulations are some additional key qualifications.

The ERM implementation was divided into two phases at Cal Poly Pomona. During phase I, which took place from Oct. 2004 to Feb. 2006, ER, contact, and license records (i.e., some of them are brief records) were created for all package databases. They comprised the majority of the library's electronic resources. ER records

for single e-journal titles that have license contracts were also created. During phase II, which took place from Mar. to Dec. 2006, coverage data purchased from Serials Solutions (SS) was added via ERM batch load to most of the package databases. Now, in addition to keeping up with regular maintenance and updates associated with coverage load, the primary objective is to fully utilize the system so that III ERM will serve as a "one stop shopping" for electronic resource management at Cal Poly Pomona.

Initially, the ERM team at Cal Poly Pomona responsible for ERM implementation consisted of two people, the AUL for technical services and an experienced LA IV. The AUL has cataloging background and the LA IV has substantial experience and expertise in both bibliographic control and III systems. Because they have other responsibilities, they devoted about 30%-40% each of their time on ERM during the implementation. This combination worked well with the initial decision-making, dictionary development, and ERM record creation during phase I. During the ERM implementation phase II, Cal Poly Pomona relied heavily on listserv help and outside contacts (i.e., University of Nevada at Reno) to help resolve some of the technical problems associated with batch load. At present, approximately 95% of the library's electronic resources are loaded into ERM (i.e., about 150 databases consisting of 10,000 e-journal titles). The ongoing maintenance of these databases includes enrichment of records, order record creation and links, and a newly created ER Unit consisting of one LA III and a LA I currently carries out routine coverage updates. This ER unit of technical services handles all electronic resource related tasks including ERM, which by estimate represents 20%-30% of the total unit tasks. The original ERM team will continue to oversee ERM operations particularly in the areas of troubleshooting and identifying future developments such as additional indices, public displays, and statistics generations.

Since ERM allows libraries to record and track substantial contractual details in the license record, and the person managing the record is most likely not the person who performs the license review, how to best arrange staff support for license record creation becomes an issue. In some academic settings, license review and approval are done by campus counsel outside of the library. Because license related work presents "unfamiliar territory" for most library staff, it would be ideal for the person responsible for the license review to create the license record once an agreement has been reached as all the details are fresh and clear (Duranceau, 2000). If that is not possible, special consideration and training need to be given to the staff performing the license record creation. At Cal Poly Pomona, this is not a problem, because one member of the ERM team is the librarian who oversees the license review process. Once the license is reviewed and approved by the dean of the university library, this librarian creates a license record in ERM immediately. The license is then scanned by a LA with an Epson scanner at the LA's workstation. The scan quality is not set to high for the following reasons: (1) the higher resolutions require more disk storage; (2) it is unlikely the library will display the license to the public; and (3) there is at least one print copy filed in the library. The librarian then saves the digitized file on Cal Poly Pomona's Intranet which is not only accessible to all university employees but also secure, has sufficient storage capacity, and is backed up regularly by campus network specialist. The Intranet URL is then recorded in the "License location" field of the license record at the end of the process.

Data Provider

In order to load and append a coverage holding record to the correct bibliographic record as well as the ER record via ERM batch load, the library needs to have a coverage data feed file (i.e., a CSV (comma-separated values) file) to begin the linking process. Some libraries generate their own files by harvesting via link resolver services like SFX or by contacting publishers directly. Most libraries, however, purchase coverage data from commercial data providers such as SS, because local creation and maintenance of coverage data is time and labor intensive. One of the most important criteria for choosing a good data provider is the scope of the provider's KB and the quality of its data including how frequently the data gets updated. A sophisticated and easy to use database interface is another crucial selection criterion. Cal Poly Pomona chose SS as its coverage data provider because: (1) SS has been exclusively providing coverage data to libraries for years; (2) based upon III ERM libraries' experience, SS provides the required data elements and seems to fit the best with III ERM; and (3) cost is reasonable as Cal Poly Pomona is under CSU/SS contract.

Creating the library's profile in the provider's database such as SS is a difficult task. Database naming convention is different from provider to provider. Elsevier, for example, not only has multiple subdatabases but also has identical names for these subdatabases like: Elsevier ScienceDirect and Elsevier SD ScienceDirect Complete, and so forth. "IEEE Xplore" is the database name Cal Poly Pomona uses, but in SS it is called IEEE Digital Library or IEEE Electronic Library Online. Thus, identifying the proper package for a target journal title can be a challenge. In addition, title activation and related coverage review are extremely time consuming and labor intensive as well. It cannot be rushed because the quality of the profile directly impacts the quality of ERM batch load. When creating Cal Poly Pomona's profile in the SS KB, the library staff had to consult several lists/sources such as the SFX KB and CSU SEIR (i.e., CSU system wide electronic information resources) to help reconcile and identify the proper database names and related coverage data. Although it took a couple of months to set up an accurate profile, the staff considers the SS client center (i.e., SS admin interface) one of the best-designed data provider databases. Many useful features such as "Package level coverage default" and "Bypass proxy" options make the edit process easier and faster. Once a profile is established with care, there will be less ongoing maintenance required and the library will be able to generate updated coverage data for all e-journal titles identified in SS at any time.

ERM Record

ERM enables libraries to have centralized and enhanced control of electronic resources not possible in the past. ER record works well with packages such as IEEE Xplore and Ebsco ASE, but does not necessarily work well with single titles outside of a package. For a single e-journal title acquired under a license contract, it is logical to use an ER record because ERM provides the ability to track and organize license related data. For a single e-journal title acquired without license contract, there are different opinions (i.e., potential solutions) among ERM libraries searching for the best practice. One suggestion advocates the creation of an umbrella ER record for all single titles, so that it resolves the batch load issue and creates a consistent public display for all e-journals. The drawback of this suggestion is the fact that this kind of ER records will not contain any common data for the individual unrelated titles. Another suggestion is the creation of an ER record for every single e-journal title that already exists in the library catalog. Some view this approach as redundant and unnecessary. Standardized Usage Statistics Harvesting Initiative (SUSHI) generation could also impact the decision on the scope of ER records, because the automatic harvesting of SUSHI statistics only applies to titles in ERM. Even if publishers were able to provide usage data based on COUNTER standard, titles outside of ERM will not generate SUSHI statistics at present. As single titles not covered by ERM represent a small portion of Cal Poly Pomona's electronic resources and most of

them are free (based upon print subscriptions through Ebsco), thus, more vulnerable in terms of access and stability, it was decided to keep them "outside" of ERM for now.

For some databases, choosing the appropriate entry for the field called "Resource name" of an ER record can be problematic. Proquest, for example, has multiple independent databases like "Safari tech books online," each having a different set of contents. Some databases are even more complex, where the provider's name, the platform's name, and the package name are all mixed together such as Scitation, the relaunch of the Online Journal Publishing Service (OJPS) of AIP. At Cal Poly Pomona, the most well known name associated with a package/database is chosen as the resource name in an ER record, regardless whether or not it is the provider's name, the platform name, or the package name. The rest of the related names are tracked as Alternative resource names, even though in some cases they are not package alternate name at all. In cases where there is confusion, "qualifiers" are added to allow for differentiation. For example, the library subscribes to Proquest products through the CSU consortium as well as the local site contract. In this case, two ER records were created in ERM, one for Proquest (CO) (i.e., Chancellor's Office) and one for Proquest (NON-CO). For complex title situations, the "unpopular" names are not only provided as alternate resource names but also explained in detail in note field(s) of the ER record.

How to best index the resource name, separately or together with the general title (i.e., as a potential indexing option), is another discussion topic among III ERM libraries. Unlike some of the III ERM libraries that prefer to index resource name together with the general titles, Cal Poly Pomona currently chose to keep it indexed separately. This decision is based upon the following reasons: (1) resource name is generally a package title, which is quite different from individual e-journal title under general title index; and (2) since Cal Poly Pomona elects not to display the

ER record in the library catalog, the title/name is mostly used by library staff. Including them in the general title index may cause unnecessary confusion for both library users and staff.

During the initial ERM implementation stage, there were times when codes needed to be defined, potentials needed to be identified, and new codes and local customizations needed to be initiated while creating ERM records. For example, "Right type" of the ER record has seven values including "Archival terms" which might require local interpretation or clarification. It is, therefore, important to set up a local data dictionary to capture what has been decided for consistency and for overall quality of the library's ERM database (i.e., for more details visit: http://www.csupomona.edu/~library/BibAccess/ermcodedic.html). For example, as a Portico member library, Cal Poly Pomona is currently recording Portico participation status in the "Archival provisions" field of a license record. This practice is recorded in the dictionary as a local practice. Some of the local customizations in place at Cal Poly Pomona include: setting up an additional index for "Resource author," using ERM display options (i.e., governed by wwwoptions) to add headers (i.e., Full text from:) and banners (i.e., "Title" and "Holdings") to improve public display, and modifying license record fixed fields such as "License code 1" to "Interlibrary loan" provision.

Batch Load

One of the major enhancements built in III ERM system is its ability to load not only MARC record but also coverage data through batch load function in minutes. A feed file such as SS review file contains information such as ISSN, EISSN, title, start date, end date, provider name, and URL. When ERM batch load finds the matching ISSN and/or title (i.e., or any other combination based upon specific criteria) in the library's catalog, it creates an e-checkin record and attaches it to the proper bibliographic record while being appended/soft-linked to the appropriate ER record. When ERM batch load does not find the matching ISSN in the library's catalog, it does one of the following two things. In the event it finds multiple identical ISSN or title, it will generate an error message in the load report indicating it failed to set up a proper e-checkin record. Or, if libraries choose to do so, it can create a mini record instantly. The mini record is created based upon a template designed specifically for the batch load. In cases where the matching is complex or problematic, a special criterion "Alt-lookup" provided in III ERM may offer additional matches. For example, Cal Poly Pomona uses the unique system generated bibliographic record number as the "Alt-lookup" value to facilitate successful matching and loading.

The best and the safest way to run ERM batch load is to start small. As the key element of soft-linking is the field in the ER record called resource ID, one must make sure the resource ID matches exactly with the resource provider name in the data feed file. Otherwise, one may choose to edit the coverage spreadsheet conversion rules file in III ERM to allow matching under different provider names (see Figure 2).

At Cal Poly Pomona, the large feed file generated by SS is divided into smaller package specific files. If any modifications have to be made, SS is updated prior to loading. After the load is completed, the load report is saved immediately as the report is session specific. Problems such as unsuccessful match, mini record errors, and display errors found in the report are then addressed. The titles that failed the batch load are usually those with similar wordings and/or ISSN especially in title change and/or multiple dates situations. For example, "Antennas and Propagation newsletter, IRE Professional Groups on" changed its title to "Antennas and Propagation Society newsletter, IEEE," then to "Newsletter (IEEE Antennas and Propagation Society)," then to "Antennas and Propagation magazine, IEEE," and finally to "IEEE antennas & propagation magazine" over

Figure 2. III ERM conversion rules

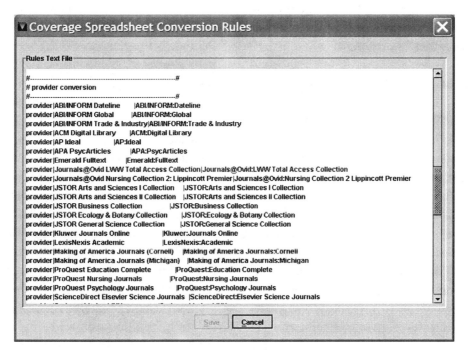

a span of 48 years. ERM cannot handle this well and logs the titles as errors. In situations like that, it is usually most helpful to avoid soft-linking all together. Creating e-checkin records and linking them to the proper ER record manually (i.e., hard linking) was the choice at Cal Poly Pomona. This method also applies to the case of multiple dates for a single title such as "IEEE proceedings. G, circuits, devices, and systems." To take advantage of the ERM batch load capability/potential, Cal Poly Pomona also loaded full text databases that were never cataloged before such as Ebsco ASE and Wilson Omni into the library catalog. As a result, there were thousands of mini records created as "by-products" of the ERM batch load and added automatically into OPAC for library users.

ERM Coverage Edit is found to be a convenient tool for batch load editing at Cal Poly Pomona. It works particularly well when: (1) editing data such as title, URL, diacritics, and coverage data; (2) deleting and breaking the soft link at both the title and the package level; and (3) browsing batch load package list and its content. Coverage Edit, however, cannot perform the following: (1) view the change result after each edit directly; (2) delete the corresponding e-checkin record in the library catalog; and (3) edit an e-checkin record created outside of batch load. Nevertheless, Coverage Edit is heavily used at Cal Poly Pomona, because it provides the most direct way to identify the proper e-checkin record for edit. In Coverage Edit mode, the staff can use natural expressions for dates such as: 20050601 (i.e., year, month, and date) instead of a fixed pattern, such as 856 |k 2001-2005, |i 01-12, |j 01-31 (i.e., for Jan. 1, 2001-Dec. 31, 2005), in cataloging mode. One can also sort by a specific column such as "title," "ISSN," "Start_date," and so forth to help identify and edit the correct title more easily, or select multiple titles for deletion by using only one click. Coverage Edit also allows the staff to get rid of a package already loaded by clicking on the package level deletion button. Because the staff cannot remove e-checkin records from the catalog in Coverage Edit, he/she will have to capture and delete those records of the package via III's "Create lists" function.

Inaccuracies and Discrepancies

Based upon Cal Poly Pomona's experience, there will always be inaccuracies and discrepancies associated with ERM batch load. Inaccurate coverage data is one of the major concerns. Data provider services such as SS get their coverage data from publishers in most cases. As the data provider's customer is the general public, most services cannot and do not distinguish library A's holding from library B's. As a result, individual libraries may need to modify the coverage data obtained from commercial data provider to match their own. Other types of inaccuracies/discrepancies also complicate ERM batch load. Different treatment in title changes and differences between the print and the online format for the same title are some examples.

In SS, there are two options a library can choose to modify coverage data for a specific database. First, at the package level, SS offers a useful feature that allows a library to set up its own default coverage. This feature is "intelligent" enough to change all related titles' coverage to the new default date (i.e., 1995) while keeping the titles that have a start date later than the new default date (i.e., 1997) intact. For titles that have start date prior to the new default date (i.e., 1993), SS will mark them and allow the staff to manually update the titles later. For example, Elsevier ScienceDirect (SD) offers a five-year contract with CSU starting in Jan. 2006 with a package in which most of the titles have a start date of 1995. The Elsevier SD package in SS, however, has titles with coverage back to the 19th century. In this case, it makes sense for Cal Poly Pomona to change the package default start date to "1995"—present," so that most of its SD titles will have an accurate coverage data. The second option to modify coverage data

is at the individual e-journal title level. This is by far more time consuming and tedious. Emerald database, for example, is "notorious" at Cal Poly Pomona because none of the titles' coverage data in SS matched. SS informed Cal Poly Pomona the discrepancy exists as Emerald generates customized coverage data for each customer. Thus, there is a big discrepancy between Cal Poly Pomona's data and SS'. In situations like this, the staff had no choice but to manually revise all Emerald titles in SS based upon Cal Poly Pomona specific coverage data before loading.

When dealing with discrepancies between the library's catalog and SS, what is already established in the catalog is given more weight. For example, the print title "IEEE transactions on parts, materials, and packaging" started in Jun. 1965 and changed its title to "IEEE transactions on parts, hybrids and packaging" in Apr. 1971. The online equivalent of the first title in IEEE Xplore started in Jan. 1965 and ended in Dec. 1971 before the second title began. Accordingly, the bibliographic records were not changed but the coverage data in the corresponding e-checkin records were updated. The print publication "Antennas and Propagation Society newsletter, IEEE" (1963-1973) changed its title to "Newsletter (IEEE Antennas and Propagation Society)" (1973-1987). Its online version has only one single title "IEEE Antennas and Propagation Society newsletter" for the entire period of 1963-1987 with one single URL. In this case, the two bibliographic records were maintained and the same URL was used for the two e-checkin records.

Despite the discrepancies, SS' data is usually accepted as is for two reasons. First, the magnitude of the editing work is usually beyond the library's ability to handle. Second, in a full text database environment, depending upon the database structure, it could be technically difficult to identify and confirm what exactly are the start date and the end date. For example, Lexis-Nexis has a start date Jan. 1, 1984 in SS, but with the way Lexis-Nexis database is organized, it is difficult to verify that Cal Poly Pomona indeed had full text access starting Jan. 1, 1984. After consulting with the reference staff, the decision was made to spot-check the package coverage data (i.e., check every other 10th title in the case of a large package) after each batch load. If there are coverage errors, they are corrected, i.e., the coverage holding data said "Jan. 1, 1995 – present," while in fact the library online access started in "Jan. 1, 2000 – present," If there are inaccurate coverage data, they are accepted as they are, that is, SS data says "Jan. 1, 1995- present" while in fact the library has "Jan. 1, 1993 – present" (i.e., more online access than indicated). In the event most of the coverage data are OK (i.e., 80% is accurate), the load is accepted as is. Otherwise, each title is fixed with the correct data. For ongoing maintenance, the library decided that databases with embargo restrictions such as Ebsco ASE will receive updates on a quarterly basis, whereas other databases such as JSTOR will be updated yearly.

CONCLUSION

ExLibris' SFX and III ERM have become important parts of the library's resource management tools at Cal Poly Pomona. Although each service brings its own set of challenges to the library staff, they are considered major and effective enhancements in providing access to electronic resources to users from the librarians' perspective.

SFX works well with most of Cal Poly Pomona's heavily used databases such as Ebsco ASE and Wilson/OmniFile Full Text Mega. Thus, the students can take advantage of SFX's context-sensitive linking functions to the fullest extent possible. However, SFX is not perfect. It does not work well with some databases such as OCLC FirstSearch ERIC, especially with ED (i.e., Eric document) files, largely due to target databases' metadata and structure limits. Also, SFX A-Z list is slow to navigate between pages because it is a large HTML file, and it only offers "title" search

capability. To remedy the situation, Cal Poly Pomona plans to add other SFX features such as "Citation Linker" and print holdings "look-up" when time permits. These features will make the search process faster and improve SFX service by connecting the A-Z list to print holdings as well as the library OPAC directly.

III ERM is considered a "rainstorm in a drought season" product for the library staff at Cal Poly Pomona, even though the staff realizes the library has yet to fully tap ERM's full potential. III ERM enables the library to add online coverage to the existing bibliographic records and to produce thousands of automatically created mini records for titles covered by full text aggregations such as Ebsco ASE. Furthermore, the close integration between III ERM and ILS presents an array of possibilities for librarians. For example, providing the best record available (i.e., print record) with the fullest information to the users instead of multiple records for aggregators is now a possibility, because the URL and the online coverage data are now delivered via an e-checkin record instead of a bibliographic record. Another possibility/potential involves utilizing batch load's automatic mini record creation function to catalog selective materials such as GPO (i.e., Government Printing Office) and Juvenile collections. For statistics gathering, the library is now able and will harvest SUSHI statistics when publishers' usage data is available. With the III ENCORE release in the making, new technologies similar to Endeca Information Access Platform (Antelman, Lynema, & Page, 2006) and the tighter integration between ILS and ERM are expected to bring about even more future possibilities. As discussed earlier, one of the major concerns associated with III ERM continues to be inaccurate coverage data issues. The inaccuracies observed are not usually caused by III ERM or SS, but are the result of a mixture of circumstances such as different bibliographic control practices between the library and the data provider, consortia specific coverage holdings derived from CSU contracts, and a library's ability to sustain quality maintenance. Thus, the inaccurate coverage data issue will most likely not be solved by III ERM and may not be resolved any time soon.

The good news is that ERM is constantly evolving. ERMI phase II, being developed under the auspices of DLF, has focused its attention in the areas of data dictionary, license expression, and usage data. From the ILS vendors' perspective, ERM is moving towards enhanced interoperability with ILS especially in the acquisitions functions (Medeiros, Miller, Chandler, & Riggio, 2007) such as renewals and payments and in the serials functions such as overlap holding comparison (Fons & Jewell, 2006). Integration between link resolver and ERM system is also being worked. From the ERM libraries' perspective, the next generation ERM is expected to have a more sophisticated public display, the capability to use complex data models and tools such as Oracle, and a single authoritative data store (Antelman, 2005). Being part of the "modularity" technology infrastructure (Calhoun, 2006), ERM will play a key role in enhancing and transforming traditional ILS functions into a library delivery system that embraces "simplicity and immediacy" (p. 2), as Riemer (2006) stated.

REFERENCES

Antelman, K. (2005). Implementing a serial work in an electronic resources management system. *Serials Librarian, 48*(3/4), 285-288.

Antelman, K., Lynema, E., & Page, A. K. (2006). Toward a twenty-first century library catalog. *Information Technology and Libraries, 25*(3), 128-139.

Association of Research Libraries (2002). Collections and access for the 21st-century scholar: changing roles of research libraries. *ARL: A bimonthly report on research library Issues and actions from ARL, CNI, and SPARC.* 225.

Retrieved November 21, 2007, from http://www.arl.org/newsltr/225/index.html

Calhoun, K. (2006). The changing nature of the catalog and its integration with other discovery tools. Retrieved November 21, 2007, from http://www.loc.gov/catdir/calhoun-report-final.pdf

Cornell University Libraries (2000). Cornell University Library digital futures plan: July 2000 to June 2002. Retrieved November 21, 2007, from http://www.library.cornell.edu/staffweb/CULDigitalFuturesPlan.html

Digital Library Federation (2006). DLF electronic resource management initiative. Retrieved November 21, 2007, from http://www.diglib.org/standards/dlf-erm02.htm

Duranceau, E. F. (2000). License tracking. *Serials Review, 26*(3), 69-73.

Fons, T., & Jewell, T. (2006, May). *Envisioning the future of ERM systems.* Paper presented at the 21st Annual NASIG Conference, Denver, Colorado.

Friedlander, A. (2002). *Dimensions and use of the scholarly information environment: Introduction to a data set assembled by the Digital Library Federation and Outsell, Inc.* Washington, D.C.: Digital Library Federation and Council on Library and Information Resources. Retrieved November 21, 2007, from http://www.clir.org/pubs/reports/pub110/contents.html

Innovative, Inc. (2006). Digital collections. Electronic resource management. Retrieved November 21, 2007, from http://www.iii.com/mill/digital.shtml#erm

Lagace, N. (2003). The OpenURL and SFX linking. *Serials Librarian, 44* (1/2), 77-89.

Medeiros, N., Miller, L., Chandler, A., & Riggio, A. (2007). White paper on interoperability between acquisitions modules of integrated library systems and electronic resource management systems: A draft for comment. Retrieved November

21, 2007, from http://www.haverford.edu/library/ DLF_ERMI2/ACQ_ERMS_white_paper.pdf

Riemer, J. J., (in press). Restrategizing bibliographic services and the one good record. *LRTS*.

Tull, L., Crum, J., Davis, T., & Strader, C. R. (2005). Integrating and streamlining electronic resources workflows via Innovative's Electronic Resource Management. *Serials Librarian, 47*(4), 103-124.

Wakimoto, J. C., Walker, D. S., & Dabbour, K. S. (2006). The myths and realities of SFX in academic libraries. *Journal of Academic Librarianship, 32*(2) 127-136.

Chapter XVIII
Panorama of Electronic Resource Management Systems

Margaret Hogarth
University of California, Riverside, USA

Vicki Bloom
University of California, Riverside, USA

ABSTRACT

Management of electronic resources requires more features and fields than legacy integrated library systems (ILS) can provide. Relationships between title, package, platform and publisher, incident and breach records, changeable holdings, license, and access restrictions cannot easily be captured. Usage combined with cost is needed for collection development and public services decisions. This chapter demonstrates how the Electronic Resource Management Initiative reports, library-developed systems, and existing and in-process standards help the continuing development of compensating electronic resource management systems and their integration into ILS. Much more work and discussion is needed in order to maximize the use of these resources and their data. Modular, extensible, standards-based tools will supplement legacy ILS and their valuable business and bibliographic data. Vendor-provided bridging tools, also based on these standards, will enable and maximize data movement between systems.

INTRODUCTION

During the last 20 years, libraries have witnessed an unprecedented growth in the availability of electronic content, particularly among serials. A survey done by Duranceau and Hepfer in 2002 of six institutions found that average e-collection growth had been 1,100% in 5 years (2002, p. 317).

In 2003, 75% of scholarly journals offered online access as did most commercial publishers (Cox & Cox, 2003).

Budgets reflected this shift in emphasis. In 1994-1995, 63 ARL libraries reported spending $11,847,577 on electronic serials; nine years later in 2003-2004, 110 ARL libraries spent $269,601,241. Over ten years ago, 82 ARL libraries reported electronic resources expenditures as 3.6% of total materials expenditures, compared with 111 ARL libraries in 2003-2004 averaging 31.33% (Kyrillidou & Young, 2005, p. 21). The numbers are most likely higher today. In an effort to cope with rising costs, libraries formed consortial buying arrangements to purchase these resources.

Where libraries had owned materials, they now provided access. This represented a shift of paradigm proportion. In the new world of electronic resources, libraries discovered that more processes, people, and data collection were involved. The straight line from the subject selector to acquisitions to cataloging and finally, the shelf no longer worked. Electronic resources demanded licenses, record-keeping of URLs and IP authentication, permissions, and new payment options such as prepayment, packages by discipline, pay per view, and micropricing (Schulz, 2001), along with many other needs. While MARC 856 fields were added to catalogs beginning in 1995, dealing with changeable holdings and updating records presented tough challenges to those managing electronic content. As electronic content became available, so did the various options for delivery. For instance, free online with the print subscription was common, as was a subsequent change in subscription to print + online at an additional charge. Technical services departments around the country bravely tried to track these resources in meaningful, useful ways. But they all discovered one common denominator: their integrated library systems were deemed inadequate for these kinds of complicated tasks.

BACKGROUND

Library catalogs have struggled to keep up with electronic resources' needs. Linking to electronic resources led to catalogs repurposed as information gateways, moving beyond an inventory list function. In response to these changes, libraries began to develop supplemental systems to ad-

dress shortfalls in online cataloging, acquisitions and other systems; these supplemental systems captured data not easily stored or easily retrievable from ILS systems. Administrative data about electronic resources was captured in paper files, spreadsheets and other receptacles, not the catalog. Permitted uses, needed by interlibrary loan and other staff, could not easily be tied to the catalog record. A-Z lists built on Web sites, spreadsheets capturing license terms, administrative information, and package information quickly became unwieldy. Usage statistics, as they began to trickle in, were not easily corralled into cost per use figures, the illusive holy grail of collection development departments everywhere (Medeiros, 2006).

LOCALLY DEVELOPED ERMS: EARLY DEVELOPMENT

Libraries began to cobble together supplemental systems and tools in an effort to shore up informational needs required by electronic resources. Using spreadsheets, paper files, databases, and combinations of these, data about electronic resources began to be consolidated on an ad hoc basis, and in response to local needs. Those institutions able to build higher level local systems or tools invested a great deal of time and resources into their projects. Often development involved partnerships between librarians and information technology staff. Development in many cases took significant time. Some systems were used then later discontinued as commercial products began to enter the market. A few systems that were created were never officially launched and others were underutilized due to inadequate data.

These initial early systems attempted to address more than one of the following functions:

1. **Listing/descriptive:** Ability to generate A-Z lists in facile ways, including titles from

Table 1.1. Locally developed ERMs:Early development

1998	2001	2002	2003	2004	2006	2007
Locally-developed systems, Phase 1 Open Source	Jewell/DLF Report OpenURL Linking	ERMI Steering Group formed Locally-developed systems, Phase 2	COUNTER	ERMI Report First integrated ERMS Commercial products with ERMS features	SUSHI ERMI-2 Steering Group formed	SERU

aggregator databases. Tie titles to package information.

2. **License:** Track and convey permitted resource uses at the point of use to patrons.
3. **Financial/purchasing:** View titles by package, publisher or interface to align subscriptions more efficiently. Monitor upcoming renewals.
4. **Process/status:** Track the processing progress of electronic resources as they are acquired, licensed, and implemented. Alert patrons when resources are temporarily unavailable.
5. **Systems/technical:** Track resource performance issues and episodes.
6. **Contact and support:** Store correspondence, service histories, and/or technical support.
7. **Usage:** Capture usage data and/or locations of publisher-produced usage data (Jewell, 2001).

All of the early systems lacked interoperability with their ILS, required dual data entry and/or downloads from the ILS or other systems and upload into the ERMs. Examples of early local systems were: Serials Cybrarian, Taylor University's TPAS, MIT's Vera, The University of Washington and Cornell's CORC, Griffith University Library's ERD, Pennsylvania State's ERLIC, Johns Hopkins HERMES, and UCLA's ERDb.

As a first step, many libraries developed Web-based lists of electronic resources geared for patron use. Examples include Serials Cybrarian and Taylor University's TPAS.

Gary O. Roberts developed Serials Cybrarian in 1998 for Alfred University in New York to maintain, search and link to e-journal holdings. A second version was developed and made publicly available for purchase in 2001. While popular with colleagues at Alfred University, the product was not commercially successful (Sitko et al., 2002). The library later chose to purchase TDNet (Cooper & Lester, 2005).

The Taylor Periodical Administration System (TPAS) was a database Web application with a search interface (Taylor Periodical List) for print and online periodicals. It also included an administrative interface for storing and managing administrative data about periodicals.

The first system, developed in 2001, was a home grown system based on ASP and Microsoft Access. It used vendor title lists combined with an Excel list of print titles. The database was maintenance intensive, requiring manual merging of title information from disparate vendor title lists, combined with print subscriptions, additions and cancellations. Even with its limits, TPAS became a critical library tool, the second most used after the library catalog.

A revision in 2003 added functionality to the administrative module. Enhanced searching allowed searches by subject and ISSN, as well as by keyword in title. Full text holdings became more reliable. Database architecture was robust and scripting language was added to address the increased traffic and system load. When SFX, ExLibris' openURL linking tool was launched, it was integrated into TPAS.

On the technical end, the process to add a periodical and compare incoming title lists with existing title lists needed simplification, as did functional output to usable file formats. Autodelete was needed in the monthly update process. Despite obvious development time and energy, TPAS still required subject fields, on-the-fly reports for management and statistics information, XML functionality, and postupdate find and replace functions (Wissman et al., 2005).

Aside from providing descriptive listings of electronic resources, the need to record and communicate license information to staff and users drove development of MIT's Vera and the University of Washington systems license database.

In response to usability test complaints about navigation and use, MIT Libraries developed a database-backed Web site, Vera, using File-Maker Pro to replace a tool developed in 1999. By 2001, Vera was being used to track licenses, manage URLs and handle proxy information for e-resources, including aggregator titles. It also associated selectors with resources. Searchable by subjects using an expanded flat list of library-generated database subjects, Vera was intended to provide one-stop access. The results screen showed title, coverage dates, format, licensing restrictions, and icons indicating online and remote availability (through shortcut persistent URLs) (Hennig, 2002).

The University of Washington's license database went a step further. In development in 2001, fields were created for vendor, status, date signed, duration, and captured permitted uses such as e-reserves, course-packs, downloading, copy, scholarly sharing, walk-ins, commercial use, special terms, and archival/ongoing access rights. Additionally, a digital registry was used to generate the production database and e-journal lists, with the ability to add subjects and categories (Jewell, Appendix B, 2001).

Several systems recorded financial and purchasing data in addition to listing and license functions. Examples include Cornell's CORC, Griffith University's ERD and Pennsylvania State's ERLIC.

Cornell's CORC (Cooperative Online Resource Catalog) system was based on 35 elements relevant to electronic resources including selector, genre, access, number of simultaneous users, price and payment history. Based on the Dublin Core resource description framework plus elements needed to describe and manage licensed electronic resources, CORC was meant to initiate some standardization among projects going on at UCLA, University of Washington, Notre Dame and Penn State University. A simple Web-based database was to be completed in 2001 (Chandler, 2000). Cornell switched to Innovative's ERM in 2005 (Medeiros et al., 2007).

In 1998, Griffith University Library in Queensland, Australia switched to using one record for both print and electronic journals. After the Griffith team saw an ERLIC presentation at NASIG in 1999, they decided to use Access stored in ORACLE architecture to develop their Electronic Resources Database (ERD). ERD was a staff tool where data could be recorded in one place. Data came from the catalog record and local subject descriptors were added (Schulz, 2001). Its management reports included a summary of journal holdings, journals by currency, by fund code, order status, by publisher and by database. ERD was thought to be a database solution until library systems could cope (Schulz, 2001).

ERLIC (Electronic Resources Licensing and Information Center) was developed for Pennsylvania State's 23-campus university system. Built in Access in 1999 for acquisitions and renewals, it evolved into a tool for ordering, access, authentication and licensing information. In 2001 they switched to a Cold Fusion base which eventually changed to Oracle. In designing the tool, they took care to assess stakeholders' information needs. They identified as their priorities the need to access data and critical documents, the ability to generate reports, update records, track problems, new products, and access privileges, and generate an e-journal list. Later, they added an optical image database for licenses. Since it is a large multicampus system, Penn State created a billboard function to alert the public of access problems, trials, and new resources (McCaslin, 2003).

As the database grew larger, ERLIC became cumbersome to update and query, taking more staff time to maintain the data. Although it was a large system, some information needs still were not being met. Some critical documentation was not handy and not available outside technical services, and acquisitions files were not secure (Alan, 2002).

Johns Hopkins University's HERMES (Hopkins Electronic Resource Management System) tracked the approval process in addition to listing, license, and process/status functions. Beginning in 1999 with a need to manage links for electronic resources, a Web-based database was built that allowed generation of alphabetic and subject-specific lists of resources, both licensed and unlicensed, on the library Web site. Elsewhere in the library, specifications for a license-tracking database were discussed. This work was folded into the project, along with workflows and approval processes. Called HERMES, this new system would automatically capture appropriate data from the ILS using XML and scheduled updates. This allowed interoperability with existing and future systems. Staff using HERMES were assigned specific functional roles allowing local changes to be made without modifying code. In 2001, planning was influenced by the information available on Web Hub. HERMES was scheduled to go live in the spring of 2003 then became open source software (Cyzyk & Robertson, 2003).

UCLA's Electronic Resources Database (ERDb) tried to address most ERMS functions.

In 2001 Sharon Farb and Angela Riggio and their team at UCLA established guiding principles for its Electronic Resources Database project:

- Know your users and uses
- Avoid unnecessary duplication
- Accommodate growth
- Design for flexibility
- Have one database but many views
- Define metadata elements
- Have the ability to implement in phases
- Provide for usage data *
  (Farb & Riggio, 2002)
  (* Note: It is not clear here whether usage data refers to the ability to collect usage data or where to access usage data.)

These principles proved to be very influential to later planning and development of ERMS by academic libraries, consortia, and vendors and other agencies.

UCLA's "one database, many views" design principle lent itself to capturing the complex nature of the electronic resource, and significantly influenced ERMS design and function for the industry. Fields communicating life cycle information, such as acquisition, implementation, product maintenance and review were presented and grouped in ways that were meaningful to staff work processes (Jewell et al., 2004).

The records set up the distinction between publisher/producer, issuing body (corporate, association, society, etc.), and access provider (supplier of information), although the information was not always easily available (UCLA, mhr and lss, 2002, Examples of publisher...) But the system, for instance, did not have a package list-building function.

Like all the other systems mentioned, UCLA's system was burdened by similar workload demands. Plain and simple, the input and editing of data increased as the number and complexity of titles, packages, exceptions, and variations increased. UCLA also had to contend with complex consortial possibilities, pricing, and problems. Data needed to be standardized for migration and synchronized with the OPAC. Most importantly, electronic resource management had not been systematized in the organization and a formal structure of workflow with clearly defined roles had not been established. (UCLA, 2004, UC survey pp. 2, 5). This severely limited the usefulness and applicability of the ERDb. UCLA and the UC campuses are exploring other systems (Medeiros et al., 2007).

THE CRY FOR STANDARDS

As the community of librarians working on electronic resource management systems grew in scope and profile, Tim Jewell and Adam Chandler of Cornell University formed Web Hub in 2001, a site for exchanging information. Information posted on Web Hub influenced projects under development (Jewell, 2006).

A group of librarians interested in electronic resource management issues met at ALA 2001. From those discussions, interested librarians organized a formal meeting at ALA Midwinter 2002. Tim Jewel of the University of Washington gave an overview of the pivotal DLF Report, *Selection and Presentation of Commercially Available Electronic Resources: Issues and Practices* to the 34 attendees. This report summarized the electronic environment, the tremendous growth in electronic resources and associated staffing

and fiscal responsibilities, and practices, coping mechanisms and tools that libraries have developed to manage these resources. It discussed effects from consortial efforts and scholarly communication reform, and the complications of managing changeable aggregated resources. After featuring ERMS efforts at various universities, the report noted the need for standards, affordable commercial systems, and the benefit of cooperative efforts.

Nathan Robertson, HERMES Committee member from Johns Hopkins, and Sharon Farb of UCLA gave presentations on local electronic resource management systems. Tim Jewell and Nicole Hennig of MIT shared information about MIT's Vera, and Lib-Lion, the next generation tool for Penn State after ERLIC.

Tim Jewell and Diane Rosolowsky discussed their "Draft Plan and Discussion Paper: Terms and Definitions for Managing Electronic Resources." Attendees requested that a metadata standard be developed for descriptive metadata, access restrictions, license details, and administrative management. Three groups were formed to focus on access, identification and licensing, to report at the 2002 ALA Annual Conference (Cyzyk & Robertson, 2003; Chandler, 2002a).

As librarians shared their systems' functions and data elements on Web Hub, it became obvious that standards would help systematize the similar issues that the libraries were building systems to address (Jewell, 2006).

From these efforts an informal steering group

Table 1.2. The cry for standards

1998	2001	2002	2003	2004	2006	2007
Locally-developed systems, Phase 1 Open Source	Jewell/DLF Report OpenURL Linking	ERMI Steering Group formed Locally-developed systems, Phase 2	COUNTER	ERMI Report First integrated ERMS Commercial products with ERMS features	SUSHI ERMI-2 Steering Group formed	SERU

grew around Jewell, Chandler, Farb, Angela Riggio (UCLA), Robertson, Ivy Anderson (Harvard), and Kimberly Parker (Yale). The steering group joined with Patricia Harris and Priscilla Caplan at NISO, and Daniel Greenstein (DLF) in efforts that led to the Workshop on Standards for Electronic Resource Management in May 2002. About 50 librarians and vendor representatives attended the workshop from EBSCO, Endeavor, ExLibris, Fretwell-Downing, Innovative Interfaces, Sirsi, and Serials Solutions. At the workshop, Jewell discussed the need for standards for data sharing; Robertson presented a model entity relationship diagram for managing license metadata, and discussed descriptive metadata. Farb discussed licensing issues and UCLA's mantra, "one database, many views." Anderson described function and data requirements for access and administration and challenges to standards development. Attendees came to consensus that it would be helpful to have standards to guide the development of ERM systems. In order to reduce duplication of effort and development costs, promote interoperability and data sharing, the steering group chose to pursue a formal collaboration that included best practices (Jewell, 2006; Chandler, 2002b).

The 2002 ALA meeting in Atlanta had a follow-up meeting, attended by 80 people, about 50 from the NISO/DLF meeting and 10-15 from ALA Midwinter. Representatives from Endeavor, ExLibris, Ebsco and other vendors were there. At that time Tim Jewel and the University of Washington were preparing to work with Innovative Interfaces (III) to build an electronic resource management stand-alone module. This tool would tie license information to the title level, group aggregator titles, and communicate to users when resources were unavailable. At the same meeting, Christa Easton of Stanford reported that they were moving a previous system into an Access database. Colorado Alliance was continuing development of Gold Rush, as was Johns Hopkins' HERMES, Nathan Robertson reported. Penn State's ERLIC2, had outgrown its Access form and was moving

to Cold Fusion/Oracle. The Tri College Consortium was building their system in Filemaker, as reported by Norm Medeiros. Emory University Library was using an MS SQL server with an Access front-end for staff and an .asp front end for patrons. Kimberly Parker of Yale University Library described moving metadata for 1700 journals into their system. Ivy Anderson of Harvard University detailed functional areas and elements for access and support and emphasized a life cycle perspective, reiterated UCLA's guiding principle, "one database, many views." Also discussed at the meeting were the roles of centralized and localized needs and practices.

At that time, Tim Jewell and the steering group were working on a proposal to the DLF in support of standards for e-license management that would result in a report on state of the art e-license management systems, specifications for metadata management, and an XML scheme (Chandler, 2002c).

ERMI

In Fall 2002, the DLF became official sponsor of the Electronic Resource Management Initiative (ERMI) project (Cyzyk & Robertson, 2003). ERMI would begin the work of standardizing access to and information about electronic resources. Reactor panels of librarians and vendors were formed to provide advice. Standards would accelerate vendor development efforts at reduced cost and risk. Products with predictable data streams were important to shops with self-developed systems that may want to transfer to a commercial system later. It was also hoped that libraries could exchange permitted uses during applicable practices such as interlibrary loan.

ERMI Deliverables

ERMI deliverables included a road map and problem definitions, workflow diagram, functional specifications, an entity relationship diagram, data elements and definitions, XML schema, and a final report. Emphasis was on the use of standards to maximize areas of common interest, to reduce vendor development costs and time investment, and the use of "predictable pathways," easing transfer of data from existing library systems (Jewell et al., 2004).

ERMI: Guiding Principles

Guiding principles for ERMS functional requirements of selection and acquisition, access, administration, user support, renewal and retention were:

- "Print and e-resource management and access should be through an integrated environment"
- "Information provided should be consistent, regardless of the path taken"
- "Each data element should have a single point of maintenance"
- "ERM systems should be sufficiently flexible to make it possible to easily add new or additional fields and data elements"

Librarians needed to see relationships between titles, packages, interfaces, and licenses. At the same time, the ability to control staff access and views to protect information integrity and to group task-related fields was important. Resource discovery was needed for collection development. The business end of electronic resources demanded tie-in with pricing, cancellation, renewal, consortial, and similar information (Jewell et al., 2004).

Main workflow processes were diagramed: Product consideration and trial processes, license negotiation, technical evaluation, business negotiation, product maintenance and review (Jewell et al., 2004). The ILS would perform ordering, budgeting, and fund accounting functions, as well as store the bibliographic record. Additional

ERMS core functions included the ability to export data from the ILS for analysis, the ability to talk to the ILS, link resolution services, and federated search tools. The system should also store and/or point to usage statistics, and record and generate URIs (Jewell, et al., 2004, 4.3.1. Functional Requirements, ¶ 14, 16-19).

Libraries would then take the information about electronic resources stored in the ERMS and use it to inform Web-based resource pages with license permissions, off-campus access, temporary access interruptions and other timely information (Jewell et al., 2004).

The data structure mapped the entity relationship diagram. The data dictionary showed element type, functionality, optimality, repeatability, suggested values, and notes (Jewell et al., 2004). A "quick-fix" set of license terms and larger set of license elements were focused on for XML deliverables once it was realized that a much broader discussion was needed for other possible data transfer functions (Jewell et al., 2004).

ERMI: Reactions

Reactions to the DLF ERMI were positive, with vendors subsequently developing systems that leaned heavily on the document's deliverables (Jewell, 2004). Still to be addressed were consortial issues, particularly when dealing with different ILS and ERMS systems, maximizing usage data, following resource succession paths, and continuation of work on data standards (Jewell et al., 2004).

LOCALLY DEVELOPED ERMS: THE SECOND PHASE

In 2002 the digital environment continued to grow exponentially. User behavior supported increased use of digital resources and fueled the demand for easier, more convenient, Google-like functionality. Electronic resources demanded more

Table 1.3. Locally developed ERMs: The second phase

1998	2001	2002	2003	2004	2006	2007
Locally-developed systems, Phase 1 Open Source	Jewell/DLF Report OpenURL Linking	ERMI Steering Group formed Locally-developed systems, Phase 2	COUNTER	ERMI Report First integrated ERMS Commercial products with ERMS features	SUSHI ERMI-2 Steering Group formed	SERU

and more management, yet ILSs were not able to capture the complex nature and relationships of these resources. Libraries continued to build local automated tools to fill the gap.

Bibliographic databases increased in numbers and size, with the complimentary need to present those resources to users in various ways (Jewell et. al., 2004). Even though vendors had begun providing A-Z lists of journals based on database holdings, these lists did not work well with the ILS. OpenURL solutions, citation-based linking in context, added a complex layer to management of electronic resources. Additionally, license agreements had supplanted copyright law, often accompanied by complex negotiations, necessitating the need to track negotiations' progress. License terms themselves were difficult to capture in a systematic, standardized way. The growth in consortial purchases had done much to complicate this picture. At the same time, staff needed to know more about electronic resources such as status, access details, permissions, and so forth. Planned, cyclical reviews of electronic resources were needed, as well as the ability to report their usage (Jewell et. al., 2004).

Despite development of tools and the initial commercial products with some ERMS functions, the need to manage e-resources far preceded the general release of the first commercial ERMS from Innovative Interfaces in 2004 (Duranceau, 2004). Local systems continued to be developed, often influenced by ERMI. Several local systems are surveyed by ERMS function below.

Listing tools continued to be developed, as exemplified by Montana State University and USC. Montana State University created a *Master Serial List* using Excel to track information in 2002. With columns for title, ISSNs, price (several years' worth), LC classification, subscription service, package, print version, electronic version, and notes, reports could be generated with package level detail, including number of titles, subscription length, notes, contact name, e-mail, and phone. Access was for staff only through a shared network drive (Marshall & Kawaski, 2005).

University of Southern California's health sciences consortial libraries had a system for populating Web sites with e-resources in place since 1999 but needed a combined database and port that met the university's standards for hardware and software. The libraries wanted one database for both systems and users to search (Brown, Nelson, & Wineburgh-Freed, 2005). Influenced by Web Hub, in particular UCLA, Washington State University, and The Tri College Consortium (Bryn Mawr, Haverford, Swarthrone), phase I duplicated the preexisting tool. Phase II, developed later, included free Web resources, licensed, paid, books, journals and databases (Brown, Nelson, & Wineburgh-Freed, 2005).

Searchable by multiple fields, changes in the database trickled down to hierarchical data. More reporting was needed, including titles by gateway and selector, and the ability to run reports without programmer intervention. Staff ability to add and delete subject categories without the programmer's involvement was also needed (Brown, Nelson, & Wineburgh-Freed, 2005).

In response to local needs, a variety of systems were developed that focused on specific ERMS functions.

In 1996 BEOnline was developed at the Library of Congress in an effort to address issues in identifying, selection and cataloging electronic resources. The process and tool included cataloging guidelines, selection criteria, workflow, and traffic manager. TrackER was developed to replace BEOnline and put into production in 2003 to assist in the distribution and tracking of electronic resources. Based on ECIP (electronic cataloging in publication), recording basic bibliographic information, TrackER virtually tracks a resource through selection, cataloging and access. The database was searchable by title, subject, catalog ID, OCLC and LCCN numbers, URL, language or access ID. TrackER was made available to libraries able to support the Oracle and UNIX architecture (Hayes & Lerner, 2004; ALCTS, 2004).

The EJournal Project, Kansas Regents Libraries version 4.0, January 2001, both a staff and public tool, allowed search by title, package, or publisher. Journals and databases were included. Results showed producer, contact information, titles licensed under the package, informational URL, number of users, package code, licensed through, access type, sent to contracts, sent on date, contract status, canceled + date, ILL information, and public notes. It is unclear where this information intersected with staff and public interfaces, but it appeared to be a robust license and package tool (The EJournal Project, 2001).

Originally developed by the Colorado Alliance of Research Libraries (CARL), Gold Rush, a resource discovery and management system, provided a public search interface for serials including an openURL link resolver, A-Z list, article finder, and browsing capabilities. Importing and exporting of data was done by Gold Rush staff. Custom field mapping was needed in order to interact with an ILS (Baker & Blocker,

2005; Machovec, 2002). Now sold by TLC, Gold Rush produces a real-time A-Z journal title list and a collection analyzer that allows comparison of titles lists from aggregators, publishers and indexing/abstracting services with or without subscriptions (TLC, 2005). This hosted service provides automated data updates and synchronization, manages URIs, IPs, license elements, usage statistics and reports on the resource and package level, and tracks price history. It also stores scanned licenses and has renewal alerts. Records are enhanced with additional Library of Congress and medical subject headings. Gold Rush does not track breach or access problems (Machovec, 2002; Meyer, 2005; Wilson, 2006).

University of North Carolina, Greensboro took a different approach with Journal Finder, whose functions included listing, usage and providing document delivery. In August 2001 Journal Finder launched and allowed, without mediation, access to any print or electronic article needed whether or not owned by the library. Journal Finder included online and print holdings, document delivery options and links to other library catalogs. Through the use of icons, the search results screen directed users to online, print or document delivery options. Usage statistics were also gathered. Data from publishers, aggregators, complimentary access, and free Websites was entered and checked periodically for accuracy.

The library used vendor title lists to populate the database, and decided against using Library of Congress subject headings, instead using a vocabulary based on the university's academic departments. Aggregator titles were not included. The database was a good interim solution until vendors could provide a product with the ability to search sets and license through a central interface (Felts, 2001).

Oklahoma University's LORA (Library Online Resource Access) tool focused on listing, license, and process/status functions, and was developed for databases, electronic journals, and resources. Patrons could search by title, type of resource, and by subject heading. Patrons could view descriptions, coverage dates, resource provider, physical location in the library, usage information, and status. There was a link to licensing information, the ability to report technical problems, a list of restrictions such as simultaneous users, a link to download an Endnote connection file, link to user guides if available, and announcements. LORA serves as a central point to license information since many librarians work on licenses (Robbins, & Smith, 2004).

Utah State University Library's ColdFusion E-Journal Database was developed in response to unwieldy hand management of journal lists. Primary functions were listing, license and tracking financial/purchasing information. Built using ColdFusion, the database incorporated aggregated titles, allowed tracking of license agreements, provided access by title, publisher, subject and keyword, and showed multiple access points and corresponding holdings. When it became available, the library subscribed to Serials Solutions to help populate the database. Even so, keeping up with data for consortial purchases remained a problem, including managing copies of license agreements, tracking renewal dates and getting accurate lists of titles included in the subscription (Brewer, Rozum, & Shrode, 2004).

The University of Illinois at Chicago used various paper and spreadsheet tools that proved inadequate and cumbersome. Mircea Stefancu (electronic services librarian) developed an electronic version in 2002, which evolved into a database, DOLLeR (Database of Library Licensed Electronic Resources), built by Jay Lambrecht (interim associate university librarian). The database had good bibliographic information, current holdings, the URL, order and payment information (including the history), vendor information, circulation information (including use statistics), licenses negotiated and maintained, contacts listed and updated, workflow and problem reports (Stefacu, Bloss, & Lambrecht, 2004).

Some systems addressed most ERMS functional requirements such as Boston College Libraries' ERMdb. Built in 2004 based on the DLF's recommended functional requirements, the system provided 2 views, a read-only and a write version, and integrates with the Aleph ILS, SFX and MetaLib. A crystal reports function allowed report viewing and exporting in Word, Excel and PDF (Boston College Libraries, n.d.; Kidd, 2004).

In building the ERMdb, Boston College followed the DLF ERM best practices, but designed their own metadata schema and cross-walked it to the DLF ERM schema. They also designed the user interface, functional requirements and workflow (Wolfe, 2005).

E-Matrix, North Carolina State was a license management tool meeting most ERMS functional requirements, was built on the DLF's data element scheme and has additional features. E-Matrix was built to support acquisition and licensing, collection management, and resource discovery. The system was built to allow migration of data into E-Matrix from existing systems. The system uses FRBR (functional requirements for bibliographic records). E-Matrix captures license, subscription information, statistics, technical support information, remote access, evaluative data, and vendor data into the administrative metadata. It leveraged the authority in the ILS database with descriptive and administrative metadata (Pace, 2004).

E-Matrix brought together print and electronic versions of the same work. It distinguished between library-selected titles and aggregated titles. The system allowed resource discovery, and could store patron queries. New lists were easily created. It used SFX, LC subjects and catalog data, including fund codes, to populate the database, and had robust reporting functionality. While implementing, they found that the technical services workflow needed radical changes, and that nonstandard data is not so bad and that standard data is not so good (Pace, 2006).

As commercial systems became available, libraries needed to weigh the advantages of maintaining a home grown system with the costs of populating a new system. Over time, more and more libraries have chosen to go with commercial systems due to staff and resource demands.

ERMI 2

The DLF Electronic Resource Management Initiative, Phase II (ERMI 2), currently in progress, continues work started in phase 1. ERMI 2's steering group comprises chair, Timothy Jewell (University of Washington), Ivy Anderson (California Digital Library), Adam Chandler (Cornell), Trisha Davis (Ohio State University), Sharon Farb and Angela Riggio (UCLA), Linda Miller (Library of Congress), and Nathan Robertson (University of Maryland Law Library) (Digital Library Federation, 2005, General Strategy, Oversight, and Outreach, ¶ 1). http://dlfermi.blogspot.com/

ERMI 2 activities are focused in three major areas:

1. Reviewing and revising the *data dictionary* for consistency and extensibility.
2. Incorporating standardized licensing terms (based upon EDItEUR/ONIX transmission standard-based license messaging standard and digital rights expression efforts by NISO for museums and archives frames) with the

hope that they can be based on ERMI data elements.
3. Extracting and analyzing usage data using ARL E-metrics and Project COUNTER and SUSHI.
(Digital Library Federation, 2005)

As part of the ERMI2 effort, a draft white paper on the "Interoperability between Acquisitions Modules of Integrated Library Systems and Electronic Resource Management Systems" was released for comment in January 2007 http://www.haverford.edu/library/DLF_ERMI2/ACQ_ERMS_white_paper.pdf. The effort focuses on the need to automate how acquisitions data moves from the ILS to the ERMS. The paper updates conversions of ERMS at four libraries and describes workflows (Medeiros et al., 2007). We can anticipate interesting developments as these efforts continue.

COMMERCIAL SYSTEMS

With libraries' increasingly demanding ways to harness electronic resources, commercial enterprises began to step in and fill the void. Systems ranged from serial vendors, serial data vendors, ERMS to publication access management systems (PAMS) and openURL linking. While these vendors based their systems on ERMI functional requirements, most did not include all ERMS

Table 1.4. ERMI 2

1998	2001	2002	2003	2004	2006	2007
Locally-developed systems, Phase 1 Open Source	Jewell/DLF Report OpenURL Linking	ERMI Steering Group formed Locally-developed systems, Phase 2	COUNTER	ERMI Report First integrated ERMS Commercial products with ERMS features	SUSHI ERMI-2 Steering Group formed	SERU

Table 1.5. Commercial systems

1998	2001	2002	2003	2004	2006	2007
Locally-developed systems, Phase 1 Open Source	Jewell/DLF Report OpenURL Linking	ERMI Steering Group formed Locally-developed systems, Phase 2	COUNTER	ERMI Report First integrated ERMS Commercial products with ERMS features	SUSHI ERMI-2 Steering Group formed	SERU

functions. Most, however, did integrate print and electronic holdings and provide an access and activation service for journals, A-Z listing, and openURL linker. Frequently, they offered management of license status and a repository for signed licenses. A few offered resource management workflows, incident reports, ways to store contact information, and trialed resources. It was the rare system (e.g., HERMIS) that tracked statistics' site information. All the commercial systems were Web based and in most cases, commercially hosted (Duranceau, 2005).

Examples include: TDNet, JournalWebCite, HERMIS, EbscoNet, SFX, and SerialsSolutions' ERMS. Associated tools include LibSGR (Villanova University).

The University of South Carolina had been maintaining e-resources both in the library catalog and on their Web site, a tedious and difficult process. By investing in TDNet, they had hoped to streamline the workflow yet expand their source of data. Their aggregator titles, for example, had not been included in the catalog and were difficult to find. Retrieval of usage statistics was also difficult. Launched at the university library in 2000, TDNet allowed access to ejournals, electronic indexes and other resources at the Library (McMullen & Wilmott, 2005). Modular in design, TDNet had multiple components, and has been purchased by a broad spectrum of libraries worldwide. Its E-journal management (EJM) component provided an A-Z list, coverage, database/vendor information, print holdings and tables of content. The

EJM results included additional services for "ask a librarian" and ILL. TDNet included: TES, an eContent searcher; CMS, a catalog maintenance service; and TOUR, an openURL resolver. TOUR became available in 2003 (McMullen & Wilmott, 2005; Duranceau, 2005).

OpenURL resolvers usually provide an A-Z listing service in addition to resolving openURLs, linking citations within context. Resolvers are bundled with many database products, are locally developed and come as stand-alone products. Herbert Van de Sompel developed SFX and the openURL framework at the University of Ghent. SFX was first available in 2001, introducing the concept of context-sensitive linking. Now a NISO standard, users can link from a "source" (Abstracting & Indexing) database to a target (full text) (Wakimoto, Walker, & Dabbour, 2006).

SFX transmits metadata for resources in the knowledge base on the following fields: full text (including DOIs), holdings, ILL, reviews, abstract, table of contents, author/cited author, reference/cited reference, cited book, cited genome, cited record, author e-mail, Web search, and Web services such as links to order services, request forms, or other Web forms that can use bibliographic information (ExLibris, 2006,). The depth and variety of linking depends on the degree to which the metadata is supported by vendors, publishers and hosting services. Like many other systems, SFX offers browsing and searching of subscribed/licensed titles (including aggregated titles) and Citation Linker. Citation Linker's title search is dependent on exact title, which can be problematic. Keyword searching was incorporated in the version 3 release. SFX also permits Z39.50 searching of the library catalog (Holman, 2005). Local items and holdings can be added and their syntax checked. Furthermore, titles can be manually added to a publisher portfolio (Ives, 2005).

SFX supports various tools that maximize the value of the data in the knowledge base including overlap analysis and exporting in various formats for other systems. Exports can be saved for comparison, lessening maintenance efforts. ONIX import tool (for licenses) is available in command-line form. Mapping is available for SOH files from EBSCO Information Systems (ExLibris, 2006).

The large serials vendor, EBSCO added several modules to its EBSCONet product, the self-named serials management system for ordering, searching, claiming and renewing periodicals. The EJS basic interface allows search and access to subscribed e-journals whereas the enhanced EJS provides statistical reports for subscribed services. It includes a customizable journal title list for print and electronic journals and easy to generate usage reports. EBSCONet also has its own URL link resolver named LinkSource, and is widely purchased in the library industry. Customers, however, found maintenance of the title list labor intensive. Recommendations for future enhancements included more sophisticated alphabetization and the addition of MeSH and LOC subject headings (Lingle, 2005).

HERMIS is a serials subscription agent that has begun to embed ERM-like services in its subscription services (Duranceau, 2005). It is available in two levels of service versions of OttoSerials 3.0, the serials management system. The hosted staff tool notifies clients of publisher/vendor changes, including policy changes. It provides an ordering/payment/renewal/cancellation service and links to publishers' licenses. The system stores scanned licenses, too. Libraries create an activation profile with contact and IP information that

HERMIS staff use to activate titles. Data can be exported to other systems. The product supports resource identification and evaluation, ordering and payment, renewals and cancellations, licensing, activation, and technical access management. COUNTER-compliant usage tracking is available to higher-level customers. A-Z lists or openURL linking is not provided, but is offered through industry partnerships (Collins, 2005; Harrassowitz, 2006; Library Technology Reports, 2006).

Developed by Ben Adams and Jefferson H. Clark in 2001, JournalWebCite was meant to be a one-stop access point for electronic journals whether single titles, in a package, or as part of an aggregated database. Print and microform holdings could be incorporated as well. JournalWebCite could provide XML, HTML, CSV and MARC-ready exports for incorporation into library catalogs. Reports included subscription, journal, database, collection development overlap, provider cost, database cost, expiration, usage statistics (90 days), global usage statistics (end of year), and top ten targets. In 2002 it was noted that publisher embargo periods by title were not easily available. The tool included Library of Congress subject headings (Sitko et al., 2002). In early 2003 TDNet took over the JournalWebCite customer base (EContent, 2003).

LibSGR is a tool focused solely on managing usage statistics. Developed by Andrew Nagy, LibSGR compiles usage statistics for journals. His work influenced ERUS, an open source program focused initially on indexing and abstracting database statistics gathering. Tables include journal, vendor, publisher, and department. Fields include: title, ISSN, call number, format, vendor, publisher, holdings, microholdings, status, department, location, and cost. It appears to still be in use (Anderson, 2004; LibSGR, n.d.).

Serials Solutions' ERMS addresses many ERMS functions. The Serials Solutions' listing service was first developed by Peter McCracken and his brothers and released in 2005. The data was leveraged into a fully-functioned ERMS.

This hosted service is closely integrated into the other products of the company (Duranceau, 2005; Library Technology Reports, 2006; Sitko et al., 2002; Szcyrbak & Pierce, 2003)

ERMS allows for discovery, overlap analysis, trials, access, click-through and search statistics, and status management. Features include an A-Z list, subject browsing, title searching and journal linker, exportable data files, proxy management, and custom metadata. Print holdings can be included (Sitko, et al., 2005, p. 178). While library data must initially be imported into Serials Solutions ERMS, the brief MARC records that libraries add to incorporate aggregate holdings into the catalog must be manually deleted if journals are discontinued (Szcyrbak & Pierce, 2003). Libraries can add notes, include non-journal resources, contacts, manage licenses, display terms of use, monitor acquisition workflow, record incident reports and usage statistic benchmarking, allowing comparison between institutions, and manage vendor usage statistics (Duranceau, 2005; Serials Solutions, n.d). Unmediated database updating with the datafeed (Ives, 2005) was not available. Bought by Proquest in 2004, Serials Solution continued development of a license management module and e-journal workflow tracking (Collins, 2005) and in the summer of 2006 merged with SirsiDynix with the goal to produce a suite of ERM products for their ILS systems (Breeding, 2006).

Many of these products enjoyed and still receive wide support in the library community because libraries could easily justify their procurement without re-thinking their approach holistically or waiting for the appropriate integrated ERMS to be available. Many of the commercial projects, in addition, meet the needs of institutions who are concerned about the costs of full blown systems or do not use the larger ILS vendors which are developing ERMS. In the meantime, these products provide vital services that are an intrinsic part of library for both patrons and staff.

INTEGRATED SYSTEMS

Integrated systems, those systems associated with integrated library systems, include ExLibris' Verde, Innovative Interface's ERM, and VTLS' Verify. All are ERMI compliant. Horizon Information Management System from SirsiDynix is in development and will be targeted to libraries or consortia (SirsiDynix, 2006).

Endeavor's Meridian is Web-based, uses an Oracle database and tracks selection, evaluation, acquisition, maintenance, and access in accordance with license terms. The system manages restrictions, users, trials (including evaluations), history and renewals. A stand-alone, Meridian is available as a hosted or on-site installation and integrates with linking and metasearch systems. Rules are assigned at the package level, and the system shows hierarchical relationships. Usage restrictions can be displayed in the OPAC or on

Table 1.6. Integrated systems

1998	2001	2002	2003	2004	2006	2007
Locally-developed systems, Phase 1 Open Source	Jewell/DLF Report OpenURL Linking	ERMI Steering Group formed Locally-developed systems, Phase 2	COUNTER	ERMI Report First integrated ERMS Commercial products with ERMS features	SUSHI ERMI-2 Steering Group formed	SERU

A-Z lists. Web services are used to pull data from the ILS; periodic updates will be needed.

Future support of SUSHI and storage of usage statistics is in development, as is a tagged license function. An SQL reporting tool using the Cog-Nos business intelligence-reporting program is bundled with the system, and mapped to canned, schedulable queries. Reports are e-mailed. Queries allow the use of wild cards, and left, right and center truncation. It is possible to give selected faculty read rights for collection development purposes (Jones, 2006; Duranceau, 2004).

Verde from Ex Libris maximizes use of the data in the knowledge base to manage evaluation, selection, acquisition, processing, and cancellation. It has the ability to track perpetual access, management history, incidents and breaches. Verde is a stand-alone staff product that works well with SFX and Ex Libris' ILS, Aleph. Data is sent using SOAP and Web services to other systems. Workflows are set to role-based authentication and can be customized.

Based on the following entities, interface, package, e-constituent (e-journal, e-book), contacts and tasks (both external and internal), roles, management, and license permissions (140-150 terms), characteristics and terms are inheritable. Verde allows cross-institutional search and retrieval.

Future development will include consortial searching, SUSHI retrieval, vertical calculation (an e-constituent used in the context of a package and interface) and horizontal calculation (use of an e-journal from all sources). Cross-consortium workflow and voting, and cost per package and per e-title will be added (Koppel, 2006a).

In 2002 the University of Washington Libraries formed a development partnership with Innovative Interfaces (III), along with Glasgow University, Ohio State University, and the University of Western Australia to develop an ERM that would integrate licensing and purchasing details using a single interface, streamline workflows, eliminate the need to maintain separate spreadsheets

and databases, and store and selectively display information in the online catalog for staff and patrons. ERM's functions are: selection, licensing, purchase, maintenance, user support, public access, collection analysis, holdings' overlap analysis, and tasks in one GUI interface with the ILS. Used as both a staff and public tool, ERM was released in Spring 2004, and was the first ERM on the market (Duranceau, 2004; Fons, 2006; Tull et al., 2005).

ERM's entities are resource, license, and contact. The ERM tracks renewal dates, authentication, proxy data, and content descriptions. As a standalone it maintains resources, track licenses, and manages coverage data. Integrated with Millenium, it is used as a portal for all digital subscriptions. Data is stored in one central database, and is fed to staff and public modules. ERM supports journal 1 COUNTER-compliant statistics, and automated e-mail. ERM has reporting capability, a real-time A-Z list, e-resource search tool, and can be integrated with WebBridge (an openURL linking tool). ERM is able to operate in a consortia environment, supports SUSHI, and calculates cost-per-use information, combined with SUSHI use data. XML server support allows delivery of bibliographic information in XML format, although not yet to the license level. Mock bibliographic records are used for packages. ERM works with ScholaryStats. Future reports will include usage reports by subject by cost analysis. Library of Congress subject headings will be incorporated. A tool for export and re-import of data in batch is planned (Fons, 2006, Innovative Interfaces, 2006; Tull et al., 2005).

VTLS' Verify is a standalone or ILS-integrated tool for trial, selection, ordering, contracting, installation, licensing, training, and public accessibility, including workflow and the approvals process through 400 data elements. Verify sends e-mail alerts for renewal, review, or event notifications, and has fields for cost information, payment information including invoice and check numbers, agreement start and end dates, modes of access, restrictions, links to resources or metadata records, copyright restrictions, contracts and licenses (entry, storage, display of digital copies), registered IP addresses, holdings, including print runs, and shows the relationship between aggregators and publishers. Comments on trial resources can be captured. There are separate record views for public (Web-based) and staff (GUI); views can be customized by user class. On the single interface, patrons can view access restrictions, copyright information, printing and ILL permissions. Information is organized in hierarchical tree structure in the spirit of FRBR (functional requirements for bibliographic records) http://www.frbr.org/.

All data elements can be reported on, including usage statistics on number and time of access to each e-resource. Verify data supports MySQL and Oracle databases and has consortial enhancements. Language and interface translation can be done using the Unicode UTF-8 character set (Duranceau, 2005; VTLS, n.d., 2004).

With these products, ILS producers hope to leverage the huge investment in time, staffing and funds that libraries have poured into ILS systems. The vendors continue development.

OPEN SOURCE

Open source programs, those programs that are freely available and encourage adaptation, are an alternative to libraries without the budget, but with the IT resources necessary to develop these resources. There are several open source tools that have ERM or related functionality: ERUS, Request Tracker, jake, PubList, HERMES, and ERTS.

ERUS, Electronic Resource Usage Statistics, developed by Trinity College, Villanova University and Simmons was to be used for collecting, managing, and analyzing electronic resource usage statistics. The process began in the fall of 2004 at Simmons using PHP and MySQL by Megan Fox and Dr. Gary Geisler, and expanded to include Lori Stethers at Trinity College and Andrew Nagy at Villanova University. Development included assessing the current practices for data collection, analysis and utilization of e-resources statistics. They identified challenges and ideal conditions for managing usage statistics and gathered insight into a model for providing access via a single, database-backed Web interface. Automation, standardization and compliance quickly became primary foci.

Database design was slow as the process was hung up on the discussion of entities. The software learning curve was steep. Functionality focused on running reports and importing data. Data collection continued to be difficult. Scripts to extract data sent by e-mail still required customization. By the end of 2004 database development was stated as being "actively begun" (Anderson, 2004).

Request Tracker, an open source software program, creates e-mail tickets for incident reporting and resolution caption. It enhances communica-

Table 1.7. Open source

1998	2001	2002	2003	2004	2006	2007
Locally-developed systems, Phase 1 Open Source	Jewell/DLF Report OpenURL Linking	ERMI Steering Group formed Locally-developed systems, Phase 2	COUNTER	ERMI Report First integrated ERMS Commercial products with ERMS features	SUSHI ERMI-2 Steering Group formed	SERU

tion and management statistics, and supports evaluation of e-resources. Further standardization is needed (McCaslin, 2003,).

PubList and jake are open source efforts to address listing needs. jake was created at Yale University School of Medicine in early 1999 in an effort to track relationships between titles, databases and vendors in a cooperative effort. Jake was freely available through the GNU general public license (GPL), and organizations were encouraged to use, copy and modify jake while observing the GPL. Using title lists from vendors and publishers, they added coverage dates, id codes, URL construction rules, title abbreviations, and Library of Congress and Dewey classifications. A typical record showed which resource the title, volume, issue, and pages appeared in, linked to the resource and provider, and showed whether it included citations and/or fulltext. Users could download title lists from resources with and without the jakeid, and generate simple MARC records.

The creators realized how valuable the information could be for collection development. Publisher details planned to be added. Institutions could add other information to their implementation of jake such as technical support contacts, key license agreement terms, technical requirements, remote access information, usage statistics (where to get them, how to process them, where they are stored), and local link information. Maintenance to jake stopped in 2002 (Chudnov et al., 2000; Notess, 2000).

PubList is a free resource based on Ulrich's international periodicals directory data, launched in 1998, and owned by Infotrieve since 2000. Infotrieve's proprietary services are available through the site, also. Free registration allows searching by title, publisher, subject, circulation data (said to be in development on the site), and ISSN. Records have fields for title, publication type, frequency, ISSN, country, language, editor, publisher and contact information. Missing are price information, first year published, Dewey

and LC call numbers, and parallel and ceased title information. Errors are not uncommon, but PubList might be useful as a free resource for organizations with limited resources where currency is not crucial (Jasco, 2003; Notess, 2000; PubList, 1998-2001).

HERMES and ERTS are more fully functioned ERMS open source tools. In 2000 the HERMES (The Hopkins Electronic Resource Management System) committee formed and set functional requirements for a new system. The system was for patrons to identify and access electronic resources of Johns Hopkins University Libraries, and to help staff facilitate the process of selecting, purchasing, and managing these resources. A full workflow and approvals process to support selection, procurement, and implementation of e-resources was needed, with dynamic lists for public display. Staff needed automatic notification of changes in status and scope to e-resource ordering and licensing, and link management for e-resources, automatic update of URLs in the backend database, campus proxy server, library Web site, and so forth. They wanted a single interface for staff viewing, updating, reporting and administering e-resources, and robust, custom report generation. They needed to appropriately restrict use, yet have the system be interoperable with present and future systems.

HERMES automatically captured data from the ILS through XML DTD for bibliographic data import. It could also be used as a stand-alone system. The system was designed around functional roles, tasks, rights, and responsibilities. Inserting additional workflow steps was a simple process.

HERMES was released as open source software for other libraries to customize and use. Currently, Johns Hopkins Libraries are using Dynix for their catalog and SFX for the A-Z list (Cyzyk & Robertson, 2003,).

Developed in 2001 for the Tri-College Consortium (Bryn Mawr, Haverford, & Swarthmore), the Electronic Resources Tracking System (ERTS) had several goals: allow access to license information, provide statistical reports not available from the ILS, and notify staff when e-resources are about to expire.

License information was particularly important. ERTS stored ILL, print and reserve restrictions, number of simultaneous users, e-mail notification when new content becomes available, archival guarantee, license, and comments.

ERTS was made available as freeware. Plans for a workflow model were in process, as was a database to handle trials. ERTS did not provide access to any resources and would outgrow its humble origins to be decommissioned in 2004. The Tri-College Consortium chose VTLS' Verify in 2005 (Medeiros et al., 2003; Medeiros, 2006; Medeiros et al., 2007; Tri-College Consortium, 2003).

For most libraries, open source will not be a viable solution: the data is simply too vast and changeable, and library talent must be used elsewhere. For libraries without funding support some tools may be a possible option. As standards, modularity, and facile systems increase, open source tools may become more commonplace.

EVALUATION OF ERMS

When acquiring an ERMS it is important to define the institution's goals for the ERM and to understand its capabilities. ERMS are not acquisitions systems but will need to work closely with the ILS covering those functions. Cooper and Lester (2005, pp. 29, 31, 33, 34) suggested the following goals for the ERMS:

1. An accurate representation of ejournals inside aggregator databases
2. A representation of ejournals that are subscribed to and free journals
3. One-stop shopping for serials regardless of format
4. Usage statistics at the database and title level

Also important:

- The ability to view permitted uses (staff and patrons)
- The ability to view collections of other institutions in the consortium
- The ability to export data using Web services to other library services
- The ability to generate reports that will inform library decision making; these reports will combine traits of the various database entities.

Meyer (2005, p. 20) and Cooper and Lester (2005, pp. 29, 31, 33, 34) offer some suggestions to ask when evaluating ERMS. Purchasing and contract details that could be asked:

- When was the product released?
- What is the pricing structure, including initial price and costs for continuing operation and maintenance?
- What is the estimated amount of time from contract signing to live system?
- Is it available as a stand-alone, or as a component of one of your other products?
- Where is the system hosted?
- What is the primary market (academic, public, school, corporate)?
- How many systems are in place?
- How many systems are fully implemented? This could provide insight into how ready a system is for widespread use.

Technical details to be considered:

- Does it have operating system compatibility (Windows, Mac, Unix, Linux)?
- How frequently will system updates be made?
- Can the vendor provide additional services beyond the A-Z list?
- Do you want or need additional serials management services? It is best to think

about ERMS in holistic terms of needs and functions.

- o Full or brief catalog records
- o Notification of changes in titles in the system
- o Tables of contents alerting service
- o OpenURL link resolver
- o Federated searching over all electronic databases and the online catalog
- o Statistical reports on usage of titles and databases
- Which data management capabilities does it support? URI management, data import/export in ONIX, library-defined data elements, IP address management, individual license data elements, usage statistics management, storage and retrieval, COUNTER-compliant usage statistics?
- What data import/export formats are available? Data import and export can be incredibly time and labor consuming.
- What communication protocols are available?
- What interface options are available (Web-based HTML, Web-based Java, Windows, Mac, interface based on ILS or existing system)?

Interoperability with other systems can be a major stumbling block. One may want to clarify:

- Does it integrate with your knowledgebase or PAMS product?
- Does it integrate with openURL link resolvers?
- Does it integrate with federated searching tools?
- Does it integrate with public access tools (OPACs, A-Z lists, etc.)?
- Does it provide automated data updates and synchronization?
- Does it integrate with ILS's from other vendors?

Functional requirements depend on what the organization would like to capture. In significant combination, data from an ERMS can inform many decisions. Some requirements that will help the planning effort can include:

- What are the available reporting options: resource level, package level, custom reports, reporting with usage statistics, reports with evaluative elements?
- Does it provide different user permissions and access levels?
- Does it track subscription life cycles?
- Does it tract contact history for license negotiation?
- Does it track price history?
- Does it provide automated notification for renewals?
- Does it provide access to e-resource holdings data?
- Does it provide access to print holdings data when both print and electronic copies are held?
- Does it support breach logs or tracking for access problems?

It is important for an institution to understand what the system is capable of, and how the library's needs intersect with the system's functionality. Be careful not to assume that the ERMS will solve all information needs. It may solve some, but much depends on the institution's data and its quality. Being realistic will cultivate much better buy-in from the stakeholders.

IMPLEMENTATION OF ERMS

Preparing for an ERM is labor and time intensive. Unfortunately, the system is only as good as the completeness of its data. It takes time, discipline and perseverance to get the initial data in, difficult tasks when staff are busy. Many libraries with ERMS struggle to maintain disciplined data entry. This is complicated by the fact that multiple staff are often responsible for entering particular entities. A generic task and timeline are listed below to help libraries anticipate implementation needs for an ERMS.

- List entities in the database, and then the fields for those entities
- Determine which fields your institution will use, which will be required fields, and, if applicable, the possible values for those fields
- Interpret institution data and populate Excel spreadsheets with fields and data
- Prepare staff for the ERM and build buy-in
- Upload data
- Test uploaded data
- Define staff roles and set permissions
- Set tasks and workflow
- Test staff and permissions data
- Set drop-dead date when new system will be functional, and where data maintenance changes need to take place
- Train staff
- Release system to staff
- Provide a mechanism for staff feedback
- Modify workflows with staff input
- De-brief staff on implementation process; incorporate feedback into institutional change mechanisms

- For the first year, add the ERMS to meeting agendas so staff can provide feedback and stay informed
- Incorporate usage data into regular review of resources
- Set up audit calendar, and link checking mechanism

STANDARDS

Several existing standards and those in-process contribute to the matrix of tools that begin to address electronic resources and their management. SERU (shared e-resource understanding), in draft form March 2007, is a shared set of understandings to which publishers and libraries can point when negotiating the sale of electronic content http://www.niso.org/committees/SERU/. It is hoped that this standard will reduce the negotiation burden for both libraries and publishers. ONIX for Serials including SPS (serials products and subscriptions), SOH (serials online holdings), SRN (serials release notification), ONIX for licensing terms (in process), COUNTER and SUSHI help, but more standards are needed.

Ted Koppel, Verde Product Manager, ExLibris, (2006, Visions of ERM; 2006, Electronic Resource Management) suggests several more standards as being useful:

Table 1.8. Standards

1998	2001	2002	2003	2004	2006	2007
Locally-developed systems, Phase 1 Open Source	Jewell/DLF Report OpenURL Linking	ERMI Steering Group formed Locally-developed systems, Phase 2	COUNTER	ERMI Report First integrated ERMS Commercial products with ERMS features	SUSHI ERMI-2 Steering Group formed	SERU

- A standard for communicating IP address changes to content providers
- A standard for vendors to communicate real-time availability
- A sub-library unique library identifier (for branches)
- A unique collection identifier for aggregators and databases, like an ISBN per e-package/collection
- A standard for exchange of acquisitions order record, invoice record and vendor information
- A standard for open access and other pricing models for the ERM

Other useful standards would include:

- A standard for title and subject list generation
- A standard for holdings information, including enumeration, with post-application to ILS systems
- A standard for exchange of acquisitions renewal and trial records
- A standard to help capture Association of Research Libraries (ARL) statistics
- A standard for capture, storage, and querying usage statistics by title, publisher, vendor and platform
- A standard to integrate openURL linkers into the ILS

(Fons, 2006)

All standards need to be compatible with ERMI standards, and based on Web services.

FUTURE TRENDS

The necessity of ERMS will affect libraries in myriad ways. The transformative tendencies of the industry will offer new directions as companies merge. For example, the mergers such as that of Endeavor with ExLibris in 2006 will have

unknown effects on libraries with traditional ILS products. ERMS will demand new staffing models, a shift of staffing from the print to electronic workflow, and further drive outsourcing of some acquisition processes. The fiscal fallout is still unknown. The implementation of an ERMS will funnel huge staff needs and efforts into an intense setup period. Industry factors such as the evolution of additional services offered by vendors that are associated with emerging standards will be a certainty.

Patrick Jones of Endeavor (2006) predicts that vendors will begin to ask libraries to pay for usage statistics. Vendors will then add value to usage statistics by integrating impact factors, relative value for money between resources and subject-based analysis of usage and costs. Integration of citation analysis would also be useful, as ISI is doing with the Web of Knowledge JUR trial.

Ted Fons, innovative product manager of Innovative Interfaces (2006, *Future of ERM Systems*) points out that very few vendors have SUSHI servers. Integration of ERMs into the ILS is a necessity. He predicts that there will be increased use of the coverage data in the knowledge base using vendor-neutral data since patrons benefit from access information scope notes, announcements, new features and content will be integrated into resources. Promotion of library sponsorship of access will increase. Access based on license terms will be the norm.

Automation of administrative tasks will increase, as SUSHI proves, and tools to allow collection analysis will be offered as part of a suite of services. Areas with potential for automation include IP registration, trial administration, activation, renewal, incident reporting, sample license review, and license exchange. Renewals, payments, contributions to cost, and cost-per-use calculations will be provided by incorporating SUSHI and COUNTER data into the acquisitions system. A system for comparing print and electronic serials holdings is needed. Vendor-independent integration systems should provide tools for integration of data using Web services. These changes would require cooperation between system developers and content providers.

Ted Koppel (2006a) predicts there will be a move away from aggregators to more title selection with more truth in pricing. The ILS will reform around the ERM, discovery tools and digital objects. There will be demands on content providers for SUSHI, and license expression transmission. Additionally, there will be increased transparency for content providers on pricing, and the demise of aggregator packages. There will be a blurring of lines between electronic resource management and digital resource management. There will be pay-per-view support and tracking within the ERM. The ERM will serve as the nexus between legacy systems and the e-product world. The ERM will supplant the ILS for many back-room functions.

Timothy Jewell, in a presentation given December 15, 2005 to Rutgers University Libraries' Electronic Resources Access and Integration Task Force, also stated that a future function of ERMS is to serve as an institution registry. Established by a third party but maintained by participating libraries, vendors would be notified of changes systematically by the registry (Smulewitz, 2005).

For the future, standardization will be key to maximizing the business and holdings data in ILS and the detail needed in ERMs. If standards are not developed and embraced by vendors, data loading and translation will be a time-consuming and labor intensive process. Interoperability, particularly with legacy ILS systems will be vital for success. A modular approach is needed so that institutions can maintain their ILS but use different interfaces to display information as needs arise. There is great potential for standards-based bridging systems between legacy ILS and ERMs. Hopefully, the synergy of librarians producing standards and the industry responding will continue.

CONCLUSION

Integrated library systems (ILS) have not kept pace with the record keeping, functionality and information demands of electronic resources. ILS do not adequately record the relationships between package, journal, interface, and e-product. The print acquisition record and workflow is not sufficient to capture the demands of licensing, implementation, tracking and maintaining electronic resources. Usage statistics have become more accessible and standardized, but the ILS lacks an entity to record them. With exponential growth in electronic resources, libraries began developing local systems in an effort to cope with management and maintenance of these resources. Tim Jewell's report *Selection and Presentation of Commercially Available Electronic Resources: Issues and Practices* illustrating libraries' similar approaches to electronic resource management practices, workflow and staffing needs, paved the way for the Digital Library's (DLF's) *Electronic Resource Management Initiative* (ERMI). The report is a road map for functional requirements, XML schemas, document type definitions, workflows and the electronic resource life cycle.

The impact of this report cannot be underestimated. Unprecedented in the information environment, it resulted in vendors developing tools according to specifications from librarians. The resultant series of tools from integrated library system and other vendors, subscription agents, publication access management services (PAMS) and nonprofit organizations have addressed various ERMS functions.

Electronic resource management systems need to be standards-based, modular, extensible, interoperable with existing tools, have data import/export capabilities, and integrate with Web services so data can be displayed in catalogs, Web sites, portals, and other preexisting services. The perfect ERMS is an abstraction depending on the relationship with the ILS, interoperability, data completeness, and staff buy-in to evolved workflows.

Continuing development is needed. With the sheer volume of electronic resources and fluidity of holdings and link data, manageable automation techniques are needed that maintain data authority and control. Best practices and/or standards need to be developed for loading and transferring data into an ERM, as its functionality is only as good and as complete as its data. Libraries will continue to struggle with the tension between proprietary information products and their adherence to standards and interoperability needs. Synergistic efforts of librarians, standards organizations, publishers and vendors will result in new products and services.

REFERENCES

Alan, R. (2002). *Keeping track of electronic resources to keep them on track.* NASIG 2002. Retrieved November 22, 2007 from http://www.library.cornell.edu/cts/elicensestudy/pennstate/PSUN/ASigPresentation2002.ppt

ALCTS (2004, December). LC announces Track-ER software availability and specifications. *ALCTS Newsletter Online, 15,* 6. Retrieved November 22, 2007, from http://www.ala.org/ala/alcts/alctspubs/alctsnewsletter/v15n6/tracker.htm

Anderson, C. (2004, December). ERUS December 2004 report. Retrieved November 22, 2007, from http://web.simmons.edu/~andersoc/erus/report-dec04.html

Baker, G., & Blocker, L. (2005). Electronic resource management systems (ERMS). PowerPoint presentation. Retrieved November 22, 2007, from http://www.lib.utk.edu/~elecser/ts-erms.ppt

Boston College Libraries (n.d.). ERM database documentation. Retrieved November 22, 2007, from http://www.bc.edu/bc_org/avp_ulib/staff/erm/erm-db

Breeding, M. (July, 2006). Strategic development: SirsiDynix and Serials Solutions. *Smart Libraries Newsletter, Library Technology Guides.* Retrieved November 22, 2007, from http://www.librarytechnology.org/ltg-displaytext.pl?RC=12102

Brewer, K., Rozum, B., & Shrode, F. (2004). Developing a database for e-journals that improves both access and management. In D. C. Fowler (Ed.), *E-serials collection management: Transitions, trends, and technicalities* (pp. 253-264). Binghamton, NY: Haworth Information Press.

Brown, J. F., Nelson, J. L., & Wineburgh-Freed, M. (2005). Customized electronic resources management system. *Serials Librarian, 47*(4), 89-102.

Chandler, A. (2000). An application profile and prototype metatdata management system for licensed electronic resources. Retrieved November 22, 2007, from http://www.library.cornell.edu/cts/elicensestudy/ApplicationProfile.htm

Chandler, A. (2002a, January 30). ALA midwinter 2002 meeting. Retrieved November 22, 2007, from http://www.library.cornell.edu/elicensestudy/alamidwinter2002.htm

Chandler, A. (2002b, May 20). Notes, NISO/Digital Library Federation workshop, May 10, 2002. Retrieved November 22, 2007, from http://www.library.cornell.edu/elicensestudy/nisodlf/home.htm

Chandler, A. (2002c, June 14). ALCTS-sponsored meeting on e-resource management metadata at ALA, June 14, 2002. Retrieved November 22, 2007, from http://www.library.cornell.edu/elicensestudy/alaannual2002/home.htm

Chudnov, D. et al. (2000). Jake: Overview and status report [Jointly administered knowledge environment, Electronic journal database at Yale University]. *Serials Review, 26*(4), 12-17.

Collins, M. (2005). Electronic resource management systems: Understanding the players and how to make the right choice for your library. *Serials Review, 31,* 124-140.

Cooper, P. S., & Lester, D. (2005). One-stop serials management with TDNet. *The Serials Librarian, 47*(4), 27-34.

Cox, J., & Cox, L. (2003). *Scholarly publishing practice: The ALPSP report on academic journal publishers' policies and practices in online publishing.* Rookwood, UK: John Cox Associates.

Cyzyk, M., & Robertson, N. (2003). HERMES: The Hopkins Electronic Resource Management System. *Information Technology and Libraries, 22*(1), 12-17.

Digital Library Federation (2005). DLF electronic resource management initiative, Phase II. Retrieved November 22, 2007, from http://www.diglib.org/standards/dlf-erm05.htm

Duranceau, E. F. (2004). Electronic resource management systems from ILS vendors. *Against the Grain, 16*(4), 91-94.

Duranceau, E. F. (2005). Electronic resource management systems, part II: Offerings from serial vendors and serial data vendors. *Against the Grain, 17*(3), 59-60.

Duranceau, E. F., & Hepfer, C. (2002) Staffing for electronic resource management: The results of a survey. *Serials Review, 28*, 316-320.

EContent (2003, Feb 18). TDNet takes over JournalWebCite customer base. *EContent: Digital content strategies & resources.* Retrieved November 22, 2007, from http://www.econtentmag.com/Articles/ArticleReader.aspx?ArticleID=4057

The EJournal Project (2001). (Tool Web site). Retrieved November 22, 2007, from http://www.lib.ksu.edu/databases/ejournal/search.jsp?searchletter=A

ExLibris (2006). *Users Guide.*

Farb, S. E., & Riggio, A. (2002). *UCLA electronic resources database project overview.* PowerPoint, ALA Midwinter Meeting, 2002. Retrieved November 22, 2007, from http://www.library.cornell.edu/cts/elicensestudy/ucla/ALAMidwinter2002.ppt

Felts, J. W., Jr. (2001). Now you can get there from here: Creating an interactive web application for accessing full-text journal articles from any location. *Library Collections, Acquisitions, & Technical Services, 25*(3), 281-290.

Fons, T. (2006). Future of ERM systems (PowerPoint Presentation) California Digital Library Institute. *Electronic Resource Management*, presenter, November 10, 2006. Representative of Innovative Interfaces.

Harrassowitz (2006). Electronic journal services, HERMIS 3.0. Retrieved November 22, 2007, from http://www.harrassowitz.de/periodicals_e-journals.html

Hayes, A., & Lerner, S. (2004). Tracking electronic resources at the Library of Congress (PowerPoint presentation). Retrieved November 22, 2007, from http://www.loc.gov/catdir/TrackERALA2004.ppt

Hennig, N. (2002). Improving access to e-journals and databases at the MIT libraries: Building a database-backed web site called "Vera." *The Serials Librarian, 41*(3-4), 227-254.

Holman, J. (2005). Can SFX replace your home-grown periodical holdings list? *Serials Librarian, 47*(4), 79-88.

Innovative Interfaces (2006). Electronic Resource Management. [brochure]

Ives, G. (2005). Transition to e-journals at Texas A&M University, 1995-2004. *Serials Librarian, 47*(4), 71-78.

Jasco, P. (2003). Peter's picks and pans. *Online, 27*(2), 72-74.

Jewell, T. D. (2001). Appendix B: Functions and data elements for managing electronic resources. Retrieved November 22, 2007, from http://www.library.cornell.edu/elicensestudy/u-washington/FinalAppendixB.xls

Jewell, T. D. (2001). Selection and presentation of commercially available electronic resources: Issues and practices. Retrieved November 22, 2007, from http://www.clir.org/pubs/reports/pub99/contents.html

Jewell, T. (2006). Electronic resource management systems: What should they do? In P. M. Bluh & C. Hepfer (Eds.), *Managing electronic resources: Contemporary problems and emerging issues* (pp. 9-34). Chicago: Association for Library Collections & Technical Services.

Jewell, T. D., et al. (2004). *Electronic resource management: Report of the DLF electronic resource management initiative.* Washington, D.C.: Digital Library Federation.

Jones, P. (2006). California Digital Library Institute: *Electronic Resource Management*, presenter, November 10, 2006. Representative of Endeavor Meridian.

Kidd, K. (2004). Local e-resource management systems: Boston college libraries. Retrieved November 22, 2007, from http://www.library.cornell.edu/cts/elicensestudy/webhubarchive.html

Koppel, T. (2006a). California Digital Library Institute: *Electronic Resource Management*, presenter, November 10, 2006. Representative of ExLibris.

Koppel, T. (2006b). *Visions of ERM.* Presentation at NISO Managing Electronic collections, Strategies from Content to User, Denver, Colorado, September 28-20, 2006.

Kyrillidou, M., & Young, M. (Eds.) (2005). *ARL statistics, 2003-2004.* Washington, D.C.: Association of Research Libraries.

Library Technology Reports (2006). The ERMI and its offspring (Chapter 2). *Library Technology Reports, 42*(2), 14-21.

LibSGR (n.d.) LibSGR: Library statistics gathering and reporting (tool Web site). Retrieved November 22, 2007, from http://liboffice.villanova.edu/libsgr/index.php

Lingle, V. (2005). Implementing EBSCO's A-to-Z... *Serials Librarian, 47*(4), 43-54.

Machovec, G. S. (2002). Gold rush: Electronic resource discovery and management system. *The Charleston Advisor, 4*(1). Retrieved November 22, 2007, from http://www.charlestonco.com/features.cfm?id=98&type=np

Marshall, S., & Kawasaki, J. L. (2005). The master serial list at Montana State University: A simple, easy to use approach. *The Serials Librarian, 47*(4), 3-15.

McCaslin, S. (Recorder) (2003). Alan, R., & Hsiung, L.Y., presenters. Web-based tracking systems for electronic resources management. *The Serials Librarian, 44*(3/4), 293-297.

McMullen, K., & Wilmott, D. (2005). Taming the e-journal jungle: The University of South Carolina's experience with TDNet. *Serials Librarian, 47*(4), 35-42.

Medeiros, N. (2006). House of horrors: Exorcising electronic resources. In P. M. Bluh, & C. Hepfer (Eds.), *Managing electronic resources: Contemporary problems and emerging issues* (pp. 56-66). Chicago: Association for Library Collections & Technical Services.

Medeiros, N., et al. (2003). Managing administrative metadata: The tri-college consortium's electronic resources tracking system (ERTS). *Library and Technical Services, 47*(1), 28-25.

Medeiros, N., et al. (2007). White paper on interoperability between acquisitions modules of integrated library systems and electronic resource management systems: A draft for comment. Retrieved November 22, 2007, from http://www.haverford.edu/library/DLF_ERMI2/ACQ_ERMS_white_paper.pdf

Meyer, S. (2005) Helping you buy: Electronic resource management systems. *Computers in Libraries*, November/December, 19-24.

Notess, G. R. (2000, Oct/Nov). PubList and jake: Free periodical reference sources [review of two databases]. *Econtent, 23*:5, 64-66.

Pace, A. K. (2004). *Disintegrated library systems and electronic resource management: Dismantling library systems.* Presentation at ALA, 2004. Retrieved November 22, 2007, from http://www.lib.ncsu.edu/presentations/2004ala/IRRT_pace.ppt

Pace, A. K. (2006). *E-matrix: Electronic resource management at NCSU.* PowerPoint presented to Amigos, May 11, 2006. Retrieved November 22, 2007, from http://www.lib.ncsu.edu/presentations/2006Amigos/ematrix.ppt

PubList (1998-2001). About PubList.com. Retrieved November 22, 2007, from http://www.publist.com/about.html

Robbins, S., & Smith, M. (2004). Managing e-resources: A database-driven approach. In D.C. Fowler (Ed.), *E-serials collection management: Transitions, trends, and technicalities* (pp. 239-251). Binghamton, NY: Haworth Information Press.

Schulz, N. (2001). E-journal databases: A long-term solution? *Library Collections, Acquisitions, and Technical Services, 25*, 449-459.

Serials Solutions (n.d.). ERMS electronic management system. Retrieved November 22, 2007, from http://www.serialsolutions.com/promotion/ERMS/images/ErMS.pdf

SirsiDynix (2006). Horizon information management system. Retrieved November 22, 2007, from http://www.dynix.com/products/erm/ .

Sitko, M. et al. (2002). E-journal management systems: Trends, trials, and trade-offs. *Serials Review, 28*(3), 176-194.

Smulewitz, G. (recorder). (2005). Minutes of december 14, 2005 meeting. Rutgers University Libraries' Electronic Resource Access and Integration Task Force. Retrieved November 22, 2007, from http://www.libraries.rutgers.edu/rul/staff/groups/eratf/minutes/eratf_05_12_14.shmtl

Stefancu, M., Bloss, A., & Lambrecht, J. (2004). All about DOLLeR: Managing electronic resources at the UCI library. Preprint of *Serials Review, 30*(3), 194-205. Retrieved November 22, 2007, from http://www.library.cornell.edu/cts/elicensestudy/uic/AllAboutDOLLeR_web.html

Swets Information Services (2004). Retrieved November 22, 2007, from http://informationservices.swets.com

Szczyrbak, G., & Pierce, L. (2003). E-journal subscription management systems and beyond. *The Serials Librarian, 44*(3/4), 57-162.

TLC (2005). Gold rush: A discovery and management tool for electronic Resources. Retrieved November 22, 2007, from http://www.tlcdelivers.com/tlb/pdf/goldrush.pdf

Tri-College Consortium (2003). Electronic resources tracking System (ERTS). Retrieved November 22, 2007, from http://www.haverford.edu/library/erts

Tull, L., Crum J., Davis, T., & Strader, C. R. (2005). Integrating and streamlining electronic resources workflows via innovative's electronic resource management. *Serials Librarian, 47*(4), 103-124.

University of California, Los Angeles (2004). UC electronic resources management planning meeting campus/CDL survey: Electronic resources management at UCLA, March 4, 2004. Retrieved November 22, 2007, from http://libraries.universityofcalifornia.edu/sopag/appen06surveyfinalucal.doc

University of California, Los Angeles, mhr and lss (2002). ERBd examples of publisher, Issued by and access provider. Retrieved November 22, 2007, from http://www.library.cornell.edu/elicensestudy/ucla/2003/Examples%20of%20Publisher,%20Issued%20By%20&%20Access%20Provider%2012-19-02.doc

VTLS (n.d.). Verify [brochure]. Retrieved November 22, 2007, from http://www.vtls.com/brochures/verify.pdf

VTLS (2004.) Verify: Verify for yourself, e-resource management can be easy! Retrieved November 22, 2007, from http://www.vtls.com/Products/verify.shtml

Wakimoto, J. C., Walker, D. S., & Dabbour, K. S. (2006). The myths and realities of SFX in academic libraries. *Journal of Academic Librarianship*, *32*(2), 27-136.

Wilson, H. W. (2006). Gold rush quick facts. Retrieved November 22, 2007, from http://www.hwwilson.com/documentation/WilsonWeb/goldrush-quickfacts.htm

Wissman, M. et al. (2005). Taylor Periodical Administration System. Retrieved November 22, 2007, from http://www2.taylor.edu/library/upland/sjo/tpas.html

Wolfe, R. H. W. (2005) Managing the metadata morass: Applying cataloging skills beyond the traditional catalog: Boston College Library Catalogers. *Metametametadata*. Retrieved November 22, 2007, from http://www.metametadata.net/mt/archives/2005_04.html

Chapter XIX
The Impact of Locally Developed Electronic Resource Management Systems

Marie R. Kennedy
University of Southern California, USA

ABSTRACT

As libraries dramatically increased their numbers of licensed electronic resources in the 1990s, such as online journals and databases, they realized the need for a record-keeping system that would help manage the details of acquiring and maintaining them. Since no off-the-shelf product existed, some libraries developed their own tools to manage electronic resources. This chapter discusses the development of locally designed electronic resource management systems; the process of developing the tools at several academic institutions is traced, with a focus on the aspects of the systems unique to each university. Locally developed electronic resource management systems have lead academic institutions to engage with other institutions and vendors building similar tools. As a result, community-wide efforts in identifying key elements for managing electronic resources have begun to emerge. These efforts lay the foundation for the future successful development of tools and standards to assist in electronic resource management.

INTRODUCTION

In the 1990s libraries began to see a dramatic increase in publication of and patron interest in electronic resources. Delivering materials to a user's computer desktop in digital form brought with it a multitude of considerations for providers of information in academic settings. Due to the rapid acquisition of electronic resources libraries had to quickly create new workflows for technical processes such as managing and renewing license agreements and "processing" virtual products, as well as develop new communication structures and staffing workflows related to electronic resources (Gardner, 2001).

As libraries acquired an increased number of electronic resources, such as online journals and databases, they realized the pressing need for a recordkeeping system that would help manage the details of maintaining the resources. Since no off-the-shelf product existed, and traditional serials vendors did not provide management services for electronic resources, some libraries began developing their own tools to assist them in managing electronic resources.

In this chapter we will recount the impetus for the creation of several locally developed electronic resource management systems. The process of building such tools will be described in detail, as reported by the libraries that developed them (Cyzyk & Robertson, 2003; Farb & Riggio, 2002; Hennig, 2002; Loghry & Shannon, 2000). In addition to the creation of the management system itself, the administrative and staffing changes will be discussed, as evidenced in the literature (Duranceau & Hepfer, 2002; Gardner, 2001; Loghry & Shannon, 2000; Montgomery & Sparks, 2000).

As the idea of locally designed and built electronic resource management systems became more accepted, academic institutions began to seek assistance outside their universities to build their own systems. Examples of universities collaborating with other universities as well as commercial vendors and their impact on effective group management design will be presented (Chandler & Jewell, 2005; Digital Library Federation, 2004; Digital Library Federation, 2006; Dublin Core Metadata Initiative, 2006; Johns Hopkins University, 2004). The development of the individual management systems and the by-products of those systems, such as administrative metadata and the automatic exchange of serials data, will be noted (Chandler & Jewell, 2005; Jones, 2002). The process of developing these electronic resource management systems, and their eventual expansion, will be discussed as a possible model for organizing effective future library tools (Conger, 2004).

THE STATE OF LIBRARY ACQUISITIONS AS ELECTRONIC RESOURCES EMERGE

The delivery of electronic resources has transitioned from physical formats such as tapes, 3.5" floppy disks, and CD-ROMs (CD) and DVDs to remote databases and the currently common format of delivery via the Internet. Since large amounts of data could be stored on a CD, companies began to offer their proprietary resources in this format rather than in print or on earlier electronic formats such as floppy disks. The CDs acted as early databases, allowing users to "search" the CD for data. The CDs were either used at individual workstations or networked to allow for simultaneous searching by multiple patrons. The acquisitions department had to begin working more closely with their systems or technology department in order to ensure that the material delivered on CD was made appropriately available. In contrast with today's current expansive publishing on the Internet, relatively few publishers and vendors produced CD products, so the workflow paths that were initially developed were addressed at an ad hoc level.

As users grew comfortable with accessing content on their desktops rather than in print, publishers explored other options that would allow them to provide more frequent updates to their content, with quicker production times, and took advantage of an Internet-based format for delivery of materials. The move from CD- and remote database-delivered material to delivery via the Internet quickly gained popularity among library users; libraries nationwide cite a sudden and dramatic increase in purchases of electronic resources (Montgomery & Sparks, 2000, p. 13). In 2003 the Association of Research Libraries reported that in just ten years the average percentage of a member institution's total budget on electronic resources grew from 3.6% to 25% (Young & Kyrillidou, 2004).

The issues surrounding the increase of publication of electronic journals were compounded for library staff, as no mechanism was in place for their management. The issues were diverse, with large issues such as deciding who had negotiating and signing authority for the license agreements required to lease the electronic content delivered over the Internet, to smaller issues such as figuring out how to organize large electronic journal packages and conceiving a mechanism to remind staff to renew electronic journal subscriptions so that patron access to the material was seamless and uninterrupted.

CHANGES IN STAFFING AS A RESULT OF LICENSE AGREEMENTS

As the steps for securing access to an electronic resource are complicated, so are the staffing needs. Whereas a print purchase requires action only within the acquisitions department, an electronic resource lease or purchase may require action both within and outside of the acquisitions department. Jewell notes that these new requirements mean that library staff are playing "new and important specialized roles" to ensure success in the acquisition of each electronic resource (Jewell & Mitchell, 2005, p. 139). In this new role, the acquisitions staff member maintains communication with other required parties during this negotiation process, keeping all stakeholders informed of the progress. After the purchase, the acquisitions staff member may contact the library's systems department to verify access to the resource or to plan its maintenance. In this way, the acquisitions member acts as a liaison throughout the life of the resource in the library. Gardner's 2001 survey identifies the following departments that may play a role in resolving a license agreement: acquisitions, the library director, collection development, the assistant director, and systems (Gardner, 2001).

The effect of electronic resources on other departments is also evident after the resource has been leased. In Duranceau and Hepfer's informal survey reported in 2002 they note that "we find few, if any, 'routine' tasks related to digital resource management" (Duranceau & Hepfer, 2002, p. 317). Montgomery and Sparks note that a shift toward more electronic resources affects a variety of library departments and resources. Circulation/access services see a decreased need for reshelving and manual statistics gathering. Reserves are affected as students' access materials electronically rather than in print. Information services are affected as seemingly fewer reference questions are asked; and the systems department is pressed for more assistance with infrastructure needs (Montgomery & Sparks, 2000).

CREATING LOCALLY DEVELOPED ELECTRONIC RESOURCE MANAGEMENT SYSTEMS

As library staff expressed a need for a mechanism for clear communication about the status of a license being negotiated, an active resource needing maintenance, or a report of funds spent, most libraries began a series of paper lists or worksheets to assist them (Kennedy, Crump, & Kiker, 2004; Loghry & Shannon, 2000). As the number of electronic resources grew it became clear that the paper lists could not be effectively shared among the staff needing access to them. Library staff needed a computer program that was designed to hold all the information related to an electronic resource so that it could be viewed from all the stakeholders' computer desktops, yet no such software existed. Without an off-the-shelf program available to assist them in organizing their resources, many libraries turned to their own library or university staff for assistance in creating one.

Many universities attempted to create their own electronic resource management systems, with varying degrees of success. Some created complete systems to manage many aspects of electronic resources processing at their libraries, while others focused their efforts just on specific aspects of managing the resources. Of the known electronic resource management systems and initiatives, three stand out as pioneers: Massachusetts Institute of Technology's VERA, Pennsylvania State University's ERLIC, and University of California Los Angeles's ERDb. There are other notable systems, such as Gold Rush, HERMES and the Tri-College Consortium's ERTS, which will also be discussed in detail.

Massachusetts Institute of Technology's VERA

The Massachusetts Institute of Technology (MIT) library launched VERA (Virtual Electronic Resource Access) in 2000. The program was developed to respond to two specific issues that had been identified at MIT: the library staff needed a centralized location in which to store information about eight aspects of license management, and the library needed an improved access point for patrons (Duranceau, 2000; Hennig, 2002). Until VERA was created, staff had to input information about licenses and access using a variety of tools; VERA gave them one centralized data tool. More importantly, MIT also wanted to improve user access to its licensed electronic resources; VERA was designed to make lists of its electronic titles easier to use.

The VERA program was created using File-Maker Pro software. MIT decided to use this database software because they had a site license for it and staff members were already familiar with its use (Hennig, 2002). Using a known software program to build the new system proved to be a smart decision because: (1) staff were likely to use VERA since they were familiar with its software; and (2) the developers could focus solely on the design of the tool instead of having to learn a software program and develop a new tool at the same time (Kennedy, 2004).

VERA was designed to be both a front-end and back-end system. The front-end, or patron view, allows searches by title, subject, keyword, or provider. The back-end, or staff view, allows staff to enter data into the Web-enabled version of FileMaker Pro. Since it is Web-based, staff outside of acquisitions can make changes to the title database from their own workstations without having to download software to their computers. The changes made are available to the public the following day, as the "working copy" of the program is uploaded each night to replace the existing live version (Hennig, 2002, p. 251).

Other than the ability to view text, patrons are presented with several icons with their search result (Massachusetts Institute of Technology Libraries, 2006). If the information is relevant to the search result, then the icon is displayed in the "More" field of the results screen. A legend of icons appears on the search results screen, assisting the patron to understand the access restrictions and permissions in a visual format. Staff activate the appropriate icons from the back-end view of VERA in order to display them to the public.

Pennsylvania State University's ERLIC

Pennsylvania State University's (PSU) Electronic Resources Licensing and Information Center (ERLIC) was constructed in 1999 as a way to track orders. The system was designed for acquisitions functions, and so the Microsoft Access-based program was initially populated with data related to acquisitions processes. In a 2000 conference presentation, Cochenour notes that though ERLIC was originally constructed in order to track and claim invoices for electronic resources it quickly grew to encompass information about license agreements and to share information about the resources (Cochenour, 2000).

ERLIC grew quickly once the stakeholders of the PSU electronic resources were identified. PSU identified the stakeholders as staff in the following departments: acquisitions, cataloging, collection development, public service and systems. In order to meet the demands of these staff members ERLIC was designed to house information about funds and budgets, the status of orders and license agreements, and electronic resources access points. Microsoft Access was chosen as the development tool due to its relational database nature; views for different stakeholders could be customized to display only the elements relevant to that department. Cochenour commented in 2000 that the program had not spurred major changes in the daily workflows of the various stakeholders; this smooth incorporation of a system into the daily activities of a group is the result of considerate design based on a careful needs assessment that was conducted before beginning to build ERLIC (Cochenour, 2000). In 2001 the library added Cold Fusion Web pages to provide better license tracking and user authentication (Alan, 2002).

University of California Los Angeles's ERDb

The University of California Los Angeles's (UCLA) Electronic Resources Database (ERDb) was drawn from several working principles, the first of which is to "know your users" (Farb & Riggio, 2002). In designing their ERDb UCLA first developed a staff working group known as the Steering Committee on Access to Electronic Resources (SCAER) (University of California Los Angeles Library, 2006). The documents of this committee are freely available and include reports on its vision of the electronic resource management system, a list of contacts in each department that report to the SCAER, and a month by month timeline of steps to be completed in the development of the ERDb (available at http://staff.library.ucla.edu/groups/scaer/).

The architecture of the staff view of the system is constructed on Microsoft Access software, and is served to the public view through Cold Fusion (University of California Los Angeles Library,

2002). The ERDb has a staff view back-end and a patron view front-end. The back end has multiple fields for text entry and many pull down options for choosing keyword descriptors for a particular resource. A particularly useful feature of the ERDb is found on the troubleshooting screen, which houses problem reports for each resource. This trouble history tracks the problems of a resource over time and offers help in correcting a problem when similar issues occur (Farb & Riggio, 2002).

SOME SUCCESSFUL ELECTRONIC RESOURCE MANAGEMENT SYSTEMS, WITH A SPECIALIZED FOCUS

The electronic resource management systems discussed to this point focus on tools developed for a specific university setting. There are three additional locally developed systems that are notable for their successes in other areas. Gold Rush was locally developed and then made commercial, HERMES was locally developed and then made available as freeware, and the Tri-College Consortium's ERTS was created as a consortial management system; each will be briefly described.

Gold Rush

The Colorado Alliance of Research Libraries, a nonprofit group, developed the electronic resource management system called Gold Rush. It was created as a result of information gleaned from various academic institutions about what elements an ideal electronic resource management system would contain; from this information the stand-alone system was built (Collins, 2005). Stockton and Machovec note that the alliance hoped that by being constructed as a consortial tool Gold Rush would act as a "database of databases" (Stockton & Machovec, 2001, p. 53).

Gold Rush is a Web-driven system that is hosted remotely, so that libraries that use it do not have to download any software. It contains a variety of modules: subscription management, openURL link resolver, a public interface to allow A-Z searching, and a reporting feature for collection development assistance (Gold Rush, 2006). Of particular note is an email feature, which notifies a defined group of people when a license agreement will be coming due for renewal. This feature is customizable, with the ability to alert different groups of people for different resources, if desired. There are also several "views" available, giving each staff member access only to relevant modules of the system. Gold Rush does not integrate with a library's catalog, though the data can be drawn out of or into the program to reduce double keying. The system is available for an annual licensing fee.

HERMES

The electronic resource management system, HERMES, was designed at Johns Hopkins University throughout 2000, and was built in 2001. It was developed in PostgreSQL and served through Cold Fusion (Jewell, 2005). It is constructed of modules, to which staff may be given access to few or many. The available modules are: authorization, selection, acquisitions, catalog interface, catalog, library computing services, public display, administrative search, report, scheduled notifications (Cyzyk & Robertson, 2003). Since the system is open source, another library may choose to add or delete modules to suit its needs.

An interesting feature of this system is the automated subject indexing. Based on a bibliographic record's subject headings, the cataloging interface allows a mapping to HERMES's subject schema. The cataloger enters the mapping for the first entry, and thereafter the system uses a look-up table to determine if the newly entered bibliographic record has a similar mapping structure; if it does it is automatically entered into the system.

The developers of HERMES defined particular roles, or groups, that would enter data into the system. These roles were identified in order to make certain that only necessary staff would be allowed access to the material. The roles include license management, budget management, purchasing, and cataloging, to name a few (Cyzyk & Robertson, 2003).

The Tri-College Consortium's ERTS

The Tri-College Consortium developed their Electronic Resources Tracking System (ERTS) because the "paper files maintained by Serials Librarians have proven inadequate in both accessibility and organization" (Medeiros & Pascale, 2003). The Tri-College Consortium, made up of the libraries of Bryn Mawr, Haverford, and Swarthmore Colleges, shares many electronic resources, but paper files maintained at one college are not useful to the libraries of the remaining two schools. The design of this system, therefore, was planned to serve the consortium in managing the resources licensed by all three colleges.

The ERTS began construction in 2001 using FileMaker Pro and is shared with the other colleges in the consortium by the use of FileMaker's sharing feature. The system contains a public view and a technical services view; the public view is made available through the Web. In addition, a design focus serves the function of generating reports that cannot be derived from the individual colleges' integrated library systems. The reports available are: 60-day expiration alert, purchase type, pay date, expenditure comparison by purchase type, and acquisition count (Medeiros & Pascale, 2003).

The program is constructed of four modules: licensors, purchases, vendors, titles. Each college adds information to the modules, reusing existing data, if possible. For example, their stated intent of the licensing module is "to have one licensor record for all libraries that use that license, even if our terms differ slightly" (Medeiros & Pascale,

2003). Sharing this administrative metadata at the consortial level enables the three college libraries to have the same information if they need to contact technical support for a resource, request a new license agreement, or renegotiate a price upon renewal. The construction of a database with shared information reflects the efforts of three colleges that have gone to great lengths to accomplish this community effort. The consortium has constructed a suggested workflow for how to best handle licensing electronic resources in each library. The ERTS is available for download as shareware.

CHARACTERISTICS OF AN IDEAL ELECTRONIC RESOURCE MANAGEMENT SYSTEM

As locally developed electronic resource management systems cropped up across the academic library community it became evident that each served the needs of a particular institution, but was not necessarily effective in another setting. In evaluating the locally developed electronic resource management systems and the literature about them, authors attempted to identify the characteristics of an ideal system (Jewell, 2001; Jewell, 2005; Kennedy, 2004). In 2004 Kennedy suggested that the "dream" program would contain the following functions: notify appropriate staff before licenses expire, integrate with library management system to eliminate double keying, maintain current/appropriate vendor contact information, track funds used to purchase resources, eliminate paper shuffling from one office to another, track consortia purchases, update in real time, and produce ad hoc reports (Kennedy, 2004). The Digital Library Federation has since defined 47 requirements to construct a comprehensive system, and a Council on Library and Information Resources report lists nearly 150 functions or data elements (Jewell, 2001; Jewell, 2005). More recent focus in this area has concentrated on further identifying elements that would enable methods for capturing and delivering usage statistics (Digital Library Federation, 2004; Fons & Jewell, 2006).

THE LIMITATIONS OF LOCALLY DEVELOPED ELECTRONIC RESOURCE MANAGEMENT SYSTEMS

Each of the six locally developed electronic resource management systems that have been discussed may be considered successful because of their approach to design. Each was constructed to specifically address the particular needs of its institution, or a perceived user group, but may not encompass all aspects of an ideal electronic resource management system. Appendix B of a Council on Library and Information Resources report which lists the data elements for MIT's VERA, PSU's ERLIC, and UCLA's ERDb, shows clearly that though there is some overlap in the elements these systems encompass, they are distinctly different from one another (Jewell, 2001).

Although they created successful programs, the universities that developed in-house programs are slowly migrating away from them, in favor of commercial products (see Pennsylvania State University, 2006, for example). Much work has been done within the library and vendor communities to co-develop new tools and work together to add functionality where individual in-house programs cannot. The in-house programs have provided a time-limited solution for these universities, and as academic institutions move toward more consortial purchasing, continuing to heartily develop the in-house programs is not time efficient. Most of the in-house tools developed failed with some interoperability problems, the consistent issues being a lack of integration with the library catalog, requiring redundancy of data, and scalability issues. Solutions for some of these issues were generated by librarians and vendors working together to create community-wide initiatives.

COMMUNITY-WIDE EFFORTS IN MANAGING ELECTRONIC RESOURCES

As institutions sought communication related to the development of electronic resource management systems outside their university boundaries several impressive initiatives were constructed. The Digital Library Federation created an initiative called the Electronic Resource Management Initiative, run by a steering group of members from seven academic institutions; information sharing initiatives such as the Open Digital Rights Language and the Dublin Core Metadata Initiative were developed; and interest in creating standardized license agreement language became evident. These and a number of additional community efforts will be discussed in this section.

Electronic Resource Management Initiative

As institutions realized that effective communication about their common problem of managing electronic resources could lead to satisfying solutions they began to seek discussion outside their own academic institutions. The "Web hub for developing administrative metadata for electronic resource management" was constructed to facilitate the sharing of information about institutions developing their own electronic resource management systems (Chandler & Jewell, 2005). The Web hub was a Web site managed by Adam Chandler and Tim Jewell (no longer updated as of February 2005), which listed the names of the universities that were building systems or creating initiatives to address their own electronic resource management needs. The site also listed descriptions of the systems and contact persons at each university. The site was built so that uni-

versities could read how other institutions were developing their tools, and could communicate with those universities if they had similar needs. The Web hub was a successful facilitator for those institutions that were considering building their own electronic resource management systems but needed more information or support before beginning their projects.

The creators of the Web hub started the Digital Library Federation's Electronic Resource Management Initiative steering group in 2001. The purpose of the Electronic Resource Management Initiative (ERMI) was to define an essential list of data elements that would construct a full and complete electronic resource management system (Chang, 2003). In addition to defining the data elements, the group sought to develop workflows and promote standards for the management of the data (Digital Library Federation, 2006). The Web hub served as a fertile space from which the ERMI could pull information to begin their discussions.

In the final report of the Digital Library Federation's ERMI seven functional areas required to construct a comprehensive management system are identified: "listing and descriptive;" "license-related;" "financial and purchasing;" "process and status;" "systems and technical;" "contact and support;" and "usage" (Digital Library Federation, 2004, p. 4). By identifying these functional areas the ERMI hopes to convey accurately to vendors or others wishing to build management systems what elements are needed (Chandler, 2004).

As the Digital Library Federation's ERMI outlined its own goals it also included conversations with library vendors. By communicating with the vendors the ERMI created a successful ongoing rapport about what was needed to develop a complete electronic resource management system. By including vendors in this discussion the ERMI could provide the data backbone of a system that could then be developed by the vendors; in this way libraries could depend on vendors for development support and collaboration rather than acting as independent system creators.

Standardized License Agreements

Another area of electronic resource management that has had community-wide efforts to streamline is in developing standardized license agreements. A major challenge to the timely management of electronic resources is the often ambiguous or difficult language in which license agreements are worded. These agreements are legally binding, yet many librarians in charge of implementing them often have little or no training in how to interpret their language. As a result license agreements at some libraries are forwarded from a library's acquisition department to a legal signatory for the university, stopping the acquisitions process until the license has been rewritten to have agreeable terms for both the publisher/vendor and the university. This time lag is a major problem for an acquisitions department that is used to a standardized, on-time workflow. In addition to the break in workflow, tracking the progress of a license agreement that is passed back and forth from vendor/publisher to the legal signatory for the university is a challenge.

To counter this difficulty there have been attempts to simplify the language of a license agreement so that they can be quickly agreed upon and signed, providing patrons with prompt access to the materials licensed. In 2000, John Cox constructed five model license agreements, the development of which were sponsored by subscription vendors (Cox, 2000). These licenses are in the public domain and are meant to be altered to fit the specific needs of a particular licensing situation. Yale also offered a standard license agreement, written under sponsorship by the Council on Library and Information Resources and the Digital Library Federation. Yale's license notes, in brackets, the sections of the license that the library is to complete (Yale University Library, 2001). They also offer a best practices short form of the license.

As of 2007 the National Information Standards Organization is sponsoring a working group titled Shared E-Resource Understanding. This group is charged with developing some guidelines that publishers and licensors of electronic resources can use to establish a fiscal relationship without the inclusion of a written license agreement. Negating the requirement for a written license in favor of simply agreeing in principle on how electronic resources will be used is a step toward more open and collegial working relationships between publishers and their resource licensors.

The Open Digital Rights Language

An effort to disambiguate the language used in license agreements about what users may/may not do with the information, the open digital rights language has created a data dictionary that defines the rights and limitations. Written as an XML document, the language is meant to be interoperable, meaning that the terms used in one instantiation mean the same as in another. The language can be used for a variety of electronic resources, whether they are describing the rights and limitations of a traditional electronic journal or a digital image, audio, or movie (Iannella, 2002).

The Dublin Core Metadata Initiative

Dublin Core is a metadata schema that was designed to help describe data in a consistent way across platforms. It is similar to the open digital rights language (ODRL), yet its focus is on broad resource description, rather than focusing specifically on rights and limitations. The Dublin Core has proven itself to be an internationally successful tool due to its scalability; it is constructed of only 15 elements, each of which is optional, and all may be repeated (Dublin Core Metadata Initiative, 2006). This flexible set of descriptors can be applied to almost any kind of resource. One of the descriptors particularly relevant to this discussion is the element "rights." This field can hold information regarding licensing rights and limitations for a particular resource or for a group of resources. To promote maximum interoperability, the ODRL and the Dublin Core Metadata Initiative teamed together as of 2005 to begin discussions about how to merge the access rights elements of their two vocabularies.

Other Concepts

As a result of broad discussion surrounding electronic resources the standardization of administrative metadata became an important topic. Administrative metadata can be loosely defined as information about electronic resources that facilitates their management. Data such as resource title, rights and limitations, license terms and dates, and budgeting information may be considered administrative metadata. As more of this metadata is created inside electronic resource management systems it has become clear that a standardization of the information would be beneficial for comparison across resources. Another standardization effort that would assist in sharing data is the automatic exchange of serials data (Jones, 2002). If the metadata about serials could be standardized then the data could be shared between systems without any extra keying, allowing for more accurate data (no typing errors) and freeing staff to pursue other tasks. Usage statistics is a current effort in standardization as well, with hopes that counting web page visits and article downloads can be standardized to facilitate usage comparison between different publications (Fons & Jewell, 2006).

CHANGING COMMUNICATION PATTERNS DUE TO LOCALLY DEVELOPED ELECTRONIC RESOURCE MANAGEMENT SYSTEMS

It is clear that the problem of managing electronic resources motivated librarians to act outside of

their usual environment into a more public role. This movement outside of the normal work setting occurred when license agreements began to be required for the leasing of electronic resources. This necessity pushed some librarians to collaborate with university offices (often general counsel) in order to negotiate and sign the license. The format of the resource itself also required that librarians communicate with systems or technical staff to ensure that it was activated correctly. Acquisitions librarians who may not have had much communication with patrons before also learned to clarify and correct access problems with the electronic resources. These new models of communicating outside of the normal work environment may have had a positive effect on the development of the community-wide efforts in managing electronic resources.

Within one's university setting one acts in one's role; in this way librarians are tied to existing power structures and role expectations. By first working to develop local solutions to electronic resource management and then community-wide solutions librarians took themselves out of their traditional roles. Librarians who had gained enough knowledge about how to develop their own locally designed electronic resource management systems contributed to the wider discussion of developing a management system at the national level. By working outside of their libraries' hierarchies, thrusting themselves instead into peer collaboration with librarians from institutions across the United States, librarians may have created an ideal development environment. Conger suggests that this collaborative, rather than hierarchical, working environment may have contributed to the successes of community-wide development of electronic resource management systems (Conger, 2004, p. 29).

These collaborations on defining elements of a successful electronic resource management system have not included just librarians, but vendor representatives as well. By including the vendor community in defining key elements of an electronic resource management system, the Digital Library Federation's Electronic Resource Management Initiative (ERMI) steering group was able to negotiate early on what roles each would play in the future development of such systems. The librarians and vendors brought their own expertise to the discussion, broadening it with a variety of approaches and ideas. Systems vendors have, in fact, begun constructing electronic resource management modules that follow the data elements outlined in their collaborations with the ERMI (Grover & Fons, 2004; Meyer, 2005). In this way, system vendors and ERMI members may be viewed as co-developers of these new systems. By creating this kind of diverse, creative working group the members naturally developed a sense of ownership in the outcome. They defined not only a management system but also a model for future successful communications with each other.

SUMMARY

Tasking themselves with identifying new ways in which to manage electronic resources has given librarians alternate communication models from which to work. Creating locally developed electronic resource management systems helped to unify the library communities at Massachusetts Institute of Technology, Pennsylvania State University, and the University of California Los Angeles. Then as those groups began to work outside their institutions they developed what Emery calls a "library enterprise network," or library groups that act as nodes in a wider network, collaborating on a specific task (Emery, 2005). It is this wider network that librarians have learned to create for themselves, and it predicts future successes in forthcoming development tasks.

REFERENCES

Alan, R. (2002). Keeping track of electronic resources to keep them on track. Retrieved November 22, 2007, from http://www.library.cornell.edu/cts/elicensestudy/pennstate/PSUNASIGPresentation2002.ppt

Chandler, A. (2004). Electronic resource management. Retrieved November 22, 2007, from http://metadata-wg.mannlib.cornell.edu/forum/index.php?date=2004-09-24

Chandler, A., & Jewell, T. D. (2005). A web hub for developing administrative metadata for electronic resource management. Retrieved November 23, 2007, from http://www.library.cornell.edu/cts/elicensestudy/

Chang, S. (2003). The DLF electronic resource management initiative. *OCLC Systems & Services, 19*(2), 45-47.

Cochenour, D. (2000). Taming the octopus: Getting a grip on electronic resources. *Serials Librarian, 38*(3/4), 363-368.

Collins, M. (2005). Electronic resource management systems: Understanding the players and how to make the right choice for your library. *Serials Review, 31*, 125-140.

Conger, J. E. (2004). *Collaborative electronic resource management*. Westport, CT: Libraries Unlimited.

Cox, J. (2000). Model generic licenses: Cooperation and competition. *Serials Review, 26*(1), 3-9.

Cyzyk, M., & Robertson, N. (2003). HERMES: The Hopkins Electronic Resource Management System. *Information Technology and Libraries, 22*(1), 12-17.

Digital Library Federation (2004). Electronic resource management: Final report of the DLF initiative. Retrieved November 23, 2007, from http://www.library.cornell.edu/elicensestudy/dlfdeliverables/DLF-ERMI-FinalReport.pdf

Digital Library Federation. (2006). DLF electronic resource management initiative. Retrieved November 23, 2007, from http://www.diglib.org/standards/dlf-erm02.htm

Dublin Core Metadata Initiative (2006). DCMI metadata terms. Retrieved November 23, 2007, from http://dublincore.org/documents/dcmi-terms/

Duranceau, E. F. (2000). License tracking. *Serials Review, 26*(3), 69-73.

Duranceau, E. F., & Hepfer, C. (2002). Staffing for electronic resource management: The results of a survey. *Serials Review, 28*(4), 316-320.

Emery, J. (2005). Beginning to see the light: Developing a discourse for electronic resource management. *Serials Librarian, 47*(4), 137-147.

Farb, S., & Riggio, A. (2002). UCLA electronic resources database project overview. Retrieved November 23, 2007, from http://www.library.cornell.edu/cts/elicensestudy/ucla/ALAMidwinter2002.ppt

Fons, T., & Jewell, T. (2006). *Envisioning the future of ERM systems.* Paper presented at the meeting of the North American Serials Interest Group, Denver, CO.

Gardner, S. (2001). The impact of electronic journals on library staff at ARL member institutions: A survey and a critique of the survey methodology. *Serials Review, 27*(3-4), 17-32.

Gold Rush (2006). Welcome to Gold Rush. Retrieved November 23, 2007, from http://grweb.coalliance.org/

Grover, D., & Fons, T. (2004). The Innovative electronic resource management system: A development partnership. *Serials Review, 30,* 110-116.

Hennig, N. (2002). Improving access to e-journals and databases at the MIT libraries: Building a database-backed web site called "VERA". In J. Cole, & W. Jones (Eds.), *E-serials cataloging: Access to continuing and integrating resources via the catalog and the web* (pp. 227-254). Binghamton, NY: Haworth.

Iannella, R. (2002). Open Digital Rights Language (ODRL) version 1.1. Retrieved November 23, 2007, from http://www.w3.org/TR/odrl/

Jewell, T. D. (2001). *Selection and presentation of commercially available electronic resources: Issues and practices.* Washington, DC: Council on Library and Information Resources.

Jewell, T. D. (2005). E-resource management systems: Past, present, and future. Retrieved November 23, 2007, from http://www.sirsidynix-institute.com/Resources/Attachments/Slides/jewell_20051207.pdf

Jewell, T. D., & Mitchell, A. (2005). Electronic resource management: The quest for systems and standards. *Serials Librarian, 48*(1/2), 137-163.

Johns Hopkins University. (2004). HERMES. Retrieved November 23, 2007, from http://hermes.mse.jhu.edu:8008/hermesdocs/

Jones, E. (2002). *The exchange of serials subscription information.* Bethesda, MD: National Information Standards Organization.

Kennedy, M. R. (2004). Dreams of perfect programs: Managing the acquisition of electronic resources. *Library Collections, Acquisitions, and Technical Services, 28*(4), 449-458.

Kennedy, M. R., Crump, M. J., & Kiker, D. (2004). Paper to PDF: Making license agreements accessible through the OPAC. *Library Resources & Technical Services, 48*(1), 20-25.

Loghry, P. A., & Shannon, A. W. (2000). Managing selection and implementation of electronic products: One tiny step in organization, one giant step for the University of Nevada, Reno. *Serials Review, 26*(3), 32-44.

Massachusetts Institute of Technology Libraries. (2006). VERA: Virtual electronic resource access. Retrieved November 23, 2007, from http://libraries.mit.edu/vera

Medeiros, N., & Pascale, C. (2003). The Tri-College Consortium's electronic resource tracking system (ERTS). Retrieved November 23, 2007, from http://www.haverford.edu/library/erts/

Meyer, S. (2005). Helping you buy: Electronic resource management systems. *Computers in Libraries, 25*(10), 19-24.

Montgomery, C. H., & Sparks, J. L. (2000). The transition to an electronic journal collection: Managing the organizational changes. *Serials Review, 26*(3), 4-18.

Pennsylvania State University Libraries. (2006). Serials and acquisitions services tactical plan 05/06-07/08. Retrieved November 23, 2007, from http://www.libraries.psu.edu/admin/adup/tactical/serials_acq_plan_rev072006.pdf

Stockton, M., & Machovec, G. (2001). Gold Rush: A digital registry of electronic journals. *Technical Services Quarterly, 19*(3), 51-59.

University of California Los Angeles Library (2002). SCAER vision of access to electronic resources. Retrieved November 23, 2007, from http://staff.library.ucla.edu/groups/scaer/vision_rept.doc

University of California Los Angeles Library (2006). Staff intranet: Steering committee on access to electronic resources (SCAER). Retrieved November 23, 2007, from http://staff.library.ucla.edu/groups/scaer/

Yale University Library (2001). CLIR/DLF model license. Retrieved November 23, 2007, from http://www.library.yale.edu/~llicense/modlic.shtml

Young, M., & Kyrillidou, M. (2004). ARL supplementary statistics 2002-03. Retrieved November 23, 2007, from http://www.arl.org/stats/pubpdf/sup03.pdf

Chapter XX
The Future of Electronic Resource Management Systems:
Inside and Out

Ted Fons
Innovative Interfaces, Inc., USA

ABSTRACT

The core functional requirements for electronic resource management systems have been identified and implemented in varying depths by commercial and library system developers. As use of these systems increases, novel needs have been revealed. These new needs reside on both sides of the end-user spectrum. Library staff have a need to analyze their electronic collections for comprehensiveness, title overlap, cost-per-use, usage distribution within journal packages and other collection analysis functions. They also have the need to automate administrative tasks like IP registration, incident reporting, activation, renewal, sample license review, and license exchange. Library patrons and public services staff have a need to understand the full range of permissions and restrictions for electronic resource use at the local and consortial levels. They also have the need to be alerted when electronic resources have been upgraded, enhanced or when system outages are planned or are on going. Those needs are manifest at all levels of access: the discovery services platform, online public access catalog, the link resolver, the metasearch environment, A-Z list, and so forth. Since the electronic resource management system already stores permitted and restricted uses, it is the ideal source for that data at all levels of patron access. As electronic resource management systems evolve, the functional requirements should evolve to describe the library's needs for a system that acts as a collection development and analysis tool and as the source for critical access and license data for patrons wherever they access the library's electronic resources and to support the requirements of libraries in a consortial arrangement.

INTRODUCTION

Electronic resource management (ERM) systems have followed a traditional path in library system development. As the workflow impact and overall importance of electronic resources grew in the late 1990's and early 2000's, library staff developed local systems to meet specific functional requirements. As the workflow and overall impact of electronic resources increased, library professionals collaborated on formalizing functional requirements and the ideal data elements for ERM systems. This effort took the form of the *Electronic Resource Management: Report of the DLF Electronic Resource Management Initiative* (Jewell et al., 2004). Over time, the locally developed systems could not adequately meet staff needs or could not be maintained and enhanced over the long term. In the early 2000's, library professionals approached commercial system developers to build systems to match the now-formal functional requirements and data elements. It was widely understood that the commercial system developers had the development resources and long-term commitment to providing systems that would meet the needs of electronic resources librarians. These systems were to varying degrees integrated with integrated library systems and other systems already in use by the library (Fons & Grover, 2004). As the middle 2000's approached, a robust market of competing systems grew and libraries began to implement the commercial systems at the local and consortial levels. As these systems were developed and the core functional requirements were met, new functional requirements have evolved and pressure is now being applied to system developers to build systems that can grow with the evolving requirements.

The new functional requirements for staff cluster around the need to make routine administrative tasks more efficient through automation and interface development and improved data analysis and reporting.

Usage statistics harvesting is a prime example of the need for automation of routine administrative tasks (Chandler & Jewell, 2006). A critical need is integration with other local systems like the integrated library system (ILS), the link resolver engine and knowledgebase and perhaps most importantly, integration with the administrative functions of the content providers and subscription agents that provide access and licensing services. Another critical need is for standardized license data to facilitate the review of terms for proposed resources and automated population of the ERM system (NISO, n.d.). Librarians are also looking for enhanced reporting functions that maximize the value of harvested usage data and other locally held data such as cost. Access to acquisitions data within the ERM system for enhanced reporting and troubleshooting has arisen as a functional need for ERM systems (Digital Library Federation, Acquisitions Interoperability Subcommittee, 2007).

As the primary functional requirements for staff have been met, the need to provide data from the ERM system to library patrons has become an increasingly important functional requirement. Libraries are looking to provide the terms and conditions of use at all points of access to content. These access points include link resolver displays, A-Z lists of electronic journals, the online public access catalog, metasearch environments and the new discovery services platforms such as Encore from Innovative Interfaces and Primo from ExLibris that provide an enhanced resource discovery and delivery experience for patrons.

BACKGROUND

Before the appearance of commercial ERM systems, electronic resource management was typically handled by a combination of automated and non-automated solutions. Libraries used analog management systems to track contact information and the printed versions of contracts. Some libraries used the integrated library system unmodified for tracking electronic resources (Tull, Crum, Davis, & Strader, 2005). Finally, other libraries developed local systems for tracking their electronic resources (Jewell, 2001). UCLA's ERDb, North Carolina State University's E-Matrix and MIT's Vera are notable examples. The Electronic Resource Management Initiative (ERMI) documents authors took advantage of that collective experience to document the critical data elements and functional requirements for the ideal ERM system. The commercial vendors responded strongly to this effort. Beginning in 2004 when Innovative Interfaces introduced its Electronic Resource Management product, there followed a series of releases from other commercial vendors. The ILS vendor Endeavor developed Meridian and Ex Libris developed Verde. The publication access management service Serials Solutions introduced their Electronic Resource Management System. Noncommercial organizations such as the Colorado Alliance ("Gold Rush") also appeared in the market during this period (Duranceau, 2004).

First-generation commercial ERM systems were developed to create a single system that would serve as the database of record for metadata related to electronic resources. They were built to describe the components of an electronic resource including the electronic product, interface, resource, contacts and license (Jewell et al., 2004). To facilitate an efficient workflow they were designed to record details of the steps in the acquisition and licensing of the resource—including recording the details of the administrative tasks such as IP registration, activation and other stages of the administrative process. Title lists for journal packages and article databases along with access metadata like linking rules, embargo periods, coverage dates, and static URLs were also a core feature of these systems. Knowledgebase data and methods of maintaining data currency provided users with a list of available titles and access points for link resolvers and public displays where they were available. Acquisitions

details like pricing models; negotiation notes and quotes were also stored in the ERM. Workflow paths and responsibilities and tasks were a basic functional requirement along with contact details for platform vendors, publishers, data providers, and consortium partners were all important components of the first generation ERM functional requirements.

To varying degrees all of these systems have satisfied the core functional requirements and matched the data elements recommended by the ERMI model. As these systems have been implemented by libraries; the need for a new set of functional requirements has been exposed. The following section describes a new set of useful functional requirements for ERM systems.

STAFF NEEDS

The evolving staff needs within ERM systems fall into three categories:

- **Automation:** The need for enhanced efficiency through automation of routine administrative tasks and interface development.
- **Analysis:** The need for sophisticated analysis of existing data to provide a deeper understanding of library holdings to and make informed decisions about the return on investment for electronic resources.
- **Consortium requirements:** The need to track license terms at the appropriate level and to manage title metadata that is shared and unique in a consortial environment.

Automation

As ERM systems have matured, libraries have sought new efficiencies through standardization of data. The License Expression Working Group has been convened to develop an industry standard for the description of the license terms that govern a licensed resource (NISO, n.d.). The need for such a standard lies in the library's time-consuming task of analyzing license documents and coding them according to the features of the local ERM system. This has proven to be a labor-intensive task that requires the skills of a staff member deeply familiar with license terms. The evolved functional requirement is a feature built into the ERM system that will accept a feed of license data and populate the ERM system with the appropriate terms of use and other license elements as profiled by the library. Additionally, ERM systems should offer a view of license terms for resources that are not currently licensed—such as those that are undergoing a trial or other resource selection review process. The ideal application would connect to the system of the content provider or a clearinghouse of license documents and allow the selector to review the proposed license terms before purchase or at any time during the evaluation process. A Web-services based request and response model should be in place and integrated with the ERM application. This would allow the user to make real-time, just-in-time requests for licensed or under-trial electronic resources. An industry-standard license description format would provide the backbone for this model.

The automation of routine administrative tasks provides a rich source of new functional requirements for ERM systems. Interfaces between ERM systems and content provider or subscription agent administration systems would facilitate the automation of administration functions such as:

IP Registration

As local networks grow or are reconfigured, libraries must broadcast a list of IP address ranges to their content providers. This is particularly true for libraries in a consortial arrangement or agreements with partner institutions and affiliated institutions. This task is required in addition to the registration of IPs when new resources are licensed. Current methods are labor intensive and the actual registration mechanism can vary from provider to provider. As libraries look to the new generation of ERM systems they want to see a single model for IP registration enabled by standards-based protocols within the ERM system.

Activation

As with IP registration, this critical part of the workflow varies from provider to provider. A single activation mechanism enabled by a standard protocol among all providers could have the effect of avoiding service problems and improve overall efficiency. Automating this activity would have the additional benefit of blending the activation action itself with the recording of the event in the ERM system—thereby contributing to overall efficiency.

Renewal

While renewal might involve a review of license terms or renegotiation of some aspects of the license, where the license is being accepted without revision, it should be possible to indicate an intent to renew or to commit to renewal via communication between the ERM system and the content provider or licensing agency. Where both parties agree to a standard protocol, the amount of staff administrative activity should be attenuated by the automated system.

Incident Reporting

Incident reporting is the activity whereby the library notifies the publisher or platform provider that there is a problem with access to an electronic resource or one of its components. It is the administrative function that is perhaps in the greatest need of automation. Current ERM systems allow staff to record the details of a service incident at a detailed level—including title details for journal packages and the reporter and reportee. The fact that this process is not automated contributes to inefficiency. Library staff are forced to report incidents through provider-specific mechanism and then record the details of the incident in the ERM system for long term analysis and to seed follow up tools provided by the ERM system. This should be a single event with a feedback loop based on an agreed-upon protocol.

License Review

As described above, there is a need for a request and response protocol for license terms. This would facilitate the review process for not-yet-licensed resources and allow the library to review current or proposed standard license terms for renewing licenses. This mechanism would create the foundation for an automated method for populating the ERM system with license terms.

What is needed here is a standard model for communication between the ERM system and the content provider or subscription agent's administrative system. Each of these administrative functions shares the same identifiers; the only difference between the exchanges is in the administrative data transferred. See Table 1.

While no model currently exists for this data exchange, a Web services model with a common

request and response syntax could be developed between ERM system developers and content providers or subscription agents.

Analysis

ERM systems have a number of data elements that make them an ideal source for advanced data analysis. They contain or have access to the knowledgebase of titles, links, embargo periods and coverage dates for all licensed and unlicensed ejournal content available to the library. Some ERM systems have contain cost data provided by the acquisitions system from an integrated library system or loaded through interfaces. Combined, all of this data can serve as the input for advanced analytical tools. Libraries need these tools to inform decisions on subscription renewals, aggregation and publisher-direct cost/benefit comparisons and as evidence for challenging the principles of title bundling—particularly with the bundled ejournal packages. Data-informed analysis tools could provide libraries with concrete evidence of the use pattern within packages and a detailed understanding of the value for money for the little-used titles within a package.

Standard statistical methods can provide valuable tools in the analysis of the patterns of use

Table 1. Core data elements for automation of administrative tasks

Administrative Function	Identifiers	Request or Report (Client)	Response (Server)
IP registration	Institution identifier Resource identifier	IP addresses	Confirmation
Activation	Institution identifier Resource identifier	Activation request	Confirmation
Renewal	Institution identifier Resource identifier	Renewal request	Confirmation
Incident report	Institution identifier Resource identifier	Incident description	Confirmation
License review	Institution identifier Resource identifier	License request	License data

within a package. The spread of usage of journals within a package can be analyzed by the following statistical measures:

- **Mean** to measure average usage within a collection
- **Median** to identify the middle point in usage within a collection
- **Skewness** to identify asymmetry of the distribution of usage values within a collection

Quantile analysis to group journals into one hundred bins (percentiles) or ten bins (deciles) where journals are arranged from least usage to highest usage and then divided into the bins. This arrangement facilitates histogram views and percentage of usage calculation.

Using these measures, libraries could understand how much on average resources are used (mean), the abstract distribution of usage within a package (median) and test for unequal distribution of usage with a package (skewness and quantile analysis). These latter tools can provide perhaps the most revealing analysis of distribution of usage. Quantile analysis can be used to expose unequal distribution of usage within a package. For example, if a set of journals are arranged in equal groups of deciles from least usage to highest usage, it possible to quickly calculate and analyze the share percentage of each decile. If usage is highly unequal, then the greatest share of total usage will be in the top deciles. In extreme cases, this analysis will show that a few of the most highly used journals comprise the majority of total usage within a package. To illustrate the potential usefulness of this analysis, sample usage data from three ejournal collections licensed by an ARL library were analyzed using the Stata statistical analysis tool. See Tables 2-4.

In the case of the American Chemical Society, the top decile comprises 30.11% of the total usage—under a third. For the Ovid journals the share of the top decile is 46.72%—just under

Table 2. American Chemical Society: Quantile analysis of 2006 usage

American Chemical Society, 2006 Usage		
Quantile Group	Quantile	Share
1	51.00	0.48%
2	83.00	1.02%
3	152.00	2.06%
4	281.00	3.74%
5	426.00	4.05%
6	440.00	6.26%
7	561.00	7.46%
8	1127.00	13.24%
9	2687.00	31.57%
10		30.11%

Table 3. Ovid journals: Quantile analysis of 2006 usage

Ovid Journals - Lippincott Williams & Wilkins, 2006 Usage		
Quantile Group	Quantile	Share
1	2.00	0.45%
2	4.00	0.80%
3	8.00	2.03%
4	12.00	3.10%
5	17.00	3.16%
6	25.00	5.58%
7	37.00	8.39%
8	53.00	11.82%
9	88.00	17.95%
10		46.72%

half. The most extreme case is Science Direct where 68.33% of total usage (approaching three quarters) is accounted for by the top ten percent of the journals.

Skewness is simply a statistical description of the curve that describes the usage. Again, if a set of journals are arranged in deciles and a graph of the usage is produced, a highly unequal distribution

Table 4. Science Direct: Quantile analysis of 2006 usage

Elsevier – Science Direct, 2006 Usage		
Quantile Group	Quantile	Share
1	4.00	0.09%
2	12.00	0.37%
3	22.00	0.79%
4	37.00	1.32%
5	60.00	2.24%
6	88.00	3.27%
7	125.00	4.69%
8	199.00	7.34%
9	341.00	11.55%
10		68.33%

of usage will show a highly negative skew—that is most of the usage will be crowded within the top deciles. This provides an easily comparable measure of the inequality of usage distribution among packages. A gradually rising curve that does not deviate significantly from the median value would demonstrate a more even distribution of usage among journals and an extremely low skewness score would be assigned. See Table 5 for mean, spread of usage for journals within the package and skewness analysis for the same packages analyzed above.

These data show that there is tremendous variation in usage of journals within a package and the distribution of usage within the deciles can be highly unequal. As an analytical tool, these measures could provide electronic resource management staff a concrete measure of the true usage of bundled journal packages.

Collection Analysis Tools

The utility of ERM systems is expanded dramatically when collection analysis tools are present. The most useful tools and candidates for new functional requirements are:

Cost-Per-Use Analysis

When cost figures are available to the ERM system, the ERM system can use the payment data to support electronic resource collection analysis functions—especially cost-per-use figures. For example, where title-level usage data is stored in the ERM system, payments for those titles stored on the system can be used to calculate cost-per-use figures for each. Those same usage and payment figures can then be combined to calculate average resource- or package-level costs-per-use. This would allow libraries to make meaningful comparisons across content platforms offering similar content. The goal of these calculations is typically not to determine extremely high or low cost amounts, rather it is to provide concrete cost figures at the use level for reporting to faculty, staff, funders, selectors or other analysts of the relative cost of the library's licensed resources (Fons & Jewell, in press).

Table 5. Statistical summary for sample packages

Package	Mean	Smallest Usage Count	Largest Usage Count	Skewness Score
American Chemical Society, 2006 Usage	745.6071	20	3337	1.636924
Ovid Journals - Lippincott Williams & Wilkins, 2006 Usage	37.98857	1	352	2.790133
Elsevier – Science Direct, 2006 Usage	221.7717	0	56811	25.14667

Overlap Analysis With Cost-Per-Use Analysis

Where packages contain identical titles, it is useful to understand the degree to which titles overlap and the holdings ranges overlap. When identifying candidates for selection review, it is useful to understand the degree to which titles are available in other packages. Overlap analysis tools should generate percentages for unambiguous analysis. Where possible, resource-level cost-per-use figures should be included to provide a value-for-money dimension. Relative cost-per-use can be a valuable tool in understanding which of multiple resources provides the maximum value for money spent.

Usage Statistics Harvesting

The development of the Standardized Usage Statistics Harvesting Initiative (SUSHI) or Z39.93 standard at last provides libraries with an efficient method for gathering usage statistics across all of their COUNTER-compliant content providers, and thereby to support and streamline these kinds of analyses. SUSHI harvesting capability should be a baseline functional requirement for all ERM systems. In addition to cost and usage data, future ERM systems should have access to bibliographic data elements like subject and publisher to provide the full range of analysis tools (Fons & Jewell, in press).

Acquisitions Data

As previously discussed in the section on cost-per-use analysis, acquisitions data can be useful in the ERM context. In the ERM system, acquisitions data can support cost analysis and a set of use cases related to supporting the electronic resource lifecycle. These include payment verification for resources that have been reported as unavailable by users and the relative cost at the journal level for aggregated journals and publisher-direct subscriptions.

The most significant challenge to making acquisitions data available to the ERM system is the location of the acquisitions system of record for the institution. The majority of ERM systems are offered as parallel applications to the ILS. Where the acquisitions and ERM systems are built on the same platform, it possible to have direct access to the cost data described above. Where these systems exist in parallel there are no existing standards for the automated exchange of cost data. The Acquisitions Interoperability Subcommittee of the DLF's ERMI phase II project has identified the core data elements for exchange between systems (Digital Library Federation, Acquisitions Interoperability Subcommittee, 2007). The challenge for ERM system developers is to build interfaces to acquisitions systems to import that data. The ideal application would allow requests carrying the appropriate institutional credentials and specific resource identifiers. The return data would follow an industry standard for processing into the ERM system. Until such a model can be developed, ERM systems should accept data in proprietary formats from a variety of sources.

Consortium Requirements

Managing electronic resources that are available through the library's consortial memberships has become an important requirement for ERM systems. Both at the library and the consortial level, it is important to track these components:

- **View of consortial (shared) resources.** Here it is critical to track the license terms as they apply to each member of the consortium. Libraries need to understand the terms and conditions that apply to the use of the shared resources and to what extent they can share the resources with their extended user community.
- **View of library-specific resources.** In a system that tracks consortial resources it must be possible to filter searches and views

to the resources that are made available exclusively through the library's funds.

- **Proposed and trialed resources.** Libraries in consortia want a mechanism to publish resources that are under consideration for purchase. A feedback mechanism for each library's purchase preference is a useful component of this feature.

Libraries have pursued consortial arrangements because of the perception that the buying power of a collection of libraries offers a wider range of resources than could be acquired by each library acting independently. These arrangements have allowed libraries to expand their resources through the "big deal" from resources that they license directly to resources that they license collectively and to resources that are available outside of their specific subscriptions, but are available through the consortial configuration. These resources that are not owned directly, but are available for use through consortial negotiations are not tracked well in current ERM systems. The requirements above combine to provide a rich area for improvement with next-generation ERM systems.

PATRON AND PUBLIC SERVICES NEEDS

Current ERM systems have been designed to support the acquisitions workflow, collection analysis and on-going management of electronic resources. However, the need for a tool for public services staff in supporting electronic resources for library patrons and for the library patrons themselves remains significant. Library public services staff frequently support inquiries about the current status of and access parameters of electronic resources. The ERM system is designed to store information about resource status, incident status and the specific terms and conditions for use. This information should be exposed at all points of description and access. More importantly, it is not uncommon for licenses to require the library's best efforts to express the terms and conditions to the end user. Therefore, all public points of access should display:

Terms and Conditions of Use

Perhaps the most critical data for public services staff. The ability for public services staff to consult an easily-accessible interface that describes the terms and conditions such as authorized categories of users and terms of core activities like interlibrary loan allows faster resolution of access problems and rapid resolution of patron inquiries.

Resource Availability and Advisory, With Forecast for Problem Resolution When System Outage is Ongoing

When resources are not available because of scheduled outage, unscheduled outages or administrative error, it is critical for public services staff to be able to communicate the current status of the issue to library patrons and to have a resource to consult when library patrons inquire about the status of a resource. The public display component of the ERM system is the ideal location for this information. Coupling these displays with the incident reporting functionality described above would maximize efficiency within the system.

The advisory component of the public display would allow the library to go beyond the simple service outage notification feature. The advisory component would also allow the library to promote some aspect of the resource that might be relevant to the moment or to broadcast new content sponsored by the library or library consortium. For example, the library could promote the recent addition of new titles or other enhanced content and to provide credit to the funding agency.

Resource Scope/Description

As with appropriate resource selection where there are multiple resource options, a scope note displaying at the point of discovery or access, the ERM system becomes both the system of record for all metadata about a resource and a reference tool for library patrons. Resource scope notes and general description has the potential to help a user determine the type of resource being accessed (journal collection, article database, index, etc.). It can also help the user determine the depth of treatment of topics, for example general knowledge/multidisciplinary or specialized resource.

Technical Requirements for Access

As Web browsers mature and incorporate helper applications, this component is less critical than it has been in the past. However, the broadcast of technical requirements for access can be useful for specialized databases where specific helper applications are required for file types included in the resource.

The advantage of including information from the ERM system in public access applications extends beyond the description of access terms and resource descriptions. It also provides the library with the opportunity to centralize all information about the electronic resource including resource features, enhancements, and library value-adds and library sponsorship of research-related content.

Discovery Services Platform, Link Resolver and Metasearch Views

The value of ERM data in public views is not restricted to the online public access catalog and A-Z lists of resources and journals. It extends to external points of access such as the discovery services platform (Encore and Primo are examples), link resolver and metasearch environment. Library patrons accessing licensed content should

have a clear understanding of access rights and restrictions as well as relevant administrative data describing the nature and availability of the desired content. Particular attention should be paid to providing information about the technical requirements for full text access to content. This includes browser versions required and suggestions on secondary applications required for accessing content. All of this data should be available in the ERM system. Where the ERM system and the link resolver share the same platform, these linkages should be built in. Where the systems do not, interoperability methods should be developed between systems to allow the real-time request for the appropriate data elements.

Exposing ERM data to public interfaces share some of the same challenges that we saw in making cost data available to the ERM system. The ERM system often does not share the same platform as the public interfaces and no standards exist for the query and supply of the data elements identified previously. The development of an industry-standard model for the request of this data is a positive direction for the development of the next generation of ERM systems.

CONCLUSION

The rapid development and implementation of ERM systems in the library marketplace shows that ERM systems are important components of the contemporary library management toolset. ERM systems were important enough to libraries that they evolved from locally developed systems to commercial products sold by commercial software vendors. However, ERM systems must evolve to provide features beyond those provided by the first-generation commercial ERM systems. The SUSHI standard demonstrates that it is not only possible, but highly desirable, to develop new standards to bring greater efficiency to electronic resource management. As SUSHI used Web services technology, that same technology could be used to bring new efficiencies to routine administrative tasks such as IP registration, activation, renewal, incident reporting and license review. Data standards for license data will further facilitate those interfaces. Standard statistical techniques should be applied to the analysis of ejournal packages to give electronic resource professionals the tools they need to make informed decisions about electronic resource purchases and the quantitative analysis data required to successfully negotiate with electronic resource providers. And finally, new technologies and intra-industry cooperation should be sought for the sharing of ERM data with the critical public interfaces. In all, there is much room for growth in electronic resource management systems and their profiles as a critical tool for professional management of the library's most critical resources will continue to grow.

REFERENCES

Chandler, A., & Jewell, T. D. (2006) Standards – Libraries, data providers and SUSHI: The standardized usage statistics harvesting initiative. *Against the Grain, 18*(2), 82-3.

DLF Electronic Resource Management Initiative, Phase II, Acquisitions Interoperability Subcommittee (2007). White paper on interoperability between acquisitions modules of integrated library systems and electronic resource management systems: A draft for comment. Retrieved November 23, 2007, from http://www.haverford.edu/library/DLF_ERMI2/ACQ_ERMS_white_paper.pdf

Duranceau, E. F. (2004). Electronic resource management systems from ILS vendors. *Against the Grain, 16*(4), 91-94.

Fons, T. & Grover, D. (2004). The innovative electronic resource management system: A development partnership. *Serials Review, 30*(2), 110-116.

Fons, T. & Jewell, T. D. (in press). Envisioning the future of ERM systems—NASIG 2006 Proceedings. *The Serials Librarian.*

Jewell, T. D. (2001). *Selection and presentation of commercially available electronic resources: Issues and practices.* Washington, D.C.: Digital Library Federation.

Jewell, T. D. et al. (2004). Electronic resource management: Report of the DLF electronic resource management initiative. Retrieved November 23, 2007, from http://www.diglib.org/pubs/dlf102/ERMFINAL.pdf

NISO, License Expression Working Group (n.d.). Retrieved November 23, 2007, from http://www.niso.org/committees/License_Expression/LicenseEx_comm.html

Tull, L., Crum, J., Davis, T., & Strader, C. R. (2005). Integrating and streamlining electronic resources workflows via innovative's electronic resource management. *The Serials Librarian, 47*(4), 103-124.

Chapter XXI
In the Eye of the Storm:
ERM Systems are Guiding Libraries' Future

Ted Koppel
Ex Libris Inc, USA

INTRODUCTION

Electronic resource management (ERM), as a tool for library management, grows in importance every day. The ERM industry has matured greatly over the past decade. Just ten years ago, the first journals began to be published on the Web in significant volume; by 2007, many smaller colleges and some large research libraries have moved to complete or nearly complete electronic-only access (Ives, 2006). The Association of Research Libraries reports that the average ARL research library now spends over 31% of its materials budget on electronic resources, with a large proportion of these libraries spending more than 50% of their materials budget on electronic resources (Kyrillidou & Young, 2006).

In a relatively short period of time, libraries have struggled to redesign not just the nitty-gritty of policies, procedures, systems for managing their resources, but especially their roles in the information delivery process, to meet the demands and opportunities of a digital landscape for information seeking and research. Changes

have been revolutionary, but libraries and publishers have adjusted rapidly and there are now systems, best practices documents, and evolving standards on which to build future enhancements Libraries are working with less chaos and more confidence in managing e-resources. But this calm is deceptive—libraries are in the eye of the growing storm that will soon reveal more revolutionary change.

In this chapter, we will examine the most significant of these changes, show how they present challenges for libraries, and suggest how electronic resource management systems (ERMs) could evolve to help libraries meet these challenges. We conclude that ERMs represent just a step towards the "new ILS" (integrated library system)—that the next "heart" of library management will be something past the ERM, and believe that it is imperative that libraries work carefully to push ERM system development in ways that support and advance, rather than undercut, the libraries' missions.

This chapter will examine following major trends in electronic resource management and look at critical opportunities for ERM system use and development in each area:

- Ubiquity of high speed communication platforms and inexpensive mass storage
- Changes in user behavior / increased competition from non library search engines and content sources, user-centric design; the need to get metadata where users are, rather than asking them to come to library Web sites or tools.
- Disintegration of the ILS: End of ILS as the gateway/gatekeeper. The case for integration and/or interoperability; and incorporation of user-generated content in end-user tools and services.
- Evolving pricing and access models, including changing fortunes of the Big Deal and the associated practical and philosophical issues; open access; usage-based pricing; and cost-effectiveness measures for e-resources, pay per view.
- Intellectual property struggle: Digital rights management models, licensing concerns and trends
- Technical, as well as philosophical archiving issues, including the development of third party cooperative archiving

In addressing these key trends in e-resource management, we will look at how the emergence of local and then commercial ERM systems relate to these trends, and how the mission of the ERM system has expanded to encompass many library functions (e.g., serials control, acquisitions, license metadata storage). We will examine the differing expectations for ERM systems from various players in the market (libraries, publishers, and ERM system vendors) and how "mission creep" should be addressed, including the specter of ERM systems as digital rights management delivery mechanism.

RECENT MAJOR TRENDS IN ELECTRONIC RESOURCE MANAGEMENT

Hardware and Software Changes

Three major hardware and software advancements during the last ten years have enabled the library world to rapidly adapt to electronic resources are the primary means of information delivery to their constituencies. Lacking any of these three, electronic resources would not have been able to flourish to the extent that they have, but the late 1990's and early 2000's delivered a "perfect storm" of technological advancement.

Assisted by the 1996 U.S. Telecommunications Act that continued deregulation of communications companies, a number of telephone, cable, and other participants in the telecom industry began an orgy of fiber-optic data line construction across the United States (and indeed, the rest of the world participated as well). Millions of miles of "dark fiber" (referring to excess capacity in a carrier's fiber optic lines) were buried in anticipation of future use. Telephone companies developed ambitious business plans to carry huge amounts of data, based on predictions of data transmission demand multiplying for years.

The dot-com bust (2000-2001) resulted in a huge oversupply of fiber data carrying capacity. Lack of demand for data transmission, the oversupply of capacity, and advances in multiplexing and data communications hardware combined to make high-speed data transmission extremely inexpensive. Colleges and universities rewired their campuses to take advantage of new, faster data transmission. New offerings for the end-user consumer, such as cable modems, DSL, and broadband Internet service, brought high speed data to almost all locations in the United States. A 2004 map showed almost the entire United States, with the exception of some small areas in northern Alaska and northwestern Utah, having access to at least one high speed or broadband provider.

Some areas of the country have access to as many as four providers (High Speed, 2004).

Inexpensive mass storage is a second factor contributing to the "perfect storm" of technological change in the last decade. Server hard disk drives tumbled in price. Advances in technology allowed for storage capacities to become exponentially larger while costing less and less. Fault tolerance (or 100% uptime) guaranteed by RAID (redundant array of inexpensive disks) became affordable. Data storage—formerly a major and limiting cost to providing large scale information retrieval—became cheap and commoditized. Using inexpensive storage, content providers were better able to make the economic case for investing in, publishing, and delivering their products electronically.

Perhaps the most important technological factor enabling electronic resources as an industry to succeed was the creation and broad acceptance of a common platform for computers of all types—the Web browser. Prior to the Web browser, information retrieval was most often done using a line-by-line (telnet) interface, or, in some cases, with a dedicated client that handled communication with a content provider's server.

Netscape 1.0 was released in late 1994, and Internet Explorer in early 1995. By version 4 (1997-1998)—after several software revisions and technology enhancements—Web browsing became an integral part of our environment. Additional browsers—both for Windows and for different hardware platforms—were developed. Although minor differences between the browsers remain even in 2007, Web browsing as a platform for the delivery of information services is a completely accepted and standard means of access. Line-based information retrieval is virtually nonexistent at this time, and very few client-based systems still exist.

User Behavior and Expectations

Much has been written concerning the ways that end users approach the Web in order to find in-

formation. To the dismay of many in the library world, library catalogs are used (as the starting point of information gathering) by only 3% of information seekers (OCLC, 2005). Search engines (Google and others) are the launching point for 86% of all queries. Some groups in the library world have looked inward, trying to understand where and why libraries have failed to be relevant in the information delivery process. Other groups have taken a defensive stance, castigating Google and its brethren as part of the "evil empire" and casting aspersions as to the completeness and quality of search engine retrieval. However, general consensus has evolved in the last year or two to be as follows: first, the large search engines are here to stay—they are not going to disappear, and therefore let us coopt them or work with the, rather than fight them. Second, the success of search engines such as Google shows that their approach is doing something right, and therefore the library world may be able to learn something from it.

Internet users have become used to entering their search in a single box on an uncrowded screen. They expect a search that will bring back "some" results. They expect that the search results will be ranked and presented in an order that reflects relevance to their search argument. Users do not want to be bothered with prequalifying sets or completing a screen full of search parameters—they want to enter a simple argument and rapidly receive useful results. Many users draw no distinction between the 8 billion pages that are indexed and free on Google and the multitude of expensive electronic products that are paid for and provided by the library.

Further, users are no longer willing to go into a library to retrieve the information they need. The personal computer workstation acts as an enabler—the user feels that he should be able to find the information he needs whether he is at home, in the classroom, on the beach, or in a restaurant. Information (and access to that information) is moving from the library to the user.

From a service delivery standpoint, the library has a greater burden, because it may not even see its users. The users, however, have an expectation that the library will server them.

Disintegration of the ILS

The integrated library system—for decades the way that library automation systems were designed and delivered—is in the process of falling apart. Early library automation practice was for one systems vendor to provide for the entire library's management needs—one unified set of modules controlled circulation, an OPAC, acquisitions, serials control, and sometimes interlibrary loan. This was largely due to the way that the ILS industry evolved—Innovative Interfaces' original product was an acquisitions system, TLC/CARL's was a public access catalog, NOTIS' was a circulation system, etc.

The move towards disintegration accelerated in the early 2000's as a result of three different trends. First, a number of systems vendors began to develop automation products that were agnostic—that is, they were designed to work with, and complement another vendor's ILS system. Examples include ExLibris' SFX link resolver and MetaLib metasearch module, TLC's Online Selection and Acquisitions (Web-based acquisitions service), TLC's AuthorityWorks (Web-based authority control for any ILS), AquaBrowser (an OPAC graphic front-end), and to some degree resource sharing systems such as SirsiDynix's URSA (Universal Resource Sharing Application) and Innovative Interface's INNReach. Each of these systems was designed with interoperability in mind. As a result of this trend, libraries are able to choose the "best of breed" in each different functional area with the (not-always-realized) expectation that they will all work together.

A second trend pushing the disintegration of the ILS is the technical maturity and sophistication of libraries and library staff. Twenty years ago, library automation was considered something

akin to magic. In contrast to that era, powerful personal computers are used by (and understood by) hundreds of millions of users. Network management is no longer mystical when consumers and library users can install their own home routers and wireless networks. Graphic user interfaces are so ubiquitous—almost every application uses one—that libraries and users alike have little patience for a poorly designed interface. Computing, Web page development and management, and similar skills are far more accessible than ever before. As a result, libraries feel that they can act as their own systems integrators instead of purchasing services and software from a single vendor.

The third trend, as mentioned earlier and elsewhere in this book, was the rise of e-products as a major service delivered by the library. Library processes are changing (and will continue to do so) as the electronic products are purchased by libraries in greater numbers. The line between serials acquisitions, monographic acquisitions, and electronic resource processing is becoming increasingly blurry. Traditional technical processing will evolve as physical items become a smaller percentage of library procurement and electronic products a much larger proportion.

Pricing

Pricing of electronic products continues to be controversial. The mission of libraries is to collect and distribute information in whatever form it takes, and make it available to the libraries' clientele. Academic and research libraries need to subscribe to a broad range of journals to fulfill their mission. Publishers are, of course, aware of the library's mission, and have for years—long before the advent of electronic resources—priced their journals at rates considered exorbitant by libraries. As electronic resources consume a larger percentage of a library's materials budget, publishers have tried to defend their subscription base by tying access to an e-journal to the continued subscription of a paper journal, and vice versa. Further, publishers introduced the concept of the "Big Deal" in which a library would receive large portions of a publisher's electronic journal output in exchange for severe limitations on that library's ability to manage its collection and cancel titles that it no longer needs. Various models of the "Big Deal" exist within today's electronic product market, each with different bundles of e-products and with different terms that affect the library.

Many libraries are satisfied with "Big Deal" pricing, because it allows them to continue to receive (and in many cases, expand the number of) journals—paper and electronic—in their collection. Other libraries have opted away from the "Big Deal" because they felt publisher product bundling ran counter to the library's responsibility to purchase wisely only those titles that were consistent with the university's curriculum. Further, restrictions on Big Deal titles (e.g., restricting interlibrary loan) prevent a library from fulfilling its traditional sharing role in the academic community.

Partially in reaction to the "Big Deal," but largely to apply some rationality to electron journal pricing, several different no-cost or low-cost alternatives have been started. The Public Library of Science (www.plos.org) "is a nonprofit organization of scientists and physicians committed to making the world's scientific and medical literature a freely available public resource." PLoS, a private, nonprofit organization, makes journals freely available online without use or distribution restrictions. In a similar way, the Directory of Open Access Journals (www.doaj.org) lists and links to almost 3000 electronic journals that are freely available for use.

Open access publishing is very much an evolving phenomenon in academia. Some open access models required that the articles' authors pay a certain amount in order to have their articles peer reviewed and made available to the public. PLoS, for example, charges the author $2500 per article

submitted. Other open access models charge nothing (because of external funding support) or are hybrids.

Another approach to high electronic resource product pricing is the "pay per use" or "pay per view" model, in which article citation information is made freely available. A user wishing to use a particular full text resource must pay an a'la-carte price for the article; the price is usually set by the publisher. Financial arrangements can be made between the library and the publisher for more efficient user interaction. Pay per view's appeal to the library is clear—the library need not subscribe to a journal—the end user pays for what he wants. Even in cases where libraries subsidize article purchases, there is the assumption that the single-article purchase prices will not total the amount that a subscription would have cost.

Pay-per-use has its disadvantages as well. Besides being expensive, most pay-per-use library models deliver the document to the one person who requested it. No one else; least of all the library, benefits from the purchase. The articles are not collected or shared; there is no net addition to the library's collection on behalf of future users.

Intellectual Property

Intellectual property and digital rights management in the era of electronic resources management is increasingly complex as well. Although many publishers are attempting to secure the reprint and resale from their authors, this is by no means common and successful across the industry. Publishers and aggregators make available what they are legally allowed to deliver, which can make for inconsistent or spotty delivery of full text of certain publications. This becomes particularly acute in the aggregation and delivery of backfiles of older material, because publishers a decade or two ago did not attempt to secure rights to electronic publication and distribution. Some publishers have gone back to article authors to retroactively secure those rights, while others have not.

Most ERMs do not have a role to play in the protection or delivery if intellectually property other than to act as a higher-level gateway to the material itself. On an administrative level, an ERM system may chose to store information about the level of completeness of a title's (or package's) full text delivery, but this has not yet become a major factor in ERM user.

In some areas, the library appears to be blurring the line between an ERM system and a DRM (digital rights management) system. DRM systems concern themselves primarily with digital objects, their description, and their rules for use. Generally DRM system-manage their data on an object level, since each object (a film clip, sound bite, or perhaps a photograph) will have distinct metadata differences from one another. However, most ERM systems can be, with a little imagination, made applicable to management of digital sets as well as e-journals and e-books. After all, sets of digital objects are often "packaged" in a similar way as e-journals. Therefore, DRM expectations will be imputed onto ERM systems, causing them to begin to change.

Perpetual Access and Archiving

Libraries worry that e-books or e-journals may disappear from availability over time. This may be because a publisher or aggregator loses the rights to distribute that title, or it may because the title is no longer economically viable, for example. In any case, several different alternatives have arisen to attempt to ensure that electronic journals continue exist and be available in an online form even after the publisher may have ceased publishing the title.

Note that in this chapter we are *not* discussing perpetual access to titles that the library may have subscribed to but for which they have dropped the subscription. That situation is a contractual/legal one which may allow the library ongoing access to the years for which it was a subscriber. This discussion is about those titles which are no longer

being published, where otherwise access would be permanently denied.

Several approaches have developed to archive electronic manifestations of journals. LOCKSS (for "Lots of copies keep stuff safe") is open source software that provides librarians with an easy and inexpensive way to collect, store, preserve, and provide access to their own, local copy of authorized content they purchase. LOCKSS, as the name implies, is distributed (local) software that enables libraries to make immediate and contemporaneous copies for their own use, and maintain those collections ad infinitum. Further cooperative agreements between LOCKSS members can allow distributed collecting and shared use of LOCKSS-stored materials. LOCKSS libraries are audited to ensure that appropriate publisher permission has been received and that usage and distribution rules are being followed.

Another archiving-preservation approach has been developed by JSTOR (www.jstor.org). JSTOR is a not-for-profit organization with a dual mission to create and maintain a trusted archive of important scholarly journals, and to provide access to these journals as widely as possible. JSTOR offers researchers the ability to retrieve high-resolution, scanned images of journal issues and pages as they were originally designed, printed, and illustrated. JSTOR scans and archivally stores scholarly journals in various collections (arts and sciences, health and general science, biological science, etc.). Citations are indexed and searchable from within the JSTOR interface; libraries can access the journals for which they have contracted. JSTOR's collection and coverage are continually growing; however, their selection criteria call for complete (or near-complete) journal runs.

Portico, a more recent entrant in the preservation field, performs a similar task. From the Portico Web page: "The Portico service offers a permanent archive of electronic scholarly journals, thereby providing protection against the potential loss of access to e-literature integral to a library's collection." Portico provides all libraries supporting the archive with campus-wide access to archived content when specific trigger events occur, and when titles are no longer available from the publisher or other source. Trigger events include:

- A publisher stops operations
- A publisher ceases to publish a title
- A publisher no longer offers back issues
- Upon catastrophic and sustained failure of a publisher's delivery platform

Portico also provides a reliable means to secure perpetual access, if participating publishers choose to designate Portico as a provider of post-cancellation access. In addition, select librarians at participating libraries are granted password-controlled access for verification and audit purposes only.

Other preservation and archival centers exist, and still other new ones are in formation. Although not all will survive the economic tests being demanded of a perpetual archive, one can assume that many will, and that there will be consistent availability of titles that would otherwise have disappeared for various reasons.

LOOKING TO THE FUTURE

This concluding chapter will try and predict the future of electronic resources management:

1. More demands for interoperability between systems of all types: ERM systems are in some ways a catalyst for interoperability in the future. They need to share data with computers and servers of all types; this will become increasingly more of a demand as time goes on. Therefore, it is possible to foresee interoperability requirements with:
   a. **Publishers:** In addition to SUSHI and license expressions, the ability for publishers to announce uptime and downtime (in real time). Also, the ability for libraries to directly update the publishers with new or changed IP addresses
   b. **Agents:** The ability for serials subscription agents' servers to directly download payment and pricing information from their servers to the libraries' ERM systems for immediate updating
   c. **ILS:** Direct data exchange between libraries' ERM systems and their ILS software, whether or not they are supplied by the same company. Specifically, companies that try to sell an integrated ERM-ILS solution will find themselves losing in the marketplace.
   d. Direct interaction between ERMs, accounts payable, and other budget management systems
   e. Interoperability with third party systems such as copyright agencies and rights management concerns, to ensure that copyright fees are assessed and collected in a consistent way
2. More pressure on subscription agents to add value to the ERM process
   a. Subscription agents have had less of a role as the number of paper subscriptions has diminished and the number of e-subscriptions has increased. Aggregation and billing services are somewhat less in demand than previously.
   b. As a result, subscription agents will need to (and are trying to!) find a value-add role in the e-product supply chain. These new roles may include:
      i. Billing aggregators
      ii. Statistics collection and distribution aggregators using SUSHI or other mechanisms
      iii. License collection aggregators
      iv. Data feeds to ERM systems
      v. Full text or document delivery purveyors

3. Opportunities for niche players to find a role in the ERM process

   a. As the ERM industry matures, opportunities will arise for niche players to develop businesses around management areas that are not handled by any parties. An early example can be seen in ScholarlyStats, who have developed a business in collection, normalization, and repackaging of statistical data. Perhaps this is not a glamorous area, but it is an important one and libraries are willing to pay for the high quality output.

   b. Some of 'enhanced MARC record' supply (made available by ExLibris' MARCit and Serials Solutions) are examples of niche products for which there is a market and a supplier, It is difficult to predict what the next one(s) will be, but it is safe to assume that there will be places in the market for a number of different services.

4. Pricing transparency from vendors

   a. ERM systems provide a hitherto unavailable degree of incisive and analytical information about usage, duplication, and pricing of the resources that they are purchasing. As libraries become savvy to the power of, and begin to use these new tools to affect their subscription negotiations, it is possible that we will see the following:

      i. For vendors of aggregated packages and some selected packages: truth in pricing. Prices that show value.

      ii. Less padding of packages with low-use and low-value titles, and real pricing for valuable titles.

      iii. Ultimately, potentially the breakup of the aggregated package and a move towards per-title pricing where the customer, not the vendor, makes the choice.

5. Vastly increased use of pay-per-view pricing

   a. As the traditional aggregator model ceases to exist, libraries will still want occasional access to titles that do not meet their criteria for ongoing subscriptions. Pay-per-view, now a very small percentage of electronic resources use, will grow as an alternative means of e-resource delivery.

6. A slow move towards rational and consistent copyright and licensing terms, systematically applied across academic libraries. Rather than each publisher or aggregator pushing its own idiosyncratic and inconsistent set of copyright rules and fees to the market, there will be movement towards flattening and rationalizing these terms across the industry. This will come as a result of customer pressure and negotiation with publishers.

7. New standards for new functions. We have already seen new standards such as SUSHI and the (nascent) License Expression Working Group. As the ERM industry matures and interoperability (see above) becomes more important, additional standards will be needed:

   a. Acquisitions data exchange format (for sharing of fund, invoice, cost, price, and other information)

   b. Unique identifiers (across the industry) for packages and collections

   c. A protocol for the exchange of uptime and downtime information

   d. A protocol for the delivery of IP address changes from library to vendor

   e. A pay-per-view data sharing protocol for PPV transactions

8. The ERM (and the novel concept of ERAMS) will cease to exist. ERMs and ERAMS take too narrow a view of library resources, in that they deprecate the value of paper and other nonelectronic resources. The phrase: "Electronic Resource Access and Manage-

ment Systems" (or ERAMS) is attributed to Martha Whittaker, then of Serials Solutions, by Lorcan Dempsey in his blog (Dempsey, 2007). The ERM, combined with the disintegration of the traditional ILS and the reshaping of the library around discovery and delivery, will evolve into the RM (that is, generalized resource manager) or perhaps the URM (the universal resource manager). The "electronic" focus of ERM will stop being a delineator of library function, and become an adjective—one of many categories in the greater world of resource management.

REFERENCES

Dempsey, L. (2007). Lorcan Dempsey's weblog. Retrieved November 23, 2007, from orweblog. oclc.org/archives/001250.html

High Speed Providers by Zip Code (2004). Retrieved November 23, 2007, from www.cable-modem.net/images/coverage_map.gif

Ives, Gary (2006). Transition to E-Journals at Texas A&M University, 1995-2004. *Serials Librarian, 47*(4), 71-78.

Kyrillidou, M., & Young, M. (2006). ARL library trends 2003-04. Retrieved November 23, 2007, from www.arl.org/stats/arlstat/04pub/04intro. html

OCLC Inc. (2005). Perceptions of libraries and information resources: A report to the OCLC membership. Retrieved November 23, 2007, from www.oclc.org/reports/pdfs/Percept_all.pdf

Compilation of References

17 U.S.C. §107-122 (2001 & Supp. 2005).

21st Century Department of Justice Appropriations Authorization Act. (2002). Retrieved November 17, 2007, from http://www.copyright.gov/legislation/pl107-273.html

Alabama Commission on Higher Education (2006, December 12). NAAL index. Retrieved November 12, 2007, from http://www.ache.state.al.us/NAAL/

Alan, R. (2002). Keeping track of electronic resources to keep them on track. Retrieved November 22, 2007, from http://www.library.cornell.edu/cts/elicensestudy/pennstate/PSUNASIGPresentation2002.ppt

Albitz, R. S. (2002). Electronic resource librarians in academic libraries: A position announcement analysis, 1996-2001. *Portal: Libraries and the Academy, 2*(4), 589-600.

ALCTS (2004, December). LC announces TrackER software availability and specifications. *ALCTS Newsletter Online, 15*, 6. Retrieved November 22, 2007, from http://www.ala.org/ala/alcts/alctspubs/alctsnewsletter/v15n6/tracker.htm

Alford, D. E. (2002). Negotiating and analyzing electronic license agreements. *Law Library Journal, 94*, 621-644.

Alford, L. (2000). *The impact of digital resources on organization and management of collection development and acquisitions.* Paper presented at the IFLA Conference Proceedings, Jerusalem, Israel. Retrieved November 12, 2007, from http://www.ifla.org/IV/ifla66/papers/168-180e.htm

Allgood, J.E. (2006). Friend or foe?—Digital resources within library collections. *Against the Grain, 18*(2), 24-30.

Allison, D., & McNeil, B. (2000). Database selection: One size does not fit all. *College & Research Libraries, 61*(1), 56.

American Association of Law Libraries (2001). Competencies of law librarianship. Retrieved November 17, 2007, from http://www.aallnet.org/prodev/competencies.asp

American Association of Law Libraries (2004). Principles for licensing electronic resources. Retrieved November 17, 2007, from http://www.aallnet.org/committee/reports/LicensingPrinciplesElecResources.pdf

American Association of Law Libraries, American Library Association, Association of Academic Health Sciences Libraries, Association of Research Libraries, Medical Library Association, Special Libraries Association (1997). Principles for licensing electronic resources. Retrieved November 21, 2007, from http://www.arl.org/sc/licensing/licprinciples.shtml

American Law Institute (1981-2006). *Restatement of the law second, Contracts 2d: As adopted and promulgated by the American Law Institute at Washington, D.C.* St. Paul, MN: American Law Institute Publishers.

American Library Association (2004). Policy concerning confidentiality of personally identifiable information about library users. Retrieved November 21, 2007, from http://www.ala.org/alaorg/oif/pol_user.html

American Library Association (2005). Draft core competencies. Retrieved November 17, 2007, from http://www.

ala.org/ala/accreditationb/Draft_Core_Competencies_07_05.pdf

American Library Association (2006). UCITA: Impact on libraries. Retrieved November 18, 2007, from http://www.ala.org/ala/washoff/WOissues/copyrightb/ucita/impact.htm

American Library Association (2006). UCITA: UCITA & related legislation in your state. Retrieved November 18, 2007, from http://www.ala.org/ala/washoff/WOissues/copyrightb/ucita/states.htm

Anderson, B. (1999). Web lists or OPACs: Can we have our cake and eat it, too? *Library Computing, 18*(4), 312-316.

Anderson, B., & Hawkins, L. (1996). Development of CONSER cataloguing policies for remote access computer file serials. *The Public-Access Computer Systems Review, 7*(1). Retrieved November 21, 2007, from http://epress.lib.uh.edu/pr/v7/n1/adne7n1.html

Anderson, C. (2004, December). ERUS December 2004 report. Retrieved November 22, 2007, from http://web.simmons.edu/~andersoc/erus/reportdec04.html

Anglo-American cataloguing rules (2nd ed.) (2002). Ottawa: Canadian Library Association, the Chartered Institute of Library and Information Professionals, and the American Library Association.

Antelman, K. (2005). Implementing a serial work in an electronic resources management system. *Serials Librarian, 48*(3/4), 285-288.

Antelman, K., Lynema, E., & Pace, A. K. (2006). Toward a twenty-first century library catalog. *Information Technology and Libraries, 25*(3), 128-139.

Apps, A., & MacIntyre, R. (2006, November 9). Why OpenURL? *D-Lib Magazine, 12*(5).

Arms, C. (1999). Enabling access in digital libraries: A report on a workshop on access management. Retrieved November 21, 2007, from http://www.clir.org/pubs/reports/arms-79/contents.html

Association of Research Libraries (1997). Principles for licensing electronic resources, final draft, July 15, 1997, by the American Association of Law Libraries, the American Library Association, the Association of Academic Health Sciences Libraries, the Association of Research Libraries, the Medical Library Association, and the Special Libraries Association. Retrieved November 17, 2007, from http://www.arl.org/scomm/licensing/principles.html

Association of Research Libraries (2002). Collections and access for the 21st-century scholar: changing roles of research libraries. *ARL: A bimonthly report on research library Issues and actions from ARL, CNI, and SPARC.* 225. Retrieved November 21, 2007, from http://www.arl.org/newsltr/225/index.html

Avram, H.D. (1968). MARC: The first two years. *Library Resources & Technical Services, 12*(3), 245-250.

Awasthi, S., Beardmore, J., Clark, J., Hadridge, P., Madani, H., & Marusic, A., et al. (2005). Five futures for academic medicine. *PLoS Medicine, 2*(7), e207 OP.

Bader, S. A., & Thompson, L. L. (1989). Analyzing in-house journal utilization: An added dimension in decision making. *Bulletin of the Medical Library Association, 77*(2), 216-218.

Baker, G., & Blocker, L. (2005). Electronic resource management systems (ERMS). PowerPoint presentation. Retrieved November 22, 2007, from http://www.lib.utk.edu/~elecser/ts-erms.ppt

Balas, J. L. (2005). Blogging is so last year-now podcasting is hot. *Computers in Libraries, 25*(10), 29.

Balas, J. L. (2006). The "magic" of wireless access in the library. *Computers in Libraries, 26*(3), 32.

Balas, J. L. (2006). What's in their pockets? Mobile electronics. *Computers in Libraries, 26*(4), 32.

Beck, M. (1995). *CONSER cataloging manual: Module 31, Remote access computer file serials.* Washington, D.C.: Library of Congress.

Bednarek-Michalska, B. (2002). Creating a job description for an electronic resources librarian. *Library Management, 23*(8/9), 378-383.

Beile, P. M., & Adams, M. M. (2000). Other duties as assigned: Emerging trends in the academic library job market. *College & Research Libraries, 61*(4), 336-347.

Beit-Arie, & Oren, Caplan, Priscilla, et al. (2001). Linking to the appropriate copy: Report of a DOI-based prototype [Electronic version]. *D-Lib Magazine, 7*(9).

Bellsouth Advertising & Publishing Corp. vs. Donnelley Information Publishing, Inc. 999 F.2d 1436 (11th Cir.). (1993). Retrieved November 17, 2007, from http://www.coolcopyright.com/cases/chp4/bellsouthdonnelley.htm

Bergman, B. (2005). Looking at electronic resources librarians: Is there gender equity within this emerging specialty? *New Library World, 106*(1210/1211), 116-127.

Berkman Center for Internet and Society, Harvard Law School. (2003, January 15). Openlaw site: Eldred v. Ashcroft. Retrieved November 17, 2007, from http://cyber.law.harvard.edu/eldredvreno/

Berners-Lee, T. (1996). The world wide web: Past, present and future. Retrieved November 17, 2007, from http://www.w3.org/People/Berners-Lee/1996/ppf.html

Bertot, J. C., McClure, C. R., & Ryan, J. (2000). *Developing national public library statistics and performance measures for the networked environment: final report* (ERIC Document Reproduction Service No. ED447803). Washington, D.C.: Institute of Museum and Library Services.

Bevis, M. D., & Graham, J. B. (2003). The evolution of an integrated electronic journals collection. *Journal of Academic Librarianship, 24*(2), 115-119.

Bevis, M. D., & McAbee, S. L. (1994). NOTIS as an impetus for change in technical services departmental staffing. *Technical Services Quarterly, 12*(2), 29-43.

Bhatt, J. (2005). Blogging as a tool: Innovative approaches to information access. *Library Hi Tech News Incorporating Online and CD Notes, 22*(9), 28(5).

Bielefield, A., & Cheeseman, L. (1999). *Interpreting and negotiating licensing agreements: A guidebook for the library, research, and teaching professions.* New York: Neal-Schuman Publishers, Inc.

Bjorner, S., & Ardito, S.C. (2003). Online before the Internet: Early pioneers tell their stories [Electronic version]. *Searcher, 11*(6), 36-46.

Black, S. (2006). Bibliographic control of serials. *Serials in libraries: Issues and practices* (pp. 83-102). Westport, CT: Libraries Unlimited.

Blackwell-Synergy (2006). Terms and conditions. Retrieved November 18, 2007, from http://www.blackwell-synergy.com/help?context=terms_and_conditions

Bluh, P. M. (2001). *Managing electronic serials: Essays based on the ALCTS electronic serials institutes, 1997-1999.* Chicago: American Library Association.

Bordeaux, A., Kraemer, A. B., & Sullenger, P. (2005). Making the most of your usage statistics. *The Serials Librarian, 48*(3/4), 295-299.

Boss, R.W. (1989). Current uses of automated systems: A review and status report. In A.P. Trezza (Ed.) *Changing technology: Opportunity and challenge* (pp. 99-102). Boston: G.K. Hall & Co.

Boss, R.W., & Marcum, D.B. (1980, September-October). The library catalog: COM and on-line options. *Library Technology Reports, 16*, 443-527.

Boss, S. C., & Nelson, M. L. (2005). Federated Search Tools: The next step in the quest for one-stop-shopping. *The Reference Librarian,* (91/92), 139-160.

Boston College Libraries (n.d.). ERM database documentation. Retrieved November 22, 2007, from http://www.bc.edu/bc_org/avp_ulib/staff/erm/erm-db

Bothmann, R.L., & Holmberg, M. (2006). *Electronic resources planning and management.* Unpublished electronic survey conducted on ERIL from 27 November to 1 December 2006.

Bourne, C. P., & Bellardo Hahn, T. (2003). *A history of online information services, 1963-1976.* Boston: MIT Press.

Bracke, P. J. (2001). Access to remote electronic resources at the University of Arizona. *Science & Technology Libraries, 20*(2/3), 5-14.

Breeding, M. (2004). The many facets of managing electronic resources. *Computers in libraries.* Retrieved November 14, 2007, from http://www.infotoday.com/cilmag/jan04/breeding.shtml

Breeding, M. (2006). Musings on the state of the ILS in 2006. *Computers in Libraries, 26*(3), 26-28.

Breeding, M. (July, 2006). Strategic development: Sirsi-Dynix and Serials Solutions. *Smart Libraries Newsletter, Library Technology Guides.* Retrieved November 22, 2007, from http://www.librarytechnology.org/ltg-displaytext.pl?RC=12102

Brewer, K., Rozum, B., & Shrode, F. (2004). Developing a database for e-journals that improves both access and management. In D. C. Fowler (Ed.), *E-serials collection management: Transitions, trends, and technicalities* (pp. 253-264). Binghamton, NY: Haworth Information Press.

Briscoe, G., Selden, K., & Nyberg, C. R. (2003). The catalog vs. the home page? Best practices in connecting to online resources. *Law Library Journal, 95*(2), 151-174.

Brisson, R. (1999). Online documentation in library technical services. *Technical Services Quarterly, 16*(3), 1-19.

Brown, J. F., Nelson, J. L., & Wineburgh-Freed, M. (2005). Customized electronic resources management system. *Serials Librarian, 47*(4), 89-102.

Brown, J.F., Nelson, J.L., & Wineburgh-Freed, M. (2005.) Customized electronic resources management system for a multi-library university: Viewpoint from one library. In G. Ives (Ed.), *Electronic journal management systems: Experiences from the field* (pp. 89-102). New York: Haworth Information Press.

Brown, M. E. (1995). By any other name: Accounting for failure in the naming of subject categories. *Library and Information Science Research, 17*(4), 347-385.

Burrows, S. (2006). A review of electronic journal acquisition, management, and use in health sciences libraries. *Journal of the Medical Library Association, 24*(1), 67-74.

Calhoun, K. (2006). The changing nature of the catalog and its integration with other discovery tools. Retrieved November 21, 2007, from http://www.loc.gov/catdir/calhoun-report-final.pdf

California Digital Library (2005). Assessment. Retrieved November 18, 2007, from the California Digital Library Web site: http://www.cdlib.org/inside/assess/

California Digital Library (2005). CDL resource liaison charge. Retrieved November 18, 2007, from the California Digital Library Web site: http://www.cdlib.org/inside/groups/Resource liaison/charge.html

California Digital Library (2006). CDL resource liaison meetings. Retrieved November 18, 2007, from the California Digital Library Web site: http://www.cdlib.org/inside/groups/rl/meetings.html

California Digital Library (2006). Information About CDL-Licensed Resources. Retrieved November 18, 2007, from the California Digital Library Web site: http://www.cdlib.org/inside/resources/licensed/index.html

California Digital Library (2006). Instructional materials. Retrieved November 18, 2007, from the California Digital Library Web site: http://www.cdlib.org/inside/instruct/

California Digital Library (2006). Metadata requirements for OpenURLs. Retrieved November 18, 2007, from the California Digital Library Web site: http://www.cdlib.org/vendors/Metadata_requirements.pdf

California Digital Library (2006). Resource selection criteria. Retrieved November 18, 2007, from the California Digital Library Web site: http://www.cdlib.org/inside/resources/licensed/resource_selection_criteria.rtf

California Digital Library (2006). Vendors and content providers. Retrieved November 18, 2007, from the California Digital Library Web site: http://www.cdlib.org/vendors/

California Digital Library (2006, April). California digital library technical requirements for database vendors. Retrieved November 18, 2007, from the California Digital Library Web site: http://www.cdlib.org/vendors/CDL_ejournal_Vendor_Req.rtf

California Digital Library (2006, April). California digital library technical requirements for e-journal vendors. Retrieved November 18, 2007, from the California Digital Library Web site: http://www.cdlib.org/vendors/CDL_DB_Vendor_Req.rtf

California Digital Library (n.d.). Checklist of points to be addressed in a CDL License Agreement. Retrieved November 17, 2007, from http://www.cdlib.org/vendors/checklist.html

California Digital Library. (2003, June). User Interface Principles. Retrieved November 18, 2007, from the California Digital Library Web site: http://www.cdlib.org/vendors/Interface_Principles.rtf

California School Library Association. (2006). Legislation and advocacy. Retrieved November 17, 2007, from http://www.schoolibrary.org/leg/

Cambridge Journals Online (2006). Online terms of use. Retrieved November 17, 2007, from http://journals.cambridge.org/action/terms

Carstens, T., & Buchanan, H. (2004). The future of the catalog: A user-friendly academic search engine. *Technical Services Quarterly, 22*(2), 37-47.

Champy, J. (2006). People and process. *Queue, 4*(2), 34-38. Retrieved November 14, 2007, from http://doi.acm.org/10.1145/1122674.1122687

Chandler, A. (2000). An application profile and prototype metatdata management system for licensed electronic resources. Retrieved November 22, 2007, from http://www.library.cornell.edu/cts/elicensestudy/Application-Profile.htm

Chandler, A. (2002, January 30). ALA midwinter 2002 meeting. Retrieved November 22, 2007, from http://www.library.cornell.edu/elicensestudy/alamidwinter2002.htm

Chandler, A. (2002, May 20). Notes, NISO/Digital Library Federation workshop, May 10, 2002. Retrieved November 22, 2007, from http://www.library.cornell.edu/elicensestudy/nisodlf/home.htm

Chandler, A. (2002, June 14). ALCTS-sponsored meeting on e-resource management metadata at ALA, June 14, 2002. Retrieved November 22, 2007, from http://www.library.cornell.edu/elicensestudy/alaannual2002/home.htm

Chandler, A. (2004). Electronic resource management. Retrieved November 22, 2007, from http://metadata-wg.mannlib.cornell.edu/forum/index.php?date=2004-09-24

Chandler, A., & Jewell, T. (2006). Standards – libraries, data providers, and SUSHI: The Standardized Usage Statistics Harvesting Initiative. *Against the Grain, 18*(2), 1-2.

Chandler, A., & Jewell, T. D. (2005). A web hub for developing administrative metadata for electronic resource management. Retrieved November 23, 2007, from http://www.library.cornell.edu/cts/elicensestudy/

Chang, S. (2003). The DLF electronic resource management initiative. *OCLC Systems & Services, 19*(2), 45-47.

Chapman, L. (2004). *Managing acquisitions in library and information services* (Rev. ed.). London: Facet.

Chen, C. C. (1972). The use patterns of physics journals in a large academic research library. *Journal of the American Society for Information Science, 23*(4), 254-265.

Chen, X., Colgan, L., Greene, C., Lowe, E., & Winke, C. (2004). E-resource cataloging practices: A survey of academic libraries and consortia. *Serials Librarian, 47*(1/2), 153-179.

Christian, R. (1978). *The electronic library: Bibliographic data bases, 1978-1979.* White Plains, NY: Knowledge Industry Publications, Inc.

Chrzastojwski, T. E. (1999). E-journal access: The online catalog (856 field), web lists, and "the principle of least effort". *Library Computing, 18*(4), 317-322.

Chudnov, D. et al. (2000). Jake: Overview and status report [Jointly administered knowledge environment, Electronic journal database at Yale University]. *Serials Review, 26*(4), 12-17.

Chudnov, D., Cameron, R., Frumkin, J., Singer, R., & Yee, R. (2005, May 24). Opening up OpenURLs with autodiscovery. *Ariadne* (43). Retrieved November 18, 2007, from http://www.ariadne.ac.uk/issue43/chudnov/

Cochenour, D. (2000). Taming the octopus: Getting a grip on electronic resources. *Serials Librarian, 38*(3/4), 363-368.

Cohen, B. (2006). E-reserve use of e-journal content. Email on SERIALST listserv. Retrieved November 17, 2007.

Cohen, L. B. (2005). Finding scholarly content on the web: From google scholar to RSS feeds. *CHOICE: Current Reviews for Academic Libraries, 42*(SPECIAL), 7-17.

Cole, J. (2003). Impacts of the abandonment of catalog records for electronic serials. *The Serials Librarian, 45*(1), 27-33.

Cole, Jim E. & Williams, J. W. (1992). *Serials cataloging: Modern perspectives and international developments.* New York: Haworth Press.

Cole, L. (2004). Back to basics: What is the e-journal? *The Serials Librarian, 47*(1/2), 77-87.

Coleridge, S. T. (1798). The rime of the ancient mariner. Retrieved November 12, 2007, from LitFINDER database.

Collantes, L. (1995). Degree of agreement in naming objects and concepts for information retrieval. *Journal of the American Society for Information Science, 46*(2), 116-132.

Collins, M. (2005). Electronic resource management systems: Understanding the players and how to make the right choice for your library. *Serials Review, 31*, 125-140.

Collins, M. (2005). Electronic resource management systems: Understanding the players and how to make the right choice for your library. *Serials Review, 31*, 124-140.

Collins, M. (2005). The effects of e-journal management tools and services on serials cataloging. *Serials Review, 31*(4), 291-297.

Conger, J. E. (2004). *Collaborative electronic resource management.* Westport, CT: Libraries Unlimited.

Conger, J. E. (2004). *Collaborative electronic resource management: From acquisitions to assessment.* Englewood, CO: Libraries Unlimited.

Congleton, R. (2002). Re-evaluating technical services workflow for integrated library systems. *Library Collections, Acquisitions, & Technical Services, 26*(4), 337-341.

Conhaim, W. W. (2006). Blogging: A modern tool for an age-old quest. *Information Today, 23*(2), 27-29.

CONSER (2006). *CONSER cataloging manual: Module 31, Remote access electronic serials (online serials).* Washington, D.C.: Library of Congress. Retrieved November 21, 2007, from http://www.loc.gov/acq/conser/module31.html

CONTU (National Commission on New Technological Uses of Copyright Works) (1979). *Final report of the national commission on new technological uses of copyright works.* Washington, D.C.: Library of Congress.

Convey, J. (1992). *Online information retrieval: An introductory manual to principles and practice* (4th ed.). London: Library Association Publishing.

Cooper, M. D., & McGregor, G. F. (1994). Using article photocopy data in bibliographic models for journal collection management. *Library Quarterly, 64*(4), 386-413.

Cooper, P. S., & Lester, D. (2005). One-stop serials management with TDNet. *The Serials Librarian, 47*(4), 27-34.

Copeland, A. W. (1997). The demand for serials catalogers: An analysis of job advertisements, 1980-1995. *The Serials Librarian, 32*(1/2), 27-37.

Copeland, A. W. (2002). E-serials cataloging in the 1990s: A review of the literature. *The Serials Librarian, 41*(3/4), 7-29.

Corbett, L. (2006). Serials: Review of the literature 2000-2003. *Library Resources & Technical Services, 50*(1), 16-30.

Corbin, J. (1993). Competencies for electronic information services. *Public-Access Computer Systems Review, 4*(6), 5-22. Retrieved November 17, 2007, from http://epress.lib.uh.edu/pr/v4/n6/corbin.4n6

Cornell University Libraries (2000). Cornell University Library digital futures plan: July 2000 to June 2002. Retrieved November 21, 2007, from http://www.library.cornell.edu/staffweb/CULDigitalFuturesPlan.html

Cornell University. (2006, September 19). Cornell University and publishers announce new copyright guidelines governing use of digital course materials. Retrieved November 17, 2007, from http://www.news.cornell.edu/pressoffice/Sept06/AAPCopyright.shtml

COUNTER (2005, April). Release 2 of the COUNTER code of practice for journals and databases. Retrieved November 18, 2007, from the Project COUNTER Web site: http://www.projectcounter.org/code_practice.html

COUNTER (n.d.). About. Retrieved November 18, 2007 from the Project COUNTER Web site: http://www.projectcounter.org/about.html

COUNTER: Counting Online Usage of NeTworked Electronic Resources (n.d.). Retrieved November 11, 2007, from http://www.projectcounter.org

Cox, J. (2000). Model generic licenses: Cooperation and competition. *Serials Review, 26*(1), 3-9.

Cox, J., & Cox, L. (2003). *Scholarly publishing practice: The ALPSP report on academic journal publishers' policies and practices in online publishing.* Rookwood, UK: John Cox Associates.

CQ Press. (2006). Terms of service for the online services at cqpress.com. Retrieved November 18, 2007, from http://www.cqpress.com/TermsOfUse/general.htm

Creative Commons (2007). About us. Retrieved November 18, 2007, from http://creativecommons.org/about/history

Creative Commons (2007). Creative commons licenses. Retrieved November 18, 2007, from http://creativecommons.org/about/licenses/meet-the-licenses

Creative Commons. (2006). License your work. Retrieved November 17, 2007, from http://creativecommons.org/license/

Creative Commons. (2007). Main page. Retrieved November 17, 2007, from http://creativecommons.org/license

Croneis, K. S. & Henderson, P. (2002). Electronic and digital librarian positions: A content analysis of announcements from 1990 through 2000. *Journal of Academic Librarianship, 28*(4), 232-237.

Curtis, A. (2005). Why federated search? *Knowledge Quest, 33*(3), 35-37.

Curtis, D. (2005). *E-journals: A how-to-do-it manual for building, managing, and supporting electronic journal collections.* New York: Neal-Schuman Publishers.

Curtis, D., Scheschy, V.M., & Tarango, A.R. (2000). *Developing and managing electronic journal collections: A how-to-do-it manual for librarians.* New York: Neal-Schuman Publishers.

Cyzyk, M., & Robertson, N. (2003). HERMES: The Hopkins Electronic Resource Management System. *Information Technology and Libraries, 22*(1), 12-17.

Data Farm University of Pennsylvania Library (n.d.). Retrieved November 11, 2007, from http://metrics.library.upenn.edu/prototype/about/indexHTML

Davis, P. M. (2002). Patterns in electronic journal usage: Challenging the composition of geographic consortia. *College and Research Libraries, 63*(6), 484-497. http://www.ala.org/ala/acrl/acrlpubs/crljournal/backissues2002b/november02/davisPDF

Davis, P. M., & Price, J. S. (2006). eJournal interface can influence usage statistics: Implications for libraries, publishers, and Project COUNTER. *Journal of the American Society for Information Science and Technology, 57*(9), 1243-1248.

Davis, P. M., & Solla, L. R. (2003). An IP-level analysis of usage statistics for electronic journals in chemistry: Making inferences about user behavior. *Journal of the American Society for Information Science and Technology, 54*(11), 1062-1068.

De Jong, P. (2006). Going with the flow. *Queue, 4*(2), 24-32, Retrieved November 14, 2007, from http://doi.acm.org/10.1145/1122674.1122686

De Rosa, C., Dempsey, L., & Wilson, A. (2004). *The 2003 OCLC environmental scan: Pattern recognition: A report to the OCLC membership.* Dublin, OH: OCLC Online Computer Library Center. Retrieved November 18, 2007, from http://www.oclc.org/reports/escan/

Deeken, J., & Thomas, D. (2006). Technical services job ads: Changes since 1995. *College & Research Libraries, 67*(2), 136-145.

Deming, W. E. (1986). *Out of the crisis.* Cambridge: Massachusetts Institute of Technology, Center for Advanced Engineering Study.

Dempsey, L. (2006). Libraries and the long tail: Some thoughts about libraries in a network age. *D-Lib Magazine, 12*(4). Retrieved November 18, 2007, from http://www.dlib.org/dlib/april06/dempsey/04dempsey.html

Dempsey, L. (2007). Lorcan Dempsey's weblog. Retrieved November 23, 2007, from orweblog.oclc.org/archives/001250.html

Dewey, B. I., DeBlois, P. B., & the 2006 EDUCAUSE Current Issues Committee (2006). Top-ten IT issues, 2006. Retrieved November 18, 2007, from the EDUCAUSE Web site: http://www.educause.edu/ir/library/pdf/ERM0633.pdf

Dialog invented online information services. (2006). Retrieved November 10, 2007, from http://www.dialog.com/about/

Digital Library Federation (2004). *DLF electronic resources management initiative.* Retrieved November 14, 2007, from http://www.diglib.org/standards/dlf-erm02.htm

Digital Library Federation (2004). Electronic resource management: Final report of the DLF initiative. Retrieved November 23, 2007, from www.library.cornell.edu/elicensestudy/dlfdeliverables/DLF-ERMI-Final-Report.pdf

Digital Library Federation (2005). DLF electronic resource management initiative, Phase II. Retrieved November 22, 2007, from http://www.diglib.org/standards/dlf-erm05.htm

Digital Library Federation (2006). DLF electronic resource management initiative. Retrieved November 21, 2007, from http://www.diglib.org/standards/dlf-erm02.htm

Digital Library Federation. (2006). DLF electronic resource management initiative. Retrieved November 23, 2007, from http://www.diglib.org/standards/dlf-erm02.htm

DLF Electronic Resource Management Initiative, Phase II, Acquisitions Interoperability Subcommittee (2007). White paper on interoperability between acquisitions modules of integrated library systems and electronic resource management systems: A draft for comment. Retrieved November 23, 2007, from http://www.haverford.edu/library/DLF_ERMI2/ACQ_ERMS_white_paper.pdf

Dole, W. V., Hurych, J. M., & Liebst, A. (2005). Assessment: A core competency for library leaders. *Library Administration & Management, 19*(3), 125-132.

Dublin Core Metadata Initiative (2006). DCMI metadata terms. Retrieved November 23, 2007, from http://dublincore.org/documents/dcmi-terms/

Dupuis, J. & Ryan, P. (2002). Bridging the two cultures: A collaborative approach to managing electronic resources. *Issues in Science and Technology Librarianship, 34.* Retrieved November 12, 2007, from http://www.istl.org/02-spring/article1.html

Duranceau, E. F. (1998). Beyond print: Revisioning serials acquisitions for the digital age. *The Serials Librarian, 33*(1/2), 83-106.

Duranceau, E. F. (2000). License tracking. *Serials Review, 26*(3), 69-73.

Duranceau, E. F. (2002). Staffing for electronic resource management: The results of a survey. *Serials Review, 28*(4), 316-320.

Duranceau, E. F. (2004). Electronic resource management systems from ILS vendors. *Against the Grain, 16*(4), 91-94.

Duranceau, E. F. (2005). Electronic resource management systems, part II: Offerings from serial vendors and serial data vendors. *Against the Grain, 17*(3), 59-60.

Duranceau, E. F., & Hepfer, C. (2002) Staffing for electronic resource management: The results of a survey. *Serials Review, 28*, 316-320.

Dureanceau, E. F., & Hepfer, C. (2002). Electronic journal forum: Staffing for electronic resource management: The results of a survey (Column). *Serials Review, 28*(4), 316-320.

Dusollier, S. (2006). The master's tools v. the master's house: Creative commons v. copyright. *Columbia Journal of Law & the Arts, 29*(3), 271-293.

Duy, J., & Vaughan, L. (2006). Can electronic journal usage data replace citation data as a measure of journal use? An empirical examination. *The Journal of Academic Librarianship, 32*(5), 512-517.

Eaton, N.L., MacDonald, L.B., & Saule, M.R. (1989). *CD-ROM and other optical information systems: Implementation issues for libraries.* Phoenix, AZ: Oryx Press.

EContent (2003, Feb 18). TDNet takes over JournalWebCite customer base. *EContent: Digital content strategies & resources.* Retrieved November 22, 2007, from http://www.econtentmag.com/Articles/ArticleReader.aspx?ArticleID=4057

EDUCAUSE, The New Media Consortium (NMC) (2006). The horizon report, 2006 edition. Retrieved November 18, 2007, from the EDUCAUSE Web site: http://www.educause.edu/ir/library/pdf/CSD4387.pdf

Eduserv Technologies Limited (n.d.). Eduserv athens. Retrieved November 21, 2007, from http://www.athensams.net/

Elkin-Koren, N. (2005). What contracts cannot do: The limits of private ordering in facilitating a creative commons. *Fordham Law Review, 74*(2), 375-422.

Emery, J. (2005). Beginning to see the light: Developing a discourse for electronic resource management. *Serials Librarian, 47*(4), 137-147.

Engineering Libraries Division, American Society for Engineering Education (2005, May). Punch list of best practices for electronic resources. Retrieved November 18, 2007, from the Engineering Libraries Division of American Society for Engineering Education Web site: http://eld.lib.ucdavis.edu/punchlist/PunchlistRevision2005.pdf

European Commission. (2006). About this site. Retrieved November 17, 2007, from http://ec.europa.eu/about_en.htm

ExLibris (2006). *Users Guide.*

Farb, S. (2006). Libraries, licensing and the challenge of stewardship. *First Monday, 11*(7). Retrieved November 14, 2007, from http://www.firstmonday.org/

Farb, S. E., & Riggio, A. (2002). *UCLA electronic resources database project overview.* PowerPoint, ALA Midwinter Meeting, 2002. Retrieved November 22, 2007, from http://www.library.cornell.edu/cts/elicensestudy/ucla/ALAMidwinter2002.ppt

Farnsworth, E. A. (1999). *United States contract law* (Rev. ed.). Huntington, NY: Juris Publishing.

Feist Publications, Inc. vs. Rural Telephone Service Co., 499 U.S. 340. (1991). Retrieved November 17, 2007, from http://www.coolcopyright.com/cases/chp2/feistrural.htm

Felt, E. C. (1999). Holland library's electronic resource librarians: A profile of these positions. *The Reference Librarian, 64*, 75-113.

Felts, J. W., Jr. (2001). Now you can get there from here: Creating an interactive web application for accessing full-text journal articles from any location. *Library Collections, Acquisitions, & Technical Services, 25*(3), 281-290.

Ferguson, C. L., Collins, M. D. D., & Grogg, J. E. (2006). Finding the perfect e-journal access solution... the hard way. *Technical Services Quarterly, 23*(4), 27-50.

Fescemyer, K. (2005). Serials clutter in online catalogs. *Serials Review, 31*(1), 14-19.

Ficher, K., & Barton, H. (2005). The landscape of E-journal management. *Journal of Electronic Resources in Medical Libraries, 2*(3), 57.

Fichter, D. (2005). Intranet librarian - intranets, wikis, blikis, and collaborative working. *Online, 29*(5), 47.

Fichter, D. (2006). Doing the monster mashup. *Online, 30*(4), 48.

FindLaw for Legal Professionals. (2001, June 25). New York Times Co., Inc. et al. v. Tasini et al. Retrieved November 17, 2007, from http://caselaw.lp.findlaw.com/scripts/getcase.pl?court=US&vol=000&invol=00-201

First Options of Chicago, Inc. v. Kaplan, 514 U.S. 938 (1995).

Fischer, K.S., & Barton, H. (2005). The landscape of e-journal management. *Journal of Electronic Resources in Medical Libraries, 2*(3), 57-63.

Fisher, W. (2001). Core competencies for the acquisitions librarian: Analysis of position announcements. *Library Collections, Acquisitions, & Technical Services, 25*(2), 179- 190.

Fisher, W. (2003). The electronic resources librarian position: A public services phenomenon? *Library Collections, Acquisitions, & Technical Services*, 27, (1), 3-17.

Flanders, B.L. (1990). Spinning the hits: CD-ROM networks in libraries [Electronic version]. *American Libraries, 21*(11), 1032-1033.

Flint, E. (2000). Introducing the Baen Free Library. Retrieved November 11, 2007, from http://www.baen.com/library/home.htm

Fons, T. & Grover, D. (2004). The innovative electronic resource management system: A development partnership. *Serials Review, 30*(2), 110-116.

Fons, T. & Jewell, T. D. (in press). Envisioning the future of ERM systems—NASIG 2006 Proceedings. *The Serials Librarian.*

Fons, T. (2006). Future of ERM systems (PowerPoint Presentation) California Digital Library Institute. *Electronic Resource Management*, presenter, November 10, 2006. Representative of Innovative Interfaces.

Fons, T., & Jewell, T. (2006, May). *Envisioning the future of ERM systems.* Paper presented at the 21ˢᵗ Annual NASIG Conference, Denver, Colorado.

Foote, M. (1997). The systems librarian in U.S. academic libraries: A survey of announcements from *College & Research Libraries News*, 1990-1994. *College & Research Libraries, 58*, 517-26.

Foudy, G., & McManus, A. (2005). Using a decision grid process to build consensus in electronic resources cancellation decisions. *Journal of Academic Librarianship, 31*(6), 533-538.

Fowler, D.C. (Ed.). (2004). *E-serials collection management: Transitions, trends, and technicalities.* New York: Haworth Information Press.

Frazier, K. (2001). The librarians' dilemma: Contemplating the costs of the "big deal". *D-Lib Magazine, 7*(3). Retrieved November 18, 2007, from http://www.dlib.org/dlib/march01/frazier/03frazier.html

Freedom of Information Act (Michigan), Mich. Comp. Laws Ann. § 15.231 *et seq.* (West 2004 & Supp. 2006).

Freedom of Information Act, 5 U.S.C. § 552 (2001 & Supp. 2005).

Frick, R., Duncan, C. J., & Walsh, W. D. (2005). Nuts and bolts of linking: Understanding context sensitive linking services and implementation. *The Serials Librarian, 48*(3/4), 257-264.

Friedlander, A. (2002). *Dimensions and use of the scholarly information environment: Introduction to a data set assembled by the Digital Library Federation and Outsell, Inc.* Washington, D.C.: Digital Library Federation and Council on Library and Information Resources. Retrieved November 21, 2007, from http://www.clir.org/pubs/reports/pub110/contents.html

Gall, J.E. (2005). Dispelling five myths about e-books [Electronic version]. *Information Technology and Libraries, 24*(1), 25-31.

Gardner, S. (2001). The impact of electronic journals on library staff at ARL member institutions: A survey and a critique of the survey methodology. *Serials Review, 27*(3-4), 17-32.

Gargano, J., Glenn A., Graham, R., Gurnani, S., Houser, L., Millman, D., et al. (2000). A digital library authentication and authorization architecture. Retrieved November 21, 2007, from http://www.cdlib.org/inside/groups/stas/links.html

General overview. (n.d.). Retrieved November 11, 2007, from, http://muse.jhu.edu/about/muse/overview.html

Gerald, N. (2000). Collection development and organization of electronic resources. *Collection Management, 25*(1/2), 97-113.

Gerhand, K. (1998). Coordination and collaboration: A model for electronic resources management. *The Serials Librarian, 33*(3/4), 279-286.

Ghaphery, J., Kesselman, M., & Watstein, S. B. (2001). Personalized information clients: Short answers to simple questions about "my library" services. *Reference Services Review, 29*(4), 276.

Giles, V. (2003). Single or multiple records for print and electronic serials titles: When less is more (more or less). *The Serials Librarian, 45*(1), 35-45.

Ginanni, K. (2006). Talk about: E-resources librarian to the rescue? Creating the über librarian: Turning model job descriptions into practical positions. *The Serials Librarian, 50*(1/2), 173-177.

GNU. (2006, August 3). What is copyleft? Retrieved November 17, 2007, from http://www.gnu.org/copyleft/copyleft.html

Gold Rush (2006). Welcome to Gold Rush. Retrieved November 23, 2007, from http://grweb.coalliance.org/

Google milestones. (2006). Retrieved November 11, 2007, from http://www.google.com/corporate/history.html#2005

Gorman, G. E., & Miller, R. H. (Eds.). (1997). *Collection management for the 21st century: A handbook for librarians.* Westport, CT: Greenwood Press.

Grahame, V., McAdam, T., & Association of Research Libraries. Office of Leadership and Management Services. (2004). *Managing electronic resources.* Washington, D.C.: Association of Research Libraries, Office of Leadership and Management Services

Graves, T., & Arthur, M. A. (2006). Developing a crystal clear future for the serials unit in an electronic environment: Results of a workflow analysis. *Serials Review, 32*(4), 238-246.

Graves, T., & Arthur, M.A. (2006). Developing a crystal clear future for the serials unit in an electronic environment: Results of a workflow analysis. *Serials Review, 32*(4), 238-246.

Gregory, V. L., & Hanson, A. (2006). *Selecting and managing electronic resources: A how-to-do-it manual for librarians* (Rev. ed.). New York: Neal Schuman Publishers.

Grogg, J. E. (2004). Linking in the traditional online world. *Searcher, 12*(6), 34.

Grogg, J. E. (2005). Land of linking. *The Serials Librarian, 49*(3), 177.

Grogg, J. E. (2006). Innovative uses of the openURL. *Library Technology Reports, 42*(1), 35.

Grogg, J. E. (2006). Other linking issues. *Library Technology Reports, 42*(1), 38.

Grogg, J. E. (2006). The development of context-sensitive linking. *Library Technology Reports, 42*(1), 14.

Grogg, J. E., & Tenopir, C. (2000, Nov/Dec). Linking to full text in scholarly journals: Here a link, there a link, everywhere a link. *Searcher, 8*(10),

Grover, D., & Fons, T. (2004). The innovative electronic resource management system: A development partnership. *Serials Review, 30*(2), 110-116.

Guenther, K. (2005). Socializing your web site with wikis, twikis, and blogs. (web site management methods using webcasting). *Online, 29*(6), 51(3).

Guidelines for classroom copying of books and periodicals. (2001, August 9). Retrieved November 17, 2007, from http://www.utsystem.edu/OGC/INTELLECTU-ALPROPERTY/clasguid.htm

Hahn, K. L., & Faulkner, L. A. (2002). Evaluative usage-based metrics for the selection of e-journals. *College and Research Libraries, 63*(3), 215-227.

Hammer, M., & Champy, J. (1993). *Reengineering the corporation: A manifesto for business revolution.* New York: HarperBusiness.

Harrassowitz (2006). Electronic journal services, HERMIS 3.0. Retrieved November 22, 2007, from http://www.harrassowitz.de/periodicals_e-journals.html

Harris, L. E. (2002). *Licensing digital content: A practical guide for librarians.* Chicago: American Library Association.

Hart, M. (1992). Gutenberg: The history and philosophy of Project Gutenberg by Michael Hart. Retrieved November 11, 2007, from http://www.gutenberg.org/wiki/Gutenberg:The_History_and_Philosophy_of_Project_Gutenberg_by_Michael_Hart

Harvell, T. (2005). Electronic resources management systems: The experience of beta testing and implementation. *Serials Librarian, 47*(4).

Harvell, T.A. (2005). Electronic resources management systems: The experience of beta testing and implementation. In G. Ives (Ed.), *Electronic journal management systems: Experiences from the field* (pp. 125-136). New York: Haworth Information Press.

Haworth Press (2006). The Haworth Press multi-site online terms. Retrieved November 18, 2007, from http://www.haworthpress.com/pdfs/Multi-SiteLicense.pdf

Hawthorne, D. (2003/0). Administrative metadata to support the acquisition of continuing e-resources. *Serials Review, 29*(4), 276-281.

Hayes, A., & Lerner, S. (2004). Tracking electronic resources at the Library of Congress (PowerPoint presentation). Retrieved November 22, 2007, from http://www.loc.gov/catdir/TrackERALA2004.ppt

Hayes, J., & Sullivan, M. (2003). Mapping the process: Engaging staff in work redesign. *Library Administration & Management, 17*(2), 87-93.

Hellman, E. (2005). OpenURL COinS: A convention to embed bibliographic metadata in HTML. Retrieved November 18, 2007, from http://ocoins.info/

Hennig, N. (2002). Improving access to e-journals and databases at the MIT libraries: Building a database-backed web site called "VERA". In J. Cole, & W. Jones (Eds.), *E-serials cataloging: Access to continuing and integrating resources via the catalog and the web* (pp. 227-254). Binghamton, NY: Haworth.

Hennig, N. (2002). Improving access to e-journals and databases at the MIT libraries: Building a database-backed web site called "Vera." *The Serials Librarian, 41*(3-4), 227-254.

High Speed Providers by Zip Code (2004). Retrieved November 23, 2007, from www.cable-modem.net/images/coverage_map.gif

Ho, J. (2005). Enhancing access to resources through the online catalog and the library website: A collaboration between public and technical services at Texas A&M University Libraries. *Technical Services Quarterly, 22*(4), 19-37.

Holleman, C. (2000). Electronic resources: Are basic criteria for the selection of materials changing? *Library Trends, 48*(4), 694.

Holman, J. (2005). Can SFX replace your homegrown periodical holdings list? *Serials Librarian, 47*(4), 79-88.

Hood, A., & Howard, M. (2006). Adding value to the catalog in an open access world. *The Serials Librarian, 50*(3/4), 249-252.

Horny, K.L. (1982). Online catalogs: Coping with the choices. *The Journal of Academic Librarianship, 8*(1), 14-19.

Iannella, R. (2002). Open digital rights language (ODRL) version 1.1. Retrieved November 23, 2007, from http://www.w3.org/TR/odrl/

ICOLC (2006, October). Revised guidelines for statistical measures of usage of web-based information resources. Retrieved November 18, 2007, from the ICOLC Web site: http://www.library.yale.edu/consortia/webstats06.htm

ICOLC guidelines and preferred practices for selection and purchase of electronic resources (2001). *Online Libraries & Microcomputers, 19*(12), 1.

Innovative Interfaces (2006). Electronic Resource Management. [brochure]

Innovative, Inc. (2006). Digital collections. Electronic resource management. Retrieved November 21, 2007, from http://www.iii.com/mill/digital.shtml#erm

International Coalition of Library Consortia (1997). Statement of current perspective and preferred practices for the selection and purchase of electronic information. Retrieved November 21, 2007, from http://www.library.yale.edu/consortia/statement.html

International Coalition of Library Consortia (1998). Statement of current perspective and preferred practices for the selection and purchase of electronic information. Retrieved November 17, 2007, from http://www.library.yale.edu/consortia/statement.html

International Coalition of Library Consortia (2002). Privacy guidelines for electronic resources vendors. Retrieved November 21, 2007 from http://www.library.yale.edu/consortia/2002privacyguidelines.html

International Coalition of Library Consortia (ICOLC) (1998, November). Guidelines for statistical measures of usage of web-based indexed, abstracted, and full text resources. Retrieved November 11 2007, from http://www.library.yale.edu/consortia/webstatsHTML

International Federation of Library Association Committee on Copyright and Other Legal Matters (2001).

Licensing principles. Retrieved November 17, 2007, from http://www.ifla.org/V/ebpb/copy.htm

International Federation of Library Associations and Institutions (2001). Licensing principles. Retrieved November 21, 2007, from http://www.ifla.org/V/ebpb/copy.htm

Internet2 (n.d.). Shibboleth - Internet2 middleware. Retrieved November 21, 2007, from http://shibboleth.internet2.edu/

Irlam, G. (1995). Naming. Retrieved November 21, 2007, from http://www.gordoni.com/web/naming.html

Islam, M.S., & Chowdhury, M.A.K. (2006). Organisation and management issues for electronic journals: A Bangladesh perspective. *Malaysian Journal of Library & Information Science, 11*(1), 61-74.

Ives, G. (2005). Transition to e-journals at Texas A&M University, 1995-2004. *Serials Librarian, 47*(4), 71-78.

Jaguszewski, J. M., & Probst, L. K. (2000). The impact of electronic resources on serial cancellations and remote storage decisions in academic research libraries. *Library Trends, 48*(4), 799.

Jasco, P. (2003). Peter's picks and pans. *Online, 27*(2), 72-74.

Jasper, R. P. (2002). Collaborative roles in managing electronic publications. *Library Collections, Acquisitions, & Technical Services, 26*, 355-361.

Jasper, R.P., & Sheble, L. (2005). Evolutionary approach to managing e-resources. In G. Ives (Ed.), *Electronic journal management systems: Experiences from the field* (pp. 55-70). New York: Haworth Information Press.

Java Architectures Special Interest Group (n.d.). CAS overview. Retrieved November 21, 2007, from http://www.ja-sig.org/products/cas/overview/index.html

Jewell, T. (2006). Electronic resource management systems: What should they do? In P. M. Bluh & C. Hepfer (Eds.), *Managing electronic resources: Contemporary problems and emerging issues* (pp. 9-34). Chicago: Association for Library Collections & Technical Services.

Jewell, T. D. (2001). Appendix B: Functions and data elements for managing electronic resources. Retrieved November 22, 2007, from http://www.library.cornell.edu/elicensestudy/u-washington/FinalAppendixB.xls

Jewell, T. D. (2001). *Selection and presentation of commercially available electronic resources: Issues and practices.* Washington, DC.: Council on Library and Information Resources.

Jewell, T. D. (2005). E-resource management systems: Past, present, and future. Retrieved November 23, 2007, from http://www.sirsidynixinstitute.com/Resources/Attachments/Slides/jewell_20051207.pdf

Jewell, T. D. et al. (2004). Electronic resource management: Report of the DLF electronic resource management initiative. Retrieved November 23, 2007, from http://www.diglib.org/pubs/dlf102/ERMFINAL.pdf

Jewell, T. D., & Mitchell, A. (2005). Electronic resource management: The quest for systems and standards. *Serials Librarian, 48*(1/2), 137-163.

Jewell, T. D., et al. (2004). *Electronic resource management: Report of the DLF electronic resource management initiative.* Washington, D.C.: Digital Library Federation.

Jewell, T., Anderson, I., Chandler, A., Farb, S. E., Parker, K., Riggio, A., et al. (2004). *Electronic resource management. Report of the DLF ERM Initiative.* Washington, DC. Digital Library Federation. Retrieved November 14, 2007, from http://www.diglib.org/pubs/dlf102/

JISC (n.d.). Usage statistics working group. About usage statistics working group. Retrieved November 11, 2007, from http://www.jisc.ac.uk/aboutus/committees/working_groups/working_groups_disbanded/usage_stats_group.aspx

JISC infoNet. infoKits (n.d.). Process mapping. Retrieved November 14, 2007, from http://www.jiscinfonet.ac.uk/InfoKits/process-review/process-review-9.4

Johns Hopkins University. (2004). HERMES. Retrieved November 23, 2007, from http://hermes.mse.jhu.edu:8008/hermesdocs/

Johnson, K., & Manoff, M. (2003). Report of the death of the catalog is greatly exaggerated: The E-journal access journey at the University of Tennessee. *The Serials Librarian, 44*(3/4), 285-292.

Johnson, P. (2004). *Fundamentals of collection development & management.* Chicago: American Library Association.

Joint Steering Committee for Revision of AACR (1999). *Revising AACR2 to accommodate seriality.* Ottawa: Library and Archives Canada. Retrieved November 21, 2007, from http://www.collectionscanada.ca/jsc/serrep6.html

Jones, E. (2002). *The exchange of serials subscription information.* Bethesda, MD: National Information Standards Organization.

Jones, P. (2006). California Digital Library Institute: *Electronic Resource Management*, presenter, November 10, 2006. Representative of Endeavor Meridian.

Jones, W. (2003). A personal mini-history of e-serials cataloging. *The Serials Librarian, 43*(3), 21-24.

JSTOR (2006). Terms and conditions of use. Retrieved November 18, 2007, from http://www.jstor.org/about/terms.html

JSTOR Web Statistics Task Force (1998, April). Guidelines for statistical measures of usage of web-based resources. Retrieved November 11, 2007, from http://www.library.yale.edu/~kparker/WebStatsHTML

Katz, Z. (2006). Pitfalls of open licensing: An analysis of creative commons licensing. *IDEA, 46*(3), 391-413.

Kennedy, M. R. (2004). Dreams of perfect programs: Managing the acquisition of electronic resources. *Library Collections, Acquisitions, and Technical Services, 28*(4), 449-458.

Kennedy, M. R., Crump, M. J., & Kiker, D. (2004). Paper to PDF: Making license agreements accessible through the OPAC. *Library Resources & Technical Services, 48*(1), 20.

Kent, S. T., & Millett L. I. (Eds.) (2003). *Who goes there?: Authentication through the lens of privacy*. Washington, D.C.: National Academy Press.

Kichuk, D. (2000). *Library space study*. Unpublished internal report, University of Saskatchewan Library, Saskatoon.

Kidd, K. (2004). Local e-resource management systems: Boston college libraries. Retrieved November 22, 2007, from http://www.library.cornell.edu/cts/elicensestudy/webhubarchive.html

King, D. W., Tenopir, C., Montgomery, C. H., & Aerni, S. E., (2003). *Patterns of journal use by faculty at three diverse universities. D-Lib Magazine, 9*(10).

Klughist, A. C. (2000). LIBER licensing principles for electronic information. *Journal of Academic Librarianship, 26(3),* 199-201.

Kohl, D. F., & Sanville, T. (2006). More bang for the buck: Increasing the effectiveness of library expenditures through cooperation. *Library Trends, 54*(3), 394-410.

Konopasek, K., & O'Brien, N. P. (1982). A survey of journal use within the undergraduate library at the University of Illinois at Urbana-Champaign. ED 225601.

Koppel, T. (2006). *An Introduction to the rapidly changing world of ERM standards*. Ex Libris White Paper. Retrieved November 21, 2007, from http://www.exlibrisgroup.com/resources/various/Koppel_ERM_Standards.doc

Koppel, T. (2006). California Digital Library Institute: *Electronic Resource Management*, presenter, November 10, 2006. Representative of ExLibris.

Koppel, T. (2006). *Visions of ERM*. Presentation at NISO Managing Electronic collections, Strategies from Content to User, Denver, Colorado, September 28-20, 2006.

Kovacs, D. (2000). *Building electronic library collections: The essential guide to selection criteria and core subject collections*. New York: Neal-Schuman Publishers.

Krug, S. (2006). *Don't make me think: A common sense approach to web usability* (2nd ed.). Berkeley, CA: New Riders.

Kutten, L. J. (2003-2006). *Computer software: Protection/liability/law/forms* (2003 Recompiled ed.). St. Paul, MN: Thomson/West.

Kyrillidou, M., & Young, M. (2006). ARL library trends 2003-04. Retrieved November 23, 2007, from www.arl.org/stats/arlstat/04pub/04intro.html

Kyrillidou, M., & Young, M. (2006). ARL statistics 2004-05: A compilation of the statistics from the one hundred and twenty-three members of the Association of Research Libraries. Retrieved November 21, 2007, from http://www.arl.org/stats/annualsurveys/arlstats/index.shtml

Kyrillidou, M., & Young, M. (Eds.) (2005). *ARL statistics, 2003-2004*. Washington, D.C.: Association of Research Libraries.

Lagace, N. (2003). The OpenURL and SFX linking. S*erials Librarian, 44* (1/2), 77-89.

Larkin, M. R. T. (2006). AACR3 is coming—what is it? [Report on a presentation by P. J. Weiss] *Serials Librarian, 50*(3/4), 285-294.

Leiner, B. M. et al. (2005, October 31). *A brief history of the internet*. Reston, VA: Internet Society. Retrieved November 17, 2007, from http://www.isoc.org/internet/history/brief.shtml

Lerner, R. M. (2006) At the forge: Extending web services using other web services. *Linux Journal, 2006*(144), 9.

LexisNexis (1996). Terms & conditions of use for the LexisNexis services. Retrieved November 18, 2007, from http://www.lexisnexis.com/terms/general/

Librarian…educator…historian…entrepreneur. (2006). *NextSpace, 3,* 2-7.

Library of Congress. (2006). The section 108 study group. Retrieved November 17, 2007, from http://www.loc.gov/section108/

Library Technology Reports (2006). The ERMI and its offspring (Chapter 2). *Library Technology Reports, 42*(2), 14-21.

LibSGR (n.d.) LibSGR: Library statistics gathering and reporting (tool Web site). Retrieved November 22, 2007, from http://liboffice.villanova.edu/libsgr/index.php

Ligue des Bibliothèques Européennes de Recherche (1998). Licensing principles. Retrieved November 17, 2007, from http://www.kb.dk/liber/currentinitiatives/licensing.htm

Lingle, V. (2005). Implementing EBSCO's A-to-Z... *Serials Librarian, 47*(4), 43-54.

Loghry, P. A., & Shannon, A. W. (2000). Managing selection and implementation of electronic products: One tiny step in organization, one giant step for the University of Nevada, Reno. *Serials Review, 26*(3), 32-44.

Lugg, R., & Fischer, R. (2005). Acquisitions' next step. *Library Journal, 130*(12), 30-32.

Luther, J. (2000). *White paper on electronic journal usage statistics.* Washington, D.C.: Council on Library and Information Resources. http://www.clir.org/PUBS/reports/pub94/contentsHTML

Lynch, B., & Smith, K. R. (2001). The changing nature of work in academic libraries. *College & Research Libraries, 62*(5), 407-420.

Lynch, C. (1998). A white paper on authentication and access management issues in cross-organizational use of networked information resources. Retrieved November 21, 2007, from http://www.cni.org/projects/authentication/authentication-wp.html

Lynch, C.A., & Preston, C.M. (1990). Internet access to information resources. In M.E. Williams (Ed.), *Annual review of information science and technology* (Vol. 25, pp. 263-312). Amsterdam: Elsevier Science Publishing B.V.

Ma, W., & Cole, T. W. (2000). Genesis of an electronic database expert system. *Reference Services Review, 28*(3), 207.

Machovec, G. S. (2002). Gold rush: Electronic resource discovery and management system. *The Charleston Advisor, 4*(1). Retrieved November 22, 2007, from http://www.charlestonco.com/features.cfm?id=98&type=np

Maharana, B., & Chandra Panda, K. (2001). Planning business process reengineering (BPR) in academic libraries. *Malaysian Journal of Library and Information Science, 6*(1), 105-111.

Managing electronic resources at Yale University library (2006). Retrieved November 12, 2007, from http://www.library.yale.edu/ecollections/eresmanage.html

Manoff, M. (2000). Hybridity, mutability, multiplicity: Theorizing electronic library collections. *Library Trends, 49*(1), 857-876.

Marshall, S., & Kawasaki, J. L. (2005). The master serial list at Montana State University: A simple, easy to use approach. *The Serials Librarian, 47*(4), 3-15.

Marshall, S.P., & Kawasaki, J.L. (2005). The master serial list at Montana State University: A simple, easy to use approach. In G. Ives (Ed.), *Electronic journal management systems: Experiences from the field* (pp. 3-15). New York: Haworth Information Press.

Martin, C. K., & Hoffman, P. S. (2002). Do we catalog or not? How research libraries provide bibliographic access to electronic journals in aggregated databases. *The Serials Librarian, 43*(1), 61-77.

Massachusetts Institute of Technology Libraries. (2006). VERA: Virtual electronic resource access. Retrieved November 23, 2007, from http://libraries.mit.edu/vera

McCain, K. W., & Bobick, J. E. (1981). Patterns of journal use in a departmental library: A citation analysis. *Journal of the American Society for Information Science, 32*(4), 257-267.

McCaslin, S. (Recorder) (2003). Alan, R., & Hsiung, L.Y., presenters. Web-based tracking systems for electronic resources management. *The Serials Librarian, 44*(3/4), 293-297.

McCracken, P. (2003). Beyond title lists: Incorporating ejournals into the OPAC. *The Serials Librarian, 45*(3), 101-108.

McCracken, P. (2004). The OPAC reborn. *Library Journal NetConnect, 129*, 32.

McElfresh, L. K. (2005). Accessing E-journals through link resolvers. *Technicalities, 25*(6), 3.

McGinnis, S. D. (2000). *Electronic collection management.* Binghamton, NY: Haworth Information Press.

McGinnis, S., & Kemp, J. H. (1998/0). The electronic resources group: Using the cross-functional team approach to the challenge of acquiring electronic resources. *Library Acquisitions: Practice & Theory, 22*(3), 295-301.

McMullen, K., & Wilmott, D. (2005). Taming the e-journal jungle: The University of South Carolina's experience with TDNet. *Serials Librarian, 47*(4), 35-42.

McNeil, B. (Comp). (2002). *SPEC kit #270: Core competencies.* Washington, D.C.: Association of Research Libraries.

Medeiros, N. (2005). Electronic resources management: An update. *OCLC Systems & Services, 21*(2), 92-94.

Medeiros, N. (2006). House of horrors: Exorcising electronic resources. In P. M. Bluh, & C. Hepfer (Eds.), *Managing electronic resources: Contemporary problems and emerging issues* (pp. 56-66). Chicago: Association for Library Collections & Technical Services.

Medeiros, N., & Pascale, C. (2003). The tri-college consortium's electronic resource tracking system (ERTS). Retrieved November 23, 2007, from http://www.haverford.edu/library/erts/

Medeiros, N., et al. (2003). Managing administrative metadata: The tri-college consortium's electronic resources tracking system (ERTS). *Library and Technical Services, 47*(1), 28-25.

Medeiros, N., Miller, L., Adam, C., et al. (2007). White paper on interoperability between acquisitions modules of integrated library systems and electronic resource management systems: A draft for comment. Retrieved November 21, 2007, from www.haverford.edu/library/DLF_ERMI2/ACQ_ERMS_white_paper.pdf

Mencik, S. (2001). How single sign-on work. Retrieved November 21, 2007, from shttp://searchsecurity.techtarget.com/ateQuestionNResponse/0,289625,sid14_cid391596_tax285453,00.html

Mercer, L. S. (2000). Measuring the use and value of electronic journals and books. *Issues in Science and Technology Librarianship, 25.* http://www.istl.org/00-winter/article1HTML

Merriam-Webster's Dictionary of Law (1996). Springfield, MA: Merriam-Webster.

Metz, P. (2000). Principles of selection for electronic resources. *Library Trends, 48*(4), 711.

Meyer, S. (2005). Helping you buy: Electronic resource management systems. *Computers in Libraries, 25*(10), 19-24.

Mi, J., & Sullenger, P. (2006). Examining workflows and redefining roles: Auburn University and the College of New Jersey. *The Serials Librarian, 50*(3/4), 279-283.

Miles-Board, T., Carr, L., & Hall, W. (2002). Looking for linking: Associative links on the web. In *Proceedings of the Thirteenth ACM Conference on Hypertext and Hypermedia,* College Park, Maryland (pp. 76-77).

Miller, R. G. (2002). Shaping digital library content. *Journal of Academic Librarianship, 28*(3), 97.

Miller, R. H. (2000). Electronic resources and academic libraries, 1980-2000: A historical perspective. *Library Trends, 48*(4), 645.

Mitchell, A. M., & Surratt, B. E. (2005). *Cataloging and organizing digital resources: A how-to-do-it manual for librarians.* New York: Neal-Schuman Publishers.

Montgomery, C. H., & Sparks, J. L. (2000). The transition to an electronic journal collection: Managing the organizational changes. *Serials Review, 26*(3), 4-18.

Montgomery, C.H. (2000). "Fast track" transition to an electronic collection: A case study. *New Library World, 101*(1159), 294-302.

Moore, C.W. (1981). User reactions to online catalogs: An exploratory study. *College & Research Libraries, 12*(4), 295-302.

Mullin, C. (2002). A funny thing happened on the way to the e-book [Electronic version]. *PNLA Quarterly, 67*(1), 20-27.

Munson, K. I., & Frisque, M. (2004). How we treated our clients' need for remote access through a single interface. *Computers In Libraries, 24*(9), 10-15.

Murphy, M. (1991). Preface. *Future Competencies of the Information Professional* (pp. v-vi). Washington, D.C.: Special Libraries Association.

Murray, J. E., Jr. (2001). *Murray on contracts* (4th ed.) New York: LexisNexis.

Netscape (1996). Navigator proxy auto-config file format. Retrieved November 21, 2007, from http://wp.netscape.com/eng/mozilla/2.0/relnotes/demo/proxy-live.html

Newman, G. (2000). Collection development and organization of electronic resources. *Collection Management, 25*(1/2), 97-113.

Nicholas, D., Huntington, P., & Watkinson, A. (2003). Digital journals, big deals and online searching behaviour: A pilot study. *ASLIB Proceedings, 55*(1/2), 84-109.

Nicholson, S. (2005). Bibliomining: Data mining for libraries. Retrieved November 11, 2007, from http://www.bibliomining.com/

Nicholson, S. (2006, May 15). *Balancing evidence-based librarianship and protecting patron privacy through the bibliomining process.* Paper presented at the Eastern New York ACRL Chapter 2006 Spring Conference. Retrieved November 11, 2007, from http://www.enyacrl.org/acrlkeynote.ppt

Nicklen, J. E. (2003). *Serials cataloguing and harmonisation. A briefing session paper.* UKSG Conference, April 7-9, 2003, Edinburgh. Retrieved November 21, 2007, from http://www.uksg.org.uk/presentations3/nicklen.pdf

NISO (2006). NISO standardized usage statistics harvesting initiative. Retrieved November 18, 2007, from the NISO Web site: http://www.niso.org/committees/SUSHI/SUSHI_comm.html

NISO (n.d.). FAQ for the standardized usage statistics harvesting initiative (SUSHI) (Draft). Retrieved November 11, 2007, from http://docs.google.com/View.aspx?docid=d2dhjwd_63tkkwf

NISO (n.d.). *NISO RP-2006-02, NISO Metasearch XML Gateway implementers guide.* Retrieved November 18, 2007, from http://www.niso.org/standards/resources/RP-2006-02.pdf

NISO (n.d.). NISO standardized usage statistics harvesting initiative (SUSHI). National Information Standards Organization. Retrieved November 11, 2007, from http://www.niso.org/committees/SUSHI/SUSHI_comm.html

NISO (n.d.). *NISO Z39.92-200X.* Information retrieval service description specification DRAFT STANDARD FOR TRIAL USE. Period: November 1, 2005 – October 31, 2006

NISO MetaSearch initiative (2005). Retrieved November 18, 2007, from http://www.niso.org/committees/MS_initiative.html

NISO Metasearch Initiative Task Group 1 (2005*).* Ranking of authentication and access methods available to the metasearch environment. Retrieved November 21, 2007, from http://www.niso.org/standards/resources/MI-Access_Management.pdf

NISO, License Expression Working Group (n.d.). Retrieved November 23, 2007, from http://www.niso.org/committees/License_Expression/LicenseEx_comm.html

Nissley, M. (1990). CD-ROMs, licenses and librarians. In M. Nissley & N.M. Nelson (Eds.), *CD-ROM licensing and copyright issues for libraries* (pp. 1-17). Westport, CT: Meckler Corporation.

Nofsinger, M. M. (1999). Training and retraining reference professionals: Core competencies for the 21st century. *The Reference Librarian, 64*, 9-19.

Norden, D.J., & Lawrence, G.H. (1981). Public terminal use in an online catalog: Some preliminary results. *College & Research Libraries, 12*(4), 308-316.

North American Free Trade Agreement. (1992). Office of NAFTA and inter-American affairs: Intellectual property rights. Retrieved November 17, 2007, from http://www.sice.oas.org/TRADE/NAFTA/naftatce.asp

NorthEast Research Libraries (n.d.). Licensing guidelines. Retrieved November 17, 2007, from http://www.library.yale.edu/NERLpublic/licensingprinciples.html

Notess, G. R. (2000, Oct/Nov). PubList and jake: Free periodical reference sources [review of two databases]. *Econtent, 23*:5, 64-66.

Notess, G. R. (2005). Casting the net: Podcasting and screencasting. *Online, 29*(6), 43-45.

Notess, G. R. (2006). On the net - the terrible twos: Web 2.0, library 2.0, and more. *Online, 30*(3), 40.

Novotny, E. (2004). I don't think I click: A protocol analysis study of use of a library online catalog in the internet age. *College & Research Libraries, 65*(6), 525-537.

O'Neill, J. M. (2006, November 20). Professors get "F" in copyright protection knowledge. *Seattle Post-Intelligencer.* Retrieved November 17, 2007, from http://www.google.com/search?sourceid=navclient&ie=UTF-8&rls=RNWE,RNWE:2004-50,RNWE:en&q=professors+get+f

OCLC Inc. (2005). Perceptions of libraries and information resources: A report to the OCLC membership. Retrieved November 23, 2007, from www.oclc.org/reports/pdfs/Percept_all.pdf

OCLC OpenURL resolver registry (2006). Retrieved November 18, 2007, from http://www.oclc.org/productworks/urlresolver.htm

Office of Descriptive Cataloging Policy, Library of Congress (1989). *Library of Congress rule interpretations.* Washington, D.C.: Cataloging Distribution Service, Library of Congress.

Ojala, M. (1993). Core competencies for special library managers of the future. *Special Libraries, 84*, 230-234.

Okerson, A. (1996). What academic libraries need in electronic content licenses. Retrieved November 18, 2007, from http://www.library.yale.edu/~okerson/stm.html

Okerson, A. (1997). Copyright or contract? *Library Journal, 122*(14), 136-139.

Okerson, A. S., Stenlake, R. & Harper, G. (2006). LIBLICENSE: Authorized use of license materials. Retrieved November 18, 2007, from http://www.library.yale.edu/~llicense/usecls.shtml

Okerson, A. S., Stenlake, R., & Harper, G. (2006). LIBLICENSE: Amendment. Retrieved November 18, 2007, from http://www.library.yale.edu/~llicense/amendgen.shtml

Okerson, A. S., Stenlake, R., & Harper, G. (2006). LIBLICENSE: Confidentiality. Retrieved November 18, 2007, from http://www.library.yale.edu/~llicense/confgen.shtml

Okerson, A. S., Stenlake, R., & Harper, G. (2006). LIBLICENSE: Fees. Retrieved November 18, 2007, from http://www.library.yale.edu/~llicense/paygen.shtml

Okerson, A. S., Stenlake, R., & Harper, G. (2006). LIBLICENSE: Governing law; Dispute resolution. Retrieved November 18, 2007, from http://www.library.yale.edu/~llicense/remgen.shtml

Okerson, A. S., Stenlake, R., & Harper, G. (2006). LIBLICENSE: Warranties; Indemnities; Limitations on warranties. Retrieved November 17, 2007, from http://www.library.yale.edu/~llicense/warrgen.shtml

OpenURL referrer (2006). Dublin, OH: OCLC Openly Informatics. Retrieved November 18, 2007, from http://www.openly.com/openurlref/

Osmus, L. L. (1996). The transformation of serials cataloging 1965-1990. *Technical services management, 1965-1990.* (pp. 171-190). Haworth Press.

Osorio, N. L. (1999). An analysis of science-engineering academic library positions in the last three decades. *Issues in Science and Technology Librarianship.* Retrieved November 17, 2007, from http://www.istl.org/99-fall/article2.html

Pace, A. K. (2003). *The ultimate digital library: Where the new information players meet.* Chicago: American Library Association.

Pace, A. K. (2004). *Disintegrated library systems and electronic resource management: Dismantling library systems*. Presentation at ALA, 2004. Retrieved November 22, 2007, from http://www.lib.ncsu.edu/presentations/2004ala/IRRT_pace.ppt

Pace, A. K. (2006). *E-matrix: Electronic resource management at NCSU*. PowerPoint presented to Amigos, May 11, 2006. Retrieved November 22, 2007, from http://www.lib.ncsu.edu/presentations/2006Amigos/ematrix.ppt

Parker, K., Anderson, I., Chandler, A., Farb, S. E., Jewell, T., Riggio, A., & Robertson, N. D. M. (2004). *Electronic resource management: Report of the DLF ERM Initiative, Appendix E: Electronic resource management system data structure*. Washington, D.C.: Digital Library Federation. Retrieved November 21, 2007, from http://www.diglib.org/pubs/dlf102/

Pattie, L. W., & Cox, B. J. (1996). *Electronic resources: Selection and bibliographic control*. Binghamton, NY: Haworth Press.

Pennsylvania State University Libraries. (2006). Serials and acquisitions services tactical plan 05/06-07/08. Retrieved November 23, 2007, from http://www.libraries.psu.edu/admin/adup/tactical/serials_acq_plan_rev072006.pdf

Pesch, O. (2004). Usage statistics: Taking e-metrics to the next level. *The Serials Librarian, 46*(1/2), 143-154.

Plum, T., & Bleiler, R. (2001). *User authentication. SPEC Kit. 267*. Washington, D.C.: Association of Research Libraries.

Pooley, C. G. (1990). CD-ROM licensing issues. In M. Nissley & N.M. Nelson (Eds.), *CD-ROM licensing and copyright issues for libraries* (pp. 31-43). Westport, CT: Meckler Corporation.

Primich, T., & Richardson, C. (2006). The integrated library system: From innovation to relegation to innovation again. In A. Fenner (Ed.), *Integrating print and digital resources in library collections* (pp. 119-133). New York: Haworth Press.

Program for Cooperative Cataloging / BIBCO (Revision) (2005). *Integrating resources: A cataloging manual. Appendix A to the BIBCO participants' manual and Module*

35 of the CONSER cataloging manual. Washington, D.C.: PCC/BIBCO. Retrieved November 21, 2007, from http://www.loc.gov/catdir/pcc/bibco/irman.pdf

Public Knowledge. (2006, September 11). H.R. 6052: Copyright modernization act of 2006. Retrieved November 17, 2007, from http://www.publicknowledge.org/node/621

PubList (1998-2001). About PubList.com. Retrieved November 22, 2007, from http://www.publist.com/about.html

Quint, B. (2004, December 20). Google and research libraries launch massive digitization project. *Information Today*. Retrieved November 17, 2007, from http://www.infotoday.com/newsbreaks/nb041220-2.shtml

Ragouzis, N., Hughes, J., Philpott, R., & Maler, E. (Eds.) (2006). Security assertion markup language (SAML) V2.0 technical overview. Working Draft 10. Retrieved November 21, 2007, from http://www.oasis-open.org/committees/security/docs/draft-sstc-saml-01.pdf

Ranganathan, S.R. (1963). *The five laws of library science*. Bombay, India: Asia Publishing House.

Reagan, B. (2006, December). The digital ice age [Electronic version]. *Popular Mechanics, 183*(12), 97-94, 139.

Reference and User Services Association (RUSA), American Library Association (2003). Professional competencies for reference and user services librarians. Retrieved November 17, 2007 from, http://www.ala.org/ala/rusa/rusaprotools/referenceguide/professional.htm

Reidy, K. (2004). Succesful messaging services: SMS [& MMS] 4 biz 2day. *EContent, 27*(9), 30.

Reser. D. W., & Schuneman, A. P. (1992). The academic library job market: A content analysis comparing public and technical services. *College & Research Libraries, 53*, 49-59.

Rice, B. A. (1979). Science periodicals use study. *Serials Librarian, 4*(1) 35-47.

Rice, D. A. (2002). Legal-technological regulation of information access. In T. A. Lipinski (Ed.), *Libraries, museums, and archives: Legal issues and ethical challenges in the new information era* (pp. 275-294). Lanham, MD: Scarecrow Press.

Richards, R. (2001). Licensing agreements: Contracts, the eclipse of copyright, and the promise of cooperation. *Acquisitions Librarian, 13*(26), 89-107.

Riemer, J. J., (in press). Restrategizing bibliographic services and the one good record. *LRTS*.

Riemer, J., Declerck, L., Kautzman, A., Martin, P., & Ryan, T. (2005, December). Bibliographic services task force final report. Retrieved November 18, 2007, from the University of California Libraries Web site: http://libraries.universityofcalifornia.edu/sopag/BSTF/Final.pdf

Riggio, A. et al. (n.d.). Report of the DLF electronic resource management initiative, Appendix D: Data element dictionary. Retrieved November 21, 2007, from http://www.library.cornell.edu/cts/elicensestudy/dlfdeliverables/DLF-ERMI-AppendixD.pdf

Robbins, S., & Smith, M. (2004). Managing e-resources: A database-driven approach. In D.C. Fowler (Ed.), *E-serials collection management: Transitions, trends, and technicalities* (pp. 239-251). Binghamton, NY: Haworth Information Press.

Roose, T. (1988, October 15). Computerized reference tools of the next decade: Taking the plunge with CD-ROM. *Library Journal, 113*, 56-61.

Sadeh, T. & Ellingsen, M. (2005). Electronic resource management systems: The need and the realization. *New Library World, 106*(1212/1213), 208-218.

Schiff, S. (2006, July 31). Know it all. *The New Yorker, 82*, 36-43.

Schmidt, A. (2005). The young & the wireless. *School Library Journal, 51*(10), 44.

Schneider, K. G. (2006). How OPACs suck, Part 1: Relevance rank (or the lack of it). Retrieved November 18, 2007, from http://www.techsource.ala.org/blog/2006/03/how-opacs-suck-part-1-relevance-rank-or-the-lack-of-it.html

Schneider, K. G. (2006). How OPACs suck, Part 2: The checklist of shame. Retrieved November 18, 2007, from http://www.techsource.ala.org/blog/2006/04/how-opacs-suck-part-2-the-checklist-of-shame.html

Schneider, K. G. (2006). How OPACs suck, Part 3: The big picture. Retrieved November 18, 2007, from http://www.techsource.ala.org/blog/2006/05/how-opacs-suck-part-3-the-big-picture.html

Scholarly Publishing and Academic Resources Coalition. (2006). About SPARC. Retrieved November 17, 2007, from http://www.arl.org/sparc/about/index.html

Schottlaender, B. (1998). The development of national principles to guide librarians in licensing electronic resources. *Library Acquisitions: Practice and Theory, 22*(1), 49-54.

Schulz, N. (2001). E-journal databases: A long-term solution? *Library Collections, Acquisitions, and Technical Services, 25*, 449-459.

Scigliano, M. (2002). Consortium purchases: Case study for a cost-benefit analysis. *The Journal of Academic Librarianship, 28*(6), 393-399.

Seelye, K. Q. (2005). Snared in the web of a wikipedia liar. (Week in review desk)(rewriting history). *The New York Times,* WK1(L).

Sennema, G. (2004). Our e-journal journey: Where to next? *Serials Librarian, 47*(3), 35-43.

Serials Solutions (2006, December 12). *Products – Access and management suite*. Retrieved November 12, 2007, from http://serialssolutions.com/ams.asp

Serials Solutions (n.d.). ERMS electronic management system. Retrieved November 22, 2007, from http://www.serialsolutions.com/promotion/ERMS/images/ErMS.pdf

Shadle, S. (2006). FRBR and serials: An overview and analysis. *The Serials Librarian, 50*(1/2), 83-103.

Shepherd, P. T. (2004). COUNTER: Towards reliable vendor usage statistics. *VINE, 34*(4), 184-189.

SHERPA (2006). SHERPA RoMEO publisher copyright policies and self-archiving. Retrieved November 18, 2007, from the SHERPA Web site: http://www.sherpa.ac.uk/romeo.php

Shim, W., McClure, C. R., Fraser, B. T., Bertot, J. C., Dagli, A., & Leahy, E. H. (2001). *Measures and statistics for research library networked services: Procedures and issues. ARL E-metrics phase II report.* Washington, D.C.: Association of Research Libraries. Retrieved November 11, 2007, from http://www.arl.org/stats/newmeas/emetrics/phasetwopreface.pdf

Shorten, J. (2006). What do libraries really do with electronic resources? The practice in 2003. In A. Fenner (Ed.), *Integrating print and digital resources in library collections* (pp. 55-73). New York: Haworth Information Press.

SirsiDynix (2006). Horizon information management system. Retrieved November 22, 2007, from http://www.dynix.com/products/erm/ .

Sitko, M. et al. (2002). E-journal management systems: Trends, trials, and trade-offs. *Serials Review, 28*(3), 176-194.

Skaggs, B., Poe, J. W., & Stevens, K. W. (2006). One-stop shopping: A perspective on the evolution of electronic resources management. *OCLC Systems and Services: International Digital Library Perspective, 22*(3), 192-206.

Smulewitz, G. (recorder). (2005). Minutes of december 14, 2005 meeting. Rutgers University Libraries' Electronic Resource Access and Integration Task Force. Retrieved November 22, 2007, from http://www.libraries.rutgers.edu/rul/staff/groups/eratf/minutes/eratf_05_12_14.shmtl

Snavely, L., & Clark, K. (1996). What users really think: How they see and find serials in the arts and sciences. *Library Resources & Technical Services 40*, 49-51.

Special Libraries Association (2003). Competencies for information professionals of the 21st century. Retrieved November 17, 2007 from, http://www.sla.org/content/learn/comp2003/index.cfm

Sproles, C., & Ratledge, D. (2004). An analysis of entry-level librarian ads published in *American Libraries*, 1982-2002. *Electronic Journal of Academic and Special Librarianship, 5* (2-3). Retrieved November 17, 2007, from http://southernlibrarianship.icaap.org/content/v05n02/sprolesc01.htm

Srivastava, S., & Taglienti, P. (2005). E-journal management: An online survey evaluation. *Serials Review, 31*(1), 28-38.

Stange, K. (2006). Caught between print and electronic. *IFLA Journal, 32*(3), 237-239.

Stefancu, M., Bloss, A., & Lambrecht, J. (2004). All about DOLLeR: Managing electronic resources at the UCI library. Preprint of *Serials Review, 30*(3), 194-205. Retrieved November 22, 2007, from http://www.library.cornell.edu/cts/elicensestudy/uic/AllAboutDOLLeR_web.html

Stockton, M., & Machovec, G. (2001). Gold Rush: A digital registry of electronic journals. *Technical Services Quarterly, 19*(3), 51-59.

Subcommittee on the Source of Title Note for Internet Resources, Cataloging Policy Committee (CAPC) (2005). *Source of title note for internet resources (3rd ed).* Online Audiovisual Catalogers, Inc. (OLAC). Retrieved November 21, 2007, from http://ublib.buffalo.edu/libraries/units/cts/olac/capc/stnir.html

SUSHI for librarians and content providers. Recording of Webinar presented May 17, 2006. Retrieved November 11, 2007, from https://niso.webex.com/niso/onstage/tool/record/viewrecording1.php?EventID=277481065

Sutherland, N. R., & Adams, V. P. (2004). Territorial invasion or symbiotic relationship? Technical services and reference cooperation. *College & Research Libraries News, 65*(1), 12-15.

Swank Motion Pictures, Inc. (2006). Home page. Retrieved November 17, 2007, from http://www.swank.com

Swets Information Services (2004). Retrieved November 22, 2007, from http://informationservices.swets.com

Szczyrbak, G., & Pierce, L. (2003). E-journal subscription management systems and beyond. *The Serials Librarian, 44*(3/4), 57-162.

Tashbook, L. (2004). *Survey on licensing.* Buffalo, NY: Williams S. Hein & Co., Inc.

Taylor & Francis (2003). Terms and conditions of access. Retrieved November 18, 2007, from http://public.metapress.com/download/profiles/taylorandfrancis/terms-and-conditions-of-access.pdf

Taylor & Francis Group Journals. (2006, January). Terms and conditions of access. Retrieved November 17, 2007, from http://www.tandf.co.uk/journals/pdf/terms.pdf

Taylor, A. G. (2004). *Wynar's introduction to cataloging and classification.* Englewood, CO: Libraries Unlimited.

Teets, M., & Murray, P. (n.d.). Metasearch authentication and access management. *D-Lib Magazine.* Retrieved November 21, 2007, from http://www.dlib.org/dlib/june06/teets/06teets.html

Tennant, R. (2005). Lipstick on a pig. *Library Journal, 130*(7), 34.

Tenopir, C. (1986, March 1). Databases on CD-ROM. *Library Journal, 111,* 68-69.

Tenopir, C., & King, D. W. (2000). *Towards electronic journals. Realities for scientists, librarians, and publishers.* Washington, D.C.: SLA Publishing.

The Charleston Advisor (2007). TCA review scorecard. Retrieved November 18, 2007, from the Charleston Advisor Web site: http://www.charlestonco.com/scorecard.cfm

The EJournal Project (2001). (Tool Web site). Retrieved November 22, 2007, from http://www.lib.ksu.edu/databases/ejournal/search.jsp?searchletter=A

TLC (2005). Goldrush: A discovery and management tool for electronic Resources. Retrieved November 22, 2007, from http://www.tlcdelivers.com/tlb/pdf/goldrush.pdf

Tobia, R. C. (2001). Electronic journals: Experiences of an academic health sciences library. *Serials Review, 27*(1), 3-17.

Tonkery, D. (2006, May 8). Best of show—what's a serial when you are running on internet time. *Liveserials* [blog]. Retrieved November 21, 2007, from http://liveserials.blogspot.com/2006/05/best-of-show-whats-serial-when-you-are.html

Torkington, R.B. (1974). MARC and its application to library automation. In M.J. Voigt (Vol. Ed.), *Advances in librarianship* (Vol. 4, pp. 1-23). New York: Academic Press Inc.

Traill, S., & Huismann, M. (2004, September). *Beyond books: Blogs at the University of Minnesota.* Unpublished work; poster presentation at the 2004 OLAC Conference, Montréal, Canada.

Tri-College Consortium (2003). Electronic resources tracking System (ERTS). Retrieved November 22, 2007, from http://www.haverford.edu/library/erts

Tull, L., Crum J., Davis, T., & Strader, C. R. (2005). Integrating and streamlining electronic resources workflows via innovative's electronic resource management. *Serials Librarian, 47*(4), 103-124.

Turoff, M., & Hiltz, S.R. (1982). The electronic journal: A progress report [Electronic version]. *Journal of the American Society for Information Science, 33*(4), 195-202.

U.S. Copyright Act. 17 U.S.C. §101 et seq.

Uniform Computer Information Transactions Act (2002-2006). *Uniform laws annotated* (Vol. 7, Part II). Minneapolis, MN: Thomson/West.

United States Copyright Office. (1998). *Circular 21: Reproduction of copyrighted works by educators and librarians.* Washington, D.C: Library of Congress, Copyright Office.

United States Copyright Office. (1998, December). The digital millennium copyright act of 1998: A U.S. copyright office summary. Retrieved November 17, 2007, from http://www.copyright.gov/legislation/dmca.pdf

United States Copyright Office. (2006, November 22). Statement of the librarian of congress relating to section 1201 rulemaking. Retrieved November 17, 2007, from http://www.copyright.gov/1201/docs/2006_statement.html

United States. (1787, September 17). Constitution Article 1, Section 8. Retrieved November 17, 2007, from http://www.law.emory.edu/cms/site/index.php?id=3080

University of California Libraries (n.d.). Principles for acquiring and licensing information in digital formats. Retrieved November 17, 2007, from http://libraries.universityofcalifornia.edu/cdc/principlesforacquiring.html

University of California Los Angeles Library (2002). SCAER vision of access to electronic resources. Retrieved November 23, 2007, from http://staff.library.ucla.edu/groups/scaer/vision_rept.doc

University of California Los Angeles Library (2006). Staff intranet: Steering committee on access to electronic resources (SCAER). Retrieved November 23, 2007, from http://staff.library.ucla.edu/groups/scaer/

University of California, Berkeley Library (2007). *Proxy server setup instructions.* Retrieved November 21, 2007, from http://proxy.lib.berkeley.edu/instructions.html

University of California, Los Angeles (2004). UC electronic resources management planning meeting campus/CDL survey: Electronic resources management at UCLA, March 4, 2004. Retrieved November 22, 2007, from http://libraries.universityofcalifornia.edu/sopag/appen06surveyfinalucal.doc

University of California, Los Angeles (2002). ERBd examples of publisher, Issued by and access provider. Retrieved November 22, 2007, from http://www.library.cornell.edu/elicensestudy/ucla/2003/Examples%20of%20Publisher,%20Issued%20By%20&%20Access%20Provider%2012-19-02.doc

University of Chicago Press Journals Division (2006). Electronic access to astronomy journals. Retrieved November 18, 2007, from http://www.journals.uchicago.edu/sitedocs.pdf

University of Texas System. (1997). CONFU: The conference on fair use. Retrieved November 17, 2007, from

http://www.utsystem.edu/ogc/INTELLECTUALPROPERTY/confu.htm

University of Texas System. (2004, November 22). Offsite: Fair use. Retrieved November 17, 2007, from http://www.utsystem.edu/ogc/INTELLECTUALPROPERTY/offsite.htm#fair

Van de Sompel, H., & Beit-Arie, O. (2001). Open linking in the scholarly information environment using the OpenURL framework. *D-Lib Magazine, 7*(3). Retrieved November 21, 2007, from http://www.dlib.org/dlib/march01/vandesompel/03vandesompel.html

VTLS (2004.) Verify: Verify for yourself, e-resource management can be easy! Retrieved November 22, 2007, from http://www.vtls.com/Products/verify.shtml

VTLS (n.d.). Verify [brochure]. Retrieved November 22, 2007, from http://www.vtls.com/brochures/verify.pdf

Wakimoto, J. C., Walker, D. S., & Dabbour, K. S. (2006). The myths and realities of SFX in academic libraries. *Journal of Academic Librarianship, 32*(2), 27-136.

Wakimoto, J. C., Walker, D. S., & Dabbour, K. S. (2006). The myths and realities of SFX in academic libraries. *Journal of Academic Librarianship, 32*(2) 127-136.

Walter, P. L. (1996). A journal use study: Checkouts and in-house use. *Bulletin of the Medical Library Association, 84*(4), 461-467.

Wang, H. (2006). From "user" to "customer": TQM in academic libraries? *Library Management, 27*(9)

Welch, J. M. (2002/0). Hey! what about us?! Changing roles of subject specialists and reference librarians in the age of electronic resources. *Serials Review, 28*(4), 283-286.

White, G. (1999). Academic subject specialist positions in the United States: A content analysis of announcements from 1990 through 1998. *The Journal of Academic Librarianship, 25*(5), 372-382.

White, G. (2000). Head of reference positions in academic libraries: A survey of job announcements from 1990 through 1999. *Reference & User Services Quarterly, 39*(3), 265-272.

White, H. (2005). Documentation in technical services. *The Serials Librarian, 49*(3), 47-55.

White, J. (2005). Effecting change in periodicals service: Management models and a process. *Serials Review, 32*(1), 22-25.

Wikipedia, the free encyclopedia. (2006, December 27). Central Authentication Service. Retrieved November 21, 2007, from http://en.wikipedia.org/wiki/Central_Authentication_Service

Wikipedia, the free encyclopedia. (2007, January 18). Shibboleth. Retrieved November 21, 2007, from http://en.wikipedia.org/wiki/Shibboleth

Wikipedia, the free encyclopedia. (2007, January 30). Single sign-on. Retrieved November 21, 2007, from http://en.wikipedia.org/wiki/Single_sign-on

Wikipedia. (2006). Five laws of library science. Retrieved November 18, 2007, from http://en.wikipedia.org/wiki/Five_laws_of_library_science

Wikipedia. (2006, December 31). Retrieved November 17, 2007, from http://en.wikipedia.org/wiki/Wikipedia:Copyrights

Wilkinson, F. C., & Lewis, L. K. (2003). *The complete guide to acquisitions management.* London: Libraries Unlimited.

Williams, J. W. (1997). Serials cataloging, 1991-1996: A review. *The Serials Librarian, 32*(1-2), 3-26.

Wilson, H. W. (2006). Gold rush quick facts. Retrieved November 22, 2007, from http://www.hwwilson.com/documentation/WilsonWeb/goldrush-quickfacts.htm

Wisniewski, J. (2006, March/April). Getting a handle on content. *Online*, 52-54.

Wissman, M. et al. (2005). Taylor Periodical Administration System. Retrieved November 22, 2007, from http://www2.taylor.edu/library/upland/sjo/tpas.html

Wolfe, R. H. W. (2005) Managing the metadata morass: Applying cataloging skills beyond the traditional catalog: Boston College Library Catalogers. *Metametametadata.* Retrieved November 22, 2007, from http://www.metametadata.net/mt/archives/2005_04.html

Wolverton, R. E. (2003). E-journal licensing and legal issues: A panel report. *The Serials Librarian, 45*(2), 153-156.

World Intellectual Property Organization. (2006). Home page. Retrieved November 17, 2007, from http://www.wipo.int/portal/index.html.en

Wright, C. A. (1994). *The law of federal courts* (5th ed.). St. Paul, MN: West.

Wusteman, J., & O'hlceadha, P. (2006). Using Ajax to empower dynamic searching. *Information Technology and Libraries, 25*(2), 57.

Xu, H. (1996). The impact of automation on job requirements and qualifications for catalogers and reference librarians in academic libraries. *Library Resources and Technical Services, 40*(1), 9-31.

Yale University Library (2001). CLIR/DLF model license. Retrieved November 23, 2007, from http://www.library.yale.edu/~llicense/modlic.shtml

Young, M., & Kyrillidou, M. (2004). ARL supplementary statistics 2002-03. Retrieved November 23, 2007, from http://www.arl.org/stats/pubpdf/sup03.pdf

Zagar, C. (2000, January 24). Proxy server vs. URL rewriter for authentication. Message posted to Web4lib listserv. Retrieved November 21, 2007, from http://lists.webjunction.org/wjlists/web4lib/2000-January/030233.html

Zagar, C. (2007). URL rewrting. Retrieved November 21, 2007, from http://www.usefulutilities.com/support/rewrite.html

Zeter, M. J., Thunell, A., & Maguire, J. (2003). Success in searching for serials: What is the MAGIC solution? *Serials Librarian, 44*(3/4), 201-207.

Zhou, Y. (1996). Analysis of trends in demand for computer-related skills for academic librarians from 1974 to 1994. *College & Research Libraries, 57*, 259-272.

Zhu, Q. (2006). The nuts and bolts of delivering new technical reports via database-generated RSS FEEDS. *Computers in Libraries, 26*(2), 24.

Zuidema, K. (1999). Reengineering technical services processes. *Library Resources & Technical Services, 43*(1), 37-52.

About the Contributors

Marianne Afifi is the associate dean of the University Library at California State University, Northridge. She is responsible for access services, special collections, archives and emergency planning. She also participates in strategic planning, decision-making and fundraising. In previous positions, she managed electronic information resources and developed systems, digital library and online learning objects. She has presented and published locally, nationally, and internationally. She serves on the board of directors of ASIST and holds membership in ALA and ACM. She has an MBA from USC and MLS in information systems design from UCLA.

Mary Bevis is the serials and acquisitions librarian for the Houston Cole Library at Jacksonville State University. She holds the rank of full professor. Ms. Bevis received a Bachelor of science in business administration from Jacksonville State University, a Master's in instructional media from Jacksonville State University, and an EdS in library and information sciences from the University of Alabama.

Vicki Bloom has been head of the Rivera Library Reference Services department at the University of California Riverside Libraries since 1995. She is chair of the UC Reference Bibliographers group and active in ALA RUSA CODES. She has a broad background in reference, instruction, management, collection development, and online/print product review. Prior to her position at UCR, Vicki was the associate director of the Green-Field National Alzheimer's Library and Resource Center in Chicago and search services coordinator/science Librarian at Loyola University Chicago. She has a MLS from Wayne State University.

George Boston is the electronic resources and serials librarian at Western Michigan University, holding several positions in the Acquisitions and Serials Department at Western Michigan University since 1990. Prior to that, he held various positions at the Kalamazoo Public Library, Southwest Michigan Library Cooperative, and Western Michigan University. He possesses an MA and a MLS from Western Michigan University and a BS from Central Michigan University.

Robert L. Bothmann is electronic access/catalog librarian, associate professor at Minnesota State University, Mankato (MSU) where he is a cataloger for electronic and print monographs and journals. He serves on the editorial board of *Cataloging & Classification Quarterly*, is the vice president/president elect (2007-2009) of the OnLine Audiovisual Catalogers, and the 2007 recipient of the Esther J. Piercy award. He is active in leadership roles for the Consortium of MnPALS Libraries, a consortium of Minnesota libraries using Aleph. He holds an MLIS from the University of Wisconsin—Milwaukee and an MS in geography and english technical communication from MSU.

Kincaid Brown is the american and electronic services librarian and Webmaster for the University of Law Library. He received his BA in history from the University of Michigan in 1994; his JD from the University of Michigan Law School in 1996; and, his MSI with a specialization in library and information services from the University of Michigan School of Information in 1998.

Heather Christenson has led the California Digital Library (CDL) Resource Liaison Program for the past four years. In addition, she recently led CDL's NSDL-grant funded project to develop an integrated search service which incorporated metasearch, OpenURL linking, and OAI-harvested metadata. Heather is a coauthor of CDL's 2003 analysis of solutions for capture, curation, and preservation of government information on the Web. She is currently CDL's project manager for implementation of University of California libraries' system-wide electronic resources management system. Prior to joining CDL, Heather worked on commercial Web search tools, and was a news librarian, law librarian, and cataloger. She received her MLIS from the University of California, Berkeley.

Janet Crum received her MLS from the University of Washington in 1992 and is currently head of library systems & cataloging at Oregon Health & Science University in Portland, OR. In her current position, she supports OHSU's integrated library system and manages the library's cataloging, computer support, digital resources, electronic resources management, and Web development sections. She led the teams that implemented OHSU's link resolver and co-led the team that beta tested and implemented the electronic resources management product from Innovative Interfaces, Inc.

Trisha L. Davis is an associate professor and head, Serials and Electronic Resources Department at the Ohio State University Libraries. She also serves as an adjunct faculty member for the Kent State University School of Library and Information Science, Columbus Program. Since 1997, Ms. Davis has served as the visiting program officer for licensing of electronic products at the Association of Research Libraries. She is actively involved in committee work for the American Library Association.

Debra Engel holds an MLS from the University of Arizona. Since 2001, she has worked as the director of Public Services for the University of Oklahoma Libraries. Prior to 2001, Ms. Engel worked as the assistant director for the Pioneer Library System in Norman, Oklahoma. She is a member of the Oklahoma Library Association, the American Library Association, the Association of College and Research Libraries and the Library Administration and Management Association. To contact: dhengel@ou.edu.

Celeste Feather is the electronic resources librarian at the Ohio State University Libraries. Prior to accepting this position in 2005, she was the associate librarian at the University of Connecticut School of Law Library and the access services librarian at the Georgetown University Law Library. She holds a BA from Oberlin College, an MA from George Washington University, and an MLS from the University of Maryland, College Park.

Donna L. Ferullo is director of the Purdue University Copyright Office and associate professor of library science. Ms. Ferullo holds a BA from Boston College, an MLS from the University of Maryland and a JD from Suffolk University Law School. She is former chair of the ACRL Copyright Committee. Ms. Ferullo has published articles on copyright and its impact on higher education and libraries.

She has also given presentations for the American Library Association; the Association of College and Research Libraries; the Association of Research Libraries; and many other groups in higher education and libraries.

Ted Fons is the senior product manager at Innovative Interfaces. He is responsible for the management of Innovative's Electronic Resource Management, Acquisitions, Serials, WebBridge LR and Pathfinder Pro products. His most recent development project was to bring to general release the first Standardized Usage Statistics Harvesting Initiative (SUSHI) client in an electronic resource management system. Theodore has been with Innovative since 1996. He has an MLS from Syracuse University and has worked in acquisitions, cataloging and reference in academic libraries.

Randle Gedeon is the monographic acquisitions and gifts librarian at Western Michigan University, holding several positions in the Acquisitions and Serials Department at Western Michigan University since 2000. Prior to that, he held public service positions at Western Michigan, Northeastern State University (Tahlequah, Oklahoma), and John Carroll University. He possesses an MLS from Kent State University, a MAEd from Baldwin-Wallace College and a BA from Muskingum College. He has published on topics related to library acquisitions and instruction.

John-Bauer Graham is the head of public Services for the Houston Cole Library at Jacksonville State University. He holds the rank of Associate Professor. Mr. Graham received a BA in History from Auburn University, a MA in History from JSU, a MLIS from the University of Alabama, and is currently pursuing a Doctorate in higher education administration from the University of Alabama.

Dalene Hawthorne began working with electronic resources as an indexer at Information Access Company, now part of the Gale Group, in 1989. Ms. Hawthorne became an editor of magazine index in 1991 and manager of serials acquisitions in 1992. She became a customer sales consultant for Innovative Interfaces in 1998. Ms. Hawthorne worked for various special libraries from 1999 to 2002, when she became serials librarian at Stanford University Libraries. She holds a MLIS from San Jose State University. Ms. Hawthorne is currently head of systems and technical services at Emporia State University.

Margaret Hogarth has been electronic resources coordinator for the University of California, Riverside Libraries since 2004. Prior to this, she was interim library Web coordinator at California State University, Fullerton and a pool librarian at Rio Hondo College and California State Polytechnic University, Pomona. She has an MLIS from San Jose State University and a Master's in environmental studies from California State University, Fullerton.

Melissa Holmberg is the electronic resources librarian, associate professor at Minnesota State University, Mankato (MSU), where she staffs the reference desk on a weekly rotation, conducts collection development activities and instruction sessions for the physical sciences, and manages electronic resources, including federated search, OpenURL, and dynamic Web pages for accessing over 200 databases. She holds an MLS from the University of Missouri-Columbia and an MS in english technical communication from MSU.

Patricia Hults, a practicing librarian for over 20 years, currently serves as coordinator of technical services at Rensselaer Polytechnic Institute. Prior to this she was digital resources librarian at the same institution. In both positions she has been intimately involved in collecting and using electronic statistics. She worked for fifteen years in the State University of New York system in serials, reference, and public services. She earned an Associate degree in applied sciences, computer information systems from SUNY Cobleskill, several years after her MLS from SUNY Albany.

Smita Joshipura is an acquisitions librarian at Fletcher Library, Arizona State University at the west campus, Phoenix, AZ, where she is responsible for acquisitions of all the formats as well as oversees the materials budget. She is currently a core member of Electronic Resources Management Implementation group. Moreover, she is chairing Fletcher Library's Diversity Initiative Team. She has an MLIS from India as well as from University of Arizona, United States.

Marie Kennedy holds an MFA in photography from the University of Texas at Austin and an MSIS from the University of North Carolina at Chapel Hill. She is the head, metadata & content management at the Norris Medical Library of the University of Southern California. Her research interests include the management of data, and the development of systems designed to assist in that endeavor.

Diana Kichuk is the electronic resources librarian at the University of Saskatchewan Library. She has also worked in public services and technical services. Prior to that, she was the regional coordinator for library services for Agriculture Canada covering the four western provinces. She has published articles on supplementary content in electronic journals and remediation in electronic resources.

Ted Koppel is Verde product marketing manager for Ex Libris, a position that builds on his significant product management and related experience in the library and information marketplace. Ted's prior experience includes working at the CARL Corporation, the UnCover Company, OCLC, and as senior product manager for standards implementation at The Library Corporation (TLC). Ted has been an active participant in standards committees throughout his career. Currently, he serves on four standards committees in the ERM and resource sharing areas. He holds a Bachelor's degree in languages from Georgetown, with a minor in Arabic. He also has an MSLS from Case Western Reserve University, Cleveland, Ohio.

Bethany Latham is the electronic resources/documents librarian for the Houston Cole Library at Jacksonville State University. She holds a rank of assistant professor. Ms. Latham received a BA in history from Jacksonville State University and a MLIS from the University of Alabama.

Jodi Poe is the distance education/electronic resources manager for the Houston Cole Library at Jacksonville State University. She holds the rank of associate professor. Ms. Poe received a BS in accounting from Jacksonville State University and a MLIS from the University of Alabama.

Sarah Robbins holds an MLIS from the University of Oklahoma. She currently works as the Web & digital initiatives coordinator for the University of Oklahoma Libraries. Ms. Robbins is actively involved in the Oklahoma Library Association and the Library and Information Technology Association and serves on a number of professional committees. To contact: srobbins@ou.edu.

Juan Carlos Rodriguez has a MLIS from UCLA with a specialization in information systems. He is currently the director of Library Systems & Information Technology Services at California State University, Sacramento (CSUS). Prior to joining CSUS, he held several positions at UC Riverside including science reference librarian and coordinator of information technology for the Science Library. His research interests include emerging information technologies and their potential use in an academic environment, information seeking behavior in an online environment and WSeb-based technologies in libraries. He has presented nationally in the areas of information retrieval of Internet resources and metadata.

Aline Soules is a library faculty member and professor at California State University, East Bay. She holds a BA (Hons.) and MA from the University of Windsor, an MSLS from Wayne State University, and an MFA from Antioch University, Los Angeles. Her current library responsibilities include instruction, reference, and collections, and she has been active in legislative and copyright issues for some years. She is a member of ACRL's legislative network and was recently chosen as one of its legislative advocates. She is also legislative liaison for CARL (California Academic and Research Libraries).

Kimberly W. Stevens is the senior catalog librarian for the Houston Cole Library at Jacksonville State University. She holds the rank of associate professor. Ms. Stevens holds a BA in english from Auburn University and the MSLS from the University of North Carolina at Chapel Hill.

Sherry Willhite is the convener of the California Digital Library (CDL) Resource Wranglers group, and the coordinator of the CDL technical requirements documents. She has been CDL's primary analyst for abstracting & indexing databases since 1996. Until 2003 she was the CDL Resource Liaison Coordinator. Sherry is currently CDL's project manager for the UC Request Service (Interlibrary loan and Document Delivery services). Before joining UC's Division of Library Automation (now the CDL) in 1993, she was the chemistry librarian at the University of California, San Diego, and a reference librarian at the Carlsbad City Library. Sherry has an MLIS from the University of California, Los Angeles and a PharmD from the University of the Pacific.

Bin Zhang is currently the digital information services librarian at California State University, Sacramento. Before this position, he was the systems librarian at Kapiʻolani College Library, University of Hawaiʻi. His background and experiences in his library career include digital library project development, electronic resources development and management, web project development and management, server administration, etc. Mr. Zhang received his BS in agriculture from Xinjiang Agricultural University, Urumqi, China, and MLIS from University of Hawaiʻi at Mānoa.

Yvonne W. Zhang In 1997 with eight years of background as a serials librarian at Northwestern University Library, she moved to California and joined Cal Poly Pomona University in the capacity of associate university librarian for technical services. Her expertise and interests lie with serials cataloging and electronic resource management, demonstrated by her professional involvement with NASIG, SCCTP, and by my numerous publications over the years including "Measuring and assessment of library electronic resources," *The Serials Librarian, 43*(3), 2002; and "Serials cataloging at the turn of the century (book review)," *Serials Review, 24*(3/4), 1998.

Index

CPSIA information can be obtained at www.ICGtesting.com
Printed in the USA
BVOW052341151211

278192BV00007B/42/P